WALLACE STEVENS

Wallace Stevens

COLLECTED POETRY AND PROSE

THE LIBRARY OF AMERICA

FRANK KERMODE AND JOAN RICHARDSON
SELECTED THE CONTENTS AND WROTE
THE NOTES FOR THIS VOLUME

Wallace Stevens' *Collected Poetry and Prose*
has been published with support from

JAMES MERRILL
(1926–1995)

and will be kept in print by a gift in his memory
to the Guardians of American Letters Fund,
established by The Library of America
to ensure that every volume in the series
will be permanently available.

Contents

POEMS ADDED TO HARMONIUM (1931)

IDEAS OF ORDER (1936)

THE MAN WITH THE BLUE GUITAR (1937)

PARTS OF A WORLD (1942)

THE AURORAS OF AUTUMN (1950)

THE ROCK (1954)

FROM THE NOTEBOOKS

JOURNALS AND LETTERS

HARMONIUM

(1923)

To
MY WIFE

Earthy Anecdote

Every time the bucks went clattering
Over Oklahoma
A firecat bristled in the way.

Wherever they went,
They went clattering,
Until they swerved
In a swift, circular line
To the right,
Because of the firecat.

Or until they swerved
In a swift, circular line
To the left,
Because of the firecat.

The bucks clattered.
The firecat went leaping,
To the right, to the left,
And
Bristled in the way.

Later, the firecat closed his bright eyes
And slept.

Invective Against Swans

The soul, O ganders, flies beyond the parks
And far beyond the discords of the wind.

A bronze rain from the sun descending marks
The death of summer, which that time endures

Like one who scrawls a listless testament
Of golden quirks and Paphian caricatures,

Bequeathing your white feathers to the moon
And giving your bland motions to the air.

Behold, already on the long parades
The crows anoint the statues with their dirt.

And the soul, O ganders, being lonely, flies
Beyond your chilly chariots, to the skies.

In the Carolinas

The lilacs wither in the Carolinas.
Already the butterflies flutter above the cabins.
Already the new-born children interpret love
In the voices of mothers.

Timeless mother,
How is it that your aspic nipples
For once vent honey?

The pine-tree sweetens my body.
The white iris beautifies me.

The Paltry Nude Starts on a Spring Voyage

But not on a shell, she starts,
Archaic, for the sea.
But on the first-found weed
She scuds the glitters,
Noiselessly, like one more wave.

She too is discontent
And would have purple stuff upon her arms,
Tired of the salty harbors,
Eager for the brine and bellowing
Of the high interiors of the sea.

The wind speeds her,
Blowing upon her hands
And watery back.
She touches the clouds, where she goes
In the circle of her traverse of the sea.

Yet this is meagre play
In the scurry and water-shine,
As her heels foam—
Not as when the goldener nude
Of a later day

Will go, like the centre of sea-green pomp,
In an intenser calm,
Scullion of fate,
Across the spick torrent, ceaselessly,
Upon her irretrievable way.

The Plot Against the Giant

First Girl

When this yokel comes maundering,
Whetting his hacker,
I shall run before him,
Diffusing the civilest odors
Out of geraniums and unsmelled flowers.
It will check him.

Second Girl

I shall run before him,
Arching cloths besprinkled with colors
As small as fish-eggs.
The threads
Will abash him.

Third Girl

Oh, la . . . le pauvre!
I shall run before him,
With a curious puffing.
He will bend his ear then.
I shall whisper
Heavenly labials in a world of gutturals.
It will undo him.

Infanta Marina

Her terrace was the sand
And the palms and the twilight.

She made of the motions of her wrist
The grandiose gestures
Of her thought.

The rumpling of the plumes
Of this creature of the evening
Came to be sleights of sails
Over the sea.

And thus she roamed
In the roamings of her fan,

Partaking of the sea,
And of the evening,
As they flowed around
And uttered their subsiding sound.

Domination of Black

At night, by the fire,
The colors of the bushes
And of the fallen leaves,
Repeating themselves,
Turned in the room,
Like the leaves themselves
Turning in the wind.
Yes: but the color of the heavy hemlocks
Came striding.
And I remembered the cry of the peacocks.

The colors of their tails
Were like the leaves themselves
Turning in the wind,
In the twilight wind.
They swept over the room,
Just as they flew from the boughs of the hemlocks
Down to the ground.
I heard them cry—the peacocks.
Was it a cry against the twilight
Or against the leaves themselves
Turning in the wind,
Turning as the flames
Turned in the fire,
Turning as the tails of the peacocks
Turned in the loud fire,
Loud as the hemlocks
Full of the cry of the peacocks?
Or was it a cry against the hemlocks?

Out of the window,
I saw how the planets gathered
Like the leaves themselves
Turning in the wind.
I saw how the night came,
Came striding like the color of the heavy hemlocks.
I felt afraid.
And I remembered the cry of the peacocks.

The Snow Man

One must have a mind of winter
To regard the frost and the boughs
Of the pine-trees crusted with snow;

And have been cold a long time
To behold the junipers shagged with ice,
The spruces rough in the distant glitter

Of the January sun; and not to think
Of any misery in the sound of the wind,
In the sound of a few leaves,

Which is the sound of the land
Full of the same wind
That is blowing in the same bare place

For the listener, who listens in the snow,
And, nothing himself, beholds
Nothing that is not there and the nothing that is.

The Ordinary Women

Then from their poverty they rose,
From dry catarrhs, and to guitars
They flitted
Through the palace walls.

They flung monotony behind,
Turned from their want, and, nonchalant,
They crowded
The nocturnal halls.

The lacquered loges huddled there
Mumbled zay-zay and a-zay, a-zay.
The moonlight
Fubbed the girandoles.

And the cold dresses that they wore,
In the vapid haze of the window-bays,
Were tranquil
As they leaned and looked

From the window-sills at the alphabets,
At beta b and gamma g,
To study
The canting curlicues

Of heaven and of the heavenly script.
And there they read of marriage-bed.
Ti-lill-o!
And they read right long.

The gaunt guitarists on the strings
Rumbled a-day and a-day, a-day.
The moonlight
Rose on the beachy floors.

How explicit the coiffures became,
The diamond point, the sapphire point,
The sequins
Of the civil fans!

Insinuations of desire,
Puissant speech, alike in each,
Cried quittance
To the wickless halls.

Then from their poverty they rose,
From dry guitars, and to catarrhs
They flitted
Through the palace walls.

The Load of Sugar-Cane

The going of the glade-boat
Is like water flowing;

Like water flowing
Through the green saw-grass,
Under the rainbows;

Under the rainbows
That are like birds,
Turning, bedizened,

While the wind still whistles
As kildeer do,

When they rise
At the red turban
Of the boatman.

Le Monocle de Mon Oncle

I

"Mother of heaven, regina of the clouds,
O sceptre of the sun, crown of the moon,
There is not nothing, no, no, never nothing,
Like the clashed edges of two words that kill."
And so I mocked her in magnificent measure.
Or was it that I mocked myself alone?
I wish that I might be a thinking stone.
The sea of spuming thought foists up again
The radiant bubble that she was. And then
A deep up-pouring from some saltier well
Within me, bursts its watery syllable.

II

A red bird flies across the golden floor.
It is a red bird that seeks out his choir
Among the choirs of wind and wet and wing.
A torrent will fall from him when he finds.
Shall I uncrumple this much-crumpled thing?
I am a man of fortune greeting heirs;
For it has come that thus I greet the spring.
These choirs of welcome choir for me farewell.
No spring can follow past meridian.
Yet you persist with anecdotal bliss
To make believe a starry *connaissance*.

III

Is it for nothing, then, that old Chinese
Sat tittivating by their mountain pools
Or in the Yangtse studied out their beards?
I shall not play the flat historic scale.
You know how Utamaro's beauties sought
The end of love in their all-speaking braids.
You know the mountainous coiffures of Bath.
Alas! Have all the barbers lived in vain
That not one curl in nature has survived?
Why, without pity on these studious ghosts,
Do you come dripping in your hair from sleep?

IV

This luscious and impeccable fruit of life
Falls, it appears, of its own weight to earth.
When you were Eve, its acrid juice was sweet,
Untasted, in its heavenly, orchard air.
An apple serves as well as any skull
To be the book in which to read a round,
And is as excellent, in that it is composed
Of what, like skulls, comes rotting back to ground.
But it excels in this, that as the fruit
Of love, it is a book too mad to read
Before one merely reads to pass the time.

V

In the high west there burns a furious star.
It is for fiery boys that star was set
And for sweet-smelling virgins close to them.
The measure of the intensity of love
Is measure, also, of the verve of earth.
For me, the firefly's quick, electric stroke
Ticks tediously the time of one more year.
And you? Remember how the crickets came
Out of their mother grass, like little kin,
In the pale nights, when your first imagery
Found inklings of your bond to all that dust.

VI

If men at forty will be painting lakes
The ephemeral blues must merge for them in one,
The basic slate, the universal hue.
There is a substance in us that prevails.
But in our amours amorists discern
Such fluctuations that their scrivening
Is breathless to attend each quirky turn.
When amorists grow bald, then amours shrink
Into the compass and curriculum
Of introspective exiles, lecturing.
It is a theme for Hyacinth alone.

VII

The mules that angels ride come slowly down
The blazing passes, from beyond the sun.
Descensions of their tinkling bells arrive.
These muleteers are dainty of their way.
Meantime, centurions guffaw and beat
Their shrilling tankards on the table-boards.
This parable, in sense, amounts to this:
The honey of heaven may or may not come,
But that of earth both comes and goes at once.
Suppose these couriers brought amid their train
A damsel heightened by eternal bloom.

VIII

Like a dull scholar, I behold, in love,
An ancient aspect touching a new mind.
It comes, it blooms, it bears its fruit and dies.
This trivial trope reveals a way of truth.
Our bloom is gone. We are the fruit thereof.
Two golden gourds distended on our vines,
We hang like warty squashes, streaked and rayed,
Into the autumn weather, splashed with frost,
Distorted by hale fatness, turned grotesque.
The laughing sky will see the two of us
Washed into rinds by rotting winter rains.

IX

In verses wild with motion, full of din,
Loudened by cries, by clashes, quick and sure
As the deadly thought of men accomplishing
Their curious fates in war, come, celebrate
The faith of forty, ward of Cupido.
Most venerable heart, the lustiest conceit
Is not too lusty for your broadening.
I quiz all sounds, all thoughts, all everything
For the music and manner of the paladins
To make oblation fit. Where shall I find
Bravura adequate to this great hymn?

X

The fops of fancy in their poems leave
Memorabilia of the mystic spouts,
Spontaneously watering their gritty soils.
I am a yeoman, as such fellows go.
I know no magic trees, no balmy boughs,
No silver-ruddy, gold-vermilion fruits.
But, after all, I know a tree that bears
A semblance to the thing I have in mind.
It stands gigantic, with a certain tip
To which all birds come sometime in their time.
But when they go that tip still tips the tree.

XI

If sex were all, then every trembling hand
Could make us squeak, like dolls, the wished-for words.
But note the unconscionable treachery of fate,
That makes us weep, laugh, grunt and groan, and shout
Doleful heroics, pinching gestures forth
From madness or delight, without regard
To that first, foremost law. Anguishing hour!
Last night, we sat beside a pool of pink,
Clippered with lilies scudding the bright chromes,
Keen to the point of starlight, while a frog
Boomed from his very belly odious chords.

XII

A blue pigeon it is, that circles the blue sky,
On side-long wing, around and round and round.
A white pigeon it is, that flutters to the ground,
Grown tired of flight. Like a dark rabbi, I
Observed, when young, the nature of mankind,
In lordly study. Every day, I found
Man proved a gobbet in my mincing world.
Like a rose rabbi, later, I pursued,
And still pursue, the origin and course
Of love, but until now I never knew
That fluttering things have so distinct a shade.

Nuances of a Theme by Williams

*It's a strange courage
you give me, ancient star:*

*Shine alone in the sunrise
toward which you lend no part!*

I

Shine alone, shine nakedly, shine like bronze,
that reflects neither my face nor any inner part
of my being, shine like fire, that mirrors nothing.

II

Lend no part to any humanity that suffuses
you in its own light.
Be not chimera of morning,
Half-man, half-star.
Be not an intelligence,
Like a widow's bird
Or an old horse.

Metaphors of a Magnifico

Twenty men crossing a bridge,
Into a village,
Are twenty men crossing twenty bridges,
Into twenty villages,
Or one man
Crossing a single bridge into a village.

This is old song
That will not declare itself . . .

Twenty men crossing a bridge,
Into a village,
Are
Twenty men crossing a bridge
Into a village.

That will not declare itself
Yet is certain as meaning . . .

The boots of the men clump
On the boards of the bridge.
The first white wall of the village
Rises through fruit-trees.
Of what was it I was thinking?

So the meaning escapes.

The first white wall of the village . . .
The fruit-trees. . . .

Ploughing on Sunday

The white cock's tail
Tosses in the wind.
The turkey-cock's tail
Glitters in the sun.

Water in the fields.
The wind pours down.
The feathers flare
And bluster in the wind.

Remus, blow your horn!
I'm ploughing on Sunday,
Ploughing North America.
Blow your horn!

Tum-ti-tum,
Ti-tum-tum-tum!
The turkey-cock's tail
Spreads to the sun.

The white cock's tail
Streams to the moon.
Water in the fields.
The wind pours down.

Cy Est Pourtraicte, Madame
Ste Ursule, et Les Unze
Mille Vierges

Ursula, in a garden, found
A bed of radishes.
She kneeled upon the ground
And gathered them,
With flowers around,
Blue, gold, pink, and green.

She dressed in red and gold brocade
And in the grass an offering made
Of radishes and flowers.

She said, "My dear,
Upon your altars,
I have placed
The marguerite and coquelicot,
And roses
Frail as April snow;
But here," she said,
"Where none can see,
I make an offering, in the grass,
Of radishes and flowers."
And then she wept
For fear the Lord would not accept.

The good Lord in His garden sought
New leaf and shadowy tinct,
And they were all His thought.
He heard her low accord,
Half prayer and half ditty,
And He felt a subtle quiver,
That was not heavenly love,
Or pity.

This is not writ
In any book.

Hibiscus on the Sleeping Shores

I say now, Fernando, that on that day
The mind roamed as a moth roams,
Among the blooms beyond the open sand;

And that whatever noise the motion of the waves
Made on the sea-weeds and the covered stones
Disturbed not even the most idle ear.

Then it was that that monstered moth
Which had lain folded against the blue
And the colored purple of the lazy sea,

And which had drowsed along the bony shores,
Shut to the blather that the water made,
Rose up besprent and sought the flaming red

Dabbled with yellow pollen—red as red
As the flag above the old café—
And roamed there all the stupid afternoon.

Fabliau of Florida

Barque of phosphor
On the palmy beach,

Move outward into heaven,
Into the alabasters
And night blues.

Foam and cloud are one.
Sultry moon-monsters
Are dissolving.

Fill your black hull
With white moonlight.

There will never be an end
To this droning of the surf.

The Doctor of Geneva

The doctor of Geneva stamped the sand
That lay impounding the Pacific swell,
Patted his stove-pipe hat and tugged his shawl.

Lacustrine man had never been assailed
By such long-rolling opulent cataracts,
Unless Racine or Bossuet held the like.

He did not quail. A man so used to plumb
The multifarious heavens felt no awe
Before these visible, voluble delugings,

Which yet found means to set his simmering mind
Spinning and hissing with oracular
Notations of the wild, the ruinous waste,

Until the steeples of his city clanked and sprang
In an unburgherly apocalypse.
The doctor used his handkerchief and sighed.

Another Weeping Woman

Pour the unhappiness out
From your too bitter heart,
Which grieving will not sweeten.

Poison grows in this dark.
It is in the water of tears
Its black blooms rise.

The magnificent cause of being,
The imagination, the one reality
In this imagined world

Leaves you
With him for whom no phantasy moves,
And you are pierced by a death.

Homunculus et La Belle Etoile

In the sea, Biscayne, there prinks
The young emerald, evening star,
Good light for drunkards, poets, widows,
And ladies soon to be married.

By this light the salty fishes
Arch in the sea like tree-branches,
Going in many directions
Up and down.

This light conducts
The thoughts of drunkards, the feelings
Of widows and trembling ladies,
The movements of fishes.

How pleasant an existence it is
That this emerald charms philosophers,
Until they become thoughtlessly willing
To bathe their hearts in later moonlight,

Knowing that they can bring back thought
In the night that is still to be silent,
Reflecting this thing and that,
Before they sleep!

It is better that, as scholars,
They should think hard in the dark cuffs
Of voluminous cloaks,
And shave their heads and bodies.

It might well be that their mistress
Is no gaunt fugitive phantom.
She might, after all, be a wanton,
Abundantly beautiful, eager,

Fecund,
From whose being by starlight, on sea-coast,
The innermost good of their seeking
Might come in the simplest of speech.

It is a good light, then, for those
That know the ultimate Plato,
Tranquillizing with this jewel
The torments of confusion.

The Comedian as the Letter C

I

The World without Imagination

Nota: man is the intelligence of his soil,
The sovereign ghost. As such, the Socrates
Of snails, musician of pears, principium
And lex. Sed quaeritur: is this same wig
Of things, this nincompated pedagogue,
Preceptor to the sea? Crispin at sea
Created, in his day, a touch of doubt.
An eye most apt in gelatines and jupes,
Berries of villages, a barber's eye,
An eye of land, of simple salad-beds,
Of honest quilts, the eye of Crispin, hung
On porpoises, instead of apricots,
And on silentious porpoises, whose snouts
Dibbled in waves that were mustachios,
Inscrutable hair in an inscrutable world.

One eats one paté, even of salt, quotha.
It was not so much the lost terrestrial,
The snug hibernal from that sea and salt,
That century of wind in a single puff.
What counted was mythology of self,
Blotched out beyond unblotching. Crispin,
The lutanist of fleas, the knave, the thane,
The ribboned stick, the bellowing breeches, cloak
Of China, cap of Spain, imperative haw
Of hum, inquisitorial botanist,
And general lexicographer of mute
And maidenly greenhorns, now beheld himself,
A skinny sailor peering in the sea-glass.
What word split up in clickering syllables
And storming under multitudinous tones
Was name for this short-shanks in all that brunt?
Crispin was washed away by magnitude.

The whole of life that still remained in him
Dwindled to one sound strumming in his ear,
Ubiquitous concussion, slap and sigh,
Polyphony beyond his baton's thrust.

Could Crispin stem verboseness in the sea,
The old age of a watery realist,
Triton, dissolved in shifting diaphanes
Of blue and green? A wordy, watery age
That whispered to the sun's compassion, made
A convocation, nightly, of the sea-stars,
And on the clopping foot-ways of the moon
Lay grovelling. Triton incomplicate with that
Which made him Triton, nothing left of him,
Except in faint, memorial gesturings,
That were like arms and shoulders in the waves,
Here, something in the rise and fall of wind
That seemed hallucinating horn, and here,
A sunken voice, both of remembering
And of forgetfulness, in alternate strain.
Just so an ancient Crispin was dissolved.
The valet in the tempest was annulled.
Bordeaux to Yucatan, Havana next,
And then to Carolina. Simple jaunt.
Crispin, merest minuscule in the gales,
Dejected his manner to the turbulence.
The salt hung on his spirit like a frost,
The dead brine melted in him like a dew
Of winter, until nothing of himself
Remained, except some starker, barer self
In a starker, barer world, in which the sun
Was not the sun because it never shone
With bland complaisance on pale parasols,
Beetled, in chapels, on the chaste bouquets.
Against his pipping sounds a trumpet cried
Celestial sneering boisterously. Crispin
Became an introspective voyager.

Here was the veritable ding an sich, at last,
Crispin confronting it, a vocable thing,

But with a speech belched out of hoary darks
Noway resembling his, a visible thing,
And excepting negligible Triton, free
From the unavoidable shadow of himself
That lay elsewhere around him. Severance
Was clear. The last distortion of romance
Forsook the insatiable egotist. The sea
Severs not only lands but also selves.
Here was no help before reality.
Crispin beheld and Crispin was made new.
The imagination, here, could not evade,
In poems of plums, the strict austerity
Of one vast, subjugating, final tone.
The drenching of stale lives no more fell down.
What was this gaudy, gusty panoply?
Out of what swift destruction did it spring?
It was caparison of wind and cloud
And something given to make whole among
The ruses that were shattered by the large.

II

Concerning the Thunderstorms of Yucatan

In Yucatan, the Maya sonneteers
Of the Caribbean amphitheatre,
In spite of hawk and falcon, green toucan
And jay, still to the night-bird made their plea,
As if raspberry tanagers in palms,
High up in orange air, were barbarous.
But Crispin was too destitute to find
In any commonplace the sought-for aid.
He was a man made vivid by the sea,
A man come out of luminous traversing,
Much trumpeted, made desperately clear,
Fresh from discoveries of tidal skies,
To whom oracular rockings gave no rest.
Into a savage color he went on.

How greatly had he grown in his demesne,
This auditor of insects! He that saw
The stride of vanishing autumn in a park
By way of decorous melancholy; he
That wrote his couplet yearly to the spring,
As dissertation of profound delight,
Stopping, on voyage, in a land of snakes,
Found his vicissitudes had much enlarged
His apprehension, made him intricate
In moody rucks, and difficult and strange
In all desires, his destitution's mark.
He was in this as other freemen are,
Sonorous nutshells rattling inwardly.
His violence was for aggrandizement
And not for stupor, such as music makes
For sleepers halfway waking. He perceived
That coolness for his heat came suddenly,
And only, in the fables that he scrawled
With his own quill, in its indigenous dew,
Of an aesthetic tough, diverse, untamed,
Incredible to prudes, the mint of dirt,
Green barbarism turning paradigm.
Crispin foresaw a curious promenade
Or, nobler, sensed an elemental fate,
And elemental potencies and pangs,
And beautiful barenesses as yet unseen,
Making the most of savagery of palms,
Of moonlight on the thick, cadaverous bloom
That yuccas breed, and of the panther's tread.
The fabulous and its intrinsic verse
Came like two spirits parleying, adorned
In radiance from the Atlantic coign,
For Crispin and his quill to catechize.
But they came parleying of such an earth,
So thick with sides and jagged lops of green,
So intertwined with serpent-kin encoiled
Among the purple tufts, the scarlet crowns,
Scenting the jungle in their refuges,
So streaked with yellow, blue and green and red
In beak and bud and fruity gobbet-skins,

That earth was like a jostling festival
Of seeds grown fat, too juicily opulent,
Expanding in the gold's maternal warmth.

So much for that. The affectionate emigrant found
A new reality in parrot-squawks.
Yet let that trifle pass. Now, as this odd
Discoverer walked through the harbor streets
Inspecting the cabildo, the façade
Of the cathedral, making notes, he heard
A rumbling, west of Mexico, it seemed,
Approaching like a gasconade of drums.
The white cabildo darkened, the façade,
As sullen as the sky, was swallowed up
In swift, successive shadows, dolefully.
The rumbling broadened as it fell. The wind,
Tempestuous clarion, with heavy cry,
Came bluntly thundering, more terrible
Than the revenge of music on bassoons.
Gesticulating lightning, mystical,
Made pallid flitter. Crispin, here, took flight.
An annotator has his scruples, too.
He knelt in the cathedral with the rest,
This connoisseur of elemental fate,
Aware of exquisite thought. The storm was one
Of many proclamations of the kind,
Proclaiming something harsher than he learned
From hearing signboards whimper in cold nights
Or seeing the midsummer artifice
Of heat upon his pane. This was the span
Of force, the quintessential fact, the note
Of Vulcan, that a valet seeks to own,
The thing that makes him envious in phrase.

And while the torrent on the roof still droned
He felt the Andean breath. His mind was free
And more than free, elate, intent, profound
And studious of a self possessing him,
That was not in him in the crusty town
From which he sailed. Beyond him, westward, lay
The mountainous ridges, purple balustrades,

In which the thunder, lapsing in its clap,
Let down gigantic quavers of its voice,
For Crispin to vociferate again.

III

Approaching Carolina

The book of moonlight is not written yet
Nor half begun, but, when it is, leave room
For Crispin, fagot in the lunar fire,
Who, in the hubbub of his pilgrimage
Through sweating changes, never could forget
That wakefulness or meditating sleep,
In which the sulky strophes willingly
Bore up, in time, the somnolent, deep songs.
Leave room, therefore, in that unwritten book
For the legendary moonlight that once burned
In Crispin's mind above a continent.
America was always north to him,
A northern west or western north, but north,
And thereby polar, polar-purple, chilled
And lank, rising and slumping from a sea
Of hardy foam, receding flatly, spread
In endless ledges, glittering, submerged
And cold in a boreal mistiness of the moon.
The spring came there in clinking pannicles
Of half-dissolving frost, the summer came,
If ever, whisked and wet, not ripening,
Before the winter's vacancy returned.
The myrtle, if the myrtle ever bloomed,
Was like a glacial pink upon the air.
The green palmettoes in crepuscular ice
Clipped frigidly blue-black meridians,
Morose chiaroscuro, gauntly drawn.

How many poems he denied himself
In his observant progress, lesser things
Than the relentless contact he desired;
How many sea-masks he ignored; what sounds

He shut out from his tempering ear; what thoughts,
Like jades affecting the sequestered bride;
And what descants, he sent to banishment!
Perhaps the Arctic moonlight really gave
The liaison, the blissful liaison,
Between himself and his environment,
Which was, and is, chief motive, first delight,
For him, and not for him alone. It seemed
Illusive, faint, more mist than moon, perverse,
Wrong as a divagation to Peking,
To him that postulated as his theme
The vulgar, as his theme and hymn and flight,
A passionately niggling nightingale.
Moonlight was an evasion, or, if not,
A minor meeting, facile, delicate.

Thus he conceived his voyaging to be
An up and down between two elements,
A fluctuating between sun and moon,
A sally into gold and crimson forms,
As on this voyage, out of goblinry,
And then retirement like a turning back
And sinking down to the indulgences
That in the moonlight have their habitude.
But let these backward lapses, if they would,
Grind their seductions on him, Crispin knew
It was a flourishing tropic he required
For his refreshment, an abundant zone,
Prickly and obdurate, dense, harmonious
Yet with a harmony not rarefied
Nor fined for the inhibited instruments
Of over-civil stops. And thus he tossed
Between a Carolina of old time,
A little juvenile, an ancient whim,
And the visible, circumspect presentment drawn
From what he saw across his vessel's prow.

He came. The poetic hero without palms
Or jugglery, without regalia.
And as he came he saw that it was spring,

A time abhorrent to the nihilist
Or searcher for the fecund minimum.
The moonlight fiction disappeared. The spring,
Although contending featly in its veils,
Irised in dew and early fragrancies,
Was gemmy marionette to him that sought
A sinewy nakedness. A river bore
The vessel inward. Tilting up his nose,
He inhaled the rancid rosin, burly smells
Of dampened lumber, emanations blown
From warehouse doors, the gustiness of ropes,
Decays of sacks, and all the arrant stinks
That helped him round his rude aesthetic out.
He savored rankness like a sensualist.
He marked the marshy ground around the dock,
The crawling railroad spur, the rotten fence,
Curriculum for the marvellous sophomore.
It purified. It made him see how much
Of what he saw he never saw at all.
He gripped more closely the essential prose
As being, in a world so falsified,
The one integrity for him, the one
Discovery still possible to make,
To which all poems were incident, unless
That prose should wear a poem's guise at last.

IV

The Idea of a Colony

Nota: his soil is man's intelligence.
That's better. That's worth crossing seas to find.
Crispin in one laconic phrase laid bare
His cloudy drift and planned a colony.
Exit the mental moonlight, exit lex,
Rex and principium, exit the whole
Shebang. Exeunt omnes. Here was prose
More exquisite than any tumbling verse:
A still new continent in which to dwell.
What was the purpose of his pilgrimage,

Whatever shape it took in Crispin's mind,
If not, when all is said, to drive away
The shadow of his fellows from the skies,
And, from their stale intelligence released,
To make a new intelligence prevail?
Hence the reverberations in the words
Of his first central hymns, the celebrants
Of rankest trivia, tests of the strength
Of his aesthetic, his philosophy,
The more invidious, the more desired.
The florist asking aid from cabbages,
The rich man going bare, the paladin
Afraid, the blind man as astronomer,
The appointed power unwielded from disdain.

His western voyage ended and began.
The torment of fastidious thought grew slack,
Another, still more bellicose, came on.
He, therefore, wrote his prolegomena,
And, being full of the caprice, inscribed
Commingled souvenirs and prophecies.
He made a singular collation. Thus:
The natives of the rain are rainy men.
Although they paint effulgent, azure lakes,
And April hillsides wooded white and pink,
Their azure has a cloudy edge, their white
And pink, the water bright that dogwood bears.
And in their music showering sounds intone.
On what strange froth does the gross Indian dote,
What Eden sapling gum, what honeyed gore,
What pulpy dram distilled of innocence,
That streaking gold should speak in him
Or bask within his images and words?
If these rude instances impeach themselves
By force of rudeness, let the principle
Be plain. For application Crispin strove,
Abhorring Turk as Esquimau, the lute
As the marimba, the magnolia as rose.

Upon these premises propounding, he
Projected a colony that should extend

To the dusk of a whistling south below the south,
A comprehensive island hemisphere.
The man in Georgia waking among pines
Should be pine-spokesman. The responsive man,
Planting his pristine cores in Florida,
Should prick thereof, not on the psaltery,
But on the banjo's categorical gut,
Tuck tuck, while the flamingos flapped his bays.
Sepulchral señors, bibbing pale mescal,
Oblivious to the Aztec almanacs,
Should make the intricate Sierra scan.
And dark Brazilians in their cafés,
Musing immaculate, pampean dits,
Should scrawl a vigilant anthology,
To be their latest, lucent paramour.
These are the broadest instances. Crispin,
Progenitor of such extensive scope,
Was not indifferent to smart detail.
The melon should have apposite ritual,
Performed in verd apparel, and the peach,
When its black branches came to bud, belle day,
Should have an incantation. And again,
When piled on salvers its aroma steeped
The summer, it should have a sacrament
And celebration. Shrewd novitiates
Should be the clerks of our experience.

These bland excursions into time to come,
Related in romance to backward flights,
However prodigal, however proud,
Contained in their afflatus the reproach
That first drove Crispin to his wandering.
He could not be content with counterfeit,
With masquerade of thought, with hapless words
That must belie the racking masquerade,
With fictive flourishes that preordained
His passion's permit, hang of coat, degree
Of buttons, measure of his salt. Such trash
Might help the blind, not him, serenely sly.
It irked beyond his patience. Hence it was,

Preferring text to gloss, he humbly served
Grotesque apprenticeship to chance event,
A clown, perhaps, but an aspiring clown.
There is a monotonous babbling in our dreams
That makes them our dependent heirs, the heirs
Of dreamers buried in our sleep, and not
The oncoming fantasies of better birth.
The apprentice knew these dreamers. If he dreamed
Their dreams, he did it in a gingerly way.
All dreams are vexing. Let them be expunged.
But let the rabbit run, the cock declaim.

Trinket pasticcio, flaunting skyey sheets,
With Crispin as the tiptoe cozener?
No, no: veracious page on page, exact.

V

A Nice Shady Home

Crispin as hermit, pure and capable,
Dwelt in the land. Perhaps if discontent
Had kept him still the pricking realist,
Choosing his element from droll confect
Of was and is and shall or ought to be,
Beyond Bordeaux, beyond Havana, far
Beyond carked Yucatan, he might have come
To colonize his polar planterdom
And jig his chits upon a cloudy knee.
But his emprize to that idea soon sped.
Crispin dwelt in the land and dwelling there
Slid from his continent by slow recess
To things within his actual eye, alert
To the difficulty of rebellious thought
When the sky is blue. The blue infected will.
It may be that the yarrow in his fields
Sealed pensive purple under its concern.
But day by day, now this thing and now that

Confined him, while it cosseted, condoned,
Little by little, as if the suzerain soil
Abashed him by carouse to humble yet
Attach. It seemed haphazard denouement.
He first, as realist, admitted that
Whoever hunts a matinal continent
May, after all, stop short before a plum
And be content and still be realist.
The words of things entangle and confuse.
The plum survives its poems. It may hang
In the sunshine placidly, colored by ground
Obliquities of those who pass beneath,
Harlequined and mazily dewed and mauved
In bloom. Yet it survives in its own form,
Beyond these changes, good, fat, guzzly fruit.
So Crispin hasped on the surviving form,
For him, of shall or ought to be in is.

Was he to bray this in profoundest brass
Arointing his dreams with fugal requiems?
Was he to company vastest things defunct
With a blubber of tom-toms harrowing the sky?
Scrawl a tragedian's testament? Prolong
His active force in an inactive dirge,
Which, let the tall musicians call and call,
Should merely call him dead? Pronounce amen
Through choirs infolded to the outmost clouds?
Because he built a cabin who once planned
Loquacious columns by the ructive sea?
Because he turned to salad-beds again?
Jovial Crispin, in calamitous crape?
Should he lay by the personal and make
Of his own fate an instance of all fate?
What is one man among so many men?
What are so many men in such a world?
Can one man think one thing and think it long?
Can one man be one thing and be it long?
The very man despising honest quilts
Lies quilted to his poll in his despite.
For realists, what is is what should be.

And so it came, his cabin shuffled up,
His trees were planted, his duenna brought
Her prismy blonde and clapped her in his hands,
The curtains flittered and the door was closed.
Crispin, magister of a single room,
Latched up the night. So deep a sound fell down
It was as if the solitude concealed
And covered him and his congenial sleep.
So deep a sound fell down it grew to be
A long soothsaying silence down and down.
The crickets beat their tambours in the wind,
Marching a motionless march, custodians.

In the presto of the morning, Crispin trod,
Each day, still curious, but in a round
Less prickly and much more condign than that
He once thought necessary. Like Candide,
Yeoman and grub, but with a fig in sight,
And cream for the fig and silver for the cream,
A blonde to tip the silver and to taste
The rapey gouts. Good star, how that to be
Annealed them in their cabin ribaldries!
Yet the quotidian saps philosophers
And men like Crispin like them in intent,
If not in will, to track the knaves of thought.
But the quotidian composed as his,
Of breakfast ribands, fruits laid in their leaves,
The tomtit and the cassia and the rose,
Although the rose was not the noble thorn
Of crinoline spread, but of a pining sweet,
Composed of evenings like cracked shutters flung
Upon the rumpling bottomness, and nights
In which those frail custodians watched,
Indifferent to the tepid summer cold,
While he poured out upon the lips of her
That lay beside him, the quotidian
Like this, saps like the sun, true fortuner.
For all it takes it gives a humped return
Exchequering from piebald fiscs unkeyed.

VI

And Daughters with Curls

Portentous enunciation, syllable
To blessed syllable affined, and sound
Bubbling felicity in cantilene,
Prolific and tormenting tenderness
Of music, as it comes to unison,
Forgather and bell boldly Crispin's last
Deduction. Thrum with a proud douceur
His grand pronunciamento and devise.

The chits came for his jigging, bluet-eyed,
Hands without touch yet touching poignantly,
Leaving no room upon his cloudy knee,
Prophetic joint, for its diviner young.
The return to social nature, once begun,
Anabasis or slump, ascent or chute,
Involved him in midwifery so dense
His cabin counted as phylactery,
Then place of vexing palankeens, then haunt
Of children nibbling at the sugared void,
Infants yet eminently old, then dome
And halidom for the unbraided femes,
Green crammers of the green fruits of the world,
Bidders and biders for its ecstasies,
True daughters both of Crispin and his clay.
All this with many mulctings of the man,
Effective colonizer sharply stopped
In the door-yard by his own capacious bloom.
But that this bloom grown riper, showing nibs
Of its eventual roundness, puerile tints
Of spiced and weathery rouges, should complex
The stopper to indulgent fatalist
Was unforeseen. First Crispin smiled upon
His goldenest demoiselle, inhabitant,
She seemed, of a country of the capuchins,
So delicately blushed, so humbly eyed,
Attentive to a coronal of things

Secret and singular. Second, upon
A second similar counterpart, a maid
Most sisterly to the first, not yet awake
Excepting to the motherly footstep, but
Marvelling sometimes at the shaken sleep.
Then third, a thing still flaxen in the light,
A creeper under jaunty leaves. And fourth,
Mere blusteriness that gewgaws jollified,
All din and gobble, blasphemously pink.
A few years more and the vermeil capuchin
Gave to the cabin, lordlier than it was,
The dulcet omen fit for such a house.
The second sister dallying was shy
To fetch the one full-pinioned one himself
Out of her botches, hot embosomer.
The third one gaping at the orioles
Lettered herself demurely as became
A pearly poetess, peaked for rhapsody.
The fourth, pent now, a digit curious.
Four daughters in a world too intricate
In the beginning, four blithe instruments
Of differing struts, four voices several
In couch, four more personæ, intimate
As buffo, yet divers, four mirrors blue
That should be silver, four accustomed seeds
Hinting incredible hues, four self-same lights
That spread chromatics in hilarious dark,
Four questioners and four sure answerers.

Crispin concocted doctrine from the rout.
The world, a turnip once so readily plucked,
Sacked up and carried overseas, daubed out
Of its ancient purple, pruned to the fertile main,
And sown again by the stiffest realist,
Came reproduced in purple, family font,
The same insoluble lump. The fatalist
Stepped in and dropped the chuckling down his craw,
Without grace or grumble. Score this anecdote
Invented for its pith, not doctrinal

In form though in design, as Crispin willed,
Disguised pronunciamento, summary,
Autumn's compendium, strident in itself
But muted, mused, and perfectly revolved
In those portentous accents, syllables,
And sounds of music coming to accord
Upon his law, like their inherent sphere,
Seraphic proclamations of the pure
Delivered with a deluging onwardness.
Or if the music sticks, if the anecdote
Is false, if Crispin is a profitless
Philosopher, beginning with green brag,
Concluding fadedly, if as a man
Prone to distemper he abates in taste,
Fickle and fumbling, variable, obscure,
Glozing his life with after-shining flicks,
Illuminating, from a fancy gorged
By apparition, plain and common things,
Sequestering the fluster from the year,
Making gulped potions from obstreperous drops,
And so distorting, proving what he proves
Is nothing, what can all this matter since
The relation comes, benignly, to its end?

So may the relation of each man be clipped.

From the Misery of Don Joost

I have finished my combat with the sun;
And my body, the old animal,
Knows nothing more.

The powerful seasons bred and killed,
And were themselves the genii
Of their own ends.

Oh, but the very self of the storm
Of sun and slaves, breeding and death,
The old animal,

The senses and feeling, the very sound
And sight, and all there was of the storm,
Knows nothing more.

O, Florida, Venereal Soil

A few things for themselves,
Convolvulus and coral,
Buzzards and live-moss,
Tiestas from the keys,
A few things for themselves,
Florida, venereal soil,
Disclose to the lover.

The dreadful sundry of this world,
The Cuban, Polodowsky,
The Mexican women,
The negro undertaker
Killing the time between corpses
Fishing for crayfish . . .
Virgin of boorish births,

Swiftly in the nights,
In the porches of Key West,
Behind the bougainvilleas,
After the guitar is asleep,
Lasciviously as the wind,
You come tormenting,
Insatiable,

When you might sit,
A scholar of darkness,
Sequestered over the sea,
Wearing a clear tiara

Of red and blue and red,
Sparkling, solitary, still,
In the high sea-shadow.

Donna, donna, dark,
Stooping in indigo gown
And cloudy constellations,
Conceal yourself or disclose
Fewest things to the lover—
A hand that bears a thick-leaved fruit,
A pungent bloom against your shade.

Last Looks at the Lilacs

To what good, in the alleys of the lilacs,
O caliper, do you scratch your buttocks
And tell the divine ingénue, your companion,
That this bloom is the bloom of soap
And this fragrance the fragrance of vegetal?

Do you suppose that she cares a tick,
In this hymeneal air, what it is
That marries her innocence thus,
So that her nakedness is near,
Or that she will pause at scurrilous words?

Poor buffo! Look at the lavender
And look your last and look still steadily,
And say how it comes that you see
Nothing but trash and that you no longer feel
Her body quivering in the Floréal

Toward the cool night and its fantastic star,
Prime paramour and belted paragon,
Well-booted, rugged, arrogantly male,
Patron and imager of the gold Don John,
Who will embrace her before summer comes.

The Worms at Heaven's Gate

Out of the tomb, we bring Badroulbadour,
Within our bellies, we her chariot.
Here is an eye. And here are, one by one,
The lashes of that eye and its white lid.
Here is the cheek on which that lid declined,
And, finger after finger, here, the hand,
The genius of that cheek. Here are the lips,
The bundle of the body and the feet.

　　　　·　　·　　·　　·　　·　　·　　·

Out of the tomb we bring Badroulbadour.

The Jack-Rabbit

In the morning,
The jack-rabbit sang to the Arkansaw.
He carolled in caracoles
On the feat sandbars.

The black man said,
"Now, grandmother,
Crochet me this buzzard
On your winding-sheet,
And do not forget his wry neck
After the winter."

The black man said,
"Look out, O caroller,
The entrails of the buzzard
Are rattling."

Valley Candle

My candle burned alone in an immense valley.
Beams of the huge night converged upon it,
Until the wind blew.
Then beams of the huge night
Converged upon its image,
Until the wind blew.

Anecdote of Men by the Thousand

The soul, he said, is composed
Of the external world.

There are men of the East, he said,
Who are the East.
There are men of a province
Who are that province.
There are men of a valley
Who are that valley.

There are men whose words
Are as natural sounds
Of their places
As the cackle of toucans
In the place of toucans.

The mandoline is the instrument
Of a place.

Are there mandolines of western mountains?
Are there mandolines of northern moonlight?

The dress of a woman of Lhassa,
In its place,
Is an invisible element of that place
Made visible.

The Silver Plough-Boy

A black figure dances in a black field.
It seizes a sheet, from the ground, from a bush, as if spread
  there by some wash-woman for the night.
It wraps the sheet around its body, until the black figure is
  silver.
It dances down a furrow, in the early light, back of a crazy
  plough, the green blades following.
How soon the silver fades in the dust! How soon the black
  figure slips from the wrinkled sheet! How softly the
  sheet falls to the ground!

The Apostrophe to Vincentine

I

I figured you as nude between
Monotonous earth and dark blue sky.
It made you seem so small and lean
And nameless,
Heavenly Vincentine.

II

I saw you then, as warm as flesh,
Brunette,
But yet not too brunette,
As warm, as clean.
Your dress was green,
Was whited green,
Green Vincentine.

III

Then you came walking,
In a group
Of human others,
Voluble.

Yes: you came walking,
Vincentine.
Yes: you came talking.

IV

And what I knew you felt
Came then.
Monotonous earth I saw become
Illimitable spheres of you,
And that white animal, so lean,
Turned Vincentine,
Turned heavenly Vincentine,
And that white animal, so lean,
Turned heavenly, heavenly Vincentine.

Floral Decorations for Bananas

Well, nuncle, this plainly won't do.
These insolent, linear peels
And sullen, hurricane shapes
Won't do with your eglantine.
They require something serpentine.
Blunt yellow in such a room!

You should have had plums tonight,
In an eighteenth-century dish,
And pettifogging buds,
For the women of primrose and purl,
Each one in her decent curl.
Good God! What a precious light!

But bananas hacked and hunched . . .
The table was set by an ogre,
His eye on an outdoor gloom
And a stiff and noxious place.
Pile the bananas on planks.
The women will be all shanks
And bangles and slatted eyes.

And deck the bananas in leaves
Plucked from the Carib trees,
Fibrous and dangling down,
Oozing cantankerous gum
Out of their purple maws,
Darting out of their purple craws
Their musky and tingling tongues.

Anecdote of Canna

Huge are the canna in the dreams of
X, the mighty thought, the mighty man.
They fill the terrace of his capitol.

His thought sleeps not. Yet thought that wakes
In sleep may never meet another thought
Or thing. . . . Now day-break comes. . . .

X promenades the dewy stones,
Observes the canna with a clinging eye,
Observes and then continues to observe.

Of the Manner of Addressing Clouds

Gloomy grammarians in golden gowns,
Meekly you keep the mortal rendezvous,
Eliciting the still sustaining pomps
Of speech which are like music so profound
They seem an exaltation without sound.
Funest philosophers and ponderers,
Their evocations are the speech of clouds.
So speech of your processionals returns
In the casual evocations of your tread
Across the stale, mysterious seasons. These
Are the music of meet resignation; these

The responsive, still sustaining pomps for you
To magnify, if in that drifting waste
You are to be accompanied by more
Than mute bare splendors of the sun and moon.

Of Heaven Considered as a Tomb

What word have you, interpreters, of men
Who in the tomb of heaven walk by night,
The darkened ghosts of our old comedy?
Do they believe they range the gusty cold,
With lanterns borne aloft to light the way,
Freemen of death, about and still about
To find whatever it is they seek? Or does
That burial, pillared up each day as porte
And spiritous passage into nothingness,
Foretell each night the one abysmal night,
When the host shall no more wander, nor the light
Of the steadfast lanterns creep across the dark?
Make hue among the dark comedians,
Halloo them in the topmost distances
For answer from their icy Elysée.

Of the Surface of Things

I

In my room, the world is beyond my understanding;
But when I walk I see that it consists of three or four
    hills and a cloud.

II

From my balcony, I survey the yellow air,
Reading where I have written,
"The spring is like a belle undressing."

III

The gold tree is blue.
The singer has pulled his cloak over his head.
The moon is in the folds of the cloak.

Anecdote of the Prince of Peacocks

In the moonlight
I met Berserk,
In the moonlight
On the bushy plain.
Oh, sharp he was
As the sleepless!

And, "Why are you red
In this milky blue?"
I said.
"Why sun-colored,
As if awake
In the midst of sleep?"

"You that wander,"
So he said,
"On the bushy plain,
Forget so soon.
But I set my traps
In the midst of dreams."

I knew from this
That the blue ground
Was full of blocks
And blocking steel.
I knew the dread
Of the bushy plain,

And the beauty
Of the moonlight
Falling there,
Falling
As sleep falls
In the innocent air.

A High-Toned Old Christian Woman

Poetry is the supreme fiction, madame.
Take the moral law and make a nave of it
And from the nave build haunted heaven. Thus,
The conscience is converted into palms,
Like windy citherns hankering for hymns.
We agree in principle. That's clear. But take
The opposing law and make a peristyle,
And from the peristyle project a masque
Beyond the planets. Thus, our bawdiness,
Unpurged by epitaph, indulged at last,
Is equally converted into palms,
Squiggling like saxophones. And palm for palm,
Madame, we are where we began. Allow,
Therefore, that in the planetary scene
Your disaffected flagellants, well-stuffed,
Smacking their muzzy bellies in parade,
Proud of such novelties of the sublime,
Such tink and tank and tunk-a-tunk-tunk,
May, merely may, madame, whip from themselves
A jovial hullabaloo among the spheres.
This will make widows wince. But fictive things
Wink as they will. Wink most when widows wince.

The Place of the Solitaires

Let the place of the solitaires
Be a place of perpetual undulation.

Whether it be in mid-sea
On the dark, green water-wheel,
Or on the beaches,
There must be no cessation
Of motion, or of the noise of motion,
The renewal of noise
And manifold continuation;

And, most, of the motion of thought
And its restless iteration,

In the place of the solitaires,
Which is to be a place of perpetual undulation.

The Weeping Burgher

It is with a strange malice
That I distort the world.

Ah! that ill humors
Should mask as white girls.
And ah! that Scaramouche
Should have a black barouche.

The sorry verities!
Yet in excess, continual,
There is cure of sorrow.

Permit that if as ghost I come
Among the people burning in me still,
I come as belle design
Of foppish line.

And I, then, tortured for old speech,
A white of wildly woven rings;
I, weeping in a calcined heart,
My hands such sharp, imagined things.

The Curtains in the House
of the Metaphysician

It comes about that the drifting of these curtains
Is full of long motions; as the ponderous
Deflations of distance; or as clouds
Inseparable from their afternoons;
Or the changing of light, the dropping
Of the silence, wide sleep and solitude
Of night, in which all motion
Is beyond us, as the firmament,
Up-rising and down-falling, bares
The last largeness, bold to see.

Banal Sojourn

Two wooden tubs of blue hydrangeas stand at the foot of
    the stone steps.
The sky is a blue gum streaked with rose. The trees are
    black.
The grackles crack their throats of bone in the smooth air.
Moisture and heat have swollen the garden into a slum of
    bloom.
Pardie! Summer is like a fat beast, sleepy in mildew,
Our old bane, green and bloated, serene, who cries,
"That bliss of stars, that princox of evening heaven!"
    reminding of seasons,
When radiance came running down, slim through the
    bareness.
And so it is one damns that green shade at the bottom of
    the land.
For who can care at the wigs despoiling the Satan ear?
And who does not seek the sky unfuzzed, soaring to the
    princox?
One has a malady, here, a malady. One feels a malady.

Depression Before Spring

The cock crows
But no queen rises.

The hair of my blonde
Is dazzling,
As the spittle of cows
Threading the wind.

Ho! Ho!

But ki-ki-ri-ki
Brings no rou-cou,
No rou-cou-cou.

But no queen comes
In slipper green.

The Emperor of Ice-Cream

Call the roller of big cigars,
The muscular one, and bid him whip
In kitchen cups concupiscent curds.
Let the wenches dawdle in such dress
As they are used to wear, and let the boys
Bring flowers in last month's newspapers.
Let be be finale of seem.
The only emperor is the emperor of ice-cream.

Take from the dresser of deal,
Lacking the three glass knobs, that sheet
On which she embroidered fantails once
And spread it so as to cover her face.
If her horny feet protrude, they come
To show how cold she is, and dumb.
Let the lamp affix its beam.
The only emperor is the emperor of ice-cream.

The Cuban Doctor

I went to Egypt to escape
The Indian, but the Indian struck
Out of his cloud and from his sky.

This was no worm bred in the moon,
Wriggling far down the phantom air,
And on a comfortable sofa dreamed.

The Indian struck and disappeared.
I knew my enemy was near—I,
Drowsing in summer's sleepiest horn.

Tea at the Palaz of Hoon

Not less because in purple I descended
The western day through what you called
The loneliest air, not less was I myself.

What was the ointment sprinkled on my beard?
What were the hymns that buzzed beside my ears?
What was the sea whose tide swept through me there?

Out of my mind the golden ointment rained,
And my ears made the blowing hymns they heard.
I was myself the compass of that sea:

I was the world in which I walked, and what I saw
Or heard or felt came not but from myself;
And there I found myself more truly and more strange.

Exposition of the Contents of a Cab

Victoria Clementina, negress,
Took seven white dogs
To ride in a cab.

Bells of the dogs chinked.
Harness of the horses shuffled
Like brazen shells.

Oh-hé-hé! Fragrant puppets
By the green lake-pallors,
She too is flesh,

And a breech-cloth might wear,
Netted of topaz and ruby
And savage blooms;

Thridding the squawkiest jungle
In a golden sedan,
White dogs at bay.

What breech-cloth might you wear,
Except linen, embroidered
By elderly women?

Disillusionment of Ten O'Clock

The houses are haunted
By white night-gowns.
None are green,
Or purple with green rings,
Or green with yellow rings,
Or yellow with blue rings.
None of them are strange,
With socks of lace
And beaded ceintures.
People are not going

To dream of baboons and periwinkles.
Only, here and there, an old sailor,
Drunk and asleep in his boots,
Catches tigers
In red weather.

Sunday Morning

I

Complacencies of the peignoir, and late
Coffee and oranges in a sunny chair,
And the green freedom of a cockatoo
Upon a rug mingle to dissipate
The holy hush of ancient sacrifice.
She dreams a little, and she feels the dark
Encroachment of that old catastrophe,
As a calm darkens among water-lights.
The pungent oranges and bright, green wings
Seem things in some procession of the dead,
Winding across wide water, without sound.
The day is like wide water, without sound,
Stilled for the passing of her dreaming feet
Over the seas, to silent Palestine,
Dominion of the blood and sepulchre.

II

Why should she give her bounty to the dead?
What is divinity if it can come
Only in silent shadows and in dreams?
Shall she not find in comforts of the sun,
In pungent fruit and bright, green wings, or else
In any balm or beauty of the earth,
Things to be cherished like the thought of heaven?
Divinity must live within herself:
Passions of rain, or moods in falling snow;
Grievings in loneliness, or unsubdued
Elations when the forest blooms; gusty

Emotions on wet roads on autumn nights;
All pleasures and all pains, remembering
The bough of summer and the winter branch.
These are the measures destined for her soul.

III

Jove in the clouds had his inhuman birth.
No mother suckled him, no sweet land gave
Large-mannered motions to his mythy mind.
He moved among us, as a muttering king,
Magnificent, would move among his hinds,
Until our blood, commingling, virginal,
With heaven, brought such requital to desire
The very hinds discerned it, in a star.
Shall our blood fail? Or shall it come to be
The blood of paradise? And shall the earth
Seem all of paradise that we shall know?
The sky will be much friendlier then than now,
A part of labor and a part of pain,
And next in glory to enduring love,
Not this dividing and indifferent blue.

IV

She says, "I am content when wakened birds,
Before they fly, test the reality
Of misty fields, by their sweet questionings;
But when the birds are gone, and their warm fields
Return no more, where, then, is paradise?"
There is not any haunt of prophesy,
Nor any old chimera of the grave,
Neither the golden underground, nor isle
Melodious, where spirits gat them home,
Nor visionary south, nor cloudy palm
Remote on heaven's hill, that has endured
As April's green endures; or will endure
Like her remembrance of awakened birds,
Or her desire for June and evening, tipped
By the consummation of the swallow's wings.

V

She says, "But in contentment I still feel
The need of some imperishable bliss."
Death is the mother of beauty; hence from her,
Alone, shall come fulfilment to our dreams
And our desires. Although she strews the leaves
Of sure obliteration on our paths,
The path sick sorrow took, the many paths
Where triumph rang its brassy phrase, or love
Whispered a little out of tenderness,
She makes the willow shiver in the sun
For maidens who were wont to sit and gaze
Upon the grass, relinquished to their feet.
She causes boys to pile new plums and pears
On disregarded plate. The maidens taste
And stray impassioned in the littering leaves.

VI

Is there no change of death in paradise?
Does ripe fruit never fall? Or do the boughs
Hang always heavy in that perfect sky,
Unchanging, yet so like our perishing earth,
With rivers like our own that seek for seas
They never find, the same receding shores
That never touch with inarticulate pang?
Why set the pear upon those river-banks
Or spice the shores with odors of the plum?
Alas, that they should wear our colors there,
The silken weavings of our afternoons,
And pick the strings of our insipid lutes!
Death is the mother of beauty, mystical,
Within whose burning bosom we devise
Our earthly mothers waiting, sleeplessly.

VII

Supple and turbulent, a ring of men
Shall chant in orgy on a summer morn

Their boisterous devotion to the sun,
Not as a god, but as a god might be,
Naked among them, like a savage source.
Their chant shall be a chant of paradise,
Out of their blood, returning to the sky;
And in their chant shall enter, voice by voice,
The windy lake wherein their lord delights,
The trees, like serafin, and echoing hills,
That choir among themselves long afterward.
They shall know well the heavenly fellowship
Of men that perish and of summer morn.
And whence they came and whither they shall go
The dew upon their feet shall manifest.

VIII

She hears, upon that water without sound,
A voice that cries, "The tomb in Palestine
Is not the porch of spirits lingering.
It is the grave of Jesus, where he lay."
We live in an old chaos of the sun,
Or old dependency of day and night,
Or island solitude, unsponsored, free,
Of that wide water, inescapable.
Deer walk upon our mountains, and the quail
Whistle about us their spontaneous cries;
Sweet berries ripen in the wilderness;
And, in the isolation of the sky,
At evening, casual flocks of pigeons make
Ambiguous undulations as they sink,
Downward to darkness, on extended wings.

The Virgin Carrying a Lantern

There are no bears among the roses,
Only a negress who supposes
Things false and wrong

About the lantern of the beauty
Who walks, there, as a farewell duty,
Walks long and long.

The pity that her pious egress
Should fill the vigil of a negress
With heat so strong!

Stars at Tallapoosa

The lines are straight and swift between the stars.
The night is not the cradle that they cry,
The criers, undulating the deep-oceaned phrase.
The lines are much too dark and much too sharp.

The mind herein attains simplicity,
There is no moon, no single, silvered leaf.
The body is no body to be seen
But is an eye that studies its black lid.

Let these be your delight, secretive hunter,
Wading the sea-lines, moist and ever-mingling,
Mounting the earth-lines, long and lax, lethargic.
These lines are swift and fall without diverging.

The melon-flower nor dew nor web of either
Is like to these. But in yourself is like:
A sheaf of brilliant arrows flying straight,
Flying and falling straightway for their pleasure,

Their pleasure that is all bright-edged and cold;
Or, if not arrows, then the nimblest motions,
Making recoveries of young nakedness
And the lost vehemence the midnights hold.

Explanation

Ach, Mutter,
This old, black dress,
I have been embroidering
French flowers on it.

Not by way of romance,
Here is nothing of the ideal,
Nein,
Nein.

It would have been different,
Liebchen,
If I had imagined myself,
In an orange gown,
Drifting through space,
Like a figure on the church-wall.

Six Significant Landscapes

I

An old man sits
In the shadow of a pine tree
In China.
He sees larkspur,
Blue and white,
At the edge of the shadow,
Move in the wind.
His beard moves in the wind.
The pine tree moves in the wind.
Thus water flows
Over weeds.

II

The night is of the color
Of a woman's arm:

Night, the female,
Obscure,
Fragrant and supple,
Conceals herself.
A pool shines,
Like a bracelet
Shaken in a dance.

III

I measure myself
Against a tall tree.
I find that I am much taller,
For I reach right up to the sun,
With my eye;
And I reach to the shore of the sea
With my ear.
Nevertheless, I dislike
The way the ants crawl
In and out of my shadow.

IV

When my dream was near the moon,
The white folds of its gown
Filled with yellow light.
The soles of its feet
Grew red.
Its hair filled
With certain blue crystallizations
From stars,
Not far off.

V

Not all the knives of the lamp-posts,
Nor the chisels of the long streets,
Nor the mallets of the domes
And high towers,
Can carve
What one star can carve,
Shining through the grape-leaves.

VI

Rationalists, wearing square hats,
Think, in square rooms,
Looking at the floor,
Looking at the ceiling.
They confine themselves
To right-angled triangles.
If they tried rhomboids,
Cones, waving lines, ellipses—
As for example, the ellipse of the half-moon—
Rationalists would wear sombreros.

Bantams in Pine-Woods

Chieftain Iffucan of Azcan in caftan
Of tan with henna hackles, halt!

Damned universal cock, as if the sun
Was blackamoor to bear your blazing tail.

Fat! Fat! Fat! Fat! I am the personal.
Your world is you. I am my world.

You ten-foot poet among inchlings. Fat!
Begone! An inchling bristles in these pines,

Bristles, and points their Appalachian tangs,
And fears not portly Azcan nor his hoos.

Anecdote of the Jar

I placed a jar in Tennessee,
And round it was, upon a hill.
It made the slovenly wilderness
Surround that hill.

The wilderness rose up to it,
And sprawled around, no longer wild.
The jar was round upon the ground
And tall and of a port in air.

It took dominion everywhere.
The jar was gray and bare.
It did not give of bird or bush,
Like nothing else in Tennessee.

Palace of the Babies

The disbeliever walked the moonlit place,
Outside of gates of hammered serafin,
Observing the moon-blotches on the walls.

The yellow rocked across the still façades,
Or else sat spinning on the pinnacles,
While he imagined humming sounds and sleep.

The walker in the moonlight walked alone,
And each blank window of the building balked
His loneliness and what was in his mind:

If in a shimmering room the babies came,
Drawn close by dreams of fledgling wing,
It was because night nursed them in its fold.

Night nursed not him in whose dark mind
The clambering wings of birds of black revolved,
Making harsh torment of the solitude.

The walker in the moonlight walked alone,
And in his heart his disbelief lay cold.
His broad-brimmed hat came close upon his eyes.

Frogs Eat Butterflies. Snakes Eat Frogs.
Hogs Eat Snakes. Men Eat Hogs

It is true that the rivers went nosing like swine,
Tugging at banks, until they seemed
Bland belly-sounds in somnolent troughs,

That the air was heavy with the breath of these swine,
The breath of turgid summer, and
Heavy with thunder's rattapallax,

That the man who erected this cabin, planted
This field, and tended it awhile,
Knew not the quirks of imagery,

That the hours of his indolent, arid days,
Grotesque with this nosing in banks,
This somnolence and rattapallax,

Seemed to suckle themselves on his arid being,
As the swine-like rivers suckled themselves
While they went seaward to the sea-mouths.

Jasmine's Beautiful Thoughts
Underneath the Willow

My titillations have no foot-notes
And their memorials are the phrases
Of idiosyncratic music.

The love that will not be transported
In an old, frizzled, flambeaued manner,
But muses on its eccentricity,

Is like a vivid apprehension
Of bliss beyond the mutes of plaster,
Or paper souvenirs of rapture,

Of bliss submerged beneath appearance,
In an interior ocean's rocking
Of long, capricious fugues and chorals.

Cortège for Rosenbloom

Now, the wry Rosenbloom is dead
And his finical carriers tread,
On a hundred legs, the tread
Of the dead.
Rosenbloom is dead.

They carry the wizened one
Of the color of horn
To the sullen hill,
Treading a tread
In unison for the dead.

Rosenbloom is dead.
The tread of the carriers does not halt
On the hill, but turns
Up the sky.
They are bearing his body into the sky.

It is the infants of misanthropes
And the infants of nothingness
That tread
The wooden ascents
Of the ascending of the dead.

It is turbans they wear
And boots of fur
As they tread the boards
In a region of frost,
Viewing the frost.

To a chirr of gongs
And a chitter of cries
And the heavy thrum
Of the endless tread
That they tread.

To a jangle of doom
And a jumble of words
Of the intense poem
Of the strictest prose
Of Rosenbloom.

And they bury him there,
Body and soul,
In a place in the sky.
The lamentable tread!
Rosenbloom is dead.

Tattoo

The light is like a spider.
It crawls over the water.
It crawls over the edges of the snow.
It crawls under your eyelids
And spreads its webs there—
Its two webs.

The webs of your eyes
Are fastened
To the flesh and bones of you
As to rafters or grass.

There are filaments of your eyes
On the surface of the water
And in the edges of the snow.

The Bird with the Coppery, Keen Claws

Above the forest of the parakeets,
A parakeet of parakeets prevails,
A pip of life amid a mort of tails.

(The rudiments of tropics are around,
Aloe of ivory, pear of rusty rind.)
His lids are white because his eyes are blind.

He is not paradise of parakeets,
Of his gold ether, golden alguazil.
Except because he broods there and is still,

Panache upon panache, his tails deploy
Upward and outward, in green-vented forms,
His tip a drop of water full of storms.

But though the turbulent tinges undulate
As his pure intellect applies its laws,
He moves not on his coppery, keen claws.

He munches a dry shell while he exerts
His will, yet never ceases, perfect cock,
To flare, in the sun-pallor of his rock.

Life Is Motion

In Oklahoma,
Bonnie and Josie,
Dressed in calico,
Danced around a stump.
They cried,
"Ohoyaho,
Ohoo" . . .
Celebrating the marriage
Of flesh and air.

Architecture

I

What manner of building shall we build?
Let us design a chastel de chasteté.
De pensée. . . .
Never cease to deploy the structure.
Keep the laborers shouldering plinths.
Pass the whole of life earing the clink of the
Chisels of the stone-cutters cutting the stones.

II

In this house, what manner of utterance shall there be?
What heavenly dithyramb
And cantilene?
What niggling forms of gargoyle patter?
Of what shall the speech be,
In that splay of marble
And of obedient pillars?

III

And how shall those come vested that come there?
In their ugly reminders?
Or gaudy as tulips?
As they climb the stairs
To the group of Flora Coddling Hecuba?
As they climb the flights
To the closes
Overlooking whole seasons?

IV

Let us build the building of light.
Push up the towers
To the cock-tops.
These are the pointings of our edifice,
Which, like a gorgeous palm,

Shall tuft the commonplace.
These are the window-sill
On which the quiet moonlight lies.

V

How shall we hew the sun,
Split it and make blocks,
To build a ruddy palace?
How carve the violet moon
To set in nicks?
Let us fix portals, east and west,
Abhorring green-blue north and blue-green south.
Our chiefest dome a demoiselle of gold.
Pierce the interior with pouring shafts,
In diverse chambers.
Pierce, too, with buttresses of coral air
And purple timbers,
Various argentines,
Embossings of the sky.

VI

And, finally, set guardians in the grounds,
Gray, gruesome grumblers.
For no one proud, nor stiff,
No solemn one, nor pale,
No chafferer, may come
To sully the begonias, nor vex
With holy or sublime ado
The kremlin of kermess.

VII

Only the lusty and the plenteous
Shall walk
The bronze-filled plazas
And the nut-shell esplanades.

The Wind Shifts

This is how the wind shifts:
Like the thoughts of an old human,
Who still thinks eagerly
And despairingly.
The wind shifts like this:
Like a human without illusions,
Who still feels irrational things within her.
The wind shifts like this:
Like humans approaching proudly,
Like humans approaching angrily.
This is how the wind shifts:
Like a human, heavy and heavy,
Who does not care.

Colloquy with a Polish Aunt

*Elle savait toutes les légendes du Paradis et tous les contes
de la Pologne.*   *Revue des Deux Mondes*

She

How is it that my saints from Voragine,
In their embroidered slippers, touch your spleen?

He

Old pantaloons, duenna of the spring!

She

Imagination is the will of things. . . .
Thus, on the basis of the common drudge,
You dream of women, swathed in indigo,
Holding their books toward the nearer stars,
To read, in secret, burning secrecies. . . .

Gubbinal

That strange flower, the sun,
Is just what you say.
Have it your way.

The world is ugly,
And the people are sad.

That tuft of jungle feathers,
That animal eye,
Is just what you say.

That savage of fire,
That seed,
Have it your way.

The world is ugly,
And the people are sad.

Two Figures in Dense Violet Night

I had as lief be embraced by the porter at the hotel
As to get no more from the moonlight
Than your moist hand.

Be the voice of night and Florida in my ear.
Use dusky words and dusky images.
Darken your speech.

Speak, even, as if I did not hear you speaking,
But spoke for you perfectly in my thoughts,
Conceiving words,

As the night conceives the sea-sounds in silence,
And out of their droning sibilants makes
A serenade.

Say, puerile, that the buzzards crouch on the ridge-pole
And sleep with one eye watching the stars fall
Below Key West.

Say that the palms are clear in a total blue,
Are clear and are obscure; that it is night;
That the moon shines.

Theory

I am what is around me.

Women understand this.
One is not duchess
A hundred yards from a carriage.

These, then are portraits:
A black vestibule;
A high bed sheltered by curtains.

These are merely instances.

To the One of Fictive Music

Sister and mother and diviner love,
And of the sisterhood of the living dead
Most near, most clear, and of the clearest bloom,
And of the fragrant mothers the most dear
And queen, and of diviner love the day
And flame and summer and sweet fire, no thread
Of cloudy silver sprinkles in your gown
Its venom of renown, and on your head
No crown is simpler than the simple hair.

Now, of the music summoned by the birth
That separates us from the wind and sea,
Yet leaves us in them, until earth becomes,
By being so much of the things we are,

Gross effigy and simulacrum, none
Gives motion to perfection more serene
Than yours, out of our imperfections wrought,
Most rare, or ever of more kindred air
In the laborious weaving that you wear.

For so retentive of themselves are men
That music is intensest which proclaims
The near, the clear, and vaunts the clearest bloom,
And of all vigils musing the obscure,
That apprehends the most which sees and names,
As in your name, an image that is sure,
Among the arrant spices of the sun,
O bough and bush and scented vine, in whom
We give ourselves our likest issuance.

Yet not too like, yet not so like to be
Too near, too clear, saving a little to endow
Our feigning with the strange unlike, whence springs
The difference that heavenly pity brings.
For this, musician, in your girdle fixed
Bear other perfumes. On your pale head wear
A band entwining, set with fatal stones.
Unreal, give back to us what once you gave:
The imagination that we spurned and crave.

Hymn from a Watermelon Pavilion

You dweller in the dark cabin,
To whom the watermelon is always purple,
Whose garden is wind and moon,

Of the two dreams, night and day,
What lover, what dreamer, would choose
The one obscured by sleep?

Here is the plantain by your door
And the best cock of red feather
That crew before the clocks.

A feme may come, leaf-green,
Whose coming may give revel
Beyond revelries of sleep,

Yes, and the blackbird spread its tail,
So that the sun may speckle,
While it creaks hail.

You dweller in the dark cabin,
Rise, since rising will not waken,
And hail, cry hail, cry hail.

Peter Quince at the Clavier

I

Just as my fingers on these keys
Make music, so the self-same sounds
On my spirit make a music, too.

Music is feeling, then, not sound;
And thus it is that what I feel,
Here in this room, desiring you,

Thinking of your blue-shadowed silk,
Is music. It is like the strain
Waked in the elders by Susanna;

Of a green evening, clear and warm,
She bathed in her still garden, while
The red-eyed elders, watching, felt

The basses of their beings throb
In witching chords, and their thin blood
Pulse pizzicati of Hosanna.

II

In the green water, clear and warm,
Susanna lay.
She searched
The touch of springs,
And found
Concealed imaginings.
She sighed,
For so much melody.

Upon the bank, she stood
In the cool
Of spent emotions.
She felt, among the leaves,
The dew
Of old devotions.

She walked upon the grass,
Still quavering.
The winds were like her maids,
On timid feet,
Fetching her woven scarves,
Yet wavering.

A breath upon her hand
Muted the night.
She turned—
A cymbal crashed,
And roaring horns.

III

Soon, with a noise like tambourines,
Came her attendant Byzantines.

They wondered why Susanna cried
Against the elders by her side;

And as they whispered, the refrain
Was like a willow swept by rain.

Anon, their lamps' uplifted flame
Revealed Susanna and her shame.

And then, the simpering Byzantines
Fled, with a noise like tambourines.

IV

Beauty is momentary in the mind—
The fitful tracing of a portal;
But in the flesh it is immortal.

The body dies; the body's beauty lives.
So evenings die, in their green going,
A wave, interminably flowing.
So gardens die, their meek breath scenting
The cowl of winter, done repenting.
So maidens die, to the auroral
Celebration of a maiden's choral.

Susanna's music touched the bawdy strings
Of those white elders; but, escaping,
Left only Death's ironic scraping.
Now, in its immortality, it plays
On the clear viol of her memory,
And makes a constant sacrament of praise.

Thirteen Ways of Looking at a Blackbird

I

Among twenty snowy mountains,
The only moving thing
Was the eye of the black bird.

II

I was of three minds,
Like a tree
In which there are three blackbirds.

III

The blackbird whirled in the autumn winds.
It was a small part of the pantomime.

IV

A man and a woman
Are one.
A man and a woman and a blackbird
Are one.

V

I do not know which to prefer,
The beauty of inflections
Or the beauty of innuendoes,
The blackbird whistling
Or just after.

VI

Icicles filled the long window
With barbaric glass.
The shadow of the blackbird
Crossed it, to and fro.
The mood
Traced in the shadow
An indecipherable cause.

VII

O thin men of Haddam,
Why do you imagine golden birds?
Do you not see how the blackbird
Walks around the feet
Of the women about you?

VIII

I know noble accents
And lucid, inescapable rhythms;
But I know, too,

That the blackbird is involved
In what I know.

IX

When the blackbird flew out of sight,
It marked the edge
Of one of many circles.

X

At the sight of blackbirds
Flying in a green light,
Even the bawds of euphony
Would cry out sharply.

XI

He rode over Connecticut
In a glass coach.
Once, a fear pierced him,
In that he mistook
The shadow of his equipage
For blackbirds.

XII

The river is moving.
The blackbird must be flying.

XIII

It was evening all afternoon.
It was snowing
And it was going to snow.
The blackbird sat
In the cedar-limbs.

Nomad Exquisite

As the immense dew of Florida
Brings forth
The big-finned palm
And green vine angering for life,

As the immense dew of Florida
Brings forth hymn and hymn
From the beholder,
Beholding all these green sides
And gold sides of green sides,

And blessed mornings,   ·
Meet for the eye of the young alligator,
And lightning colors
So, in me, come flinging
Forms, flames, and the flakes of flames.

Tea

When the elephant's-ear in the park
Shrivelled in frost,
And the leaves on the paths
Ran like rats,
Your lamp-light fell
On shining pillows,
Of sea-shades and sky-shades,
Like umbrellas in Java.

To the Roaring Wind

What syllable are you seeking,
Vocalissimus,
In the distances of sleep?
Speak it.

POEMS ADDED TO
HARMONIUM

(1931)

The Man Whose Pharynx Was Bad

The time of year has grown indifferent.
Mildew of summer and the deepening snow
Are both alike in the routine I know.
I am too dumbly in my being pent.

The wind attendant on the solstices
Blows on the shutters of the metropoles,
Stirring no poet in his sleep, and tolls
The grand ideas of the villages.

The malady of the quotidian. . . .
Perhaps, if winter once could penetrate
Through all its purples to the final slate,
Persisting bleakly in an icy haze,

One might in turn become less diffident,
Out of such mildew plucking neater mould
And spouting new orations of the cold.
One might. One might. But time will not relent.

The Death of a Soldier

Life contracts and death is expected,
As in a season of autumn.
The soldier falls.

He does not become a three-days personage,
Imposing his separation,
Calling for pomp.

Death is absolute and without memorial,
As in a season of autumn,
When the wind stops,

When the wind stops and, over the heavens,
The clouds go, nevertheless,
In their direction.

Negation

Hi! The creator too is blind,
Struggling toward his harmonious whole,
Rejecting intermediate parts,
Horrors and falsities and wrongs;
Incapable master of all force,
Too vague idealist, overwhelmed
By an afflatus that persists.
For this, then, we endure brief lives,
The evanescent symmetries
From that meticulous potter's thumb.

The Surprises of the Superhuman

The palais de justice of chambermaids
Tops the horizon with its colonnades.

If it were lost in Übermenschlichkeit,
Perhaps our wretched state would soon come right.

For somehow the brave dicta of its kings
Make more awry our faulty human things.

Sea Surface Full of Clouds

I

In that November off Tehuantepec,
The slopping of the sea grew still one night
And in the morning summer hued the deck

And made one think of rosy chocolate
And gilt umbrellas. Paradisal green
Gave suavity to the perplexed machine

Of ocean, which like limpid water lay.
Who, then, in that ambrosial latitude
Out of the light evolved the moving blooms,

Who, then, evolved the sea-blooms from the clouds
Diffusing balm in that Pacific calm?
C'était mon enfant, mon bijou, mon âme.

The sea-clouds whitened far below the calm
And moved, as blooms move, in the swimming green
And in its watery radiance, while the hue

Of heaven in an antique reflection rolled
Round those flotillas. And sometimes the sea
Poured brilliant iris on the glistening blue.

II

In that November off Tehuantepec
The slopping of the sea grew still one night.
At breakfast jelly yellow streaked the deck

And made one think of chop-house chocolate
And sham umbrellas. And a sham-like green
Capped summer-seeming on the tense machine

Of ocean, which in sinister flatness lay.
Who, then, beheld the rising of the clouds
That strode submerged in that malevolent sheen,

Who saw the mortal massives of the blooms
Of water moving on the water-floor?
C'était mon frère du ciel, ma vie, mon or.

The gongs rang loudly as the windy booms
Hoo-hooed it in the darkened ocean-blooms.
The gongs grew still. And then blue heaven spread

Its crystalline pendentives on the sea
And the macabre of the water-glooms
In an enormous undulation fled.

III

In that November off Tehuantepec,
The slopping of the sea grew still one night
And a pale silver patterned on the deck

And made one think of porcelain chocolate
And pied umbrellas. An uncertain green,
Piano-polished, held the tranced machine

Of ocean, as a prelude holds and holds.
Who, seeing silver petals of white blooms
Unfolding in the water, feeling sure

Of the milk within the saltiest spurge, heard, then,
The sea unfolding in the sunken clouds?
Oh! C'était mon extase et mon amour.

So deeply sunken were they that the shrouds,
The shrouding shadows, made the petals black
Until the rolling heaven made them blue,

A blue beyond the rainy hyacinth,
And smiting the crevasses of the leaves
Deluged the ocean with a sapphire blue.

IV

In that November off Tehuantepec
The night-long slopping of the sea grew still.
A mallow morning dozed upon the deck

And made one think of musky chocolate
And frail umbrellas. A too-fluent green
Suggested malice in the dry machine

Of ocean, pondering dank stratagem.
Who then beheld the figures of the clouds
Like blooms secluded in the thick marine?

Like blooms? Like damasks that were shaken off
From the loosed girdles in the spangling must.
C'était ma foi, la nonchalance divine.

The nakedness would rise and suddenly turn
Salt masks of beard and mouths of bellowing,
Would—But more suddenly the heaven rolled

Its bluest sea-clouds in the thinking green,
And the nakedness became the broadest blooms,
Mile-mallows that a mallow sun cajoled.

V

In that November off Tehuantepec
Night stilled the slopping of the sea. The day
Came, bowing and voluble, upon the deck,

Good clown. . . . One thought of Chinese chocolate
And large umbrellas. And a motley green
Followed the drift of the obese machine

Of ocean, perfected in indolence.
What pistache one, ingenious and droll,
Beheld the sovereign clouds as jugglery

And the sea as turquoise-turbaned Sambo, neat
At tossing saucers—cloudy-conjuring sea?
C'était mon esprit bâtard, l'ignominie.

The sovereign clouds came clustering. The conch
Of loyal conjuration trumped. The wind
Of green blooms turning crisped the motley hue

To clearing opalescence. Then the sea
And heaven rolled as one and from the two
Came fresh transfigurings of freshest blue.

The Revolutionists Stop for Orangeade

Capitán profundo, capitán geloso,
Ask us not to sing standing in the sun,
Hairy-backed and hump-armed,
Flat-ribbed and big-bagged.
There is no pith in music
Except in something false.

Bellissimo, pomposo,
Sing a song of serpent-kin,
Necks among the thousand leaves,
Tongues around the fruit.
Sing in clownish boots
Strapped and buckled bright.

Wear the breeches of a mask,
Coat half-flare and half galloon;
Wear a helmet without reason,
Tufted, tilted, twirled, and twisted.
Start the singing in a voice
Rougher than a grinding shale.

Hang a feather by your eye,
Nod and look a little sly.
This must be the vent of pity,
Deeper than a truer ditty
Of the real that wrenches,
Of the quick that's wry.

New England Verses

I

The Whole World Including the Speaker

Why nag at the ideas of Hercules, Don Don?
Widen your sense. All things in the sun are sun.

II

The Whole World Excluding the Speaker

I found between moon-rising and moon-setting
The world was round. But not from my begetting.

III

Soupe Aux Perles

Health-o, when ginger and fromage bewitch
The vile antithesis of poor and rich.

IV

Soupe Sans Perles

I crossed in '38 in the *Western Head*.
It depends which way you crossed, the tea-belle said.

V

Boston with a Note-book

Lean encyclopædists, inscribe an Iliad.
There's a weltanschauung of the penny pad.

VI

Boston without a Note-book

Let us erect in the Basin a lofty fountain.
Suckled on ponds, the spirit craves a watery mountain.

VII

Artist in Tropic

Of Phœbus Apothicaire the first beatitude:
Blessed, who is his nation's multitude.

VIII

Artist in Arctic

And of Phœbus the Tailor the second saying goes:
Blessed, whose beard is cloak against the snows.

IX

Statue against a Clear Sky

Ashen man on ashen cliff above the salt halloo,
O ashen admiral of the hale, hard blue. . . .

X

Statue against a Cloudy Sky

Scaffolds and derricks rise from the reeds to the clouds
Meditating the will of men in formless crowds.

XI

Land of Locust

Patron and patriarch of couplets, walk
In fragrant leaves heat-heavy yet nimble in talk.

XII

Land of Pine and Marble

Civilization must be destroyed. The hairy saints
Of the North have earned this crumb by their complaints.

XIII

The Male Nude

Dark cynic, strip and bathe and bask at will.
Without cap or strap, you are the cynic still.

XIV

The Female Nude

Ballatta dozed in the cool on a straw divan
At home, a bit like the slenderest courtesan.

XV

Scène Flétrie

The purple dress in autumn and the belfry breath
Hinted autumnal farewells of academic death.

XVI

Scène Fleurie

A perfect fruit in perfect atmosphere.
Nature as Pinakothek. Whist! Chanticleer. . . .

Lunar Paraphrase

The moon is the mother of pathos and pity.

When, at the wearier end of November,
Her old light moves along the branches,
Feebly, slowly, depending upon them;
When the body of Jesus hangs in a pallor,
Humanly near, and the figure of Mary,
Touched on by hoar-frost, shrinks in a shelter
Made by the leaves, that have rotted and fallen;

When over the houses, a golden illusion
Brings back an earlier season of quiet
And quieting dreams in the sleepers in darkness—

The moon is the mother of pathos and pity.

Anatomy of Monotony

I

If from the earth we came, it was an earth
That bore us as a part of all the things
It breeds and that was lewder than it is.
Our nature is her nature. Hence it comes,
Since by our nature we grow old, earth grows
The same. We parallel the mother's death.
She walks an autumn ampler than the wind
Cries up for us and colder than the frost
Pricks in our spirits at the summer's end,
And over the bare spaces of our skies
She sees a barer sky that does not bend.

II

The body walks forth naked in the sun
And, out of tenderness or grief, the sun
Gives comfort, so that other bodies come,
Twinning our phantasy and our device,
And apt in versatile motion, touch and sound
To make the body covetous in desire
Of the still finer, more implacable chords.
So be it. Yet the spaciousness and light
In which the body walks and is deceived,
Falls from that fatal and that barer sky,
And this the spirit sees and is aggrieved.

The Public Square

A slash of angular blacks
Like a fractured edifice
That was buttressed by blue slants
In a coma of the moon.

A slash and the edifice fell,
Pylon and pier fell down.
A mountain-blue cloud arose
Like a thing in which they fell,

Fell slowly as when at night
A languid janitor bears
His lantern through colonnades
And the architecture swoons.

It turned cold and silent. Then
The square began to clear.
The bijou of Atlas, the moon,
Was last with its porcelain leer.

Sonatina to Hans Christian

If any duck in any brook,
Fluttering the water
For your crumb,
Seemed the helpless daughter

Of a mother
Regretful that she bore her;
Or of another,
Barren, and longing for her;

What of the dove,
Or thrush, or any singing mysteries?
What of the trees
And intonations of the trees?

What of the night
That lights and dims the stars?
Do you know, Hans Christian,
Now that you see the night?

In the Clear Season of Grapes

The mountains between our lands and the sea—
This conjunction of mountains and sea and our lands—
Have I stopped and thought of its point before?

When I think of our lands I think of the house
And the table that holds a platter of pears,
Vermilion smeared over green, arranged for show.

But this gross blue under rolling bronzes
Belittles those carefully chosen daubs.
Flashier fruits! A flip for the sun and moon,

If they mean no more than that. But they do.
And mountains and the sea do. And our lands.
And the welter of frost and the fox cries do.

Much more than that. Autumnal passages
Are overhung by the shadows of the rocks
And his nostrils blow out salt around each man.

Two at Norfolk

Mow the grass in the cemetery, darkies,
Study the symbols and the requiescats,
But leave a bed beneath the myrtles.
This skeleton had a daughter and that, a son.

In his time, this one had little to speak of,
The softest word went gurrituck in his skull.
For him the moon was always in Scandinavia
And his daughter was a foreign thing.

And that one was never a man of heart.
The making of his son was one more duty.
When the music of the boy fell like a fountain,
He praised Johann Sebastian, as he should.

The dark shadows of the funereal magnolias
Are full of the songs of Jamanda and Carlotta;
The son and the daughter, who come to the darkness,
He for her burning breast and she for his arms.

And these two never meet in the air so full of summer
And touch each other, even touching closely,
Without an escape in the lapses of their kisses.
Make a bed and leave the iris in it.

Indian River

The trade-wind jingles the rings in the nets around the racks
    by the docks on Indian River.
It is the same jingle of the water among the roots under the
    banks of the palmettoes,
It is the same jingle of the red-bird breasting the orange-
    trees out of the cedars.
Yet there is no spring in Florida, neither in boskage perdu,
    nor on the nunnery beaches.

IDEAS OF ORDER

(1936)

Farewell to Florida

Go on, high ship, since now, upon the shore,
The snake has left its skin upon the floor.
Key West sank downward under massive clouds
And silvers and greens spread over the sea. The moon
Is at the mast-head and the past is dead.
Her mind will never speak to me again.
I am free. High above the mast the moon
Rides clear of her mind and the waves make a refrain
Of this: that the snake has shed its skin upon
The floor. Go on through the darkness. The waves fly back.

II

Her mind had bound me round. The palms were hot
As if I lived in ashen ground, as if
The leaves in which the wind kept up its sound
From my North of cold whistled in a sepulchral South,
Her South of pine and coral and coraline sea,
Her home, not mine, in the ever-freshened Keys,
Her days, her oceanic nights, calling
For music, for whisperings from the reefs.
How content I shall be in the North to which I sail
And to feel sure and to forget the bleaching sand . . .

III

I hated the weathery yawl from which the pools
Disclosed the sea floor and the wilderness
Of waving weeds. I hated the vivid blooms
Curled over the shadowless hut, the rust and bones,
The trees like bones and the leaves half sand, half sun.
To stand here on the deck in the dark and say
Farewell and to know that that land is forever gone
And that she will not follow in any word
Or look, nor ever again in thought, except
That I loved her once . . . Farewell. Go on, high ship.

IV

My North is leafless and lies in a wintry slime
Both of men and clouds, a slime of men in crowds.
The men are moving as the water moves,
This darkened water cloven by sullen swells
Against your sides, then shoving and slithering,
The darkness shattered, turbulent with foam.
To be free again, to return to the violent mind
That is their mind, these men, and that will bind
Me round, carry me, misty deck, carry me
To the cold, go on, high ship, go on, plunge on.

Ghosts as Cocoons

The grass is in seed. The young birds are flying.
Yet the house is not built, not even begun.

The vetch has turned purple. But where is the bride?
It is easy to say to those bidden—But where,

Where, butcher, seducer, bloodman, reveller,
Where is sun and music and highest heaven's lust,

For which more than any words cries deeplier?
This mangled, smutted semi-world hacked out

Of dirt . . . It is not possible for the moon
To blot this with its dove-winged blendings.

She must come now. The grass is in seed and high.
Come now. Those to be born have need

Of the bride, love being a birth, have need to see
And to touch her, have need to say to her,

"The fly on the rose prevents us, O season
Excelling summer, ghost of fragrance falling

On dung." Come now, pearled and pasted, bloomy-leafed,
While the domes resound with chant involving chant.

Sailing After Lunch

It is the word *pejorative* that hurts.
My old boat goes round on a crutch
And doesn't get under way.
It's the time of the year
And the time of the day.

Perhaps it's the lunch that we had
Or the lunch that we should have had.
But I am, in any case,
A most inappropriate man
In a most unpropitious place.

Mon Dieu, hear the poet's prayer.
The romantic should be here.
The romantic should be there.
It ought to be everywhere.
But the romantic must never remain,

Mon Dieu, and must never again return.
This heavy historical sail
Through the mustiest blue of the lake
In a really vertiginous boat
Is wholly the vapidest fake. . . .

It is least what one ever sees.
It is only the way one feels, to say
Where my spirit is I am,
To say the light wind worries the sail,
To say the water is swift today,

To expunge all people and be a pupil
Of the gorgeous wheel and so to give

That slight transcendence to the dirty sail,
By light, the way one feels, sharp white,
And then rush brightly through the summer air.

Sad Strains of a Gay Waltz

The truth is that there comes a time
When we can mourn no more over music
That is so much motionless sound.

There comes a time when the waltz
Is no longer a mode of desire, a mode
Of revealing desire and is empty of shadows.

Too many waltzes have ended. And then
There's that mountain-minded Hoon,
For whom desire was never that of the waltz,

Who found all form and order in solitude,
For whom the shapes were never the figures of men.
Now, for him, his forms have vanished.

There is order in neither sea nor sun.
The shapes have lost their glistening.
There are these sudden mobs of men,

These sudden clouds of faces and arms,
An immense suppression, freed,
These voices crying without knowing for what,

Except to be happy, without knowing how,
Imposing forms they cannot describe,
Requiring order beyond their speech.

Too many waltzes have ended. Yet the shapes
For which the voices cry, these, too, may be
Modes of desire, modes of revealing desire.

Too many waltzes—The epic of disbelief
Blares oftener and soon, will soon be constant.
Some harmonious skeptic soon in a skeptical music

Will unite these figures of men and their shapes
Will glisten again with motion, the music
Will be motion and full of shadows.

Dance of the Macabre Mice

In the land of turkeys in turkey weather
At the base of the statue, we go round and round.
What a beautiful history, beautiful surprise!
Monsieur is on horseback. The horse is covered with mice.

This dance has no name. It is a hungry dance.
We dance it out to the tip of Monsieur's sword,
Reading the lordly language of the inscription,
Which is like zithers and tambourines combined:

The Founder of the State. Whoever founded
A state that was free, in the dead of winter, from mice?
What a beautiful tableau tinted and towering,
The arm of bronze outstretched against all evil!

Meditation Celestial & Terrestrial

The wild warblers are warbling in the jungle
Of life and spring and of the lustrous inundations,
Flood on flood, of our returning sun.

Day after day, throughout the winter,
We hardened ourselves to live by bluest reason
In a world of wind and frost,

And by will, unshaken and florid
In mornings of angular ice,
That passed beyond us through the narrow sky.

But what are radiant reason and radiant will
To warblings early in the hilarious trees
Of summer, the drunken mother?

Lions in Sweden

No more phrases, Swenson: I was once
A hunter of those sovereigns of the soul
And savings banks, Fides, the sculptor's prize,
All eyes and size, and galled Justitia,
Trained to poise the tables of the law,
Patientia forever soothing wounds
And mighty Fortitudo, frantic bass.
But these shall not adorn my souvenirs,
These lions, these majestic images.
If the fault is with the soul, the sovereigns
Of the soul must likewise be at fault, and first.
If the fault is with the souvenirs, yet these
Are the soul itself. And the whole of the soul, Swenson,
As every man in Sweden will concede,
Still hankers after lions, or, to shift,
Still hankers after sovereign images.
If the fault is with the lions, send them back
To Monsieur Dufy's Hamburg whence they came.
The vegetation still abounds with forms.

How To Live. What To Do

Last evening the moon rose above this rock
Impure upon a world unpurged.
The man and his companion stopped
To rest before the heroic height.

Coldly the wind fell upon them
In many majesties of sound:
They that had left the flame-freaked sun
To seek a sun of fuller fire.

Instead there was this tufted rock
Massively rising high and bare
Beyond all trees, the ridges thrown
Like giant arms among the clouds.

There was neither voice nor crested image,
No chorister, nor priest. There was
Only the great height of the rock
And the two of them standing still to rest.

There was the cold wind and the sound
It made, away from the muck of the land
That they had left, heroic sound
Joyous and jubilant and sure.

Some Friends from Pascagoula

Tell me more of the eagle, Cotton,
And you, black Sly,
Tell me how he descended
Out of the morning sky.

Describe with deepened voice
And noble imagery
His slowly-falling round
Down to the fishy sea.

Here was a sovereign sight,
Fit for a kinky clan.
Tell me again of the point
At which the flight began,

Say how his heavy wings,
Spread on the sun-bronzed air,
Turned tip and tip away,
Down to the sand, the glare

Of the pine trees edging the sand,
Dropping in sovereign rings
Out of his fiery lair.
Speak of the dazzling wings.

Waving Adieu, Adieu, Adieu

That would be waving and that would be crying,
Crying and shouting and meaning farewell,
Farewell in the eyes and farewell at the centre,
Just to stand still without moving a hand.

In a world without heaven to follow, the stops
Would be endings, more poignant than partings,
        profounder,
And that would be saying farewell, repeating farewell,
Just to be there and just to behold.

To be one's singular self, to despise
The being that yielded so little, acquired
So little, too little to care, to turn
To the ever-jubilant weather, to sip

One's cup and never to say a word,
Or to sleep or just to lie there still,
Just to be there, just to be beheld,
That would be bidding farewell, be bidding farewell.

One likes to practice the thing. They practice,
Enough, for heaven. Ever-jubilant,
What is there here but weather, what spirit
Have I except it comes from the sun?

The Idea of Order at Key West

She sang beyond the genius of the sea.
The water never formed to mind or voice,
Like a body wholly body, fluttering
Its empty sleeves; and yet its mimic motion
Made constant cry, caused constantly a cry,
That was not ours although we understood,
Inhuman, of the veritable ocean.

The sea was not a mask. No more was she.
The song and water were not medleyed sound
Even if what she sang was what she heard,
Since what she sang was uttered word by word.
It may be that in all her phrases stirred
The grinding water and the gasping wind;
But it was she and not the sea we heard.

For she was the maker of the song she sang.
The ever-hooded, tragic-gestured sea
Was merely a place by which she walked to sing.
Whose spirit is this? we said, because we knew
It was the spirit that we sought and knew
That we should ask this often as she sang.

If it was only the dark voice of the sea
That rose, or even colored by many waves;
If it was only the outer voice of sky
And cloud, of the sunken coral water-walled,
However clear, it would have been deep air,
The heaving speech of air, a summer sound
Repeated in a summer without end
And sound alone. But it was more than that,
More even than her voice, and ours, among
The meaningless plungings of water and the wind,
Theatrical distances, bronze shadows heaped
On high horizons, mountainous atmospheres
Of sky and sea.

　　　　　　　　It was her voice that made
The sky acutest at its vanishing.
She measured to the hour its solitude.
She was the single artificer of the world
In which she sang. And when she sang, the sea,
Whatever self it had, became the self
That was her song, for she was the maker. Then we,
As we beheld her striding there alone,
Knew that there never was a world for her
Except the one she sang and, singing, made.

Ramon Fernandez, tell me, if you know,
Why, when the singing ended and we turned
Toward the town, tell why the glassy lights,
The lights in the fishing boats at anchor there,
As the night descended, tilting in the air,
Mastered the night and portioned out the sea,
Fixing emblazoned zones and fiery poles,
Arranging, deepening, enchanting night.

Oh! Blessed rage for order, pale Ramon,
The maker's rage to order words of the sea,
Words of the fragrant portals, dimly-starred,
And of ourselves and of our origins,
In ghostlier demarcations, keener sounds.

The American Sublime

How does one stand
To behold the sublime,
To confront the mockers,
The mickey mockers
And plated pairs?

When General Jackson
Posed for his statue
He knew how one feels.
Shall a man go barefoot
Blinking and blank?

But how does one feel?
One grows used to the weather,
The landscape and that;
And the sublime comes down
To the spirit itself,

The spirit and space,
The empty spirit
In vacant space.
What wine does one drink?
What bread does one eat?

Mozart, 1935

Poet, be seated at the piano.
Play the present, its hoo-hoo-hoo,
Its shoo-shoo-shoo, its ric-a-nic,
Its envious cachinnation.

If they throw stones upon the roof
While you practice arpeggios,
It is because they carry down the stairs
A body in rags.
Be seated at the piano.

That lucid souvenir of the past,
The divertimento;
That airy dream of the future,
The unclouded concerto . . .
The snow is falling.
Strike the piercing chord.

Be thou the voice,
Not you. Be thou, be thou
The voice of angry fear,
The voice of this besieging pain.

Be thou that wintry sound
As of the great wind howling,
By which sorrow is released,
Dismissed, absolved
In a starry placating.

We may return to Mozart.
He was young, and we, we are old.
The snow is falling
And the streets are full of cries.
Be seated, thou.

Snow and Stars

The grackles sing avant the spring
Most spiss—oh! Yes, most spissantly.
They sing right puissantly.

This robe of snow and winter stars,
The devil take it, wear it, too.
It might become his hole of blue.

Let him remove it to his regions,
White and star-furred for his legions,
And make much bing, high bing.

It would be ransom for the willow
And fill the hill and fill it full
Of ding, ding, dong.

The Sun This March

The exceeding brightness of this early sun
Makes me conceive how dark I have become,

And re-illumines things that used to turn
To gold in broadest blue, and be a part

Of a turning spirit in an earlier self.
That, too, returns from out the winter's air,

Like an hallucination come to daze
The corner of the eye. Our element,

Cold is our element and winter's air
Brings voices as of lions coming down.

Oh! Rabbi, rabbi, fend my soul for me
And true savant of this dark nature be.

Botanist on Alp (No. 1)

Panoramas are not what they used to be.
Claude has been dead a long time
And apostrophes are forbidden on the funicular.
Marx has ruined Nature,
For the moment.

For myself, I live by leaves,
So that corridors of clouds,
Corridors of cloudy thoughts,
Seem pretty much one:
I don't know what.

But in Claude how near one was
(In a world that was resting on pillars,
That was seen through arches)
To the central composition,
The essential theme.

What composition is there in all this:
Stockholm slender in a slender light,

An adriatic *riva* rising,
Statues and stars,
Without a theme?

The pillars are prostrate, the arches are haggard,
The hotel is boarded and bare.
Yet the panorama of despair
Cannot be the specialty
Of this ecstatic air.

Botanist on Alp (No. 2)

The crosses on the convent roofs
Gleam sharply as the sun comes up.

What's down below is in the past
Like last night's crickets, far below.

And what's above is in the past
As sure as all the angels are.

Why should the future leap the clouds
The bays of heaven, brighted, blued?

Chant, O ye faithful, in your paths
The poem of long celestial death;

For who could tolerate the earth
Without that poem, or without

An earthier one, tum, tum-ti-tum,
As of those crosses, glittering,

And merely of their glittering,
A mirror of a mere delight?

Evening Without Angels

the great interests of man: air and light, the joy of having a
body, the voluptuousness of looking.   MARIO ROSSI

Why seraphim like lutanists arranged
Above the trees? And why the poet as
Eternal *chef d'orchestre*?

Air is air.
Its vacancy glitters round us everywhere.
Its sounds are not angelic syllables
But our unfashioned spirits realized
More sharply in more furious selves.

And light
That fosters seraphim and is to them
Coiffeur of haloes, fecund jeweller—
Was the sun concoct for angels or for men?
Sad men made angels of the sun, and of
The moon they made their own attendant ghosts,
Which led them back to angels, after death.

Let this be clear that we are men of sun
And men of day and never of pointed night,
Men that repeat antiquest sounds of air
In an accord of repetitions. Yet,
If we repeat, it is because the wind
Encircling us, speaks always with our speech.

Light, too, encrusts us making visible
The motions of the mind and giving form
To moodiest nothings, as, desire for day
Accomplished in the immensely flashing East,
Desire for rest, in that descending sea
Of dark, which in its very darkening
Is rest and silence spreading into sleep.

. . . Evening, when the measure skips a beat
And then another, one by one, and all
To a seething minor swiftly modulate.
Bare night is best. Bare earth is best. Bare, bare,
Except for our own houses, huddled low
Beneath the arches and their spangled air,
Beneath the rhapsodies of fire and fire,
Where the voice that is in us makes a true response,
Where the voice that is great within us rises up,
As we stand gazing at the rounded moon.

The Brave Man

The sun, that brave man,
Comes through boughs that lie in wait,
That brave man.

Green and gloomy eyes
In dark forms of the grass
Run away.

The good stars,
Pale helms and spiky spurs,
Run away.

Fears of my bed,
Fears of life and fears of death,
Run away.

That brave man comes up
From below and walks without meditation,
That brave man.

A Fading of the Sun

Who can think of the sun costuming clouds
When all people are shaken

Or of night endazzled, proud,
When people awaken
And cry and cry for help?

The warm antiquity of self,
Everyone, grows suddenly cold.
The tea is bad, bread sad.
How can the world so old be so mad
That the people die?

If joy shall be without a book
It lies, themselves within themselves,
If they will look
Within themselves
And will not cry for help,

Within as pillars of the sun,
Supports of night. The tea,
The wine is good. The bread,
The meat is sweet.
And they will not die.

Gray Stones and Gray Pigeons

The archbishop is away. The church is gray.
He has left his robes folded in camphor
And, dressed in black, he walks
Among fireflies.

The bony buttresses, the bony spires
Arranged under the stony clouds
Stand in a fixed light.
The bishop rests.

He is away. The church is gray.
This is his holiday.
The sexton moves with a sexton's stare
In the air.

A dithery gold falls everywhere.
It wets the pigeons,
It goes and the birds go,
Turn dry,

Birds that never fly
Except when the bishop passes by,
Globed in today and tomorrow,
Dressed in his colored robes.

Winter Bells

The Jew did not go to his synagogue
To be flogged.
But it was solemn,
That church without bells.

He preferred the brightness of bells,
The *mille fiori* of vestments,
The voice of centuries
On the priestly gramophones.

It was the custom
For his rage against chaos
To abate on the way to church,
In regulations of his spirit.
How good life is, on the basis of propriety,
To be followed by a platter of capon!

Yet he kept promising himself
To go to Florida one of these days,
And in one of the little arrondissements
Of the sea there,
To give this further thought.

Academic Discourse at Havana

I

Canaries in the morning, orchestras
In the afternoon, balloons at night. That is
A difference, at least, from nightingales,
Jehovah and the great sea-worm. The air
Is not so elemental nor the earth
So near.
          But the sustenance of the wilderness
Does not sustain us in the metropoles.

II

Life is an old casino in a park.
The bills of the swans are flat upon the ground.
A most desolate wind has chilled Rouge-Fatima
And a grand decadence settles down like cold.

III

The swans . . . Before the bills of the swans fell flat
Upon the ground, and before the chronicle
Of affected homage foxed so many books,
They warded the blank waters of the lakes
And island canopies which were entailed
To that casino. Long before the rain
Swept through its boarded windows and the leaves
Filled its encrusted fountains, they arrayed
The twilights of the mythy goober khan.
The centuries of excellence to be
Rose out of promise and became the sooth
Of trombones floating in the trees.

                              The toil
Of thought evoked a peace eccentric to
The eye and tinkling to the ear. Gruff drums
Could beat, yet not alarm the populace.
The indolent progressions of the swans
Made earth come right; a peanut parody
For peanut people.

And serener myth
Conceiving from its perfect plenitude,
Lusty as June, more fruitful than the weeks
Of ripest summer, always lingering
To touch again the hottest bloom, to strike
Once more the longest resonance, to cap
The clearest woman with apt weed, to mount
The thickest man on thickest stallion-back,
This urgent, competent, serener myth
Passed like a circus.

Politic man ordained
Imagination as the fateful sin.
Grandmother and her basketful of pears
Must be the crux for our compendia.
That's world enough, and more, if one includes
Her daughters to the peached and ivory wench
For whom the towers are built. The burgher's breast,
And not a delicate ether star-impaled,
Must be the place for prodigy, unless
Prodigious things are tricks. The world is not
The bauble of the sleepless nor a word
That should import a universal pith
To Cuba. Jot these milky matters down.
They nourish Jupiters. Their casual pap
Will drop like sweetness in the empty nights
When too great rhapsody is left annulled
And liquorish prayer provokes new sweats: so, so:
Life is an old casino in a wood.

IV

Is the function of the poet here mere sound,
Subtler than the ornatest prophecy,
To stuff the ear? It causes him to make
His infinite repetition and alloys
Of pick of ebon, pick of halcyon.
It weights him with nice logic for the prim.
As part of nature he is part of us.
His rarities are ours: may they be fit

And reconcile us to our selves in those
True reconcilings, dark, pacific words,
And the adroiter harmonies of their fall.
Close the cantina. Hood the chandelier.
The moonlight is not yellow but a white
That silences the ever-faithful town.
How pale and how possessed a night it is,
How full of exhalations of the sea . . .
All this is older than its oldest hymn,
Has no more meaning than tomorrow's bread.
But let the poet on his balcony
Speak and the sleepers in their sleep shall move,
Waken, and watch the moonlight on their floors.
This may be benediction, sepulcher,
And epitaph. It may, however, be
An incantation that the moon defines
By mere example opulently clear.
And the old casino likewise may define
An infinite incantation of our selves
In the grand decadence of the perished swans.

Nudity at the Capital

But nakedness, woolen massa, concerns an innermost atom.
If that remains concealed, what does the bottom matter?

Nudity in the Colonies

Black man, bright nouveautés leave one, at best,
    pseudonymous.
Thus one is most disclosed when one is most
    anonymous.

Re-statement of Romance

The night knows nothing of the chants of night.
It is what it is as I am what I am:
And in perceiving this I best perceive myself

And you. Only we two may interchange
Each in the other what each has to give.
Only we two are one, not you and night,

Nor night and I, but you and I, alone,
So much alone, so deeply by ourselves,
So far beyond the casual solitudes,

That night is only the background of our selves,
Supremely true each to its separate self,
In the pale light that each upon the other throws.

The Reader

All night I sat reading a book,
Sat reading as if in a book
Of sombre pages.

It was autumn and falling stars
Covered the shrivelled forms
Crouched in the moonlight.

No lamp was burning as I read,
A voice was mumbling, "Everything
Falls back to coldness,

Even the musky muscadines,
The melons, the vermilion pears
Of the leafless garden."

The sombre pages bore no print
Except the trace of burning stars
In the frosty heaven.

Mud Master

The muddy rivers of spring
Are snarling
Under muddy skies.
The mind is muddy.

As yet, for the mind, new banks
Of bulging green
Are not;
Sky-sides of gold
Are not.
The mind snarls.

Blackest of pickanines,
There is a master of mud.
The shaft of light
Falling, far off, from sky to land,
That is he—

The peach-bud maker,
The mud master,
The master of the mind.

Anglais Mort à Florence

A little less returned for him each spring.
Music began to fail him. Brahms, although
His dark familiar, often walked apart.

His spirit grew uncertain of delight,
Certain of its uncertainty, in which
That dark companion left him unconsoled

For a self returning mostly memory.
Only last year he said that the naked moon
Was not the moon he used to see, to feel

(In the pale coherences of moon and mood
When he was young), naked and alien,
More leanly shining from a lankier sky.

Its ruddy pallor had grown cadaverous.
He used his reason, exercised his will,
Turning in time to Brahms as alternate

In speech. He was that music and himself.
They were particles of order, a single majesty:
But he remembered the time when he stood alone.

He stood at last by God's help and the police;
But he remembered the time when he stood alone.
He yielded himself to that single majesty;

But he remembered the time when he stood alone,
When to be and delight to be seemed to be one,
Before the colors deepened and grew small.

The Pleasures of Merely Circulating

The garden flew round with the angel,
The angel flew round with the clouds,
And the clouds flew round and the clouds flew round
And the clouds flew round with the clouds.

Is there any secret in skulls,
The cattle skulls in the woods?
Do the drummers in black hoods
Rumble anything out of their drums?

Mrs. Anderson's Swedish baby
Might well have been German or Spanish,
Yet that things go round and again go round
Has rather a classical sound.

Like Decorations in a Nigger Cemetery

FOR ARTHUR POWELL

I

In the far South the sun of autumn is passing
Like Walt Whitman walking along a ruddy shore.
He is singing and chanting the things that are part of him,
The worlds that were and will be, death and day.
Nothing is final, he chants. No man shall see the end.
His beard is of fire and his staff is a leaping flame.

II

Sigh for me, night-wind, in the noisy leaves of the oak.
I am tired. Sleep for me, heaven over the hill.
Shout for me, loudly and loudly, joyful sun, when you rise.

III

It was when the trees were leafless first in November
And their blackness became apparent, that one first
Knew the eccentric to be the base of design.

IV

Under the mat of frost and over the mat of clouds.
But in between lies the sphere of my fortune
And the fortunes of frost and of clouds,
All alike, except for the rules of the rabbis,
Happy men, distinguishing frost and clouds.

V

If ever the search for a tranquil belief should end,
The future might stop emerging out of the past,
Out of what is full of us; yet the search
And the future emerging out of us seem to be one.

VI

We should die except for Death
In his chalk and violet robes.
Not to die a parish death.

VII

How easily the feelings flow this afternoon
Over the simplest words:
It is too cold for work, now, in the fields.

VIII

Out of the spirit of the holy temples,
Empty and grandiose, let us make hymns
And sing them in secrecy as lovers do.

IX

In a world of universal poverty
The philosophers alone will be fat
Against the autumn winds
In an autumn that will be perpetual.

X

Between farewell and the absence of farewell,
The final mercy and the final loss,
The wind and the sudden falling of the wind.

XI

The cloud rose upward like a heavy stone
That lost its heaviness through that same will,
Which changed light green to olive then to blue.

XII

The sense of the serpent in you, Ananke,
And your averted stride
Add nothing to the horror of the frost
That glistens on your face and hair.

XIII

The birds are singing in the yellow patios,
Pecking at more lascivious rinds than ours,
From sheer Gemütlichkeit.

XIV

The leaden pigeon on the entrance gate
Must miss the symmetry of a leaden mate,
Must see her fans of silver undulate.

XV

Serve the rouged fruits in early snow.
They resemble a page of Toulet
Read in the ruins of a new society,
Furtively, by candle and out of need.

XVI

If thinking could be blown away
Yet this remain the dwelling-place
Of those with a sense for simple space.

XVII

The sun of Asia creeps above the horizon
Into this haggard and tenuous air,
A tiger lamed by nothingness and frost.

XVIII

Shall I grapple with my destroyers
In the muscular poses of the museums?
But my destroyers avoid the museums.

XIX

An opening of portals when night ends,
A running forward, arms stretched out as drilled.
Act I, Scene 1, at a German Staats-Oper.

XX

Ah, but the meaningless, natural effigy!
The revealing aberration should appear,
The agate in the eye, the tufted ear,
The rabbit fat, at last, in glassy grass.

XXI

She was a shadow as thin in memory
As an autumn ancient underneath the snow,
Which one recalls at a concert or in a café.

XXII

The comedy of hollow sounds derives
From truth and not from satire on our lives.
Clog, therefore, purple Jack and crimson Jill.

XXIII

The fish are in the fishman's window,
The grain is in the baker's shop,
The hunter shouts as the pheasant falls.
Consider the odd morphology of regret.

XXIV

A bridge above the bright and blue of water
And the same bridge when the river is frozen.
Rich Tweedle-dum, poor Tweedle-dee.

XXV

From oriole to crow, note the decline
In music. Crow is realist. But, then,
Oriole, also, may be realist.

XXVI

This fat pastiche of Belgian grapes exceeds
The total gala of auburn aureoles.
Cochon! Master, the grapes are here and now.

XXVII

John Constable they could never quite transplant
And our streams rejected the dim Academy.
Granted the Picts impressed us otherwise
In the taste for iron dogs and iron deer.

XXVIII

A pear should come to the table popped with juice,
Ripened in warmth and served in warmth. On terms
Like these, autumn beguiles the fatalist.

XXIX

Choke every ghost with acted violence,
Stamp down the phosphorescent toes, tear off
The spittling tissues tight across the bones.
The heavy bells are tolling rowdy-dow.

XXX

The hen-cock crows at midnight and lays no egg,
The cock-hen crows all day. But cockerel shrieks,
Hen shudders: the copious egg is made and laid.

XXXI

A teeming millpond or a furious mind.
Gray grasses rolling windily away
And bristling thorn-trees spinning on the bank.
The actual is a deft beneficence.

XXXII

Poetry is a finikin thing of air
That lives uncertainly and not for long
Yet radiantly beyond much lustier blurs.

XXXIII

For all his purple, the purple bird must have
Notes for his comfort that he may repeat
Through the gross tedium of being rare.

XXXIV

A calm November. Sunday in the fields.
A reflection stagnant in a stagnant stream.
Yet invisible currents clearly circulate.

XXXV

Men and the affairs of men seldom concerned
This pundit of the weather, who never ceased
To think of man the abstraction, the comic sum.

XXXVI

The children will be crying on the stair,
Half-way to bed, when the phrase will be spoken,
The starry voluptuary will be born.

XXXVII

Yesterday the roses were rising upward,
Pushing their buds above the dark green leaves,
Noble in autumn, yet nobler than autumn.

XXXVIII

The album of Corot is premature.
A little later when the sky is black.
Mist that is golden is not wholly mist.

XXXIX

Not the ocean of the virtuosi
But the ugly alien, the mask that speaks
Things unintelligible, yet understood.

XL

Always the standard repertoire in line
And that would be perfection, if each began
Not by beginning but at the last man's end.

XLI

The chrysanthemums' astringent fragrance comes
Each year to disguise the clanking mechanism
Of machine within machine within machine.

XLII

God of the sausage-makers, sacred guild,
Or possibly, the merest patron saint
Ennobled as in a mirror to sanctity.

XLIII

It is curious that the density of life
On a given plane is ascertainable
By dividing the number of legs one sees by two.
At least the number of people may thus be fixed.

XLIV

Freshness is more than the east wind blowing round one.
There is no such thing as innocence in autumn,
Yet, it may be, innocence is never lost.

XLV

Encore un instant de bonheur. The words
Are a woman's words, unlikely to satisfy
The taste of even a country connoisseur.

XLVI

Everything ticks like a clock. The cabinet
Of a man gone mad, after all, for time, in spite
Of the cuckoos, a man with a mania for clocks.

XLVII

The sun is seeking something bright to shine on.
The trees are wooden, the grass is yellow and thin.
The ponds are not the surfaces it seeks.
It must create its colors out of itself.

XLVIII

Music is not yet written but is to be.
The preparation is long and of long intent
For the time when sound shall be subtler than we ourselves.

XLIX

It needed the heavy nights of drenching weather
To make him return to people, to find among them
Whatever it was that he found in their absence,
A pleasure, an indulgence, an infatuation.

L

Union of the weakest develops strength
Not wisdom. Can all men, together, avenge
One of the leaves that have fallen in autumn?
But the wise man avenges by building his city in snow.

A Postcard from the Volcano

Children picking up our bones
Will never know that these were once
As quick as foxes on the hill;

And that in autumn, when the grapes
Made sharp air sharper by their smell
These had a being, breathing frost;

And least will guess that with our bones
We left much more, left what still is
The look of things, left what we felt

At what we saw. The spring clouds blow
Above the shuttered mansion-house,
Beyond our gate and the windy sky

Cries out a literate despair.
We knew for long the mansion's look
And what we said of it became

A part of what it is . . . Children,
Still weaving budded aureoles,
Will speak our speech and never know,

Will say of the mansion that it seems
As if he that lived there left behind
A spirit storming in blank walls,

A dirty house in a gutted world,
A tatter of shadows peaked to white,
Smeared with the gold of the opulent sun.

Autumn Refrain

The skreak and skritter of evening gone
And grackles gone and sorrows of the sun,
The sorrows of sun, too, gone . . . the moon and moon,
The yellow moon of words about the nightingale
In measureless measures, not a bird for me
But the name of a bird and the name of a nameless air
I have never—shall never hear. And yet beneath
The stillness of everything gone, and being still,
Being and sitting still, something resides,
Some skreaking and skrittering residuum,
And grates these evasions of the nightingale
Though I have never—shall never hear that bird.
And the stillness is in the key, all of it is,
The stillness is all in the key of that desolate sound.

A Fish-Scale Sunrise

Melodious skeletons, for all of last night's music
Today is today and the dancing is done.

Dew lies on the instruments of straw that you were playing,
The ruts in your empty road are red.

You Jim and you Margaret and you singer of La Paloma,
The cocks are crowing and crowing loud,

And although my mind perceives the force behind the
        moment,
The mind is smaller than the eye.

The sun rises green and blue in the fields and in the
        heavens.
The clouds foretell a swampy rain.

Gallant Chateau

Is it bad to have come here
And to have found the bed empty?

One might have found tragic hair,
Bitter eyes, hands hostile and cold.

There might have been a light on a book
Lighting a pitiless verse or two.

There might have been the immense solitude
Of the wind upon the curtains.

Pitiless verse? A few words tuned
And tuned and tuned and tuned.

It is good. The bed is empty,
The curtains are stiff and prim and still.

Delightful Evening

A very felicitous eve,
Herr Doktor, and that's enough,
Though the brow in your palm may grieve

At the vernacular of light
(Omitting reefs of cloud):
Empurpled garden grass;

The spruces' outstretched hands;
The twilight overfull
Of wormy metaphors.

THE MAN
WITH THE BLUE GUITAR

(1937)

The Man with the Blue Guitar

I

The man bent over his guitar,
A shearsman of sorts. The day was green.

They said, "You have a blue guitar,
You do not play things as they are."

The man replied, "Things as they are
Are changed upon the blue guitar."

And they said then, "But play, you must,
A tune beyond us, yet ourselves,

A tune upon the blue guitar
Of things exactly as they are."

II

I cannot bring a world quite round,
Although I patch it as I can.

I sing a hero's head, large eye
And bearded bronze, but not a man,

Although I patch him as I can
And reach through him almost to man.

If to serenade almost to man
Is to miss, by that, things as they are,

Say that it is the serenade
Of a man that plays a blue guitar.

III

Ah, but to play man number one,
To drive the dagger in his heart,

135

To lay his brain upon the board
And pick the acrid colors out,

To nail his thought across the door,
Its wings spread wide to rain and snow,

To strike his living hi and ho,
To tick it, tock it, turn it true,

To bang it from a savage blue,
Jangling the metal of the strings . . .

IV

So that's life, then: things as they are?
It picks its way on the blue guitar.

A million people on one string?
And all their manner in the thing,

And all their manner, right and wrong,
And all their manner, weak and strong?

The feelings crazily, craftily call,
Like a buzzing of flies in autumn air,

And that's life, then: things as they are,
This buzzing of the blue guitar.

V

Do not speak to us of the greatness of poetry,
Of the torches wisping in the underground,

Of the structure of vaults upon a point of light.
There are no shadows in our sun,

Day is desire and night is sleep.
There are no shadows anywhere.

The earth, for us, is flat and bare.
There are no shadows. Poetry

Exceeding music must take the place
Of empty heaven and its hymns,

Ourselves in poetry must take their place,
Even in the chattering of your guitar.

VI

A tune beyond us as we are,
Yet nothing changed by the blue guitar;

Ourselves in the tune as if in space,
Yet nothing changed, except the place

Of things as they are and only the place
As you play them, on the blue guitar,

Placed, so, beyond the compass of change,
Perceived in a final atmosphere;

For a moment final, in the way
The thinking of art seems final when

The thinking of god is smoky dew.
The tune is space. The blue guitar

Becomes the place of things as they are,
A composing of senses of the guitar.

VII

It is the sun that shares our works.
The moon shares nothing. It is a sea.

When shall I come to say of the sun,
It is a sea; it shares nothing;

The sun no longer shares our works
And the earth is alive with creeping men,

Mechanical beetles never quite warm?
And shall I then stand in the sun, as now

I stand in the moon, and call it good,
The immaculate, the merciful good,

Detached from us, from things as they are?
Not to be part of the sun? To stand

Remote and call it merciful?
The strings are cold on the blue guitar.

VIII

The vivid, florid, turgid sky,
The drenching thunder rolling by,

The morning deluged still by night,
The clouds tumultuously bright

And the feeling heavy in cold chords
Struggling toward impassioned choirs,

Crying among the clouds, enraged
By gold antagonists in air—

I know my lazy, leaden twang
Is like the reason in a storm;

And yet it brings the storm to bear.
I twang it out and leave it there.

IX

And the color, the overcast blue
Of the air, in which the blue guitar

Is a form, described but difficult,
And I am merely a shadow hunched

Above the arrowy, still strings,
The maker of a thing yet to be made;

The color like a thought that grows
Out of a mood, the tragic robe

Of the actor, half his gesture, half
His speech, the dress of his meaning, silk

Sodden with his melancholy words,
The weather of his stage, himself.

X

Raise reddest columns. Toll a bell
And clap the hollows full of tin.

Throw papers in the streets, the wills
Of the dead, majestic in their seals.

And the beautiful trombones—behold
The approach of him whom none believes,

Whom all believe that all believe,
A pagan in a varnished car.

Roll a drum upon the blue guitar.
Lean from the steeple. Cry aloud,

"Here am I, my adversary, that
Confront you, hoo-ing the slick trombones,

Yet with a petty misery
At heart, a petty misery,

Ever the prelude to your end,
The touch that topples men and rock."

XI

Slowly the ivy on the stones
Becomes the stones. Women become

The cities, children become the fields
And men in waves become the sea.

It is the chord that falsifies.
The sea returns upon the men,

The fields entrap the children, brick
Is a weed and all the flies are caught,

Wingless and withered, but living alive.
The discord merely magnifies.

Deeper within the belly's dark
Of time, time grows upon the rock.

XII

Tom-tom, c'est moi. The blue guitar
And I are one. The orchestra

Fills the high hall with shuffling men
High as the hall. The whirling noise

Of a multitude dwindles, all said,
To his breath that lies awake at night.

I know that timid breathing. Where
Do I begin and end? And where,

As I strum the thing, do I pick up
That which momentously declares

Itself not to be I and yet
Must be. It could be nothing else.

XIII

The pale intrusions into blue
Are corrupting pallors . . . ay di mi,

Blue buds or pitchy blooms. Be content—
Expansions, diffusions—content to be

The unspotted imbecile revery,
The heraldic center of the world

Of blue, blue sleek with a hundred chins,
The amorist Adjective aflame . . .

XIV

First one beam, then another, then
A thousand are radiant in the sky.

Each is both star and orb; and day
Is the riches of their atmosphere.

The sea appends its tattery hues.
The shores are banks of muffling mist.

One says a German chandelier—
A candle is enough to light the world.

It makes it clear. Even at noon
It glistens in essential dark.

At night, it lights the fruit and wine,
The book and bread, things as they are,

In a chiaroscuro where
One sits and plays the blue guitar.

XV

Is this picture of Picasso's, this "hoard
Of destructions", a picture of ourselves,

Now, an image of our society?
Do I sit, deformed, a naked egg,

Catching at Good-bye, harvest moon,
Without seeing the harvest or the moon?

Things as they are have been destroyed.
Have I? Am I a man that is dead

At a table on which the food is cold?
Is my thought a memory, not alive?

Is the spot on the floor, there, wine or blood
And whichever it may be, is it mine?

XVI

The earth is not earth but a stone,
Not the mother that held men as they fell

But stone, but like a stone, no: not
The mother, but an oppressor, but like

An oppressor that grudges them their death,
As it grudges the living that they live.

To live in war, to live at war,
To chop the sullen psaltery,

To improve the sewers in Jerusalem,
To electrify the nimbuses—

Place honey on the altars and die,
You lovers that are bitter at heart.

XVII

The person has a mould. But not
Its animal. The angelic ones

Speak of the soul, the mind. It is
An animal. The blue guitar—

On that its claws propound, its fangs
Articulate its desert days.

The blue guitar a mould? That shell?
Well, after all, the north wind blows

A horn, on which its victory
Is a worm composing in a straw.

XVIII

A dream (to call it a dream) in which
I can believe, in face of the object,

A dream no longer a dream, a thing,
Of things as they are, as the blue guitar

After long strumming on certain nights
Gives the touch of the senses, not of the hand,

But the very senses as they touch
The wind-gloss. Or as daylight comes,

Like light in a mirroring of cliffs,
Rising upward from a sea of ex.

XIX

That I may reduce the monster to
Myself, and then may be myself

In face of the monster, be more than part
Of it, more than the monstrous player of

One of its monstrous lutes, not be
Alone, but reduce the monster and be,

Two things, the two together as one,
And play of the monster and of myself,

Or better not of myself at all,
But of that as its intelligence,

Being the lion in the lute
Before the lion locked in stone.

XX

What is there in life except one's ideas,
Good air, good friend, what is there in life?

Is it ideas that I believe?
Good air, my only friend, believe,

Believe would be a brother full
Of love, believe would be a friend,

Friendlier than my only friend,
Good air. Poor pale, poor pale guitar . . . .

XXI

A substitute for all the gods:
This self, not that gold self aloft,

Alone, one's shadow magnified,
Lord of the body, looking down,

As now and called most high,
The shadow of Chocorua

In an immenser heaven, aloft,
Alone, lord of the land and lord

Of the men that live in the land, high lord.
One's self and the mountains of one's land,

Without shadows, without magnificence,
The flesh, the bone, the dirt, the stone.

XXII

Poetry is the subject of the poem,
From this the poem issues and

To this returns. Between the two,
Between issue and return, there is

An absence in reality,
Things as they are. Or so we say.

But are these separate? Is it
An absence for the poem, which acquires

Its true appearances there, sun's green,
Cloud's red, earth feeling, sky that thinks?

From these it takes. Perhaps it gives,
In the universal intercourse.

XXIII

A few final solutions, like a duet
With the undertaker: a voice in the clouds,

Another on earth, the one a voice
Of ether, the other smelling of drink,

The voice of ether prevailing, the swell
Of the undertaker's song in the snow

Apostrophizing wreaths, the voice
In the clouds serene and final, next

The grunted breath serene and final,
The imagined and the real, thought

And the truth, Dichtung und Wahrheit, all
Confusion solved, as in a refrain

One keeps on playing year by year,
Concerning the nature of things as they are.

XXIV

A poem like a missal found
In the mud, a missal for that young man,

That scholar hungriest for that book,
The very book, or, less, a page

Or, at the least, a phrase, that phrase,
A hawk of life, that latined phrase:

To know; a missal for brooding-sight.
To meet that hawk's eye and to flinch

Not at the eye but at the joy of it.
I play. But this is what I think.

XXV

He held the world upon his nose
And this-a-way he gave a fling.

His robes and symbols, ai-yi-yi—
And that-a-way he twirled the thing.

Sombre as fir-trees, liquid cats
Moved in the grass without a sound.

They did not know the grass went round.
The cats had cats and the grass turned gray

And the world had worlds, ai, this-a-way:
The grass turned green and the grass turned gray.

And the nose is eternal, that-a-way.
Things as they were, things as they are,

Things as they will be by and by . . .
A fat thumb beats out ai-yi-yi.

XXVI

The world washed in his imagination,
The world was a shore, whether sound or form

Or light, the relic of farewells,
Rock, of valedictory echoings,

To which his imagination returned,
From which it sped, a bar in space,

Sand heaped in the clouds, giant that fought
Against the murderous alphabet:

The swarm of thoughts, the swarm of dreams
Of inaccessible Utopia.

A mountainous music always seemed
To be falling and to be passing away.

XXVII

It is the sea that whitens the roof.
The sea drifts through the winter air.

It is the sea that the north wind makes.
The sea is in the falling snow.

This gloom is the darkness of the sea.
Geographers and philosophers,

Regard. But for that salty cup,
But for the icicles on the eaves—

The sea is a form of ridicule.
The iceberg settings satirize

The demon that cannot be himself,
That tours to shift the shifting scene.

XXVIII

I am a native in this world
And think in it as a native thinks,

Gesu, not native of a mind
Thinking the thoughts I call my own,

Native, a native in the world
And like a native think in it.

It could not be a mind, the wave
In which the watery grasses flow

And yet are fixed as a photograph,
The wind in which the dead leaves blow.

Here I inhale profounder strength
And as I am, I speak and move

And things are as I think they are
And say they are on the blue guitar.

XXIX

In the cathedral, I sat there, and read,
Alone, a lean Review and said,

"These degustations in the vaults
Oppose the past and the festival.

What is beyond the cathedral, outside,
Balances with nuptial song.

So it is to sit and to balance things
To and to and to the point of still,

To say of one mask it is like,
To say of another it is like,

To know that the balance does not quite rest,
That the mask is strange, however like."

The shapes are wrong and the sounds are false.
The bells are the bellowings of bulls.

Yet Franciscan don was never more
Himself than in this fertile glass.

XXX

From this I shall evolve a man.
This is his essence: the old fantoche

Hanging his shawl upon the wind,
Like something on the stage, puffed out,

His strutting studied through centuries.
At last, in spite of his manner, his eye

A-cock at the cross-piece on a pole
Supporting heavy cables, slung

Through Oxidia, banal suburb,
One-half of all its installments paid.

Dew-dapper clapper-traps, blazing
From crusty stacks above machines.

Ecce, Oxidia is the seed
Dropped out of this amber-ember pod,

Oxidia is the soot of fire,
Oxidia is Olympia.

XXXI

How long and late the pheasant sleeps . . .
The employer and employee contend,

Combat, compose their droll affair.
The bubbling sun will bubble up,

Spring sparkle and the cock-bird shriek.
The employer and employee will hear

And continue their affair. The shriek
Will rack the thickets. There is no place,

Here, for the lark fixed in the mind,
In the museum of the sky. The cock

Will claw sleep. Morning is not sun,
It is this posture of the nerves,

As if a blunted player clutched
The nuances of the blue guitar.

It must be this rhapsody or none,
The rhapsody of things as they are.

XXXII

Throw away the lights, the definitions,
And say of what you see in the dark

That it is this or that it is that,
But do not use the rotted names.

How should you walk in that space and know
Nothing of the madness of space,

Nothing of its jocular procreations?
Throw the lights away. Nothing must stand

Between you and the shapes you take
When the crust of shape has been destroyed.

You as you are? You are yourself.
The blue guitar surprises you.

XXXIII

That generation's dream, aviled
In the mud, in Monday's dirty light,

That's it, the only dream they knew,
Time in its final block, not time

To come, a wrangling of two dreams.
Here is the bread of time to come,

Here is its actual stone. The bread
Will be our bread, the stone will be

Our bed and we shall sleep by night.
We shall forget by day, except

The moments when we choose to play
The imagined pine, the imagined jay.

Owl's Clover

I. The Old Woman & the Statue

I

Another evening in another park,
A group of marble horses rose on wings
In the midst of a circle of trees, from which the leaves
Raced with the horses in bright hurricanes.

II

So much the sculptor had foreseen: autumn,
The sky above the plaza widening
Before the horses, clouds of bronze imposed
On clouds of gold, and green engulfing bronze,
The marble leaping in the storms of light.
So much he had devised: white forelegs taut
To the muscles' very tip for the vivid plunge,
The heads held high and gathered in a ring
At the center of the mass, the haunches low,
Contorted, staggering from the thrust against
The earth as the bodies rose on feathery wings,
Clumped carvings, circular, like blunted fans,
Arranged for phantasy to form an edge
Of crisping light along the statue's rim.
More than his muddy hand was in the manes,
More than his mind in the wings. The rotten leaves
Swirled round them in immense autumnal sounds.

III

But her he had not foreseen: the bitter mind
In a flapping cloak. She walked along the paths
Of the park with chalky brow scratched over black
And black by thought that could not understand
Or, if it understood, repressed itself
Without any pity in a somnolent dream.
The golden clouds that turned to bronze, the sounds

Descending, did not touch her eye and left
Her ear unmoved. She was that tortured one,
So destitute that nothing but herself
Remained and nothing of herself except
A fear too naked for her shadow's shape.
To search for clearness all an afternoon
And without knowing, and then upon the wind
To hear the stroke of one's certain solitude,
What sound could comfort away the sudden sense?
What path could lead apart from what she was
And was to be? Could it happen to be this,
This atmosphere in which the horses rose,
This atmosphere in which her musty mind
Lay black and full of black misshapen? Wings
And light lay deeper for her than her sight.

IV

The mass of stone collapsed to marble hulk,
Stood stiffly, as if the black of what she thought,
Conflicting with the moving colors there,
Changed them, at last, to its triumphant hue,
Triumphant as that always upward wind
Blowing among the trees its meaningless sound.
The space above the trees might still be bright
Yet the light fell falsely on the marble skulls,
Manes matted of marble across the air, the light
Fell falsely on the matchless skeletons,
A change so felt, a fear in her so known,
Now felt, now known as this. The clouds of bronze
Slowly submerging in flatness disappeared.
If the sky that followed, smaller than the night,
Still eked out luminous wrinklings on the leaves,
Whitened, again, forms formless in the dark,
It was as if transparence touched her mind.
The statue stood in stars like water-spheres,
Washed over by their green, their flowing blue.
A mood that had become so fixed it was
A manner of the mind, a mind in a night
That was whatever the mind might make of it,
A night that was that mind so magnified

It lost the common shape of night and came
To be the sovereign shape in a world of shapes.
A woman walking in the autumn leaves,
Thinking of heaven and earth and of herself
And looking at the place in which she walked,
As a place in which each thing was motionless
Except the thing she felt but did not know.

V

Without her, evening like a budding yew
Would soon be brilliant, as it was, before
The harridan self and ever-maladive fate
Went crying their desolate syllables, before
Their voice and the voice of the tortured wind were one,
Each voice within the other, seeming one,
Crying against a need that pressed like cold,
Deadly and deep. It would become a yew
Grown great and grave beyond imagined trees,
Branching through heavens heavy with the sheen
And shadowy hanging of it, thick with stars
Of a lunar light, dark-belted sorcerers
Dazzling by simplest beams and soothly still,
The space beneath it still, a smooth domain,
Untroubled by suffering, which fate assigns
To the moment. There the horses would rise again,
Yet hardly to be seen and again the legs
Would flash in air, and the muscular bodies thrust
Hoofs grinding against the stubborn earth, until
The light wings lifted through the crystal space
Of night. How clearly that would be defined!

II. The Statue at the World's End

I

The thing is dead . . . . . Everything is dead
Except the future. Always everything
That is is dead except what ought to be.
All things destroy themselves or are destroyed.

These are not even Russian animals.
They are horses as they were in the sculptor's mind.
They might be sugar or paste or citron-skin
Made by a cook that never rode the back
Of his angel through the skies. They might be mud
Left here by moonlit muckers when they fled
At the burst of day, crepuscular images
Made to remember a life they never lived
In the witching wilderness, night's witchingness,
Made to affect a dream they never had,
Like a word in the mind that sticks at artichoke
And remains inarticulate, horses with cream.
The statue seems a thing from Schwarz's, a thing
Of the dank imagination, much below
Our crusted outlines hot and huge with fact,
Ugly as an idea, not beautiful
As sequels without thought. In the rudest red
Of autumn, these horses should go clattering
Along the thin horizons, nobly more
Than this jotting-down of the sculptor's foppishness
Long after the worms and the curious carvings of
Their snouts.

II

Come, all celestial paramours,
Whether in-dwelling haughty clouds, frigid
And crisply musical, or holy caverns temple-toned,
Entwine your arms and moving to and fro,
Now like a ballet infantine in awkward steps,
Chant sibilant requiems for this effigy.
Bring down from nowhere nothing's wax-like blooms,
Calling them what you will but loosely-named
In a mortal lullaby, like porcelain.
Then, while the music makes you, make, yourselves,
Long autumn sheens and pittering sounds like sounds
On pattering leaves and suddenly with lights,
Astral and Shelleyan, diffuse new day;
And on this ring of marble horses shed
The rainbow in its glistening serpentines

Made by the sun ascending seventy seas.
Agree: the apple in the orchard, round
And red, will not be redder, rounder then
Than now. No: nor the ploughman in his bed
Be free to sleep there sounder, for the plough
And the dew and the ploughman still will best be one.
But this gawky plaster will not be here.

III

The stones
That will replace it shall be carved, *"The Mass
Appoints These Marbles Of Itself To Be
Itself."* No more than that, no subterfuge,
No memorable muffing, bare and blunt.

IV

At some gigantic, solitary urn,
A trash can at the end of the world, the dead
Give up dead things and the living turn away.
There buzzards pile their sticks among the bones
Of buzzards and eat the bellies of the rich,
Fat with a thousand butters, and the crows
Sip the wild honey of the poor man's life,
The blood of his bitter brain; and there the sun
Shines without fire on columns intercrossed,
White slapped on white, majestic, marble heads,
Severed and tumbled into seedless grass,
Motionless, knowing neither dew nor frost.
There lies the head of the sculptor in which the thought
Of lizards, in its eye, is more acute
Than the thought that once was native to the skull;
And there are the white-maned horses' heads, beyond
The help of any wind or any sky:
Parts of the immense detritus of a world
That is completely waste, that moves from waste
To waste, out of the hopeless waste of the past
Into a hopeful waste to come. There even
The colorless light in which this wreckage lies

Has faint, portentous lustres, shades and shapes
Of rose, or what will once more rise to rose,
When younger bodies, because they are younger, rise
And chant the rose-points of their birth, and when
For a little time, again, rose-breasted birds
Sing rose-beliefs. Above that urn two lights
Commingle, not like the commingling of sun and moon
At dawn, nor of summer-light and winter-light
In an autumn afternoon, but two immense
Reflections, whirling apart and wide away.

V

Mesdames, it is not enough to be reconciled
Before the strange, having wept and having thought
And having said farewell. It is not enough
That the vista retain ploughmen, peacocks, doves,
However tarnished, companions out of the past,
And that, heavily, you move with them in the dust.
It is not enough that you are indifferent,
Because time moves on columns intercrossed
And because the temple is never quite composed,
Silent and turquoised and perpetual,
Visible over the sea. It is only enough
To live incessantly in change. See how
On a day still full of summer, when the leaves
Appear to sleep within a sleeping air,
They suddenly fall and the leafless sound of the wind
Is no longer a sound of summer. So great a change
Is constant. The time you call serene descends
Through a moving chaos that never ends. Mesdames,
Leaves are not always falling and the birds
Of chaos are not always sad nor lost
In melancholy distances. You held
Each other moving in a chant and danced
Beside the statue, while you sang. Your eyes
Were solemn and your gowns were blown and grief
Was under every temple-tone. You sang
A tragic lullaby, like porcelain.
But change composes, too, and chaos comes

To momentary calm, spectacular flocks
Of crimson and hoods of Venezuelan green
And the sound of z in the grass all day, though these
Are chaos and of archaic change. Shall you,
Then, fear a drastic community evolved
From the whirling, slowly and by trial; or fear
Men gathering for a mighty flight of men,
An abysmal migration into a possible blue?

III. The Greenest Continent

I

Large-leaved and many-footed shadowing,
What god rules over Africa, what shape,
What avuncular cloud-man beamier than spears?

II

The heaven of Europe is empty. But there was
A heaven once, a heaven all selves. It was
The spirit's episcopate, hallowed and high,
To which the spirit ascended, to increase
Itself, beyond the utmost increase come
From youngest day or oldest night and far
Beyond thought's regulation. There each man,
Through long cloud-cloister-porches, walked alone,
Noble within perfecting solitude,
Like a solitude of the sun, in which the mind
Acquired transparence and beheld itself
And beheld the source from which transparence came;
And there he heard the voices that were once
The confusion of men's voices, intricate
Made extricate by meanings, meanings made
Into a music never touched to sound.
There, too, he saw, since he must see, the domes
Of azure round an upper dome, brightest
Because it rose above them all, stippled

By waverings of stars, the joy of day
And its immaculate fire, the middle dome,
The temple of the altar where each man
Beheld the truth and knew it to be true.

III

That was never the heaven of Africa, which had
No heaven, had death without a heaven, death
In a heaven of death. Beneath the heavy foils,
Beneath the spangling greens, fear might placate
And the serpent might become a god, quick-eyed,
Rising from indolent coils. If the statue rose,
If once the statue were to rise, if it stood,
Thinly, among the elephantine palms,
Sleekly the serpent would draw himself across.
The horses are part of a northern sky
Too starkly pallid for the jaguar's light,
In which he and the lion and the serpent hide
Even in sleep, deep in the grass of sleep,
Deep grass that totters under the weight of light.
There sleep and waking fill with jaguar-men
And lion-men and the flicking serpent-kin
In flowery nations, crashing and alert.
No god rules over Africa, no throne,
Single, of burly ivory, inched of gold,
Disposed upon the central of what we see,
That purges the wrack or makes the jungle shine,
As brilliant as mystic, as mystic as single, all
In one, except a throne raised up beyond
Men's bones, beyond their breaths, the black sublime,
Toward which, in the nights, the glittering serpents climb,
Dark-skinned and sinuous, winding upwardly,
Winding and waving, slowly, waving in air,
Darting envenomed eyes about, like fangs,
Hissing, across the silence, puissant sounds.
Death, only, sits upon the serpent throne
In silence: death, the herdsman of elephants,
To whom the jaguars cry and lions roar
Their petty dirges of fallen forest-men,

Forever hunting or hunted, rushing through
Endless pursuit or endlessly pursued,
Until each tree, each evil-blossomed vine,
Each fretful fern drops down a fear like dew
And Africa, basking in antiquest sun,
Contains for its children not a gill of sweet.

IV

Forth from their tabernacles once again
The angels come, armed, gloriously to slay
The black and ruin his sepulchral throne.
Hé quoi! Angels go pricking elephants?
Wings spread and whirling over jaguar-men?
Angels tiptoe upon the snowy cones
Of palmy peaks sighting machine-guns? These,
Seraphim of Europe? Pouring out of dawn,
Fresh from the sacred clarities, chanters
Of the pith of mind, cuirassiers against
The milkiest bowmen. This makes a new design,
Filleted angels over flapping ears,
Combatting bushmen for a patch of gourds,
Loosing black slaves to make black infantry,
Angels returning after war with belts
And beads and bangles of gold and trumpets raised,
Racking the world with clarion puffs. This must
Be merely a masquerade or else a rare
Tractatus, of military things, with plates,
Miraculously preserved, full fickle-fine,
Of an imagination flashed with irony
And by a hand of certitude to cut
The heavenly cocks, the bowmen, and the gourds,
The oracular trumpets round and roundly hooped,
In Leonardo's way, to magnify
Concentric bosh. To their tabernacles, then,
Remoter than Athos, the effulgent hordes
Return, affecting roseate aureoles,
To contemplate time's golden paladin
And purpose, to hear the wild bee drone, to feel
The ecstasy of sense in a sensuous air.

V

But could the statue stand in Africa?
The marble was imagined in the cold.
Its edges were taken from tumultuous wind
That beat out slimmest edges in the ear,
Made of the eye an insatiable intellect,
Its surfaces came from distant fire; and it
Was meant to stand, not in a tumbling green,
Intensified and grandiose, but among
The common-places of which it formed a part
And there, by feat extenuations, to make
A visible clear cap, a visible wreath
To men, to houses, streets and the squalid whole.
There it would be of the mode of common dreams,
A ring of horses rising from memory
Or rising in the appointments of desire,
The spirit's natural images, carriers,
The drafts of gay beginnings and bright ends,
Majestic bearers or solemn haulers trapped
In endless elegies. But in Africa
The memory moves on leopards' feet, desire
Appoints its florid messengers with wings
Wildly curvetted, color-scarred, so beaked,
With tongues unclipped and throats so stuffed with thorns,
So clawed, so sopped with sun, that in these things
The message is half-borne. Could marble still
Be marble after the drenching reds, the dark
And drenching crimsons, or endure? It came
If not from winter, from a summer like
A winter's noon, in which the colors sprang
From snow, and would return again to snow,
As summer would return to weazened days.

VI

Fatal Ananke is the common god.
He looks upon the statue, where it is,
And the sun and the sun-reek piled and peaked above
The jostled ferns, where it might be, having eyes
Of the shape of eyes, like blunt intaglios,

And nothing more. He sees but not by sight.
He does not hear by sound. His spirit knows
Each look and each necessitous cry, as a god
Knows, knowing that he does not care, and knows,
Knowing and meaning that he cannot care.
He sees the angel in the nigger's mind
And hears the nigger's prayer in motets, belched
From pipes that swarm clerestory walls. The voice
In the jungle is a voice in Fontainebleau.
The long recessional at parish eves wails round
The cuckoo trees and the widow of Madrid
Weeps in Segovia. The beggar in Rome
Is the beggar in Bogotá. The kraal
Chants a death that is a medieval death . . .
Fateful Ananke is the final god.
His hymn, his psalm, his cithern song of praise
Is the exile of the disinherited,
Life's foreigners, pale aliens of the mud,
Those whose Jerusalem is Glasgow-frost
Or Paris-rain. He thinks of the noble lives
Of the gods and, for him, a thousand litanies
Are like the perpetual verses in a poet's mind.
He is that obdurate ruler who ordains
For races, not for men, powerful beyond
A grace to nature, a changeless element.
His place is large and high, an ether flamed
By his presence, the seat of his ubiquitous will.
He, only, caused the statue to be made
And he shall fix the place where it will stand.
Be glory to this unmerciful pontifex,
Lord without any deviation, lord
And origin and resplendent end of law,
Sultan of African sultans, starless crown.

IV. A Duck for Dinner

I

The Bulgar said, "After pineapple with fresh mint
We went to walk in the park; for, after all,

The workers do not rise, as Venus rose,
Out of a violet sea. They rise a bit
On summer Sundays in the park, a duck
To a million, a duck with apples and without wine."

II

Buckskins and broad-brims, crossers of divides,
For whom men were to be ends in themselves,
Are the cities to breed as the mountains bred? For you
Day came upon the spirit as life comes
And deep winds flooded you; for these, day comes,
A penny sun in a tinsel sky, unrhymed,
And the spirit writhes to be wakened, writhes
To see, once more, this hacked-up world of tools.
In their cadaverous Eden, they desire
The same down-dropping fruit in yellow leaves.
The scholar's outline that you had, the print
Of poets, the Italian lives preserved
For poverty are gaudy o to these.
Their destiny is just as much machine
As death itself. It will, it will be changed,
Time's fortune near, the sleepless sleepers moved
By the torture of things that will be realized,
Will, will, but how and all of them asking how.
These lives are not your lives, O free, O bold
That rode your horses straight away.

III

                    Again
The acrid Bulgar said, "There are more things
Than poodles in Pomerania. These men,
Infected by unreality, rapt round
By dense unreason, irreproachable force,
Are cast in pandemonium, flittered, howled
By harmonies beyond known harmony.
These bands, these swarms, these motions, what of them?
Of what are they thinking, of what, in spite of the duck,
Are they being part, of what are they feeling the strength,
Seeing the fulgent shadows upward heaped,

Spelling out pandects and haggard institutes?
Is each man thinking his separate thoughts or, for once,
Are all men thinking together as one, thinking
Each other's thoughts, thinking a single thought,
Disclosed in everything, transcended, poised
For the syllable, poised for the touch? But that
Apocalypse was not contrived for parks,
Geranium budgets, pay-roll water-falls,
The clank of the carrousel and, under the trees,
The sheep-like falling-in of distances,
Converging on the statue, white and high."

IV

Then Basilewsky in the band-stand played
"Concerto for Airplane and Pianoforte,"
The newest Soviet réclame. Profound
Abortion, fit for the enchanting of basilisks.
They chanced to think: suppose the future fails.
If platitude and inspiration are alike
As evils, and if reason, fatuous fire,
Is only another egoist wearing a mask,
What man of folk-lore shall rebuild the world,
What lesser man shall measure sun and moon,
What super-animal dictate our fates?
As the man the state, not as the state the man.
But man means more, means the million and the duck.
It cannot mean a sea-wide country strewn
With squalid cells. It means, at least, this mob.
The man in the band-stand could be orator,
Some pebble-chewer practiced in Tyrian speech,
An apparition, twanging instruments
Within us hitherto unknown, he that
Confounds all opposites and spins a sphere
Created, like a bubble, of bright sheens,
With a tendency to bulge as it floats away.
Basilewsky's bulged before it floated, turned
Caramel and would not, could not float. And yet
In an age of concentric mobs would any sphere
Escape all deformation, much less this,

This source and patriarch of other spheres,
This base of every future, vibrant spring,
The volcano Apostrophe, the sea Behold?
Suppose, instead of failing, it never comes,
This future, although the elephants pass and the blare,
Prolonged, repeated and once more prolonged,
Goes off a little on the side and stops.
Yet to think of the future is a genius,
To think of the future is a thing and he
That thinks of it is inscribed on walls and stands
Complete in bronze on enormous pedestals.

V

The statue is white and high, white brillianter
Than the color white and high beyond any height
That rises in the air. The sprawlers on the grass
See more than marble in their eyes, see more
Than the horses quivering to be gone, flashed through
With senses chiseled on bright stone. They see
The metropolitan of mind, they feel
The central of the composition, in which
They live. They see and feel themselves, seeing
And feeling the world in which they live. The manes,
The leaping bodies, come from the truculent hand,
The stubborn eye, of the conformer who conforms
The manes to his image of the flying wind,
The leaping bodies to his strength, convulsed
By tautest pinions lifted through his thought.
The statue is the sculptor not the stone.
In this he carved himself, he carved his age,
He carved the feathery walkers standing by,
Twitching a little with crude souvenirs
Of young identities, Aprilian stubs.
Exceeding sex, he touched another race,
Above our race, yet of ourselves transformed,
Don Juan turned furious divinity,
Ethereal compounder, pater patriae,
Great mud-ancestor, oozer and Abraham,
Progenitor wearing the diamond crown of crowns,

He from whose beard the future springs, elect.
More of ourselves in a world that is more our own,
For the million, perhaps, two ducks instead of one;
More of ourselves, the mood of life made strong
As by a juicier season; and more our own
As against each other, the dead, the phantomesque.

VI

If these were theoretical people, like
Small bees of spring, sniffing the coldest buds
Of a time to come—A shade of horror turns
The bees to scorpions blackly-barbed, a shade
Of fear changes the scorpions to skins
Concealed in glittering grass, dank reptile skins.
The civil fiction, the calico idea,
The Johnsonian composition, abstract man,
All are evasions like a repeated phrase,
Which, by its repetition, comes to bear
A meaning without a meaning. These people have
A meaning within the meaning they convey,
Walking the paths, watching the gilding sun,
To be swept across them when they are revealed,
For a moment, once each century or two.
The future for them is always the deepest dome,
The darkest blue of the dome and the wings around
The giant Phosphor of their earliest prayers.
Once each century or two. But then so great,
So epical a twist, catastrophe
For Isaac Watts: the diverting of the dream
Of heaven from heaven to the future, as a god,
Takes time and tinkering, melodious
And practical. The envoi to the past
Is largely another winding of the clock.
The tempo, in short, of this complicated shift,
With interruptions by vast hymns, blood odes,
Parades of whole races with attendant bands,
And the bees, the scorpions, the men that think,
The summer Sundays in the park, must be
A leaden ticking circular in width.

How shall we face the edge of time? We walk
In the park. We regret we have no nightingale.
We must have the throstle on the gramophone.
Where shall we find more than derisive words?
When shall lush chorals spiral through our fire
And daunt that old assassin, heart's desire?

V. Sombre Figuration

I

There is a man whom rhapsodies of change,
Of which he is the cause, have never changed
And never will, a subman under all
The rest, to whom in the end the rest return,
The man below the man below the man,
Steeped in night's opium, evading day.

II

We have grown weary of the man that thinks.
He thinks and it is not true. The man below
Imagines and it is true, as if he thought
By imagining, anti-logician, quick
With a logic of transforming certitudes.
It is not that he was born in another land,
Powdered with primitive lights, and lives with us
In glimpses, on the edge or at the tip.
He was born within us as a second self,
A self of parents who have never died,
Whose lives return, simply, upon our lips,
Their word and ours; in what we see, their hues
Without a season, unstinted in livery,
And ours, of rigid measure, a miser's paint;
And most in what we hear, sound brushed away,
A mumbling at the elbow, turgid tunes,
As of insects or cloud-stricken birds, away
And away, dialogues between incognitos.
He dwells below, the man below, in less
Than body and in less than mind, ogre,

Inhabitant, in less than shape, of shapes
That are dissembled in vague memory
Yet still retain resemblances, remain
Remembrances, a place of a field of lights,
As a church is a bell and people are an eye,
A cry, the pallor of a dress, a touch.
He turns us into scholars, studying
The masks of music. We perceive each mask
To be the musician's own and, thence, become
An audience to mimics glistening
With meanings, doubled by the closest sound,
Mimics that play on instruments discerned
In the beat of the blood.
          Green is the path we take
Between chimeras and garlanded the way,
The down-descent into November's void.
The spontaneities of rain or snow
Surprise the sterile rationalist who sees
Maidens in bloom, bulls under sea, the lark
On urns and oak-leaves twisted into rhyme.
The man, but not the man below, for whom
The pheasant in a field was pheasant, field,
Until they changed to eagle in white air,
Lives in a fluid, not on solid rock.
The solid was an age, a period
With appropriate, largely English, furniture,
Barbers with charts of the only possible modes,
Cities that would not wash away in the mist,
Each man in his asylum maundering,
Policed by the hope of Christmas. Summer night,
Night gold, and winter night, night silver, these
Were the fluid, the cat-eyed atmosphere, in which
The man and the man below were reconciled,
The east wind in the west, order destroyed,
The cycle of the solid having turned.

III

High up in heaven a sprawling portent moves,
As if it bears all darkness in its bulk.

But this we cannot see. The shaggy top
Broods in tense meditation, constantly,
On the city, on which it leans, the people there,
Its shadow on their houses, on their walls,
Their beds, their faces drawn in distant sleep.
This is invisible. The supporting arms
Reach from the horizons, rim to rim,
While the shaggy top collects itself to do
And the shoulders turn, breathing immense intent.
All this is hidden from sight.
                                        It is the form
Of a generation that does not know itself,
Still questioning if to crush the soaring stacks.
The man below beholds the portent poised,
An image of his making, beyond the eye.
The year's dim elongations stretch below
To tumbled rock, its bright projections lie
The shallowest iris on the emptiest eye.
The future must bear within it every past,
Not least the pasts destroyed, magniloquent
Syllables, pewter on ebony, yet still
A board for bishops' grapes, the happy form
That revolution takes for connoisseurs:
The portent may itself be memory;
And memory may itself be time to come
And must be, when the portent, changed, takes on
A mask up-gathered brilliantly from the dirt,
And memory's lord is the lord of prophesy
And steps forth, priestly in severity,
Yet lord, a mask of flame, the darkest form
A wandering orb upon a path grown clear.

IV

High up in heaven the sprawling portent moves.
The statue in a crow's perspective of trees
Stands brimming white, chiaroscuro scaled
To space. To space? The statue scaled to space
Would be a ring of heads and haunches, torn
From size, backs larger than the eye, not flesh

In marble, but marble massive as the thrust
Of that which is not seen and cannot be.
The portent would become man-haggard to
A race of dwarfs, the meditative arms
And head a shadow trampled under hoofs,
Man-misty to a race star-humped, astride
In a clamor thudding up from central earth.
Not the space in camera of the man below,
Immeasurable, the space in which he knows
The locust's titter and the turtle's sob.
The statue stands in true perspective. Crows
Give only their color to the leaves. The trees
Are full of fanfares of farewell, as night
And the portent end in night, composed, before
Its wheel begins to turn.
                              The statue stands
In hum-drum space, farewell, farewell, by day
The green, white, blue of the ballad-eye, by night
The mirror of other nights combined in one.
The spring is hum-drum like an instrument,
That a man without passion plays in an aimless way.
Even imagination has an end,
When the statue is not a thing imagined, a stone,
The flight of emblemata through his mind,
Thoughts by descent. To flourish the great cloak we wear
At night, to turn away from the abominable
Farewells and, in the darkness, to feel again
The reconciliation, the rapture of a time
Without imagination, without past
And without future, a present time, is that
The passion, indifferent to the poets' hum,
That we conceal? A passion to fling the cloak,
Adorned for a multitude, in a gesture spent
In the gesture's whim, a passion merely to be
For the gaudium of being, Jocundus instead
Of the black-blooded scholar, the man of the cloud, to be
The medium man among other medium men,
The cloak to be clipped, the night to be redesigned,
Its land-breath to be stifled, its color changed,
Night and the imagination being one.

A Thought Revolved

I. The Mechanical Optimist

A lady dying of diabetes
Listened to the radio,
Catching the lesser dithyrambs.
So heaven collects its bleating lambs.

Her useless bracelets fondly fluttered,
Paddling the melodic swirls,
The idea of god no longer sputtered
At the roots of her indifferent curls.

The idea of the Alps grew large,
Not yet, however, a thing to die in.
It seemed serener just to die,
To float off on the floweriest barge,

Accompanied by the exegesis
Of familiar things in a cheerful voice,
Like the night before Christmas and all the carols.
Dying lady, rejoice, rejoice!

II. Mystic Garden & Middling Beast

The poet striding among the cigar stores,
Ryan's lunch, hatters, insurance and medicines,
Denies that abstraction is a vice except
To the fatuous. These are his infernal walls,
A space of stone, of inexplicable base
And peaks outsoaring possible adjectives.
One man, the idea of man, that is the space,
The true abstract in which he promenades.
The era of the idea of man, the cloak
And speech of Virgil dropped, that's where he walks,
That's where his hymns come crowding, hero-hymns,
Chorals for mountain voices and the moral chant,

Happy rather than holy but happy-high,
Day hymns instead of constellated rhymes,
Hymns of the struggle of the idea of god
And the idea of man, the mystic garden and
The middling beast, the garden of paradise
And he that created the garden and peopled it.

III. Romanesque Affabulation

He sought an earthly leader who could stand
Without panache, without cockade,
Son only of man and sun of men,
The outer captain, the inner saint,

The pine, the pillar and the priest,
The voice, the book, the hidden well,
The faster's feast and heavy-fruited star,
The father, the beater of the rigid drums,

He that at midnight touches the guitar,
The solitude, the barrier, the Pole
In Paris, celui qui chante et pleure,
Winter devising summer in its breast,

Summer assaulted, thundering, illumed,
Shelter yet thrower of the summer spear,
With all his attributes no god but man
Of men whose heaven is in themselves,

Or else whose hell, foamed with their blood
And the long echo of their dying cry,
A fate intoned, a death before they die,
The race that sings and weeps and knows not why.

IV. The Leader

Behold the moralist hidalgo
Whose whore is Morning Star

Dressed in metal, silk and stone,
Syringa, cicada, his flea.

In how severe a book he read,
Until his nose grew thin and taut
And knowledge dropped upon his heart
Its pitting poison, half the night.

He liked the nobler works of man,
The gold façade round early squares,
The bronzes liquid through gay light.
He hummed to himself at such a plan.

He sat among beggars wet with dew,
Heard the dogs howl at barren bone,
Sat alone, his great toe like a horn,
The central flaw in the solar morn.

The Men That Are Falling

God and all angels sing the world to sleep,
Now that the moon is rising in the heat

And crickets are loud again in the grass. The moon
Burns in the mind on lost remembrances.

He lies down and the night wind blows upon him here.
The bells grow longer. This is not sleep. This is desire.

Ah! Yes, desire . . . this leaning on his bed,
This leaning on his elbows on his bed,

Staring, at midnight, at the pillow that is black
In the catastrophic room . . . beyond despair,

Like an intenser instinct. What is it he desires?
But this he cannot know, the man that thinks,

Yet life itself, the fulfilment of desire
In the grinding ric-rac, staring steadily

At a head upon the pillow in the dark,
More than sudarium, speaking the speech

Of absolutes, bodiless, a head
Thick-lipped from riot and rebellious cries,

The head of one of the men that are falling, placed
Upon the pillow to repose and speak,

Speak and say the immaculate syllables
That he spoke only by doing what he did.

God and all angels, this was his desire,
Whose head lies blurring here, for this he died.

Taste of the blood upon his martyred lips,
O pensioners, O demagogues and pay-men!

This death was his belief though death is a stone.
This man loved earth, not heaven, enough to die.

The night wind blows upon the dreamer, bent
Over words that are life's voluble utterance.

PARTS OF A WORLD

(1942)

Parochial Theme

Long-tailed ponies go nosing the pine-lands,
Ponies of Parisians shooting on the hill.

The wind blows. In the wind, the voices
Have shapes that are not yet fully themselves,

Are sounds blown by a blower into shapes,
The blower squeezed to the thinnest *mi* of falsetto.

The hunters run to and fro. The heavy trees,
The grunting, shuffling branches, the robust,

The nocturnal, the antique, the blue-green pines
Deepen the feelings to inhuman depths.

These are the forest. This health is holy,
This halloo, halloo, halloo heard over the cries

Of those for whom a square room is a fire,
Of those whom the statues torture and keep down.

This health is holy, this descant of a self,
This barbarous chanting of what is strong, this blare.

But salvation here? What about the rattle of sticks
On tins and boxes? What about horses eaten by wind?

When spring comes and the skeletons of the hunters
Stretch themselves to rest in their first summer's sun,

The spring will have a health of its own, with none
Of autumn's halloo in its hair. So that closely, then,

Health follows after health. Salvation there:
There's no such thing as life; or if there is,

It is faster than the weather, faster than
Any character. It is more than any scene:

Of the guillotine or of any glamorous hanging.
Piece the world together, boys, but not with your hands.

Poetry Is a Destructive Force

That's what misery is,
Nothing to have at heart.
It is to have or nothing.

It is a thing to have,
A lion, an ox in his breast,
To feel it breathing there.

Corazon, stout dog,
Young ox, bow-legged bear,
He tastes its blood, not spit.

He is like a man
In the body of a violent beast.
Its muscles are his own . . .

The lion sleeps in the sun.
Its nose is on its paws.
It can kill a man.

The Poems of Our Climate

I

Clear water in a brilliant bowl,
Pink and white carnations. The light
In the room more like a snowy air,
Reflecting snow. A newly-fallen snow
At the end of winter when afternoons return.
Pink and white carnations—one desires
So much more than that. The day itself
Is simplified: a bowl of white,
Cold, a cold porcelain, low and round,
With nothing more than the carnations there.

II

Say even that this complete simplicity
Stripped one of all one's torments, concealed
The evilly compounded, vital I
And made it fresh in a world of white,
A world of clear water, brilliant-edged,
Still one would want more, one would need more,
More than a world of white and snowy scents.

III

There would still remain the never-resting mind,
So that one would want to escape, come back
To what had been so long composed.
The imperfect is our paradise.
Note that, in this bitterness, delight,
Since the imperfect is so hot in us,
Lies in flawed words and stubborn sounds.

Prelude to Objects

I

If he will be heaven after death,
If, while he lives, he hears himself
Sounded in music, if the sun,
Stormer, is the color of a self
As certainly as night is the color
Of a self, if, without sentiment,
He is what he hears and sees and if,
Without pathos, he feels what he hears
And sees, being nothing otherwise,
Having nothing otherwise, he has not
To go to the Louvre to behold himself.
Granted each picture is a glass,

That the walls are mirrors multiplied,
That the marbles are gluey pastiches, the stairs
The sweep of an impossible elegance,
And the notorious views from the windows
Wax wasted, monarchies beyond
The S.S. *Normandie*, granted
One is always seeing and feeling oneself,
That's not by chance. It comes to this:
That the guerilla I should be booked
And bound. Its nigger mystics should change
Foolscap for wigs. Academies
As of a tragic science should rise.

II

Poet, patting more nonsense foamed
From the sea, conceive for the courts
Of these academies, the diviner health
Disclosed in common forms. Set up
The rugged black, the image. Design
The touch. Fix quiet. Take the place
Of parents, lewdest of ancestors.
We are conceived in your conceits.

Study of Two Pears

I

Opusculum paedagogum.
The pears are not viols,
Nudes or bottles.
They resemble nothing else.

II

They are yellow forms
Composed of curves
Bulging toward the base.
They are touched red.

III

They are not flat surfaces
Having curved outlines.
They are round
Tapering toward the top.

IV

In the way they are modelled
There are bits of blue.
A hard dry leaf hangs
From the stem.

V

The yellow glistens.
It glistens with various yellows,
Citrons, oranges and greens
Flowering over the skin.

VI

The shadows of the pears
Are blobs on the green cloth.
The pears are not seen
As the observer wills.

The Glass of Water

That the glass would melt in heat,
That the water would freeze in cold,
Shows that this object is merely a state,
One of many, between two poles. So,
In the metaphysical, there are these poles.

Here in the centre stands the glass. Light
Is the lion that comes down to drink. There
And in that state, the glass is a pool.

Ruddy are his eyes and ruddy are his claws
When light comes down to wet his frothy jaws

And in the water winding weeds move round.
And there and in another state—the refractions,
The *metaphysica*, the plastic parts of poems
Crash in the mind—But, fat Jocundus, worrying
About what stands here in the centre, not the glass,

But in the centre of our lives, this time, this day,
It is a state, this spring among the politicians
Playing cards. In a village of the indigenes,
One would have still to discover. Among the dogs and
    dung,
One would continue to contend with one's ideas.

Add This to Rhetoric

It is posed and it is posed.
But in nature it merely grows.
Stones pose in the falling night;
And beggars dropping to sleep,
They pose themselves and their rags.
Shucks . . . lavender moonlight falls.
The buildings pose in the sky
And, as you paint, the clouds,
Grisaille, impearled, profound,
Pftt . . . In the way you speak
You arrange, the thing is posed,
What in nature merely grows.

To-morrow when the sun,
For all your images,
Comes up as the sun, bull fire,
Your images will have left
No shadow of themselves.
The poses of speech, of paint,
Of music—Her body lies

Worn out, her arm falls down,
Her fingers touch the ground.
Above her, to the left,
A brush of white, the obscure,
The moon without a shape,
A fringed eye in a crypt.
The sense creates the pose.
In this it moves and speaks.
This is the figure and not
An evading metaphor.

Add this. It is to add.

Dry Loaf

It is equal to living in a tragic land
To live in a tragic time.
Regard now the sloping, mountainous rocks
And the river that batters its way over stones,
Regard the hovels of those that live in this land.

That was what I painted behind the loaf,
The rocks not even touched by snow,
The pines along the river and the dry men blown
Brown as the bread, thinking of birds
Flying from burning countries and brown sand shores,

Birds that came like dirty water in waves
Flowing above the rocks, flowing over the sky,
As if the sky was a current that bore them along,
Spreading them as waves spread flat on the shore,
One after another washing the mountains bare.

It was the battering of drums I heard
It was hunger, it was the hungry that cried
And the waves, the waves were soldiers moving,
Marching and marching in a tragic time
Below me, on the asphalt, under the trees.

It was soldiers went marching over the rocks
And still the birds came, came in watery flocks,
Because it was spring and the birds had to come.
No doubt that soldiers had to be marching
And that drums had to be rolling, rolling, rolling.

Idiom of the Hero

I heard two workers say, "This chaos
Will soon be ended."

This chaos will not be ended,
The red and the blue house blended,

Not ended, never and never ended,
The weak man mended,

The man that is poor at night
Attended

Like the man that is rich and right.
The great men will not be blended . . .

I am the poorest of all.
I know that I cannot be mended,

Out of the clouds, pomp of the air,
By which at least I am befriended.

The Man on the Dump

Day creeps down. The moon is creeping up.
The sun is a corbeil of flowers the moon Blanche
Places there, a bouquet. Ho-ho . . . The dump is full
Of images. Days pass like papers from a press.
The bouquets come here in the papers. So the sun,

And so the moon, both come, and the janitor's poems
Of every day, the wrapper on the can of pears,
The cat in the paper-bag, the corset, the box
From Esthonia: the tiger chest, for tea.

The freshness of night has been fresh a long time.
The freshness of morning, the blowing of day, one says
That it puffs as Cornelius Nepos reads, it puffs
More than, less than or it puffs like this or that.
The green smacks in the eye, the dew in the green
Smacks like fresh water in a can, like the sea
On a cocoanut—how many men have copied dew
For buttons, how many women have covered themselves
With dew, dew dresses, stones and chains of dew, heads
Of the floweriest flowers dewed with the dewiest dew.
One grows to hate these things except on the dump.

Now, in the time of spring (azaleas, trilliums,
Myrtle, viburnums, daffodils, blue phlox),
Between that disgust and this, between the things
That are on the dump (azaleas and so on)
And those that will be (azaleas and so on),
One feels the purifying change. One rejects
The trash.

          That's the moment when the moon creeps up
To the bubbling of bassoons. That's the time
One looks at the elephant-colorings of tires.
Everything is shed; and the moon comes up as the moon
(All its images are in the dump) and you see
As a man (not like an image of a man),
You see the moon rise in the empty sky.

One sits and beats an old tin can, lard pail.
One beats and beats for that which one believes.
That's what one wants to get near. Could it after all
Be merely oneself, as superior as the ear
To a crow's voice? Did the nightingale torture the ear,
Pack the heart and scratch the mind? And does the ear
Solace itself in peevish birds? Is it peace,

Is it a philosopher's honeymoon, one finds
On the dump? Is it to sit among mattresses of the dead,
Bottles, pots, shoes and grass and murmur *aptest eve*:
Is it to hear the blatter of grackles and say
Invisible priest; is it to eject, to pull
The day to pieces and cry *stanza my stone*?
Where was it one first heard of the truth? The the.

On the Road Home

It was when I said,
"There is no such thing as the truth,"
That the grapes seemed fatter.
The fox ran out of his hole.

You . . . You said,
"There are many truths,
But they are not parts of a truth."
Then the tree, at night, began to change,

Smoking through green and smoking blue.
We were two figures in a wood.
We said we stood alone.

It was when I said,
"Words are not forms of a single word.
In the sum of the parts, there are only the parts.
The world must be measured by eye";

It was when you said,
"The idols have seen lots of poverty,
Snakes and gold and lice,
But not the truth";

It was at that time, that the silence was largest
And longest, the night was roundest,
The fragrance of the autumn warmest,
Closest and strongest.

The Latest Freed Man

Tired of the old descriptions of the world,
The latest freed man rose at six and sat
On the edge of his bed. He said,
                            "I suppose there is
A doctrine to this landscape. Yet, having just
Escaped from the truth, the morning is color and mist,
Which is enough: the moment's rain and sea,
The moment's sun (the strong man vaguely seen),
Overtaking the doctrine of this landscape. Of him
And of his works, I am sure. He bathes in the mist
Like a man without a doctrine. The light he gives—
It is how he gives his light. It is how he shines,
Rising upon the doctors in their beds
And on their beds. . . ."
                         And so the freed man said.
It was how the sun came shining into his room:
To be without a description of to be,
For a moment on rising, at the edge of the bed, to be,
To have the ant of the self changed to an ox
With its organic boomings, to be changed
From a doctor into an ox, before standing up,
To know that the change and that the ox-like struggle
Come from the strength that is the strength of the sun,
Whether it comes directly or from the sun.
It was how he was free. It was how his freedom came.
It was being without description, being an ox.
It was the importance of the trees outdoors,
The freshness of the oak-leaves, not so much
That they were oak-leaves, as the way they looked.
It was everything being more real, himself
At the centre of reality, seeing it.
It was everything bulging and blazing and big in itself,
The blue of the rug, the portrait of Vidal,
Qui fait fi des joliesses banales, the chairs.

United Dames of America

Je tâche, en restant exact, d'être poète.
                                    —JULES RENARD

There are not leaves enough to cover the face
It wears. This is the way the orator spoke:
"The mass is nothing. The number of men in a mass
Of men is nothing. The mass is no greater than

The singular man of the mass. Masses produce
Each one its paradigm." There are not leaves
Enough to hide away the face of the man
Of this dead mass and that. The wind might fill

With faces as with leaves, be gusty with mouths,
And with mouths crying and crying day by day.
Could all these be ourselves, sounding ourselves,
Our faces circling round a central face

And then nowhere again, away and away?
Yet one face keeps returning (never the one),
The face of the man of the mass, never the face
That hermit on reef sable would have seen,

Never the naked politician taught
By the wise. There are not leaves enough to crown,
To cover, to crown, to cover—let it go—
The actor that will at last declaim our end.

Country Words

I sang a canto in a canton,
Cunning-coo, O, cuckoo cock,
In a canton of Belshazzar
To Belshazzar, putrid rock,

Pillar of a putrid people,
Underneath a willow there
I stood and sang and filled the air.

It was an old rebellious song,
An edge of song that never clears;
But if it did . . . If the cloud that hangs
Upon the heart and round the mind
Cleared from the north and in that height
The sun appeared and reddened great
Belshazzar's brow, O, ruler, rude
With rubies then, attend me now.

What is it that my feeling seeks?
I know from all the things it touched
And left beside and left behind.
It wants the diamond pivot bright.
It wants Belshazzar reading right
The luminous pages on his knee,
Of being, more than birth or death.
It wants words virile with his breath.

The Dwarf

Now it is September and the web is woven.
The web is woven and you have to wear it.

The winter is made and you have to bear it,
The winter web, the winter woven, wind and wind,

For all the thoughts of summer that go with it
In the mind, pupa of straw, moppet of rags.

It is the mind that is woven, the mind that was jerked
And tufted in straggling thunder and shattered sun.

It is all that you are, the final dwarf of you,
That is woven and woven and waiting to be worn,

Neither as mask nor as garment but as a being,
Torn from insipid summer, for the mirror of cold,

Sitting beside your lamp, there citron to nibble
And coffee dribble . . . Frost is in the stubble.

A Rabbit as King of the Ghosts

The difficulty to think at the end of day,
When the shapeless shadow covers the sun
And nothing is left except light on your fur—

There was the cat slopping its milk all day,
Fat cat, red tongue, green mind, white milk
And August the most peaceful month.

To be, in the grass, in the peacefullest time,
Without that monument of cat,
The cat forgotten in the moon;

And to feel that the light is a rabbit-light,
In which everything is meant for you
And nothing need be explained;

Then there is nothing to think of. It comes of itself;
And east rushes west and west rushes down,
No matter. The grass is full

And full of yourself. The trees around are for you,
The whole of the wideness of night is for you,
A self that touches all edges,

You become a self that fills the four corners of night.
The red cat hides away in the fur-light
And there you are humped high, humped up,

You are humped higher and higher, black as stone—
You sit with your head like a carving in space
And the little green cat is a bug in the grass.

Loneliness in Jersey City

The deer and the dachshund are one.
Well, the gods grow out of the weather.
The people grow out of the weather;
The gods grow out of the people.
Encore, encore, encore les dieux . . .

The distance between the dark steeple
And cobble ten thousand and three
Is more than a seven-foot inchworm
Could measure by moonlight in June.

Kiss, cats: for the deer and the dachshund
Are one. My window is twenty-nine three
And plenty of window for me.
The steeples are empty and so are the people,
There's nothing whatever to see
Except Polacks that pass in their motors
And play concertinas all night.
They think that things are all right,
Since the deer and the dachshund are one.

Anything Is Beautiful If You Say It Is

Under the eglantine
The fretful concubine
Said, "Phooey! Phoo!"
She whispered, "Pfui!"

The demi-monde
On the mezzanine
Said, "Phooey!" too,
And a "Hey-de-i-do!"

The bee may have all sweet
For his honey-hive-o,
From the eglantine-o.

And the chandeliers are neat . . .
But their mignon, marblish glare!
We are cold, the parrots cried,
In a place so debonair.

The Johannisberger, Hans.
I love the metal grapes,
The rusty, battered shapes
Of the pears and of the cheese

And the window's lemon light,
The very will of the nerves,
The crack across the pane,
The dirt along the sill.

A Weak Mind in the Mountains

There was the butcher's hand.
He squeezed it and the blood
Spurted from between the fingers
And fell to the floor.
And then the body fell.

So afterward, at night,
The wind of Iceland and
The wind of Ceylon,
Meeting, gripped my mind,
Gripped it and grappled my thoughts.

The black wind of the sea
And the green wind
Whirled upon me.
The blood of the mind fell
To the floor. I slept.

Yet there was a man within me
Could have risen to the clouds,

Could have touched these winds,
Bent and broken them down,
Could have stood up sharply in the sky.

The Bagatelles the Madrigals

Where do you think, serpent,
Where do you lie, beneath snow,
And with eyes closed
Breathe in a crevice of earth?

In what camera do you taste
Poison, in what darkness set
Glittering scales and point
The tipping tongue?

And where is it, you, people,
Where is it that you think, baffled
By the trash of life,
Through winter's meditative light?

In what crevice do you find
Forehead's cold, spite of the eye
Seeing that which is refused,
Vengeful, shadowed by gestures

Of the life that you will not live,
Of days that will be wasted,
Of nights that will not be more than
Surly masks and destroyers?

(This is one of the thoughts
Of the mind that forms itself
Out of all the minds,
One of the songs of that dominance.)

Girl in a Nightgown

Lights out. Shades up.
A look at the weather.
There has been a booming all the spring,
A refrain from the end of the boulevards.

This is the silence of night,
This is what could not be shaken,
Full of stars and the images of stars—
And that booming wintry and dull,

Like a tottering, a falling and an end,
Again and again, always there,
Massive drums and leaden trumpets,
Perceived by feeling instead of sense,

A revolution of things colliding.
Phrases! But of fear and of fate.
The night should be warm and fluters' fortune
Should play in the trees when morning comes.

Once it was, the repose of night,
Was a place, strong place, in which to sleep.
It is shaken now. It will burst into flames,
Either now or tomorrow or the day after that.

Connoisseur of Chaos

I

A.   A violent order is disorder; and
B.   A great disorder is an order. These
Two things are one. (Pages of illustrations.)

II

If all the green of spring was blue, and it is;
If the flowers of South Africa were bright

On the tables of Connecticut, and they are;
If Englishmen lived without tea in Ceylon, and they do;
And if it all went on in an orderly way,
And it does; a law of inherent opposites,
Of essential unity, is as pleasant as port,
As pleasant as the brush-strokes of a bough,
An upper, particular bough in, say, Marchand.

III

After all the pretty contrast of life and death
Proves that these opposite things partake of one,
At least that was the theory, when bishops' books
Resolved the world. We cannot go back to that.
The squirming facts exceed the squamous mind,
If one may say so. And yet relation appears,
A small relation expanding like the shade
Of a cloud on sand, a shape on the side of a hill.

IV

A.   Well, an old order is a violent one.
This proves nothing. Just one more truth, one more
Element in the immense disorder of truths.
B.   It is April as I write. The wind
Is blowing after days of constant rain.
All this, of course, will come to summer soon.
But suppose the disorder of truths should ever come
To an order, most Plantagenet, most fixed . . .
A great disorder is an order. Now, A
And B are not like statuary, posed
For a vista in the Louvre. They are things chalked
On the sidewalk so that the pensive man may see.

V

The pensive man . . . He sees that eagle float
For which the intricate Alps are a single nest.

The Blue Buildings in the Summer Air

I

Cotton Mather died when I was a boy. The books
He read, all day, all night and all the nights,
Had got him nowhere. There was always the doubt,
That made him preach the louder, long for a church
In which his voice would roll its cadences,
After the sermon, to quiet that mouse in the wall.

II

Over wooden Boston, the sparkling Byzantine
Was everything that Cotton Mather was
And more. Yet the eminent thunder from the mouse,
The grinding in the arches of the church,
The plaster dropping, even dripping, down,
The mouse, the moss, the woman on the shore . . .

III

If the mouse should swallow the steeple, in its time . . .
It was a theologian's needle, much
Too sharp for that. The shore, the sea, the sun,
Their brilliance through the lattices, crippled
The chandeliers, their morning glazes spread
In opal blobs along the walls and floor.

IV

Look down now, Cotton Mather, from the blank.
Was heaven where you thought? It must be there.
It must be where you think it is, in the light
On bed-clothes, in an apple on a plate.
It is the honey-comb of the seeing man.
It is the leaf the bird brings back to the boat.

V

Go, mouse, go nibble at Lenin in his tomb.
Are you not le plus pur, you ancient one?

Cut summer down to find the honey-comb.
You are one . . . Go hunt for honey in his hair.
You are one of the not-numberable mice
Searching all day, all night, for the honey-comb.

Dezembrum

I

Tonight there are only the winter stars.
The sky is no longer a junk-shop,
Full of javelins and old fire-balls,
Triangles and the names of girls.

II

Over and over again you have said,
This great world, it divides itself in two,
One part is man, the other god:
Imagined man, the monkish mask, the face.

III

Tonight the stars are like a crowd of faces
Moving round the sky and singing
And laughing, a crowd of men,
Whose singing is a mode of laughter,

IV

Never angels, nothing of the dead,
Faces to people night's brilliancy,
Laughing and singing and being happy,
Filling the imagination's need.

V

In this rigid room, an intenser love,
Not toys, not thing-a-ma-jigs—
The reason can give nothing at all
Like the response to desire.

Poem Written at Morning

A sunny day's complete Poussiniana
Divide it from itself. It is this or that
And it is not.
                    By metaphor you paint
A thing. Thus, the pineapple was a leather fruit,
A fruit for pewter, thorned and palmed and blue,
To be served by men of ice.
                              The senses paint
By metaphor. The juice was fragranter
Than wettest cinnamon. It was cribled pears
Dripping a morning sap.
                         The truth must be
That you do not see, you experience, you feel,
That the buxom eye brings merely its element
To the total thing, a shapeless giant forced
Upward.
          Green were the curls upon that head.

Life on a Battleship

I

The rape of the bourgeoisie accomplished, the men
Returned on board *The Masculine*. That night,
The captain said,
                    "The war between classes is
A preliminary, provincial phase,
Of the war between individuals. In time,
When earth has become a paradise, it will be
A paradise full of assassins. Suppose I seize
The ship, make it my own and, bit by bit,
Seize yards and docks, machinery and men,
As others have, and then, unlike the others,
Instead of building ships, in numbers, build
A single ship, a cloud on the sea, the largest
Possible machine, a divinity of steel,
Of which I am captain. Given what I intend,

The ship would become the centre of the world.
My cabin as the centre of the ship and I
As the centre of the cabin, the centre of
The divinity, the divinity's mind, the mind
Of the world would have only to ring and ft!
It would be done. If, only to please myself,
I said that men should wear stone masks and, to make
The word respected, fired ten thousand guns
In mid-Atlantic, bellowing, to command,
It would be done. And once the thing was done,
Once the assassins wore stone masks and did
As I wished, once they fell backward when my breath
Blew against them or bowed from the hips, when I turned
My head, the sorrow of the world, except
As man is natural, would be at an end."

II

So posed, the captain drafted rules of the world,
Regulae mundi, as apprentice of
Descartes:
           First. The grand simplifications reduce
Themselves to one.
                 Of this the Captain said,
"It is a lesser law than the one itself,
Unless it is the one itself, or unless
The Masculine, much magnified, that cloud
On the sea, is both law and evidence in one,
As the final simplification is meant to be.
It is clear that it is not a moral law.
It appears to be what there is of life compressed
Into its own illustration, a divinity
Like any other, rex by right of the crown,
The jewels in his beard, the mystic wand,
And imperator because of death to oppose
The illustrious arms, the symbolic horns, the red
For battle, the purple for victory. But if
It is the absolute why must it be
This immemorial grandiose, why not
A cockle-shell, a trivial emblem great

With its final force, a thing invincible
In more than phrase? There's the true masculine,
The spirit's ring and seal, the naked heart.
It was a rabbi's question. Let the rabbis reply.
It implies a flaw in the battleship, a defeat
As of a make-believe.

III

Second. The part
Is the equal of the whole.
The captain said,
"The ephebi say that there is only the whole,
The race, the nation, the state. But society
Is a phase. We approach a society
Without a society, the politicians
Gone, as in Calypso's isle or in Citare,
Where I or one or the part is the equal of
The whole. The sound of a dozen orchestras
May rush to extinguish the theme, the basses thump
And the fiddles smack, the horns yahoo, the flutes
Strike fire, but the part is the equal of the whole,
Unless society is a mystical mass.
This is a thing to twang a philosopher's sleep,
A vacuum for the dozen orchestras
To fill, the grindstone of antiquest time,
Breakfast in Paris, music and madness and mud,
The perspective squirming as it tries to take
A shape, the vista twisted and burning, a thing
Kicked through the roof, caressed by the river-side.
On *The Masculine* one asserts and fires the guns.
But one lives to think of this growing, this pushing life,
The vine, at the roots, this vine of Key West, splurging,
Covered one morning with blue, one morning with white,
Coming from the East, forcing itself to the West,
The jungle of tropical part and tropical whole."

IV

The first and second rules are reconciled
In a Third: The whole cannot exist without

The parts. Thus: Out of the number of his thoughts
The thinker knows. The gunman of the commune
Kills the commune.
                     Captain, high captain, how is it, now,
With our affair, our destiny, our hash?
Your guns are not rhapsodic strophes, red
And true. The good, the strength, the sceptre moves
From constable to god, from earth to air,
The circle of the sceptre growing large
And larger as it moves, moving toward
A hand that fails to seize it. High captain, the grand
Simplifications approach but do not touch
The ultimate one, though they are parts of it.
Without them it could not exist. That's our affair,
That's this grandiose battleship of yours and your
Regulae mundi . . . That much is out of the way.
If the sceptre returns to earth, still moving, still
Precious from the region of the hand, still bright
With saintly imagination and the stains
Of martyrs, to be arrogant in our need,
It will be all we have. Our fate is our own:
Our good, from this the rhapsodic strophes flow,
Through prophets and succeeding prophets, whose
    prophecies
Grow large and larger. Our fate is our own. The hand,
It must be the hand of one, it must be the hand
Of a man, that seizes our strength, will seize it to be
Merely the centre of a circle, spread
To the final full, an end without rhetoric.

The Woman That Had More Babies Than That

I

An acrobat on the border of the sea
Observed the waves, the rising and the swell
And the first line spreading up the beach; again,
The rising and the swell, the preparation

And the first line foaming over the sand; again,
The rising and the swell, the first line's glitter,
Like a dancer's skirt, flung round and settling down.
This was repeated day by day. The waves
Were mechanical, muscular. They never changed,
They never stopped, a repetition repeated
Continually— There is a woman has had
More babies than that. The merely revolving wheel
Returns and returns, along the dry, salt shore.
There is a mother whose children need more than that.
She is not the mother of landscapes but of those
That question the repetition on the shore,
Listening to the whole sea for a sound
Of more or less, ascetically sated
By amical tones.
                    The acrobat observed
The universal machine. There he perceived
The need for a thesis, a music constant to move.

II

Berceuse, transatlantic. The children are men, old men,
Who, when they think and speak of the central man,
Of the humming of the central man, the whole sound
Of the sea, the central humming of the sea,
Are old men breathed on by a maternal voice,
Children and old men and philosophers,
Bald heads with their mother's voice still in their ears.
The self is a cloister full of remembered sounds
And of sounds so far forgotten, like her voice,
That they return unrecognized. The self
Detects the sound of a voice that doubles its own,
In the images of desire, the forms that speak,
The ideas that come to it with a sense of speech.
The old men, the philosophers, are haunted by that
Maternal voice, the explanation at night.
They are more than parts of the universal machine.
Their need in solitude: that is the need,
The desire, for the fiery lullaby.

III

                    If her head
Stood on a plain of marble, high and cold;
If her eyes were chinks in which the sparrows built;
If she was deaf with falling grass in her ears—
But there is more than a marble, massive head.
They find her in the crackling summer night,
In the *Duft* of towns, beside a window, beside
A lamp, in a day of the week, the time before spring,
A manner of walking, yellow fruit, a house,
A street. She has a supernatural head.
On her lips familiar words become the words
Of an elevation, an elixir of the whole.

Thunder by the Musician

Sure enough, moving, the thunder became men,
Ten thousand, men hewn and tumbling,
Mobs of ten thousand, clashing together,
This way and that.

Slowly, one man, savager than the rest,
Rose up, tallest, in the black sun,
Stood up straight in the air, struck off
The clutch of the others.

And, according to the composer, this butcher,
Held in his hand the suave egg-diamond
That had flashed (like vicious music that ends
In transparent accords).

It would have been better, the time conceived,
To have had him holding—what?
His arm would be trembling, he would be weak,
Even though he shouted.

The sky would be full of bodies like wood.
There would have been the cries of the dead

And the living would be speaking,
As a self that lives on itself.

It would have been better for his hands
To be convulsed, to have remained the hands
Of one wilder than the rest (like music blunted,
Yet the sound of that).

The Common Life

That's the down-town frieze,
Principally the church steeple,
A black line beside a white line;
And the stack of the electric plant,
A black line drawn on flat air.

It is a morbid light
In which they stand,
Like an electric lamp
On a page of Euclid.

In this light a man is a result,
A demonstration, and a woman,
Without rose and without violet,
The shadows that are absent from Euclid,
Is not a woman for a man.

The paper is whiter
For these black lines.
It glares beneath the webs
Of wire, the designs of ink,
The planes that ought to have genius,
The volumes like marble ruins
Outlined and having alphabetical
Notations and footnotes.
The paper is whiter.
The men have no shadows
And the women have only one side.

The Sense of the Sleight-of-Hand Man

One's grand flights, one's Sunday baths,
One's tootings at the weddings of the soul
Occur as they occur. So bluish clouds
Occurred above the empty house and the leaves
Of the rhododendrons rattled their gold,
As if someone lived there. Such floods of white
Came bursting from the clouds. So the wind
Threw its contorted strength around the sky.

Could you have said the bluejay suddenly
Would swoop to earth? It is a wheel, the rays
Around the sun. The wheel survives the myths.
The fire eye in the clouds survives the gods.
To think of a dove with an eye of grenadine
And pines that are cornets, so it occurs,
And a little island full of geese and stars:
It may be that the ignorant man, alone,
Has any chance to mate his life with life
That is the sensual, pearly spouse, the life
That is fluent in even the wintriest bronze.

The Candle a Saint

Green is the night, green kindled and apparelled.
It is she that walks among astronomers.

She strides above the rabbit and the cat,
Like a noble figure, out of the sky,

Moving among the sleepers, the men,
Those that lie chanting *green is the night.*

Green is the night and out of madness woven,
The self-same madness of the astronomers

And of him that sees, beyond the astronomers,
The topaz rabbit and the emerald cat,

That sees above them, that sees rise up above them,
The noble figure, the essential shadow,

Moving and being, the image at its source,
The abstract, the archaic queen. Green is the night.

A Dish of Peaches in Russia

With my whole body I taste these peaches,
I touch them and smell them. Who speaks?

I absorb them as the Angevine
Absorbs Anjou. I see them as a lover sees,

As a young lover sees the first buds of spring
And as the black Spaniard plays his guitar.

Who speaks? But it must be that I,
That animal, that Russian, that exile, for whom

The bells of the chapel pullulate sounds at
Heart. The peaches are large and round,

Ah! and red; and they have peach fuzz, ah!
They are full of juice and the skin is soft.

They are full of the colors of my village
And of fair weather, summer, dew, peace.

The room is quiet where they are.
The windows are open. The sunlight fills

The curtains. Even the drifting of the curtains,
Slight as it is, disturbs me. I did not know

That such ferocities could tear
One self from another, as these peaches do.

Arcades of Philadelphia the Past

Only the rich remember the past,
The strawberries once in the Apennines,
Philadelphia that the spiders ate.

There they sit, holding their eyes in their hands.
Queer, in this Vallombrosa of ears,
That they never hear the past. To see,
To hear, to touch, to taste, to smell, that's now,
That's this. Do they touch the thing they see,
Feel the wind of it, smell the dust of it?
They do not touch it. Sounds never rise
Out of what they see. They polish their eyes
In their hands. The lilacs came long after.
But the town and the fragrance were never one,
Though the blue bushes bloomed—and bloom,
Still bloom in the agate eyes, red blue,
Red purple, never quite red itself.
The tongue, the fingers, and the nose
Are comic trash, the ears are dirt,
But the eyes are men in the palm of the hand.

This? A man must be very poor
With a single sense, though he smells clouds,
Or to see the sea on Sunday, or
To touch a woman cadaverous,
Of poorness as an earth, to taste
Dry seconds and insipid thirds,
To hear himself and not to speak.

The strawberries once in the Apennines . . .
They seem a little painted, now.
The mountains are scratched and used, clear fakes.

Of Hartford in a Purple Light

A long time you have been making the trip
From Havre to Hartford, Master Soleil,
Bringing the lights of Norway and all that.

A long time the ocean has come with you,
Shaking the water off, like a poodle,
That splatters incessant thousands of drops,

Each drop a petty tricolor. For this,
The aunts in Pasadena, remembering,
Abhor the plaster of the western horses,

Souvenirs of museums. But, Master, there are
Lights masculine and lights feminine.
What is this purple, this parasol,

This stage-light of the Opera?
It is like a region full of intonings.
It is Hartford seen in a purple light.

A moment ago, light masculine,
Working, with big hands, on the town,
Arranged its heroic attitudes.

But now as in an amour of women
Purple sets purple round. Look, Master,
See the river, the railroad, the cathedral . . .

When male light fell on the naked back
Of the town, the river, the railroad were clear.
Now, every muscle slops away.

Hi! Whisk it, poodle, flick the spray
Of the ocean, ever-freshening,
On the irised hunks, the stone bouquet.

Cuisine Bourgeoise

These days of disinheritance, we feast
On human heads. True, birds rebuild
Old nests and there is blue in the woods.
The church bells clap one night in the week.
But that's all done. It is what used to be,
As they used to lie in the grass, in the heat,
Men on green beds and women half of sun.
The words are written, though not yet said.

It is like the season when, after summer,
It is summer and it is not, it is autumn
And it is not, it is day and it is not,
As if last night's lamps continued to burn,
As if yesterday's people continued to watch
The sky, half porcelain, preferring that
To shaking out heavy bodies in the glares
Of this present, this science, this unrecognized,

This outpost, this douce, this dumb, this dead, in which
We feast on human heads, brought in on leaves,
Crowned with the first, cold buds. On these we live,
No longer on the ancient cake of seed,
The almond and deep fruit. This bitter meat
Sustains us . . . Who, then, are they, seated here?
Is the table a mirror in which they sit and look?
Are they men eating reflections of themselves?

Forces, the Will & the Weather

At the time of nougats, the peer yellow
Sighed in the evening that he lived
Without ideas in a land without ideas,
The pair yellow, the peer.

It was at the time, the place, of nougats.
There the dogwoods, the white ones and the pink ones,
Bloomed in sheets, as they bloom, and the girl,
A pink girl took a white dog walking.

The dog had to walk. He had to be taken.
The girl had to hold back and lean back to hold him,
At the time of the dogwoods, handfuls thrown up
To spread colors. There was not an idea

This side of Moscow. There were anti-ideas
And counter-ideas. There was nothing one had. There were
No horses to ride and no one to ride them
In the woods of the dogwoods,

No large white horses. But there was the fluffy dog.
There were the sheets high up on older trees,
Seeming to be liquid as leaves made of cloud,
Shells under water. These were nougats.

It had to be right: nougats. It was a shift
Of realities, that, in which it could be wrong.
The weather was like a waiter with a tray.
One had come early to a crisp café.

On an Old Horn

I

The bird kept saying that birds had once been men,
Or were to be, animals with men's eyes,
Men fat as feathers, misers counting breaths,

Women of a melancholy one could sing.
Then the bird from his ruddy belly blew
A trumpet round the trees. Could one say that it was
A baby with the tail of a rat?
                                        The stones
Were violet, yellow, purple, pink. The grass
Of the iris bore white blooms. The bird then boomed.
Could one say that he sang the colors in the stones,
False as the mind, instead of the fragrance, warm
With sun?
                In the little of his voice, or the like,
Or less, he found a man, or more, against
Calamity, proclaimed himself, was proclaimed.

II

If the stars that move together as one, disband,
Flying like insects of fire in a cavern of night,
Pipperoo, pippera, pipperum . . . The rest is rot.

Bouquet of Belle Scavoir

I

It is she alone that matters.
She made it. It is easy to say
The figures of speech, as why she chose
This dark, particular rose.

II

Everything in it is herself.
Yet the freshness of the leaves, the burn
Of the colors, are tinsel changes,
Out of the changes of both light and dew.

III

How often had he walked
Beneath summer and the sky

To receive her shadow into his mind . . .
Miserable that it was not she.

IV

The sky is too blue, the earth too wide.
The thought of her takes her away.
The form of her in something else
Is not enough.

V

The reflection of her here, and then there,
Is another shadow, another evasion,
Another denial. If she is everywhere,
She is nowhere, to him.

VI

But this she has made. If it is
Another image, it is one she has made.
It is she that he wants, to look at directly,
Someone before him to see and to know.

Variations on a Summer Day

I

Say of the gulls that they are flying
In light blue air over dark blue sea.

II

A music more than a breath, but less
Than the wind, sub-music like sub-speech,
A repetition of unconscious things,
Letters of rock and water, words
Of the visible elements, and of ours.

III

The rocks of the cliffs are the heads of dogs
That turn into fishes and leap
Into the sea.

IV

Star over Monhegan, Atlantic star,
Lantern without a bearer, you drift,
You, too, are drifting, in spite of your course;
Unless in the darkness, brightly-crowned,
You are the will, if there is a will,
Or the portent of a will that was,
One of the portents of the will that was.

V

The leaves of the sea are shaken and shaken.
There was a tree that was a father,
We sat beneath it and sang our songs.

VI

It is cold to be forever young,
To come to tragic shores and flow,
In sapphire, round the sun-bleached stones,
Being, for old men, time of their time.

VII

One sparrow is worth a thousand gulls,
When it sings. The gull sits on chimney-tops.
He mocks the guinea, challenges
The crow, inciting various modes.
The sparrow requites one, without intent.

VIII

An exercise in viewing the world.
On the motive! But one looks at the sea
As one improvises, on the piano.

IX

This cloudy world, by aid of land and sea,
Night and day, wind and quiet, produces
More nights, more days, more clouds, more worlds.

X

To change nature, not merely to change ideas,
To escape from the body, so to feel
Those feelings that the body balks,
The feelings of the natures round us here:
As a boat feels when it cuts blue water.

XI

Now, the timothy at Pemaquid
That rolled in heat is silver-tipped
And cold. The moon follows the sun like a French
Translation of a Russian poet.

XII

Everywhere the spruce trees bury soldiers:
Hugh March, a sergeant, a redcoat, killed,
With his men, beyond the barbican.
Everywhere spruce trees bury spruce trees.

XIII

Cover the sea with the sand rose. Fill
The sky with the radiantiana
Of spray. Let all the salt be gone.

XIV

Words add to the senses. The words for the dazzle
Of mica, the dithering of grass,
The Arachne integument of dead trees,
Are the eye grown larger, more intense.

XV

The last island and its inhabitant,
The two alike, distinguish blues,
Until the difference between air
And sea exists by grace alone,
In objects, as white this, white that.

XVI

Round and round goes the bell of the water
And round and round goes the water itself
And that which is the pitch of its motion,
The bell of its dome, the patron of sound.

XVII

Pass through the door and through the walls,
Those bearing balsam, its field fragrance,
Pine-figures bringing sleep to sleep.

XVIII

Low tide, flat water, sultry sun.
One observes profoundest shadows rolling.
Damariscotta da da doo.

XIX

One boy swims under a tub, one sits
On top. Hurroo, the man-boat comes,
In a man-makenesse, neater than Naples.

XX

You could almost see the brass on her gleaming,
Not quite. The mist was to light what red
Is to fire. And her mainmast tapered to nothing,
Without teetering a millimeter's measure.
The beads on her rails seemed to grasp at transparence.
It was not yet the hour to be dauntlessly leaping.

Yellow Afternoon

It was in the earth only
That he was at the bottom of things
And of himself. There he could say
Of this I am, this is the patriarch,
This it is that answers when I ask,
This is the mute, the final sculpture
Around which silence lies on silence.
This reposes alike in springtime
And, arbored and bronzed, in autumn.

He said I had this that I could love,
As one loves visible and responsive peace,
As one loves one's own being,
As one loves that which is the end
And must be loved, as one loves that
Of which one is a part as in a unity,
A unity that is the life one loves,
So that one lives all the lives that comprise it
As the life of the fatal unity of war.

Everything comes to him
From the middle of his field. The odor
Of earth penetrates more deeply than any word.
There he touches his being. There as he is
He is. The thought that he had found all this
Among men, in a woman—she caught his breath—
But he came back as one comes back from the sun
To lie on one's bed in the dark, close to a face
Without eyes or mouth, that looks at one and speaks.

Martial Cadenza

I

Only this evening I saw again low in the sky
The evening star, at the beginning of winter, the star
That in spring will crown every western horizon,
Again . . . as if it came back, as if life came back,
Not in a later son, a different daughter, another place,
But as if evening found us young, still young,
Still walking in a present of our own.

II

It was like sudden time in a world without time,
This world, this place, the street in which I was,
Without time: as that which is not has no time,
Is not, or is of what there was, is full
Of the silence before the armies, armies without
Either trumpets or drums, the commanders mute, the arms
On the ground, fixed fast in a profound defeat.

III

What had this star to do with the world it lit,
With the blank skies over England, over France
And above the German camps? It looked apart.
Yet it is this that shall maintain—Itself
Is time, apart from any past, apart
From any future, the ever-living and being,
The ever-breathing and moving, the constant fire,

IV

The present close, the present realized,
Not the symbol but that for which the symbol stands,
The vivid thing in the air that never changes,
Though the air change. Only this evening I saw it again,
At the beginning of winter, and I walked and talked
Again, and lived and was again, and breathed again
And moved again and flashed again, time flashed again.

Man and Bottle

The mind is the great poem of winter, the man,
Who, to find what will suffice,
Destroys romantic tenements
Of rose and ice

In the land of war. More than the man, it is
A man with the fury of a race of men,
A light at the centre of many lights,
A man at the centre of men.

It has to content the reason concerning war,
It has to persuade that war is part of itself,
A manner of thinking, a mode
Of destroying, as the mind destroys,

An aversion, as the world is averted
From an old delusion, an old affair with the sun,
An impossible aberration with the moon,
A grossness of peace.

It is not the snow that is the quill, the page.
The poem lashes more fiercely than the wind,
As the mind, to find what will suffice, destroys
Romantic tenements of rose and ice.

Of Modern Poetry

The poem of the mind in the act of finding
What will suffice. It has not always had
To find: the scene was set; it repeated what
Was in the script.
                    Then the theatre was changed
To something else. Its past was a souvenir.

It has to be living, to learn the speech of the place.
It has to face the men of the time and to meet

The women of the time. It has to think about war
And it has to find what will suffice. It has
To construct a new stage. It has to be on that stage
And, like an insatiable actor, slowly and
With meditation, speak words that in the ear,
In the delicatest ear of the mind, repeat,
Exactly, that which it wants to hear, at the sound
Of which, an invisible audience listens,
Not to the play, but to itself, expressed
In an emotion as of two people, as of two
Emotions becoming one. The actor is
A metaphysician in the dark, twanging
An instrument, twanging a wiry string that gives
Sounds passing through sudden rightnesses, wholly
Containing the mind, below which it cannot descend,
Beyond which it has no will to rise.
                                        It must
Be the finding of a satisfaction, and may
Be of a man skating, a woman dancing, a woman
Combing. The poem of the act of the mind.

Arrival at the Waldorf

Home from Guatemala, back at the Waldorf.
This arrival in the wild country of the soul,
All approaches gone, being completely there,

Where the wild poem is a substitute
For the woman one loves or ought to love,
One wild rhapsody a fake for another.

You touch the hotel the way you touch moonlight
Or sunlight and you hum and the orchestra
Hums and you say "The world in a verse,

A generation sealed, men remoter than mountains,
Women invisible in music and motion and color,"
After that alien, point-blank, green and actual Guatemala.

Landscape with Boat

An anti-master-man, floribund ascetic.

He brushed away the thunder, then the clouds,
Then the colossal illusion of heaven. Yet still
The sky was blue. He wanted imperceptible air.
He wanted to see. He wanted the eye to see
And not be touched by blue. He wanted to know,
A naked man who regarded himself in the glass
Of air, who looked for the world beneath the blue,
Without blue, without any turquoise tint or phase,
Any azure under-side or after-color. Nabob
Of bones, he rejected, he denied, to arrive
At the neutral centre, the ominous element,
The single-colored, colorless, primitive.

It was not as if the truth lay where he thought,
Like a phantom, in an uncreated night.
It was easier to think it lay there. If
It was nowhere else, it was there and because
It was nowhere else, its place had to be supposed,
Itself had to be supposed, a thing supposed
In a place supposed, a thing that he reached
In a place that he reached, by rejecting what he saw
And denying what he heard. He would arrive.
He had only not to live, to walk in the dark,
To be projected by one void into
Another.

            It was his nature to suppose,
To receive what others had supposed, without
Accepting. He received what he denied.
But as truth to be accepted, he supposed
A truth beyond all truths.

                        He never supposed
That he might be truth, himself, or part of it,
That the things that he rejected might be part
And the irregular turquoise, part, the perceptible blue
Grown denser, part, the eye so touched, so played

Upon by clouds, the ear so magnified
By thunder, parts, and all these things together,
Parts, and more things, parts. He never supposed divine
Things might not look divine, nor that if nothing
Was divine then all things were, the world itself,
And that if nothing was the truth, then all
Things were the truth, the world itself was the truth.

Had he been better able to suppose:
He might sit on a sofa on a balcony
Above the Mediterranean, emerald
Becoming emeralds. He might watch the palms
Flap green ears in the heat. He might observe
A yellow wine and follow a steamer's track
And say, "The thing I hum appears to be
The rhythm of this celestial pantomime."

On the Adequacy of Landscape

The little owl flew through the night,
As if the people in the air
Were frightened and he frightened them,
By being there,

The people that turned off and came
To avoid the bright, discursive wings,
To avoid the hap-hallow hallow-ho
Of central things,

Nor in their empty hearts to feel
The blood-red redness of the sun,
To shrink to an insensible,
Small oblivion,

Beyond the keenest diamond day
Of people sensible to pain,
When cocks wake, clawing at their beds
To be again,

And who, for that, turn toward the cocks
And toward the start of day and trees
And light behind the body of night
And sun, as if these

Were what they are, the sharpest sun:
The sharpest self, the sensible range,
The extent of what they are, the strength
That they exchange,

So that he that suffers most desires
The red bird most and the strongest sky—
Not the people in the air that hear
The little owl fly.

Les Plus Belles Pages

The milkman came in the moonlight and the moonlight
Was less than moonlight. Nothing exists by itself.
The moonlight seemed to.

                    Two people, three horses, an ox
And the sun, the waves together in the sea.

The moonlight and Aquinas seemed to. He spoke,
Kept speaking, of God. I changed the word to man.
The automaton, in logic self-contained,
Existed by itself. Or did the saint survive?
Did several spirits assume a single shape?

Theology after breakfast sticks to the eye.

Poem with Rhythms

The hand between the candle and the wall
Grows large on the wall.

The mind between this light or that and space,
(This man in a room with an image of the world,
That woman waiting for the man she loves,)
Grows large against space:

There the man sees the image clearly at last.
There the woman receives her lover into her heart
And weeps on his breast, though he never comes.

It must be that the hand
Has a will to grow larger on the wall,
To grow larger and heavier and stronger than
The wall; and that the mind
Turns to its own figurations and declares,
"This image, this love, I compose myself
Of these. In these, I come forth outwardly.
In these, I wear a vital cleanliness,
Not as in air, bright-blue-resembling air,
But as in the powerful mirror of my wish and will."

Woman Looking at a Vase of Flowers

It was as if thunder took form upon
The piano, that time: the time when the crude
And jealous grandeurs of sun and sky
Scattered themselves in the garden, like
The wind dissolving into birds,
The clouds becoming braided girls.
It was like the sea poured out again
In east wind beating the shutters at night.

Hoot, little owl within her, how
High blue became particular
In the leaf and bud and how the red,
Flicked into pieces, points of air,
Became—how the central, essential red
Escaped its large abstraction, became,
First, summer, then a lesser time,
Then the sides of peaches, of dusky pears.

Hoot how the inhuman colors fell
Into place beside her, where she was,
Like human conciliations, more like
A profounder reconciling, an act,
An affirmation free from doubt.
The crude and jealous formlessness
Became the form and the fragrance of things
Without clairvoyance, close to her.

The Well Dressed Man with a Beard

After the final no there comes a yes
And on that yes the future world depends.
No was the night. Yes is this present sun.
If the rejected things, the things denied,
Slid over the western cataract, yet one,
One only, one thing that was firm, even
No greater than a cricket's horn, no more
Than a thought to be rehearsed all day, a speech
Of the self that must sustain itself on speech,
One thing remaining, infallible, would be
Enough. Ah! douce campagna of that thing!
Ah! douce campagna, honey in the heart,
Green in the body, out of a petty phrase,
Out of a thing believed, a thing affirmed:
The form on the pillow humming while one sleeps,
The aureole above the humming house . . .

It can never be satisfied, the mind, never.

Of Bright & Blue Birds & the Gala Sun

Some things, niño, some things are like this,
That instantly and in themselves they are gay
And you and I are such things, O most miserable . . .

For a moment they are gay and are a part
Of an element, the exactest element for us,
In which we pronounce joy like a word of our own.

It is there, being imperfect, and with these things
And erudite in happiness, with nothing learned,
That we are joyously ourselves and we think

Without the labor of thought, in that element,
And we feel, in a way apart, for a moment, as if
There was a bright *scienza* outside of ourselves,

A gaiety that is being, not merely knowing,
The will to be and to be total in belief,
Provoking a laughter, an agreement, by surprise.

Mrs. Alfred Uruguay

So what said the others and the sun went down
And, in the brown blues of evening, the lady said,
In the donkey's ear, "I fear that elegance
Must struggle like the rest." She climbed until
The moonlight in her lap, mewing her velvet,
And her dress were one and she said, "I have said no
To everything, in order to get at myself.
I have wiped away moonlight like mud. Your innocent ear
And I, if I rode naked, are what remain."

The moonlight crumbled to degenerate forms,
While she approached the real, upon her mountain,
With lofty darkness. The donkey was there to ride,
To hold by the ear, even though it wished for a bell,
Wished faithfully for a falsifying bell.
Neither the moonlight could change it. And for her,
To be, regardless of velvet, could never be more
Than to be, she could never differently be,
Her no and no made yes impossible.

Who was it passed her there on a horse all will,
What figure of capable imagination?
Whose horse clattered on the road on which she rose,
As it descended, blind to her velvet and
The moonlight? Was it a rider intent on the sun,
A youth, a lover with phosphorescent hair,
Dressed poorly, arrogant of his streaming forces,
Lost in an integration of the martyrs' bones,
Rushing from what was real; and capable?

The villages slept as the capable man went down,
Time swished on the village clocks and dreams were alive,
The enormous gongs gave edges to their sounds,
As the rider, no chevalere and poorly dressed,
Impatient of the bells and midnight forms,
Rode over the picket rocks, rode down the road,
And, capable, created in his mind,
Eventual victor, out of the martyrs' bones,
The ultimate elegance: the imagined land.

Asides on the Oboe

The prologues are over. It is a question, now,
Of final belief. So, say that final belief
Must be in a fiction. It is time to choose.

I

That obsolete fiction of the wide river in
An empty land; the gods that Boucher killed;
And the metal heroes that time granulates—
The philosophers' man alone still walks in dew,
Still by the sea-side mutters milky lines
Concerning an immaculate imagery.
If you say on the hautboy man is not enough,
Can never stand as god, is ever wrong
In the end, however naked, tall, there is still
The impossible possible philosophers' man,

The man who has had the time to think enough,
The central man, the human globe, responsive
As a mirror with a voice, the man of glass,
Who in a million diamonds sums us up.

II

He is the transparence of the place in which
He is and in his poems we find peace.
He sets this peddler's pie and cries in summer,
The glass man, cold and numbered, dewily cries,
"Thou art not August unless I make thee so."
Clandestine steps upon imagined stairs
Climb through the night, because his cuckoos call.

III

One year, death and war prevented the jasmine scent
And the jasmine islands were bloody martyrdoms.
How was it then with the central man? Did we
Find peace? We found the sum of men. We found,
If we found the central evil, the central good.
We buried the fallen without jasmine crowns.
There was nothing he did not suffer, no; nor we.

It was not as if the jasmine ever returned.
But we and the diamond globe at last were one.
We had always been partly one. It was as we came
To see him, that we were wholly one, as we heard
Him chanting for those buried in their blood,
In the jasmine haunted forests, that we knew
The glass man, without external reference.

Extracts from Addresses
to the Academy of Fine Ideas

I

A crinkled paper makes a brilliant sound.
The wrinkled roses tinkle, the paper ones,

And the ear is glass, in which the noises pelt,
The false roses—Compare the silent rose of the sun
And rain, the blood-rose living in its smell,
With this paper, this dust. That states the point.

                                        Messieurs,
It is an artificial world. The rose
Of paper is of the nature of its world.
The sea is so many written words; the sky
Is blue, clear, cloudy, high, dark, wide and round;
The mountains inscribe themselves upon the walls.
And, otherwise, the rainy rose belongs
To naked men, to women naked as rain.

Where is that summer warm enough to walk
Among the lascivious poisons, clean of them,
And in what covert may we, naked, be
Beyond the knowledge of nakedness, as part
Of reality, beyond the knowledge of what
Is real, part of a land beyond the mind?

Rain is an unbearable tyranny. Sun is
A monster-maker, an eye, only an eye,
A shapener of shapes for only the eye,
Of things no better than paper things, of days
That are paper days. The false and true are one.

                    II

The eye believes and its communion takes.
The spirit laughs to see the eye believe
And its communion take. And now of that.
Let the Secretary for Porcelain observe
That evil made magic, as in catastrophe,
If neatly glazed, becomes the same as the fruit
Of an emperor, the egg-plant of a prince.
The good is evil's last invention. Thus
The maker of catastrophe invents the eye
And through the eye equates ten thousand deaths

With a single well-tempered apricot, or, say,
An egg-plant of good air.

                        My beards, attend
To the laughter of evil: the fierce ricanery
With the ferocious chu-chot-chu between, the sobs
For breath to laugh the louder, the deeper gasps
Uplifting the completest rhetoric
Of sneers, the fugues commencing at the toes
And ending at the finger-tips. . . . It is death
That is ten thousand deaths and evil death.
Be tranquil in your wounds. It is good death
That puts an end to evil death and dies.
Be tranquil in your wounds. The placating star
Shall be the gentler for the death you die
And the helpless philosophers say still helpful things.
Plato, the reddened flower, the erotic bird.

III

The lean cats of the arches of the churches,
That's the old world. In the new, all men are priests.

They preach and they are preaching in a land
To be described. They are preaching in a time
To be described. Evangelists of what?
If they could gather their theses into one,
Collect their thoughts together into one,
Into a single thought, thus: into a queen,
An intercessor by innate rapport,
Or into a dark-blue king, *un roi tonnerre*,
Whose merely being was his valiance,
Panjandrum and central heart and mind of minds—
If they could! Or is it the multitude of thoughts,
Like insects in the depths of the mind, that kill
The single thought? The multitudes of men
That kill the single man, starvation's head,
One man, their bread and their remembered wine?

The lean cats of the arches of the churches
Bask in the sun in which they feel transparent,
As if designed by X, the per-noble master.
They have a sense of their design and savor
The sunlight. They bear brightly the little beyond
Themselves, the slightly unjust drawing that is
Their genius: the exquisite errors of time.

IV

On an early Sunday in April, a feeble day,
He felt curious about the winter hills
And wondered about the water in the lake.
It had been cold since December. Snow fell, first,
At New Year and, from then until April, lay
On everything. Now it had melted, leaving
The gray grass like a pallet, closely pressed;
And dirt. The wind blew in the empty place.
The winter wind blew in an empty place—
There was that difference between the and an,
The difference between himself and no man,
No man that heard a wind in an empty place.
It was time to be himself again, to see
If the place, in spite of its witheredness, was still
Within the difference. He felt curious
Whether the water was black and lashed about
Or whether the ice still covered the lake. There was still
Snow under the trees and on the northern rocks,
The dead rocks not the green rocks, the live rocks. If,
When he looked, the water ran up the air or grew white
Against the edge of the ice, the abstraction would
Be broken and winter would be broken and done,
And being would be being himself again,
Being, becoming seeing and feeling and self,
Black water breaking into reality.

V

The law of chaos is the law of ideas,
Of improvisations and seasons of belief.

Ideas are men. The mass of meaning and
The mass of men are one. Chaos is not

The mass of meaning. It is three or four
Ideas or, say, five men or, possibly, six.

In the end, these philosophic assassins pull
Revolvers and shoot each other. One remains.

The mass of meaning becomes composed again.
He that remains plays on an instrument

A good agreement between himself and night,
A chord between the mass of men and himself,

Far, far beyond the putative canzones
Of love and summer. The assassin sings

In chaos and his song is a consolation.
It is the music of the mass of meaning.

And yet it is a singular romance,
This warmth in the blood-world for the pure idea,

This inability to find a sound,
That clings to the mind like that right sound, that song

Of the assassin that remains and sings
In the high imagination, triumphantly.

VI

Of systematic thinking . . . Ercole,
O, skin and spine and hair of you, Ercole,
Of what do you lie thinking in your cavern?
To think it is to think the way to death . . .

That other one wanted to think his way to life,
Sure that the ultimate poem was the mind,

Or of the mind, or of the mind in these
Elysia, these days, half earth, half mind;
Half sun, half thinking of the sun; half sky,
Half desire for indifference about the sky.

He, that one, wanted to think his way to life,
To be happy because people were thinking to be.
They had to think it to be. He wanted that,
To face the weather and be unable to tell
How much of it was light and how much thought,
In these Elysia, these origins,
This single place in which we are and stay,
Except for the images we make of it,
And for it, and by which we think the way,
And, being unhappy, talk of happiness
And, talking of happiness, know that it means
That the mind is the end and must be satisfied.

It cannot be half earth, half mind; half sun,
Half thinking; until the mind has been satisfied,
Until, for him, his mind is satisfied.
Time troubles to produce the redeeming thought.
Sometimes at sleepy mid-days it succeeds,
Too vaguely that it be written in character.

VII

To have satisfied the mind and turn to see,
(That being as much belief as we may have,)
And turn to look and say there is no more
Than this, in this alone I may believe,
Whatever it may be; then one's belief
Resists each past apocalypse, rejects
Ceylon, wants nothing from the sea, *la belle
Aux crinolines*, smears out mad mountains.

                                                    What
One believes is what matters. Ecstatic identities
Between one's self and the weather and the things
Of the weather are the belief in one's element,

The casual reunions, the long-pondered
Surrenders, the repeated sayings that
There is nothing more and that it is enough
To believe in the weather and in the things and men
Of the weather and in one's self, as part of that
And nothing more. So that if one went to the moon,
Or anywhere beyond, to a different element,
One would be drowned in the air of difference,
Incapable of belief, in the difference.
And then returning from the moon, if one breathed
The cold evening, without any scent or the shade
Of any woman, watched the thinnest light
And the most distant, single color, about to change,
And naked of any illusion, in poverty,
In the exactest poverty, if then
One breathed the cold evening, the deepest inhalation
Would come from that return to the subtle centre.

VIII

We live in a camp . . . Stanzas of final peace
Lie in the heart's residuum . . . Amen.
But would it be amen, in choirs, if once
In total war we died and after death
Returned, unable to die again, fated
To endure thereafter every mortal wound,
Beyond a second death, as evil's end?

It is only that we are able to die, to escape
The wounds. Yet to lie buried in evil earth,
If evil never ends, is to return
To evil after death, unable to die
Again and fated to endure beyond
Any mortal end. The chants of final peace
Lie in the heart's residuum.

How can
We chant if we live in evil and afterward
Lie harshly buried there?

                              If earth dissolves
Its evil after death, it dissolves it while
We live. Thence come the final chants, the chants
Of the brooder seeking the acutest end
Of speech: to pierce the heart's residuum
And there to find music for a single line,
Equal to memory, one line in which
The vital music formulates the words.

Behold the men in helmets borne on steel,
Discolored, how they are going to defeat.

Montrachet-le-Jardin

What more is there to love than I have loved?
And if there be nothing more, O bright, O bright,
The chick, the chidder-barn and grassy chives

And great moon, cricket-impresario,
And, hoy, the impopulous purple-plated past,
Hoy, hoy, the blue bulls kneeling down to rest.

Chome! clicks the clock, if there be nothing more.
But if, but if there be something more to love,
Something in now a senseless syllable,

A shadow in the mind, a flourisher
Of sounds resembling sounds, efflorisant,
Approaching the feelings or come down from them,

These other shadows, not in the mind, players
Of aphonies, tuned in from zero and
Beyond, futura's fuddle-fiddling lumps,

But if there be something more to love, amen,
Amen to the feelings about familiar things,
The blessed regal dropped in daggers' dew,

Amen to thought, our singular skeleton,
Salt-flicker, amen to our accustomed cell,
The moonlight in the cell, words on the wall.

To-night, night's undeciphered murmuring
Comes close to the prisoner's ear, becomes a throat
The hand can touch, neither green bronze nor marble,

The hero's throat in which the words are spoken,
From which the chant comes close upon the ear,
Out of the hero's being, the deliverer

Delivering the prisoner by his words,
So that the skeleton in the moonlight sings,
Sings of an heroic world beyond the cell,

No, not believing, but to make the cell
A hero's world in which he is the hero.
Man must become the hero of his world.

The salty skeleton must dance because
He must, in the aroma of summer nights,
Licentious violet and lascive rose,

Midsummer love and softest silences,
Weather of night creatures, whistling all day, too,
And echoing rhetorics more than our own.

He hears the earliest poems of the world
In which man is the hero. He hears the words,
Before the speaker's youngest breath is taken!

Fear never the brute clouds nor winter-stop
And let the water-belly of ocean roar,
Nor feel the x malisons of other men,

Since in the hero-land to which we go,
A little nearer by each multitude,
To which we come as into bezeled plain,

The poison in the blood will have been purged,
An inner miracle and sun-sacrament,
One of the major miracles, that fall

As apples fall, without astronomy,
One of the sacraments between two breaths,
Magical only for the change they make.

The skeleton said it is a question of
The naked man, the naked man as last
And tallest hero and plus gaudiest vir.

Consider how the speechless, invisible gods
Ruled us before, from over Asia, by
Our merest apprehension of their will.

There must be mercy in Asia and divine
Shadows of scholars bent upon their books,
Divine orations from lean sacristans

Of the good, speaking of good in the voice of men.
All men can speak of it in the voice of gods.
But to speak simply of good is like to love,

To equate the root-man and the super-man,
The root-man swarming, tortured by his mass,
The super-man friseured, possessing and possessed.

A little while of Terra Paradise
I dreamed, of autumn rivers, silvas green,
Of sanctimonious mountains high in snow,

But in that dream a heavy difference
Kept waking and a mournful sense sought out,
In vain, life's season or death's element.

Bastard chateaux and smoky demoiselles,
No more. I can build towers of my own,
There to behold, there to proclaim, the grace

And free requiting of responsive fact,
To project the naked man in a state of fact,
As acutest virtue and ascetic trove.

Item: The cocks crow and the birds cry and
The sun expands, like a repetition on
One string, an absolute, not varying

Toward an inaccessible, pure sound.
Item: The wind is never rounding O
And, imageless, it is itself the most,

Mouthing its constant smatter throughout space.
Item: The green fish pensive in green reeds
Is an absolute. Item: The cataracts

As facts fall like rejuvenating rain,
Fall down through nakedness to nakedness,
To the auroral creature musing in the mind.

Item: Breathe, breathe upon the centre of
The breath life's latest, thousand senses.
But let this one sense be the single main.

And yet what good were yesterday's devotions?
I affirm and then at midnight the great cat
Leaps quickly from the fireside and is gone.

The News and the Weather

I

The blue sun in his red cockade
Walked the United States today,

Taller than any eye could see,
Older than any man could be.

He caught the flags and the picket-lines
Of people, round the auto-works:

His manner slickened them. He milled
In the rowdy serpentines. He drilled.

His red cockade topped off a parade.
His manner took what it could find,

In the greenish greens he flung behind
And the sound of pianos in his mind.

II

Solange, the magnolia to whom I spoke,
A nigger tree and with a nigger name,

To which I spoke, near which I stood and spoke,
I am Solange, euphonious bane, she said.

I am a poison at the winter's end,
Taken with withered weather, crumpled clouds,

To smother the wry spirit's misery.
Inhale the purple fragrance. It becomes

Almost a nigger fragment, a *mystique*
For the spirit left helpless by the intelligence.

There's a moment in the year, Solange,
When the deep breath fetches another year of life.

Metamorphosis

Yillow, yillow, yillow,
Old worm, my pretty quirk,
How the wind spells out
Sep - tem - ber. . . .

Summer is in bones.
Cock-robin's at Caracas.
Make o, make o, make o,
Oto - otu - bre.

And the rude leaves fall.
The rain falls. The sky
Falls and lies with the worms.
The street lamps

Are those that have been hanged,
Dangling in an illogical
To and to and fro
Fro Niz - nil - imbo.

Contrary Theses (I)

Now grapes are plush upon the vines.
A soldier walks before my door.

The hives are heavy with the combs.
Before, before, before my door.

And seraphs cluster on the domes,
And saints are brilliant in fresh cloaks.

Before, before, before my door.
The shadows lessen on the walls.

The bareness of the house returns.
An acid sunlight fills the halls.

Before, before. Blood smears the oaks.
A soldier stalks before my door.

Phosphor Reading by His Own Light

It is difficult to read. The page is dark.
Yet he knows what it is that he expects.

The page is blank or a frame without a glass
Or a glass that is empty when he looks.

The greenness of night lies on the page and goes
Down deeply in the empty glass . . .

Look, realist, not knowing what you expect.
The green falls on you as you look,

Falls on and makes and gives, even a speech.
And you think that that is what you expect,

That elemental parent, the green night,
Teaching a fusky alphabet.

The Search for Sound Free from Motion

All afternoon the gramaphone
Parl-parled the West-Indian weather.
The zebra leaves, the sea
And it all spoke together.

The many-stanzaed sea, the leaves
And it spoke all together.
But you, you used the word,
Your self its honor.

All afternoon the gramaphoon,
All afternoon the gramaphoon,
The world as word,
Parl-parled the West-Indian hurricane.

The world lives as you live,
Speaks as you speak, a creature that
Repeats its vital words, yet balances
The syllable of a syllable.

Jumbo

The trees were plucked like iron bars
And jumbo, the loud general-large
Singsonged and singsonged, wildly free.

Who was the musician, fatly soft
And wildly free, whose clawing thumb
Clawed on the ear these consonants?

Who the transformer, himself transformed,
Whose single being, single form
Were their resemblances to ours?

The companion in nothingness,
Loud, general, large, fat, soft
And wild and free, the secondary man,

Cloud-clown, blue painter, sun as horn,
Hill-scholar, man that never is,
The bad-bespoken lacker,

Ancestor of Narcissus, prince
Of the secondary men. There are no rocks
And stones, only this imager.

Contrary Theses (II)

One chemical afternoon in mid-autumn,
When the grand mechanics of earth and sky were near,
Even the leaves of the locust were yellow then,

He walked with his year-old boy on his shoulder.
The sun shone and the dog barked and the baby slept.
The leaves, even of the locust, the green locust.

He wanted and looked for a final refuge,
From the bombastic intimations of winter
And the martyrs à la mode. He walked toward

An abstract, of which the sun, the dog, the boy
Were contours. Cold was chilling the wide-moving swans.
The leaves were falling like notes from a piano.

The abstract was suddenly there and gone again.
The negroes were playing football in the park.
The abstract that he saw, like the locust-leaves, plainly:

The premiss from which all things were conclusions,
The noble, Alexandrine verve. The flies
And the bees still sought the chrysanthemums' odor.

The Hand as a Being

In the first canto of the final canticle,
Too conscious of too many things at once,
Our man beheld the naked, nameless dame,

Seized her and wondered: why beneath the tree
She held her hand before him in the air,
For him to see, wove round her glittering hair.

Too conscious of too many things at once,
In the first canto of the final canticle,
Her hand composed him and composed the tree.

The wind had seized the tree and ha, and ha,
It held the shivering, the shaken limbs,
Then bathed its body in the leaping lake.

Her hand composed him like a hand appeared,
Of an impersonal gesture, a stranger's hand.
He was too conscious of too many things

In the first canto of the final canticle.
Her hand took his and drew him near to her.
Her hair fell on him and the mi-bird flew

To the ruddier bushes at the garden's end.
Of her, of her alone, at last he knew
And lay beside her underneath the tree.

Oak Leaves Are Hands

In Hydaspia, by Howzen
Lived a lady, Lady Lowzen,
For whom what is was other things.

Flora she was once. She was florid
A bachelor of feen masquerie,
Evasive and metamorphorid.

Mac Mort she had been, ago,
Twelve-legged in her ancestral hells,
Weaving and weaving many arms.

Even now, the centre of something else,
Merely by putting hand to brow,
Brooding on centuries like shells.

As the acorn broods on former oaks
In memorials of Northern sound,
Skims the real for its unreal,

So she in Hydaspia created
Out of the movement of few words,
Flora Lowzen invigorated

Archaic and future happenings,
In glittering seven-colored changes,
By Howzen, the chromatic Lowzen.

Examination of the Hero in a Time of War

I

Force is my lot and not pink-clustered
Roma ni Avignon ni Leyden,
And cold, my element. Death is my
Master and, without light, I dwell. There
The snow hangs heavily on the rocks, brought
By a wind that seeks out shelter from snow. Thus
Each man spoke in winter. Yet each man spoke of
The brightness of arms, said Roma wasted
In its own dirt, said Avignon was
Peace in a time of peace, said Leyden
Was always the other mind. The brightness
Of arms, the will opposed to cold, fate
In its cavern, wings subtler than any mercy,
These were the psalter of their sybils.

II

The Got whome we serve is able to deliver
Us. Good chemistry, good common man, what
Of that angelic sword? Creature of
Ten times ten times dynamite, convulsive
Angel, convulsive shatterer, gun,
Click, click, the Got whom we serve is able,
Still, still to deliver us, still magic,
Still moving yet motionless in smoke, still
One with us, in the heaved-up noise, still
Captain, the man of skill, the expert
Leader, the creator of bursting color
And rainbow sortilege, the savage weapon
Against enemies, against the prester,
Presto, whose whispers prickle the spirit.

III

They are sick of each old romance, returning,
Of each old revolving dance, the music
Like a euphony in a museum
Of euphonies, a skin from Nubia,
A helio-horn. How strange the hero
To this accurate, exacting eye. Sight
Hangs heaven with flash drapery. Sight
Is a museum of things seen. Sight,
In war, observes each man profoundly.
Yes. But these sudden sublimations
Are to combat what his exaltations
Are to the unaccountable prophet or
What any fury to its noble centre.

IV

To grasp the hero, the eccentric
On a horse, in a plane, at the piano—
At the piano, scales, arpeggios
And chords, the morning exercises,
The afternoon's reading, the night's reflection,
That's how to produce a virtuoso.
The drill of a submarine. The voyage
Beyond the oyster-beds, indigo
Shadow, up the great sea and downward
And darkly beside the vulcanic
Sea-tower, sea-pinnacles, sea-mountain.
The signal . . . The sea-tower, shaken,
Sways slightly and the pinnacles frisson.
The mountain collapses. Chopiniana.

V

The common man is the common hero.
The common hero is the hero.
Imprimatur. But then there's common fortune,
Induced by what you will: the entrails
Of a cat, twelve dollars for the devil,
A kneeling woman, a moon's farewell;

And common fortune, induced by nothing,
Unwished for, chance, the merest riding
Of the wind, rain in a dry September,
The improvisations of the cuckoos
In a clock-shop. . . . Soldier, think, in the darkness,
Repeating your appointed paces
Between two neatly measured stations,
Of less neatly measured common-places.

VI

Unless we believe in the hero, what is there
To believe? Incisive what, the fellow
Of what good. Devise. Make him of mud,
For every day. In a civiler manner,
Devise, devise, and make him of winter's
Iciest core, a north star, central
In our oblivion, of summer's
Imagination, the golden rescue:
The bread and wine of the mind, permitted
In an ascetic room, its table
Red as a red table-cloth, its windows
West Indian, the extremest power
Living and being about us and being
Ours, like a familiar companion.

VII

Gazette Guerrière. A man might happen
To prefer *L'Observateur de la Paix,* since
The hero of the *Gazette* and the hero
Of *L'Observateur,* the classic hero
And the bourgeois, are different, much.
The classic changed. There have been many.
And there are many bourgeois heroes.
There are more heroes than marbles of them.
The marbles are pinchings of an idea,
Yet there is that idea behind the marbles,
The idea of things for public gardens,
Of men suited to public ferns . . . The hero

Glides to his meeting like a lover
Mumbling a secret, passionate message.

VIII

The hero is not a person. The marbles
Of Xenophon, his epitaphs, should
Exhibit Xenophon, what he was, since
Neither his head nor horse nor knife nor
Legend were part of what he was, forms
Of a still-life, symbols, brown things to think of
In brown books. The marbles of what he was stand
Like a white abstraction only, a feeling
In a feeling mass, a blank emotion,
An anti-pathos, until we call it
Xenophon, its implement and actor.
Obscure Satanas, make a model
Of this element, this force. Transfer it
Into a barbarism as its image.

IX

If the hero is not a person, the emblem
Of him, even if Xenophon, seems
To stand taller than a person stands, has
A wider brow, large and less human
Eyes and bruted ears: the man-like body
Of a primitive. He walks with a defter
And lither stride. His arms are heavy
And his breast is greatness. All his speeches
Are prodigies in longer phrases.
His thoughts begotten at clear sources,
Apparently in air, fall from him
Like chantering from an abundant
Poet, as if he thought gladly, being
Compelled thereto by an innate music.

X

And if the phenomenon, magnified, is
Further magnified, sua voluntate,

Beyond his circumstance, projected
High, low, far, wide, against the distance,
In parades like several equipages,
Painted by mad-men, seen as magic,
Leafed out in adjectives as private
And peculiar and appropriate glory,
Even enthroned on rainbows in the sight
Of the fishes of the sea, the colored
Birds and people of this too voluminous
Air-earth—Can we live on dry descriptions,
Feel everything starving except the belly
And nourish ourselves on crumbs of whimsy?

XI

But a profane parade, the basso
Preludes a-rub, a-rub-rub, for him that
Led the emperor astray, the tom trumpets
Curling round the steeple and the people,
The elephants of sound, the tigers
In trombones roaring for the children,
Young boys resembling pastry, hip-hip,
Young men as vegetables, hip-hip,
Home and the fields give praise, hurrah, hip,
Hip, hip, hurrah. Eternal morning . . .
Flesh on the bones. The skeleton throwing
His crust away eats of this meat, drinks
Of this tabernacle, this communion,
Sleeps in the sun no thing recalling.

XII

It is not an image. It is a feeling.
There is no image of the hero.
There is a feeling as definition.
How could there be an image, an outline,
A design, a marble soiled by pigeons?
The hero is a feeling, a man seen
As if the eye was an emotion,
As if in seeing we saw our feeling

In the object seen and saved that mystic
Against the sight, the penetrating,
Pure eye. Instead of allegory,
We have and are the man, capable
Of his brave quickenings, the human
Accelerations that seem inhuman.

XIII

These letters of him for the little,
The imaginative, ghosts that dally
With life's salt upon their lips and savor
The taste of it, secrete within them
Too many references. The hero
Acts in reality, adds nothing
To what he does. He is the heroic
Actor and act but not divided.
It is a part of his conception,
That he be not conceived, being real.
Say that the hero is his nation,
In him made one, and in that saying
Destroy all references. This actor
Is anonymous and cannot help it.

XIV

A thousand crystals' chiming voices,
Like the shiddow-shaddow of lights revolving
To momentary ones, are blended,
In hymns, through iridescent changes,
Of the apprehending of the hero.
These hymns are like a stubborn brightness
Approaching in the dark approaches
Of time and place, becoming certain,
The organic centre of responses,
Naked of hindrance, a thousand crystals.
To meditate the highest man, not
The highest supposed in him and over,
Creates, in the blissfuller perceptions,
What unisons create in music.

XV

The highest man with nothing higher
Than himself, his self, the self that embraces
The self of the hero, the solar single,
Man-sun, man-moon, man-earth, man-ocean,
Makes poems on the syllable *fa* or
Jumps from the clouds or, from his window,
Sees the petty gildings on February . . .
The man-sun being hero rejects that
False empire . . . These are the works and pastimes
Of the highest self: he studies the paper
On the wall, the lemons on the table.
This is his day. With nothing lost, he
Arrives at the man-man as he wanted.
This is his night and meditation.

XVI

Each false thing ends. The bouquet of summer
Turns blue and on its empty table
It is stale and the water is discolored.
True autumn stands then in the doorway.
After the hero, the familiar
Man makes the hero artificial.
But was the summer false? The hero?
How did we come to think that autumn
Was the veritable season, that familiar
Man was the veritable man? So
Summer, jangling the savagest diamonds and
Dressed in its azure-doubled crimsons,
May truly bear its heroic fortunes
For the large, the solitary figure.

T HE immense poetry of war and the poetry of a work of the imagination are two different things. In the presence of the violent reality of war, consciousness takes the place of the imagination. And consciousness of an immense war is a consciousness of fact. If that is true, it follows that the poetry of war as a consciousness of the victories and defeats of nations, is a consciousness of fact, but of heroic fact, of fact on such a scale that the mere consciousness of it affects the scale of one's thinking and constitutes a participating in the heroic.

It has been easy to say in recent times that everything tends to become real, or, rather, that everything moves in the direction of reality, that is to say, in the direction of fact. We leave fact and come back to it, come back to what we wanted fact to be, not to what it was, not to what it has too often remained. The poetry of a work of the imagination constantly illustrates the fundamental and endless struggle with fact. It goes on everywhere, even in the periods that we call peace. But in war, the desire to move in the direction of fact as we want it to be and to move quickly is overwhelming.

Nothing will ever appease this desire except a consciousness of fact as everyone is at least satisfied to have it be.

W.S.

TRANSPORT TO SUMMER

(1947)

God Is Good. It Is a Beautiful Night

Look round, brown moon, brown bird, as you rise to fly,
Look round at the head and zither
On the ground.

Look round you as you start to rise, brown moon,
At the book and shoe, the rotted rose
At the door.

This was the place to which you came last night,
Flew close to, flew to without rising away.
Now, again,

In your light, the head is speaking. It reads the book.
It becomes the scholar again, seeking celestial
Rendezvous,

Picking thin music on the rustiest string,
Squeezing the reddest fragrance from the stump
Of summer.

The venerable song falls from your fiery wings.
The song of the great space of your age pierces
The fresh night.

Certain Phenomena of Sound

I

The cricket in the telephone is still.
A geranium withers on the window-sill.

Cat's milk is dry in the saucer. Sunday song
Comes from the beating of the locust's wings,

That do not beat by pain, but calendar,
Nor meditate the world as it goes round.

Someone has left for a ride in a balloon
Or in a bubble examines the bubble of air.

The room is emptier than nothingness.
Yet a spider spins in the left shoe under the bed—

And old John Rocket dozes on his pillow.
It is safe to sleep to a sound that time brings back.

II

So you're home again, Redwood Roamer, and ready
To feast . . . Slice the mango, Naaman, and dress it

With white wine, sugar and lime juice. Then bring it,
After we've drunk the Moselle, to the thickest shade

Of the garden. We must prepare to hear the Roamer's
Story . . . The sound of that slick sonata,

Finding its way from the house, makes music seem
To be a nature, a place in which itself

Is that which produces everything else, in which
The Roamer is a voice taller than the redwoods,

Engaged in the most prolific narrative,
A sound producing the things that are spoken.

III

Eulalia, I lounged on the hospital porch,
On the east, sister and nun, and opened wide
A parasol, which I had found, against
The sun. The interior of a parasol,
It is a kind of blank in which one sees.
So seeing, I beheld you walking, white,
Gold-shined by sun, perceiving as I saw
That of that light Eulalia was the name.
Then I, Semiramide, dark-syllabled,
Contrasting our two names, considered speech.

You were created of your name, the word
Is that of which you were the personage.
There is no life except in the word of it.
I write *Semiramide* and in the script
I am and have a being and play a part.
You are that white Eulalia of the name.

The Motive for Metaphor

You like it under the trees in autumn,
Because everything is half dead.
The wind moves like a cripple among the leaves
And repeats words without meaning.

In the same way, you were happy in spring,
With the half colors of quarter-things,
The slightly brighter sky, the melting clouds,
The single bird, the obscure moon—

The obscure moon lighting an obscure world
Of things that would never be quite expressed,
Where you yourself were never quite yourself
And did not want nor have to be,

Desiring the exhilarations of changes:
The motive for metaphor, shrinking from
The weight of primary noon,
The A B C of being,

The ruddy temper, the hammer
Of red and blue, the hard sound—
Steel against intimation—the sharp flash,
The vital, arrogant, fatal, dominant X.

Gigantomachia

They could not carry much, as soldiers.
There was no past in their forgetting,
No self in the mass: the braver being,
The body that could never be wounded,
The life that never would end, no matter
Who died, the being that was an abstraction,
A giant's heart in the veins, all courage.

But to strip off the complacent trifles,
To expel the ever-present seductions,
To reject the script for its lack-tragic,
To confront with plainest eye the changes,
That was to look on what war magnified.
It was increased, enlarged, made simple,
Made single, made one. This was not denial.

Each man himself became a giant,
Tipped out with largeness, bearing the heavy
And the high, receiving out of others,
As from an inhuman elevation
And origin, an inhuman person,
A mask, a spirit, an accoutrement.
For soldiers, the new moon stretches twenty feet.

Dutch Graves in Bucks County

Angry men and furious machines
Swarm from the little blue of the horizon
To the great blue of the middle height.
Men scatter throughout clouds.
The wheels are too large for any noise.

And you, my semblables, in sooty residence
Tap skeleton drums inaudibly.

There are shouts and voices.
There are men shuffling on foot in air.

Men are moving and marching
And shuffling lightly, with the heavy lightness
Of those that are marching, many together.

And you, my semblables—the old flag of Holland
Flutters in tiny darkness.

There are circles of weapons in the sun.
The air attends the brightened guns,
As if sounds were forming
Out of themselves, a saying,
An expressive on-dit, a profession.

And you, my semblables, are doubly killed
To be buried in desert and deserted earth.

The flags are natures newly found.
Rifles grow sharper on the sight.
There is a rumble of autumnal marching,
From which no soft sleeve relieves us.
Fate is the present desperado.

And you, my semblables, are crusts that lie
In the shrivellings of your time and place.

There is a battering of the drums. The bugles
Cry loudly, cry out in the powerful heart.
A force gathers that will cry loudlier
Than the most metal music, loudlier,
Like an instinctive incantation.

And you, my semblables, in the total
Of remembrance share nothing of ourselves.

An end must come in a merciless triumph,
An end of evil in a profounder logic,
In a peace that is more than a refuge,
In the will of what is common to all men,
Spelled from spent living and spent dying.

And you, my semblables, in gaffer-green,
Know that the past is not part of the present.

There were other soldiers, other people,
Men came as the sun comes, early children
And late wanderers creeping under the barb of night,
Year, year and year, defeated at last and lost
In an ignorance of sleep with nothing won.

And you, my semblables, know that this time
Is not an early time that has grown late.

But these are not those rusted armies.
There are the lewdest and the lustiest,
The hullaballoo of health and have,
The much too many disinherited
In a storm of torn-up testaments.

And you, my semblables, know that your children
Are not your children, not your selves.

Who are the mossy cronies muttering,
Monsters antique and haggard with past thought?
What is this crackling of voices in the mind,
This pitter-patter of archaic freedom,
Of the thousands of freedoms except our own?

And you, my semblables, whose ecstasy
Was the glory of heaven in the wilderness—

Freedom is like a man who kills himself
Each night, an incessant butcher, whose knife
Grows sharp in blood. The armies kill themselves,
And in their blood an ancient evil dies—
The action of incorrigible tragedy.

And you, my semblables, behold in blindness
That a new glory of new men assembles.

This is the pit of torment that placid end
Should be illusion, that the mobs of birth

Avoid our stale perfections, seeking out
Their own, waiting until we go
To picnic in the ruins that we leave.

So that the stars, my semblables, chimeres,
Shine on the very living of those alive.

These violent marchers of the present,
Rumbling along the autumnal horizon,
Under the arches, over the arches, in arcs
Of a chaos composed in more than order,
March toward a generation's centre.

Time was not wasted in your subtle temples.
No: nor divergence made too steep to follow down.

No Possum, No Sop, No Taters

He is not here, the old sun,
As absent as if we were asleep.

The field is frozen. The leaves are dry.
Bad is final in this light.

In this bleak air the broken stalks
Have arms without hands. They have trunks

Without legs or, for that, without heads.
They have heads in which a captive cry

Is merely the moving of a tongue.
Snow sparkles like eyesight falling to earth,

Like seeing fallen brightly away.
The leaves hop, scraping on the ground.

It is deep January. The sky is hard.
The stalks are firmly rooted in ice.

It is in this solitude, a syllable,
Out of these gawky flitterings,

Intones its single emptiness,
The savagest hollow of winter-sound.

It is here, in this bad, that we reach
The last purity of the knowledge of good.

The crow looks rusty as he rises up.
Bright is the malice in his eye . . .

One joins him there for company,
But at a distance, in another tree.

So-and-So Reclining on Her Couch

On her side, reclining on her elbow.
This mechanism, this apparition,
Suppose we call it Projection A.

She floats in air at the level of
The eye, completely anonymous,
Born, as she was, at twenty-one,

Without lineage or language, only
The curving of her hip, as motionless gesture,
Eyes dripping blue, so much to learn.

If just above her head there hung,
Suspended in air, the slightest crown
Of Gothic prong and practick bright,

The suspension, as in solid space,
The suspending hand withdrawn, would be
An invisible gesture. Let this be called

Projection B. To get at the thing
Without gestures is to get at it as
Idea. She floats in the contention, the flux

Between the thing as idea and
The idea as thing. She is half who made her.
This is the final Projection, C.

The arrangement contains the desire of
The artist. But one confides in what has no
Concealed creator. One walks easily

The unpainted shore, accepts the world
As anything but sculpture. Good-bye,
Mrs. Pappadopoulos, and thanks.

Chocorua to Its Neighbor

I

To speak quietly at such a distance, to speak
And to be heard is to be large in space,
That, like your own, is large, hence, to be part
Of sky, of sea, large earth, large air. It is
To perceive men without reference to their form.

II

The armies are forms in number, as cities are.
The armies are cities in movement. But a war
Between cities is a gesticulation of forms,
A swarming of number over number, not
One foot approaching, one uplifted arm.

III

At the end of night last night a crystal star,
The crystal-pointed star of morning, rose

And lit the snow to a light congenial
To this prodigious shadow, who then came
In an elemental freedom, sharp and cold.

IV

The feeling of him was the feel of day,
And of a day as yet unseen, in which
To see was to be. He was the figure in
A poem for Liadoff, the self of selves:
To think of him destroyed the body's form.

V

He was a shell of dark blue glass, or ice,
Or air collected in a deep essay,
Or light embodied, or almost, a flash
On more than muscular shoulders, arms and chest,
Blue's last transparence as it turned to black,

VI

The glitter of a being, which the eye
Accepted yet which nothing understood,
A fusion of night, its blue of the pole of blue
And of the brooding mind, fixed but for a slight
Illumination of movement as he breathed.

VII

He was as tall as a tree in the middle of
The night. The substance of his body seemed
Both substance and non-substance, luminous flesh
Or shapely fire: fire from an underworld,
Of less degree than flame and lesser shine.

VIII

Upon my top he breathed the pointed dark.
He was not man yet he was nothing else.
If in the mind, he vanished, taking there
The mind's own limits, like a tragic thing
Without existence, existing everywhere.

IX

He breathed in crystal-pointed change the whole
Experience of night, as if he breathed
A consciousness from solitude, inhaled
A freedom out of silver-shaping size,
Against the whole experience of day.

X

The silver-shapeless, gold-encrusted size
Of daylight came while he sat thinking. He said,
"The moments of enlargement overlook
The enlarging of the simplest soldier's cry
In what I am, as he falls. Of what I am,

XI

The cry is part. My solitaria
Are the meditations of a central mind.
I hear the motions of the spirit and the sound
Of what is secret becomes, for me, a voice
That is my own voice speaking in my ear.

XII

There lies the misery, the coldest coil
That grips the centre, the actual bite, that life
Itself is like a poverty in the space of life,
So that the flapping of wind around me here
Is something in tatters that I cannot hold."

XIII

In spite of this, the gigantic bulk of him
Grew strong, as if doubt never touched his heart.
Of what was this the force? From what desire
And from what thinking did his radiance come?
In what new spirit had his body birth?

XIV

He was more than an external majesty,
Beyond the sleep of those that did not know,

More than a spokesman of the night to say
Now, time stands still. He came from out of sleep.
He rose because men wanted him to be.

XV

They wanted him by day to be, image,
But not the person, of their power, thought,
But not the thinker, large in their largeness, beyond
Their form, beyond their life, yet of themselves,
Excluding by his largeness their defaults.

XVI

Last night at the end of night his starry head,
Like the head of fate, looked out in darkness, part
Thereof and part desire and part the sense
Of what men are. The collective being knew
There were others like him safely under roof:

XVII

The captain squalid on his pillow, the great
Cardinal, saying the prayers of earliest day;
The stone, the categorical effigy;
And the mother, the music, the name; the scholar,
Whose green mind bulges with complicated hues:

XVIII

True transfigurers fetched out of the human mountain,
True genii for the diminished, spheres,
Gigantic embryos of populations,
Blue friends in shadows, rich conspirators,
Confiders and comforters and lofty kin.

XIX

To say more than human things with human voice,
That cannot be; to say human things with more
Than human voice, that, also, cannot be;

To speak humanly from the height or from the depth
Of human things, that is acutest speech.

XX

Now, I, Chocorua, speak of this shadow as
A human thing. It is an eminence,
But of nothing, trash of sleep that will disappear
With the special things of night, little by little,
In day's constellation, and yet remain, yet be,

XXI

Not father, but bare brother, megalfrere,
Or by whatever boorish name a man
Might call the common self, interior fons.
And fond, the total man of glubbal glub,
Political tramp with an heraldic air,

XXII

Cloud-casual, metaphysical metaphor,
But resting on me, thinking in my snow,
Physical if the eye is quick enough,
So that, where he was, there is an enkindling, where
He is, the air changes and grows fresh to breathe.

XXIII

The air changes, creates and re-creates, like strength,
And to breathe is a fulfilling of desire,
A clearing, a detecting, a completing,
A largeness lived and not conceived, a space
That is an instant nature, brilliantly.

XXIV

Integration for integration, the great arms
Of the armies, the solid men, make big the fable.
This is their captain and philosopher,
He that is fortelleze, though he be
Hard to perceive and harder still to touch.

XXV

Last night at the end of night and in the sky,
The lesser night, the less than morning light,
Fell on him, high and cold, searching for what
Was native to him in that height, searching
The pleasure of his spirit in the cold.

XXVI

How singular he was as man, how large,
If nothing more than that, for the moment, large
In my presence, the companion of presences
Greater than mine, of his demanding, head
And, of human realizings, rugged roy . . .

Poesie Abrutie

The brooks are bristling in the field,
Now, brooks are bristling in the fields
And gelid Januar has gone to hell.

II

The water puddles puddles are
And ice is still in Februar.
It still is ice in Februar.

III

The figures of the past go cloaked.
They walk in mist and rain and snow
And go, go slowly, but they go.

IV

The greenhouse on the village green
Is brighter than the sun itself.
Cinerarias have a speaking sheen.

The Lack of Repose

A young man seated at his table
Holds in his hand a book you have never written
Staring at the secretions of the words as
They reveal themselves.

It is not midnight. It is mid-day,
The young man is well-disclosed, one of the gang,
Andrew Jackson Something. But this book
Is a cloud in which a voice mumbles.

It is a ghost that inhabits a cloud,
But a ghost for Andrew, not lean, catarrhal
And pallid. It is the grandfather he liked,
With an understanding compounded by death

And the associations beyond death, even if only
Time. What a thing it is to believe that
One understands, in the intense disclosures
Of a parent in the French sense.

And not yet to have written a book in which
One is already a grandfather and to have put there
A few sounds of meaning, a momentary end
To the complication, is good, is a good.

Somnambulisma

On an old shore, the vulgar ocean rolls
Noiselessly, noiselessly, resembling a thin bird,
That thinks of settling, yet never settles, on a nest.

The wings keep spreading and yet are never wings.
The claws keep scratching on the shale, the shallow shale,
The sounding shallow, until by water washed away.

The generations of the bird are all
By water washed away. They follow after.
They follow, follow, follow, in water washed away.

Without this bird that never settles, without
Its generations that follow in their universe,
The ocean, falling and falling on the hollow shore,

Would be a geography of the dead: not of that land
To which they may have gone, but of the place in which
They lived, in which they lacked a pervasive being,

In which no scholar, separately dwelling,
Poured forth the fine fins, the gawky beaks, the personalia,
Which, as a man feeling everything, were his.

Crude Foyer

Thought is false happiness: the idea
That merely by thinking one can,
Or may, penetrate, not may,
But can, that one is sure to be able—

That there lies at the end of thought
A foyer of the spirit in a landscape
Of the mind, in which we sit
And wear humanity's bleak crown;

In which we read the critique of paradise
And say it is the work
Of a comedian, this critique;
In which we sit and breathe

An innocence of an absolute,
False happiness, since we know that we use
Only the eye as faculty, that the mind
Is the eye, and that this landscape of the mind

Is a landscape only of the eye; and that
We are ignorant men incapable
Of the least, minor, vital metaphor, content,
At last, there, when it turns out to be here.

Repetitions of a Young Captain

I

A tempest cracked on the theatre. Quickly,
The wind beat in the roof and half the walls.
The ruin stood still in an external world.

It had been real. It was something overseas
That I remembered, something that I remembered
Overseas, that stood in an external world.

It had been real. It was not now. The rip
Of the wind and the glittering were real now,
In the spectacle of a new reality.

II

The people sat in the theatre, in the ruin,
As if nothing had happened. The dim actor spoke.
His hands became his feelings. His thick shape

Issued thin seconds glibly gapering.
Then faintly encrusted, a tissue of the moon
Walked toward him on the stage and they embraced.

They polished the embracings of a pair
Born old, familiar with the depths of the heart,
Like a machine left running, and running down.

It was a blue scene washing white in the rain,
Like something I remembered overseas.
It was something overseas that I remembered.

III

Millions of major men against their like
Make more than thunder's rural rumbling. They make
The giants that each one of them becomes

In a calculated chaos: he that takes form
From the others, being larger than he was,
Accoutred in a little of the strength

That sweats the sun up on its morning way
To giant red, sweats up a giant sense
To the make-matter, matter-nothing mind,

Until this matter-makes in years of war.
This being in a reality beyond
The finikin spectres in the memory,

This elevation, in which he seems to be tall,
Makes him rise above the houses, looking down.
His route lies through an image in his mind:

My route lies through an image in my mind,
It is the route that milky millions find,
An image that leaves nothing much behind.

IV

If these were only words that I am speaking
Indifferent sounds and not the heraldic-ho
Of the clear sovereign that is reality,

Of the clearest reality that is sovereign,
How should I repeat them, keep repeating them,
As if they were desperate with a know-and-know,

Central responses to a central fear,
The adobe of the angels? Constantly,
At the railway station, a soldier steps away,

Sees a familiar building drenched in cloud
And goes to an external world, having
Nothing of place. There is no change of place

Nor of time. The departing soldier is as he is,
Yet in that form will not return. But does
He find another? The giant of sense remains

A giant without a body. If, as giant,
He shares a gigantic life, it is because
The gigantic has a reality of its own.

V

On a few words of what is real in the world
I nourish myself. I defend myself against
Whatever remains. Of what is real I say,

Is it the old, the roseate parent or
The bride come jingling, kissed and cupped, or else
The spirit and all ensigns of the self?

A few words, a memorandum voluble
Of the giant sense, the enormous harnesses
And writhing wheels of this world's business,

The drivers in the wind-blows cracking whips,
The pulling into the sky and the setting there
Of the expanses that are mountainous rock and sea;

And beyond the days, beyond the slow-foot litters
Of the nights, the actual, universal strength,
Without a word of rhetoric—there it is.

A memorandum of the people sprung
From that strength, whose armies set their own expanses.
A few words of what is real or may be

Or of glistening reference to what is real,
The universe that supplements the manqué,
The soldier seeking his point between the two,

The organic consolation, the complete
Society of the spirit when it is
Alone, the half-arc hanging in mid-air

Composed, appropriate to the incomplete,
Supported by a half-arc in mid-earth.
Millions of instances of which I am one.

VI

And if it be theatre for theatre,
The powdered personals against the giants' rage,
Blue and its deep inversions in the moon

Against gold whipped reddened in big-shadowed black,
Her vague "Secrete me from reality,"
His "That reality secrete itself,"

The choice is made. Green is the orator
Of our passionate height. He wears a tufted green,
And tosses green for those for whom green speaks.

Secrete us in reality. It is there
My orator. Let this giantness fall down
And come to nothing. Let the rainy arcs

And pathetic magnificences dry in the sky.
Secrete us in reality. Discover
A civil nakedness in which to be,

In which to bear with the exactest force
The precisions of fate, nothing fobbed off, nor changed
In a beau language without a drop of blood.

The Creations of Sound

If the poetry of *X* was music,
So that it came to him of its own,
Without understanding, out of the wall

Or in the ceiling, in sounds not chosen,
Or chosen quickly, in a freedom
That was their element, we should not know

That *X* is an obstruction, a man
Too exactly himself, and that there are words
Better without an author, without a poet,

Or having a separate author, a different poet,
An accretion from ourselves, intelligent
Beyond intelligence, an artificial man

At a distance, a secondary expositor,
A being of sound, whom one does not approach
Through any exaggeration. From him, we collect.

Tell X that speech is not dirty silence
Clarified. It is silence made still dirtier.
It is more than an imitation for the ear.

He lacks this venerable complication.
His poems are not of the second part of life.
They do not make the visible a little hard

To see nor, reverberating, eke out the mind
On peculiar horns, themselves eked out
By the spontaneous particulars of sound.

We do not say ourselves like that in poems.
We say ourselves in syllables that rise
From the floor, rising in speech we do not speak.

Holiday in Reality

I

It was something to see that their white was different,
Sharp as white paint in the January sun;

Something to feel that they needed another yellow,
Less Aix than Stockholm, hardly a yellow at all,

A vibrancy not to be taken for granted, from
A sun in an almost colorless, cold heaven.

They had known that there was not even a common speech,
Palabra of a common man who did not exist.

Why should they not know they had everything of their
        own
As each had a particular woman and her touch?

After all, they knew that to be real each had
To find for himself his earth, his sky, his sea.

And the words for them and the colors that they possessed.
It was impossible to breathe at Durand-Ruel's.

II

The flowering Judas grows from the belly or not at all.
The breast is covered with violets. It is a green leaf.

Spring is umbilical or else it is not spring.
Spring is the truth of spring or nothing, a waste, a fake.

These trees and their argentines, their dark-spiced branches,
Grow out of the spirit or they are fantastic dust.

The bud of the apple is desire, the down-falling gold,
The catbird's gobble in the morning half-awake—

These are real only if I make them so. Whistle
For me, grow green for me and, as you whistle and grow
        green,

Intangible arrows quiver and stick in the skin
And I taste at the root of the tongue the unreal of what is
        real.

Esthétique du Mal

He was at Naples writing letters home
And, between his letters, reading paragraphs
On the sublime. Vesuvius had groaned
For a month. It was pleasant to be sitting there,
While the sultriest fulgurations, flickering,
Cast corners in the glass. He could describe
The terror of the sound because the sound
Was ancient. He tried to remember the phrases: pain
Audible at noon, pain torturing itself,
Pain killing pain on the very point of pain.
The volcano trembled in another ether,
As the body trembles at the end of life.

It was almost time for lunch. Pain is human.
There were roses in the cool café. His book
Made sure of the most correct catastrophe.
Except for us, Vesuvius might consume
In solid fire the utmost earth and know
No pain (ignoring the cocks that crow us up
To die). This is a part of the sublime
From which we shrink. And yet, except for us,
The total past felt nothing when destroyed.

At a town in which acacias grew, he lay
On his balcony at night. Warblings became
Too dark, too far, too much the accents of
Afflicted sleep, too much the syllables
That would form themselves, in time, and communicate
The intelligence of his despair, express
What meditation never quite achieved.

The moon rose up as if it had escaped
His meditation. It evaded his mind.
It was part of a supremacy always

277

Above him. The moon was always free from him,
As night was free from him. The shadow touched
Or merely seemed to touch him as he spoke
A kind of elegy he found in space:

It is pain that is indifferent to the sky
In spite of the yellow of the acacias, the scent
Of them in the air still hanging heavily
In the hoary-hanging night. It does not regard
This freedom, this supremacy, and in
Its own hallucination never sees
How that which rejects it saves it in the end.

III

His firm stanzas hang like hives in hell
Or what hell was, since now both heaven and hell
Are one, and here, O terra infidel.

The fault lies with an over-human god,
Who by sympathy has made himself a man
And is not to be distinguished, when we cry

Because we suffer, our oldest parent, peer
Of the populace of the heart, the reddest lord,
Who has gone before us in experience.

If only he would not pity us so much,
Weaken our fate, relieve us of woe both great
And small, a constant fellow of destiny,

A too, too human god, self-pity's kin
And uncourageous genesis . . . It seems
As if the health of the world might be enough.

It seems as if the honey of common summer
Might be enough, as if the golden combs
Were part of a sustenance itself enough,

As if hell, so modified, had disappeared,
As if pain, no longer satanic mimicry,
Could be borne, as if we were sure to find our way.

IV

Livre de Toutes Sortes de Fleurs D'Après Nature.
All sorts of flowers. That's the sentimentalist.
When B. sat down at the piano and made
A transparence in which we heard music, made music,
In which we heard transparent sounds, did he play
All sorts of notes? Or did he play only one
In an ecstasy of its associates,
Variations in the tones of a single sound,
The last, or sounds so single they seemed one?

And then that Spaniard of the rose, itself
Hot-hooded and dark-blooded, rescued the rose
From nature, each time he saw it, making it,
As he saw it, exist in his own especial eye.
Can we conceive of him as rescuing less,
As muffing the mistress for her several maids,
As foregoing the nakedest passion for barefoot
Philandering? . . . The genius of misfortune
Is not a sentimentalist. He is
That evil, that evil in the self, from which
In desperate hallow, rugged gesture, fault
Falls out on everything: the genius of
The mind, which is our being, wrong and wrong,
The genius of the body, which is our world,
Spent in the false engagements of the mind.

V

Softly let all true sympathizers come,
Without the inventions of sorrow or the sob
Beyond invention. Within what we permit,
Within the actual, the warm, the near,
So great a unity, that it is bliss,
Ties us to those we love. For this familiar,

This brother even in the father's eye,
This brother half-spoken in the mother's throat
And these regalia, these things disclosed,
These nebulous brilliancies in the smallest look
Of the being's deepest darling, we forego
Lament, willingly forfeit the ai-ai

Of parades in the obscurer selvages.
Be near me, come closer, touch my hand, phrases
Compounded of dear relation, spoken twice,
Once by the lips, once by the services
Of central sense, these minutiae mean more
Than clouds, benevolences, distant heads.
These are within what we permit, in-bar
Exquisite in poverty against the suns
Of ex-bar, in-bar retaining attributes
With which we vested, once, the golden forms
And the damasked memory of the golden forms
And ex-bar's flower and fire of the festivals
Of the damasked memory of the golden forms,
Before we were wholly human and knew ourselves.

VI

The sun, in clownish yellow, but not a clown,
Brings the day to perfection and then fails. He dwells
In a consummate prime, yet still desires
A further consummation. For the lunar month
He makes the tenderest research, intent
On a transmutation which, when seen, appears
To be askew. And space is filled with his
Rejected years. A big bird pecks at him
For food. The big bird's boney appetite
Is as insatiable as the sun's. The bird
Rose from an imperfection of its own
To feed on the yellow bloom of the yellow fruit
Dropped down from turquoise leaves. In the landscape of
The sun, its grossest appetite becomes less gross,
Yet, when corrected, has its curious lapses,
Its glitters, its divinations of serene
Indulgence out of all celestial sight.

The sun is the country wherever he is. The bird
In the brightest landscape downwardly revolves
Disdaining each astringent ripening,
Evading the point of redness, not content
To repose in an hour or season or long era
Of the country colors crowding against it, since
The yellow grassman's mind is still immense,
Still promises perfections cast away.

VII

How red the rose that is the soldier's wound,
The wounds of many soldiers, the wounds of all
The soldiers that have fallen, red in blood,
The soldier of time grown deathless in great size.

A mountain in which no ease is ever found,
Unless indifference to deeper death
Is ease, stands in the dark, a shadows' hill,
And there the soldier of time has deathless rest.

Concentric circles of shadows, motionless
Of their own part, yet moving on the wind,
Form mystical convolutions in the sleep
Of time's red soldier deathless on his bed.

The shadows of his fellows ring him round
In the high night, the summer breathes for them
Its fragrance, a heavy somnolence, and for him,
For the soldier of time, it breathes a summer sleep,

In which his wound is good because life was.
No part of him was ever part of death.
A woman smoothes her forehead with her hand
And the soldier of time lies calm beneath that stroke.

VIII

The death of Satan was a tragedy
For the imagination. A capital

Negation destroyed him in his tenement
And, with him, many blue phenomena.
It was not the end he had foreseen. He knew
That his revenge created filial
Revenges. And negation was eccentric.
It had nothing of the Julian thunder-cloud:
The assassin flash and rumble . . . He was denied.
Phantoms, what have you left? What underground?
What place in which to be is not enough
To be? You go, poor phantoms, without place
Like silver in the sheathing of the sight,
As the eye closes . . . How cold the vacancy
When the phantoms are gone and the shaken realist
First sees reality. The mortal no
Has its emptiness and tragic expirations.
The tragedy, however, may have begun,
Again, in the imagination's new beginning,
In the yes of the realist spoken because he must
Say yes, spoken because under every no
Lay a passion for yes that had never been broken.

IX

Panic in the face of the moon—round effendi
Or the phosphored sleep in which he walks abroad
Or the majolica dish heaped up with phosphored fruit
That he sends ahead, out of the goodness of his heart,
To anyone that comes—panic, because
The moon is no longer these nor anything
And nothing is left but comic ugliness
Or a lustred nothingness. Effendi, he
That has lost the folly of the moon becomes
The prince of the proverbs of pure poverty.
To lose sensibility, to see what one sees,
As if sight had not its own miraculous thrift,
To hear only what one hears, one meaning alone,
As if the paradise of meaning ceased
To be paradise, it is this to be destitute.
This is the sky divested of its fountains.
Here in the west indifferent crickets chant

Through our indifferent crises. Yet we require
Another chant, an incantation, as in
Another and later genesis, music
That buffets the shapes of its possible halcyon
Against the haggardie . . . A loud, large water
Bubbles up in the night and drowns the crickets' sound.
It is a declaration, a primitive ecstasy,
Truth's favors sonorously exhibited.

X

He had studied the nostalgias. In these
He sought the most grossly maternal, the creature
Who most fecundly assuaged him, the softest
Woman with a vague moustache and not the mauve
Maman. His anima liked its animal
And liked it unsubjugated, so that home
Was a return to birth, a being born
Again in the savagest severity,
Desiring fiercely, the child of a mother fierce
In his body, fiercer in his mind, merciless
To accomplish the truth in his intelligence.
It is true there were other mothers, singular
In form, lovers of heaven and earth, she-wolves
And forest tigresses and women mixed
With the sea. These were fantastic. There were homes
Like things submerged with their englutted sounds,
That were never wholly still. The softest woman,
Because she is as she was, reality,
The gross, the fecund, proved him against the touch
Of impersonal pain. Reality explained.
It was the last nostalgia: that he
Should understand. That he might suffer or that
He might die was the innocence of living, if life
Itself was innocent. To say that it was
Disentangled him from sleek ensolacings.

XI

Life is a bitter aspic. We are not
At the centre of a diamond. At dawn,

The paratroopers fall and as they fall
They mow the lawn. A vessel sinks in waves
Of people, as big bell-billows from its bell
Bell-bellow in the village steeple. Violets,
Great tufts, spring up from buried houses
Of poor, dishonest people, for whom the steeple,
Long since, rang out farewell, farewell, farewell.

Natives of poverty, children of malheur,
The gaiety of language is our seigneur.

A man of bitter appetite despises
A well-made scene in which paratroopers
Select adieux; and he despises this:
A ship that rolls on a confected ocean,
The weather pink, the wind in motion; and this:
A steeple that tip-tops the classic sun's
Arrangements; and the violets' exhumo.

The tongue caresses these exacerbations.
They press it as epicure, distinguishing
Themselves from its essential savor,
Like hunger that feeds on its own hungriness.

XII

He disposes the world in categories, thus:
The peopled and the unpeopled. In both, he is
Alone. But in the peopled world, there is,
Besides the people, his knowledge of them. In
The unpeopled, there is his knowledge of himself.
Which is more desperate in the moments when
The will demands that what he thinks be true?

Is it himself in them that he knows or they
In him? If it is himself in them, they have
No secret from him. If it is they in him,
He has no secret from them. This knowledge
Of them and of himself destroys both worlds,
Except when he escapes from it. To be
Alone is not to know them or himself.

This creates a third world without knowledge,
In which no one peers, in which the will makes no
Demands. It accepts whatever is as true,
Including pain, which, otherwise, is false.
In the third world, then, there is no pain. Yes, but
What lover has one in such rocks, what woman,
However known, at the centre of the heart?

XIII

It may be that one life is a punishment
For another, as the son's life for the father's.
But that concerns the secondary characters.
It is a fragmentary tragedy
Within the universal whole. The son
And the father alike and equally are spent,
Each one, by the necessity of being
Himself, the unalterable necessity
Of being this unalterable animal.
This force of nature in action is the major
Tragedy. This is destiny unperplexed,
The happiest enemy. And it may be
That in his Mediterranean cloister a man,
Reclining, eased of desire, establishes
The visible, a zone of blue and orange
Versicolorings, establishes a time
To watch the fire-feinting sea and calls it good,
The ultimate good, sure of a reality
Of the longest meditation, the maximum,
The assassin's scene. Evil in evil is
Comparative. The assassin discloses himself,
The force that destroys us is disclosed, within
This maximum, an adventure to be endured
With the politest helplessness. Ay-mi!
One feels its action moving in the blood.

XIV

Victor Serge said, "I followed his argument
With the blank uneasiness which one might feel
In the presence of a logical lunatic."

He said it of Konstantinov. Revolution
Is the affair of logical lunatics.
The politics of emotion must appear
To be an intellectual structure. The cause
Creates a logic not to be distinguished
From lunacy . . . One wants to be able to walk
By the lake at Geneva and consider logic:
To think of the logicians in their graves
And of the worlds of logic in their great tombs.
Lakes are more reasonable than oceans. Hence,
A promenade amid the grandeurs of the mind,
By a lake, with clouds like lights among great tombs,
Gives one a blank uneasiness, as if
One might meet Konstantinov, who would interrupt
With his lunacy. He would not be aware of the lake.
He would be the lunatic of one idea
In a world of ideas, who would have all the people
Live, work, suffer and die in that idea
In a world of ideas. He would not be aware of the clouds,
Lighting the martyrs of logic with white fire.
His extreme of logic would be illogical.

XV

The greatest poverty is not to live
In a physical world, to feel that one's desire
Is too difficult to tell from despair. Perhaps,
After death, the non-physical people, in paradise,
Itself non-physical, may, by chance, observe
The green corn gleaming and experience
The minor of what we feel. The adventurer
In humanity has not conceived of a race
Completely physical in a physical world.
The green corn gleams and the metaphysicals
Lie sprawling in majors of the August heat,
The rotund emotions, paradise unknown.

This is the thesis scrivened in delight,
The reverberating psalm, the right chorale.

One might have thought of sight, but who could think
Of what it sees, for all the ill it sees?
Speech found the ear, for all the evil sound,
But the dark italics it could not propound.
And out of what one sees and hears and out
Of what one feels, who could have thought to make
So many selves, so many sensuous worlds,
As if the air, the mid-day air, was swarming
With the metaphysical changes that occur,
Merely in living as and where we live.

The Bed of Old John Zeller

This structure of ideas, these ghostly sequences
Of the mind, result only in disaster. It follows,
Casual poet, that to add your own disorder to disaster

Makes more of it. It is easy to wish for another structure
Of ideas and to say as usual that there must be
Other ghostly sequences and, it would be, luminous

Sequences, thought of among spheres in the old peak of
    night:
This is the habit of wishing, as if one's grandfather lay
In one's heart and wished as he had always wished,
    unable

To sleep in that bed for its disorder, talking of ghostly
Sequences that would be sleep and ting-tang tossing, so
    that
He might slowly forget. It is more difficult to evade

That habit of wishing and to accept the structure
Of things as the structure of ideas. It was the structure
Of things at least that was thought of in the old peak of
    night.

Less and Less Human, O Savage Spirit

If there must be a god in the house, must be,
Saying things in the rooms and on the stair,

Let him move as the sunlight moves on the floor,
Or moonlight, silently, as Plato's ghost

Or Aristotle's skeleton. Let him hang out
His stars on the wall. He must dwell quietly.

He must be incapable of speaking, closed,
As those are: as light, for all its motion, is;

As color, even the closest to us, is;
As shapes, though they portend us, are.

It is the human that is the alien,
The human that has no cousin in the moon.

It is the human that demands his speech
From beasts or from the incommunicable mass.

If there must be a god in the house, let him be one
That will not hear us when we speak: a coolness,

A vermilioned nothingness, any stick of the mass
Of which we are too distantly a part.

Wild Ducks, People and Distances

The life of the world depends on that he is
Alive, on that people are alive, on that
There is village and village of them, without regard
To that be-misted one and apart from her.

Did we expect to live in other lives?
We grew used so soon, too soon, to earth itself,
As an element; to the sky, as an element.
People might share but were never an element,

Like earth and sky. Then he became nothing else
And they were nothing else. It was late in the year.
The wild ducks were enveloped. The weather was cold.
Yet, under the migrations to solitude,

There remained the smoke of the villages. Their fire
Was central in distances the wild ducks could
Not span, without any weather at all, except
The weather of other lives, from which there could

Be no migrating. It was that they were there
That held the distances off: the villages
Held off the final, fatal distances,
Between us and the place in which we stood.

The Pure Good of Theory

I

All the Preludes to Felicity

It is time that beats in the breast and it is time
That batters against the mind, silent and proud,
The mind that knows it is destroyed by time.

Time is a horse that runs in the heart, a horse
Without a rider on a road at night.
The mind sits listening and hears it pass.

It is someone walking rapidly in the street.
The reader by the window has finished his book
And tells the hour by the lateness of the sounds.

Even breathing is the beating of time, in kind:
A retardation of its battering,
A horse grotesquely taut, a walker like

A shadow in mid-earth . . . If we propose
A large-sculptured, platonic person, free from time,
And imagine for him the speech he cannot speak,

A form, then, protected from the battering, may
Mature: A capable being may replace
Dark horse and walker walking rapidly.

Felicity, ah! Time is the hooded enemy,
The inimical music, the enchantered space
In which the enchanted preludes have their place.

II

Description of a Platonic Person

Then came Brazil to nourish the emaciated
Romantic with dreams of her avoirdupois, green glade
Of serpents like z rivers simmering,

Green glade and holiday hotel and world
Of the future, in which the memory had gone
From everything, flying the flag of the nude,

The flag of the nude above the holiday hotel.
But there was one invalid in that green glade
And beneath that handkerchief drapeau, severe,

Signal, a character out of solitude,
Who was what people had been and still were,
Who lay in bed on the west wall of the sea,

Ill of a question like a malady,
Ill of a constant question in his thought,
Unhappy about the sense of happiness.

Was it that—a sense and beyond intelligence?
Could the future rest on a sense and be beyond
Intelligence? On what does the present rest?

This platonic person discovered a soul in the world
And studied it in his holiday hotel.
He was a Jew from Europe or might have been.

III

Fire-Monsters in the Milky Brain

Man, that is not born of woman but of air,
That comes here in the solar chariot,
Like rhetoric in a narration of the eye—

We knew one parent must have been divine,
Adam of beau regard, from fat Elysia,
Whose mind malformed this morning metaphor,

While all the leaves leaked gold. His mind made morning,
As he slept. He woke in a metaphor: this was
A metamorphosis of paradise,

Malformed, the world was paradise malformed . . .
Now, closely the ear attends the varying
Of this precarious music, the change of key

Not quite detected at the moment of change
And, now, it attends the difficult difference.
To say the solar chariot is junk

Is not a variation but an end.
Yet to speak of the whole world as metaphor
Is still to stick to the contents of the mind

And the desire to believe in a metaphor.
It is to stick to the nicer knowledge of
Belief, that what it believes in is not true.

IV

Dry Birds Are Fluttering in Blue Leaves—

It is never the thing but the version of the thing:
The fragrance of the woman not her self,
Her self in her manner not the solid block,

The day in its color not perpending time,
Time in its weather, our most sovereign lord,
The weather in words and words in sounds of sound.

These devastations are the divertissements
Of a destroying spiritual that digs-a-dog,
Whines in its hole for puppies to come see,

Springs outward, being large, and, in the dust,
Being small, inscribes ferocious alphabets,
Flies like a bat expanding as it flies,

Until its wings bear off night's middle witch;
And yet remains the same, the beast of light,
Groaning in half-exploited gutturals

The need of its element, the final need
Of final access to its element—
Of access like the page of a wiggy book,

Touched suddenly by the universal flare
For a moment, a moment in which we read and repeat
The eloquences of light's faculties.

A Word with José Rodríguez-Feo

As one of the secretaries of the moon,
The queen of ignorance, you have deplored
How she presides over imbeciles. The night
Makes everything grotesque. Is it because

Night is the nature of man's interior world?
Is lunar Habana the Cuba of the self?

We must enter boldly that interior world
To pick up relaxations of the known.
For example, this old man selling oranges
Sleeps by his basket. He snores. His bloated breath
Bursts back. What not quite realized transit
Of ideas moves wrinkled in a motion like

The cry of an embryo? The spirit tires,
It has, long since, grown tired, of such ideas.
It says there is an absolute grotesque.
There is a nature that is grotesque within
The boulevards of the generals. Why should
We say that it is man's interior world

Or seeing the spent, unconscious shapes of night,
Pretend they are shapes of another consciousness?
The grotesque is not a visitation. It is
Not apparition but appearance, part
Of that simplified geography, in which
The sun comes up like news from Africa.

Paisant Chronicle

What are the major men? All men are brave.
All men endure. The great captain is the choice
Of chance. Finally, the most solemn burial
Is a paisant chronicle.

Men live to be
Admired by men and all men, therefore, live
To be admired by all men. Nations live
To be admired by nations. The race is brave.
The race endures. The funeral pomps of the race
Are a multitude of individual pomps
And the chronicle of humanity is the sum
Of paisant chronicles.

The major men—
That is different. They are characters beyond
Reality, composed thereof. They are
The fictive man created out of men.
They are men but artificial men. They are
Nothing in which it is not possible
To believe, more than the casual hero, more
Than Tartuffe as myth, the most Molière,
The easy projection long prohibited.

The baroque poet may see him as still a man
As Virgil, abstract. But see him for yourself,
The fictive man. He may be seated in
A café. There may be a dish of country cheese
And a pineapple on the table. It must be so.

Sketch of the Ultimate Politician

He is the final builder of the total building,
The final dreamer of the total dream,
Or will be. Building and dream are one.

There is a total building and there is
A total dream. There are words of this,
Words, in a storm, that beat around the shapes.

There is a storm much like the crying of the wind,
Words that come out of us like words within,
That have rankled for many lives and made no sound.

He can hear them, like people on the walls,
Running in the rises of common speech,
Crying as that speech falls as if to fail.

There is a building stands in a ruinous storm,
A dream interrupted out of the past,
From beside us, from where we have yet to live.

Flyer's Fall

This man escaped the dirty fates,
Knowing that he did nobly, as he died.

Darkness, nothingness of human after-death,
Receive and keep him in the deepnesses of space—

Profundum, physical thunder, dimension in which
We believe without belief, beyond belief.

Jouga

The physical world is meaningless tonight
And there is no other. There is Ha-eé-me, who sits
And plays his guitar. Ha-eé-me is a beast.

Or perhaps his guitar is a beast or perhaps they are
Two beasts. But of the same kind—two conjugal beasts.
Ha-eé-me is the male beast . . . an imbecile,

Who knocks out a noise. The guitar is another beast
Beneath his tip-tap-tap. It is she that responds.
Two beasts but two of a kind and then not beasts.

Yet two not quite of a kind. It is like that here.
There are many of these beasts that one never sees,
Moving so that the foot-falls are slight and almost nothing.

This afternoon the wind and the sea were like that—
And after a while, when Ha-eé-me has gone to sleep,
A great jaguar running will make a little sound.

Debris of Life and Mind

There is so little that is close and warm.
It is as if we were never children.

Sit in the room. It is true in the moonlight
That it is as if we had never been young.

We ought not to be awake. It is from this
That a bright red woman will be rising

And, standing in violent golds, will brush her hair.
She will speak thoughtfully the words of a line.

She will think about them not quite able to sing.
Besides, when the sky is so blue, things sing themselves,

Even for her, already for her. She will listen
And feel that her color is a meditation,

The most gay and yet not so gay as it was.
Stay here. Speak of familiar things a while.

Description Without Place

I

It is possible that to seem—it is to be,
As the sun is something seeming and it is.

The sun is an example. What it seems
It is and in such seeming all things are.

Thus things are like a seeming of the sun
Or like a seeming of the moon or night

Or sleep. It was a queen that made it seem
By the illustrious nothing of her name.

Her green mind made the world around her green.
The queen is an example . . . This green queen

In the seeming of the summer of her sun
By her own seeming made the summer change.

In the golden vacancy she came, and comes,
And seems to be on the saying of her name.

Her time becomes again, as it became,
The crown and week-day coronal of her fame.

II

Such seemings are the actual ones: the way
Things look each day, each morning, or the style

Peculiar to the queen, this queen or that,
The lesser seeming original in the blind

Forward of the eye that, in its backward, sees
The greater seeming of the major mind.

An age is a manner collected from a queen.
An age is green or red. An age believes

Or it denies. An age is solitude
Or a barricade against the singular man

By the incalculably plural. Hence
Its identity is merely a thing that seems,

In the seeming of an original in the eye,
In the major manner of a queen, the green

The red, the blue, the argent queen. If not,
What subtlety would apparition have?

In flat appearance we should be and be,
Except for delicate clinkings not explained.

These are the actual seemings that we see,
Hear, feel and know. We feel and know them so.

III

There are potential seemings, arrogant
To be, as on the youngest poet's page,

Or in the dark musician, listening
To hear more brightly the contriving chords.

There are potential seemings turbulent
In the death of a soldier, like the utmost will,

The more than human commonplace of blood,
The breath that gushes upward and is gone,

And another breath emerging out of death,
That speaks for him such seemings as death gives.

There might be, too, a change immenser than
A poet's metaphors in which being would

Come true, a point in the fire of music where
Dazzle yields to a clarity and we observe,

And observing is completing and we are content,
In a world that shrinks to an immediate whole,

That we do not need to understand, complete
Without secret arrangements of it in the mind.

There might be in the curling-out of spring
A purple-leaping element that forth

Would froth the whole heaven with its seeming-so,
The intentions of a mind as yet unknown,

The spirit of one dwelling in a seed,
Itself that seed's ripe, unpredictable fruit.

Things are as they seemed to Calvin or to Anne
Of England, to Pablo Neruda in Ceylon,

To Nietzsche in Basel, to Lenin by a lake.
But the integrations of the past are like

A *Museo Olimpico*, so much
So little, our affair, which is the affair

Of the possible: seemings that are to be,
Seemings that it is possible may be.

IV

Nietzsche in Basel studied the deep pool
Of these discolorations, mastering

The moving and the moving of their forms
In the much-mottled motion of blank time.

His revery was the deepness of the pool,
The very pool, his thoughts the colored forms,

The eccentric souvenirs of human shapes,
Wrapped in their seemings, crowd on curious crowd,

In a kind of total affluence, all first,
All final, colors subjected in revery

To an innate grandiose, an innate light,
The sun of Nietzsche gildering the pool,

Yes: gildering the swarm-like manias
In perpetual revolution, round and round . . .

Lenin on a bench beside a lake disturbed
The swans. He was not the man for swans.

The slouch of his body and his look were not
In suavest keeping. The shoes, the clothes, the hat

Suited the decadence of those silences,
In which he sat. All chariots were drowned. The swans

Moved on the buried water where they lay.
Lenin took bread from his pocket, scattered it—

The swans fled outward to remoter reaches,
As if they knew of distant beaches; and were

Dissolved. The distances of space and time
Were one and swans far off were swans to come.

The eye of Lenin kept the far-off shapes.
His mind raised up, down-drowned, the chariots.

And reaches, beaches, tomorrow's regions became
One thinking of apocalyptic legions.

V

If seeming is description without place,
The spirit's universe, then a summer's day,

Even the seeming of a summer's day,
Is description without place. It is a sense

To which we refer experience, a knowledge
Incognito, the column in the desert,

On which the dove alights. Description is
Composed of a sight indifferent to the eye.

It is an expectation, a desire,
A palm that rises up beyond the sea,

A little different from reality:
The difference that we make in what we see

And our memorials of that difference,
Sprinklings of bright particulars from the sky.

The future is description without place,
The categorical predicate, the arc.

It is a wizened starlight growing young,
In which old stars are planets of morning, fresh

In the brilliantest descriptions of new day,
Before it comes, the just anticipation

Of the appropriate creatures, jubilant,
The forms that are attentive in thin air.

VI

Description is revelation. It is not
The thing described, nor false facsimile.

It is an artificial thing that exists,
In its own seeming, plainly visible,

Yet not too closely the double of our lives,
Intenser than any actual life could be,

A text we should be born that we might read,
More explicit than the experience of sun

And moon, the book of reconciliation,
Book of a concept only possible

In description, canon central in itself,
The thesis of the plentifullest John.

VII

Thus the theory of description matters most.
It is the theory of the word for those

For whom the word is the making of the world,
The buzzing world and lisping firmament.

It is a world of words to the end of it,
In which nothing solid is its solid self.

As, men make themselves their speech: the hard hidalgo
Lives in the mountainous character of his speech;

And in that mountainous mirror Spain acquires
The knowledge of Spain and of the hidalgo's hat—

A seeming of the Spaniard, a style of life,
The invention of a nation in a phrase,

In a description hollowed out of hollow-bright,
The artificer of subjects still half night.

It matters, because everything we say
Of the past is description without place, a cast

Of the imagination, made in sound;
And because what we say of the future must portend,

Be alive with its own seemings, seeming to be
Like rubies reddened by rubies reddening.

Two Tales of Liadoff

I

Do you remember how the rocket went on
And on, at night, exploding finally
In an ovation of resplendent forms—

Ovation on ovation of large blue men
In pantaloons of fire and of women hatched,
Like molten citizens of the vacuum?

Do you remember the children there like wicks,
That constantly sparkled their small gold? The town
Had crowded into the rocket and touched the fuse.

That night, Liadoff, a long time after his death,
At a piano in a cloud sat practicing,
On a black piano practiced epi-tones.

Do you remember what the townsmen said,
As they fell down, as they heard Liadoff's cloud
And its tragical, its haunted arpeggios?

And is it true that what they said, as they fell,
Was repeated by Liadoff in a narration
Of incredible colors ex, ex and ex and out?

II

The feeling of Liadoff was changed. It is
The instant of the change that was the poem,
When the cloud pressed suddenly the whole return

From thought, like a violent pulse in the cloud itself,
As if Liadoff no longer remained a ghost
And, being straw, turned green, lived backward, shared

The fantastic fortune of fantastic blood,
Until his body smothered him, until
His being felt the need of soaring, the need

Of air . . . But then that cloud, that piano placed
Just where it was, oh beau caboose . . . It was part
Of the instant to perceive, after the shock,

That the rocket was only an inferior cloud.
There was no difference between the town
And him. Both wanted the same thing. Both sought

His epi-tones, the colors of the ear,
The sounds that soon become a voluble speech—
Voluble but archaic and hard to hear.

Analysis of a Theme

Theme

How happy I was the day I told the young Blandina of
three-legged giraffes . . .

Analysis

In the conscious world, the great clouds
Potter in the summer sky.
It is a province—

Of ugly, subconscious time, in which
There is no beautiful eye
And no true tree,

There being no subconscious place,
Only Indyterranean
Resemblances

Of place: time's haggard mongrels.
Yet in time's middle deep,
In its abstract motion,

Its immaterial monsters move,
Without physical pedantry
Or any name.

Invisible, they move and are,
Not speaking worms, nor birds
Of mutable plume,

Pure coruscations, that lie beyond
The imagination, intact
And unattained,

Even in Paris, in the Gardens
Of Acclimatization,
On a holiday.

The knowledge of bright-ethered things
Bears us toward time, on its
Perfective wings.

We enjoy the ithy oonts and long-haired
Plomets, as the Herr Gott
Enjoys his comets.

Late Hymn from the Myrrh-Mountain

Unsnack your snood, madanna, for the stars
Are shining on all brows of Neversink.

Already the green bird of summer has flown
Away. The night-flies acknowledge these planets,

Predestined to this night, this noise and the place
Of summer. Tomorrow will look like today,

Will appear like it. But it will be an appearance,
A shape left behind, with like wings spreading out,

Brightly empowered with like colors, swarmingly,
But not quite molten, not quite the fluid thing,

A little changed by tips of artifice, changed
By the glints of sound from the grass. These are not

The early constellations, from which came the first
Illustrious intimations—uncertain love,

The knowledge of being, sense without sense of time.
Take the diamonds from your hair and lay them down.

The deer-grass is thin. The timothy is brown.
The shadow of an external world comes near.

Man Carrying Thing

The poem must resist the intelligence
Almost successfully. Illustration:

A brune figure in winter evening resists
Identity. The thing he carries resists

The most necessitous sense. Accept them, then,
As secondary (parts not quite perceived

Of the obvious whole, uncertain particles
Of the certain solid, the primary free from doubt,

Things floating like the first hundred flakes of snow
Out of a storm we must endure all night,

Out of a storm of secondary things),
A horror of thoughts that suddenly are real.

We must endure our thoughts all night, until
The bright obvious stands motionless in cold.

Pieces

Tinsel in February, tinsel in August.
There are things in a man besides his reason.
Come home, wind, he kept crying and crying.

Snow glistens in its instant in the air,
Instant of millefiori bluely magnified—
Come home, wind, he said as he climbed the stair—

Crystal on crystal until crystal clouds
Become an over-crystal out of ice,
Exhaling these creations of itself.

There is a sense in sounds beyond their meaning.
The tinsel of August falling was like a flame
That breathed on ground, more blue than red, more red

Than green, fidgets of all-related fire.
The wind is like a dog that runs away.
But it is like a horse. It is like motion

That lives in space. It is a person at night,
A member of the family, a tie,
An ethereal cousin, another milleman.

A Completely New Set of Objects

From a Schuylkill in mid-earth there came emerging
Flotillas, willed and wanted, bearing in them

Shadows of friends, of those he knew, each bringing
From the water in which he believed and out of desire

Things made by mid-terrestrial, mid-human
Makers without knowing, or intending, uses.

These figures verdant with time's buried verdure
Came paddling their canoes, a thousand thousand,

Carrying such shapes, of such alleviation,
That the beholder knew their subtle purpose,

Knew well the shapes were the exactest shaping
Of a vast people old in meditation . . .

Under Tinicum or small Cohansey,
The fathers of the makers may lie and weather.

Adult Epigram

The romance of the precise is not the elision
Of the tired romance of imprecision.
It is the ever-never-changing same,
An appearance of Again, the diva-dame.

Two Versions of the Same Poem

That Which Cannot Be Fixed

I

Once more he turned to that which could not be fixed,
By the sea, insolid rock, stentor, and said:

Lascar, is there a body, turbulent
With time, in wavering water lies, swollen

With thought, through which it cannot see? Does it
Lie lengthwise like the cloud of sleep, not quite

Reposed? And does it have a puissant heart
To toll its pulses, vigors of its self?

Lascar, and water-carcass never-named,
These vigors make, thrice-triple-syllabled,

The difficult images of possible shapes,
That cannot now be fixed. Only there is

A beating and a beating in the centre of
The sea, a strength that tumbles everywhere,

Like more and more becoming less and less,
Like space dividing its blue and by division

Being changed from space to the sailor's metier,
Or say from that which was conceived to that

Which was realized, like reason's constant ruin.
Sleep deep, good eel, in your perverse marine.

II

The human ocean beats against this rock
Of earth, rises against it, tide by tide,

Continually. And old John Zeller stands
On his hill, watching the rising and falling, and says:

Of what are these the creatures, what element
Or—yes: what elements, unreconciled

Because there is no golden solvent here?
If they were creatures of the sea alone,

But singular, they would, like water, scale
The uptopping top and tip of things, borne up

By the cadaver of these caverns, half-asleep.
But if they are of sea, earth, sky—water

And fire and air and things not discomposed
From ignorance, not an undivided whole,

It is an ocean of watery images
And shapes of fire, and wind that bears them down.

Perhaps these forms are seeking to escape
Cadaverous undulations. Rest, old mould . . .

Men Made Out of Words

What should we be without the sexual myth,
The human revery or poem of death?

Castratos of moon-mash—Life consists
Of propositions about life. The human

Revery is a solitude in which
We compose these propositions, torn by dreams,

By the terrible incantations of defeats
And by the fear that defeats and dreams are one.

The whole race is a poet that writes down
The eccentric propositions of its fate.

Thinking of a Relation
Between the Images of Metaphors

The wood-doves are singing along the Perkiomen.
The bass lie deep, still afraid of the Indians.

In the one ear of the fisherman, who is all
One ear, the wood-doves are singing a single song.

The bass keep looking ahead, upstream, in one
Direction, shrinking from the spit and splash

Of waterish spears. The fisherman is all
One eye, in which the dove resembles the dove.

There is one dove, one bass, one fisherman.
Yet coo becomes rou-coo, rou-coo. How close

To the unstated theme each variation comes . . .
In that one ear it might strike perfectly:

State the disclosure. In that one eye the dove
Might spring to sight and yet remain a dove.

The fisherman might be the single man
In whose breast, the dove, alighting, would grow still.

Chaos in Motion and Not in Motion

Oh, that this lashing wind was something more
Than the spirit of Ludwig Richter . . .

The rain is pouring down. It is July.
There is lightning and the thickest thunder.

It is a spectacle. Scene 10 becomes 11,
In Series X, Act IV, et cetera.

People fall out of windows, trees tumble down,
Summer is changed to winter, the young grow old,

The air is full of children, statues, roofs
And snow. The theatre is spinning round,

Colliding with deaf-mute churches and optical trains.
The most massive sopranos are singing songs of scales.

And Ludwig Richter, turbulent Schlemihl,
Has lost the whole in which he was contained,

Knows desire without an object of desire,
All mind and violence and nothing felt.

He knows he has nothing more to think about,
Like the wind that lashes everything at once.

The House Was Quiet and the World Was Calm

The house was quiet and the world was calm.
The reader became the book; and summer night

Was like the conscious being of the book.
The house was quiet and the world was calm.

The words were spoken as if there was no book,
Except that the reader leaned above the page,

Wanted to lean, wanted much most to be
The scholar to whom his book is true, to whom

The summer night is like a perfection of thought.
The house was quiet because it had to be.

The quiet was part of the meaning, part of the mind:
The access of perfection to the page.

And the world was calm. The truth in a calm world,
In which there is no other meaning, itself

Is calm, itself is summer and night, itself
Is the reader leaning late and reading there.

Continual Conversation with a Silent Man

The old brown hen and the old blue sky,
Between the two we live and die—
The broken cartwheel on the hill.

As if, in the presence of the sea,
We dried our nets and mended sail
And talked of never-ending things,

Of the never-ending storm of will,
One will and many wills, and the wind,
Of many meanings in the leaves,

Brought down to one below the eaves,
Link, of that tempest, to the farm,
The chain of the turquoise hen and sky

And the wheel that broke as the cart went by.
It is not a voice that is under the eaves.
It is not speech, the sound we hear

In this conversation, but the sound
Of things and their motion: the other man,
A turquoise monster moving round.

A Woman Sings a Song for a Soldier Come Home

The wound kills that does not bleed.
It has no nurse nor kin to know
Nor kin to care.

And the man dies that does not fall.
He walks and dies. Nothing survives
Except what was,

Under the white clouds piled and piled
Like gathered-up forgetfulness,
In sleeping air.

The clouds are over the village, the town,
To which the walker speaks
And tells of his wound,

Without a word to the people, unless
One person should come by chance,
This man or that,

So much a part of the place, so little
A person he knows, with whom he might
Talk of the weather—

And let it go, with nothing lost,
Just out of the village, at its edge,
In the quiet there.

The Pediment of Appearance

Young men go walking in the woods,
Hunting for the great ornament,
The pediment of appearance.

They hunt for a form which by its form alone,
Without diamond—blazons or flashing or
Chains of circumstance,

By its form alone, by being right,
By being high, is the stone
For which they are looking:

The savage transparence. They go crying
The world is myself, life is myself,
Breathing as if they breathed themselves,

Full of their ugly lord,
Speaking the phrases that follow the sight
Of this essential ornament

In the woods, in this full-blown May,
The month of understanding. The pediment
Lifts up its heavy scowl before them.

Burghers of Petty Death

These two by the stone wall
Are a slight part of death.
The grass is still green.

But there is a total death,
A devastation, a death of great height
And depth, covering all surfaces,
Filling the mind.

These are the small townsmen of death,
A man and a woman, like two leaves
That keep clinging to a tree,
Before winter freezes and grows black—

Of great height and depth
Without any feeling, an imperium of quiet,
In which a wasted figure, with an instrument,
Propounds blank final music.

Human Arrangement

Place-bound and time-bound in evening rain
And bound by a sound which does not change,

Except that it begins and ends,
Begins again and ends again—

Rain without change within or from
Without. In this place and in this time

And in this sound, which do not change,
In which the rain is all one thing,

In the sky, an imagined, wooden chair
Is the clear-point of an edifice,

Forced up from nothing, evening's chair,
Blue-strutted curule, true—unreal,

The center of transformations that
Transform for transformation's self,

In a glitter that is a life, a gold
That is a being, a will, a fate.

The Good Man Has No Shape

Through centuries he lived in poverty.
God only was his only elegance.

Then generation by generation he grew
Stronger and freer, a little better off.

He lived each life because, if it was bad,
He said a good life would be possible.

At last the good life came, good sleep, bright fruit,
And Lazarus betrayed him to the rest,

Who killed him, sticking feathers in his flesh
To mock him. They placed with him in his grave

Sour wine to warm him, an empty book to read;
And over it they set a jagged sign,

Epitaphium to his death, which read,
The Good Man Has No Shape, as if they knew.

The Red Fern

The large-leaved day grows rapidly,
And opens in this familiar spot
Its unfamiliar, difficult fern,
Pushing and pushing red after red.

There are doubles of this fern in clouds,
Less firm than the paternal flame,
Yet drenched with its identity,
Reflections and off-shoots, mimic-motes

And mist-mites, dangling seconds, grown
Beyond relation to the parent trunk:

The dazzling, bulging, brightest core,
The furiously burning father-fire . . .

Infant, it is enough in life
To speak of what you see. But wait
Until sight wakens the sleepy eye
And pierces the physical fix of things.

From the Packet of Anacharsis

In his packet Anacharsis found the lines:
"The farm was fat and the land in which it lay
Seemed in the morning like a holiday."

He had written them near Athens. The farm was white.
The buildings were of marble and stood in marble light.
It was his clarity that made the vista bright.

A subject for Puvis. He would compose
The scene in his gray-rose with violet rocks.
And Bloom would see what Puvis did, protest

And speak of the floridest reality . . .
In the punctual centre of all circles white
Stands truly. The circles nearest to it share

Its color, but less as they recede, impinged
By difference and then by definition
As a tone defines itself and separates

And the circles quicken and crystal colors come
And flare and Bloom with his vast accumulation
Stands and regards and repeats the primitive lines.

The Dove in the Belly

The whole of appearance is a toy. For this,
The dove in the belly builds his nest and coos,

Selah, tempestuous bird. How is it that
The rivers shine and hold their mirrors up,

Like excellence collecting excellence?
How is it that the wooden trees stand up

And live and heap their panniers of green
And hold them round the sultry day? Why should

These mountains being high be, also, bright,
Fetched up with snow that never falls to earth?

And this great esplanade of corn, miles wide,
Is something wished for made effectual

And something more. And the people in costumes,
Though poor, though raggeder than ruin, have that

Within them right for terraces—oh, brave salut!
Deep dove, placate you in your hiddenness.

Mountains Covered with Cats

The sea full of fishes in shoals, the woods that let
One seed alone grow wild, the railway-stops
In Russia at which the same statue of Stalin greets
The same railway passenger, the ancient tree
In the centre of its cones, the resplendent flights
Of red facsimiles through related trees,
White houses in villages, black communicants—
The catalogue is too commodious.

Regard the invalid personality
Instead, outcast, without the will to power

And impotent, like the imagination seeking
To propagate the imagination or like
War's miracle begetting that of peace.

Freud's eye was the microscope of potency.
By fortune, his gray ghost may meditate
The spirits of all the impotent dead, seen clear,
And quickly understand, without their flesh,
How truly they had not been what they were.

The Prejudice Against the Past

Day is the children's friend.
It is Marianna's Swedish cart.
It is that and a very big hat.

Confined by what they see,
Aquiline pedants treat the cart,
As one of the relics of the heart.

They treat the philosopher's hat,
Left thoughtlessly behind,
As one of the relics of the mind . . .

Of day, then, children make
What aquiline pedants take
For souvenirs of time, lost time,

Adieux, shapes, images—
No, not of day, but of themselves,
Not of perpetual time.

And, therefore, aquiline pedants find
The philosopher's hat to be part of the mind,
The Swedish cart to be part of the heart.

Extraordinary References

The mother ties the hair-ribbons of the child
And she has peace. *My Jacomyntje!*
Your great-grandfather was an Indian fighter.

The cool sun of the Tulpehocken refers
To its barbed, barbarous rising and has peace.
These earlier dissipations of the blood

And brain, as the extraordinary references
Of ordinary people, places, things,
Compose us in a kind of eulogy.

My Jacomyntje! This first spring after the war,
In which your father died, still breathes for him
And breathes again for us a fragile breath.

In the inherited garden, a second-hand
Vertumnus creates an equilibrium.
The child's three ribbons are in her plaited hair.

Attempt to Discover Life

At San Miguel de los Baños,
The waitress heaped up black Hermosas
In the magnificence of a volcano.
Round them she spilled the roses
Of the place, blue and green, both streaked,
And white roses shaded emerald on petals
Out of the deadliest heat.

There entered a cadaverous person,
Who bowed and, bowing, brought, in her mantilla,
A woman brilliant and pallid-skinned,
Of fiery eyes and long thin arms.

She stood with him at the table,
Smiling and wetting her lips
In the heavy air.

The green roses drifted up from the table
In smoke. The blue petals became
The yellowing fomentations of effulgence,
Among fomentations of black bloom and of white bloom.
The cadaverous persons were dispelled.
On the table near which they stood
Two coins were lying—dos centavos.

A Lot of People Bathing in a Stream

It was like passing a boundary to dive
Into the sun-filled water, brightly leafed
And limbed and lighted out from bank to bank.

That's how the stars shine during the day. There, then,
The yellow that was yesterday, refreshed,
Became to-day, among our children and

Ourselves, in the clearest green—well, call it green.
We bathed in yellow green and yellow blue
And in these comic colors dangled down,

Like their particular characters, addicts
To blotches, angular anonymids
Gulping for shape among the reeds. No doubt,

We were the appropriate conceptions, less
Than creatures, of the sky between the banks,
The water flowing in the flow of space.

It was passing a boundary, floating without a head
And naked, or almost so, into the grotesque
Of being naked, or almost so, in a world

Of nakedness, in the company of the sun,
Good-fortuner of the grotesque, patroon,
A funny foreigner of meek address.

How good it was at home again at night
To prepare for bed, in the frame of the house, and move
Round the rooms, which do not ever seem to change . . .

Credences of Summer

I

Now in midsummer come and all fools slaughtered
And spring's infuriations over and a long way
To the first autumnal inhalations, young broods
Are in the grass, the roses are heavy with a weight
Of fragrance and the mind lays by its trouble.

Now the mind lays by its trouble and considers.
The fidgets of remembrance come to this.
This is the last day of a certain year
Beyond which there is nothing left of time.
It comes to this and the imagination's life.

There is nothing more inscribed nor thought nor felt
And this must comfort the heart's core against
Its false disasters—these fathers standing round,
These mothers touching, speaking, being near,
These lovers waiting in the soft dry grass.

II

Postpone the anatomy of summer, as
The physical pine, the metaphysical pine.
Let's see the very thing and nothing else.
Let's see it with the hottest fire of sight.
Burn everything not part of it to ash.

Trace the gold sun about the whitened sky
Without evasion by a single metaphor.

Look at it in its essential barrenness
And say this, this is the centre that I seek.
Fix it in an eternal foliage

And fill the foliage with arrested peace,
Joy of such permanence, right ignorance
Of change still possible. Exile desire
For what is not. This is the barrenness
Of the fertile thing that can attain no more.

III

It is the natural tower of all the world,
The point of survey, green's green apogee,
But a tower more precious than the view beyond,
A point of survey squatting like a throne,
Axis of everything, green's apogee

And happiest folk-land, mostly marriage-hymns.
It is the mountain on which the tower stands,
It is the final mountain. Here the sun,
Sleepless, inhales his proper air, and rests.
This is the refuge that the end creates.

It is the old man standing on the tower,
Who reads no book. His ruddy ancientness
Absorbs the ruddy summer and is appeased,
By an understanding that fulfils his age,
By a feeling capable of nothing more.

IV

One of the limits of reality
Presents itself in Oley when the hay,
Baked through long days, is piled in mows. It is
A land too ripe for enigmas, too serene.
There the distant fails the clairvoyant eye

And the secondary senses of the ear
Swarm, not with secondary sounds, but choirs,
Not evocations but last choirs, last sounds

With nothing else compounded, carried full,
Pure rhetoric of a language without words.

Things stop in that direction and since they stop
The direction stops and we accept what is
As good. The utmost must be good and is
And is our fortune and honey hived in the trees
And mingling of colors at a festival.

V

One day enriches a year. One woman makes
The rest look down. One man becomes a race,
Lofty like him, like him perpetual.
Or do the other days enrich the one?
And is the queen humble as she seems to be,

The charitable majesty of her whole kin?
The bristling soldier, weather-foxed, who looms
In the sunshine is a filial form and one
Of the land's children, easily born, its flesh,
Not fustian. The more than casual blue

Contains the year and other years and hymns
And people, without souvenir. The day
Enriches the year, not as embellishment.
Stripped of remembrance, it displays its strength—
The youth, the vital son, the heroic power.

VI

The rock cannot be broken. It is the truth.
It rises from land and sea and covers them.
It is a mountain half way green and then,
The other immeasurable half, such rock
As placid air becomes. But it is not

A hermit's truth nor symbol in hermitage.
It is the visible rock, the audible,
The brilliant mercy of a sure repose,
On this present ground, the vividest repose,
Things certain sustaining us in certainty.

It is the rock of summer, the extreme,
A mountain luminous half-way in bloom
And then half way in the extremest light
Of sapphires flashing from the central sky,
As if twelve princes sat before a king.

VII

Far in the woods they sang their unreal songs,
Secure. It was difficult to sing in face
Of the object. The singers had to avert themselves
Or else avert the object. Deep in the woods
They sang of summer in the common fields.

They sang desiring an object that was near,
In face of which desire no longer moved,
Nor made of itself that which it could not find . . .
Three times the concentred self takes hold, three times
The thrice concentred self, having possessed

The object, grips it in savage scrutiny,
Once to make captive, once to subjugate
Or yield to subjugation, once to proclaim
The meaning of the capture, this hard prize,
Fully made, fully apparent, fully found.

VIII

The trumpet of morning blows in the clouds and through
The sky. It is the visible announced,
It is the more than visible, the more
Than sharp, illustrious scene. The trumpet cries
This is the successor of the invisible.

This is its substitute in stratagems
Of the spirit. This, in sight and memory,
Must take its place, as what is possible
Replaces what is not. The resounding cry
Is like ten thousand tumblers tumbling down

To share the day. The trumpet supposes that
A mind exists, aware of division, aware

Of its cry as clarion, its diction's way
As that of a personage in a multitude:
Man's mind grown venerable in the unreal.

IX

Fly low, cock bright, and stop on a bean pole. Let
Your brown breast redden, while you wait for warmth.
With one eye watch the willow, motionless.
The gardener's cat is dead, the gardener gone
And last year's garden grows salacious weeds.

A complex of emotions falls apart,
In an abandoned spot. Soft, civil bird,
The decay that you regard: of the arranged
And of the spirit of the arranged, *douceurs*,
Tristesses, the fund of life and death, suave bush

And polished beast, this complex falls apart.
And on your bean pole, it may be, you detect
Another complex of other emotions, not
So soft, so civil, and you make a sound,
Which is not part of the listener's own sense.

X

The personae of summer play the characters
Of an inhuman author, who meditates
With the gold bugs, in blue meadows, late at night.
He does not hear his characters talk. He sees
Them mottled, in the moodiest costumes,

Of blue and yellow, sky and sun, belted
And knotted, sashed and seamed, half pales of red,
Half pales of green, appropriate habit for
The huge decorum, the manner of the time,
Part of the mottled mood of summer's whole,

In which the characters speak because they want
To speak, the fat, the roseate characters,
Free, for a moment, from malice and sudden cry,
Completed in a completed scene, speaking
Their parts as in a youthful happiness.

A Pastoral Nun

Finally, in the last year of her age,
Having attained a present blessedness,
She said poetry and apotheosis are one.

This is the illustration that she used:
If I live according to this law I live
In an immense activity, in which

Everything becomes morning, summer, the hero,
The enraptured woman, the sequestered night,
The man that suffered, lying there at ease,

Without his envious pain in body, in mind,
The favorable transformations of the wind
As of a general being or human universe.

There was another illustration, in which
The two things compared their tight resemblances:
Each matters only in that which it conceives.

The Pastor Caballero

The importance of its hat to a form becomes
More definite. The sweeping brim of the hat
Makes of the form Most Merciful Capitan,

If the observer says so: grandiloquent
Locution of a hand in a rhapsody.
Its line moves quickly with the genius

Of its improvisation until, at length,
It enfolds the head in a vital ambiance,
A vital, linear ambiance. The flare

In the sweeping brim becomes the origin
Of a human evocation, so disclosed
That, nameless, it creates an affectionate name,

Derived from adjectives of deepest mine.
The actual form bears outwardly this grace,
An image of the mind, an inward mate,

Tall and unfretted, a figure meant to bear
Its poisoned laurels in this poisoned wood,
High in the height that is our total height.

The formidable helmet is nothing now.
These two go well together, the sinuous brim
And the green flauntings of the hours of peace.

Notes Toward a Supreme Fiction

To Henry Church

And for what, except for you, do I feel love?
Do I press the extremest book of the wisest man
Close to me, hidden in me day and night?
In the uncertain light of single, certain truth,
Equal in living changingness to the light
In which I meet you, in which we sit at rest,
For a moment in the central of our being,
The vivid transparence that you bring is peace.

It Must Be Abstract

I

Begin, ephebe, by perceiving the idea
Of this invention, this invented world,
The inconceivable idea of the sun.

You must become an ignorant man again
And see the sun again with an ignorant eye
And see it clearly in the idea of it.

Never suppose an inventing mind as source
Of this idea nor for that mind compose
A voluminous master folded in his fire.

How clean the sun when seen in its idea,
Washed in the remotest cleanliness of a heaven
That has expelled us and our images . . .

The death of one god is the death of all.
Let purple Phoebus lie in umber harvest,
Let Phoebus slumber and die in autumn umber,

Phoebus is dead, ephebe. But Phoebus was
A name for something that never could be named.
There was a project for the sun and is.

There is a project for the sun. The sun
Must bear no name, gold flourisher, but be
In the difficulty of what it is to be.

II

It is the celestial ennui of apartments
That sends us back to the first idea, the quick
Of this invention; and yet so poisonous

Are the ravishments of truth, so fatal to
The truth itself, the first idea becomes
The hermit in a poet's metaphors,

Who comes and goes and comes and goes all day.
May there be an ennui of the first idea?
What else, prodigious scholar, should there be?

The monastic man is an artist. The philosopher
Appoints man's place in music, say, today.
But the priest desires. The philosopher desires.

And not to have is the beginning of desire.
To have what is not is its ancient cycle.
It is desire at the end of winter, when

It observes the effortless weather turning blue
And sees the myosotis on its bush.
Being virile, it hears the calendar hymn.

It knows that what it has is what is not
And throws it away like a thing of another time,
As morning throws off stale moonlight and shabby sleep.

III

The poem refreshes life so that we share,
For a moment, the first idea . . . It satisfies
Belief in an immaculate beginning

And sends us, winged by an unconscious will,
To an immaculate end. We move between these points:
From that ever-early candor to its late plural

And the candor of them is the strong exhilaration
Of what we feel from what we think, of thought
Beating in the heart, as if blood newly came,

An elixir, an excitation, a pure power.
The poem, through candor, brings back a power again
That gives a candid kind to everything.

We say: At night an Arabian in my room,
With his damned hoobla-hoobla-hoobla-how,
Inscribes a primitive astronomy

Across the unscrawled fores the future casts
And throws his stars around the floor. By day
The wood-dove used to chant his hoobla-hoo

And still the grossest iridescence of ocean
Howls hoo and rises and howls hoo and falls.
Life's nonsense pierces us with strange relation.

IV

The first idea was not our own. Adam
In Eden was the father of Descartes
And Eve made air the mirror of herself,

Of her sons and of her daughters. They found themselves
In heaven as in a glass; a second earth;
And in the earth itself they found a green—

The inhabitants of a very varnished green.
But the first idea was not to shape the clouds
In imitation. The clouds preceded us.

There was a muddy centre before we breathed.
There was a myth before the myth began,
Venerable and articulate and complete.

From this the poem springs: that we live in a place
That is not our own and, much more, not ourselves
And hard it is in spite of blazoned days.

We are the mimics. Clouds are pedagogues.
The air is not a mirror but bare board,
Coulisse bright-dark, tragic chiaroscuro

And comic color of the rose, in which
Abysmal instruments make sounds like pips
Of the sweeping meanings that we add to them.

V

The lion roars at the enraging desert,
Reddens the sand with his red-colored noise,
Defies red emptiness to evolve his match,

Master by foot and jaws and by the mane,
Most supple challenger. The elephant
Breaches the darkness of Ceylon with blares,

The glitter-goes on surfaces of tanks,
Shattering velvetest far-away. The bear,
The ponderous cinnamon, snarls in his mountain

At summer thunder and sleeps through winter snow.
But you, ephebe, look from your attic window,
Your mansard with a rented piano. You lie

In silence upon your bed. You clutch the corner
Of the pillow in your hand. You writhe and press
A bitter utterance from your writhing, dumb,

Yet voluble of dumb violence. You look
Across the roofs as sigil and as ward
And in your centre mark them and are cowed . . .

These are the heroic children whom time breeds
Against the first idea—to lash the lion,
Caparison elephants, teach bears to juggle.

VI

Not to be realized because not to
Be seen, not to be loved nor hated because
Not to be realized. Weather by Franz Hals,

Brushed up by brushy winds in brushy clouds,
Wetted by blue, colder for white. Not to
Be spoken to, without a roof, without

First fruits, without the virginal of birds,
The dark-blown ceinture loosened, not relinquished.
Gay is, gay was, the gay forsythia

And yellow, yellow thins the Northern blue.
Without a name and nothing to be desired,
If only imagined but imagined well.

My house has changed a little in the sun.
The fragrance of the magnolias comes close,
False flick, false form, but falseness close to kin.

It must be visible or invisible,
Invisible or visible or both:
A seeing and unseeing in the eye.

The weather and the giant of the weather,
Say the weather, the mere weather, the mere air:
An abstraction blooded, as a man by thought.

VII

It feels good as it is without the giant,
A thinker of the first idea. Perhaps
The truth depends on a walk around a lake,

A composing as the body tires, a stop
To see hepatica, a stop to watch
A definition growing certain and

A wait within that certainty, a rest
In the swags of pine-trees bordering the lake.
Perhaps there are times of inherent excellence,

As when the cock crows on the left and all
Is well, incalculable balances,
At which a kind of Swiss perfection comes

And a familiar music of the machine
Sets up its Schwärmerei, not balances
That we achieve but balances that happen,

As a man and woman meet and love forthwith.
Perhaps there are moments of awakening,
Extreme, fortuitous, personal, in which

We more than awaken, sit on the edge of sleep,
As on an elevation, and behold
The academies like structures in a mist.

VIII

Can we compose a castle-fortress-home,
Even with the help of Viollet-le-Duc,
And set the MacCullough there as major man?

The first idea is an imagined thing.
The pensive giant prone in violet space
May be the MacCullough, an expedient,

Logos and logic, crystal hypothesis,
Incipit and a form to speak the word
And every latent double in the word,

Beau linguist. But the MacCullough is MacCullough.
It does not follow that major man is man.
If MacCullough himself lay lounging by the sea,

Drowned in its washes, reading in the sound,
About the thinker of the first idea,
He might take habit, whether from wave or phrase,

Or power of the wave, or deepened speech,
Or a leaner being, moving in on him,
Of greater aptitude and apprehension,

As if the waves at last were never broken,
As if the language suddenly, with ease,
Said things it had laboriously spoken.

IX

The romantic intoning, the declaimed clairvoyance
Are parts of apotheosis, appropriate
And of its nature, the idiom thereof.

They differ from reason's click-clack, its applied
Enflashings. But apotheosis is not
The origin of the major man. He comes,

Compact in invincible foils, from reason,
Lighted at midnight by the studious eye,
Swaddled in revery, the object of

The hum of thoughts evaded in the mind,
Hidden from other thoughts, he that reposes
On a breast forever precious for that touch,

For whom the good of April falls tenderly,
Falls down, the cock-birds calling at the time.
My dame, sing for this person accurate songs.

He is and may be but oh! he is, he is,
This foundling of the infected past, so bright,
So moving in the manner of his hand.

Yet look not at his colored eyes. Give him
No names. Dismiss him from your images.
The hot of him is purest in the heart.

X

The major abstraction is the idea of man
And major man is its exponent, abler
In the abstract than in his singular,

More fecund as principle than particle,
Happy fecundity, flor-abundant force,
In being more than an exception, part,

Though an heroic part, of the commonal.
The major abstraction is the commonal,
The inanimate, difficult visage. Who is it?

What rabbi, grown furious with human wish,
What chieftain, walking by himself, crying
Most miserable, most victorious,

Does not see these separate figures one by one,
And yet see only one, in his old coat,
His slouching pantaloons, beyond the town,

Looking for what was, where it used to be?
Cloudless the morning. It is he. The man
In that old coat, those sagging pantaloons,

It is of him, ephebe, to make, to confect
The final elegance, not to console
Nor sanctify, but plainly to propound.

It Must Change

I

The old seraph, parcel-gilded, among violets
Inhaled the appointed odor, while the doves
Rose up like phantoms from chronologies.

The Italian girls wore jonquils in their hair
And these the seraph saw, had seen long since,
In the bandeaux of the mothers, would see again.

The bees came booming as if they had never gone,
As if hyacinths had never gone. We say
This changes and that changes. Thus the constant

Violets, doves, girls, bees and hyacinths
Are inconstant objects of inconstant cause
In a universe of inconstancy. This means

Night-blue is an inconstant thing. The seraph
Is satyr in Saturn, according to his thoughts.
It means the distaste we feel for this withered scene

Is that it has not changed enough. It remains,
It is a repetition. The bees come booming
As if— The pigeons clatter in the air.

An erotic perfume, half of the body, half
Of an obvious acid is sure what it intends
And the booming is blunt, not broken in subtleties.

II

The President ordains the bee to be
Immortal. The President ordains. But does
The body lift its heavy wing, take up,

Again, an inexhaustible being, rise
Over the loftiest antagonist
To drone the green phrases of its juvenal?

Why should the bee recapture a lost blague,
Find a deep echo in a horn and buzz
The bottomless trophy, new hornsman after old?

The President has apples on the table
And barefoot servants round him, who adjust
The curtains to a metaphysical t

And the banners of the nation flutter, burst
On the flag-poles in a red-blue dazzle, whack
At the halyards. Why, then, when in golden fury

Spring vanishes the scraps of winter, why
Should there be a question of returning or
Of death in memory's dream? Is spring a sleep?

This warmth is for lovers at last accomplishing
Their love, this beginning, not resuming, this
Booming and booming of the new-come bee.

III

The great statue of the General Du Puy
Rested immobile, though neighboring catafalques
Bore off the residents of its noble Place.

The right, uplifted foreleg of the horse
Suggested that, at the final funeral,
The music halted and the horse stood still.

On Sundays, lawyers in their promenades
Approached this strongly-heightened effigy
To study the past, and doctors, having bathed

Themselves with care, sought out the nerveless frame
Of a suspension, a permanence, so rigid
That it made the General a bit absurd,

Changed his true flesh to an inhuman bronze.
There never had been, never could be, such
A man. The lawyers disbelieved, the doctors

Said that as keen, illustrious ornament,
As a setting for geraniums, the General,
The very Place Du Puy, in fact, belonged

Among our more vestigial states of mind.
Nothing had happened because nothing had changed.
Yet the General was rubbish in the end.

IV

Two things of opposite natures seem to depend
On one another, as a man depends
On a woman, day on night, the imagined

On the real. This is the origin of change.
Winter and spring, cold copulars, embrace
And forth the particulars of rapture come.

Music falls on the silence like a sense,
A passion that we feel, not understand.
Morning and afternoon are clasped together

And North and South are an intrinsic couple
And sun and rain a plural, like two lovers
That walk away as one in the greenest body.

In solitude the trumpets of solitude
Are not of another solitude resounding;
A little string speaks for a crowd of voices.

The partaker partakes of that which changes him.
The child that touches takes character from the thing,
The body, it touches. The captain and his men

Are one and the sailor and the sea are one.
Follow after, O my companion, my fellow, my self,
Sister and solace, brother and delight.

V

On a blue island in a sky-wide water
The wild orange trees continued to bloom and to bear,
Long after the planter's death. A few limes remained,

Where his house had fallen, three scraggy trees weighted
With garbled green. These were the planter's turquoise
And his orange blotches, these were his zero green,

A green baked greener in the greenest sun.
These were his beaches, his sea-myrtles in
White sand, his patter of the long sea-slushes.

There was an island beyond him on which rested,
An island to the South, on which rested like
A mountain, a pine-apple pungent as Cuban summer.

And là-bas, là-bas, the cool bananas grew,
Hung heavily on the great banana tree,
Which pierces clouds and bends on half the world.

He thought often of the land from which he came,
How that whole country was a melon, pink
If seen rightly and yet a possible red.

An unaffected man in a negative light
Could not have borne his labor nor have died
Sighing that he should leave the banjo's twang.

VI

Bethou me, said sparrow, to the crackled blade,
And you, and you, bethou me as you blow,
When in my coppice you behold me be.

Ah, ké! the bloody wren, the felon jay,
Ké-ké, the jug-throated robin pouring out,
Bethou, bethou, bethou me in my glade.

There was such idiot minstrelsy in rain,
So many clappers going without bells,
That these bethous compose a heavenly gong.

One voice repeating, one tireless chorister,
The phrases of a single phrase, ké-ké,
A single text, granite monotony,

One sole face, like a photograph of fate,
Glass-blower's destiny, bloodless episcopus,
Eye without lid, mind without any dream—

These are of minstrels lacking minstrelsy,
Of an earth in which the first leaf is the tale
Of leaves, in which the sparrow is a bird

Of stone, that never changes. Bethou him, you
And you, bethou him and bethou. It is
A sound like any other. It will end.

VII

After a lustre of the moon, we say
We have not the need of any paradise,
We have not the need of any seducing hymn.

It is true. Tonight the lilacs magnify
The easy passion, the ever-ready love
Of the lover that lies within us and we breathe

An odor evoking nothing, absolute.
We encounter in the dead middle of the night
The purple odor, the abundant bloom.

The lover sighs as for accessible bliss,
Which he can take within him on his breath,
Possess in his heart, conceal and nothing known.

For easy passion and ever-ready love
Are of our earthy birth and here and now
And where we live and everywhere we live,

As in the top-cloud of a May night-evening,
As in the courage of the ignorant man,
Who chants by book, in the heat of the scholar, who writes

The book, hot for another accessible bliss:
The fluctuations of certainty, the change
Of degrees of perception in the scholar's dark.

VIII

On her trip around the world, Nanzia Nunzio
Confronted Ozymandias. She went
Alone and like a vestal long-prepared.

I am the spouse. She took her necklace off
And laid it in the sand. As I am, I am
The spouse. She opened her stone-studded belt.

I am the spouse, divested of bright gold,
The spouse beyond emerald or amethyst,
Beyond the burning body that I bear.

I am the woman stripped more nakedly
Than nakedness, standing before an inflexible
Order, saying I am the contemplated spouse.

Speak to me that, which spoken, will array me
In its own only precious ornament.
Set on me the spirit's diamond coronal.

Clothe me entire in the final filament,
So that I tremble with such love so known
And myself am precious for your perfecting.

Then Ozymandias said the spouse, the bride
Is never naked. A fictive covering
Weaves always glistening from the heart and mind.

IX

The poem goes from the poet's gibberish to
The gibberish of the vulgate and back again.
Does it move to and fro or is it of both

At once? Is it a luminous flittering
Or the concentration of a cloudy day?
Is there a poem that never reaches words

And one that chaffers the time away?
Is the poem both peculiar and general?
There's a meditation there, in which there seems

To be an evasion, a thing not apprehended or
Not apprehended well. Does the poet
Evade us, as in a senseless element?

Evade, this hot, dependent orator,
The spokesman at our bluntest barriers,
Exponent by a form of speech, the speaker

Of a speech only a little of the tongue?
It is the gibberish of the vulgate that he seeks.
He tries by a peculiar speech to speak

The peculiar potency of the general,
To compound the imagination's Latin with
The lingua franca et jocundissima.

                         X

A bench was his catalepsy, Theatre
Of Trope. He sat in the park. The water of
The lake was full of artificial things,

Like a page of music, like an upper air,
Like a momentary color, in which swans
Were seraphs, were saints, were changing essences.

The west wind was the music, the motion, the force
To which the swans curveted, a will to change,
A will to make iris frettings on the blank.

There was a will to change, a necessitous
And present way, a presentation, a kind
Of volatile world, too constant to be denied,

The eye of a vagabond in metaphor
That catches our own. The casual is not
Enough. The freshness of transformation is

The freshness of a world. It is our own,
It is ourselves, the freshness of ourselves,
And that necessity and that presentation

Are rubbings of a glass in which we peer.
Of these beginnings, gay and green, propose
The suitable amours. Time will write them down.

It Must Give Pleasure

I

To sing jubilas at exact, accustomed times,
To be crested and wear the mane of a multitude
And so, as part, to exult with its great throat,

To speak of joy and to sing of it, borne on
The shoulders of joyous men, to feel the heart
That is the common, the bravest fundament,

This is a facile exercise. Jerome
Begat the tubas and the fire-wind strings,
The golden fingers picking dark-blue air:

For companies of voices moving there,
To find of sound the bleakest ancestor,
To find of light a music issuing

Whereon it falls in more than sensual mode.
But the difficultest rigor is forthwith,
On the image of what we see, to catch from that

Irrational moment its unreasoning,
As when the sun comes rising, when the sea
Clears deeply, when the moon hangs on the wall

Of heaven-haven. These are not things transformed.
Yet we are shaken by them as if they were.
We reason about them with a later reason.

II

The blue woman, linked and lacquered, at her window
Did not desire that feathery argentines
Should be cold silver, neither that frothy clouds

Should foam, be foamy waves, should move like them,
Nor that the sexual blossoms should repose
Without their fierce addictions, nor that the heat

Of summer, growing fragrant in the night,
Should strengthen her abortive dreams and take
In sleep its natural form. It was enough

For her that she remembered: the argentines
Of spring come to their places in the grape leaves
To cool their ruddy pulses; the frothy clouds

Are nothing but frothy clouds; the frothy blooms
Waste without puberty; and afterward,
When the harmonious heat of August pines

Enters the room, it drowses and is the night.
It was enough for her that she remembered.
The blue woman looked and from her window named

The corals of the dogwood, cold and clear,
Cold, coldly delineating, being real,
Clear and, except for the eye, without intrusion.

III

A lasting visage in a lasting bush,
A face of stone in an unending red,
Red-emerald, red-slitted-blue, a face of slate,

An ancient forehead hung with heavy hair,
The channel slots of rain, the red-rose-red
And weathered and the ruby-water-worn,

The vines around the throat, the shapeless lips,
The frown like serpents basking on the brow,
The spent feeling leaving nothing of itself,

Red-in-red repetitions never going
Away, a little rusty, a little rouged,
A little roughened and ruder, a crown

The eye could not escape, a red renown
Blowing itself upon the tedious ear.
An effulgence faded, dull cornelian

Too venerably used. That might have been.
It might and might have been. But as it was,
A dead shepherd brought tremendous chords from hell

And bade the sheep carouse. Or so they said.
Children in love with them brought early flowers
And scattered them about, no two alike.

IV

We reason of these things with later reason
And we make of what we see, what we see clearly
And have seen, a place dependent on ourselves.

There was a mystic marriage in Catawba,
At noon it was on the mid-day of the year
Between a great captain and the maiden Bawda.

This was their ceremonial hymn: Anon
We loved but would no marriage make. Anon
The one refused the other one to take,

Foreswore the sipping of the marriage wine.
Each must the other take not for his high,
His puissant front nor for her subtle sound,

The shoo-shoo-shoo of secret cymbals round.
Each must the other take as sign, short sign
To stop the whirlwind, balk the elements.

The great captain loved the ever-hill Catawba
And therefore married Bawda, whom he found there,
And Bawda loved the captain as she loved the sun.

They married well because the marriage-place
Was what they loved. It was neither heaven nor hell.
They were love's characters come face to face.

V

We drank Meursault, ate lobster Bombay with mango
Chutney. Then the Canon Aspirin declaimed
Of his sister, in what a sensible ecstasy

She lived in her house. She had two daughters, one
Of four, and one of seven, whom she dressed
The way a painter of pauvred color paints.

But still she painted them, appropriate to
Their poverty, a gray-blue yellowed out
With ribbon, a rigid statement of them, white,

With Sunday pearls, her widow's gayety.
She hid them under simple names. She held
Them closelier to her by rejecting dreams.

The words they spoke were voices that she heard.
She looked at them and saw them as they were
And what she felt fought off the barest phrase.

The Canon Aspirin, having said these things,
Reflected, humming an outline of a fugue
Of praise, a conjugation done by choirs.

Yet when her children slept, his sister herself
Demanded of sleep, in the excitements of silence
Only the unmuddled self of sleep, for them.

VI

When at long midnight the Canon came to sleep
And normal things had yawned themselves away,
The nothingness was a nakedness, a point,

Beyond which fact could not progress as fact.
Thereon the learning of the man conceived
Once more night's pale illuminations, gold

Beneath, far underneath, the surface of
His eye and audible in the mountain of
His ear, the very material of his mind.

So that he was the ascending wings he saw
And moved on them in orbits' outer stars
Descending to the children's bed, on which

They lay. Forth then with huge pathetic force
Straight to the utmost crown of night he flew.
The nothingness was a nakedness, a point

Beyond which thought could not progress as thought.
He had to choose. But it was not a choice
Between excluding things. It was not a choice

Between, but of. He chose to include the things
That in each other are included, the whole,
The complicate, the amassing harmony.

VII

He imposes orders as he thinks of them,
As the fox and snake do. It is a brave affair.
Next he builds capitols and in their corridors,

Whiter than wax, sonorous, fame as it is,
He establishes statues of reasonable men,
Who surpassed the most literate owl, the most erudite

Of elephants. But to impose is not
To discover. To discover an order as of
A season, to discover summer and know it,

To discover winter and know it well, to find,
Not to impose, not to have reasoned at all,
Out of nothing to have come on major weather,

It is possible, possible, possible. It must
Be possible. It must be that in time
The real will from its crude compoundings come,

Seeming, at first, a beast disgorged, unlike,
Warmed by a desperate milk. To find the real,
To be stripped of every fiction except one,

The fiction of an absolute— Angel,
Be silent in your luminous cloud and hear
The luminous melody of proper sound.

VIII

What am I to believe? If the angel in his cloud,
Serenely gazing at the violent abyss,
Plucks on his strings to pluck abysmal glory,

Leaps downward through evening's revelations, and
On his spredden wings, needs nothing but deep space,
Forgets the gold centre, the golden destiny,

Grows warm in the motionless motion of his flight,
Am I that imagine this angel less-satisfied?
Are the wings his, the lapis-haunted air?

Is it he or is it I that experience this?
Is it I then that keep saying there is an hour
Filled with expressible bliss, in which I have

No need, am happy, forget need's golden hand,
Am satisfied without solacing majesty,
And if there is an hour there is a day,

There is a month, a year, there is a time
In which majesty is a mirror of the self:
I have not but I am and as I am, I am.

These external regions, what do we fill them with
Except reflections, the escapades of death,
Cinderella fulfilling herself beneath the roof?

IX

Whistle aloud, too weedy wren. I can
Do all that angels can. I enjoy like them,
Like men besides, like men in light secluded,

Enjoying angels. Whistle, forced bugler,
That bugles for the mate, nearby the nest,
Cock bugler, whistle and bugle and stop just short,

Red robin, stop in your preludes, practicing
Mere repetitions. These things at least comprise
An occupation, an exercise, a work,

A thing final in itself and, therefore, good:
One of the vast repetitions final in
Themselves and, therefore, good, the going round

And round and round, the merely going round,
Until merely going round is a final good,
The way wine comes at a table in a wood.

And we enjoy like men, the way a leaf
Above the table spins its constant spin,
So that we look at it with pleasure, look

At it spinning its eccentric measure. Perhaps,
The man-hero is not the exceptional monster,
But he that of repetition is most master.

X

Fat girl, terrestrial, my summer, my night,
How is it I find you in difference, see you there
In a moving contour, a change not quite completed?

You are familiar yet an aberration.
Civil, madam, I am, but underneath
A tree, this unprovoked sensation requires

That I should name you flatly, waste no words,
Check your evasions, hold you to yourself.
Even so when I think of you as strong or tired,

Bent over work, anxious, content, alone,
You remain the more than natural figure. You
Become the soft-footed phantom, the irrational

Distortion, however fragrant, however dear.
That's it: the more than rational distortion,
The fiction that results from feeling. Yes, that.

They will get it straight one day at the Sorbonne.
We shall return at twilight from the lecture
Pleased that the irrational is rational,

Until flicked by feeling, in a gildered street,
I call you by name, my green, my fluent mundo.
You will have stopped revolving except in crystal.

———————

Soldier, there is a war between the mind
And sky, between thought and day and night. It is
For that the poet is always in the sun,

Patches the moon together in his room
To his Virgilian cadences, up down,
Up down. It is a war that never ends.

Yet it depends on yours. The two are one.
They are a plural, a right and left, a pair,
Two parallels that meet if only in

The meeting of their shadows or that meet
In a book in a barrack, a letter from Malay.
But your war ends. And after it you return

With six meats and twelve wines or else without
To walk another room . . . Monsieur and comrade,
The soldier is poor without the poet's lines,

His petty syllabi, the sounds that stick,
Inevitably modulating, in the blood.
And war for war, each has its gallant kind.

How simply the fictive hero becomes the real;
How gladly with proper words the soldier dies,
If he must, or lives on the bread of faithful speech.

THE AURORAS OF AUTUMN

(1950)

The Auroras of Autumn

I

This is where the serpent lives, the bodiless.
His head is air. Beneath his tip at night
Eyes open and fix on us in every sky.

Or is this another wriggling out of the egg,
Another image at the end of the cave,
Another bodiless for the body's slough?

This is where the serpent lives. This is his nest,
These fields, these hills, these tinted distances,
And the pines above and along and beside the sea.

This is form gulping after formlessness,
Skin flashing to wished-for disappearances
And the serpent body flashing without the skin.

This is the height emerging and its base
These lights may finally attain a pole
In the midmost midnight and find the serpent there,

In another nest, the master of the maze
Of body and air and forms and images,
Relentlessly in possession of happiness.

This is his poison: that we should disbelieve
Even that. His meditations in the ferns,
When he moved so slightly to make sure of sun,

Made us no less as sure. We saw in his head,
Black beaded on the rock, the flecked animal,
The moving grass, the Indian in his glade.

II

Farewell to an idea . . . A cabin stands,
Deserted, on a beach. It is white,
As by a custom or according to

An ancestral theme or as a consequence
Of an infinite course. The flowers against the wall
Are white, a little dried, a kind of mark

Reminding, trying to remind, of a white
That was different, something else, last year
Or before, not the white of an aging afternoon,

Whether fresher or duller, whether of winter cloud
Or of winter sky, from horizon to horizon.
The wind is blowing the sand across the floor.

Here, being visible is being white,
Is being of the solid of white, the accomplishment
Of an extremist in an exercise . . .

The season changes. A cold wind chills the beach.
The long lines of it grow longer, emptier,
A darkness gathers though it does not fall

And the whiteness grows less vivid on the wall.
The man who is walking turns blankly on the sand.
He observes how the north is always enlarging the change,

With its frigid brilliances, its blue-red sweeps
And gusts of great enkindlings, its polar green,
The color of ice and fire and solitude.

III

Farewell to an idea . . . The mother's face,
The purpose of the poem, fills the room.
They are together, here, and it is warm,

With none of the prescience of oncoming dreams.
It is evening. The house is evening, half dissolved.
Only the half they can never possess remains,

Still-starred. It is the mother they possess,
Who gives transparence to their present peace.
She makes that gentler that can gentle be.

And yet she too is dissolved, she is destroyed.
She gives transparence. But she has grown old.
The necklace is a carving not a kiss.

The soft hands are a motion not a touch.
The house will crumble and the books will burn.
They are at ease in a shelter of the mind

And the house is of the mind and they and time,
Together, all together. Boreal night
Will look like frost as it approaches them

And to the mother as she falls asleep
And as they say good-night, good-night. Upstairs
The windows will be lighted, not the rooms.

A wind will spread its windy grandeurs round
And knock like a rifle-butt against the door.
The wind will command them with invincible sound.

IV

Farewell to an idea . . . The cancellings,
The negations are never final. The father sits
In space, wherever he sits, of bleak regard,

As one that is strong in the bushes of his eyes.
He says no to no and yes to yes. He says yes
To no; and in saying yes he says farewell.

He measures the velocities of change.
He leaps from heaven to heaven more rapidly
Than bad angels leap from heaven to hell in flames.

But now he sits in quiet and green-a-day.
He assumes the great speeds of space and flutters them
From cloud to cloudless, cloudless to keen clear

In flights of eye and ear, the highest eye
And the lowest ear, the deep ear that discerns,
At evening, things that attend it until it hears

The supernatural preludes of its own,
At the moment when the angelic eye defines
Its actors approaching, in company, in their masks.

Master O master seated by the fire
And yet in space and motionless and yet
Of motion the ever-brightening origin,

Profound, and yet the king and yet the crown,
Look at this present throne. What company,
In masks, can choir it with the naked wind?

V

The mother invites humanity to her house
And table. The father fetches tellers of tales
And musicians who mute much, muse much, on the tales.

The father fetches negresses to dance,
Among the children, like curious ripenesses
Of pattern in the dance's ripening.

For these the musicians make insidious tones,
Clawing the sing-song of their instruments.
The children laugh and jangle a tinny time.

The father fetches pageants out of air,
Scenes of the theatre, vistas and blocks of woods
And curtains like a naive pretence of sleep.

Among these the musicians strike the instinctive poem.
The father fetches his unherded herds,
Of barbarous tongue, slavered and panting halves

Of breath, obedient to his trumpet's touch.
This then is Chatillon or as you please.
We stand in the tumult of a festival.

What festival? This loud, disordered mooch?
These hospitaliers? These brute-like guests?
These musicians dubbing at a tragedy,

A-dub, a-dub, which is made up of this:
That there are no lines to speak? There is no play.
Or, the persons act one merely by being here.

VI

It is a theatre floating through the clouds,
Itself a cloud, although of misted rock
And mountains running like water, wave on wave,

Through waves of light. It is of cloud transformed
To cloud transformed again, idly, the way
A season changes color to no end,

Except the lavishing of itself in change,
As light changes yellow into gold and gold
To its opal elements and fire's delight,

Splashed wide-wise because it likes magnificence
And the solemn pleasures of magnificent space.
The cloud drifts idly through half-thought-of forms.

The theatre is filled with flying birds,
Wild wedges, as of a volcano's smoke, palm-eyed
And vanishing, a web in a corridor

Or massive portico. A capitol,
It may be, is emerging or has just
Collapsed. The denouement has to be postponed . . .

This is nothing until in a single man contained,
Nothing until this named thing nameless is
And is destroyed. He opens the door of his house

On flames. The scholar of one candle sees
An Arctic effulgence flaring on the frame
Of everything he is. And he feels afraid.

VII

Is there an imagination that sits enthroned
As grim as it is benevolent, the just
And the unjust, which in the midst of summer stops

To imagine winter? When the leaves are dead,
Does it take its place in the north and enfold itself,
Goat-leaper, crystalled and luminous, sitting

In highest night? And do these heavens adorn
And proclaim it, the white creator of black, jetted
By extinguishings, even of planets as may be,

Even of earth, even of sight, in snow,
Except as needed by way of majesty,
In the sky, as crown and diamond cabala?

It leaps through us, through all our heavens leaps,
Extinguishing our planets, one by one,
Leaving, of where we were and looked, of where

We knew each other and of each other thought,
A shivering residue, chilled and foregone,
Except for that crown and mystical cabala.

But it dare not leap by chance in its own dark.
It must change from destiny to slight caprice.
And thus its jetted tragedy, its stele

And shape and mournful making move to find
What must unmake it and, at last, what can,
Say, a flippant communication under the moon.

VIII

There may be always a time of innocence.
There is never a place. Or if there is no time,
If it is not a thing of time, nor of place,

Existing in the idea of it, alone,
In the sense against calamity, it is not
Less real. For the oldest and coldest philosopher,

There is or may be a time of innocence
As pure principle. Its nature is its end,
That it should be, and yet not be, a thing

That pinches the pity of the pitiful man,
Like a book at evening beautiful but untrue,
Like a book on rising beautiful and true.

It is like a thing of ether that exists
Almost as predicate. But it exists,
It exists, it is visible, it is, it is.

So, then, these lights are not a spell of light,
A saying out of a cloud, but innocence.
An innocence of the earth and no false sign

Or symbol of malice. That we partake thereof,
Lie down like children in this holiness,
As if, awake, we lay in the quiet of sleep,

As if the innocent mother sang in the dark
Of the room and on an accordion, half-heard,
Created the time and place in which we breathed . . .

IX

And of each other thought—in the idiom
Of the work, in the idiom of an innocent earth,
Not of the enigma of the guilty dream.

We were as Danes in Denmark all day long
And knew each other well, hale-hearted landsmen,
For whom the outlandish was another day

Of the week, queerer than Sunday. We thought alike
And that made brothers of us in a home
In which we fed on being brothers, fed

And fattened as on a decorous honeycomb.
This drama that we live—We lay sticky with sleep.
This sense of the activity of fate—

The rendezvous, when she came alone,
By her coming became a freedom of the two,
An isolation which only the two could share.

Shall we be found hanging in the trees next spring?
Of what disaster in this the imminence:
Bare limbs, bare trees and a wind as sharp as salt?

The stars are putting on their glittering belts.
They throw around their shoulders cloaks that flash
Like a great shadow's last embellishment.

It may come tomorrow in the simplest word,
Almost as part of innocence, almost,
Almost as the tenderest and the truest part.

X

An unhappy people in a happy world—
Read, rabbi, the phases of this difference.
An unhappy people in an unhappy world—

Here are too many mirrors for misery.
A happy people in an unhappy world—
It cannot be. There's nothing there to roll

On the expressive tongue, the finding fang.
A happy people in a happy world—
Buffo! A ball, an opera, a bar.

Turn back to where we were when we began:
An unhappy people in a happy world.
Now, solemnize the secretive syllables.

Read to the congregation, for today
And for tomorrow, this extremity,
This contrivance of the spectre of the spheres,

Contriving balance to contrive a whole,
The vital, the never-failing genius,
Fulfilling his meditations, great and small.

In these unhappy he meditates a whole,
The full of fortune and the full of fate,
As if he lived all lives, that he might know,

In hall harridan, not hushful paradise,
To a haggling of wind and weather, by these lights
Like a blaze of summer straw, in winter's nick.

Page from a Tale

In the hard brightness of that winter day
The sea was frozen solid and Hans heard,
By his drift-fire, on the shore, the difference
Between loud water and loud wind, between that
Which has no accurate syllables and that
Which cries *so blau* and cries again *so lind*
Und so lau, between sound without meaning and speech,
Of clay and wattles made as it ascends
And *hear it* as it falls *in the deep heart's core*
A steamer lay near him, foundered in the ice.

So blau, so blau . . . Hans listened by the fire.
New stars that were a foot across came out
And shone. *And a small cabin build there.*
So lind. The wind blazed as they sang. *So lau.*
The great ship, Balayne, lay frozen in the sea.
The one-foot stars were couriers of its death
To the wild limits of its habitation.
These were not tepid stars of torpid places
But bravest at midnight and in lonely spaces,
They looked back at Hans' look with savage faces.

The wet weed sputtered, the fire died down, the cold
Was like a sleep. The sea was a sea he dreamed.
Yet Hans lay wide awake. *And live alone*
In the bee-loud glade. Lights on the steamer moved.
Men would be starting at dawn to walk ashore.
They would be afraid of the sun: what it might be,
Afraid of the country angels of those skies,
The finned flutterings and gaspings of the ice,
As if whatever in water strove to speak
Broke dialect in a break of memory.

The sun might rise and it might not and if
It rose, ashen and red and yellow, each
Opaque, in orange circlet, nearer than it
Had ever been before, no longer known,
No more that which most of all brings back the known,
But that which destroys it completely by this light
For that, or a motion not in the astronomies,
Beyond the habit of sense, anarchic shape
Afire—it might and it might not in that
Gothic blue, speed home its portents to their ends.

It might become a wheel spoked red and white
In alternate stripes converging at a point
Of flame on the line, with a second wheel below,
Just rising, accompanying, arranged to cross,
Through weltering illuminations, humps
Of billows, downward, toward the drift-fire shore.
It might come bearing, out of chaos, kin
Smeared, smoked, and drunken of thin potencies,
Lashing at images in the atmosphere,
Ringed round and barred, with eyes held in their hands,

And capable of incapably evil thought:
Slight gestures that could rend the palpable ice,
Or melt Arcturus to ingots dropping drops,
Or spill night out in brilliant vanishings,
Whirlpools of darkness in whirlwinds of light . . .
The miff-maff-muff of water, the vocables
Of the wind, the glassily-sparkling particles

Of the mind—They would soon climb down the side of the
 ship.
They would march single file, with electric lamps, alert
For a tidal undulation underneath.

Large Red Man Reading

There were ghosts that returned to earth to hear his
 phrases,
As he sat there reading, aloud, the great blue tabulae.
They were those from the wilderness of stars that had
 expected more.

There were those that returned to hear him read from the
 poem of life,
Of the pans above the stove, the pots on the table, the
 tulips among them.
They were those that would have wept to step barefoot into
 reality,

That would have wept and been happy, have shivered in the
 frost
And cried out to feel it again, have run fingers over leaves
And against the most coiled thorn, have seized on what was
 ugly

And laughed, as he sat there reading, from out of the purple
 tabulae,
The outlines of being and its expressings, the syllables of its
 law:
Poesis, poesis, the literal characters, the vatic lines,

Which in those ears and in those thin, those spended hearts,
Took on color, took on shape and the size of things as they
 are
And spoke the feeling for them, which was what they had
 lacked.

This Solitude of Cataracts

He never felt twice the same about the flecked river,
Which kept flowing and never the same way twice, flowing

Through many places, as if it stood still in one,
Fixed like a lake on which the wild ducks fluttered,

Ruffling its common reflections, thought-like Monadnocks.
There seemed to be an apostrophe that was not spoken.

There was so much that was real that was not real at all.
He wanted to feel the same way over and over.

He wanted the river to go on flowing the same way,
To keep on flowing. He wanted to walk beside it,

Under the buttonwoods, beneath a moon nailed fast.
He wanted his heart to stop beating and his mind to rest

In a permanent realization, without any wild ducks
Or mountains that were not mountains, just to know how it
      would be,

Just to know how it would feel, released from destruction,
To be a bronze man breathing under archaic lapis,

Without the oscillations of planetary pass-pass,
Breathing his bronzen breath at the azury center of time.

In the Element of Antagonisms

If it is a world without a genius,
It is most happily contrived. Here, then,

We ask which means most, for us, all the genii
Or one man who, for us, is greater than they,

On his gold horse striding, like a conjured beast,
Miraculous in its panache and swish?

Birds twitter pandemoniums around
The idea of the chevalier of chevaliers,

The well-composed in his burnished solitude,
The tower, the ancient accent, the wintry size.

And the north wind's mighty buskin seems to fall
In an excessive corridor, alas!

In a Bad Time

How mad would he have to be to say, "He beheld
An order and thereafter he belonged
To it"? He beheld the order of the northern sky.

But the beggar gazes on calamity
And thereafter he belongs to it, to bread
Hard found, and water tasting of misery.

For him cold's glacial beauty is his fate.
Without understanding, he belongs to it
And the night, and midnight, and after, where it is.

What has he? What he has he has. But what?
It is not a question of captious repartee.
What has he that becomes his heart's strong core?

He has his poverty and nothing more.
His poverty becomes his heart's strong core—
A forgetfulness of summer at the pole.

Sordid Melpomene, why strut bare boards,
Without scenery or lights, in the theatre's bricks,
Dressed high in heliotrope's inconstant hue,

The muse of misery? Speak loftier lines.
Cry out, "I am the purple muse." Make sure
The audience beholds you, not your gown.

The Beginning

So summer comes in the end to these few stains
And the rust and rot of the door through which she went.

The house is empty. But here is where she sat
To comb her dewy hair, a touchless light,

Perplexed by its darker iridescences.
This was the glass in which she used to look

At the moment's being, without history,
The self of summer perfectly perceived,

And feel its country gaiety and smile
And be surprised and tremble, hand and lip.

This is the chair from which she gathered up
Her dress, the carefulest, commodious weave

Inwoven by a weaver to twelve bells . . .
The dress is lying, cast-off, on the floor.

Now, the first tutoyers of tragedy
Speak softly, to begin with, in the eaves.

The Countryman

Swatara, Swatara, black river,
Descending, out of the cap of midnight,
Toward the cape at which
You enter the swarthy sea,

Swatara, Swatara, heavy the hills
Are, hanging above you, as you move,
Move blackly and without crystal.
A countryman walks beside you.

He broods of neither cap nor cape,
But only of your swarthy motion,
But always of the swarthy water,
Of which Swatara is the breathing,

The name. He does not speak beside you.
He is there because he wants to be
And because being there in the heavy hills
And along the moving of the water—

Being there is being in a place,
As of a character everywhere,
The place of a swarthy presence moving,
Slowly, to the look of a swarthy name.

The Ultimate Poem Is Abstract

This day writhes with what? The lecturer
On This Beautiful World Of Ours composes himself
And hems the planet rose and haws it ripe,

And red, and right. The particular question—here
The particular answer to the particular question
Is not in point—the question is in point.

If the day writhes, it is not with revelations.
One goes on asking questions. That, then, is one
Of the categories. So said, this placid space

Is changed. It is not so blue as we thought. To be blue,
There must be no questions. It is an intellect
Of windings round and dodges to and fro,

Writhings in wrong obliques and distances,
Not an intellect in which we are fleet: present
Everywhere in space at once, cloud-pole

Of communication. It would be enough
If we were ever, just once, at the middle, fixed
In This Beautiful World Of Ours and not as now,

Helplessly at the edge, enough to be
Complete, because at the middle, if only in sense,
And in that enormous sense, merely enjoy.

Bouquet of Roses in Sunlight

Say that it is a crude effect, black reds,
Pink yellows, orange whites, too much as they are
To be anything else in the sunlight of the room,

Too much as they are to be changed by metaphor,
Too actual, things that in being real
Make any imaginings of them lesser things.

And yet this effect is a consequence of the way
We feel and, therefore, is not real, except
In our sense of it, our sense of the fertilest red,

Of yellow as first color and of white,
In which the sense lies still, as a man lies,
Enormous, in a completing of his truth.

Our sense of these things changes and they change,
Not as in metaphor, but in our sense
Of them. So sense exceeds all metaphor.

It exceeds the heavy changes of the light.
It is like a flow of meanings with no speech
And of as many meanings as of men.

We are two that use these roses as we are,
In seeing them. This is what makes them seem
So far beyond the rhetorician's touch.

The Owl in the Sarcophagus

I

Two forms move among the dead, high sleep
Who by his highness quiets them, high peace
Upon whose shoulders even the heavens rest,

Two brothers. And a third form, she that says
Good-by in the darkness, speaking quietly there,
To those that cannot say good-by themselves.

These forms are visible to the eye that needs,
Needs out of the whole necessity of sight.
The third form speaks, because the ear repeats,

Without a voice, inventions of farewell.
These forms are not abortive figures, rocks,
Impenetrable symbols, motionless. They move

About the night. They live without our light,
In an element not the heaviness of time,
In which reality is prodigy.

There sleep the brother is the father, too,
And peace is cousin by a hundred names
And she that in the syllable between life

And death cries quickly, in a flash of voice,
Keep you, keep you, I am gone, oh keep you as
My memory, is the mother of us all,

The earthly mother and the mother of
The dead. Only the thought of those dark three
Is dark, thought of the forms of dark desire.

II

There came a day, there was a day—one day
A man walked living among the forms of thought
To see their lustre truly as it is

And in harmonious prodigy to be,
A while, conceiving his passage as into a time
That of itself stood still, perennial,

Less time than place, less place than thought of place
And, if of substance, a likeness of the earth,
That by resemblance twanged him through and through,

Releasing an abysmal melody,
A meeting, an emerging in the light,
A dazzle of remembrance and of sight.

III

There he saw well the foldings in the height
Of sleep, the whiteness folded into less,
Like many robings, as moving masses are,

As a moving mountain is, moving through day
And night, colored from distances, central
Where luminous agitations come to rest,

In an ever-changing, calmest unity,
The unique composure, harshest streakings joined
In a vanishing-vanished violet that wraps round

The giant body the meanings of its folds,
The weaving and the crinkling and the vex,
As on water of an afternoon in the wind

After the wind has passed. Sleep realized
Was the whiteness that is the ultimate intellect,
A diamond jubilance beyond the fire,

That gives its power to the wild-ringed eye.
Then he breathed deeply the deep atmosphere
Of sleep, the accomplished, the fulfilling air.

IV

There peace, the godolphin and fellow, estranged, estranged,
Hewn in their middle as the beam of leaves,
The prince of shither-shade and tinsel lights,

Stood flourishing the world. The brilliant height
And hollow of him by its brilliance calmed,
Its brightness burned the way good solace seethes.

This was peace after death, the brother of sleep,
The inhuman brother so much like, so near,
Yet vested in a foreign absolute,

Adorned with cryptic stones and sliding shines,
An immaculate personage in nothingness,
With the whole spirit sparkling in its cloth,

Generations of the imagination piled
In the manner of its stitchings, of its thread,
In the weaving round the wonder of its need,

And the first flowers upon it, an alphabet
By which to spell out holy doom and end,
A bee for the remembering of happiness.

Peace stood with our last blood adorned, last mind,
Damasked in the originals of green,
A thousand begettings of the broken bold.

This is that figure stationed at our end,
Always, in brilliance, fatal, final, formed
Out of our lives to keep us in our death,

To watch us in the summer of Cyclops
Underground, a king as candle by our beds
In a robe that is our glory as he guards.

V

But she that says good-by losing in self
The sense of self, rosed out of prestiges
Of rose, stood tall in self not symbol, quick

And potent, an influence felt instead of seen.
She spoke with backward gestures of her hand.
She held men closely with discovery,

Almost as speed discovers, in the way
Invisible change discovers what is changed,
In the way what was has ceased to be what is.

It was not her look but a knowledge that she had.
She was a self that knew, an inner thing,
Subtler than look's declaiming, although she moved

With a sad splendor, beyond artifice,
Impassioned by the knowledge that she had,
There on the edges of oblivion.

O exhalation, O fling without a sleeve
And motion outward, reddened and resolved
From sight, in the silence that follows her last word—

VI

This is the mythology of modern death
And these, in their mufflings, monsters of elegy,
Of their own marvel made, of pity made,

Compounded and compounded, life by life,
These are death's own supremest images,
The pure perfections of parental space,

The children of a desire that is the will,
Even of death, the beings of the mind
In the light-bound space of the mind, the floreate flare . . .

It is a child that sings itself to sleep,
The mind, among the creatures that it makes,
The people, those by which it lives and dies.

Saint John and the Back-Ache

The Back-Ache
        The mind is the terriblest force in the world, father,
        Because, in chief, it, only, can defend
        Against itself. At its mercy, we depend
        Upon it.
Saint John
               The world is presence and not force.
        Presence is not mind.
The Back-Ache
                  Presence is *Kinder-Scenen.*
Saint John
        It fills the being before the mind can think.
        The effect of the object is beyond the mind's
        Extremest pinch and, easily, as in
        A sudden color on the sea. But it is not
        That big-brushed green. Or in a tragic mode,
        As at the moment of the year when, tick,
        Autumn howls upon half-naked summer. But
        It is not the unravelling of her yellow shift.
        Presence is not the woman, come upon,
        Not yet accustomed, yet, at sight, humane
        To most incredible depths. I speak below
        The tension of the lyre. My point is that
        These illustrations are neither angels, no,
        Nor brilliant blows thereof, ti-rill-a-roo,
        Nor all one's luck at once in a play of strings.
        They help us face the dumbfoundering abyss
        Between us and the object, external cause,

The little ignorance that is everything,
The possible nest in the invisible tree,
Which in a composite season, now unknown,
Denied, dismissed, may hold a serpent, loud
In our captious hymns, erect and sinuous,
Whose venom and whose wisdom will be one.
Then the stale turtle will grow limp from age.
We shall be heavy with the knowledge of that day.

The Back-Ache

It may be, may be. It is possible.
Presence lies far too deep, for me to know
Its irrational reaction, as from pain.

Celle Qui Fût Héaulmiette

Out of the first warmth of spring,
And out of the shine of the hemlocks,
Among the bare and crooked trees,
She found a helping from the cold,

Like a meaning in nothingness,
Like the snow before it softened
And dwindled into patches,
Like a shelter not in an arc

But in a circle, not in the arc
Of winter, in the unbroken circle
Of summer, at the windy edge,
Sharp in the ice shadow of the sky,

Blue for all that and white and hard,
And yet with water running in the sun,
Entinselled and gilderlinged and gone,
Another American vulgarity.

Into that native shield she slid,
Mistress of an idea, child
Of a mother with vague severed arms
And of a father bearded in his fire.

Imago

Who can pick up the weight of Britain,
Who can move the German load
Or say to the French here is France again?
Imago. Imago. Imago.

It is nothing, no great thing, nor man
Of ten brilliancies of battered gold
And fortunate stone. It moves its parade
Of motions in the mind and heart,

A gorgeous fortitude. Medium man
In February hears the imagination's hymns
And sees its images, its motions
And multitudes of motions

And feels the imagination's mercies,
In a season more than sun and south wind,
Something returning from a deeper quarter,
A glacier running through delirium,

Making this heavy rock a place,
Which is not of our lives composed . . .
Lightly and lightly, O my land,
Move lightly through the air again.

A Primitive Like an Orb

I

The essential poem at the center of things,
The arias that spiritual fiddlings make,
Have gorged the cast-iron of our lives with good
And the cast-iron of our works. But it is, dear sirs,
A difficult apperception, this gorging good,
Fetched by such slick-eyed nymphs, this essential gold,

This fortune's finding, disposed and re-disposed
By such slight genii in such pale air.

II

We do not prove the existence of the poem.
It is something seen and known in lesser poems.
It is the huge, high harmony that sounds
A little and a little, suddenly,
By means of a separate sense. It is and it
Is not and, therefore, is. In the instant of speech,
The breadth of an accelerando moves,
Captives the being, widens—and was there.

III

What milk there is in such captivity,
What wheaten bread and oaten cake and kind,
Green guests and table in the woods and songs
At heart, within an instant's motion, within
A space grown wide, the inevitable blue
Of secluded thunder, an illusion, as it was,
Oh as, always too heavy for the sense
To seize, the obscurest as, the distant was . . .

IV

One poem proves another and the whole,
For the clairvoyant men that need no proof:
The lover, the believer and the poet.
Their words are chosen out of their desire,
The joy of language, when it is themselves.
With these they celebrate the central poem,
The fulfillment of fulfillments, in opulent,
Last terms, the largest, bulging still with more,

V

Until the used-to earth and sky, and the tree
And cloud, the used-to tree and used-to cloud,
Lose the old uses that they made of them,
And they: these men, and earth and sky, inform

Each other by sharp informations, sharp,
Free knowledges, secreted until then,
Breaches of that which held them fast. It is
As if the central poem became the world,

VI

And the world the central poem, each one the mate
Of the other, as if summer was a spouse,
Espoused each morning, each long afternoon,
And the mate of summer: her mirror and her look,
Her only place and person, a self of her
That speaks, denouncing separate selves, both one.
The essential poem begets the others. The light
Of it is not a light apart, up-hill.

VII

The central poem is the poem of the whole,
The poem of the composition of the whole,
The composition of blue sea and of green,
Of blue light and of green, as lesser poems,
And the miraculous multiplex of lesser poems,
Not merely into a whole, but a poem of
The whole, the essential compact of the parts,
The roundness that pulls tight the final ring

VIII

And that which in an altitude would soar,
A vis, a principle or, it may be,
The meditation of a principle,
Or else an inherent order active to be
Itself, a nature to its natives all
Beneficence, a repose, utmost repose,
The muscles of a magnet aptly felt,
A giant, on the horizon, glistening,

IX

And in bright excellence adorned, crested
With every prodigal, familiar fire,

And unfamiliar escapades: whirroos
And scintillant sizzlings such as children like,
Vested in the serious folds of majesty,
Moving around and behind, a following,
A source of trumpeting seraphs in the eye,
A source of pleasant outbursts on the ear.

X

It is a giant, always, that is evolved,
To be in scale, unless virtue cuts him, snips
Both size and solitude or thinks it does,
As in a signed photograph on a mantelpiece.
But the virtuoso never leaves his shape,
Still on the horizon elongates his cuts,
And still angelic and still plenteous,
Imposes power by the power of his form.

XI

Here, then, is an abstraction given head,
A giant on the horizon, given arms,
A massive body and long legs, stretched out,
A definition with an illustration, not
Too exactly labelled, a large among the smalls
Of it, a close, parental magnitude,
At the center on the horizon, concentrum, grave
And prodigious person, patron of origins.

XII

That's it. The lover writes, the believer hears,
The poet mumbles and the painter sees,
Each one, his fated eccentricity,
As a part, but part, but tenacious particle,
Of the skeleton of the ether, the total
Of letters, prophecies, perceptions, clods
Of color, the giant of nothingness, each one
And the giant ever changing, living in change.

Metaphor as Degeneration

If there is a man white as marble
Sits in a wood, in the greenest part,
Brooding sounds of the images of death,

So there is a man in black space
Sits in nothing that we know,
Brooding sounds of river noises;

And these images, these reverberations,
And others, make certain how being
Includes death and the imagination.

The marble man remains himself in space.
The man in the black wood descends unchanged.
It is certain that the river

Is not Swatara. The swarthy water
That flows round the earth and through the skies,
Twisting among the universal spaces,

Is not Swatara. It is being.
That is the flock-flecked river, the water,
The blown sheen—or is it air?

How, then, is metaphor degeneration,
When Swatara becomes this undulant river
And the river becomes the landless, waterless ocean?

Here the black violets grow down to its banks
And the memorial mosses hang their green
Upon it, as it flows ahead.

The Woman in Sunshine

It is only that this warmth and movement are like
The warmth and movement of a woman.

It is not that there is any image in the air
Nor the beginning nor end of a form:

It is empty. But a woman in threadless gold
Burns us with brushings of her dress

And a dissociated abundance of being,
More definite for what she is—

Because she is disembodied,
Bearing the odors of the summer fields,

Confessing the taciturn and yet indifferent,
Invisibly clear, the only love.

Reply to Papini

*In all the solemn moments of human history . . . poets rose to sing
the hymn of victory or the psalm of supplication. . . . Cease, then,
from being the astute calligraphers of congealed daydreams, the hunt-
ers of cerebral phosphorescences.*

Letter of Celestin VI, Pope, to the Poets
P.C.C. GIOVANNI PAPINI

I

Poor procurator, why do you ask someone else
To say what Celestin should say for himself?

He has an ever-living subject. The poet
Has only the formulations of midnight.

Is Celestin dislodged? The way through the world
Is more difficult to find than the way beyond it.

You know that the nucleus of a time is not
The poet but the poem, the growth of the mind

Of the world, the heroic effort to live expressed
As victory. The poet does not speak in ruins

Nor stand there making orotund consolations.
He shares the confusions of intelligence.

Giovanni Papini, by your faith, know how
He wishes that all hard poetry were true.

This pastoral of endurance and of death
Is of a nature that must be perceived

And not imagined. The removes must give,
Including the removes toward poetry.

II

Celestin, the generous, the civilized,
Will understand what it is to understand.

The world is still profound and in its depths
Man sits and studies silence and himself,

Abiding the reverberations in the vaults.
Now, once, he accumulates himself and time

For humane triumphals. But a politics
Of property is not an area

For triumphals. These are hymns appropriate to
The complexities of the world, when apprehended,

The intricacies of appearance, when perceived.
They become our gradual possession. The poet

Increases the aspects of experience,
As in an enchantment, analyzed and fixed

And final. This is the center. The poet is
The angry day-son clanging at its make:

The satisfaction underneath the sense,
The conception sparkling in still obstinate thought.

The Bouquet

I

Of medium nature, this farouche extreme
Is a drop of lightning in an inner world,
Suspended in temporary jauntiness.

The bouquet stands in a jar, as metaphor,
As lightning itself is, likewise, metaphor
Crowded with apparitions suddenly gone

And no less suddenly here again, a growth
Of the reality of the eye, an artifice,
Nothing much, a flitter that reflects itself.

II

One approaches, simply, the reality
Of the other eye. One enters, entering home,
The place of meta-men and para-things,

And yet still men though meta-men, still things
Though para-things; the meta-men for whom
The world has turned to the several speeds of glass,

For whom no blue in the sky prevents them, as
They understand, and take on potency,
By growing clear, transparent magistrates,

Bearded with chains of blue-green glitterings
And wearing hats of angular flick and fleck,
Cold with an under impotency that they know,

Now that they know, because they know. One comes
To the things of medium nature, as meta-men
Behold them, not choses of Provence, growing

In glue, but things transfixed, transpierced and well
Perceived: the white seen smoothly argentine
And plated up, dense silver shine, in a land

Without a god, O silver sheen and shape,
And movement of emotion through the air,
True nothing, yet accosted self to self.

Through the door one sees on the lake that the white duck
    swims
Away—and tells and tells the water tells
Of the image spreading behind it in idea.

The meta-men behold the idea as part
Of the image, behold it with exactness through beads
And dewy bearings of their light-locked beards.

The green bouquet comes from the place of the duck.
It is centi-colored and mille-flored and ripe,
Of dulce atmosphere, the fore of lofty scenes

But not of romance, the bitterest vulgar do
And die. It stands on a table at a window
Of the land, on a checkered cover, red and white.

The checkered squares, the skeleton of repose,
Breathe slightly, slightly move or seem to move
Toward a consciousness of red and white as one,

A vibrancy of petals, fallen, that still cling
By trivial filaments to the thing intact:
The recognizable, medium, central whole—

So near detachment, the cover's cornered squares,
And, when detached, so unimportantly gone,
So severed and so much forlorn debris.

Here the eye fastens intently to these lines
And crawls on them, as if feathers of the duck
Fell openly from the air to reappear

In other shapes, as if duck and table-cloth
And the eccentric twistings of the rapt bouquet
Exacted attention with attentive force.

A pack of cards is falling toward the floor.
The sun is secretly shining on a wall.
One remembers a woman standing in such a dress.

III

The rose, the delphinium, the red, the blue,
Are questions of the looks they get. The bouquet,
Regarded by the meta-men, is quirked

And queered by lavishings of their will to see.
It stands a sovereign of souvenirs
Neither remembered nor forgotten, nor old,

Nor new, nor in the sense of memory.
It is a symbol, a sovereign of symbols
In its interpretations voluble,

Embellished by the quicknesses of sight,
When in a way of seeing seen, an extreme,
A sovereign, a souvenir, a sign,

Of today, of this morning, of this afternoon,
Not yesterday, nor tomorrow, an appanage
Of indolent summer not quite physical

And yet of summer, the petty tones
Its colors make, the migratory daze,
The doubling second things, not mystical,

The infinite of the actual perceived,
A freedom revealed, a realization touched,
The real made more acute by an unreal.

IV

Perhaps, these colors, seen in insight, assume
In the eye a special hue of origin.
But if they do, they cast it widely round.

They cast deeply round a crystal crystal-white
And pallid bits, that tend to comply with blue,
A right red with its composites glutted full,

Like a monster that has everything and rests,
And yet is there, a presence in the way.
They cast closely round the facture of the thing

Turned para-thing, the rudiments in the jar,
The stalk, the weed, the grassy flourishes,
The violent disclosure trimly leafed,

Lean larkspur and jagged fern and rusting rue
In a stubborn literacy, an intelligence,
The prismatic sombreness of a torrent's wave.

The rudiments in the jar, farced, finikin,
Are flatly there, unversed except to be,
Made difficult by salt fragrance, intricate.

They are not splashings in a penumbra. They stand.
They are. The bouquet is a part of a dithering:
Cloud's gold, of a whole appearance that stands and is.

V

A car drives up. A soldier, an officer,
Steps out. He rings and knocks. The door is not locked.
He enters the room and calls. No one is there.

He bumps the table. The bouquet falls on its side.
He walks through the house, looks round him and then
        leaves.
The bouquet has slopped over the edge and lies on the
        floor.

World Without Peculiarity

The day is great and strong—
But his father was strong, that lies now
In the poverty of dirt.

Nothing could be more hushed than the way
The moon moves toward the night.
But what his mother was returns and cries on his breast.

The red ripeness of round leaves is thick
With the spices of red summer.
But she that he loved turns cold at his light touch.

What good is it that the earth is justified,
That it is complete, that it is an end,
That in itself it is enough?

It is the earth itself that is humanity . . .
He is the inhuman son and she,
She is the fateful mother, whom he does not know.

She is the day, the walk of the moon
Among the breathless spices and, sometimes,
He, too, is human and difference disappears

And the poverty of dirt, the thing upon his breast,
The hating woman, the meaningless place,
Become a single being, sure and true.

Our Stars Come from Ireland

I

Tom McGreevy, in America,
Thinks of Himself as a Boy

Out of him that I loved,
Mal Bay I made,
I made Mal Bay
And him in that water.

Over the top of the Bank of Ireland,
The wind blows quaintly
Its thin-stringed music,
As he heard it in Tarbert.

These things were made of him
And out of myself.
He stayed in Kerry, died there.
I live in Pennsylvania.

Out of him I made Mal Bay
And not a bald and tasselled saint.
What would the water have been,
Without that that he makes of it?

The stars are washing up from Ireland
And through and over the puddles of Swatara
And Schuylkill. The sound of him
Comes from a great distance and is heard.

II

The Westwardness of Everything

These are the ashes of fiery weather,
Of nights full of the green stars from Ireland,
Wet out of the sea, and luminously wet,
Like beautiful and abandoned refugees.

The whole habit of the mind is changed by them,
These Gaeled and fitful-fangled darknesses
Made suddenly luminous, themselves a change,
An east in their compelling westwardness,

Themselves an issue as at an end, as if
There was an end at which in a final change,
When the whole habit of the mind was changed,
The ocean breathed out morning in one breath.

Puella Parvula

Every thread of summer is at last unwoven.
By one caterpillar is great Africa devoured
And Gibraltar is dissolved like spit in the wind.

But over the wind, over the legends of its roaring,
The elephant on the roof and its elephantine blaring,
The bloody lion in the yard at night or ready to spring

From the clouds in the midst of trembling trees
Making a great gnashing, over the water wallows
Of a vacant sea declaiming with wide throat,

Over all these the mighty imagination triumphs
Like a trumpet and says, in this season of memory,
When the leaves fall like things mournful of the past,

Keep quiet in the heart, O wild bitch. O mind
Gone wild, be what he tells you to be: *Puella.*
Write *pax* across the window pane. And then

Be still. The *summarium in excelsis* begins . . .
Flame, sound, fury composed . . . Hear what he says,
The dauntless master, as he starts the human tale.

The Novel

The crows are flying above the foyer of summer.
The winds batter it. The water curls. The leaves
Return to their original illusion.

The sun stands like a Spaniard as he departs,
Stepping from the foyer of summer into that
Of the past, the rodomontadean emptiness.

Mother was afraid I should freeze in the Parisian hotels.
She had heard of the fate of an Argentine writer. At night,
He would go to bed, cover himself with blankets—

Protruding from the pile of wool, a hand,
In a black glove, holds a novel by Camus. She begged
That I stay away. These are the words of José . . .

He is sitting by the fidgets of a fire,
The first red of red winter, winter-red,
The late, least foyer in a qualm of cold.

How tranquil it was at vividest Varadero,
While the water kept running through the mouth of the
        speaker,
Saying: *Olalla blanca en el blanco,*

Lol-lolling the endlessness of poetry.
But here tranquillity is what one thinks.
The fire burns as the novel taught it how.

The mirror melts and moulds itself and moves
And catches from nowhere brightly-burning breath.
It blows a glassy brightness on the fire

And makes flame flame and makes it bite the wood
And bite the hard-bite, barking as it bites.
The arrangement of the chairs is so and so,

Not as one would have arranged them for oneself,
But in the style of the novel, its tracing
Of an unfamiliar in the familiar room,

A *retrato* that is strong because it is like,
A second that grows first, a black unreal
In which a real lies hidden and alive.

Day's arches are crumbling into the autumn night.
The fire falls a little and the book is done.
The stillness is the stillness of the mind.

Slowly the room grows dark. It is odd about
That Argentine. Only the real can be
Unreal today, be hidden and alive.

It is odd, too, how that Argentine is oneself,
Feeling the fear that creeps beneath the wool,
Lies on the breast and pierces into the heart,

Straight from the Arcadian imagination,
Its being beating heavily in the veins,
Its knowledge cold within one as one's own;

And one trembles to be so understood and, at last,
To understand, as if to know became
The fatality of seeing things too well.

What We See Is What We Think

At twelve, the disintegration of afternoon
Began, the return to phantomerei, if not
To phantoms. Till then, it had been the other way:

One imagined the violet trees but the trees stood green,
At twelve, as green as ever they would be.
The sky was blue beyond the vaultiest phrase.

Twelve meant as much as: the end of normal time,
Straight up, an élan without harrowing,
The imprescriptible zenith, free of harangue,

Twelve and the first gray second after, a kind
Of violet gray, a green violet, a thread
To weave a shadow's leg or sleeve, a scrawl

On the pedestal, an ambitious page dog-eared
At the upper right, a pyramid with one side
Like a spectral cut in its perception, a tilt

And its tawny caricature and tawny life,
Another thought, the paramount ado . . .
Since what we think is never what we see.

A Golden Woman in a Silver Mirror

Suppose this was the root of everything.
Suppose it turned out to be or that it touched
An image that was mistress of the world.

For example: Au Château. Un Salon. A glass
The sun steps into, regards and finds itself;
Or: Gawks of hay . . . Augusta Moon, before

An attic glass, hums of the old Lutheran bells
At home; or: In the woods, belle Belle alone
Rattles with fear in unreflecting leaves.

Abba, dark death is the breaking of a glass.
The dazzled flakes and splinters disappear.
The seal is as relaxed as dirt, perdu.

But the images, disembodied, are not broken.
They have, or they may have, their glittering crown,
Sound-soothing pearl and omni-diamond,

Of the most beautiful, the most beautiful maid
And mother. How long have you lived and looked,
Ababba, expecting this king's queen to appear?

The Old Lutheran Bells at Home

These are the voices of the pastors calling
In the names of St. Paul and of the halo-John
And of other holy and learned men, among them

Great choristers, propounders of hymns, trumpeters,
Jerome and the scrupulous Francis and Sunday women,
The nurses of the spirit's innocence.

These are the voices of the pastors calling
Much rough-end being to smooth Paradise,
Spreading out fortress walls like fortress wings.

Deep in their sound the stentor Martin sings.
Dark Juan looks outward through his mystic brow . . .
Each sexton has his sect. The bells have none.

These are the voices of the pastors calling
And calling like the long echoes in long sleep,
Generations of shepherds to generations of sheep.

Each truth is a sect though no bells ring for it.
And the bells belong to the sextons, after all,
As they jangle and dangle and kick their feet.

Questions Are Remarks

In the weed of summer comes this green sprout why.
The sun aches and ails and then returns halloo
Upon the horizon amid adult enfantillages.

Its fire fails to pierce the vision that beholds it,
Fails to destroy the antique acceptances,
Except that the grandson sees it as it is,

Peter the voyant, who says "Mother, what is that"—
The object that rises with so much rhetoric,
But not for him. His question is complete.

It is the question of what he is capable.
It is the extreme, the expert aetat. 2.
He will never ride the red horse she describes.

His question is complete because it contains
His utmost statement. It is his own array,
His own pageant and procession and display,

As far as nothingness permits . . . Hear him.
He does not say, "Mother, my mother, who are you,"
The way the drowsy, infant, old men do.

Study of Images I

It does no good to speak of the big, blue bush
Of day. If the study of his images
Is the study of man, this image of Saturday,

This Italian symbol, this Southern landscape, is like
A waking, as in images we awake,
Within the very object that we seek,

Participants of its being. It is, we are.
He is, we are. Ah, bella! He is, we are,
Within the big, blue bush and its vast shade

At evening and at night. It does no good.
Stop at the terraces of mandolins,
False, faded and yet inextricably there,

The pulse of the object, the heat of the body grown cold
Or cooling in late leaves, not false except
When the image itself is false, a mere desire,

Not faded, if images are all we have.
They can be no more faded than ourselves.
The blood refreshes with its stale demands.

Study of Images II

The frequency of images of the moon
Is more or less. The pearly women that drop
From heaven and float in air, like animals

Of ether, exceed the excelling witches, whence
They came. But, brown, the ice-bear sleeping in ice-month
In his cave, remains dismissed without a dream,

As if the center of images had its
Congenial mannequins, alert to please,
Beings of other beings manifold—

The shadowless moon wholly composed of shade,
Women with other lives in their live hair,
Rose—women as half-fishes of salt shine,

As if, as if, as if the disparate halves
Of things were waiting in a betrothal known
To none, awaiting espousal to the sound

Of right joining, a music of ideas, the burning
And breeding and bearing birth of harmony,
The final relation, the marriage of the rest.

An Ordinary Evening in New Haven

The eye's plain version is a thing apart,
The vulgate of experience. Of this,
A few words, an and yet, and yet, and yet—

As part of the never-ending meditation,
Part of the question that is a giant himself:
Of what is this house composed if not of the sun,

These houses, these difficult objects, dilapidate
Appearances of what appearances,
Words, lines, not meanings, not communications,

Dark things without a double, after all,
Unless a second giant kills the first—
A recent imagining of reality,

Much like a new resemblance of the sun,
Down-pouring, up-springing and inevitable,
A larger poem for a larger audience,

As if the crude collops came together as one,
A mythological form, a festival sphere,
A great bosom, beard and being, alive with age.

II

Suppose these houses are composed of ourselves,
So that they become an impalpable town, full of
Impalpable bells, transparencies of sound,

Sounding in transparent dwellings of the self,
Impalpable habitations that seem to move
In the movement of the colors of the mind,

The far-fire flowing and the dim-coned bells
Coming together in a sense in which we are poised,
Without regard to time or where we are,

In the perpetual reference, object
Of the perpetual meditation, point
Of the enduring, visionary love,

Obscure, in colors whether of the sun
Or mind, uncertain in the clearest bells,
The spirit's speeches, the indefinite,

Confused illuminations and sonorities,
So much ourselves, we cannot tell apart
The idea and the bearer-being of the idea.

III

The point of vision and desire are the same.
It is to the hero of midnight that we pray
On a hill of stones to make beau mont thereof.

If it is misery that infuriates our love,
If the black of night stands glistening on beau mont,
Then, ancientest saint ablaze with ancientest truth,

Say next to holiness is the will thereto,
And next to love is the desire for love,
The desire for its celestial ease in the heart,

Which nothing can frustrate, that most secure,
Unlike love in possession of that which was
To be possessed and is. But this cannot

Possess. It is desire, set deep in the eye,
Behind all actual seeing, in the actual scene,
In the street, in a room, on a carpet or a wall,

Always in emptiness that would be filled,
In denial that cannot contain its blood,
A porcelain, as yet in the bats thereof.

IV

The plainness of plain things is savagery,
As: the last plainness of a man who has fought
Against illusion and was, in a great grinding

Of growling teeth, and falls at night, snuffed out
By the obese opiates of sleep. Plain men in plain towns
Are not precise about the appeasement they need.

They only know a savage assuagement cries
With a savage voice; and in that cry they hear
Themselves transposed, muted and comforted

In a savage and subtle and simple harmony,
A matching and mating of surprised accords,
A responding to a diviner opposite.

So lewd spring comes from winter's chastity.
So, after summer, in the autumn air,
Comes the cold volume of forgotten ghosts,

But soothingly, with pleasant instruments,
So that this cold, a children's tale of ice,
Seems like a sheen of heat romanticized.

V

Inescapable romance, inescapable choice
Of dreams, disillusion as the last illusion,
Reality as a thing seen by the mind,

Not that which is but that which is apprehended,
A mirror, a lake of reflections in a room,
A glassy ocean lying at the door,

A great town hanging pendent in a shade,
An enormous nation happy in a style,
Everything as unreal as real can be,

In the inexquisite eye. Why, then, inquire
Who has divided the world, what entrepreneur?
No man. The self, the chrysalis of all men

Became divided in the leisure of blue day
And more, in branchings after day. One part
Held fast tenaciously in common earth

And one from central earth to central sky
And in moonlit extensions of them in the mind
Searched out such majesty as it could find.

VI

Reality is the beginning not the end,
Naked Alpha, not the hierophant Omega,
Of dense investiture, with luminous vassals.

It is the infant A standing on infant legs,
Not twisted, stooping, polymathic Z,
He that kneels always on the edge of space

In the pallid perceptions of its distances.
Alpha fears men or else Omega's men
Or else his prolongations of the human.

These characters are around us in the scene.
For one it is enough; for one it is not;
For neither is it profound absentia,

Since both alike appoint themselves the choice
Custodians of the glory of the scene,
The immaculate interpreters of life.

But that's the difference: in the end and the way
To the end. Alpha continues to begin.
Omega is refreshed at every end.

VII

In the presence of such chapels and such schools,
The impoverished architects appear to be
Much richer, more fecund, sportive and alive.

The objects tingle and the spectator moves
With the objects. But the spectator also moves
With lesser things, with things exteriorized

Out of rigid realists. It is as if
Men turning into things, as comedy,
Stood, dressed in antic symbols, to display

The truth about themselves, having lost, as things,
That power to conceal they had as men,
Not merely as to depth but as to height

As well, not merely as to the commonplace
But, also, as to their miraculous,
Conceptions of new mornings of new worlds,

The tips of cock-cry pinked out pastily,
As that which was incredible becomes,
In misted contours, credible day again.

VIII

We fling ourselves, constantly longing, on this form.
We descend to the street and inhale a health of air
To our sepulchral hollows. Love of the real

Is soft in three-four cornered fragrances
From five-six cornered leaves, and green, the signal
To the lover, and blue, as of a secret place

In the anonymous color of the universe.
Our breath is like a desperate element
That we must calm, the origin of a mother tongue

With which to speak to her, the capable
In the midst of foreignness, the syllable
Of recognition, avowal, impassioned cry,

The cry that contains its converse in itself,
In which looks and feelings mingle and are part
As a quick answer modifies a question,

Not wholly spoken in a conversation between
Two bodies disembodied in their talk,
Too fragile, too immediate for any speech.

IX

We keep coming back and coming back
To the real: to the hotel instead of the hymns
That fall upon it out of the wind. We seek

The poem of pure reality, untouched
By trope or deviation, straight to the word,
Straight to the transfixing object, to the object

At the exactest point at which it is itself,
Transfixing by being purely what it is,
A view of New Haven, say, through the certain eye,

The eye made clear of uncertainty, with the sight
Of simple seeing, without reflection. We seek
Nothing beyond reality. Within it,

Everything, the spirit's alchemicana
Included, the spirit that goes roundabout
And through included, not merely the visible,

The solid, but the movable, the moment,
The coming on of feasts and the habits of saints,
The pattern of the heavens and high, night air.

X

It is fatal in the moon and empty there.
But, here, allons. The enigmatical
Beauty of each beautiful enigma

Becomes amassed in a total double-thing.
We do not know what is real and what is not.
We say of the moon, it is haunted by the man

Of bronze whose mind was made up and who, therefore,
    died.
We are not men of bronze and we are not dead.
His spirit is imprisoned in constant change.

But ours is not imprisoned. It resides
In a permanence composed of impermanence,
In a faithfulness as against the lunar light,

So that morning and evening are like promises kept,
So that the approaching sun and its arrival,
Its evening feast and the following festival,

This faithfulness of reality, this mode,
This tendance and venerable holding-in
Make gay the hallucinations in surfaces.

XI

In the metaphysical streets of the physical town
We remember the lion of Juda and we save
The phrase . . . Say of each lion of the spirit

It is a cat of a sleek transparency
That shines with a nocturnal shine alone.
The great cat must stand potent in the sun.

The phrase grows weak. The fact takes up the strength
Of the phrase. It contrives the self-same evocations
And Juda becomes New Haven or else must.

In the metaphysical streets, the profoundest forms
Go with the walker subtly walking there.
These he destroys with wafts of wakening,

Free from their majesty and yet in need
Of majesty, of an invincible clou,
A minimum of making in the mind,

A verity of the most veracious men,
The propounding of four seasons and twelve months,
The brilliancy at the central of the earth.

XII

The poem is the cry of its occasion,
Part of the res itself and not about it.
The poet speaks the poem as it is,

Not as it was: part of the reverberation
Of a windy night as it is, when the marble statues
Are like newspapers blown by the wind. He speaks

By sight and insight as they are. There is no
Tomorrow for him. The wind will have passed by,
The statues will have gone back to be things about.

The mobile and the immobile flickering
In the area between is and was are leaves,
Leaves burnished in autumnal burnished trees

And leaves in whirlings in the gutters, whirlings
Around and away, resembling the presence of thought,
Resembling the presences of thoughts, as if,

In the end, in the whole psychology, the self,
The town, the weather, in a casual litter,
Together, said words of the world are the life of the world.

XIII

The ephebe is solitary in his walk.
He skips the journalism of subjects, seeks out
The perquisites of sanctity, enjoys

A strong mind in a weak neighborhood and is
A serious man without the serious,
Inactive in his singular respect.

He is neither priest nor proctor at low eve,
Under the birds, among the perilous owls,
In the big X of the returning primitive.

It is a fresh spiritual that he defines,
A coldness in a long, too-constant warmth,
A thing on the side of a house, not deep in a cloud,

A difficulty that we predicate:
The difficulty of the visible
To the nations of the clear invisible,

The actual landscape with its actual horns
Of baker and butcher blowing, as if to hear,
Hear hard, gets at an essential integrity.

XIV

The dry eucalyptus seeks god in the rainy cloud.
Professor Eucalyptus of New Haven seeks him
In New Haven with an eye that does not look

Beyond the object. He sits in his room, beside
The window, close to the ramshackle spout in which
The rain falls with a ramshackle sound. He seeks

God in the object itself, without much choice.
It is a choice of the commodious adjective
For what he sees, it comes in the end to that:

The description that makes it divinity, still speech
As it touches the point of reverberation—not grim
Reality but reality grimly seen

And spoken in paradisal parlance new
And in any case never grim, the human grim
That is part of the indifference of the eye

Indifferent to what it sees. The tink-tonk
Of the rain in the spout is not a substitute.
It is of the essence not yet well perceived.

XV

He preserves himself against the repugnant rain
By an instinct for a rainless land, the self
Of his self, come at upon wide delvings of wings.

The instinct for heaven had its counterpart:
The instinct for earth, for New Haven, for his room,
The gay tournamonde as of a single world

In which he is and as and is are one.
For its counterpart a kind of counterpoint
Irked the wet wallows of the water-spout.

The rain kept falling loudly in the trees
And on the ground. The hibernal dark that hung
In primavera, the shadow of bare rock,

Becomes the rock of autumn, glittering,
Ponderable source of each imponderable,
The weight we lift with the finger of a dream,

The heaviness we lighten by light will,
By the hand of desire, faint, sensitive, the soft
Touch and trouble of the touch of the actual hand.

XVI

Among time's images, there is not one
Of this present, the venerable mask above
The dilapidation of dilapidations.

The oldest-newest day is the newest alone.
The oldest-newest night does not creak by,
With lanterns, like a celestial ancientness.

Silently it heaves its youthful sleep from the sea—
The Oklahoman—the Italian blue
Beyond the horizon with its masculine,

Their eyes closed, in a young palaver of lips.
And yet the wind whimpers oldly of old age
In the western night. The venerable mask,

In this perfection, occasionally speaks
And something of death's poverty is heard.
This should be tragedy's most moving face.

It is a bough in the electric light
And exhalations in the eaves, so little
To indicate the total leaflessness.

XVII

The color is almost the color of comedy,
Not quite. It comes to the point and at the point,
It fails. The strength at the center is serious.

Perhaps instead of failing it rejects
As a serious strength rejects pin-idleness.
A blank underlies the trials of device,

The dominant blank, the unapproachable.
This is the mirror of the high serious:
Blue verdured into a damask's lofty symbol,

Gold easings and ouncings and fluctuations of thread
And beetling of belts and lights of general stones,
Like blessed beams from out a blessed bush

Or the wasted figurations of the wastes
Of night, time and the imagination,
Saved and beholden, in a robe of rays.

These fitful sayings are, also, of tragedy:
The serious reflection is composed
Neither of comic nor tragic but of commonplace.

XVIII

It is the window that makes it difficult
To say good-by to the past and to live and to be
In the present state of things as, say, to paint

In the present state of painting and not the state
Of thirty years ago. It is looking out
Of the window and walking in the street and seeing,

As if the eyes were the present or part of it,
As if the ears heard any shocking sound,
As if life and death were ever physical.

The life and death of this carpenter depend
On a fuchsia in a can—and iridescences
Of petals that will never be realized,

Things not yet true which he perceives through truth,
Or thinks he does, as he perceives the present,
Or thinks he does, a carpenter's iridescences,

Wooden, the model for astral apprentices,
A city slapped up like a chest of tools,
The eccentric exterior of which the clocks talk.

XIX

The moon rose in the mind and each thing there
Picked up its radial aspect in the night,
Prostrate below the singleness of its will.

That which was public green turned private gray.
At another time, the radial aspect came
From a different source. But there was always one:

A century in which everything was part
Of that century and of its aspect, a personage,
A man who was the axis of his time,

An image that begot its infantines,
Imaginary poles whose intelligence
Streamed over chaos their civilities.

What is the radial aspect of this place,
This present colony of a colony
Of colonies, a sense in the changing sense

Of things? A figure like Ecclesiast,
Rugged and luminous, chants in the dark
A text that is an answer, although obscure.

XX

The imaginative transcripts were like clouds,
Today; and the transcripts of feeling, impossible
To distinguish. The town was a residuum,

A neuter shedding shapes in an absolute.
Yet the transcripts of it when it was blue remain;
And the shapes that it took in feeling, the persons that

It became, the nameless, flitting characters—
These actors still walk in a twilight muttering lines.
It may be that they mingle, clouds and men, in the air

Or street or about the corners of a man,
Who sits thinking in the corners of a room.
In this chamber the pure sphere escapes the impure,

Because the thinker himself escapes. And yet
To have evaded clouds and men leaves him
A naked being with a naked will

And everything to make. He may evade
Even his own will and in his nakedness
Inhabit the hypnosis of that sphere.

XXI

But he may not. He may not evade his will,
Nor the wills of other men; and he cannot evade
The will of necessity, the will of wills—

Romanza out of the black shepherd's isle,
Like the constant sound of the water of the sea
In the hearing of the shepherd and his black forms;

Out of the isle, but not of any isle.
Close to the senses there lies another isle
And there the senses give and nothing take,

The opposite of Cythère, an isolation
At the center, the object of the will, this place,
The things around—the alternate romanza

Out of the surfaces, the windows, the walls,
The bricks grown brittle in time's poverty,
The clear. A celestial mode is paramount,

If only in the branches sweeping in the rain:
The two romanzas, the distant and the near,
Are a single voice in the boo-ha of the wind.

XXII

Professor Eucalyptus said, "The search
For reality is as momentous as
The search for god." It is the philosopher's search

For an interior made exterior
And the poet's search for the same exterior made
Interior: breathless things broodingly abreath

With the inhalations of original cold
And of original earliness. Yet the sense
Of cold and earliness is a daily sense,

Not the predicate of bright origin.
Creation is not renewed by images
Of lone wanderers. To re-create, to use

The cold and earliness and bright origin
Is to search. Likewise to say of the evening star,
The most ancient light in the most ancient sky,

That it is wholly an inner light, that it shines
From the sleepy bosom of the real, re-creates,
Searches a possible for its possibleness.

XXIII

The sun is half the world, half everything,
The bodiless half. There is always this bodiless half,
This illumination, this elevation, this future

Or, say, the late going colors of that past,
Effete green, the woman in black cassimere.
If, then, New Haven is half sun, what remains,

At evening, after dark, is the other half,
Lighted by space, big over those that sleep,
Of the single future of night, the single sleep,

As of a long, inevitable sound,
A kind of cozening and coaxing sound,
And the goodness of lying in a maternal sound,

Unfretted by day's separate, several selves,
Being part of everything come together as one.
In this identity, disembodiments

Still keep occurring. What is, uncertainly,
Desire prolongs its adventure to create
Forms of farewell, furtive among green ferns.

XXIV

The consolations of space are nameless things.
It was after the neurosis of winter. It was
In the genius of summer that they blew up

The statue of Jove among the boomy clouds.
It took all day to quieten the sky
And then to refill its emptiness again,

So that at the edge of afternoon, not over,
Before the thought of evening had occurred
Or the sound of Incomincia had been set,

There was a clearing, a readiness for first bells,
An opening for outpouring, the hand was raised:
There was a willingness not yet composed,

A knowing that something certain had been proposed,
Which, without the statue, would be new,
An escape from repetition, a happening

In space and the self, that touched them both at once
And alike, a point of the sky or of the earth
Or of a town poised at the horizon's dip.

XXV

Life fixed him, wandering on the stair of glass,
With its attentive eyes. And, as he stood,
On his balcony, outsensing distances,

There were looks that caught him out of empty air.
C'est toujours la vie qui me regarde . . . This was
Who watched him, always, for unfaithful thought.

This sat beside his bed, with its guitar,
To keep him from forgetting, without a word,
A note or two disclosing who it was.

Nothing about him ever stayed the same,
Except this hidalgo and his eye and tune,
The shawl across one shoulder and the hat.

The commonplace became a rumpling of blazons.
What was real turned into something most unreal,
Bare beggar-tree, hung low for fruited red

In isolated moments—isolations
Were false. The hidalgo was permanent, abstract,
A hatching that stared and demanded an answering look.

XXVI

How facilely the purple blotches fell
On the walk, purple and blue, and red and gold,
Blooming and beaming and voluming colors out.

Away from them, capes, along the afternoon Sound,
Shook off their dark marine in lapis light.
The sea shivered in transcendent change, rose up

As rain and booming, gleaming, blowing, swept
The wateriness of green wet in the sky.
Mountains appeared with greater eloquence

Than that of their clouds. These lineaments were the earth,
Seen as inamorata, of loving fame
Added and added out of a fame-full heart . . .

But, here, the inamorata, without distance
And thereby lost, and naked or in rags,
Shrunk in the poverty of being close,

Touches, as one hand touches another hand,
Or as a voice that, speaking without form,
Gritting the ear, whispers humane repose.

XXVII

A scholar, in his Segmenta, left a note,
As follows, "The Ruler of Reality,
If more unreal than New Haven, is not

A real ruler, but rules what is unreal."
In addition, there were draftings of him, thus:
"He is the consort of the Queen of Fact.

Sunrise is his garment's hem, sunset is hers.
He is the theorist of life, not death,
The total excellence of its total book."

Again, "The sibilance of phrases is his
Or partly his. His voice is audible,
As the fore-meaning in music is." Again,

"This man abolishes by being himself
That which is not ourselves: the regalia,
The attributions, the plume and helmet-ho."

Again, "He has thought it out, he thinks it out,
As he has been and is and, with the Queen
Of Fact, lies at his ease beside the sea."

XXVIII

If it should be true that reality exists
In the mind: the tin plate, the loaf of bread on it,
The long-bladed knife, the little to drink and her

Misericordia, it follows that
Real and unreal are two in one: New Haven
Before and after one arrives or, say,

Bergamo on a postcard, Rome after dark,
Sweden described, Salzburg with shaded eyes
Or Paris in conversation at a café.

This endlessly elaborating poem
Displays the theory of poetry,
As the life of poetry. A more severe,

More harassing master would extemporize
Subtler, more urgent proof that the theory
Of poetry is the theory of life,

As it is, in the intricate evasions of as,
In things seen and unseen, created from nothingness,
The heavens, the hells, the worlds, the longed-for lands.

XXIX

In the land of the lemon trees, yellow and yellow were
Yellow-blue, yellow-green, pungent with citron-sap,
Dangling and spangling, the mic-mac of mocking birds.

In the land of the elm trees, wandering mariners
Looked on big women, whose ruddy-ripe images
Wreathed round and round the round wreath of autumn.

They rolled their r's, there, in the land of the citrons.
In the land of big mariners, the words they spoke
Were mere brown clods, mere catching weeds of talk.

When the mariners came to the land of the lemon trees,
At last, in that blond atmosphere, bronzed hard,
They said, "We are back once more in the land of the elm
        trees,

But folded over, turned round." It was the same,
Except for the adjectives, an alteration
Of words that was a change of nature, more

Than the difference that clouds make over a town.
The countrymen were changed and each constant thing.
Their dark-colored words had redescribed the citrons.

XXX

The last leaf that is going to fall has fallen.
The robins are là-bas, the squirrels, in tree-caves,
Huddle together in the knowledge of squirrels.

The wind has blown the silence of summer away.
It buzzes beyond the horizon or in the ground:
In mud under ponds, where the sky used to be reflected.

The barrenness that appears is an exposing.
It is not part of what is absent, a halt
For farewells, a sad hanging on for remembrances.

It is a coming on and a coming forth.
The pines that were fans and fragrances emerge,
Staked solidly in a gusty grappling with rocks.

The glass of the air becomes an element—
It was something imagined that has been washed away.
A clearness has returned. It stands restored.

It is not an empty clearness, a bottomless sight.
It is a visibility of thought,
In which hundreds of eyes, in one mind, see at once.

XXXI

The less legible meanings of sounds, the little reds
Not often realized, the lighter words
In the heavy drum of speech, the inner men

Behind the outer shields, the sheets of music
In the strokes of thunder, dead candles at the window
When day comes, fire-foams in the motions of the sea,

Flickings from finikin to fine finikin
And the general fidget from busts of Constantine
To photographs of the late president, Mr. Blank,

These are the edgings and inchings of final form,
The swarming activities of the formulae
Of statement, directly and indirectly getting at,

Like an evening evoking the spectrum of violet,
A philosopher practicing scales on his piano,
A woman writing a note and tearing it up.

It is not in the premise that reality
Is a solid. It may be a shade that traverses
A dust, a force that traverses a shade.

Things of August

I

These locusts by day, these crickets by night
Are the instruments on which to play
Of an old and disused ambit of the soul
Or of a new aspect, bright in discovery—

A disused ambit of the spirit's way,
The sort of thing that August crooners sing,
By a pure fountain, that was a ghost, and is,
Under the sun-slides of a sloping mountain;

Or else a new aspect, say the spirit's sex,
Its attitudes, its answers to attitudes
And the sex of its voices, as the voice of one
Meets nakedly another's naked voice.

Nothing is lost, loud locusts. No note fails.
These sounds are long in the living of the ear.
The honky-tonk out of the somnolent grasses
Is a memorizing, a trying out, to keep.

II

We make, although inside an egg,
Variations on the words spread sail.

The morning-glories grow in the egg.
It is full of the myrrh and camphor of summer

And Adirondack glittering. The cat hawks it
And the hawk cats it and we say spread sail,

Spread sail, we say spread white, spread way.
The shell is a shore. The egg of the sea

And the egg of the sky are in shells, in walls, in skins
And the egg of the earth lies deep within an egg.

Spread outward. Crack the round dome. Break through.
Have liberty not as the air within a grave

Or down a well. Breathe freedom, oh, my native,
In the space of horizons that neither love nor hate.

III

High poetry and low:
Experience in perihelion
Or in the penumbra of summer night—

The solemn sentences,
Like interior intonations,
The speech of truth in its true solitude,
A nature that is created in what it says,
The peace of the last intelligence;

Or the same thing without desire,
He that in this intelligence
Mistakes it for a world of objects,
Which, being green and blue, appease him,
By chance, or happy chance, or happiness,
According to his thought, in the Mediterranean
Of the quiet of the middle of the night,
With the broken statues standing on the shore.

IV

The sad smell of the lilacs—one remembered it,
Not as the fragrance of Persephone,
Nor of a widow Dooley,
But as of an exhumation returned to earth,

The rich earth, of its own self made rich,
Fertile of its own leaves and days and wars,
Of its brown wheat rapturous in the wind,
The nature of its women in the air,

The stern voices of its necessitous men,
This chorus as of those that wanted to live.
The sentiment of the fatal is a part
Of filial love. Or is it the element,

An approximation of an element,
A little thing to think of on Sunday walks,
Something not to be mentioned to Mrs. Dooley,
An arrogant dagger darting its arrogance,

In the parent's hand, perhaps parental love?
One wished that there had been a season,
Longer and later, in which the lilacs opened
And spread about them a warmer, rosier odor.

V

We'll give the week-end to wisdom, to Weisheit, the rabbi,
Lucidity of his city, joy of his nation,
The state of circumstance.

The thinker as reader reads what has been written.
He wears the words he reads to look upon
Within his being,

A crown within him of crispest diamonds,
A reddened garment falling to his feet,
A hand of light to turn the page,

A finger with a ring to guide his eye
From line to line, as we lie on the grass and listen
To that which has no speech,

The voluble intentions of the symbols,
The ghostly celebrations of the picnic,
The secretions of insight.

VI

The world imagines for the beholder.
He is born the blank mechanic of the mountains,

The blank frere of fields, their matin laborer.
He is the possessed of sense not the possessor.

He does not change the sea from crumpled tinfoil
To chromatic crawler. But it is changed.

He does not raise the rousing of fresh light
On the still, black-slatted eastward shutters.

The woman is chosen but not by him,
Among the endlessly emerging accords.

The world? The inhuman as human? That which thinks not,
Feels not, resembling thought, resembling feeling?

It habituates him to the invisible,
By its faculty of the exceptional,

The faculty of ellipses and deviations,
In which he exists but never as himself.

VII

He turned from the tower to the house,
From the spun sky and the high and deadly view,
To the novels on the table,
The geraniums on the sill.

He could understand the things at home.
And being up high had helped him when up high,
As if on a taller tower
He would be certain to see

That, in the shadowless atmosphere,
The knowledge of things lay round but unperceived:
The height was not quite proper;
The position was wrong.

It was curious to have to descend
And, seated in the nature of his chair,
To feel the satisfactions
Of that transparent air.

VIII

When was it that the particles became
The whole man, that tempers and beliefs became
Temper and belief and that differences lost
Difference and were one? It had to be
In the presence of a solitude of the self,
An expanse and the abstraction of an expanse,
A zone of time without the ticking of clocks,
A color that moved us with forgetfulness.
When was it that we heard the voice of union?

Was it as we sat in the park and the archaic form
Of a woman with a cloud on her shoulder rose
Against the trees and then against the sky
And the sense of the archaic touched us at once
In a movement of the outlines of similarity?

We resembled one another at the sight.
The forgetful color of the autumn day
Was full of these archaic forms, giants
Of sense, evoking one thing in many men,
Evoking an archaic space, vanishing
In the space, leaving an outline of the size
Of the impersonal person, the wanderer,
The father, the ancestor, the bearded peer,
The total of human shadows bright as glass.

IX

A new text of the world,
A scribble of fret and fear and fate,

From a bravura of the mind,
A courage of the eye,

In which, for all the breathings
From the edge of night,
And for all the white voices
That were rosen once,

The meanings are our own—
It is a text that we shall be needing
To be the footing of noon,
The pillar of midnight,

That comes from ourselves, neither from knowing
Nor not knowing, yet free from question,
Because we wanted it so
And it had to be,

A text of intelligent men
At the center of the unintelligible,
As in a hermitage, for us to think,
Writing and reading the rigid inscription.

X

The mornings grow silent, the never-tiring wonder.
The trees are reappearing in poverty.

Without rain, there is the sadness of rain
And an air of lateness. The moon is a tricorn

Waved in pale adieu. The rex Impolitor
Will come stamping here, the ruler of less than men,

In less than nature. He is not here yet.
Here the adult one is still banded with fulgor,

Is still warm with the love with which she came,
Still touches solemnly with what she was

And willed. She has given too much, but not enough.
She is exhausted and a little old.

Angel Surrounded by Paysans

One of the countrymen:
                                        There is
    A welcome at the door to which no one comes?
The angel:
    I am the angel of reality,
    Seen for a moment standing in the door.

    I have neither ashen wing nor wear of ore
    And live without a tepid aureole,

    Or stars that follow me, not to attend,
    But, of my being and its knowing, part.

    I am one of you and being one of you
    Is being and knowing what I am and know.

    Yet I am the necessary angel of earth,
    Since, in my sight, you see the earth again,

    Cleared of its stiff and stubborn, man-locked set,
    And, in my hearing, you hear its tragic drone

    Rise liquidly in liquid lingerings,
    Like watery words awash; like meanings said

    By repetitions of half-meanings. Am I not,
    Myself, only half of a figure of a sort,

    A figure half seen, or seen for a moment, a man
    Of the mind, an apparition apparelled in

    Apparels of such lightest look that a turn
    Of my shoulder and quickly, too quickly, I am gone?

THE ROCK

(1954)

An Old Man Asleep

The two worlds are asleep, are sleeping, now.
A dumb sense possesses them in a kind of solemnity.

The self and the earth—your thoughts, your feelings,
Your beliefs and disbeliefs, your whole peculiar plot;

The redness of your reddish chestnut trees,
The river motion, the drowsy motion of the river R.

The Irish Cliffs of Moher

Who is my father in this world, in this house,
At the spirit's base?

My father's father, his father's father, his—
Shadows like winds

Go back to a parent before thought, before speech,
At the head of the past.

They go to the cliffs of Moher rising out of the mist,
Above the real,

Rising out of present time and place, above
The wet, green grass.

This is not landscape, full of the somnambulations
Of poetry

And the sea. This is my father or, maybe,
It is as he was,

A likeness, one of the race of fathers: earth
And sea and air.

The Plain Sense of Things

After the leaves have fallen, we return
To a plain sense of things. It is as if
We had come to an end of the imagination,
Inanimate in an inert savoir.

It is difficult even to choose the adjective
For this blank cold, this sadness without cause.
The great structure has become a minor house.
No turban walks across the lessened floors.

The greenhouse never so badly needed paint.
The chimney is fifty years old and slants to one side.
A fantastic effort has failed, a repetition
In a repetitiousness of men and flies.

Yet the absence of the imagination had
Itself to be imagined. The great pond,
The plain sense of it, without reflections, leaves,
Mud, water like dirty glass, expressing silence

Of a sort, silence of a rat come out to see,
The great pond and its waste of the lilies, all this
Had to be imagined as an inevitable knowledge,
Required, as a necessity requires.

One of the Inhabitants of the West

Our divinations,
Mechanisms of angelic thought,
The means of prophecy,

Alert us most
At evening's one star
And its pastoral text,

When the establishments
Of wind and light and cloud
Await an arrival,

A reader of the text,
A reader without a body,
Who reads quietly:

"Horrid figures of Medusa,
These accents explicate
The sparkling fall of night
On Europe, to the last Alp,
And the sheeted Atlantic.

These are not banlieus
Lacking men of stone,
In a well-rosed two-light
Of their own.
I am the archangel of evening and praise
This one star's blaze.
Suppose it was a drop of blood . . .
So much guilt lies buried
Beneath the innocence
Of autumn days."

Lebensweisheitspielerei

Weaker and weaker, the sunlight falls
In the afternoon. The proud and the strong
Have departed.

Those that are left are the unaccomplished,
The finally human,
Natives of a dwindled sphere.

Their indigence is an indigence
That is an indigence of the light,
A stellar pallor that hangs on the threads.

Little by little, the poverty
Of autumnal space becomes
A look, a few words spoken.

Each person completely touches us
With what he is and as he is,
In the stale grandeur of annihilation.

The Hermitage at the Center

The leaves on the macadam make a noise—
    How soft the grass on which the desired
    Reclines in the temperature of heaven—

Like tales that were told the day before yesterday—
    Sleek in a natural nakedness,
    She attends the tintinnabula—

And the wind sways like a great thing tottering—
    Of birds called up by more than the sun,
    Birds of more wit, that substitute—

Which suddenly is all dissolved and gone—
    Their intelligible twittering
    For unintelligible thought.

And yet this end and this beginning are one,
    And one last look at the ducks is a look
    At lucent children round her in a ring.

The Green Plant

Silence is a shape that has passed.
Otu-bre's lion-roses have turned to paper
And the shadows of the trees
Are like wrecked umbrellas.

The effete vocabulary of summer
No longer says anything.
The brown at the bottom of red
The orange far down in yellow,

Are falsifications from a sun
In a mirror, without heat,
In a constant secondariness,
A turning down toward finality—

Except that a green plant glares, as you look
At the legend of the maroon and olive forest,
Glares, outside of the legend, with the barbarous green
Of the harsh reality of which it is part.

Madame La Fleurie

Weight him down, O side-stars, with the great weightings of
    the end.
Seal him there. He looked in a glass of the earth and
    thought he lived in it.
Now, he brings all that he saw into the earth, to the waiting
    parent.
His crisp knowledge is devoured by her, beneath a dew.

Weight him, weight, weight him with the sleepiness of the
    moon.
It was only a glass because he looked in it. It was nothing
    he could be told.
It was a language he spoke, because he must, yet did not
    know.
It was a page he had found in the handbook of heartbreak.

The black fugatos are strumming the blacknesses of
    black . . .
The thick strings stutter the finial gutturals.
He does not lie there remembering the blue-jay, say the jay.

His grief is that his mother should feed on him, himself and
    what he saw,
In that distant chamber, a bearded queen, wicked in her
    dead light.

To an Old Philosopher in Rome

On the threshold of heaven, the figures in the street
Become the figures of heaven, the majestic movement
Of men growing small in the distances of space,
Singing, with smaller and still smaller sound,
Unintelligible absolution and an end—

The threshold, Rome, and that more merciful Rome
Beyond, the two alike in the make of the mind.
It is as if in a human dignity
Two parallels become one, a perspective, of which
Men are part both in the inch and in the mile.

How easily the blown banners change to wings . . .
Things dark on the horizons of perception,
Become accompaniments of fortune, but
Of the fortune of the spirit, beyond the eye,
Not of its sphere, and yet not far beyond,

The human end in the spirit's greatest reach,
The extreme of the known in the presence of the extreme
Of the unknown. The newsboys' muttering
Becomes another murmuring; the smell
Of medicine, a fragrantness not to be spoiled . . .

The bed, the books, the chair, the moving nuns,
The candle as it evades the sight, these are
The sources of happiness in the shape of Rome,
A shape within the ancient circles of shapes,
And these beneath the shadow of a shape

In a confusion on bed and books, a portent
On the chair, a moving transparence on the nuns,
A light on the candle tearing against the wick
To join a hovering excellence, to escape
From fire and be part only of that of which

Fire is the symbol: the celestial possible.
Speak to your pillow as if it was yourself.
Be orator but with an accurate tongue
And without eloquence, O, half-asleep,
Of the pity that is the memorial of this room,

So that we feel, in this illumined large,
The veritable small, so that each of us
Beholds himself in you, and hears his voice
In yours, master and commiserable man,
Intent on your particles of nether-do,

Your dozing in the depths of wakefulness,
In the warmth of your bed, at the edge of your chair, alive
Yet living in two worlds, impenitent
As to one, and, as to one, most penitent,
Impatient for the grandeur that you need

In so much misery; and yet finding it
Only in misery, the afflatus of ruin,
Profound poetry of the poor and of the dead,
As in the last drop of the deepest blood,
As it falls from the heart and lies there to be seen,

Even as the blood of an empire, it might be,
For a citizen of heaven though still of Rome.
It is poverty's speech that seeks us out the most.
It is older than the oldest speech of Rome.
This is the tragic accent of the scene.

And you—it is you that speak it, without speech,
The loftiest syllables among loftiest things,
The one invulnerable man among
Crude captains, the naked majesty, if you like,
Of bird-nest arches and of rain-stained-vaults.

The sounds drift in. The buildings are remembered.
The life of the city never lets go, nor do you
Ever want it to. It is part of the life in your room.
Its domes are the architecture of your bed.
The bells keep on repeating solemn names

In choruses and choirs of choruses,
Unwilling that mercy should be a mystery
Of silence, that any solitude of sense
Should give you more than their peculiar chords
And reverberations clinging to whisper still.

It is a kind of total grandeur at the end,
With every visible thing enlarged and yet
No more than a bed, a chair and moving nuns,
The immensest theatre, the pillared porch,
The book and candle in your ambered room,

Total grandeur of a total edifice,
Chosen by an inquisitor of structures
For himself. He stops upon this threshold,
As if the design of all his words takes form
And frame from thinking and is realized.

Vacancy in the Park

March . . . Someone has walked across the snow,
Someone looking for he knows not what.

It is like a boat that has pulled away
From a shore at night and disappeared.

It is like a guitar left on a table
By a woman, who has forgotten it.

It is like the feeling of a man
Come back to see a certain house.

The four winds blow through the rustic arbor,
Under its mattresses of vines.

The Poem That Took the Place of a Mountain

There it was, word for word,
The poem that took the place of a mountain.

He breathed its oxygen,
Even when the book lay turned in the dust of his table.

It reminded him how he had needed
A place to go to in his own direction,

How he had recomposed the pines,
Shifted the rocks and picked his way among clouds,

For the outlook that would be right,
Where he would be complete in an unexplained completion:

The exact rock where his inexactnesses
Would discover, at last, the view toward which they had
    edged,

Where he could lie and, gazing down at the sea,
Recognize his unique and solitary home.

Two Illustrations That the World
Is What You Make of It

I

The Constant Disquisition of the Wind

The sky seemed so small that winter day,
A dirty light on a lifeless world,
Contracted like a withered stick.

It was not the shadow of cloud and cold,
But a sense of the distance of the sun—
The shadow of a sense of his own,

A knowledge that the actual day
Was so much less. Only the wind
Seemed large and loud and high and strong.

And as he thought within the thought
Of the wind, not knowing that that thought
Was not his thought, nor anyone's,

The appropriate image of himself,
So formed, became himself and he breathed
The breath of another nature as his own,

But only its momentary breath,
Outside of and beyond the dirty light,
That never could be animal,

A nature still without a shape,
Except his own—perhaps, his own
In a Sunday's violent idleness.

II

The World Is Larger in Summer

He left half a shoulder and half a head
To recognize him in after time.

These marbles lay weathering in the grass
When the summer was over, when the change

Of summer and of the sun, the life
Of summer and of the sun, were gone.

He had said that everything possessed
The power to transform itself, or else,

And what meant more, to be transformed.
He discovered the colors of the moon

In a single spruce, when, suddenly,
The tree stood dazzling in the air

And blue broke on him from the sun,
A bullioned blue, a blue abulge,

Like daylight, with time's bellishings,
And sensuous summer stood full-height.

The master of the spruce, himself,
Became transformed. But his mastery

Left only the fragments found in the grass,
From his project, as finally magnified.

Prologues To What Is Possible

I

There was an ease of mind that was like being alone in a
    boat at sea,
A boat carried forward by waves resembling the bright backs
    of rowers,
Gripping their oars, as if they were sure of the way to their
    destination,
Bending over and pulling themselves erect on the wooden
    handles,
Wet with water and sparkling in the one-ness of their
    motion.

The boat was built of stones that had lost their weight and
    being no longer heavy
Had left in them only a brilliance, of unaccustomed origin,
So that he that stood up in the boat leaning and looking
    before him

Did not pass like someone voyaging out of and beyond the
    familiar.
He belonged to the far-foreign departure of his vessel and
    was part of it,
Part of the speculum of fire on its prow, its symbol,
    whatever it was,
Part of the glass-like sides on which it glided over the salt-
    stained water,
As he traveled alone, like a man lured on by a syllable
    without any meaning,
A syllable of which he felt, with an appointed sureness,
That it contained the meaning into which he wanted to
    enter,
A meaning which, as he entered it, would shatter the boat
    and leave the oarsmen quiet
As at a point of central arrival, an instant moment, much or
    little,
Removed from any shore, from any man or woman, and
    needing none.

II

The metaphor stirred his fear. The object with which he was
    compared
Was beyond his recognizing. By this he knew that likeness
    of him extended
Only a little way, and not beyond, unless between himself
And things beyond resemblance there was this and that
    intended to be recognized,
The this and that in the enclosures of hypotheses
On which men speculated in summer when they were half
    asleep.

What self, for example, did he contain that had not yet been
    loosed,
Snarling in him for discovery as his attentions spread,
As if all his hereditary lights were suddenly increased
By an access of color, a new and unobserved, slight
    dithering,

The smallest lamp, which added its puissant flick, to which
    he gave
A name and privilege over the ordinary of his
    commonplace—

A flick which added to what was real and its vocabulary,
The way some first thing coming into Northern trees
Adds to them the whole vocabulary of the South,
The way the earliest single light in the evening sky, in
    spring,
Creates a fresh universe out of nothingness by adding itself,
The way a look or a touch reveals its unexpected
    magnitudes.

Looking Across the Fields and Watching the Birds Fly

Among the more irritating minor ideas
Of Mr. Homburg during his visits home
To Concord, at the edge of things, was this:

To think away the grass, the trees, the clouds,
Not to transform them into other things,
Is only what the sun does every day,

Until we say to ourselves that there may be
A pensive nature, a mechanical
And slightly detestable *operandum*, free

From man's ghost, larger and yet a little like,
Without his literature and without his gods . . .
No doubt we live beyond ourselves in air,

In an element that does not do for us,
So well, that which we do for ourselves, too big,
A thing not planned for imagery or belief,

Not one of the masculine myths we used to make,
A transparency through which the swallow weaves,
Without any form or any sense of form,

What we know in what we see, what we feel in what
We hear, what we are, beyond mystic disputation,
In the tumult of integrations out of the sky,

And what we think, a breathing like the wind,
A moving part of a motion, a discovery
Part of a discovery, a change part of a change,

A sharing of color and being part of it.
The afternoon is visibly a source,
Too wide, too irised, to be more than calm,

Too much like thinking to be less than thought,
Obscurest parent, obscurest patriarch,
A daily majesty of meditation,

That comes and goes in silences of its own.
We think, then, as the sun shines or does not.
We think as wind skitters on a pond in a field

Or we put mantles on our words because
The same wind, rising and rising, makes a sound
Like the last muting of winter as it ends.

A new scholar replacing an older one reflects
A moment on this fantasia. He seeks
For a human that can be accounted for.

The spirit comes from the body of the world,
Or so Mr. Homburg thought: the body of a world
Whose blunt laws make an affectation of mind,

The mannerism of nature caught in a glass
And there become a spirit's mannerism,
A glass aswarm with things going as far as they can.

Song of Fixed Accord

Rou-cou spoke the dove,
Like the sooth lord of sorrow,
Of sooth love and sorrow,
And a hail-bow, hail-bow,
To this morrow.

She lay upon the roof,
A little wet of wing and woe,
And she rou-ed there,
Softly she piped among the suns
And their ordinary glare,

The sun of five, the sun of six,
Their ordinariness,
And the ordinariness of seven,
Which she accepted,
Like a fixed heaven,

Not subject to change . . .
Day's invisible beginner,
The lord of love and of sooth sorrow,
Lay on the roof
And made much within her.

The World as Meditation

*J'ai passé trop de temps à travailler mon violon, à voyager.
Mais l'exercice essentiel du compositeur—la méditation—rien
ne l'a jamais suspendu en moi . . . Je vis un rêve permanent,
qui ne s'arrête ni nuit ni jour.*

                                        GEORGES ENESCO

Is it Ulysses that approaches from the east,
The interminable adventurer? The trees are mended.
That winter is washed away. Someone is moving

On the horizon and lifting himself up above it.
A form of fire approaches the cretonnes of Penelope,
Whose mere savage presence awakens the world in which
    she dwells.

She has composed, so long, a self with which to welcome
    him,
Companion to his self for her, which she imagined,
Two in a deep-founded sheltering, friend and dear friend.

The trees had been mended, as an essential exercise
In an inhuman meditation, larger than her own.
No winds like dogs watched over her at night.

She wanted nothing he could not bring her by coming
    alone.
She wanted no fetchings. His arms would be her necklace
And her belt, the final fortune of their desire.

But was it Ulysses? Or was it only the warmth of the sun
On her pillow? The thought kept beating in her like her
    heart.
The two kept beating together. It was only day.

It was Ulysses and it was not. Yet they had met,
Friend and dear friend and a planet's encouragement.
The barbarous strength within her would never fail.

She would talk a little to herself as she combed her hair,
Repeating his name with its patient syllables,
Never forgetting him that kept coming constantly so near.

Long and Sluggish Lines

It makes so little difference, at so much more
Than seventy, where one looks, one has been there before.

Wood-smoke rises through trees, is caught in an upper flow
Of air and whirled away. But it has been often so.

The trees have a look as if they bore sad names
And kept saying over and over one same, same thing,

In a kind of uproar, because an opposite, a contradiction,
Has enraged them and made them want to talk it down.

What opposite? Could it be that yellow patch, the side
Of a house, that makes one think the house is laughing;

Or these—escent—issant pre-personae: first fly,
A comic infanta among the tragic drapings,

Babyishness of forsythia, a snatch of belief,
The spook and makings of the nude magnolia?

. . . Wanderer, this is the pre-history of February.
The life of the poem in the mind has not yet begun.

You were not born yet when the trees were crystal
Nor are you now, in this wakefulness inside a sleep.

A Quiet Normal Life

His place, as he sat and as he thought, was not
In anything that he constructed, so frail,
So barely lit, so shadowed over and naught,

As, for example, a world in which, like snow,
He became an inhabitant, obedient
To gallant notions on the part of cold.

It was here. This was the setting and the time
Of year. Here in his house and in his room,
In his chair, the most tranquil thought grew peaked

And the oldest and the warmest heart was cut
By gallant notions on the part of night—
Both late and alone, above the crickets' chords,

Babbling, each one, the uniqueness of its sound.
There was no fury in transcendent forms.
But his actual candle blazed with artifice.

Final Soliloquy of the Interior Paramour

Light the first light of evening, as in a room
In which we rest and, for small reason, think
The world imagined is the ultimate good.

This is, therefore, the intensest rendezvous.
It is in that thought that we collect ourselves,
Out of all the indifferences, into one thing:

Within a single thing, a single shawl
Wrapped tightly round us, since we are poor, a warmth,
A light, a power, the miraculous influence.

Here, now, we forget each other and ourselves.
We feel the obscurity of an order, a whole,
A knowledge, that which arranged the rendezvous,

Within its vital boundary, in the mind.
We say God and the imagination are one . . .
How high that highest candle lights the dark.

Out of this same light, out of the central mind,
We make a dwelling in the evening air,
In which being there together is enough.

The Rock

I

Seventy Years Later

It is an illusion that we were ever alive,
Lived in the houses of mothers, arranged ourselves
By our own motions in a freedom of air.

Regard the freedom of seventy years ago.
It is no longer air. The houses still stand,
Though they are rigid in rigid emptiness.

Even our shadows, their shadows, no longer remain.
The lives these lived in the mind are at an end.
They never were . . . The sounds of the guitar

Were not and are not. Absurd. The words spoken
Were not and are not. It is not to be believed.
The meeting at noon at the edge of the field seems like

An invention, an embrace between one desperate clod
And another in a fantastic consciousness,
In a queer assertion of humanity:

A theorem proposed between the two—
Two figures in a nature of the sun,
In the sun's design of its own happiness,

As if nothingness contained a métier,
A vital assumption, an impermanence
In its permanent cold, an illusion so desired

That the green leaves came and covered the high rock,
That the lilacs came and bloomed, like a blindness cleaned,
Exclaiming bright sight, as it was satisfied,

In a birth of sight. The blooming and the musk
Were being alive, an incessant being alive,
A particular of being, that gross universe.

II

The Poem as Icon

It is not enough to cover the rock with leaves.
We must be cured of it by a cure of the ground
Or a cure of ourselves, that is equal to a cure

Of the ground, a cure beyond forgetfulness.
And yet the leaves, if they broke into bud,
If they broke into bloom, if they bore fruit,

And if we ate the incipient colorings
Of their fresh culls might be a cure of the ground.
The fiction of the leaves is the icon

Of the poem, the figuration of blessedness,
And the icon is the man. The pearled chaplet of spring,
The magnum wreath of summer, time's autumn snood,

Its copy of the sun, these cover the rock.
These leaves are the poem, the icon and the man.
These are a cure of the ground and of ourselves,

In the predicate that there is nothing else.
They bud and bloom and bear their fruit without change.
They are more than leaves that cover the barren rock.

They bud the whitest eye, the pallidest sprout,
New senses in the engenderings of sense,
The desire to be at the end of distances,

The body quickened and the mind in root.
They bloom as a man loves, as he lives in love.
They bear their fruit so that the year is known,

As if its understanding was brown skin,
The honey in its pulp, the final found,
The plenty of the year and of the world.

In this plenty, the poem makes meanings of the rock,
Of such mixed motion and such imagery
That its barrenness becomes a thousand things

And so exists no more. This is the cure
Of leaves and of the ground and of ourselves.
His words are both the icon and the man.

III

Forms of the Rock in a Night-Hymn

The rock is the gray particular of man's life,
The stone from which he rises, up—and—ho,
The step to the bleaker depths of his descents . . .

The rock is the stern particular of the air,
The mirror of the planets, one by one,
But through man's eye, their silent rhapsodist,

Turquoise the rock, at odious evening bright
With redness that sticks fast to evil dreams;
The difficult rightness of half-risen day.

The rock is the habitation of the whole,
Its strength and measure, that which is near, point A
In a perspective that begins again

At B: the origin of the mango's rind.
It is the rock where tranquil must adduce
Its tranquil self, the main of things, the mind,

The starting point of the human and the end,
That in which space itself is contained, the gate
To the enclosure, day, the things illumined

By day, night and that which night illumines,
Night and its midnight-minting fragrances,
Night's hymn of the rock, as in a vivid sleep.

St. Armorer's Church from the Outside

St. Armorer's was once an immense success.
It rose loftily and stood massively; and to lie
In its church-yard, in the province of St. Armorer's,
Fixed one for good in geranium-colored day.

What is left has the foreign smell of plaster,
The closed-in smell of hay. A sumac grows
On the altar, growing toward the lights, inside.
Reverberations leak and lack among holes . . .

Its chapel rises from Terre Ensevelie,
An ember yes among its cindery noes,
His own: a chapel of breath, an appearance made
For a sign of meaning in the meaningless,

No radiance of dead blaze, but something seen
In a mystic eye, no sign of life but life,
Itself, the presence of the intelligible
In that which is created as its symbol.

It is like a new account of everything old,
Matisse at Vence and a great deal more than that,
A new-colored sun, say, that will soon change forms
And spread hallucinations on every leaf.

The chapel rises, his own, his period,
A civilization formed from the outward blank,
A sacred syllable rising from sacked speech,
The first car out of a tunnel en voyage

Into lands of ruddy-ruby fruits, achieved
Not merely desired, for sale, and market things
That press, strong peasants in a peasant world,
Their purports to a final seriousness—

Final for him, the acceptance of such prose,
Time's given perfections made to seem like less

Than the need of each generation to be itself,
The need to be actual and as it is.

St. Armorer's has nothing of this present,
This *vif*, this dizzle-dazzle of being new
And of becoming, for which the chapel spreads out
Its arches in its vivid element,

In the air of newness of that element,
In an air of freshness, clearness, greenness, blueness,
That which is always beginning because it is part
Of that which is always beginning, over and over.

The chapel underneath St. Armorer's walls,
Stands in a light, its natural light and day,
The origin and keep of its health and his own.
And there he walks and does as he lives and likes.

Note on Moonlight

The one moonlight, in the simple-colored night,
Like a plain poet revolving in his mind
The sameness of his various universe,
Shines on the mere objectiveness of things.

It is as if being was to be observed,
As if, among the possible purposes
Of what one sees, the purpose that comes first,
The surface, is the purpose to be seen,

The property of the moon, what it evokes.
It is to disclose the essential presence, say,
Of a mountain, expanded and elevated almost
Into a sense, an object the less; or else

To disclose in the figure waiting on the road
An object the more, an undetermined form
Between the slouchings of a gunman and a lover,
A gesture in the dark, a fear one feels

In the great vistas of night air, that takes this form,
In the arbors that are as if of Saturn-star.
So, then, this warm, wide, weatherless quietude
Is active with a power, an inherent life,

In spite of the mere objectiveness of things,
Like a cloud-cap in the corner of a looking-glass,
A change of color in the plain poet's mind,
Night and silence disturbed by an interior sound,

The one moonlight, the various universe, intended
So much just to be seen—a purpose, empty
Perhaps, absurd perhaps, but at least a purpose,
Certain and ever more fresh. Ah! Certain, for sure . . .

The Planet on the Table

Ariel was glad he had written his poems.
They were of a remembered time
Or of something seen that he liked.

Other makings of the sun
Were waste and welter
And the ripe shrub writhed.

His self and the sun were one
And his poems, although makings of his self,
Were no less makings of the sun.

It was not important that they survive.
What mattered was that they should bear
Some lineament or character,

Some affluence, if only half-perceived,
In the poverty of their words,
Of the planet of which they were part.

The River of Rivers in Connecticut

There is a great river this side of Stygia,
Before one comes to the first black cataracts
And trees that lack the intelligence of trees.

In that river, far this side of Stygia,
The mere flowing of the water is a gayety,
Flashing and flashing in the sun. On its banks,

No shadow walks. The river is fateful,
Like the last one. But there is no ferryman.
He could not bend against its propelling force.

It is not to be seen beneath the appearances
That tell of it. The steeple at Farmington
Stands glistening and Haddam shines and sways.

It is the third commonness with light and air,
A curriculum, a vigor, a local abstraction . . .
Call it, once more, a river, an unnamed flowing,

Space-filled, reflecting the seasons, the folk-lore
Of each of the senses; call it, again and again,
The river that flows nowhere, like a sea.

Not Ideas About the Thing But the Thing Itself

At the earliest ending of winter,
In March, a scrawny cry from outside
Seemed like a sound in his mind.

He knew that he heard it,
A bird's cry, at daylight or before,
In the early March wind.

The sun was rising at six,
No longer a battered panache above snow . . .
It would have been outside.

It was not from the vast ventriloquism
Of sleep's faded papier-mâché . . .
The sun was coming from outside.

That scrawny cry—it was
A chorister whose c preceded the choir.
It was part of the colossal sun,

Surrounded by its choral rings,
Still far away. It was like
A new knowledge of reality.

LATE POEMS

(1950–1955)

The Sick Man

Bands of black men seem to be drifting in the air,
In the South, bands of thousands of black men,
Playing mouth-organs in the night or, now, guitars.

Here in the North, late, late, there are voices of men,
Voices in chorus, singing without words, remote and deep,
Drifting choirs, long movements and turnings of sounds.

And in a bed in one room, alone, a listener
Waits for the unison of the music of the drifting bands
And the dissolving chorals, waits for it and imagines

The words of winter in which these two will come together,
In the ceiling of the distant room, in which he lies,
The listener, listening to the shadows, seeing them,

Choosing out of himself, out of everything within him,
Speech for the quiet, good hail of himself, good hail, good
    hail,
The peaceful, blissful words, well-tuned, well-sung,
    well-spoken.

As at a Theatre

Another sunlight might make another world,
Green, more or less, in green and blue in blue,
Like taste distasting the first fruit of a vine,
Like an eye too young to grapple its primitive,
Like the artifice of a new reality,
Like the chromatic calendar of time to come.

It might be the candle of another being,
Ragged in unkempt perceptions, that stands
And meditates an image of itself,
Studies and shapes a tallowy image, swarmed

With slight, prismatic reeks not recollected,
A bubble without a wall on which to hang.

The curtains, when pulled, might show another whole,
An azure outre-terre, oranged and rosed,
At the elbow of Copernicus, a sphere,
A universe without life's limp and lack,
Philosophers' end . . . What difference would it make,
So long as the mind, for once, fulfilled itself?

The Desire to Make Love in a Pagoda

Among the second selves, sailor, observe
The rioter that appears when things are changed,

Asserting itself in an element that is free,
In the alien freedom that such selves degustate:

In the first inch of night, the stellar summering
At three-quarters gone, the morning's prescience,

As if, alone on a mountain, it saw far-off
An innocence approaching toward its peak.

Nuns Painting Water-Lilies

These pods are part of the growth of life within life:
Part of the unpredictable sproutings, as of

The youngest, the still fuzz-eyed, odd fleurettes,
That could come in a slight lurching of the scene,

A swerving, a tilting, a little lengthening,
A few hours more of day, the unravelling

Of a ruddier summer, a birth that fetched along
The supernatural of its origin.

Inside our queer chapeaux, we seem, on this bank,
To be part of a tissue, a clearness of the air,

That matches, today, a clearness of the mind.
It is a special day. We mumble the words

Of saints not heard of until now, unnamed,
In aureoles that are over-dazzling crests . . .

We are part of a fraicheur, inaccessible
Or accessible only in the most furtive fiction.

The Role of the Idea in Poetry

Ask of the philosopher why he philosophizes,
Determined thereto, perhaps by his father's ghost,
Permitting nothing to the evening's edge.

The father does not come to adorn the chant.
One father proclaims another, the patriarchs
Of truth. They stride across and are masters of

The chant and discourse there, more than wild weather
Or clouds that hang lateness on the sea. They become
A time existing after much time has passed.

Therein, day settles and thickens round a form—
Blue-bold on its pedestal—that seems to say,
"I am the greatness of the new-found night."

Americana

The first soothsayers of the land, the man
In a field, the man on the side of a hill, all men
In a health of weather, knowing a few, old things,

(Remote from the deadly general of men,
The over-populace of the idea, the voices
Hard to be told from thoughts, the repeated drone

Of other lives becoming a total drone,
A sense separate that receives and holds the rest,
That which is human and yet final, like

A man that looks at himself in a glass and finds
It is the man in the glass that lives, not he.
He is the image, the second, the unreal,

The abstraction. He inhabits another man,
Other men, and not this grass, this valid air.
He is not himself. He is vitally deprived . . .)

These things he thinks of, as the buckskin hoop-la,
In a returning, a seeming of return,
Flaunts that first fortune, which he wanted so much.

The Souls of Women at Night

Now, being invisible, I walk without mantilla,
In the much-horned night, as its chief personage.
Owls warn me and with tuft-eared watches keep

Distance between me and the five-times-sensed,
In these stations, in which nothing has been lost,
Sight least, but metaphysical blindness gained,

The blindness in which seeing would be false,
A fantastic irruption. Salute you, cata-sisters,
Ancient amigas, knowing partisans—

Or is it I that, wandering, know, one-sensed,
Not one of the five, and keep a rendezvous,
Of the loftiest amour, in a human midnight?

A Discovery of Thought

At the antipodes of poetry, dark winter,
When the trees glitter with that which despoils them,
Daylight evaporates, like a sound one hears in sickness.

One is a child again. The gold beards of waterfalls
Are dissolved as in an infancy of blue snow.
It is an arbor against the wind, a pit in the mist,

A trinkling in the parentage of the north,
The cricket of summer forming itself out of ice.
And always at this antipodes, of leaden loaves

Held in the hands of blue men that are lead within,
One thinks that it could be that the first word spoken,
The desire for speech and meaning gallantly fulfilled,

The gathering of the imbecile against his motes
And the wry antipodes whirled round the world away—
One thinks, when the houses of New England catch the first
    sun,

The first word would be of the susceptible being arrived,
The immaculate disclosure of the secret, no more obscured.
The sprawling of winter might suddenly stand erect,

Pronouncing its new life and ours, not autumn's prodigal
    returned,
But an antipodal, far-fetched creature, worthy of birth,
The true tone of the metal of winter in what it says:

The accent of deviation in the living thing
That is its life preserved, the effort to be born
Surviving being born, the event of life.

The Course of a Particular

Today the leaves cry, hanging on branches swept by wind,
Yet the nothingness of winter becomes a little less.
It is still full of icy shades and shapen snow.

The leaves cry . . . One holds off and merely hears the cry.
It is a busy cry, concerning someone else.
And though one says that one is part of everything,

There is a conflict, there is a resistance involved;
And being part is an exertion that declines:
One feels the life of that which gives life as it is.

The leaves cry. It is not a cry of divine attention,
Nor the smoke-drift of puffed-out heroes, nor human cry.
It is the cry of leaves that do not transcend themselves,

In the absence of fantasia, without meaning more
Than they are in the final finding of the ear, in the thing
Itself, until, at last, the cry concerns no one at all.

How Now, O, Brightener . . .

Something of the trouble of the mind
Remains in the sight, and in sayings of the sight,
Of the spring of the year,

Trouble in the spillage and first sparkle of sun,
The green-edged yellow and yellow and blue and blue-
        edged green—
The trouble of the mind

Is a residue, a land, a rain, a warmth,
A time, an apparition and nourishing element
And simple love,

In which the spectra have dewy favor and live
And take from this restlessly unhappy happiness
Their stunted looks.

The Dove in Spring

Brooder, brooder, deep beneath its walls—
A small howling of the dove
Makes something of the little there,

The little and the dark, and that
In which it is and that in which
It is established. There the dove

Makes this small howling, like a thought
That howls in the mind or like a man
Who keeps seeking out his identity

In that which is and is established . . . It howls
Of the great sizes of an outer bush
And the great misery of the doubt of it,

Of stripes of silver that are strips
Like slits across a space, a place
And state of being large and light.

There is this bubbling before the sun,
This howling at one's ear, too far
For daylight and too near for sleep.

Farewell Without a Guitar

Spring's bright paradise has come to this.
Now the thousand-leaved green falls to the ground.
Farewell, my days.

The thousand-leaved red
Comes to this thunder of light
At its autumnal terminal—

A Spanish storm,
A wide, still Aragonese,
In which the horse walks home without a rider,

Head down. The reflections and repetitions,
The blows and buffets of fresh senses
Of the rider that was,

Are a final construction,
Like glass and sun, of male reality
And of that other and her desire.

The Sail of Ulysses

Under the shape of his sail, Ulysses,
Symbol of the seeker, crossing by night
The giant sea, read his own mind.
He said, "As I know, I am and have
The right to be". Guiding his boat
Under the middle stars, he said:

The place
of the poem.
Its theme.

I

"If knowledge and the thing known are one
So that to know a man is to be
That man, to know a place is to be
That place, and it seems to come to that;
And if to know one man is to know all
And if one's sense of a single spot
Is what one knows of the universe,
Then knowledge is the only life,
The only sun of the only day,
The only access to true ease,
The deep comfort of the world and fate.

To know
is to be.

II

There is a human loneliness;
A part of space and solitude,
In which knowledge cannot be denied,
In which nothing of knowledge fails,
The luminous companion, the hand,
The fortifying arm, the profound
Response, the completely answering voice,
That which is more than anything else
The right within us and about us,
Joined, the triumphant vigor, felt,
The inner direction on which we depend,
That which keeps us the little that we are,
The aid of greatness to be and the force.

To know
is the
force to be.

III

This is the true creator, the waver
Waving purpling wands, the thinker
Thinking gold thoughts in a golden mind,
Loftily jingled, radiant,
The joy of meaning in design
Wrenched out of chaos . . . The quiet lamp
For this creator is a lamp
Enlarging like a nocturnal ray
The space in which it stands, the shine
Of darkness, creating from nothingness
Such black constructions, such public shapes
And murky masonry, one wonders
At the finger that brushes this aside
Gigantic in everything but size.

The true
creator.

IV

The unnamed creator of an unknown sphere,
Unknown as yet, unknowable,
Uncertain certainty, Apollo
Imagined among the indigenes
And Eden conceived on Morningside,
The center of the self, the self

The center
of the self.

Of the future, of future man
And future place, when these are known,
A freedom at last from the mystical,
The beginning of a final order,
The order of man's right to be
As he is, the discipline of his scope
Observed as an absolute, himself.

V

A longer, deeper breath sustains
The eloquence of right, since knowing
And being are one: the right to know
And the right to be are one. We come
To knowledge when we come to life.
Yet always there is another life,
A life beyond this present knowing,
A life lighter than this present splendor,
Brighter, perfected and distant away,
Not to be reached but to be known,
Not an attainment of the will
But something illogically received,
A divination, a letting down
From loftiness, misgivings dazzlingly
Resolved in dazzling discovery.
There is no map of paradise.
The great Omnium descends on us
As a free race. We know it, one
By one, in the right of all. Each man
Is an approach to the vigilance
In which the litter of truths becomes
A whole, the day on which the last star
Has been counted, the genealogy
Of gods and men destroyed, the right
To know established as the right to be.
The ancient symbols will be nothing then.
We shall have gone behind the symbols
To that which they symbolized, away
From the rumors of the speech-full domes,

Except for
illogical
receptions.

To the chatter that is then the true legend,
Like glitter ascended into fire.

VI

Master of the world and of himself,
He came to this by knowledge or
Will come. His mind presents the world
And in his mind the world revolves.
The revolutions through day and night,
Through wild spaces of other suns and moons,
Round summer and angular winter and winds,
Are matched by other revolutions
In which the world goes round and round
In the crystal atmospheres of the mind,
Light's comedies, dark's tragedies,
Like things produced by a climate, the world
Goes round in the climates of the mind
And bears its floraisons of imagery.

Presence of an external master of knowledge.

The mind renews the world in a verse,
A passage of music, a paragraph
By a right philosopher: renews
And possesses by sincere insight
In the John-begat-Jacob of what we know,
The flights through space, changing habitudes.

In the generations of thought, man's sons
And heirs are powers of the mind,
His only testament and estate.
He has nothing but the truth to leave.
How then shall the mind be less than free
Since only to know is to be free?

VII

The living man in the present place,
Always, the particular thought
Among Plantagenet abstractions,
Always and always, the difficult inch,

Truth as fate.

On which the vast arches of space
Repose, always, the credible thought
From which the incredible systems spring,
The little confine soon unconfined
In stellar largenesses—these
Are the manifestations of a law
That bends the particulars to the abstract,
Makes them a pack on a giant's back,
A majestic mother's flocking brood,
As if abstractions were, themselves
Particulars of a relative sublime.
This is not poet's ease of mind.
It is the fate that dwells in truth.
We obey the coaxings of our end.

VIII

What is the shape of the sibyl? Not,   Shape of
For a change, the englistered woman, seated   the sibyl
In colorings harmonious, dewed and dashed   of truth.
By them: gorgeous symbol seated
On the seat of halidom, rainbowed,
Piercing the spirit by appearance,
A summing up of the loftiest lives
And their directing sceptre, the crown
And final effulgence and delving show.
It is the sibyl of the self,
The self as sibyl, whose diamond,
Whose chiefest embracing of all wealth
Is poverty, whose jewel found
At the exactest central of the earth
Is need. For this, the sibyl's shape
Is a blind thing fumbling for its form,
A form that is lame, a hand, a back,
A dream too poor, too destitute
To be remembered, the old shape
Worn and leaning to nothingness,
A woman looking down the road,
A child asleep in its own life.
As these depend, so must they use.

They measure the right to use. Need makes
The right to use. Need names on its breath
Categories of bleak necessity,
Which, just to name, is to create
A help, a right to help, a right
To know what helps and to attain,
By right of knowing, another plane.
The englistered woman is now seen
In an isolation, separate
From the human in humanity,
A part of the inhuman more,
The still inhuman more, and yet
An inhuman of our features, known
And unknown, inhuman for a little while,
Inhuman for a little, lesser time."

The great sail of Ulysses seemed,
In the breathings of this soliloquy,
Alive with an enigma's flittering . . .
As if another sail went on
Straight forwardly through another night
And clumped stars dangled all the way.

Presence of an External Master of Knowledge

Under the shape of his sail, Ulysses,
Symbol of the seeker, crossing by night
The giant sea, read his own mind.
He said, "As I know, I am and have
The right to be". He guided his boat
Beneath the middle stars and said:

"Here I feel the human loneliness
And that, in space and solitude,
Which knowledge is: the world and fate,
The right within me and about me,
Joined in a triumphant vigor,
Like a direction on which I depend . . .

A longer, deeper breath sustains
This eloquence of right, since knowing
And being are one—the right to know
Is equal to the right to be.
The great Omnium descends on me,
Like an absolute out of this eloquence."

The sharp sail of Ulysses seemed,
In the breathings of that soliloquy,
Alive with an enigma's flittering,
And bodying, and being there,
As he moved, straightly, on and on,
Through clumped stars dangling all the way.

A Child Asleep in Its Own Life

Among the old men that you know,
There is one, unnamed, that broods
On all the rest, in heavy thought.

They are nothing, except in the universe
Of that single mind. He regards them
Outwardly and knows them inwardly,

The sole emperor of what they are,
Distant, yet close enough to wake
The chords above your bed to-night.

Two Letters

I

A Letter From

Even if there had been a crescent moon
On every cloud-tip over the heavens,
Drenching the evening with crystals' light,

One would have wanted more—more—more—
Some true interior to which to return,
A home against one's self, a darkness,

An ease in which to live a moment's life,
The moment of life's love and fortune,
Free from everything else, free above all from thought.

It would have been like lighting a candle,
Like leaning on the table, shading one's eyes,
And hearing a tale one wanted intensely to hear,

As if we were all seated together again
And one of us spoke and all of us believed
What we heard and the light, though little, was enough.

II

A Letter To

She wanted a holiday
With someone to speak her dulcied native tongue,

In the shadows of a wood . . .
Shadows, woods . . . and the two of them in speech,

In a secrecy of words
Opened out within a secrecy of place,

Not having to do with love.
A land would hold her in its arms that day

Or something much like a land.
The circle would no longer be broken but closed.

The miles of distance away
From everything would end. It would all meet.

Conversation with Three Women of New England

The mode of the person becomes the mode of the world,
For that person, and, sometimes, for the world itself.
The contents of the mind become solid show
Or almost solid seem show—the way a fly bird
Fixes itself in its inevitable bush . . .
It follows that to change modes is to change the world.

Now, you, for instance, are of this mode: You say
That in that ever-dark central, wherever it is,
In the central of earth or sky or air or thought,
There is a drop that is life's element,
Sole, single source and minimum patriarch,
The one thing common to all life, the human
And inhuman same, the likeness of things unlike.

And you, you say that the capital things of the mind
Should be as natural as natural objects,
So that a carved king found in a jungle, huge
And weathered, should be part of a human landscape,
That a figure reclining among columns toppled down,
Stiff in eternal lethargy, should be,
Not the beginning but the end of artifice,
A nature of marble in a marble world.

And then, finally, it is you that say
That only in man's definitions of himself,
Only encompassed in humanity, is he
Himself. The author of man's canons is man,
Not some outer patron and imaginer.

In which one of these three worlds are the four of us
The most at home? Or is it enough to have seen
And felt and known the differences we have seen
And felt and known in the colors in which we live,
In the excellences of the air we breathe,
The bouquet of being—enough to realize

That the sense of being changes as we talk,
That talk shifts the cycle of the scenes of kings?

Dinner Bell in the Woods

He was facing phantasma when the bell rang.
The picnic of children came running then,

In a burst of shouts, under the trees
And through the air. The smaller ones

Came tinkling on the grass to the table
Where the fattest women belled the glass.

The point of it was the way he heard it,
In the green, outside the door of phantasma.

Reality Is an Activity
of the Most August Imagination

Last Friday, in the big light of last Friday night,
We drove home from Cornwall to Hartford, late.

It was not a night blown at a glassworks in Vienna
Or Venice, motionless, gathering time and dust.

There was a crush of strength in a grinding going round,
Under the front of the westward evening star,

The vigor of glory, a glittering in the veins,
As things emerged and moved and were dissolved,

Either in distance, change or nothingness,
The visible transformations of summer night,

An argentine abstraction approaching form
And suddenly denying itself away.

There was an insolid billowing of the solid.
Night's moonlight lake was neither water nor air.

On the Way to the Bus

A light snow, like frost, has fallen during the night.
Gloomily, the journalist confronts

Transparent man in a translated world,
In which he feeds on a new known,

In a season, a climate of morning, of elucidation,
A refreshment of cold air, cold breath,

A perception of cold breath, more revealing than
A perception of sleep, more powerful

Than a power of sleep, a clearness emerging
From cold, slightly irised, slightly bedazzled,

But a perfection emerging from a new known,
An understanding beyond journalism,

A way of pronouncing the word inside of one's tongue
Under the wintry trees of the terrace.

The Region November

It is hard to hear the north wind again,
And to watch the treetops, as they sway.

They sway, deeply and loudly, in an effort,
So much less than feeling, so much less than speech,

Saying and saying, the way things say
On the level of that which is not yet knowledge:

A revelation not yet intended.
It is like a critic of God, the world

And human nature, pensively seated
On the waste throne of his own wilderness.

Deeplier, deeplier, loudlier, loudlier,
The trees are swaying, swaying, swaying.

Solitaire Under the Oaks

In the oblivion of cards
One exists among pure principles.

Neither the cards nor the trees nor the air
Persist as facts. This is an escape

To principium, to meditation.
One knows at last what to think about

And thinks about it without consciousness,
Under the oak trees, completely released.

Local Objects

He knew that he was a spirit without a foyer
And that, in this knowledge, local objects become
More precious than the most precious objects of home:

The local objects of a world without a foyer,
Without a remembered past, a present past,
Or a present future, hoped for in present hope,

Objects not present as a matter of course
On the dark side of the heavens or the bright,
In that sphere with so few objects of its own.

Little existed for him but the few things
For which a fresh name always occurred, as if
He wanted to make them, keep them from perishing,

The few things, the objects of insight, the integrations
Of feeling, the things that came of their own accord,
Because he desired without quite knowing what,

That were the moments of the classic, the beautiful.
These were that serene he had always been approaching
As toward an absolute foyer beyond romance.

Artificial Populations

The centre that he sought was a state of mind,
Nothing more, like weather after it has cleared—
Well, more than that, like weather when it has cleared
And the two poles continue to maintain it

And the Orient and the Occident embrace
To form that weather's appropriate people,
The rosy men and the women of the rose,
Astute in being what they are made to be.

This artificial population is like
A healing-point in the sickness of the mind:
Like angels resting on a rustic steeple
Or a confect of leafy faces in a tree—

A health—and the faces in a summer night.
So, too, of the races of appropriate people
Of the wind, of the wind as it deepens, and late sleep,
And music that lasts long and lives the more.

A Clear Day and No Memories

No soldiers in the scenery,
No thoughts of people now dead,
As they were fifty years ago,
Young and living in a live air,
Young and walking in the sunshine,
Bending in blue dresses to touch something,
Today the mind is not part of the weather.

Today the air is clear of everything.
It has no knowledge except of nothingness
And it flows over us without meanings,
As if none of us had ever been here before
And are not now: in this shallow spectacle,
This invisible activity, this sense.

Banjo Boomer

The mulberry is a double tree.
Mulberry, shade me, shade me awhile.

A white, pink, purple berry tree,
A very dark-leaved berry tree.
Mulberry, shade me, shade me awhile.

A churchyard kind of bush as well,
A silent sort of bush, as well.
Mulberry, shade me, shade me awhile.

It is a shape of life described
By another shape without a word.
Mulberry, shade me, shade me awhile—

With nothing fixed by a single word.
Mulberry, shade me, shade me awhile.

July Mountain

We live in a constellation
Of patches and of pitches,
Not in a single world,
In things said well in music,
On the piano, and in speech,
As in a page of poetry—
Thinkers without final thoughts
In an always incipient cosmos,
The way, when we climb a mountain,
Vermont throws itself together.

———

A mythology reflects its region. Here
In Connecticut, we never lived in a time
When mythology was possible—But if we had—
That raises the question of the image's truth.
The image must be of the nature of its creator.
It is the nature of its creator increased,
Heightened. It is he, anew, in a freshened youth
And it is he in the substance of his region
Wood of his forests and stone out of his fields
Or from under his mountains.

Of Mere Being

The palm at the end of the mind,
Beyond the last thought, rises
In the bronze decor,

A gold-feathered bird
Sings in the palm, without human meaning,
Without human feeling, a foreign song.

You know then that it is not the reason
That makes us happy or unhappy.
The bird sings. Its feathers shine.

The palm stands on the edge of space.
The wind moves slowly in the branches.
The bird's fire-fangled feathers dangle down.

UNCOLLECTED POEMS

Autumn

Long lines of coral light
    And evening star,
One shade that leads the night
    On from afar.

And I keep, sorrowing,
    This sunless zone,
Waiting and resting here,
    In calm above.

1898

Who Lies Dead?

Who lies dead in the sea,
    All water 'tween him and the stars,
The keels of a myriad ships above,
    The sheets on a myriad spars?

Who lies dead in the world,
    All heavy of heart and hand,
The blaze of a myriad arms in sight,
    The sweep of a myriad band?

1898

Vita Mea

With fear I trembled in the House of Life,
Hast'ning from door to door, from room to room,
Seeking a way from that impenetrable gloom
Against whose walls my strength lay weak from strife.
All dark! All dark! And what sweet wind was rife
With earth, or sea, or star, or new sun's bloom,
Lay sick and dead within that place of doom,
Where I went raving like the winter's wife.

"In vain, in vain," with bitter lips I cried;
"In vain, in vain," along the hall-ways died
And sank in silences away. Oppressed
I wept. Lo! through those tears the window-bars
Shone bright, where Faith and Hope like long-sought stars
First gleamed upon that prison of unrest.

1898

Self-Respect

Sun in the heaven,
Thou art the cause of my mirth,
Star in the evening
Thine is my province since birth;
Depths of the sky
Yours are the depths of my worth.

1898

Sonnets

I

I strode along my beaches like a sea,
The sand before me stretching firm and fair;
No inland darkness cast its shadow there
And my long step was gloriously free.
The careless wind was happy company
That hurried past and did not question where;
Yet as I moved I felt a deep despair
And wonder of the thoughts that came to me.

For to my face the deep wind brought the scent
Of flowers I could not see upon the strand;
And in the sky a silent cloud was blent
With dreams of my soul's stillness; and the sand,
That had been naught to me, now trembled far
In mystery beneath the evening star.

II

Come, said the world, thy youth is not all play,
Upon these hills vast palaces must rise,
And over this green plain that calmly lies
In peace, a mighty city must have sway.
These weak and murmuring reeds cannot gainsay
The building of my wharves; this flood that flies
Unfathomed clear must bear my merchandise,
And sweep my burdens on their seaward way.

No, cried my heart, this thing I cannot do,
This is my home, this plain and water clear
Are my companions faultless as the sky—
I cannot, will not give them up to you.
And if you come upon them I shall fear,
And if you steal them from me I shall die.

III

When I think of all the centuries long dead,
The cities fall'n to dust, the kingdoms won
And in a moment lost again, the sun
That in a high and cloudless heaven led
Sad days of vanished beauty ere they fled,
Sad days so far and fair to muse upon,—
The earth grown grey and covered with the run
And progress of her years' unending tread.

Then my youth leaves me, and the blood
Leaps in its ardor like a flood.
Others with hot and angry pride, I cry,
Others in their thin covered dust may lie
And give their majesty to some pale bud
But not—if strength of will abides—not I.

IV

Through dreary winter had my soul endured
With futile striving and grave argument

Brief sunless days of bitter discontent,
Until, at length, to all its griefs inured
It ceased from idle turmoil, and secured
A new and rich repose; each hour was blent
With easeful visions of the Orient
And cities on uncertain hills immured.

It seemed as though upon a mournful world
A pure-voiced robin had sent forth a ray
Of long-impending beauty, to allay
Her wild desire; as though her deep unrest
Was in a moment's minstrelsy uphurled
Sweet-startling from her heavy-laden breast.

V

The rivers flow on idly in their light
The world is sleeping, and the golden dower
Of heaven is silent as a languorous flower
That spreads its deepness on the tender night.
The distant cities glimmer pale and bright
Each like a separate far and flaring bower
Noiseless and undisturbed in resting power
Filled with the semblance of a vaster might.

Upon this wide and star-kissed plain, my life
Is soon to feel the stir and heat of strife.
Let me look on then for a moment here
Before the morn wakes up my lust for wrong,
Let me look on a moment without fear
With eyes undimmed and youth both pure and strong.

VI

If we are leaves that fall upon the ground
To lose our greenness in the quiet dust
Of forest-depths; if we are flowers that must
Lie torn and creased upon a bitter mound,
No touch of sweetness in our ruins found;

If we are weeds whom no one wise can trust
To live an hour before we feel the gust
Of Death, and by our side its last keen sound

Then let a tremor through our briefness run,
Wrapping it in with mad, sweet sorcery
Of love; for in the fern I saw the sun
Take fire against the dew; the lily white
Was soft and deep at morn; the rosary
Streamed forth a wild perfume into the light.

VII

There shines the morning star! Through the forlorn
And silent spaces of cold heaven's height
Pours the bright radiance of his kingly light,
Swinging in revery before the morn.
The flush and fall of many tides have worn
Upon the coasts beneath him, in their flight
From sea to sea; yet ever on the night
His clear and splendid visage is upborne.

Like this he pondered on the world's first day,
Sweet Eden's flowers heavy with the dew;
And so he led bold Jason on his way
Sparkling forever in the galley's foam;
And still he shone most perfect in the blue
All bright and lovely on the hosts of Rome.

VIII

The soul of happy youth is never lost
In fancy on a page; nor does he dream
With pitiful eyes on tender leaves that turn
With mournful history of beings crossed
In their desires; nor is he rudely tossed
By energy of tears for the warm beam
Of endless love that doth already seem
All cold and dead with Time's destroying frost.

For his own love is better than the tale
Of other love gone by; and he doth feel
As fair as Launcelot in rustling mail,
Hard-driven flowers bright against his steel,
Passing through gloomy forests without fear
To keep sweet tryst with still-eyed Guenevere.

IX

Cathedrals are not built along the sea;
The tender bells would jangle on the hoar
And iron winds; the graceful turrets roar
With bitter storms the long night angrily;
And through the precious organ pipes would be
A low and constant murmur of the shore
That down those golden shafts would rudely pour
A mighty and a lasting melody.

And those who knelt within the gilded stalls
Would have vast outlook for their weary eyes;
There, they would see high shadows on the walls
From passing vessels in their fall and rise.
Through gaudy windows there would come too soon
The low and splendid rising of the moon.

X

Yet mystery is better than the light
That comes up briefly in the gloom, and goes
Before it well defines the thing it shows,
Leaving it doubly darkened; and the sight
That seeks to pierce a never-ending flight
Of dim and idle visions had best close
Its many lids; the heavy-petalled rose
Lies still and perfect in the depth of night.

So youth is better than weak, wrinkled age
Looking with patience on a single beam
Of fancied morn; and no disturbing gleam

Most futile and most sinister in birth
Mars the high pleasure of youth's pilgrimage
Passing with ardor through the happy earth.

XI

I found it flaming in the scarlet rose.
Hast thou not seen? I found it in the bed
Of blue forgetmenots. Hast thou not read?
And in the bluer bed of ocean goes
Its mystery forever. Yet who knows?
And down the yellow valleys to the head
Of earth, and in the breast of youth, and dead
Drear winter breaking-up in spring-time snows—

In these I found it—life's whole history—
Nor cared to guess what lay beyond, as though
This were the last—as though the mystery
Of rose-depths, or the sea, or earth, or slow
Transforming winter ended here—and did
Not point to things in greater mystery hid.

XII

I sang an idle song of happy youth,
A simple and a hopeful roundelay
That thoughtlessly ran through a sweet array
Of cadences, until I cried "Forsooth,
My song, thou art unjewelled and uncouth,
I will adorn thee like the month of May,
With loveliness and fervor; and thy way
Shall be a spiritual reach for Truth."

Ah well, my youth is ending, and the one,
Effaceless memory of its eager years
Is that I also strove to sing what none
Have sung; and that when I had calmed my fears,
Laid by my hopes and viewed what I had done,
My weary eyes were filled with bitter tears.

XIII

How sweet it is to find an asphodel
Along the margin of the winter sea;
More dear than any idle pearl could be,
Cast up in beauty of imperfect spell
From ruins of some olden caravel.
Because of it the world grows fair to me
And like it I could live forever free
From bitter thought of earthly parable.

Dear youth, thou also art a pleasant flow'r,
A tall, fair figure in the sullen plain,
With beauty rising in thee hour by hour—
Shining about thee like long-ripened grain;
And at thy feet with undiminished pow'r
Roll the huge waters of an endless main.

XIV

And even as I passed beside the booth
Of roses, and beheld them brightly twine
To damask heights, taking them as a sign
Of my own self still unconcerned with truth;
Even as I held up in hands uncouth
And drained with joy the golden-bodied wine,
Deeming it half-unworthy, half-divine,
From out the sweet-rimmed goblet of my youth;

Even in that pure hour I heard the tone
Of grievous music stir in memory,
Telling me of the time already flown
From my first youth. It sounded like the rise
Of distant echo from dead melody,
Soft as a song heard far in Paradise.

1899

Song

She loves me or loves me not,
    What care I?—
The depth of the fields is just as sweet,
    And sweet the sky.

She loves me or she loves me not,
    Is that to die?—
The green of the woods is just as fair,
    And fair the sky.

1899

———

You say this is the iris?
And that faery blue
Is the forget-me-not?
And that golden hue
Is but a heavy rose?
And these four long-stemmed blooms
Are purple tulips that enclose
So and so many leaves?
Their names are tender mumbling
For you who know
Naught else; through my own soul
Their wonders nameless go.

1899

Imitation of Sidney:

To Stella. (Miss B?)

Unnumbered thoughts my brain a captive holds:
The thought of splendid pastures by the sea
Whereon brave knights enact their chivalrie
For ladies soft applause; the thought of cold,

Cold steps to towers dim that do enfold
Sweet maidens in their forceless chastitie;
Of snowy skies above a Northern lea
In their bright shining tenderly unrolled;

Of roses peeping dimly from the green;
Of shady nooks, all thick with dull festoon
To hide the love of lovers faintly seen
By little birds upon a pleasant tree;
Of meadows looking meekly to the moon—
Yet these do all take flight at thought of thee.

1899

Quatrain

Go not, young cloud, too boldly through the sky,
    To meet the morning light;
Go not too boldly through that dome on high—
    For eastward lies the night.

1899

To the Morn

If this be night, break softly, blessed day.
Oh, let the silent throat of every bird
Swell tenderly in song, as though he heard
Some brother singing deep within thy ray!
Send but an unseen breeze aloft, away
From darkness and dull earth, to be a word,
A half-discovered sound, to make me gird
Myself, and persevere this cheerless way.

But softly, softly, thou most blessed morn.
Mine eyes too long accustomed to the dark
May fail when thou in glorious heav'n art born,

May fail against that far-entreated light,
Catch but the glimmer of a distant lark,
And drop, all blasted, at the sovereign sight.

1899

Song

Ah yes! beyond these barren walls
    Two hearts shall in a garden meet,
And while the latest robin calls,
    Her lips to his shall be made sweet.

And out above these gloomy tow'rs
    The full moon tenderly shall rise
To cast its light upon the flow'rs,
    And find him looking in her eyes.

1900

Outside the Hospital

See the blind and the lame at play,
    There on the summer lawn—
She with her graceless eyes of clay,
    Quick as a frightened fawn,
Running and tripping into his way
    Whose legs are gone.

How shall she 'scape him, where shall she fly,
    She who never sees?
Now he is near her, now she is by—
    Into his arms she flees.
Hear her gay laughter, hear her light cry
    Among the trees.

"Princess, my captive." "Master, my king,"
    "Here is a garland bright."

"Red roses, I wonder, red with the Spring,
  Red with a reddish light?"
"Red roses, my princess, I ran to bring,
  And be your knight."

1900

Street Songs

I

The Pigeons

Over the houses and into the sky
  And into the dazzling light,
Long hosts of fluttering pigeons fly
  Out of the blackened night,
Over the houses and into the sky
  On glistening wings of white.

Over the city and into the blue
  From ledge and tower and dome,
They rise and turn and turn anew,
  And like fresh clouds they roam,
Over the city and into the blue
  And into their airy home.

II

The Beggar

Yet in this morn there is a darkest night,
Where no feet dance or sweet birds ever rise,
Where fancy is a thing that soothes—and lies,
And leads on with mirages of light.
I speak of her who sits within plain sight
Upon the steps of yon cathedral. Skies
Are naught to her; and life a lord that buys
And sells life, whether sad, or dark, or bright.

The carvings and beauty of the throne
Where she is sitting, she doth meanly use
To win you and appeal. All rag and bone
She asks with her dry, withered hand a dreg
Of the world's riches. If she doth abuse
The place, pass on. It is a place to beg.

III

Statuary

The windy morn has set their feet to dancing—
    Young Dian and Apollo on the curb,
The pavement with their slender forms is glancing,
    No clatter doth their gaiety disturb.

No eyes are ever blind enough to shun them,
    Men wonder what their jubilance can be,
No passer-by but turns to look upon them—
    Then goes his way with all his fancy free.

IV

The Minstrel

The streets lead out into a mist
    Of daisies and of daffodils—
A world of green and amethyst,
    Of seas and of uplifted hills.

There bird-songs are not lost in eaves,
    Nor beaten down by cart and car,
But drifting sweetly through the leaves,
    They die upon the fields afar.

Nor is the wind a broken thing
    That faints within hot prison cells,
But rises on a silver wing
    From out among the heather bells.

1900

Ode

I

A night in May!
And the whole of us gathered into a room
To pack and bundle care away—
And not to remember that over the dark
The sea doth call—
Doth call from out an upward-rising day
For us to follow and to mark
How he doth stay
A patient workman by the city wall.
A night in May!
A night in May!

II

A time will come to join him on the shore;
A time will come when other men who bore
Forth on his breast
To distant worlds will say,
"We long for rest,
Take ye the ships and labor on the deep."
Then this one night that we are living now
Will be forgot in the exultant leap
And bound of our aspiring prow.

III

But not in May!
It is enough to hear young robins sing
To new companions
In the morn.
It is enough to feel our thoughts take wing
Into a happiness
Where none hath seen
A single, unenjoying, hopeless thing.
A life made keen
By its perfection!
All bright, all freshly glowing in the sun

That leads us into doing from what's done,
Without reflection.
Simply to gather and be one again,
To know old earth a mother,
To fill our cups and touch like men—
And be to each a brother!

IV

A golden time and golden-shining hour
From out the cloudless weather
Is such an hour and time as this
That finds us here together
In May! in May!
And we are careless of the night;
We shall be ready for the day;
We shall behold the splendid sight.
We shall set sail for near or far,
With a shout into the light,
And a hail to the morning star.

1900

Night-Song

I stand upon the hills to-night
    And see the cold March moon
Rise upward with his silver light
    And make a gentle noon.

The fields are blowing with the breeze,
    The stars are in the sky,
There is a humming through the trees,
    And one cloud passes by.

I wonder if that is the sea,
    Rid of the sun's annoy,
That sings a song all bold and free,
    Of glory and of joy.

1900

Ballade of the Pink Parasol

I pray thee where is the old-time wig,
   And where is the lofty hat?
Where is the maid on the road in her gig,
   And where is the fire-side cat?
   Never was sight more fair than that,
Outshining, outreaching them all,
   There in the night where lovers sat—
But where is the pink parasol?

Where in the pack is the dark spadille
   With scent of lavender sweet,
That never was held in the mad quadrille.
   And where are the slippered feet?
Ah! we'd have given a pound to meet
   The card that wrought our fall,
The card none other of all could beat—
   But where is the pink parasol?

Where is the roll of the old calash,
   And the jog of the light sedan?
Whence Chloe's diamond brooch would flash
   And conquer poor peeping man.
Answer me, where is the painted fan
   And the candles bright on the wall;
Where is the coat of yellow and tan—
   But where is the pink parasol?

Prince, these baubles are far away,
   In the ruin of palace and hall,
Made dark by the shadow of yesterday—
   But where is the pink parasol?

1900

Quatrain

He sought the music of the distant spheres
  By night, upon an empty plain, apart;
Nor knew they hid their singing all the years
  Within the keeping of his human heart.

1900

A Window in the Slums

I think I hear beyond the walls
  The sound of late birds singing.
Ah! what a sadness those dim calls
  To city streets are bringing.

But who will from my window lean
  May hear, neath cloud belated,
Voices far sadder intervene,
  Sweet songs with longing weighted—

Gay children in their fancied towers
  Of London, singing light
Gainst heavier bars, more gay than in their flowers
  The birds of the upclosing night

And after stars their places fill
  And no bird greets the skies;
The voices of the children still
  Up to my window rise.

1900

Sonnet

Build up the walls about me; close each door;
And fasten all the windows with your bars;
Still shall I walk abroad on Heaven's floor
And be companion to the singing stars.

Whether your prison be of greatest height
Or gloomier depth, it matters not. Though blind
I still shall look upon the burning light,
And see the flowers dancing in the wind.

Your walls will disappear; your doors will swing
Even as I command them. I shall fare
Either up hill or down, and I shall be
Beside the happy lark when he takes wing,
Striking sweet music from the empty air,
And pass immortal mornings by the sea.

1900

To Miss Gage

Froebel be hanged! And Pestalozzi—pooh!
No weazened Pedagogy can aspire
To thrill these thousands—through and through—
Or touch their thin souls with immortal fire.

Only in such as you the spirit gleams
With the rich beauty that compassions give:
Children no science—but a world of dreams
Where fearful futures of the Real live.

1902

———

If I love thee, I am thine;
But if I love thee not,
Or but a little—let the sun still shine
On palaces forgot.

For me: be thou no more
Attendant on my way.
My welcome one will not, like thee, implore
No never! He will play

Brave dulcimers and sing
In darkness, not repine;
And I shall leave all dreams and closer cling
And whisper, "I am thine."

1906–7

———

Elsie's mirror only shows
Golden hair and cheeks of rose.

It is like a glimpse of skies,
Whose early stars are Elsie's eyes;

Or like a faintly silver shade
That shines about the magic maid.

When she to Time has paid her due,
May I still be her mirror true.

1907

From a Vagabond

I

For us, these little books contain,
(as if, like flowers, we put them here,)
Three odorous summers of delight,
(With withered leaves of day and night.)

II

These poets Vagabondian airs
Recall how many of our own,
That sang themselves, without a rhyme,
To stirrings of some secret chime.

III

Our oriole sings, our wild-rose blooms
Our azure river chimes again
Our moon returns. Dear Elsie, hark!
Once more we whisper in the dark.

1907

A Book of Verses

From W. S. to E. V. M.
June, 1908.

I

One day more—
But first, the sun,
There on the water,
Swirling incessant gold—
One mammoth beam!
Oh, far Hesperides!

II

New Life

Noon, and a wind on the hill—
Come, I shall lead you away
To the good things, out of those ill,
At the height of the world to-day.

I shall show you mountains of sun,
And continents drowned in the sea;
I shall show you the world that is done,
And the face of the world to be.

III

Afield

You give to brooks a tune,
  A melody to trees.
You make the dumb field sing aloud
  Its hidden harmonies.

An echo's rumor waits
  A little while, and then,
I hear the water and the pine
  Take up their airs again.

IV

Hang up brave tapestries:
Huntsman and warrior there—
Shut out these mad, white walls.
I hate a room so bare.

And all these neighbor roofs
With chimney and chimney above—
Oh! let me hear the sound
Of soft feet that I love.

Then fetch me candles tall,
Stand them in bright array,
And go—I need such lights
And shadows when I pray.

V

In a Crowd

So much of man,
The wonder of him goes away!
The little art of him returns again
To struggling clay.

Come one, alone.
Come in a separate glory keen;
And sing, on shores of lapislazuli,
A song serene.

VI

On the Ferry

Fog, now, and a bell,
A smooth, a rolling tide.
Drone, bell, drone and tell,
Bell, what vapors hide.

Lights, there, not of fire,
Unsensual sounds, yet loud,
Shapes that to shape aspire,
In that encumbered cloud.

Toll, now, a world resolved
To unremembered form.
Toll the stale brain dissolved
In images of storm.

VII

Tides

These infinite green motions
Trouble, but to no end;
Trouble with mystic sense
Like the secretive oceans—

Or violet eve repining
Upon the glistening rocks;
Or haggard, desert hills;
Or hermit moon declining.

VIII

Winter Melody

I went into the dim wood
   And walked alone.
I heard the icy forest move
   With icy tone.

My heart leapt in the dim wood
   So cold, so bare—
And seemed to echo, suddenly,
   Old music there.

I halted in the dim wood,
   And watched, and soon,
There rose for me—a second time—
   The pageant moon.

IX

Sonnet

Explain my spirit—adding word to word,
As if that exposition gave delight.
Reveal me, lover, to myself more bright.
"You are a twilight, and a twilight bird."

Again! For all the untroubled senses stirred,
Conceived anew, like callow wings in flight,
Bearing desire toward an upper light.
"You are a twilight, and a twilight bird."

Burn in my shadows, Hesperus, my own,
And look upon me with a triumphant fire.
Behold, how glorious the dark has grown!
My wings shall beat all night against your breast,
Heavy with music—feel them there aspire
Home to your heart, as to a hidden nest.

X

Song

A month—a year—of idle work,
   And then, one song.
Oh! all that I am and all that I was
Is to that feeble music strung,
      And more.

Yes: more; for there a sound creeps in,
　A second voice,
From violet capes and forests of dusk,
That calls me to it without choice,
　　　Alone.

XI

After Music

The players pause,
The flute notes drop
To the song's end,
And, trembling, stop.

The harper's hand,
Reluctant, clings
To the hushed strain,
Of muffled strings.

The sounds die out,
And dying, free
The thoughts of all
You are to me.

XII

Twilight

Here the huge moth
Whirled in the dusk,
The wearied mammoth reared
His reddened tusk.

The rank serpent stole
Down golden alleys,
To the envenomed trees
Of jasmine valleys.

Lark's clangor rang,
In haggard light,
To giants, crouched in fear
Of fearful night.

XIII

Adagio

Drone, dove, that rounded woe again,
  When I bring her to-morrow.
The wood were a less happy place,
  But for that broken sorrow.

Tell her in undertones that Youth
  With other times must reckon;
That mist seals up the golden sun,
  And ghosts from gardens beckon.

XIV

There is my spectre,
Pink evening moon,
Haunting me, Caliban,
With its Ariel tune.

It leads me away
From the rickety town,
To the sombre hill
Of the dazzling crown.

Away from my room,
Through many a door,
Through many a field
I shall cross no more.

After man, and the seas,
And the last blue land,
At the world's rough end,
If, perchance, I should stand

To rest from long flight—
Pale evening moon,
I should never escape
That wild, starry tune.

XV

Damask

You need not speak, if that be shame.
    I need no voice.
Nor give to bright cheeks brighter flame:
    I can abide my choice.

For mutely to my muter call,
    Come magic means.
Now the enchanting measures fall—
    A spirit intervenes.

XVI

Rest

Glimpses of Eden for the tired mind,
    The misty vale, the bending palm,
Bright Orient reefs in Orient oceans rolled,
    That never lose their flooded calm.

Oh! large and glorious, the quiet star
    Lighted beyond the half-seen trees.
Sweet is their comfort, but for dear repose,
    You by my side are more than these.

XVII

In Town

    It's well enough to work there,
    When so many do;
    It's well enough to walk the street,
    When your work is through.

    It's night there that kills me,
    In a narrow room,
    Thinking of a wood I know,
    Deep in fragrant gloom.

XVIII

Meditation

There were feet upon the waters in the morning,
Like a golden mist that came from out the deep—
The feet of spirits lost in many a circle
Of winding dance, as if in wavering sleep.

They move away in quiet in the evening,
Lingering yet in a slow-ending round,
Faint lustres, rose and gray and purple,
That vanish soon in the devouring ground.

XIX

Home Again

Back within the valley—
Down from the divide,
No more flaming clouds about—
Oh! the soft hill side,
And my cottage light,
And the starry night!

XX

What have I to do with Arras
    Or its wasted star?
Are my two hands not strong enough,
    Just as they are?

Because men met with rugged spears,
    Upon the Lombard plain,
Must I go forth to them, or else
    Have served in vain?

And does the nightingale, long lost
    In vanished Shalott's dew,
Sing songs more welcome, dear, than those
    I sing to you?

Chiaroscuro

The house-fronts flare
In the blown rain,
The ghostly street-lamps
Have a pallid glare,

A wanderer beats,
With bitter droop,
Along the waste
Of vacant streets.

Suppose some glimmer
Recalled for him
An odorous room,
A fan's fleet shimmer

Of silvery spangle,
Two startled eyes,
A still-trembling hand
And its only bangle.

1908

In a Garden

Oh, what soft wings shall rise above this place,
This little garden of spiced bergamot,
Poppy and iris and forget-me-not,
On Doomsday, to the ghostly Throne of space!

The haunting wings, most like the visible trace
Of passing azure in a shadowy spot—
The wings of spirits, native to this plot,
Returning to their intermitted Grace!

And one shall mingle in her cloudy hair
Blossoms of twilight, dark as her dark eyes;

And one to Heaven upon her arm shall bear
Colors of what she was in her first birth;
And all shall carry upward through the skies
Odor and dew of the familiar earth.

1909

The Little June Book

W. S. to E. V. M.
June 5, 1909.

I

Morning Song

The blue convolvulus,
Less flower than light,
Ghostly with witchery
Of ghostly night,

Trembles with silver
And magic and dew,
And the lark sings
On twinkling wings.

O sun, O melting star,
Some sense supreme
Flashes inglorious Life
To glorious dream.

II

If only birds of sudden white,
Or opal, gold or iris hue,
Came upward through the columned light
Of morning's ocean-breathing blue;

If only songs disturbed our sleep,
Descending from that wakeful breeze,
And no great murmur of the deep
Sighed in our summer-sounding trees!

III

A Concert of Fishes

Here the grass grows,
And the wind blows;
And in the stream,
Small fishes gleam:
Blood-red and hue
Of shadowy blue,
And amber sheen,
And water-green,
And yellow flash
And diamond ash;
And the grass grows,
And the wind blows.

IV

Life is long in the desert,
On the sea, and the mountains.
Ah! but how short it is
By the radiant fountains,

By the jubilant fountains,
Of the rivers wide-sailing,
Under emerald poplars,
With round ivory paling.

V

Vignette

This, too, is part of our still world:
Night, like a cloud, upon the sea,
Far off from us, full of the stern
Possession of deep-rolling waves;
A broken ship, with empty deck,
Sinking in darkness, all night long.

VI

This is the lilac-bush
Full of the cat-bird's warble,

The singer drunken with song
Of his heart's distillation,
Falling from azure tuft,
From violet spray, and jade,
Down through the dusk of the bush,
To rest in a grassy shade.

Soon again, the happy sound
Will enchant the purple ground.

VII

Noon-Clearing

Now, the locust, tall and green,
Glitters in the light serene.

Leafy tremors shake around
Brilliant showers to the ground.

At a dart, an oriole sings,
To fluttering of yellow wings!

Sunlight in the rainy tree,
Flash Two-and-Twenty back to me.

VIII

Man from the waste evolved
The Cytherean glade;
Imposed on battering seas,
His keel's dividing blade,
And sailed there, unafraid.

The isle revealed his worth:
It was a place to sing in
And honor noble Life,
For white doves to wing in,
And roses to spring in.

IX

She that winked her sandal fan
Long ago in gray Japan—

She that heard the bell intone
Rendezvous by willowed Rhone—

How wide the spectacle of sleep,
Hands folded, eyes too still to weep!

X

Only to name again
The leafy rose—
So to forget the fading,
The purple shading,
Ere it goes.

Only to speak the name
Of Odor's bloom—
Rose! The soft sound, contending,
Falls at its ending,
To sweet doom.

XI

Shower

Pink and purple
In water-mist
And hazy leaves
Of amethyst;
Orange and green
And gray between,
And dark grass
In a shimmer
Of windy rain—
Then the glimmer—
And the robin's
Ballad of the rain.

XII

In the Sun

Down the golden mountains,
Through the golden land,

Where the golden forests lean,
And golden cities stand;

There I walked in ancient fire,
To many a shining place;
And found around me everywhere
A new, a burning race.

One from hidden capes come home,
One from incessant seas,
One from valleys lost in light,
And all with victories.

No man was hampered there at all,
But lived his visions out.
There was no god's necessity,
Nor any human doubt.

XIII

Song

This is the house of her,
 Window and wall,
More than the house of her:
 Rare omens fall

From the dark shade of it,
 Pleasant to see;
And the wide door of it
 Opens to me.

XIV

In April

Once more the long twilight
 Full of new leaves,
The blossoming pear-tree
 Where the thrush grieves;

Once more the young starlight,
    And a known mind,
Renewed, that feels its coil
    Slowly unbind—

Sweeping green Mars, beyond
    Antique Orion,
Beyond the Pleiades,
    To vivid Zion.

XV

Eclogue

Lying in the mint,
I heard an orchard bell
Call the ploughman home,
To his minty dell.

I saw him pass along.
He picked a bough to jog
His single, loathful cow,
And whistled to his dog.

I saw him cross a field,
I saw a window glint,
I heard a woman's voice,
Lying in the mint.

XVI

He sang, and, in her heart, the sound
Took form beyond the song's content.
She saw divinely, and she felt
With visionary blandishment.

Desire went deeper than his lute.
She saw her image, sweet and pale,
Invite her to simplicity,
Far off, in some relinquished vale.

XVII

I am weary of the plum and of the cherry,
And that buff moon in evening's aquarelle;
I have no heart within to make me merry,
I read of Heaven and, sometimes, fancy Hell.

All things are old: the new-born swallows fare
Through the Spring twilight on dead September's wing.
The dust of Babylon is in the air,
And settles on my lips the while I sing.

XVIII

An odorous bush I seek,
With lighted clouds hung round,
To make my golden instrument's
Wild, golden strings resound,

Resound in quiet night,
With an Arab moon above,
Easing the dark senses need,
Once more, in songs of love.

XIX

There, a rocket in the Wain
Brings primeval night again.
All the startled heavens flare
From the Shepherd to the Bear.

When the old-time dark returns,
Lo, the steadfast Lady burns
Her curious lantern to disclose
How calmly the White River flows.

XX

Pierrot

I lie dreaming 'neath the moon,
You lie dreaming under ground;

I lie singing as I dream,
You lie dreaming of the sound.

Soon I shall lie dreaming too,
Close beside you where you are—
Moon! Behold me while I sing,
Then, behold our empty star.

Colors

I

Pale orange, green and crimson, and
white, and gold and brown.

II

Lapis-lazuli and orange, and opaque green,
faun-color, black and gold.

1909

Testamentum

Plant the tea-plant on my grave,
And bury with me funerary cups,
Of which let one be such
That young Persephone will not resist.

1909

Sonnet from the Book of Regrets

by Joachim du Bellay

Happy the man who, like Ulysses, goodly ways
Hath been, or like to him that gained the fleece; and then
Is come, full of the manners and the minds of men,
To live among his kinsmen his remaining days!

When shall I see once more, alas, the smokey haze
Rise from the chimneys of my little town; and when:
What time o' the year, look on the cottage-close again,
That is a province to me, that no boundary stays?

The little house my fathers built of old, doth please
More than the emboldened front of Roman palaces:
More than substantial marble, thin slate wearing through,
More than the Latin Tiber, Loire of Angevine,
More, more, my little Lyré than the Palatine,
And more than briny air the sweetness of Anjou.

translated 1909

A Valentine

Willow soon, and vine;
But now Saint Valentine,
To whom I pray: "Speed two
Their happy winter through:
Her that I love—and then
Her Pierrot. . . . Amen."

1910

Dolls

The thought of Eve, within me, is a doll
That does what I desire, as, to perplex,
With apple-buds, the husband in her sire.

There's a pious caliph, now, who prays and sees
A vermeil cheek. He is half-conscious of
The quaint seduction of a scented veil.

Playing with dolls? A solid game, greybeards.
Think of the cherubim and seraphim,
And of Another, whom I must not name.

1913–14?

Infernale

(*A boor of night in middle earth cries out.*)
Hola! Hola! What steps are those that break
This crust of air? . . . (*He pauses.*) Can breath shake
The solid wax from which the warmth dies out? . . .

I saw a waxen woman in a smock
Fly from the black toward the purple air.
(*He shouts.*) Hola! Of that strange light, beware!
(*A woman's voice is heard, replying.*) Mock

The bondage of the Stygian concubine,
Hallooing haggler; for the wax is blown,
And downward, from this purple region, thrown;
And I fly forth, the naked Proserpine.

(*Her pale smock sparkles in a light begun
To be diffused, and, as she disappears,
The silent watcher, far below her, hears;*)
Soaring Olympus glitters in the sun.

1913–14?

———

All things imagined are of earth compact,
Strange beast and bird, strange creatures all;
Strange minds of men, unwilling slaves to fact:

Struggling with desperate clouds, they still proclaim
The rushing pearl, the whirling black,
Clearly, in well-remembered word and name.

Even the dead, when they return, return
Not as those dead, concealed away;
But their old persons move again, and burn.

1913–15?

L'Essor Saccadé

Swallows in the elderberry,
Fly to the steeple.
Then from one apple-tree
Fly to another.

Fly over the stones of the brook,
Along the stony water.
Fly over the widow's house
And around it.

Never mind the white dog
That barks in the bushes.
Fly over the pigeons
On the chimney.

1913–15?

An Exercise for Professor X

I see a camel in my mind.
I do not say to myself, in English,
"There is a camel."
I do not talk to myself.
On the contrary, I watch
And a camel passes in my mind.
This might happen to a Persian.
My mind and a Persian's
Are as much alike, then,
As moonlight on the Atlantic
Is like moonlight on the Pacific.

1913–15?

Headache

The letters of the alphabet
Are representations of parts of the head.
Ears are *q*s
*L*s are the edges of the teeth
*M*s are the wrinkled skin between the eyes
In frowns.
The nostrils and the bridge of the nose
Are *p*s or *b*s.
The mouth is *o*.
There are letters in the hair.
Worms frown, are full of mouths,
Bite, twitch their ears . . .
The maker of the alphabet
Had a headache.

1913–15?

———

I have lived so long with the rhetoricians
That when I see a pine tree
Broken by lightning
Or hear a crapulous crow
In dead boughs,
In April
These are too ready
To despise me
It is for this the good lord
Gave the rooster his lustre
And made sprats pink
Who can doubt that Confucius
Thought well of streets
In the spring-time
It is for this the rhetoricians
Wear long black equali
When they are abroad.

1913–15?

—————

The night-wind of August
Is like an old mother to me.
It comforts me.
I rest in it,
As one would rest,
If one could,
Once again—
It moves about, quietly
And attentively.
Its old hands touch me.
Its breath touches me.
But sometimes its breath is a little cold,
Just a little,
And I know
That it is only the night-wind.

1913–15?

To Madame Alda, Singing a Song, in a White Gown

So much sorrow comes to me out of your singing.
A few large, round leaves of wan pink
Float in a small space of air,
Luminously.
A white heron rises.
From its long legs, drifting, close together,
Drops of water slide
And glisten.
It drifts from sight.

1913–15?

Carnet de Voyage

I

An odor from a star
Comes to my fancy, slight,
Tenderly spiced and gay,
As if a seraph's hand
Unloosed the fragrant silks
Of some sultana, bright
In her soft sky. And pure
It is, and excellent,
As if a seraph's blue
Fell, as a shadow falls,
And his warm body shed
Sweet exhalations, void
Of our despised decay.

II

One More Sunset

The green goes from the corn,
The blue from all the lakes,
And the shadows of the mountains mingle in the sky.

Far off, the still bamboo
Grows green; the desert pool
Turns gaudy turquoise for the chanting caravan.

The changing green and blue
Flow round the changing earth;
And all the rest is empty wondering and sleep.

III

Here the grass grows,
And the wind blows.
And in the stream,
Small fishes gleam,
Blood-red and hue
Of shadowy blue,

And amber sheen,
And water-green,
And yellow flash,
And diamond ash.
And the grass grows,
And the wind blows.

IV

She that winked her sandal fan
Long ago in gray Japan—

She that heard the bell intone
Rendezvous by rolling Rhone—

How wide the spectacle of sleep,
Hands folded, eyes too still to weep!

V

I am weary of the plum and of the cherry,
And that buff moon in evening's aquarelle,
I have no heart within to make me merry.
I nod above the books of Heaven or Hell.

All things are old. The new-born swallows fare
Through the Spring twilight on dead September's wing.
The dust of Babylon is in the air,
And settles on my lips the while I sing.

VI

Man from the waste evolved
The Cytherean glade,
Imposed on battering seas
His keel's dividing blade,
And sailed there, unafraid.

The isle revealed his worth.
It was a place to sing in
And honor noble Life,
For white doves to wing in,
And roses to spring in.

VII

Chinese Rocket

There, a rocket in the Wain
Brings primeval night again.
All the startled heavens flare
From the Shepherd to the Bear—

When the old-time dark returns,
Lo, the steadfast Lady burns
Her curious lantern to disclose
How calmly the White River flows!

VIII

On an Old Guitar

It was a simple thing
For her to sit and sing,
  "Hey nonino!"

This year and that befell,
(Time saw and Time can tell),
  With a hey and a ho—

Under the peach-tree, play
Such mockery away,
  Hey nonino!

1914

From a Junk

A great fish plunges in the dark,
Its fins of rutted silver; sides,
Belabored with a foamy light;
And back, brilliant with scaly salt.
It glistens in the flapping wind,
Burns there and glistens, wide and wide,
Under the five-horned stars of night,
In wind and wave . . . It is the moon.

1914

Home Again

Back within the valley,
Down from the divide,
No more flaming clouds about,
O! the soft hillside,
And my cottage light,
And the starry night.

1914

Phases

*"La justice sans force est contredite, parce qu'il y a toujours
des méchants; la force sans la justice est accusée."*

—PASCAL

I

There was heaven,
Full of Raphael's costumes;
And earth,
A thing of shadows,
Stiff as stone,
Where Time, in fitful turns,
Resumes
His own . . .

A dead hand tapped the drum,
An old voice cried out, "Come!"
We were obedient and dumb.

II

There's a little square in Paris,
Waiting until we pass.
They sit idly there,
They sip the glass.

There's a cab-horse at the corner,
There's rain. The season grieves.
It was silver once,
And green with leaves.

There's a parrot in a window,
Will see us on parade,
Hear the loud drums roll—
And serenade.

III

This was the salty taste of glory,
That it was not
Like Agamemnon's story.
Only, an eyeball in the mud,
And Hopkins,
Flat and pale and gory!

IV

But the bugles, in the night,
Were wings that bore
To where our comfort was;

Arabesques of candle beams,
Winding
Through our heavy dreams;

Winds that blew
Where the bending iris grew;

Birds of intermitted bliss,
Singing in the night's abyss;

Vines with yellow fruit,
That fell
Along the walls
That bordered Hell.

V

Death's nobility again
Beautified the simplest men.
Fallen Winkle felt the pride
Of Agamemnon
When he died.

What could London's
Work and waste
Give him—
To that salty, sacrificial taste?

What could London's
Sorrow bring—
To that short, triumphant sting?

VI

[   ]

The crisp, sonorous epics
Mongered after every scene.
Sluggards must be quickened! Screen,

No more, the shape of false Confusion.
Bare his breast and draw the flood
Of all his Babylonian blood.

VII

Belgian Farm, October, 1914

The vaguest line of smoke, (a year ago),
Wavered in evening air, above the roof,
As if some Old Man of the Chimney, sick
Of summer and that unused hearth below,

Stretched out a shadowy arm to feel the night.
The children heard him in their chilly beds,
Mumbling and musing of the silent farm.
They heard his mumble in the morning light.

Now, soldiers, hear me: mark this very breeze,
That blows about in such a hopeless way,
Mumbling and musing like the most forlorn.
It is that Old Man, lost among the trees.

VIII

What shall we say to the lovers of freedom,
Forming their states for new eras to come?
Say that the fighter is master of men.

Shall we, then, say to the lovers of freedom
That force, and not freedom, must always prevail?
Say that the fighter is master of men.

Or shall we say to the lovers of freedom
That freedom will conquer and always prevail?
Say that the fighter is master of men.

Say, too, that freedom is master of masters,
Forming their states for new eras to come.
Say that the fighter is master of men.

IX

Life, the hangman, never came,
Near our mysteries of flame.

When we marched across his towns,
He cozened us with leafy crowns.

When we marched along his roads,
He kissed his hand to ease our loads.

Life, the hangman, kept away,
From the field where soldiers pay.

X

Peace means long, delicious valleys,
In the mode of Claude Lorraine;
Rivers of jade,
In serpentines,
About the heavy grain;

Leaning trees,
Where the pilgrim hums
Of the dear
And distant door.
Peace means these,
And all things, as before.

XI

War has no haunt except the heart,
Which envy haunts, and hate, and fear,
And malice, and ambition, near
The haunt of love. Who shall impart,

To that strange commune, strength enough
To drive the laggard phantoms out?
Who shall dispel for it the doubt
Of its own strength? Let Heaven snuff

The tapers round her futile throne.
Close tight the prophets' coffin-clamp.
Peer inward, with the spirit's lamp,
Look deep, and let the truth be known.

1914

Blanche McCarthy

Look in the terrible mirror of the sky
And not in this dead glass, which can reflect
Only the surfaces—the bending arm,
The leaning shoulder and the searching eye.

Look in the terrible mirror of the sky.
Oh, bend against the invisible; and lean
To symbols of descending night; and search
The glare of revelations going by!

Look in the terrible mirror of the sky.
See how the absent moon waits in a glade
Of your dark self, and how the wings of stars,
Upward, from unimagined coverts, fly.

1915–16?

For an Old Woman in a Wig

I

　　　. . . There is a moment's flitter
Of silvers and of blacks across the streaking.
　　　　　. . . a swarming chitter

Of crows that flap away beyond the creaking
Of wooden wagons in the mountain gutters.
. . .

The young dogs bark . . .

. . .
. . . 　　　　　It is the skeleton Virgil utters

The fates of men. Dogs bay their ghosts. The traces
Of morning grow large and all the cocks are crowing
And . . . 　　　　the sun . . . 　　　　paces

The tops of hell . . . 　　Death, . . . 　　knowing,
Grieves . . . our spirits with too poignant grieving,
　　　　　. . . keeps on showing

To our still envious memory, still believing,
The things we knew. For him the cocks awaken.
He spreads the thought of morning past deceiving

And yet deceives. There comes a mood that's taken
From water-deeps reflecting opening roses
And rounding, watery leaves, forever shaken,

And floating colors, which the mind supposes
In an imagination cut by sorrow.
Hell is not desolate Italy. It closes

　　　　　　. . . above a morrow
Of common yesterdays: a wagon's rumble,
Loud cocks and barking dogs. It does not borrow,

Except from dark forgetfulness, the mumble
Of sounds returning, or the phantom leaven
Of leaves so shaken in a water's tumble.

II

Is death in hell more death than death in heaven?
And is there never in that noon a turning—
One step descending one of all the seven

Implacable buttresses of sunlight, burning
In the great air? There must be spirits riven
From out contentment by too conscious yearning.

There must be spirits willing to be driven
To that immeasurable blackness, or . . .
To those old landscapes, endlessly regiven,

Whence hell, and heaven itself, were both begotten.
There must be spirits wandering in the valleys,
And on the green-planed hills, that find forgotten

Beggars of earth intent
On maids with aprons lifted up to carry
Red-purples home—beggars that cry out sallies

Of half-remembered songs . . .   sing, *"Tarry,
Tarry, are you gone?"* . . . Such spirits are the fellows,
In heaven, of those whom hell's illusions harry.

III

When summer ends and changing autumn mellows
The nights . . .   and moons glance
Over the dreamers . . .   and bring the yellows

Of autumn days and nights into resemblance,
The dreamers wake and watch the moonlight streaming.
They shall have much to suffer in remembrance.

They shall have much to suffer when the beaming

Of these clear moons, long afterward, returning,
Shines on them, elsewhere, in a deeper dreaming.

. . . Suns, too, shall follow them with burning
Hallucinations in their turbid sleeping . . .
. . .

O pitiful lovers of Earth, why are you keeping
Such count of beauty in the ways you wander?
Why are you so insistent on the sweeping

Poetry of sky and sea? Are you, then, fonder
Of the circumference of earth's impounding,
Than of some sphere on which the mind might blunder,

If you, with irrepressible will, abounding
In . . .　　　　　　　wish for revelation,
Sought out the unknown new in your surrounding?

1915–16?

The Florist Wears Knee-Breeches

My flowers are reflected
In your mind
As you are reflected in your glass.
When you look at them,
There is nothing in your mind
Except the reflections
Of my flowers.
But when I look at them
I see only the reflections
In your mind,
And not my flowers.
It is my desire
To bring roses,
And place them before you
In a white dish.

1916

Song

There are great things doing
In the world,
Little rabbit.
There is a damsel,
Sweeter than the sound of the willow,
Dearer than shallow water
Flowing over pebbles.
Of a Sunday,
She wears a long coat,
With twelve buttons on it.
Tell that to your mother.

1916

Inscription for a Monument

To the imagined lives
Evoked by music,
Creatures of horns, flutes, drums,
Violins, bassoons, cymbals—
Nude porters that glistened in Burma
Defiling from sight;
Island philosophers spent
By long thought beside fountains;
Big-bellied ogres curled up in the sunlight,
Stuttering dreams . . .

1916

Bowl

For what emperor
Was this bowl of Earth designed?
Here are more things
Than on any bowl of the Sungs,
Even the rarest—

Vines that take
The various obscurities of the moon,
Approaching rain
And leaves that would be loose upon the wind,
Pears on pointed trees,
The dresses of women,
Oxen . . .
I never tire
To think of this.

1916

Primordia

In the Northwest

1

All over Minnesota,
Cerise sopranos,
Walking in the snow,
Answer, humming,
The male voice of the wind in the dry leaves
Of the lake-hollows.
For one,
The syllables of the gulls and of the crows
And of the blue-bird
Meet in the name
Of Jalmar Lillygreen.
There is his motion
In the flowing of black water.

2

The child's hair is of the color of the hay in the haystack,
    around which the four black horses stand.
There is the same color in the bellies of frogs, in clays,
    withered reeds, skins, wood, sunlight.

3

The blunt ice flows down the Mississippi,
At night.
In the morning, the clear river
Is full of reflections,
Beautiful alliterations of shadows and of things shadowed.

4

The horses gnaw the bark from the trees.
The horses are hollow,
The trunks of the trees are hollow.
Why do the horses have eyes and ears?
The trees do not.
Why can the horses move about on the ground?
The trees cannot.
The horses weary themselves hunting for green grass.
The trees stand still,
The trees drink.
The water runs away from the horses.
La, la, la, la, la, la, la, la,
Dee, dum, diddle, dee, dee, diddle, dee, da.

5

The birch trees draw up whiteness from the ground.
In the swamps, bushes draw up dark red,
Or yellow.
O, boatman,
What are you drawing from the rain-pointed water?
O, boatman,
What are you drawing from the rain-pointed water?
Are you two boatmen
Different from each other?

In the South

6

Unctuous furrows,
The ploughman portrays in you

The spring about him:
Compilation of the effects
Of magenta blooming in the Judas-tree
And of purple blooming in the eucalyptus—
Map of yesterday's earth
And of to-morrow's heaven.

7

The lilacs wither in the Carolinas.
Already the butterflies flutter above the cabins.
Already the new-born children interpret love
In the voices of mothers.
Timeless mother,
How is it that your aspic nipples
For once vent honey?

The pine-tree sweetens my body.
The white iris beautifies me.

8

The black mother of eleven children
Hangs her quilt under the pine-trees.
There is a connection between the colors,
The shapes of the patches,
And the eleven children . . .
Frail princes of distant Monaco,
That paragon of a parasol
Discloses
At least one baby in you.

9

The trade-wind jingles the rings in the nets around the racks
    by the docks on Indian River.
It is the same jingle of the water among the roots under the
    banks of the palmettoes,
It is the same jingle of the red-bird breasting the orange-
    trees out of the cedars.
Yet there is no spring in Florida, neither in boskage perdu,
    nor on the nunnery beaches.

To the Roaring Wind

What syllable are you seeking,
Vocalissimus,
In the distances of sleep?
Speak it.

1917

Meditation

How long have I meditated, O Prince,
On sky and earth?
It comes to this,
That even the moon
Has exhausted its emotions.
What is it that I think of, truly?
The lines of blackberry bushes,
The design of leaves—
Neither sky nor earth
Express themselves before me . . .
Bossuet did not preach at the funerals
Of puppets.

1917

Gray Room

Although you sit in a room that is gray,
Except for the silver
Of the straw-paper,
And pick
At your pale white gown;
Or lift one of the green beads
Of your necklace,
To let it fall;
Or gaze at your green fan
Printed with the red branches of a red willow;
Or, with one finger,

Move the leaf in the bowl—
The leaf that has fallen from the branches of the
forsythia
Beside you . . .
What is all this?
I know how furiously your heart is beating.

1917

Lettres d'un Soldat
(1914–1915)

*Combattre avec ses frères, à sa place, à son rang, avec des yeux
dessillés, sans espoir de gloire et de profit, et simplement parce
que telle est la loi, voilà le commandement que donne le dieu
au guerrier Arjuna, quand celui-ci doute s'il doit se dé-
tourner de l'absolu pour le cauchemar humain de la bataille.
. . . Simplement, qu'Arjuna bande son arc avec les autres
Kshettryas!*

PRÉFACE D'ANDRÉ CHEVRILLON

I

7 septembre

*. . . Nous sommes embarqués dans l'aventure, sans aucune
sensation dominante, sauf peut-être une acceptation assez
belle de la fatalité. . . .*

Common Soldier

No introspective chaos . . . I accept:
War, too, although I do not understand.
And that, then, is my final aphorism.

I have been pupil under bishops' rods
And got my learning from the orthodox.
I mark the virtue of the common-place.

I take all things as stated—so and so
Of men and earth: I quote the line and page,
I quote the very phrase my masters used.

If I should fall, as soldier, I know well
The final pulse of blood from this good heart
Would taste, precisely, as they said it would.

II

27 septembre
Jamais la majesté de la nuit ne m'apporta autant de con-
solation qu'en cette accumulation d'épreuves. Vénus, étin-
celante, m'est une amie.

In an Ancient, Solemn Manner

The spirit wakes in the night wind—is naked.
What is it that hides in the night wind
Near by it?

Is it, once more, the mysterious beauté,
Like a woman inhibiting passion
In solace—

The multiform beauty, sinking in night wind,
Quick to be gone, yet never
Quite going?

She will leap back from the swift constellations,
As they enter the place of their western
Seclusion.

III

22 octobre
Ce qu'il faut, c'est reconnaître l'amour et la beauté triom-
phante de toute violence.

Anecdotal Revery

The streets contain a crowd
Of blind men tapping their way
By inches—
This man to complain to the grocer
Of yesterday's cheese,

This man to visit a woman,
This man to take the air.
Am I to pick my way
Through these crickets?—
I, that have a head
In the bag
Slung over my shoulder?
I have secrets
That prick
Like a heart full of pins.
Permit me, gentlemen,
I have killed the mayor,
And am escaping from you.
Get out of the way!
(*The blind men strike him down with their sticks.*)

IV

31 octobre

Jusqu'à présent j'ai possédé une sagesse de renoncement, mais maintenant je veux une Sagesse qui accepte tout, en s'orientant vers l'action future.

Morale

And so France feels. A menace that impends,
Too long, is like a bayonet that bends.

V

7 novembre

Si tu voyais la sécurité des petits animaux des bois, souris, mulots! L'autre jour, dans notre abri de feuillage, je sui-vais les évolutions de ces petites bêtes. Elles étaient jolies comme une estampe japonaise, avec l'intérieur de leurs oreilles rose comme un coquillage.

Comme Dieu Dispense de Graces

Here I keep thinking of the Primitives—
The sensitive and conscientious schemes
Of mountain pallors ebbing into air;

And I remember sharp Japonica—
The driving rain, the willows in the rain,
The birds that wait out rain in willow leaves.

Although life seems a goblin mummery,
These images return and are increased,
As for a child in an oblivion:

Even by mice—these scamper and are still;
They cock small ears, more glistening and pale
Than fragile volutes in a rose sea-shell.

VI

26 novembre
J'ai la ferme espérance, mais surtout j'ai confiance en la
justice éternelle, quelque surprise qu'elle cause à l'humaine
idée que nous en avons.

The Surprises of the Superhuman

The palais de justice of chambermaids
Tops the horizon with its colonnades.

If it were lost in Übermenschlichkeit,
Perhaps our wretched state would soon come right.

For somehow the brave dicta of its kings
Make more awry our faulty human things.

VII

29 novembre au matin, en cantonnement
Telle fut la beauté d'hier. Te parlerai-je des soirées pré-
cédentes, alors que sur la route, la lune me dessinait la
broderie des arbres, le pathétique des calvaires, l'atten-
drissement de ces maisons que l'on sait des ruines, mais
que la nuit fait surgir comme une évocation de la paix.

Lunar Paraphrase

The moon is the mother of pathos and pity.

When, at the wearier end of November,
Her old light moves along the branches,
Feebly, slowly, depending upon them;
When the body of Jesus hangs in a pallor,
Humanly near, and the figure of Mary,
Touched on by hoar-frost, shrinks in a shelter
Made by the leaves, that have rotted and fallen;
When over the houses, a golden illusion
Brings back an earlier season of quiet
And quieting dreams in the sleepers in darkness—

The moon is the mother of pathos and pity.

VIII

7 décembre

*Bien chère Mère aimée. . . . Pour ce qui est de ton coeur,
j'ai tellement confiance en ton courage, qu'à l'heure ac-
tuelle cette certitude est mon grand réconfort. Je sais que
ma mère a atteint à cette liberté d'âme qui permet de
contempler le spectacle universel.*

There is another mother whom I love,
O chère maman, another, who, in turn,
Is mother to the two of us, and more,
In whose hard service both of us endure
Our petty portion in the sacrifice.
Not France! France, also, serves the invincible eye,
That, from her helmet, terrible and bright,
Commands the armies; the relentless arm,
Devising proud, majestic issuance.
Wait now; have no rememberings of hope,
Poor penury. There will be voluble hymns
Come swelling, when, regardless of my end,
The mightier mother raises up her cry;
And little will or wish, that day, for tears.

IX

15 janvier
La seule sanction pour moi est ma conscience. Il faut nous
confier à une justice impersonnelle, indépendante de tout
facteur humain, et à une destinée utile et harmonieuse
malgré toute horreur de forme.

Negation

Hi! The creator too is blind,
Struggling toward his harmonious whole,
Rejecting intermediate parts,
Horrors and falsities and wrongs;
Incapable master of all force,
Too vague idealist, overwhelmed
By an afflatus that persists.
For this, then, we endure brief lives,
The evanescent symmetries
From that meticulous potter's thumb.

X

4 février
Hier soir, rentrant dans ma grange, ivresse, rixes, cris,
chants et hurlements. Voilà la vie!

John Smith and his son, John Smith,
 And his son's son John, and-a-one
 And-a-two and-a-three
And-a-rum-tum-tum, and-a
Lean John, and his son, lean John,
 And his lean son's John, and-a-one
 And-a-two and-a-three
And-a-drum-rum-rum, and-a
Rich John, and his son, rich John,
 And his rich son's John, and-a-one
 And-a-two and-a-three
And-a-pom-pom-pom, and-a

Wise John, and his son, wise John,
     And his wise son's John, and-a-one
     And-a-two and-a-three
And-a-fee and-a-fee and-a-fee
     And-a-fee-fo-fum—
Voilà la vie, la vie, la vie,
     And-a-rummy-tummy-tum
     And-a-rummy-tummy-tum.

XI

5 mars

La mort du soldat est près des choses naturelles.

Life contracts and death is expected,
As in a season of autumn.
The soldier falls.

He does not become a three-days personage,
Imposing his separation,
Calling for pomp.

Death is absolute and without memorial,
As in a season of autumn,
When the wind stops,

When the wind stops and, over the heavens,
The clouds go, nevertheless,
In their direction.

XII

17 mars

J'ai oublié de te dire que, l'autre fois, pendant la tempête, j'ai vu dans le soir les grues revenir. Une accalmie permettait d'entendre leur cri.

In a theatre, full of tragedy,
The stage becomes an atmosphere
Of seeping rose—banal machine
In an appointed repertoire . . .

XIII

26 mars

*Rien de nouveau sur notre hauteur que l'on continue
d'organiser. . . . De temps à autre la pioche rencontre un
pauvre mort que la guerre tourmente jusque dans la terre.*

Death was a reaper with sickle and stone,
Or swipling flail, sun-black in the sun,
A laborer.

Or Death was a rider beating his horse,
Gesturing grandiose things in the air,
Seen by a muse. . . .

Symbols of sentiment . . . Take this phrase,
Men of the line, take this new phrase
Of the truth of Death—

Death, that will never be satisfied,
Digs up the earth when want returns . . .
You know the phrase.

1917-18

Instant of Clearness

by Jean Le Roy

I feel an apparition,
at my back,
an ebon wrack,
of more than man's condition,
that leans upon me there;
and then in back, one more;
and then, still farther back,
still other men aligned;
and then, toujours plus grands, immensities of night,
who, less and less defined

by light,
stretch off in the black:

ancestors from the first days of the world.

Before me, I know more,
one smaller at the first, and then one smaller still,
and more and more, that are my son and then his sons.

They lie buried in dumb sleep,
or bury themselves in the future.

And for the time, just one exists:
I.
Just one exists and I am time,
the whole of time.
I am the whole of light.

My flesh alone, for the moment, lives,
my heart alone gives,
my eyes alone have sight.
I am emblazoned, the others, all, are black.
I am the whole of light!
And those behind and those before
are only routineers of rounding time.
In back, they lie perdu in the black: the breachless grime,
(just one exists and I am time)
in front, they lie in the ruddyings
of an incalculable ether that burns and stings.
My will alone commands me: I am time!
Behind they passed the point of man,
before they are not embryo—I, only, touch with prime.
And that will last long length of time,
think what you will!

I am between two infinite states
on the mid-line dividing,
between the infinite that waits
and the long-abiding,

at the golden spot, where the mid-line swells
and yields to a supple, quivering, deep
inundation.

What do we count? All is for us that live!
Time, even time, and the day's strength and beam.
My fellows, you that live around me,
are you not surprised to be supreme,
on the tense line, in this expanse
of dual circumstance?
And are you not surprised to be the base
on which the eternal poising turns?
To know that, without you, the scale of lives
would sink upon death's pitty under-place?
And are you not surprised to be the very poles?

Let us make signals in the air and cry aloud.
We must leave a wide noise tolling
in the night;
and, in the deep of time,
set the wide wind rolling.

                                        translated 1918

The Naked Eye of the Aunt

I peopled the dark park with gowns
In which were yellow, rancid skeletons.
Oh! How suave a purple passed me by!
But twiddling mon idée, as old men will,
And knowing the monotony of thought,
I said, "She thumbs the memories of dress."
Can I take fire from so benign an ash?
It is enough she comes upon the eye.
A maid of forty is no feathery girl.
Green bosoms and black legs, beguile
These ample lustres from the new-come moon.

*   *   *

Poets of pimpernel, unlucky pimps
Of pomp, in love and good ensample, see
How I exhort her, huckstering my woe.
"Oh, hideous, horrible, horrendous hocks!"
Is there one word of sunshine in this plaint?
Do I commend myself to leafy things
Or melancholy crows as shadowing clouds?
I grieve the pinch of her long-stiffening bones.
"Oh, lissomeness turned lagging ligaments!"
Eheu! Eheu! With what a weedy face
Black fact emerges from her swishing dreams.

1919?

Peter Parasol

Aux taureaux Dieu cornes donne
Et sabots durs aux chevaux . . . .

Why are not women fair,
All, as Andromache—
Having, each one, most praisable
Ears, eyes, soul, skin, hair?

Good God! That all beasts should have
The tusks of the elephant,
Or be beautiful
As large, ferocious tigers are.

It is not so with women.
I wish they were all fair,
And walked in fine clothes,
With parasols, in the afternoon air.

1919

Piano Practice at the Academy of the Holy Angels

The time will come for these children, seated before their
    long black instruments, to strike the themes of love—
All of them, darkened by time, moved by they know not
    what, amending the airs they play to fulfill themselves;
Seated before these shining forms, like the duskiest glass,
    reflecting the piebald of roses or what you will.
Blanche, the blonde, whose eyes are not wholly straight, in
    a room of lustres, shed by turquoise falling,
Whose heart will murmur with the music that will be a
    voice for her, speaking the dreaded change of speech;
And Rosa, the muslin dreamer of satin and cowry-kin,
    disdaining the empty keys; and the young infanta,
Jocunda, who will arrange the roses and rearrange, letting
    the leaves lie on the water-like lacquer;
And that confident one, Marie, the wearer of cheap stones,
    who will have grown still and restless;
And Crispine, the blade, reddened by some touch,
    demanding the most from the phrases
Of the well-thumbed, infinite pages of her masters, who will
    seem old to her, requiting less and less her feeling:
In the days when the mood of love will be swarming for
    solace and sink deeply into the thin stuff of being,
And these long, black instruments will be so little to them
    that will be needing so much, seeking so much in their
    music.

        1919

The Indigo Glass in the Grass

Which is real—
This bottle of indigo glass in the grass,
Or the bench with the pot of geraniums, the stained
    mattress and the washed overalls drying in the sun?
Which of these truly contains the world?

Neither one, nor the two together.

        1919

Anecdote of the Prince of Peacocks

In the land of the peacocks, the prince thereof,
Grown weary of romantics, walked alone,
In the first of evening, pondering.

"The deuce!" he cried.

And by him, in the bushes, he espied
A white philosopher.
The white one sighed—

He seemed to seek replies,
From nothingness, to all his sighs.

"My sighs are pulses in a dreamer's death!"
Exclaimed the white one, smothering his lips.

The prince's *frisson* reached his fingers' tips.

1919–20?

Anecdote of the Abnormal

He called hydrangeas purple. And they were.
Not fixed and deadly, (like a curving line
That merely makes a ring.)
It was a purple changeable to see.
And so hydrangeas came to be.

The common grass is green.
But there are regions where the grass
Assumes a pale, Italianate sheen—
Is almost Byzantine.
And there the common grass is never seen.

And in those regions one still feels the rose
And feels the grass
Because new colors make new things
And new things make old things again . . .
And so with men.

Crispin-valet, Crispin-saint!
The exhausted realist beholds
His tattered manikin arise,
Tuck in the straw,
And stalk the skies.

1919–20?

Romance for a Demoiselle Lying in the Grass

It is grass.
It is monotonous.

The monotony
Is like your port which conceals
All your characters
And their desires.

I might make many images of this
And twang nobler notes
Of larger sentiment.

But I invoke the monotony of monotonies
Free from images and change.

Why should I savor love
With tragedy or comedy?

Clasp me,
Delicatest machine.

1919–20?

Lulu Gay

Lulu sang of barbarians before the eunuchs
Of gobs, who called her orchidean,
Sniffed her and slapped heavy hands
Upon her.
She made the eunuchs ululate.
She described for them
The manners of the barbarians
What they did with their thumbs.
The eunuchs heard her
With continual ululation.
She described how the barbarians kissed her
With their wide mouths
And breaths as true
As the gum of the gum-tree.
"Olu" the eunuchs cried. "Ululalu."

                                                        1921

Lulu Morose

Is there a sharp edge?
Is there a sharp edge?
On which to lean
Like a belly puckered by a spear.

The cliffs are rough.
Are rough
And not all birds sing cuck
Sing coo, sing cuck, cuckoo.

Oh! Sal, the butcher's wife ate clams
And died amid uproarious damns.
And mother nature sick of silk
Shot lightning at the kind cow's milk.

And father nature, full of butter
Made the maelstrom oceans mutter.
Stabbing at his teat-like corns
From an ottoman of thorns.

1921

This Vast Inelegance

This vast inelegance may seem the blankest desolation,
Beginning of a green Cockaigne to be, disliked, abandoned,

In which the bliss of clouds is mark of an intended meeting
Between the matin air and color, goldenest generating,

Soother and lustier than this vexed, autumnal exhalation,
So sullen with sighing and surrender to marauding ennui.

Which choir makes the most faultless medley in its
    celebration?
The choir that choirs the first fatigue in deep bell of
    canzoni?

Or this, whose music, sweeping irradiation of a sea-night,
Piercing the tide by which it moves, is constantly within us?

Or this, whose jingling glorias, importunate of perfection,
Are the fulfilling rhapsodies that hymn it to creation?

Is any choir the whole voice of this fretful habitation,
This parlor of farcical dames, this clowns' colonnade, this
    kites' pavilion?

See, now, the ways beleaguered by black, dropsical duennas,
Young weasels racing steep horizons in pursuit of
    planets . . .

1921–22

Saturday Night at the Chiropodist's

Histoire

For simple pleasure, he beheld,
The rotting man for pleasure saw,
The new spring tumble in the sky.

The wry of neck and the wry of heart
Stood by him when the tumbler fell,
And the mighty, musty belly of tears.

Did they behold themselves in this
And see themselves as once they were,
O spirit of bones, O mountain of graves?

Take counsel, all hierophants
And sentimental roisterers,
They did not so. But in their throats

They pied and chuckled like a flock,
They were so glad to see the spring.
The rotting man was first to sing.

1922?

Mandolin and Liqueurs

La-la! The cat is in the violets
And the awnings are let down.
The cat should not be where she is
And the awnings are too brown,
Emphatically so.

If awnings were celeste and gay,
Iris and orange, crimson and green,
Blue and vermilion, purple and white,
And not this tinsmith's galaxy,
Things would be different.

The sun is gold, the moon is silver.
There must be a planet that is copper
And in whose light the roses
Would have a most singular appearance,
Or nearly so.

I love to sit and read the *Telegraph*,
That vast confect of telegrams,
And to find how much that really matters
Does not really matter
At all.

1923

The Shape of the Coroner

It was the morn
And the palms were waved
And the brass was played
Then the coroner came
In his limpid shoes.

The palms were waved
For the beau of illusions.
The termagant fans
Of his orange days
Fell, famous and flat,
And folded him round,

Folded and fell
And the brass grew cold
And the coroner's hand
Dismissed the band.

It was the coroner
Poured this elixir
Into the ground,
And a shabby man,
An eye too sleek,
And a biscuit cheek.

And the coroner bent
Over the palms.
The elysium lay
In a parlor of day.

1923

Red Loves Kit

I

Your yes her no, your no her yes. The words
Make little difference, for being wrong
And wronging her, if only as she thinks,
You never can be right. You are the man.
You brought the incredible calm in ecstasy,
Which, like a virgin visionary spent
In this spent world, she must possess. The gift
Came not from you. Shall the world be spent again,
Wasted in what would be an ultimate waste,
A deprivation muffled in eclipse,
The final theft? That you are innocent
And love her still, still leaves you in the wrong.
Where is that calm and where that ecstasy?
Her words accuse you of adulteries
That sack the sun, though metaphysical.

II

A beautiful thing, milord, is beautiful
Not only in itself but in the things
Around it. Thus it has a large expanse,
As the moon has in its moonlight, worlds away,
As the sea has in its coastal clamorings.
So she, when in her mystic aureole
She walks, triumphing humbly, should express
Her beauty in your love. She should reflect
Her glory in your passion and be proud.
Her music should repeat itself in you,

Impelled by a compulsive harmony.
Milord, I ask you, though you will to sing,
Does she will to be proud? True, you may love
And she have beauty of a kind, but such
Unhappy love reveals vast blemishes.

III

Rest, crows, upon the edges of the moon,
Cover the golden altar deepest black,
Fly upward thick in numbers, fly across
The blueness of the half-night, fill the air
And darken it, make an unbroken mat
Out of the whirl and denseness of your wings,
Spread over heaven shutting out the light.
Then turn your heads and let your spiral eyes
Look backward. Let your swiftly-flying flocks
Look suddenly downward with their shining eyes
And move the night by their intelligent motes.
Make a sidereal splendor as you fly.
And you, good galliard, to enchant black thoughts
Beseech them for an overwhelming gloom.
It will be fecund in rapt curios.

1924

Though Valentine brings love
And Spring brings beauty
They do not make me rise
To my poetic duty

But Elsie and Holly do
And do it daily—
Much more than Valentine or Spring
And very much more gaily.

1925

Metropolitan Melancholy

A purple woman with a lavender tongue
Said hic, said hac,
Said ha.

To dab things even nicely pink
Adds very little,
So I think.
Oh ha, Oh ha.

The silks they wear in all the cities
Are really much a million pities.

1928

Annual Gaiety

In the morning in the blue snow
The catholic sun, its majesty,
Pinks and pinks the ice-hard melanchole.

Wherefore those prayers to the moon?
Or is it that alligators lie
Along the edges of your eye
Basking in desert Florida?

Père Guzz, in heaven, thumb your lyre
And chant the January fire
And joy of snow and snow.

1930

Good Man, Bad Woman

You say that spite avails her nothing, that
You rest intact in conscience and intact

In self, a man of longer time than days,
Of larger company than one. Therefore,
Pure scientist, you look with nice aplomb
At this indifferent experience,
Deploring sentiment. When May came last,
And equally as scientist you walked
Among the orchards in the apple-blocks
And saw the blossoms, snow-bred pink and white,
Making your heart of brass to intercept
The childish onslaughts of such innocence,
Why was it that you cast the brass away
And bared yourself, and bared yourself in vain?
She can corrode your world, if never you.

1932

The Woman Who Blamed Life on a Spaniard

I

You do not understand her evil mood.
You think that like the moon she is obscured
But clears and clears until an open night
Reveals her, rounded in beneficence,
Pellucid love; and for that image, like
Some merciful divination, you forgive.
And you forgive dark broachings growing great
Night after night because the hemisphere
And still the final quarter, still the rim,
And still the impassioned place of it remain.
If she is like the moon, she never clears
But spreads an evil lustre whose increase
Is evil, crisply bright, disclosing you
Stooped in a night of vast inquietude.
Observe her shining in the deadly trees.

II

That tragic prattle of the fates, astute
To bring destruction, often seems high-pitched.

The babble of generations magnifies
A mot into a dictum, communal,
Of inescapable force, itself a fate.
How, then, if nothing more than vanity
Is at the bottom of her as pique-pain
And picador? Be briny-blooded bull.
Flatter her lance with your tempestuous dust,
Make melic groans and tooter at her strokes,
Rage in the ring and shake the corridors.
Perhaps at so much mastery, the bliss
She needs will come consolingly. Alas,
It is a most spectacular role, and yet
Less than contending with fictitious doom.

III

The choice twixt dove and goose is over-close.
The fowl of Venus may consist of both
And more. It may have feathery color-frets,
A paragon of lustre; may have voice
Like the mother of all nightingales; be wise
As a seraglio-parrot; feel disdain
In concert with the eagle's valiance.
Let this be as it may. It must have tears
And memory and claws: a paragon
Well-wetted; a decoying voice that sings
Arpeggi of celestial souvenirs,
A skillful apprehension and eye proud
In venting lacerations. So composed,
This hallowed visitant, chimerical,
Sinks into likeness blessedly beknown.

1932

Secret Man

The sounds of rain on the roof
Are like the sound of doves.
It is long since there have been doves
On any house of mine.

It is better for me
In the rushes of autumn wind
To embrace autumn, without turning
To remember summer.

Besides, the world is a tower.
Its winds are blue.
The rain falls at its base,
Summers sink from it.

The doves will fly round.
When morning comes
The high clouds will move,
Nobly as autumn moves.

The man of autumn,
Behind its melancholy mask,
Will laugh in the brown grass,
Will shout from the tower's rim.

1934

What They Call Red Cherry Pie

Meyer is a bum. He eats his pie.
He eats red cherry pie and never says—
He makes no choice of words—

Cherries are ri . . . He would never say that.
He could not. Neither of us could ever say that.
But Meyer is a bum.

He says "That's what I call red cherry pie."
And that's his way. And that's my way as well.
We two share that at least.

What is it that we share? Red cherry pie
When cherries are in season, or, at least
The way we speak of it.

Meyer has my five senses. I have his.
This matters most in things that matter least.
And that's red cherry pie.

1934

Hieroglyphica

People that live in the biggest houses
Often have the worst breaths.
Hey-di-ho.

Even if I had nothing else to do
I could look at flowers.
Hey-di-ho.

The humming-bird is the national bird
Of the humming-bird.
Hey-di-ho.

X understands Aristotle
Instinctively, not otherwise.
Hey-di-ho.

Let wise men piece the world together with wisdom
Or poets with holy magic.
Hey-di-ho.

1934

The Drum-Majors in the Labor Day Parade

If each of them wasn't a prig
And didn't care a fig,
They would show it.

They would throw their batons far up
To return in a glittering wheel
And make the Dagoes squeal.

But they are empty as balloons
The trombones are like baboons,
The parade's no good.

Are they really mechanical bears,
Toys of the millionaires,
Morbid and bleak?

They ought to be muscular men,
Naked and stamping the earth,
Whipping the air.

The banners should brighten the sun.
The women should sing as they march.
Let's go home.

1934

Polo Ponies Practicing

The constant cry against an old order,
An order constantly old,
Is itself old and stale.

Here is the world of a moment,
Fitted by men and horses
For hymns,

In a freshness of poetry by the sea,
In galloping hedges,
In thudding air:

Beyond any order,
Beyond any rebellion,
A brilliant air

On the flanks of horses,
On the clear grass,
On the shapes of the mind.

1934

The Widow

The cold wife lay with her husband after his death,
His ashen reliquiae contained in gold
Under her pillow, on which he had never slept.

1935?

Lytton Strachey, Also, Enters into Heaven

I care for neither fugues nor feathers.
What interests me most is the people
Who have always interested me most,
To see them without their passions
And to understand them.

Perhaps, without their passions, they will be
Men of memories explaining what they meant.
One man opposing a society
If properly misunderstood becomes a myth.
I fear the understanding.

Death ought to spare their passions.
Memory without passion would be better lost.
But memory and passion, and with these
The understanding of heaven, would be bliss,
If anything would be bliss.

How strange a thing it was to understand
And how strange it ought to be again, this time
Without the distortions of the theater,
Without the revolutions' ruin,
In the presence of the barefoot ghosts!

Perception as an act of intelligence
And perception as an act of grace
Are two quite different things, in particular
When applied to the mythical.
As for myself, I feel a doubt:

I am uncertain whether the perception
Applied on earth to those that were myths
In every various sense, ought not to be preferred
To an untried perception applied
In heaven. But I have no choice.

In this apologetic air, one well
Might muff the mighty spirit of Lenin.
That sort of thing was always rather stiff.
Let's hope for Mademoiselle de Lespinasse,
Instead, or Horace Walpole or Mrs. Thrale.

He is nothing, I know, to me nor I to him.
I had looked forward to understanding. Yet
An understanding may be troublesome.
I'd rather not. No doubt there's a quarter here,
Dixhuitième and Georgian and serene.

1935

Agenda

Whipped creams and the Blue Danube,
The lin-lan-lone of Babson,
And yet the damned thing doesn't come right.

Boston should be in the keys
Painting the saints among palms.
Charleston should be New York.

And what a good thing it would be
If Shasta roared up in Nassau,
Cooling the sugary air.

Perhaps if the orchestras stood on their heads
And dancers danced ballets on top of their beds—
We haven't tried that.

Those early centuries were full
Of very haphazard people and things,
The whole of them turning black;

Yet in trees round the College of Heralds,
No doubt, the well-tuned birds are singing,
Slowly and sweetly.

1935

Table Talk

Granted, we die for good.
Life, then, is largely a thing
Of happens to like, not should.

And that, too, granted, why
Do I happen to like red bush,
Gray grass and green-gray sky?

What else remains? But red,
Gray, green, why those of all?
That is not what I said:

Not those of all. But those.
One likes what one happens to like.
One likes the way red grows.

It cannot matter at all.
Happens to like is one
Of the ways things happen to fall.

1935?

A Room on a Garden

O stagnant east-wind, palsied mare,
Giddap! The ruby roses' hair
Must blow.

Behold how order is the end
Of everything. The roses bend
As one.

Order, the law of hoes and rakes,
May be perceived in windy quakes
And squalls.

The gardener searches earth and sky
The truth in nature to espy
In vain.

He well might find that eager balm
In lilies' stately-statued calm;
But then

He well might find it in this fret
Of lilies rusted, rotting, wet
With rain.

1935?

Owl's Clover

The Old Woman and the Statue

I

Another evening in another park,
A group of marble horses rose on wings
In the midst of a circle of trees, from which the leaves
Raced with the horses in bright hurricanes.

II

So much the sculptor had foreseen: autumn,
The sky above the plaza widening
Before the horses, clouds of bronze imposed
On clouds of gold, and green engulfing bronze,
The marble leaping in the storms of light.
So much he had devised: white forelegs taut
To the muscles' very tip for the vivid plunge,
The heads held high and gathered in a ring

At the center of the mass, the haunches low,
Contorted, staggering from the thrust against
The earth as the bodies rose on feathery wings,
Clumped carvings, circular, like blunted fans,
Arranged for phantasy to form an edge
Of crisping light along the statue's rim.
More than his muddy hand was in the manes,
More than his mind in the wings. The rotten leaves
Swirled round them in immense autumnal sounds.

III

But her he had not foreseen: the bitter mind
In a flapping cloak. She walked along the paths
Of the park with chalky brow scratched over black
And black by thought that could not understand
Or, if it understood, repressed itself
Without any pity in a somnolent dream.
The golden clouds that turned to bronze, the sounds
Descending, did not touch her eye and left
Her ear unmoved. She was that tortured one,
So destitute that nothing but herself
Remained and nothing of herself except
A fear too naked for her shadow's shape.
To search for clearness all an afternoon
And without knowing, and then upon the wind
To hear the stroke of one's certain solitude,
What sound could comfort away the sudden sense?
What path could lead apart from what she was
And was to be? Could it happen to be this,
This atmosphere in which the horses rose,
This atmosphere in which her musty mind
Lay black and full of black misshapen? Wings
And light lay deeper for her than her sight.

IV

The mass of stone collapsed to marble hulk,
Stood stiffly, as if the black of what she thought
Conflicting with the moving colors there
Changed them, at last, to its triumphant hue,

Triumphant as that always upward wind
Blowing among the trees its meaningless sound.
The space above the trees might still be bright
Yet the light fell falsely on the marble skulls,
Manes matted of marble across the air, the light
Fell falsely on the matchless skeletons,
A change so felt, a fear in her so known,
Now felt, now known as this. The clouds of bronze
Slowly submerging in flatness disappeared.
If the sky that followed, smaller than the night,
Still eked out luminous wrinklings on the leaves,
Whitened, again, forms formless in the dark,
It was as if transparence touched her mind.
The statue stood in stars like water-spheres,
Washed over by their green, their flowing blue.
A mood that had become so fixed it was
A manner of the mind, a mind in a night
That was whatever the mind might make of it,
A night that was that mind so magnified
It lost the common shape of night and came
To be the sovereign shape in a world of shapes.
A woman walking in the autumn leaves,
Thinking of heaven and earth and of herself
And looking at the place in which she walked,
As a place in which each thing was motionless
Except the thing she felt but did not know.

                              v

Without her, evening like a budding yew
Would soon be brilliant, as it was, before
The harridan self and ever-maladive fate
Went crying their desolate syllables, before
Their voice and the voice of the tortured wind were one,
Each voice within the other, seeming one,
Crying against a need that pressed like cold,
Deadly and deep. It would become a yew
Grown great and grave beyond imagined trees,
Branching through heavens heavy with the sheen
And shadowy hanging of it, thick with stars

Of a lunar light, dark-belted sorcerers
Dazzling by simplest beams and soothly still,
The space beneath it still, a smooth domain,
Untroubled by suffering, which fate assigns
To the moment. There the horses would rise again,
Yet hardly to be seen and again the legs
Would flash in air, and the muscular bodies thrust
Hoofs grinding against the stubborn earth, until
The light wings lifted through the crystal space
Of night. How clearly that would be defined!

Mr. Burnshaw and the Statue

I

The thing is dead . . . Everything is dead
Except the future. Always everything
That is is dead except what ought to be.
All things destroy themselves or are destroyed.

These are not even Russian animals.
They are horses as they were in the sculptor's mind.
They might be sugar or paste or citron-skin
Made by a cook that never rode the back
Of his angel through the skies. They might be mud
Left here by moonlit muckers when they fled
At the burst of day, crepuscular images
Made to remember a life they never lived
In the witching wilderness, night's witchingness,
Made to affect a dream they never had,
Like a word in the mind that sticks at artichoke
And remains inarticulate, horses with cream.
The statue seems a thing from Schwarz's, a thing
Of the dank imagination, much below
Our crusted outlines hot and huge with fact,
Ugly as an idea, not beautiful
As sequels without thought. In the rudest red
Of autumn, these horses should go clattering
Along the thin horizons, nobly more

Than this jotting-down of the sculptor's foppishness
Long after the worms and the curious carvings of
Their snouts.

II

Come, all celestial paramours,
Whether in-dwelling haughty clouds, frigid
And crisply musical, or holy caverns temple-toned,
Entwine your arms and moving to and fro,
Now like a ballet infantine in awkward steps,
Chant sibilant requiems for this effigy.
Bring down from nowhere nothing's wax-like blooms,
Calling them what you will but loosely-named
In a mortal lullaby, like porcelain.
Then, while the music makes you, make, yourselves,
Long autumn sheens and pittering sounds like sounds
On pattering leaves and suddenly with lights,
Astral and Shelleyan, diffuse new day;
And on this ring of marble horses shed
The rainbow in its glistening serpentines
Made by the sun ascending seventy seas.
Agree: the apple in the orchard, round
And red, will not be redder, rounder then
Than now. No: nor the ploughman in his bed
Be free to sleep there sounder, for the plough
And the dew and the ploughman still will best be one.
But this gawky plaster will not be here.

III

The stones
That will replace it shall be carved, *"The Mass
Appoints These Marbles Of Itself To Be
Itself."* No more than that, no subterfuge,
No memorable muffing, bare and blunt.

IV

Mesdames, one might believe that Shelley lies
Less in the stars than in their earthy wake,

Since the radiant disclosures that you make
Are of an eternal vista, manqué and gold
And brown, an Italy of the mind, a place
Of fear before the disorder of the strange,
A time in which the poets' politics
Will rule in a poets' world. Yet that will be
A world impossible for poets, who
Complain and prophesy, in their complaints,
And are never of the world in which they live.
Disclose the rude and ruddy at their jobs
And if you weep for peacocks that are gone
Or dance the death of doves, most sallowly,
Who knows? The ploughman may not live alone
With his plough, the peacock may abandon pride,
The dove's adagio may lose its depth
And change. If ploughmen, peacocks, doves alike
In vast disorder live in the ruins, free,
The charts destroyed, even disorder may,
So seen, have an order of its own, a peace
Not now to be perceived yet order's own.

V

A solemn voice, not Mr. Burnshaw's, says:
At some gigantic, solitary urn,
A trash can at the end of the world, the dead
Give up dead things and the living turn away.
There buzzards pile their sticks among the bones
Of buzzards and eat the bellies of the rich,
Fat with a thousand butters, and the crows
Sip the wild honey of the poor man's life,
The blood of his bitter brain; and there the sun
Shines without fire on columns intercrossed,
White slapped on white, majestic, marble heads,
Severed and tumbled into seedless grass,
Motionless, knowing neither dew nor frost.
There lies the head of the sculptor in which the thought
Of lizards, in its eye, is more acute
Than the thought that once was native to the skull;

And there are the white-maned horses' heads, beyond
The help of any wind or any sky:
Parts of the immense detritus of a world
That is completely waste, that moves from waste
To waste, out of the hopeless waste of the past
Into a hopeful waste to come. There even
The colorless light in which this wreckage lies
Has faint, portentous lustres, shades and shapes
Of rose, or what will once more rise to rose,
When younger bodies, because they are younger, rise
And chant the rose-points of their birth, and when
For a little time, again, rose-breasted birds
Sing rose-beliefs. Above that urn two lights
Commingle, not like the commingling of sun and moon
At dawn, nor of summer-light and winter-light
In an autumn afternoon, but two immense
Reflections, whirling apart and wide away.

VI

Mesdames, it is not enough to be reconciled
Before the strange, having wept and having thought
And having said farewell. It is not enough
That the vista retain ploughmen, peacocks, doves,
However tarnished, companions out of the past,
And that, heavily, you move with them in the dust.
It is not enough that you are indifferent,
Because time moves on columns intercrossed
And because the temple is never quite composed,
Silent and turquoised and perpetual,
Visible over the sea. It is only enough
To live incessantly in change. See how
On a day still full of summer, when the leaves
Appear to sleep within a sleeping air,
They suddenly fall and the leafless sound of the wind
Is no longer a sound of summer. So great a change
Is constant. The time you call serene descends
Through a moving chaos that never ends. Mesdames,
Leaves are not always falling and the birds
Of chaos are not always sad nor lost

In melancholy distances. You held
Each other moving in a chant and danced
Beside the statue, while you sang. Your eyes
Were solemn and your gowns were blown and grief
Was under every temple-tone. You sang
A tragic lullaby, like porcelain.
But change composes, too, and chaos comes
To momentary calm, spectacular flocks
Of crimson and hoods of Venezuelan green
And the sound of z in the grass all day, though these
Are chaos and of archaic change. Shall you,
Then, fear a drastic community evolved
From the whirling, slowly and by trial; or fear
Men gathering for a mighty flight of men,
An abysmal migration into a possible blue?

VII

Dance, now, and with sharp voices cry, but cry
Like damsels daubed and let your feet be bare
To touch the grass and, as you circle, turn
Your backs upon the vivid statue. Then,
Weaving ring in radiant ring and quickly, fling
Yourselves away and at a distance join
Your hands held high and cry again, but cry,
This time, like damsels captured by the sky,
Seized by that possible blue. Be maidens formed
Of the most evasive hue of a lesser blue,
Of the least appreciable shade of green
And despicable shades of red, just seen,
And vaguely to be seen, a matinal red,
A dewy flashing blanks away from fire,
As if your gowns were woven of the light
Yet were not bright, came shining as things come
That enter day from night, came mirror-dark,
With each fold sweeping in a sweeping play.
Let your golden hands wave fastly and be gay
And your braids bear brightening of crimson bands.
Conceive that while you dance the statue falls,
The heads are severed, topple, tumble, tip

In the soil and rest. Conceive that marble men
Serenely selves, transfigured by the selves
From which they came, make real the attitudes
Appointed for them and that the pediment
Bears words that are the speech of marble men.
In the glassy sound of your voices, the porcelain cries,
The alto clank of the long recitation, in these
Speak, and in these repeat: *To Be Itself*,
Until the sharply-colored glass transforms
Itself into the speech of the spirit, until
The porcelain bell-borrowings become
Implicit clarities in the way you cry
And are your feelings changed to sound, without
A change, until the waterish ditherings turn
To the tense, the maudlin, true meridian
That is yourselves, when, at last, you are yourselves,
Speaking and strutting broadly, fair and bloomed,
No longer of air but of the breathing earth,
Impassioned seducers and seduced, the pale
Pitched into swelling bodies, upward, drift
In a storm blown into glittering shapes, and flames
Wind-beaten into freshest, brightest fire.

The Greenest Continent

I

Large-leaved and many-footed shadowing,
What god rules over Africa, what shape,
What avuncular cloud-man beamier than spears?

II

The heaven of Europe is empty, like a Schloss
Abandoned because of taxes . . . It was enough:
It made up for everything, it was all selves
Become rude robes among white candle lights,
Motions of air, robes moving in torrents of air,
And through the torrents a jutting, jagged tower,
A broken wall—and it ceased to exist, became

A Schloss, an empty Schlossbibliothek, the books
For sale in Vienna and Zurich to people in Maine,
Ontario, Canton. It was the way
Things jutted up, the way the jagged stacks,
The foul immovables, came through the clouds,
Colossal blacks that leaped across the points
Of Boucher pink, the sheens of Venetian gray.
That's what did it. Everything did it at last.
The binders did it with armorial books.
And the cooks, the cooks, the bar-men and the maids,
The churches and their long parades, Seville
At Easter on a London screen, the seeds
Of Vilmorin, Verhaeren in his grave,
The flute on the gramophone, the Daimlers that
Dissolved the woods, war and the fatal farce
Of war, the rust on the steeples, these jutted up,
These streaked the mother-of-pearl, the lunar cress.
Everything did.

III

　　　　There was a heaven once,
But not that Salzburg of the skies. It was
The spirit's episcopate, hallowed and high,
To which the spirit ascended, to increase
Itself, beyond the utmost increase come
From youngest day or oldest night and far
Beyond thought's regulation. There each man,
Through long cloud-cloister-porches, walked alone,
Noble within perfecting solitude,
Like a solitude of the sun, in which the mind
Acquired transparence and beheld itself
And beheld the source from which transparence came;
And there he heard the voices that were once
The confusion of men's voices, intricate
Made extricate by meanings, meanings made
Into a music never touched to sound.
There, too, he saw, since he must see, the domes
Of azure round an upper dome, brightest
Because it rose above them all, stippled

By waverings of stars, the joy of day
And its immaculate fire, the middle dome,
The temple of the altar where each man
Beheld the truth and knew it to be true.

IV

That was never the heaven of Africa, which had
No heaven, had death without a heaven, death
In a heaven of death. Beneath the heavy foils,
Beneath the spangling greens, fear might placate
And the serpent might become a god, quick-eyed,
Rising from indolent coils. If the statue rose,
If once the statue were to rise, if it stood,
Thinly, among the elephantine palms,
Sleekly the serpent would draw himself across.
The horses are a part of a northern sky
Too starkly pallid for the jaguar's light,
In which he and the lion and the serpent hide
Even in sleep, deep in the grass of sleep,
Deep grass that totters under the weight of light.
There sleep and waking fill with jaguar-men
And lion-men and the flicking serpent-kin
In flowery nations, crashing and alert.
No god rules over Africa, no throne,
Single, of burly ivory, inched of gold,
Disposed upon the central of what we see,
That purges the wrack or makes the jungle shine,
As brilliant as mystic, as mystic as single, all
In one, except a throne raised up beyond
Men's bones, beyond their breaths, the black sublime,
Toward which, in the nights, the glittering serpents climb,
Dark-skinned and sinuous, winding upwardly,
Winding and waving, slowly, waving in air,
Darting envenomed eyes about, like fangs,
Hissing, across the silence, puissant sounds.
Death, only, sits upon the serpent throne:
Death, the herdsman of elephants,
To whom the jaguars cry and lions roar
Their petty dirges of fallen forest-men,

Forever hunting or hunted, rushing through
Endless pursuit or endlessly pursued,
Until each tree, each evil-blossomed vine,
Each fretful fern drops down a fear like dew
And Africa, backing in antiquest sun,
Contains for its children not a gill of sweet.

V

Forth from their tabernacles once again
The angels come, armed, gloriously to slay
The black and ruin his sepulchral throne.
Hé quoi! Angels go pricking elephants?
Wings spread and whirling over jaguar-men?
Angels tiptoe upon the snowy cones
Of palmy peaks sighting machine-guns? These,
Seraphim of Europe? Pouring out of dawn,
Fresh from the sacred clarities, chanters
Of the pith of mind, cuirassiers against
The milkiest bowmen. This makes a new design,
Filleted angels over flapping ears,
Combatting bushmen for a patch of gourds,
Loosing black slaves to make black infantry,
Angels returning after war with belts
And beads and bangles of gold and trumpets raised,
Racking the world with clarion puffs. This must
Be merely a masquerade or else a rare
Tractatus, of military things, with plates,
Miraculously preserved, full fickle-fine,
Of an imagination flashed with irony
And by a hand of certitude to cut
The heavenly cocks, the bowmen, and the gourds,
The oracular trumpets round and roundly hooped,
In Leonardo's way, to magnify
Concentric bosh. To their tabernacles, then,
Remoter than Athos, the effulgent hordes
Return, affecting roseate aureoles,
To contemplate time's golden paladin
And purpose, to hear the wild bee drone, to feel
The ecstasy of sense in a sensuous air.

VI

But could the statue stand in Africa?
The marble was imagined in the cold.
Its edges were taken from tumultous wind
That beat out slimmest edges in the ear,
Made of the eye an insatiable intellect.
Its surfaces came from distant fire; and it
Was meant to stand, not in a tumbling green,
Intensified and grandiose, but among
The common-places of which it formed a part
And there, by feat extenuations, to make
A visible clear cap, a visible wreath
To men, to houses, streets and the squalid whole.
There it would be of the mode of common dreams,
A ring of horses rising from memory
Or rising in the appointments of desire,
The spirit's natural images, carriers,
The drafts of gay beginnings and bright ends,
Majestic bearers or solemn haulers trapped
In endless elegies. But in Africa
The memory moves on leopards' feet, desire
Appoints its florid messengers with wings
Wildly curvetted, color-scarred, so beaked,
With tongues unclipped and throats so stuffed with thorns,
So clawed, so sopped with sun, that in these things
The message is half-borne. Could marble still
Be marble after the drenching reds, the dark
And drenching crimsons, or endure? It came
If not from winter, from a summer like
A winter's noon, in which the colors sprang
From snow, and would return again to snow,
As summer would return to weazened days.

VII

The diplomats of the cafés expound:
Fromage and coffee and cognac and no gods.
It was a mistake to paint the gods. The gold
Of constellations on the beachy air
Is difficult. It blights in the studios.

Magnificence most shiningly expressed
Is, after all, draped damask pampaluned,
Color and color brightening into one,
A majestic weavers' job, a summer's sweat.
It was a mistake to think of them. They have
No place in the sense of colonists, no place
In Africa. The serpent's throne is dust
At the unbeliever's touch. Cloud-cloisters blow
Out of the eye when the loud wind gathers up
And blows, with heaped-up shoulders loudly blows
And bares an earth that has no gods, and bares
The gods like marble figures fallen, left
In the streets. There will always be cafés and cards
And the obese proprietor, who has a son
In Capricorn. The statue has a form
That will always be and will be everywhere.
Why should it fail to stand? Victoria Platz,
To make its factories content, must have
A cavernous and a cruel past, tropic
Benitia, lapis Ville des Pins must soothe
The impoverished waste with dewy vibrancies
Of April here and May to come. Champagne
On a hot night and a long cigar and talk
About the weather and women and the way
Of things, why bother about the back of stars?
The statue belongs to the cavernous past, belongs
To April here and May to come. Why think,
Why feel the sun or, feeling, why feel more
Than purple paste of fruit, to taste, or leaves
Of purple flowers, to see? The black will still
Be free to sing, if only a sorrowful song.

                          VIII

Fatal Ananke is the common god.
He looks upon the statue, where it is,
And the sun and the sun-reek piled and peaked above
The jostled ferns, where it might be, having eyes
Of the shape of eyes, like blunt intaglios,
And nothing more. He sees but not by sight.

He does not hear by sound. His spirit knows
Each look and each necessitous cry, as a god
Knows, knowing that he does not care, and knows,
Knowing and meaning that he cannot care.
He sees the angel in the nigger's mind
And hears the nigger's prayer in motets, belched
From pipes that swarm clerestory walls. The voice
In the jungle is a voice in Fontainebleau.
The long recessional at parish eves wails round
The cuckoo trees and the widow of Madrid
Weeps in Segovia. The beggar in Rome
Is the beggar in Bogotá. The kraal
Chants a death that is a medieval death . . .
Fateful Ananke is the final god.
His hymn, his psalm, his cithern song of praise
Is the exile of the disinherited,
Life's foreigners, pale aliens of the mud,
Those whose Jerusalem is Glasgow-frost
Or Paris-rain. He thinks of the noble lives
Of the gods and, for him, a thousand litanies
Are like the perpetual verses in a poet's mind.
He is that obdurate ruler who ordains
For races, not for men, powerful beyond
A grace to nature, a changeless element.
His place is large and high, an ether flamed
By his presence, the seat of his ubiquitous will.
He, only, caused the statue to be made
And he shall fix the place where it will stand.
Be glory to this unmerciful pontifex,
Lord without any deviation, lord
And origin and resplendent end of law,
Sultan of African sultans, starless crown.

A Duck for Dinner

I

The Bulgar said, "After pineapple with fresh mint
We went to walk in the park; for, after all,

The workers do not rise, as Venus rose,
Out of a violet sea. They rise a bit
On summer Sundays in the park, a duck
To a million, a duck with apples and without wine.
They rise to the muddy, metropolitan elms,
To the camellia-chateaux and an inch beyond,
Forgetting work, not caring for angels, hunting a lift,
The triumph of the arcs of heaven's blue
For themselves, and space and time and ease for the duck.
If you caricature the way they rise, yet they rise.
True, only an inch, but an inch at a time, and inch
By inch, Sunday by Sunday, many men.
At least, conceive what these hands from Sweden mean,
These English noses and edged, Italian eyes,
Massed for a head they mean to make for themselves,
From which their grizzled voice will speak and be heard."

II

O buckskin, O crosser of snowy divides,
For whom men were to be ends in themselves,
Are the cities to breed as mountains bred, the streets
To trundle children like the sea? For you,
Day came upon the spirit as life comes
And deep winds flooded you; for these, day comes,
A penny sun in a tinsel sky, unrhymed,
And the spirit writhes to be wakened, writhes
To see, once more, this hacked-up world of tools,
The heart in slattern pinnacles, the clouds,
Which were their thoughts, squeezed into shapes, the sun
Streamed white and stoked and engined wrick-a-wrack.
In your cadaverous Eden, they desire
The same down-dropping fruit in yellow leaves,
The same return at heavy evening, love
Without any horror of the helpless loss.
The scholar's outline that you had, the print
Of London, the paper of Paris magnified
By poets, the Italian lives preserved
For poverty are gaudy bosh to these.

Their destiny is just as much machine
As death itself, and never can be changed
By print or paper, the trivial chance foregone,
And only an agony of dreams can help,
Not the agony of a single dreamer, but
The wide night mused by tell-tale muttering,
Time's fortune near, the sleepless sleepers moved
By the torture of things that will be realized,
Will, will, but how and all of them asking how
And sighing. These lives are not your lives, O free,
O bold, that rode your horses straight away.

III

Again the Bulgar said, "There are more things
Than poodles in Pomerania. This man
Is all the birds he ever heard and that,
The admiral of his race and everyman,
Infected by unreality, rapt round
By dense unreason, irreproachable force,
Is cast in pandemonium, flittered, howled
By harmonies beyond known harmony.
These bands, these swarms, these motions, what of them?
They keep to the paths of the skeleton architect
Of the park. They obey the rules of every skeleton.
But of what are they thinking, of what, in spite of the duck,
In spite of the watch-chains aus Wien, in spite
Of the Balkan shoes, the bonnets from Moldau, beards
From the steppes, are they being part, feeling the strength,
Seeing the fulgent shadows upward heaped,
Spelling out pandects and haggard institutes?
Is each man thinking his separate thoughts or, for once,
Are all men thinking together as one, thinking
Each other's thoughts, thinking a single thought,
Disclosed in everything, transcended, poised
For the syllable, poised for the touch? But that
Apocalypse was not contrived for parks,
Geranium budgets, pay-roll water-falls,
The clank of the carrousel and, under the trees,

The sheep-like falling-in of distances,
Converging on the statue, white and high."

IV

Then Basilewsky in the band-stand played
"Concerto for Airplane and Pianoforte,"
The newest Soviet réclame. Profound
Abortion, fit for the enchanting of basilisks.
They chanced to think. Suppose the future fails.
If platitude and inspiration are alike
As evils, and if reason, fatuous fire,
Is only another egoist wearing a mask,
What man of folk-lore shall rebuild the world,
What lesser man shall measure sun and moon,
What super-animal dictate our fates?
As the man the state, not as the state the man,
Perennial doctrine and most florid truth;
But man means more, means the million and the duck.
It cannot mean a sea-wide country strewn
With squalid cells, unless New York is Cocos
Or Chicago a Kaffir kraal. It means this mob.
The man in the band-stand could be orator.
It may be the future depends on an orator,
Some pebble-chewer practiced in Tyrian speech,
An apparition, twanging instruments
Within us hitherto unknown, he that
Confounds all opposites and spins a sphere
Created, like a bubble, of bright sheens,
With a tendency to bulge as it floats away.
Basilewsky's bulged before it floated, turned
Caramel and would not, could not float. And yet
In an age of concentric mobs would any sphere
Escape all deformation, much less this,
This source and patriarch of other spheres,
This base of every future, vibrant spring,
The volcano Apostrophe, the sea Behold?
Suppose, instead of failing, it never comes,
This future, although the elephants pass and the blare,
Prolonged, repeated and once more prolonged,

Goes off a little on the side and stops.
Yet to think of the future is a genius,
To think of the future is a thing and he
That thinks of it is inscribed on walls and stands
Complete in bronze on enormous pedestals.

V

The statue is white and high, white brillianter
Than the color white and high beyond any height
That rises in the air. The sprawlers on the grass
See more than marble in their eyes, see more
Than the horses quivering to be gone, flashed through
With senses chiseled on bright stone. They see
The metropolitan of mind, they feel
The central of the composition, in which
They live. They see and feel themselves, seeing
And feeling the world in which they live. The manes,
The leaping bodies, come from the truculent hand,
The stubborn eye, of the conformer who conforms
The manes to his image of the flying wind,
The leaping bodies to his strength, convulsed
By tautest pinions lifted through his thought.
The statue is the sculptor not the stone.
In this he carved himself, he carved his age,
He carved the feathery walkers standing by,
Twitching a little with crude souvenirs
Of young identities, Aprilian stubs.
Exceeding sex, he touched another race,
Above our race, yet of ourselves transformed,
Don Juan turned furious divinity,
Ethereal compounder, pater patriae,
Great mud-ancestor, oozer and Abraham,
Progenitor wearing the diamond crown of crowns,
He from whose beard the future springs, elect.
More of ourselves in a world that is more our own,
For the million, perhaps, two ducks instead of one;
More of ourselves, the mood of life made strong
As by a juicier season; and more our own
As against each other, the dead, the phantomesque.

VI

If these were theoretical people, like
Small bees of spring, sniffing the coldest buds
Of a time to come—A shade of horror turns
The bees to scorpions blackly-barbed, a shade
Of fear changes the scorpions to skins
Concealed in glittering grass, dank reptile skins.
The civil fiction, the calico idea,
The Johnsonian composition, abstract man,
All are evasions like a repeated phrase,
Which, by its repetition, comes to bear
A meaning without a meaning. These people have
A meaning within the meaning they convey,
Walking the paths, watching the gilding sun,
To be swept across them when they are revealed,
For a moment, once each century or two.
The future for them is always the deepest dome,
The darkest blue of the dome and the wings around
The giant Phosphor of their earliest prayers.
Once each century or two. But then so great,
So epical a twist, catastrophe
For Isaac Watts: the diverting of the dream
Of heaven from heaven to the future, as a god,
Takes time and tinkering, melodious
And practical. The envoi to the past
Is largely another winding of the clock.
The tempo, in short, of this complicated shift,
With interruptions by vast hymns, blood odes,
Parades of whole races with attendant bands,
And the bees, the scorpions, the men that think,
The summer Sundays in the park, must be
A leaden ticking circular in width.
How shall we face the edge of time? We walk
In the park. We regret we have no nightingale.
We must have the throstle on the gramophone.
Where shall we find more than derisive words?
When shall lush chorals spiral through our fire
And daunt that old assassin, heart's desire?

Sombre Figuration

I

There is a man whom rhapsodies of change,
Of which he is the cause, have never changed
And never will, a subman under all
The rest, to whom in the end the rest return,
The man below the man below the man,
Steeped in night's opium, evading day.

II

We have grown weary of the man that thinks.
He thinks and it is not true. The man below
Imagines and it is true, as if he thought
By imagining, anti-logician, quick
With a logic of transforming certitudes.
It is not that he was born in another land,
Powdered with primitive lights, and lives with us
In glimpses, on the edge or at the tip,
Playing a crackled reed, wind-stopped, in bleats.
He was born within us as a second self,
A self of parents who have never died,
Whose lives return, simply, upon our lips,
Their words and ours; in what we see, their hues
Without a season, unstinted in livery,
And ours, of rigid measure, a miser's paint;
And most in what we hear, sound brushed away,
A mumbling at the elbow, turgid tunes,
As of insects or cloud-stricken birds, away
And away, dialogues between incognitos.
He dwells below, the man below, in less
Than body and in less than mind, ogre,
Inhabitant, in less than shape, of shapes
That are dissembled in vague memory
Yet still retain resemblances, remain
Remembrances, a place of a field of lights,
As a church is a bell and people are an eye,
A cry, the pallor of a dress, a touch.
He turns us into scholars, studying

The masks of music. We perceive each mask
To be the musician's own and, thence, become
An audience to mimics glistening
With meanings, doubled by the closest sound,
Mimics that play on instruments discerned
In the beat of the blood.
                            Green is the path we take
Between chimeras and garlanded the way,
The down-descent into November's void.
The spontaneities of rain or snow
Surprise the sterile rationalist who sees
Maidens in bloom, bulls under sea, the lark
On urns and oak-leaves twisted into rhyme.
The man, but not the man below, for whom
The pheasant in a field was pheasant, field,
Until they changed to eagle in white air,
Lives in a fluid, not on solid rock.
The solid was an age, a period
With appropriate, largely English, furniture,
Barbers with charts of the only possible modes,
Cities that would not wash away in the mist,
Each man in his asylum maundering,
Policed by the hope of Christmas. Summer night,
Night gold, and winter night, night silver, these
Were the fluid, the cat-eyed atmosphere, in which
The man and the man below were reconciled,
The east wind in the west, order destroyed,
The cycle of the solid having turned.

III

High up in heaven a sprawling portent moves,
As if it bears all darkness in its bulk.
But this we cannot see. The shaggy top
Broods in tense meditation, constantly,
On the city, on which it leans, the people there,
Its shadow on their houses, on their walls,
Their beds, their faces drawn in distant sleep.
This is invisible. The supporting arms
Reach from the horizons, rim to rim,

While the shaggy top collects itself to do
And the shoulders turn, breathing immense intent.
All this is hidden from sight.
                              It is the form
Of a generation that does not know itself,
Still questioning if to crush the soaring stacks,
The churches, like dalmatics stooped in prayer,
And the people suddenly evil, waked, accused,
Destroyed by a vengeful movement of the arms,
A mass overtaken by the blackest sky,
Each one as part of the total wrath, obscure
In slaughter; or if to match its furious wit
Against the sleepers to re-create for them,
Out of their wilderness, a special fane,
Midmost in its design, the arms grown swift,
The body bent, like Hercules, to build.
If the fane were clear, if the city shone in mind,
If more than the wished-for ruin racked the night,
If more than pity and despair were sure,
If the flashy extravaganzas of the lean
Could ever make them fat, these are delays
For ponderous revolving, without help.
And, while revolving, ancient hyacinths
And fragrant fomentations of the spring
Come, baffling discontent. These, too, must be
Revolved.
           Which counts for most, the anger borne
In anger; or the fear that from the death
Of evil, evil springs; or catholic hope,
Young catechumen answering the worms?
The man below beholds the portent poised,
An image of his making, beyond the eye,
Poised, but poised as the mind through which a storm
Of other images blows, images of time
Like the time of the portent, images like leaves,
Except that this is an image of black spring
And those the leaves of autumn-afterwards,
Leaves of the autumns in which the man below
Lived as the man lives now, and hated, loved,
As the man hates now, loves now, the self-same things.

The year's dim elongations stretch below
To rumbled rock, its bright projections lie
The shallowest iris on the emptiest eye.
The future must bear within it every past,
Not least the pasts destroyed, magniloquent
Syllables, pewter on ebony, yet still
A board for bishops' grapes, the happy form
That revolution takes for connoisseurs:
The portent may itself be memory;
And memory may itself be time to come
And must be, when the portent, changed, takes on
A mask up-gathered brilliantly from the dirt,
And memory's lord is the lord of prophecy
And steps forth, priestly in severity,
Yet lord, a mask of flame, the sprawling form
A wandering orb upon a path grown clear.

IV

High up in heaven the sprawling portent moves.
The statue in a crow's perspective of trees
Stands brimming white, chiaroscuro scaled
To space. To space? The statue scaled to space
Would be a ring of heads and haunches, torn
From size, backs larger than the eye, not flesh
In marble, but marble massive as the thrust
Of that which is not seen and cannot be.
The portent would become man-haggard to
A race of dwarfs, the meditative arms
And head a shadow trampled under hoofs,
Man-misty to a race star-humped, astride
In a clamor thudding up from central earth.
Not the space in camera of the man below,
Immeasurable, the space in which he knows
The locust's titter and the turtle's sob.
The statue stands in true perspective. Crows
Give only their color to the leaves. The trees
Are full of fanfares of farewell, as night
And the portent end in night, composed, before

Its wheel begins to turn.
                                    The statue stands
In hum-drum space, farewell, farewell, by day
The green, white, blue of the ballad-eye, by night
The mirror of other nights combined in one.
The spring is hum-drum like an instrument,
That a man without passion plays in an aimless way.
Even imagination has an end,
When the statue is not a thing imagined, a stone
That changed in sleep. It is, it is, let be
The way it came, let be what it may become.
Even the man below, the subverter, stops
The flight of emblemata through his mind,
Thoughts by descent. To flourish the great cloak we wear
At night, to turn away from the abominable
Farewells and, in the darkness, to feel again
The reconciliation, the rapture of a time
Without imagination, without past
And without future, a present time, is that
The passion, indifferent to the poet's hum,
That we conceal? A passion to fling the cloak,
Adorned for a multitude, in a gesture spent
In the gesture's whim, a passion merely to be
For the gaudium of being, Jocundus instead
Of the black-blooded scholar, the man of the cloud, to be
The medium man among other medium men,
The cloak to be clipped, the night to be re-designed,
Its land-breath to be stifled, its color changed,
Night and the imagination being one.

                                                          1936

Communications of Meaning

The parrot in its palmy boughs
Repeats the farmer's almanac.

A duckling of the wildest blood
Convinces Athens with its quack.

Much too much thought, too little thought.
No thought at all: a guttural growl,

A snort across the silverware,
The petals flying through the air.

1937?

One of Those Hibiscuses of Damozels

She was all of her airs and, for all of her airs,
She was all of her airs and ears and hairs,
Her pearly ears, her jeweler's ears
And the painted hairs that composed her hair.

In spite of her airs, that's what she was. She was all
Of her airs, as surely cologne as that she was bone
Was what she was and flesh, sure enough, but airs;
Rather rings than fingers, rather fingers than hands.

How could you ever, how could you think that you saw her,
Knew her, how could you see the woman that wore the
      beads,
The ball-like beads, the bazzling and the bangling beads
Or hear her step in the way she walked?

This was not how she walked for she walked in a way
And the way was more than the walk and was hard to see.
You saw the eye-blue, sky-blue, eye-blue, and the powdered
      ears
And the cheeks like flower-pots under her hair.

1942

Outside of Wedlock

The strong music of hard times,
In a world forever without a plan
For itself as a world,
Must be played on the concertina.

The poor piano forte
Whimpers when the moon above East Hartford
Wakes us to the emotion, grand fortissimo,
Of our sense of evil,

Of our sense that time has been
Like water running in a gutter
Through an alley to nowhere,
Without beginning or the concept of an end.

The old woman that knocks at the door
Is not our grandiose destiny.
It is an old bitch, an old drunk,
That has been yelling in the dark.

Sing for her the seventy-fold Amen,
White February wind,
Through banks and banks of voices,
In the cathedral-shanty,

To the sound of the concertina,
Like the voice of all our ancestors,
The *pére* Benjamin, the *mére* Blandenah,
Saying we have forgot them, they never lived.

1942

Desire & the Object

It is curious that I should have spoken of Raël,
When it never existed, the order
That I desired. It could be—

Curious that I should have spoken of Jaffa
By her sexual name, saying that that high marriage
Could be, it could be.

I had not invented my own thoughts,
When I was sleeping, nor by day,
So that thinking was a madness, and is:

It was to be as mad as everyone was,
And is. Perhaps I had been moved
By feeling the like of thought in sleep,

So that feeling was a madness, and is.
Consider that I had asked
Was it desire that created Raël

Or was it Jaffa that created desire?
The origin could have its origin.
It could be, could be.

It could be that the sun shines
Because I desire it to shine or else
That I desire it to shine because it shines.

1942

This as Including That

This rock and the dry birds
Fluttering in blue leaves,

This rock and the priest,
The priest of nothingness who intones—

It is true that you live on this rock
And in it. It is wholly you.

It is true that there are thoughts
That move in the air as large as air,

That are almost not our own, but thoughts
To which we are related,

In an association like yours
With the rock and mine with you.

The iron settee is cold.
A fly crawls on the balustrades.

1944–45?

Tradition

A poem about tradition could easily be
A windy thing . . . However, since we are parts
Of tradition, cousins of the calendar,
If not of kin, suppose we identify
Its actual appearance, if we can,
By giving it a form. But the character
Of tradition does not easily take form.

It is not a set of laws. Therefore, its form
Is not lean marble, trenchant-eyed. There is
No book of the past in which time's senators
Have inscribed life's do and don't. The commanding codes
Are not tradition. To identify it
Is to define its form, to say: this image
Is its body visible to the important eye.

The bronze of the wise man seated in repose
Is not its form. Tradition is wise but not
The figure of the wise man fixed in sense.
The scholar is always distant in the space
Around him and in that distance meditates
Things still more distant. And tradition is near.
It joins and does not separate. What, then,

Is its true form? Is it the memory
That hears a pin fall in New Amsterdam
Or sees the new North River heaping up
Dutch ice on English boats? The memory
Is part of the classic imagination, posed
Too often to be more than secondhand.
Tradition is much more than the memory.

Is it experience, say, the final form
To which all other forms, at last, return,
The frame of a repeated effect, is it that?
Are we characters in an arithmetic
Or letters of a curious alphabet;
And is tradition an unfamiliar sum,
A legend scrawled in a script we cannot read?

It has a clear, a single, a solid form,
That of the son who bears upon his back
The father that he loves, and bears him from
The ruins of the past, out of nothing left,
Made noble by the honor he receives,
As if in a golden cloud. The son restores
The father. He hides his ancient blue beneath

His own bright red. But he bears him out of love,
His life made double by his father's life,
Ascending the humane. This is the form
Tradition wears, the clear, the single form,
The solid shape, Aeneas seen, perhaps,
By Nicolas Poussin, yet nevertheless
A tall figure upright in a giant's air.

The father keeps on living in the son, the world
Of the father keeps on living in the world
Of the son. These survivals out of time and space
Come to us every day. And yet they are
Merely parts of the general fiction of the mind:
Survivals of a good that we have loved,
Made eminent in a reflected seeming-so.

                                                              1945

Memorandum

The katy-dids at Ephrata return
But this time at another place.
It is the same sound, the same season,
But it is not Ephrata.

You said the dew falls in the blood.
The dew falls deep in the mind
On life itself and there the katy-dids
Keep whanging their brass wings. . . .

Say this to Pravda, tell the damned rag
That the peaches are slowly ripening.
Say that the American moon comes up
Cleansed clean of lousy Byzantium.

Say that in the clear Atlantic night
The plums are blue on the trees. The katy-dids
Bang cymbals as they used to do.
Millions hold millions in their arms.

                                                    1946

First Warmth

I wonder, have I lived a skeleton's life,
As a questioner about reality,

A countryman of all the bones in the world?
Now, here, the warmth I had forgotten becomes

Part of the major reality, part of
An appreciation of a reality;

And thus an elevation, as if I lived
With something I could touch, touch every way.

                                                    1947

As You Leave the Room

You speak. You say: Today's character is not
A skeleton out of its cabinet. Nor am I.

That poem about the pineapple, the one
About the mind as never satisfied,

The one about the credible hero, the one
About summer, are not what skeletons think about.

I wonder, have I lived a skeleton's life,
As a disbeliever in reality,

A countryman of all the bones in the world?
Now, here, the snow I had forgotten becomes

Part of a major reality, part of
An appreciation of a reality

And thus an elevation, as if I left
With something I could touch, touch every way.

And yet nothing has been changed except what is
Unreal, as if nothing had been changed at all.

1947–55?

PLAYS

Three Travelers Watch a Sunrise

The characters are three Chinese, two negroes and a girl.

The scene represents a forest of heavy trees on a hilltop in eastern Pennsylvania. To the right is a road, obscured by bushes. It is about four o'clock of a morning in August, at the present time.

When the curtain rises, the stage is dark. The limb of a tree creaks. A negro carrying a lantern passes along the road. The sound is repeated. The negro comes through the bushes, raises his lantern and looks through the trees. Discerning a dark object among the branches, he shrinks back, crosses stage, and goes out through the wood to the left.

A second negro comes through the bushes to the right. He carries two large baskets, which he places on the ground just inside of the bushes. Enter three Chinese, one of whom carries a lantern. They pause on the road.

SECOND CHINESE
>   All you need,
>   To find poetry,
>   Is to look for it with a lantern.
>> (*The Chinese laugh.*)

THIRD CHINESE
>   I could find it without,
>   On an August night,
>   If I saw no more
>   Than the dew on the barns.
>> (*The Second Negro makes a sound to attract their attention. The three Chinese come through the bushes. The first is short, fat, quizzical, and of middle age. The second is of middle height, thin and turning gray; a man of sense and sympathy. The third is a young man, intent, detached. They wear European clothes.*)

SECOND CHINESE (*Glancing at the baskets.*)
>   Dew is water to see,
>   Not water to drink:

We have forgotten water to drink.
Yet I am content
Just to see sunrise again.
I have not seen it
Since the day we left Pekin.
It filled my doorway,
Like whispering women.

FIRST CHINESE

And I have never seen it.
If we have no water,
Do find a melon for me
In the baskets.

> (*The Second Negro, who has been opening the baskets, hands the First Chinese a melon.*)

FIRST CHINESE

Is there no spring?

> (*The negro takes a water bottle of red porcelain from one of the baskets and places it near the Third Chinese.*)

SECOND CHINESE (*To Third Chinese.*)

Your porcelain water bottle.

> (*One of the baskets contains costumes of silk, red, blue and green. During the following speeches, the Chinese put on these costumes, with the assistance of the negro, and seat themselves on the ground.*)

THIRD CHINESE

This fetches its own water.

> (*Takes the bottle and places it on the ground in the center of the stage.*)

I drink from it, dry as it is,
As you from maxims, (*To Second Chinese.*)
Or you from melons. (*To First Chinese.*)

FIRST CHINESE

Not as I, from melons.
Be sure of that.

SECOND CHINESE

Well, it is true of maxims.

> (*He finds a book in the pocket of his costume, and reads from it.*)

"The court had known poverty and wretchedness; hu-

manity had invaded its seclusion, with its suffering and
its pity."

> (*The limb of the tree creaks.*)

Yes: it is true of maxims,
Just as it is true of poets,
Or wise men, or nobles,
Or jade.

FIRST CHINESE

Drink from wise men? From jade?
Is there no spring?

> (*Turning to the negro, who has taken a jug from
> one of the baskets.*)

Fill it and return.

> (*The negro removes a large candle from one of the
> baskets and hands it to the First Chinese; then takes
> the jug and the lantern and enters the trees to the
> left. The First Chinese lights the candle and places
> it on the ground near the water bottle.*)

THIRD CHINESE

There is a seclusion of porcelain
That humanity never invades.

FIRST CHINESE (*With sarcasm.*)

Porcelain!

THIRD CHINESE

It is like the seclusion of sunrise,
Before it shines on any house.

FIRST CHINESE

Pooh!

SECOND CHINESE

This candle is the sun;
This bottle is earth:
It is an illustration
Used by generations of hermits.
The point of difference from reality
Is this:
That, in this illustration,
The earth remains of one color—
It remains red,
It remains what it is.
But when the sun shines on the earth,

In reality
It does not shine on a thing that remains
What it was yesterday.
The sun rises
On whatever the earth happens to be.

THIRD CHINESE

And there are indeterminate moments
Before it rises,
Like this,
    (*With a backward gesture.*)
Before one can tell
What the bottle is going to be—
Porcelain, Venetian glass,
Egyptian . . .
Well, there are moments
When the candle, sputtering up,
Finds itself in seclusion,
    (*He raises the candle in the air.*)
And shines, perhaps, for the beauty of shining.
That is the seclusion of sunrise
Before it shines on any house.
    (*Replacing the candle.*)

FIRST CHINESE (*Wagging his head.*)

As abstract as porcelain.

SECOND CHINESE

Such seclusion knows beauty
As the court knew it.
The court woke
In its windless pavilions,
And gazed on chosen mornings,
As it gazed
On chosen porcelain.
What the court saw was always of the same color,
And well shaped,
And seen in a clear light.
    (*He points to the candle.*)
It never woke to see,
And never knew,
The flawed jars,
The weak colors,

The contorted glass.
It never knew
The poor lights.
       (*He opens his book significantly.*)
When the court knew beauty only,
And in seclusion,
It had neither love nor wisdom.
These came through poverty
And wretchedness,
Through suffering and pity.
       (*He pauses.*)
It is the invasion of humanity
That counts.
       (*The limb of the tree creaks. The First Chinese turns,*
       for a moment, in the direction of the sound.)
FIRST CHINESE (*Thoughtfully.*)
The light of the most tranquil candle
Would shudder on a bloody salver.
SECOND CHINESE (*With a gesture of disregard.*)
It is the invasion
That counts.
If it be supposed that we are three figures
Painted on porcelain
As we sit here,
That we are painted on this very bottle,
The hermit of the place,
Holding this candle to us,
Would wonder;
But if it be supposed
That we are painted as warriors,
The candle would tremble in his hands;
Or if it be supposed, for example,
That we are painted as three dead men,
He could not see the steadiest light,
For sorrow.
It would be true
If an emperor himself
Held the candle.
He would forget the porcelain
For the figures painted on it.

THIRD CHINESE (*Shrugging his shoulders.*)
    Let the candle shine for the beauty of shining.
    I dislike the invasion
    And long for the windless pavilions.
    And yet it may be true
    That nothing is beautiful
    Except with reference to ourselves,
    Nor ugly,
    Nor high,
        (*Pointing to the sky.*)
    Nor low.
        (*Pointing to the candle.*)
    No: not even sunrise.
    Can you play of this
        (*Mockingly to First Chinese.*)
    For us?
        (*He stands up.*)
FIRST CHINESE (*Hesitatingly.*)
    I have a song
    Called *Mistress and Maid.*
    It is of no interest to hermits
    Or emperors,
    Yet it has a bearing;
    For if we affect sunrise,
    We affect all things.

THIRD CHINESE
    It is a pity it is of women.
    Sing it.
        (*He takes an instrument from one of the baskets and
        hands it to the First Chinese, who sings the following
        song, accompanying himself, somewhat tunelessly, on
        the instrument. The Third Chinese takes various
        things out of the basket for tea. He arranges fruit.
        The First Chinese watches him while he plays. The
        Second Chinese gazes at the ground. The sky shows
        the first signs of morning.*)

FIRST CHINESE
    The mistress says, in a harsh voice,
      "He will be thinking in strange countries
      Of the white stones near my door,

And I—I am tired of him."
She says, sharply, to her maid,
"Sing to yourself no more."

Then the maid says, to herself,
 "He will be thinking in strange countries
 Of the white stones near her door;
 But it is me he will see
 At the window, as before.

 "He will be thinking in strange countries
 Of the green gown I wore.
 He was saying good-by to her."
The maid drops her eyes and says to her mistress,
 "I shall sing to myself no more."

THIRD CHINESE
 That affects the white stones,
 To be sure.
   (*They laugh.*)

FIRST CHINESE
 And it affects the green gown.

SECOND CHINESE
 Here comes our black man.
   (*The Second Negro returns, somewhat agitated,
   with water but without his lantern. He hands the
   jug to the Third Chinese. The First Chinese from
   time to time strikes the instrument. The Third Chi-
   nese, who faces the left, peers in the direction from
   which the negro has come.*)

THIRD CHINESE
 You have left your lantern behind you.
 It shines, among the trees,
 Like evening Venus in a cloud-top.
   (*The Second Negro grins but makes no explanation.
   He seats himself behind the Chinese to the right.*)

FIRST CHINESE
 Or like a ripe strawberry
 Among its leaves.
   (*They laugh.*)
 I heard tonight
 That they are searching the hill

For an Italian.

He disappeared with his neighbor's daughter.

SECOND CHINESE (*Confidingly.*)

    I am sure you heard

    The first eloping footfall,

    And the drum

    Of pursuing feet.

FIRST CHINESE (*Amusedly.*)

    It was not an elopement.

    The young gentleman was seen

    To climb the hill,

    In the manner of a tragedian

    Who sweats.

    Such things happen in the evening.

    He was

    Un misérable.

SECOND CHINESE

    Reach the lady quickly.

        (*The First Chinese strikes the instrument twice as a prelude to his narrative.*)

FIRST CHINESE

    There are as many points of view

    From which to regard her

    As there are sides to a round bottle.

        (*Pointing to the water bottle.*)

    She was represented to me

    As beautiful.

        (*They laugh. The First Chinese strikes the instrument, and looks at the Third Chinese, who yawns.*)

FIRST CHINESE (*Reciting.*)

    She was as beautiful as a porcelain water bottle.

        (*He strikes the instrument in an insinuating manner.*)

FIRST CHINESE

    She was represented to me

    As young.

    Therefore my song should go

    Of the color of blood.

        (*He strikes the instrument. The limb of the tree*

*creaks. The First Chinese notices it and puts his
hand on the knee of the Second Chinese, who is
seated between him and the Third Chinese, to call
attention to the sound. They are all seated so that
they do not face the spot from which the sound comes.
A dark object, hanging to the limb of the tree, be-
comes a dim silhouette. The sky grows constantly
brighter. No color is to be seen until the end of the
play.)*

SECOND CHINESE (*To First Chinese.*)
    It is only a tree
    Creaking in the night wind.
THIRD CHINESE (*Shrugging his shoulders.*)
    There would be no creaking
    In the windless pavilions.
FIRST CHINESE (*Resuming.*)
    So far the lady of the present ballad
    Would have been studied
    By the hermit and his candle
    With much philosophy;
    And possibly the emperor would have cried,
    "More light!"
    But it is a way with ballads
    That the more pleasing they are
    The worse end they come to;
    For here it was also represented
    That the lady was poor—
    The hermit's candle would have thrown
    Alarming shadows,
    And the emperor would have held
    The porcelain in one hand . . .
    She was represented as clinging
    To that sweaty tragedian,
    And weeping up the hill.
SECOND CHINESE (*With a grimace.*)
    It does not sound like an elopement.
FIRST CHINESE
    It is a doleful ballad,
    Fit for keyholes.

THIRD CHINESE
  Shall we hear more?
SECOND CHINESE
  Why not?
THIRD CHINESE
  We came for isolation,
  To rest in sunrise.
SECOND CHINESE (*Raising his book slightly.*)
  But this will be a part of sunrise,
  And can you tell how it will end?—
  Venetian,
  Egyptian,
  Contorted glass . . .
        (*He turns toward the light in the sky to the right,
        darkening the candle with his hands.*)
  In the meantime, the candle shines,
        (*Indicating the sunrise.*)
  As you say,
        (*To the Third Chinese.*)
  For the beauty of shining.
FIRST CHINESE (*Sympathetically.*)
  Oh! it will end badly.
  The lady's father
  Came clapping behind them
  To the foot of the hill.
  He came crying,
  "Anna, Anna, Anna!"
        (*Imitating.*)
  He was alone without her,
  Just as the young gentleman
  Was alone without her:
  Three beggars, you see,
  Begging for one another.
        (*The First Negro, carrying two lanterns, approaches
        cautiously through the trees. At the sight of him, the
        Second Negro, seated near the Chinese, jumps to his
        feet. The Chinese get up in alarm. The Second Ne-
        gro goes around the Chinese toward the First Negro.
        All see the body of a man hanging to the limb of the
        tree. They gather together, keeping their eyes fixed on*

it. The First Negro comes out of the trees and places the lanterns on the ground. He looks at the group and then at the body.)

FIRST CHINESE (*Moved.*)

The young gentleman of the ballad.

THIRD CHINESE (*Slowly, approaching the body.*)

And the end of the ballad.

Take away the bushes.

(*The negroes commence to pull away the bushes.*)

SECOND CHINESE

Death, the hermit,

Needs no candle

In his hermitage.

(*The Second Chinese snuffs out the candle. The First Chinese puts out the lanterns. As the bushes are pulled away, the figure of a girl, sitting half stupe-fied under the tree, suddenly becomes apparent to the Second Chinese and then to the Third Chinese. They step back. The negroes move to the left. When the First Chinese sees the girl, the instrument slips from his hands and falls noisily to the ground. The girl stirs.*)

SECOND CHINESE (*To the girl.*)

Is that you, Anna?

(*The girl starts. She raises her head, looks around slowly, leaps to her feet and screams.*)

SECOND CHINESE (*Gently.*)

Is that you, Anna?

(*She turns quickly toward the body, looks at it fixedly and totters up the stage.*)

ANNA (*Bitterly.*)

Go.

Tell my father:

He is dead.

(*The Second and Third Chinese support her. The First Negro whispers to the First Chinese, then takes the lanterns and goes through the opening to the road, where he disappears in the direction of the valley.*)

FIRST CHINESE (*To Second Negro.*)

Bring us fresh water

From the spring.

> (*The Second Negro takes the jug and enters the trees to the left. The girl comes gradually to herself. She looks at the Chinese and at the sky. She turns her back toward the body, shuddering, and does not look at it again.*)

ANNA

It will soon be sunrise.

SECOND CHINESE

One candle replaces
Another.

> (*The First Chinese walks toward the bushes to the right. He stands by the roadside, as if to attract the attention of anyone passing.*)

ANNA (*Simply.*)

When he was in his fields,
I worked in ours—
Wore purple to see;
And when I was in his garden
I wore gold ear-rings.
Last evening I met him on the road.
He asked me to walk with him
To the top of the hill.
I felt the evil,
But he wanted nothing.
He hanged himself in front of me.

> (*She looks for support. The Second and Third Chinese help her toward the road. At the roadside, the First Chinese takes the place of the Third Chinese. The girl and the two Chinese go through the bushes and disappear down the road. The stage is empty except for the Third Chinese. He walks slowly across the stage, pushing the instrument out of his way with his foot. It reverberates. He looks at the water bottle.*)

THIRD CHINESE

Of the color of blood . . .
Seclusion of porcelain . . .
Seclusion of sunrise . . .

> (*He picks up the water bottle.*)

The candle of the sun

Will shine soon
On this hermit earth.
        (*Indicating the bottle.*)
It will shine soon
Upon the trees,
And find a new thing
        (*Indicating the body.*)
Painted on this porcelain,
        (*Indicating the trees.*)
But not on this.
        (*Indicating the bottle.*)
        (*He places the bottle on the ground. A narrow cloud over the valley becomes red. He turns toward it, then walks to the right. He finds the book of the Second Chinese lying on the ground, picks it up and turns over the leaves.*)
Red is not only
The color of blood,
Or
        (*Indicating the body.*)
Of a man's eyes,
Or
        (*Pointedly.*)
Of a girl's.
And as the red of the sun
Is one thing to me
And one thing to another,
So it is the green of one tree
        (*Indicating.*)
And the green of another,
Which without it would all be black.
Sunrise is multiplied,
Like the earth on which it shines,
By the eyes that open on it,
Even dead eyes,
As red is multiplied by the leaves of trees.
        (*Toward the end of this speech, the Second Negro comes from the trees to the left, without being seen. The Third Chinese, whose back is turned toward the negro, walks through the bushes to the right and dis-*)

appears on the road. The negro looks around at the objects on the stage. He sees the instrument, seats himself before it and strikes it several times, listening to the sound. One or two birds twitter. A voice, urging a horse, is heard at a distance. There is the crack of a whip. The negro stands up, walks to the right and remains at the side of the road. The curtain falls slowly.)

Carlos Among the Candles

The stage is indistinguishable when the curtain rises.

The room represented is semi-circular. In the center, at the back, is a large round window, covered by long curtains. There is a door at the right and one at the left. Farther forward on the stage there are two long, low, wooden tables, one at the right and one at the left. The walls and the curtains over the window are of a dark reddish-purple, with a dim pattern of antique gold.

Carlos is an eccentric pedant of about forty. He is dressed in black. He wears close-fitting breeches and a close-fitting, tightly-buttoned, short coat with long tails. His hair is rumpled. He leaps upon the stage through the door at the right. Nothing is visible through the door. He has a long thin white lighted taper, which he holds high above his head as he moves, fantastically, over the stage, examining the room in which he finds himself.

When he has completed examining the room, he tip-toes to the table at the right and lights a single candle at the edge of the table nearest the front of the stage. It is a thin black candle, not less than two feet high. All the other candles are like it. They give very little light.

He speaks in a lively manner, but is over-nice in sounding his words.

As the candle begins to burn, he steps back, regarding it. Nothing else is visible on the table.

CARLOS:

How the solitude of this candle penetrates me! I light a candle in the darkness. It fills the darkness with solitude, which becomes my own. I become a part of the solitude of the candle . . . of the darkness flowing over the house and into it. . . This room . . . and the profound room outside. . . Just to go through a door, and the change . . . the becoming a part, instantly, of that profounder room . . . and equally to feel it communicating, with the same persistency, its own mood, its own influence . . . and there, too, to feel the lesser influences of the shapes of things, of exhalations,

615

sounds . . . to feel the mood of the candle vanishing and the mood of the special night coming to take its place. . .

(*He sighs. After a pause he pirouettes, and then continues.*)

I was always affected by the grand style. And yet I have been thinking neither of mountains nor of morgues. . . To think of this light and of myself . . . it is a duty. . . . Is it because it makes me think of myself in other places in such a light . . . or of other people in other places in such a light? How true that is: other people in other places in such a light. . . If I looked in at that window and saw a single candle burning in an empty room . . . but if I saw a figure. . . If, now, I felt that there was someone outside. . . The vague influence . . . the influence that clutches. . . But it is not only here and now. . . It is in the morning . . . the difference between a small window and a large window . . . a blue window and a green window. . . It is in the afternoon and in the evening . . . in effects, so drifting, that I know myself to be incalculable, since the causes of what I am are incalculable. . .

(*He springs toward the table, flourishing his taper. At the end farthest from the front of the stage, he discovers a second candle, which he lights. He goes back to his former position.*)

The solitude dissolves. . . The light of two candles has a meaning different from the light of one . . . and an effect different from the effect of one. . . And the proof that that is so, is that I feel the difference. . . The associations have drifted a little and changed, and I have followed in this change. . . If I see myself in other places in such a light, it is not as I saw myself before. If I see other people in other places in such a light, the people and places are different from the people and places I saw before. The solitude is gone. It is as if a company of two or three people had just separated, or as if they were about to gather. These candles are too far apart.

(*He flourishes his taper above the table and finds a third candle in the center of it, which he lights.*)

And yet with only two candles it would have been a cold and respectable company; for the feeling of coldness and respectability persists in the presence of three, modified a little, as if a kind of stateliness had modified into a kind of elegance. . . How far away from the isolation of the single candle, as arrogant of the vacancy around it as three are arrogant of association. . . It is no longer as if a company had just separated. It is only as if it were about to gather . . . as if one were soon to forget the room because of the people in the room . . . people tempered by the lights around them, affected by the lights around them . . . sensible that one more candle would turn this formative elegance into formative luxury.

(*He lights a fourth candle. He indulges his humor.*)

And the suggestion of luxury into the suggestion of magnificence.

(*He lights a fifth candle.*)

And the beginning of magnificence into the beginning of splendor.

(*He lights a sixth candle. He sighs deeply.*)

In how short a time have I been solitary, then respectable—in a company so cold as to be stately, then elegant, then conscious of luxury, even magnificence; and now I come, gradually, to the beginning of splendor. Truly, I am a modern.

(*He dances around the room.*)

To have changed so often and so much . . . or to have been changed . . . to have been carried by the lighting of six candles through so many lives and to have been brought among so many people. . . This grows more wonderful. Six candles burn like an adventure that has been completed. They are established. They are a city . . . six common candles . . . seven. . .

(*He lights another and another, until he has lighted twelve, saying after them, in turn:*)

Eight, nine, ten, eleven, twelve.

(*Following this, he goes on tip-toe to the center of the stage,*) *where he looks at the candles. Their brilliance has raised his spirits to the point of gaiety. He turns from the lighted table to face the dark one at the left. He holds his taper before him.*)

Darkness again . . . as if a night wind had come blowing . . . but too weakly to fling the cloth of darkness.

(*He goes to the window, draws one of the curtains a little and peers out. He sees nothing.*)

I had as lief look into night as look into the dark corner of a room. Darkness expels me.

(*He goes forward, holding his taper high above him, until he comes to the table at the left. He finds this covered with candles, like the table at the right, and lights them, with whimsical motions, one by one. When all the candles have been lighted, he runs to the center of the stage, holding his hands over his eyes. Then he returns to the window and flings aside the curtains. The light from the window falls on the tall stalks of flowers outside. The flowers are like hollyhocks, but they are unnaturally large, of gold and silver. He speaks excitedly.*)

Where now is my solitude and the lonely figure of solitude? Where now are the two stately ones that left their coldness behind them? They have taken their bareness with them. Their coldness has followed them. Here there will be silks and fans . . . the movement of arms . . . rumors of Renoir . . . coiffures . . . hands . . . scorn of Debussy . . . communications of body to body. . . There will be servants, as fat as plums, bearing pineapples from the Azores . . . because of twenty-four candles, burning together, as if their light had dispelled a phantasm, falling on silks and fans . . . the movement of arms. . . The pulse of the crowd will beat out the shallow pulses . . . it will fill me.

(*A strong gust of wind suddenly blows into the room, extinguishing several of the candles on the table at the left. He runs to the table at the left and looks, as if startled, at the extinguished candles. He buries his head in his arms.*)

That, too, was phantasm. . . The night wind came into the room. . . The fans are invisible upon the floor.

(*In a burst of feeling, he blows out all the candles that are still burning on the table at the left. He crosses the stage and stands before the table at the right. After a moment he goes slowly to the back of the stage and draws the curtains over the window. He returns to the table at the right.*)

What is there in the extinguishing of light? It is like twelve wild birds flying in autumn.

(*He blows out one of the candles.*)

It is like an eleven-limbed oak tree, brass-colored in frost. . . . Regret. . .

(*He blows out another candle.*)

It is like ten green sparks of a rocket, oscillating in air. . . The extinguishing of light . . . how closely regret follows it.

(*He blows out another candle.*)

It is like the diverging angles that follow nine leaves drifting in water, and that compose themselves brilliantly on the polished surface.

(*He blows out another candle.*)

It is like eight pears in a nude tree, flaming in twilight. . . The extinguishing of light is like that. The season is sorrowful. The air is cold.

(*He blows out another candle.*)

It is like the six Pleiades, and the hidden one, that makes them seven.

(*He blows out another candle.*)

It is like the seven Pleiades, and the hidden one, that makes them six.

(*He blows out another candle.*)

The extinguishing of light is like the five purple palmations of cinquefoil withering. . . It is full of the incipiencies of darkness . . . of desolation that rises as a feeling rises. . . Imagination wills the five purple palmations of cinquefoil. But in

this light they have the appearance of withering. . . To feel
and, in the midst of feeling, to imagine . . .

(*He blows out another candle.*)

The extinguishing of light is like the four posts of a cadaver,
two at its head and two at its feet, to-wit: its arms and legs.

(*He blows out another candle.*)

It is like three peregrins, departing.

(*He blows out another candle.*)

It is like heaven and earth in the eye of the disbeliever.

(*He blows out another candle. He dances around the room.
He returns to the single candle that remains burning.*)

The extinguishing of light is like that old Hesper, clapped
upon by clouds.

(*He stands in front of the candle, so as to obscure it.*)

The spikes of his light bristle around the edge of the bulk.
The spikes bristle among the clouds and behind them. There
is a spot where he was bright in the sky. . . It remains fixed
a little in the mind.

(*He opens the door at the right. Outside, the night is as blue
as water. He crosses the stage and opens the door at the left. Once
more he flings aside the curtains. He extinguishes his taper. He
looks out. He speaks with elation.*)

Oh, ho! Here is matter beyond invention.

(*He springs through the window. Curtain.*)

Bowl, Cat and Broomstick

Two figures sit in the circle of a spotlight, on a white bench, before a golden curtain. The rest of the stage is obscure. Their shadows are strongly reflected on the curtain. One, at the right, wears a gown falling below his knees. It is black covered with a faded silver pattern. Flat hat. Jewel in the hat. Black stockings. Small silver buckles on his shoes. He is gaunt. He is reading aloud from a book which is bound in yellow paper, like a French book. The other figure is smaller and more supple. Tight green costume. He is listening closely. The floor of the stage has a violet covering.

BOWL (*With finical importance*)
She says—m—m—she says—m. (*Patronizing Cat*) I shall continue to translate this for you. Fleurs—des fleurs—full of flowers—full of tawny flowers—

CAT (*A little bored*)
Tawny? What is the word for tawny?

BOWL
Rouges.

CAT
But, Bowl, rouges means red.

BOWL (*Coolly*)
No doubt, when it refers to something red. But when, as here, it refers to something tawny, then it means tawny.

Broomstick saunters on the stage at the left. Heavily built. Hard-looking. Elderly. He uses a stick. Blue blouse, red sash, white trousers, like a French peasant. Bowl studies his book. Cat is interested in Broomstick's appearance.

BROOMSTICK (*Brusquely*)
Bibliophiles!

CAT (*Very politely*)
Bowl is reading from the poems of Claire Dupray.

BROOMSTICK
Charming!

He seats himself on the bench.

CAT

What was the line you read last, Bowl?

BOWL (*With chilly diffidence*)

Le jardin est si plein de fleurs rouges . . . The garden is so full of tawny flowers.

BROOMSTICK

Remarkable!

CAT

He translates fleurs rouges by tawny flowers.

BROOMSTICK

Why not?

CAT

But, of course, rouges means red.

BROOMSTICK

A man with so firm a faith in the meaning of words should not listen to poetry.

CAT

Broomstick!

Bowl turns to the frontispiece of his book. Cat looks furtively at the portrait there.

BOWL

I say tawny because it is obvious that Claire Dupray means tawny.

BROOMSTICK

Her portrait tells you that?

BOWL

Yes; and her age tells me. She cannot be more than twenty-two.

CAT

And at twenty-two one does not like red flowers?

BOWL

At twenty-two, with eyes as large as those of Claire Dupray, with hair combed as a girl combs her hair—concealing in its arrangement the things it begins to disclose to her—and then, most of all, with the look she has here, one goes in for things that go with one's own mystery.

BROOMSTICK

And, of course, red flowers and one's own mystery—

BOWL

Are incongruous.

CAT

You see.

BOWL

They are incongruous at that age. It is an age when red be-
comes tawny, when blue becomes aerial—and when a girl, at
least, when a girl like Claire Dupray, becomes a poetess.

CAT

Say poet—poet. I hate poetess.

BROOMSTICK

Oh, poetess is just the word at twenty-two! What you are
thinking of is forty-two.

CAT

You are right, old Broomstick. May I see the portrait?

Bowl hands him the book.

You speak of her hair because her head is bare.

BROOMSTICK

It is only the poetess of forty-two that sits for a portrait
covered.

BOWL

I speak of her hair because in the case of a poetess, in the
sense in which that word is just and beautiful, the speaking of
it means so much to the portrait of her.

CAT

More than her nose or her chin? She has a delicate nose. She
has a good chin.

BROOMSTICK

She has a good chin! Oh, ho! She has a good chin. Has
she?

BOWL

Her hair reveals her. Three things live in the portrait of a
poetess: her hair, her eyes and her mouth. These make it pos-
sible to discover something of what she is from the image of
her. Claire Dupray has black hair. It is arranged simply, but,
for all that, it remains full of the long motions of her bare
arms. Is not that a part of her? What are we to expect from
such a poetess? Waxen odes? Skimped meditations? Let me
have the book.

Cat hands him the book.

Take this poem on twilight. What does she see in twilight? Not the commonplace end of daily momentum. She sees the light continuing to burn in stars. She says that the sun burns all night. And, in that, she sees the incessant momentum that tranquillizes because of the knowledge that it is immortal. The sun burns all night. She says that she will love as long as she lives.

CAT (*Fascinated*)
She is glorious.

BROOMSTICK
How little it would take to turn the poets into the only true comedians! There's no truer comedy than this hodge-podge of men and sunlight, women and moonlight, houses and clouds, and so on.

BOWL
Nor any truer tragedy.

BROOMSTICK
No one believes in tragedy.

CAT
At twenty-two—

BROOMSTICK
That brings us to her eyes.

BOWL
But her eyes are nothing unless you believe in tragedy.

CAT
I believe.

BROOMSTICK
Poor sensualist! You think you believe. The truth is, you believe in eyes.

CAT
Have you seen the portrait?

He hands Broomstick the book.

Now, we shall have Broomstick on eyes.

BROOMSTICK
I concede that these eyes are capable of tragedy. But that is

not the same thing as tragedy itself: and it is tragedy itself that we were speaking of.

BOWL

Then let me amend what I said: and say, instead, that her eyes are nothing unless you believe in eyes.

BROOMSTICK

A very proper amendment. But I am rather old, don't you think, to believe in eyes? I have reached the point where I don't believe in much of anything except legs. And one cannot be too sure even of legs.

CAT

Legs are art, not literature.

BROOMSTICK

They were always intended to be.

CAT

They are still intended to be.

BOWL

All the more reason for saying no more about them. It is a new thing that the eyes of a poetess should bring us to this.

BROOMSTICK (*Drily*)

Possibly. And yet it may not be so new, after all. (*He pauses.*) We are not living in the seventeenth century for nothing. (*He pauses.*) Moreover, just as the relations of man and moonlight, women and moonlight, man and mountains, women and waves, and so on, are undefined, so the relations of eyes and legs, lips and cheeks, and that kind of thing, are equally undefined. It is all part of the universal comedy, which the poets ignore, because they continue to believe in tragedy. You see tragedy in these eyes. They are capable of tragedy. Does the voice of tragedy dwell in this mouth?

BOWL

I was not thinking of that. I was thinking merely of the expression it gives to the portrait. That expression is vitally biographical.

BROOMSTICK

Vitally biographical? The book has the usual preface. Is that not biographical enough?

CAT

We shall come to that in time.

BOWL (*Making a point*)

We had agreed to skip it, for the moment, and to form our own idea of Claire Dupray from her portrait, and from her poetry. That is what we are doing.

CAT

Bowl is an idealist, you know.

BROOMSTICK

An idealist has nothing to fear from a preface.

CAT

That she has heavy, black hair, large eyes, capable of tragedy, as you say, which means, I hope, that they are brilliant and mysterious, for so I see them, and that her mouth is expressive, this seemed preface enough.

BROOMSTICK

It is the kind of preface you yourself would write and that is why you think it preface enough.

CAT (*Offended*)

What do you mean?

BROOMSTICK (*Putting him down*)

I assume that in what Bowl has been saying of this portrait he has been intending to derive from ink and paper a vivid impression of the sensibility of his poetess. You have seen only her beauty.

CAT (*As if justified*)

I make no bones about that. There is a special power in the poetry of a beauty.

BROOMSTICK

For you: yes.

CAT

For you, too.

BROOMSTICK (*Maliciously*)

Pathos, perhaps; not power. But Bowl's portrait is a failure.

BOWL

A failure?

BROOMSTICK (*Sarcastically*)

You might have been describing one of the many dark-haired and dark-eyed Peloponnesians. And what you say of the expressive quality of the mouth has been trite for a long time.

BOWL

And true for a long time.

BROOMSTICK

If it has been true for a long time, then I doubt if it is true any longer. The fact remains that your young poetess is an old poetess.

BOWL (*Querulously*)

Ought her hair to be cropped?

BROOMSTICK

Unquestionably. Something of the sort.

CAT

Adieu, Dupray!

BROOMSTICK

I do not insist on the cropped hair.

CAT

But on something of the sort. Poor Claire!

BROOMSTICK

You judge her poetry by her portrait. Very well. I judge her portrait by her poetry.

BOWL

You are prejudiced by the cant of the moment that she should be of her day.

BROOMSTICK

That is far from being the cant of the moment. It will still be the cant of the moment in the eighteenth century, and in the nineteenth century, too.

BOWL

Broomstick, it galls me to agree with you. If I submit, will you go no farther?

BROOMSTICK

I shall go as far as possible. Take the book again.

He hands the book to Bowl.

Would it have any effect if she wore black pendants in her ears? It should have. Test her poetry by that. They are wearing black pendants, you know.

Cat snatches the book out of Bowl's hands.

CAT

Would it have any effect?

He laughs heartily.

Confound it, Bowl! What was that poem about? The incessant momentum that tranquillizes because of the knowledge that it is immortal. Tranquillity and long, black pendants!

Bowl recovers the book from him.

BOWL
As you like. My portrait is not a failure. Broomstick is right. A poetess should be of her day. But he is thinking of the poetess of forty-two: the sophisticated poetess. I am thinking of the unsophisticated poetess of twenty-two. If she happens to look like one of the dark-haired and dark-eyed Peloponnesians, that is not a rococo pose. It is an unaffected disclosure of her relationship.

CAT
Dupray returns, a little.

BOWL
And besides, Broomstick, what you mean, no doubt, by being of one's day is being one's self in one's day.

BROOMSTICK
Well, Bowl, I submit to that, provided you, in turn, go no farther.

BOWL
Only to the extent of saying that Claire Dupray is simply herself in this portrait. It is true that she is not of the long, black pendant type. Nevertheless, she is of her day, in the sense in which you used that phrase.

CAT (*Succulently*)
And I may be tempted by her again?

BOWL
In the long run, you would have been tempted by her regardless of these, or any other, considerations; so that your question is not honest.

CAT (*Brazenly*)
It is honest enough. I am still a little harrowed by the poem on twilight.

BROOMSTICK
It haunts my own mind.

BOWL (*To Cat*)
You said that there was a special power in the poetry of a beauty.

CAT (*Alarmed*)
I said it. But I am not so certain of the beauty now.
BOWL
Then let me see.

He turns over the pages of the book rapidly.

Banal Sojourn:—Old Catamaran—an amazing thing in the
way it designs the catamaran on the surface of the sea: one of
the poems in which by the description of the thing seen, she
makes an image of the greatest intensity. Nothing in nature
could have revealed what her imagination and sensibility have
revealed. How true that is to my conception of Claire Dupray!
She is beautiful. Her poems are beautiful. Here are similar
poems: Les Dahlias—The Dahlias—What an extraordinary ef-
fect one gets from seeing things as they are, that is to say:
from looking at ordinary things intensely!
BROOMSTICK
But to look at ordinary things intensely, is not to see things
as they are. However, go on.
BOWL
Here, in another division of her book, is a group of poems in
which she studies herself—not the individual Claire Dupray,
but the racial Claire—
CAT
Ah! The racial Claire.
BOWL
When you think of what the study of self used to mean, and
then read these clear and thoughtful pages—
BROOMSTICK (*Impatiently*)
Read them, read them. Please do.
BOWL
I thought you might like me to explain.
BROOMSTICK
I may, bye and bye; but if these pages are as clear as you say
they are, then I am content to have you read them first.
BOWL (*Translating a la mode*)
In the motion of trees, m—m—that is, in the movement of
trees, I find my own agitation. If it be morning, the mood of
poplars, filled with sunlight, glistening in the dark west-wind,
is already my own. If it be noon, the tossing of the elm trees

in the golden sky has an identity with my own exulting. And if it be evening, the forms of trees, moving not at all, defining their beauty through the obscure air, m—m—m— These things are atrociously difficult in English. In French, they seem almost pellucid. Let me see: the forms of trees, moving not at all, outlining their beauty across the dim air, or in the midst of the dim air—the forms of trees are the only images in my mind. She means that the images in her mind are of the forms of trees and that there are no other images there.

Cat takes the book from Bowl, turns to the portrait, looks at it, as if impressed, and then returns the book to Bowl, marking his place.

BOWL

Does not such a poem, so young, so communicative, warrant the definition of the poetess made by her portrait? How new she is!

BROOMSTICK (*Astonished*)

New? But read another.

BOWL

One of The Dahlias, this time. Le Bouquet—The Bouquet. She tries to stimulate the sense of color and, therefore, her poem consists of nothing more than the names of colors. You read these rapidly and so produce in the mind a visual impression like that produced by the actual sight of dahlias.

BROOMSTICK

And that is a poem?

CAT (*Apprehensively*)

Read just as rapidly as you can.

BOWL

Are you ready?

CAT

I am.

BROOMSTICK

I am ready.

BOWL

Green, green, green—no doubt, this indicates the stalks—green, green, green, green, green, yellow, green, yellow, green, green, gray, green, yellow, yellow, white, white, white, green—

BROOMSTICK

We ought to be getting to the flowers soon.

BOWL

We're right in them now. The white, white, white indicates white flowers, white dahlias.

BROOMSTICK

I am sorry. I was thinking of a white holder. I thought we had come up the stalks and were going around the edge of the holder.

CAT (*Like a knowing person*)

This is really very promising; but not for Broomstick, I'm afraid.

BROOMSTICK

There might be some advantage in getting along.

BOWL

Shall I read another?

BROOMSTICK (*Striking the floor with his cane*)

Provided I select it.

BOWL

Nothing would please me more.

He hands the book to Broomstick, who refers to the index at the back.

BROOMSTICK (*With the hopeful manner of one consulting an index*)

The Shadow in the Trees.

BOWL

That is the one I read you a moment ago, the one beginning, "In the movement of trees, I find my own agitation."

BROOMSTICK (*With disgust*)

An index is full of pit-falls.

CAT

Why do you say that? I thought The Shadow in the Trees rather lovely.

BROOMSTICK (*Energetically*)

Pshaw! And imagine Bowl's thinking it new. Only because he wanted to think well of his poetess. She is young. Therefore she is new. Or therefore her poetry is young. That is one of the most persistent of all fallacies. Her poetry is young if her spirit is young—or whatever it is that poetry springs from.

Not otherwise. This emotional waste, like the first poem, the one about twilight, this stale monism like The Shadow of the Trees, this sophisticated green, green, green—it is all thirty years old at the least. Thirty years at the very least. I might even put it in the last century. But aside from the poems we have actually heard—and I daresay the book is full of others just like them—what I hold against Claire Dupray, above everything else, is just that she is not herself in her day. To be herself she must be free. She looks free (*looking at the portrait*). But she is not free in spirit, and therefore her portrait fails.

BOWL

Free from what? I regarded The Shadow in the Trees as an instance of good seventeenth century work. And Le Bouquet seemed fairly advanced. Such things are not myths.

BROOMSTICK

The most fascinating myths in the world. To be free, Claire Dupray must be as free from to-day as from yesterday.

CAT

Rather difficult.

BROOMSTICK

Indescribably so. Look at people the world over. The extent and degree of imitation is appalling.

BROOMSTICK

Necessarily, as a matter of convenience.

BROOMSTICK

Oh, but convenience is impossible in poetry. It is bad enough that Claire Dupray imitates at all. But it is fatal that she imitates the point of view and the feelings of a generation ago. Let her portrait be ever so charming. When all is said and done, she is a poetess in the old-maidenly sense of the word, not the brilliant and vivid creature you conceive her to be.

BOWL

In what year was her book published?

Broomstick examines the title page.

BROOMSTICK

In sixteen hundred and sixty.

CAT

If Bowl was right in supposing her to be twenty-two then, she would be twenty-nine or thirty now.

Cat makes a wry face. Bowl seems shocked. Broomstick turns a page or two.

BROOMSTICK (*With zest*)

Avant—Propos. You must help me with this, Bowl. My knowledge of French is not absolutely penetrating.

BOWL

Well, avant-propos means preface.

BROOMSTICK (*Imitating Bowl*)

Claire Madeleine Colombier Dupray, the writer of the—m— the extraordinary poems gathered together in this volume, was born—m—in Geneva, of French parents. During the first fifteen years of her life she lived with her parents in Geneva, receiving instruction from her mother, a Calvinist, a woman of pronounced devotional character, and of wide reading.

Cat goes behind Broomstick and looks over his shoulder. Bowl paces up and down the stage.

BROOMSTICK

It will interest my readers—What a nice old touch that is!— It will interest my readers to know that Madame Dupray—

BOWL (*With force*)

Madame?

Cat puts his finger on the word over Broomstick's shoulder.

CAT

Mademoiselle, mademoiselle.

BROOMSTICK

I always confuse them. It will interest my readers to know that Mademoiselle Dupray still has in her possession some of the books from which she first became acquainted with—m— literature, in her early years.

BOWL (*Protesting*)

Still has? Her early years?

CAT

Jeunesse. Youth.

BROOMSTICK

The abbott of Bellozane's translation of Plutarch's Lives, Florio's Dictionary, a volume of Du Bellay . . . There is a list of twenty or thirty in all. I shall skip them.

Bowl is visibly affected.

BROOMSTICK

I gather that the books were selected by her mother. Piquant reading for a young French poetess.

Cat takes the book from Broomstick and runs with it to Bowl.

CAT

Here is something about the portrait. Translate it, Bowl.

Bowl looks at the preface. He seems incredulous. He looks at the portrait and then at the preface, and again at the portrait. He throws the book on the floor.

BOWL

What a fool I have been!

He hurries off the stage. Cat is dumbfounded. Broomstick laughs loudly. Cat picks up the book and returns it to Broomstick.

CAT

What does it say about the portrait?

BROOMSTICK

Well, just here, skipping a few lines, the sentence you saw reads as follows: The frontispiece of this volume was etched in Amsterdam, from life, after Mademoiselle Dupray, at the age of twenty-three, in the year—

He pauses.

CAT

At the age of twenty-three, in the year—

BROOMSTICK

Sixteen hundred and thirty-seven.

CAT

Sixteen hundred and thirty-seven! If she was twenty-three in sixteen hundred and thirty-seven, she was forty-six in sixteen hundred and sixty when her poems were published. She is more than fifty now—fifty-three. She will love as long as she lives.

BROOMSTICK (*Cavalierly*)

I think you are right, after all, in your translation of *rouges*.

CAT

Oh, red, red! Acutely red! Damn all portraits of poets and poetesses.

Cat collapses. Broomstick laughs again, turning over the pages of the book.

BROOMSTICK

One should always read a preface first.

He helps Cat off the stage.

CURTAIN.

THE NECESSARY ANGEL

Essays on Reality and the Imagination

> . . . I am the necessary angel of earth,
> Since, in my sight, you see the earth again.
>
> THE AURORAS OF AUTUMN

Introduction

ONE FUNCTION of the poet at any time is to discover by his own thought and feeling what seems to him to be poetry at that time. Ordinarily he will disclose what he finds in his own poetry by way of the poetry itself. He exercises this function most often without being conscious of it, so that the disclosures in his poetry, while they define what seems to him to be poetry, are disclosures of poetry, not disclosures of definitions of poetry. The papers that have been collected here are intended to disclose definitions of poetry. In short, they are intended to be contributions to the theory of poetry and it is this and this alone that binds them together.

Obviously, they are not the carefully organized notes of systematic study. Except for the paper on one of Miss Moore's poems, they were written to be spoken and this affects their character. While all of them were published, after they had served the purposes for which they were written, I had no thought of making a book out of them. Several years ago, when this was suggested, I felt that their occasional and more or less informal character made it desirable at least to postpone coming to a decision. The theory of poetry, as a subject of study, was something with respect to which I had nothing but the most ardent ambitions. It seemed to me to be one of the great subjects of study. I do not mean one more *Ars Poetica* having to do, say, with the techniques of poetry and perhaps with its history. I mean poetry itself, the naked poem, the imagination manifesting itself in its domination of words. The few pages that follow are, now, alas! the only realization possible to me of those excited ambitions.

But to their extent they are a realization; and it is because that is true, that is to say, because they seem to me to communicate to the reader the portent of the subject, if nothing more, that they are presented here. Only recently I spoke of certain poetic acts as subtilizing experience and varying appearance: "The real is constantly being engulfed in the unreal. . . . [Poetry] is an illumination of a surface, the movement of a self in the rock." A force capable of bringing about fluctuations in reality in words free from mysticism is a force independent of one's desire to elevate it. It needs no elevation. It has only to be presented, as best one is able to present it. These are not pages of criticism nor of philosophy. Nor are they merely literary pages. They are pages that have to do with one of the enlargements of life. They are without pretence beyond my desire to add my own definition to poetry's many existing definitions.

WALLACE STEVENS

Contents

The Noble Rider
and the Sound of Words

IN THE *Phaedrus*, Plato speaks of the soul in a figure. He says:

> Let our figure be of a composite nature—a pair of winged horses and a charioteer. Now the winged horses and the charioteer of the gods are all of them noble, and of noble breed, while ours are mixed; and we have a charioteer who drives them in a pair, and one of them is noble and of noble origin, and the other is ignoble and of ignoble origin; and, as might be expected, there is a great deal of trouble in managing them. I will endeavor to explain to you in what way the mortal differs from the immortal creature. The soul or animate being has the care of the inanimate, and traverses the whole heaven in divers forms appearing;—when perfect and fully winged she soars upward, and is the ruler of the universe; while the imperfect soul loses her feathers, and drooping in her flight at last settles on the solid ground.

We recognize at once, in this figure, Plato's pure poetry; and at the same time we recognize what Coleridge called Plato's dear, gorgeous nonsense. The truth is that we have scarcely read the passage before we have identified ourselves with the charioteer, have, in fact, taken his place and, driving his winged horses, are traversing the whole heaven. Then suddenly we remember, it may be, that the soul no longer exists and we droop in our flight and at last settle on the solid ground. The figure becomes antiquated and rustic.

I

What really happens in this brief experience? Why does this figure, potent for so long, become merely the emblem of a mythology, the rustic memorial of a belief in the soul and in a distinction between good and evil? The answer to these questions is, I think, a simple one.

I said that suddenly we remember that the soul no longer exists and we droop in our flight. For that matter, neither charioteers nor chariots any longer exist. Consequently, the figure does not become unreal because we are troubled about the soul. Besides, unreal things have a reality of their own, in poetry as elsewhere. We do not hesitate, in poetry, to yield ourselves to the unreal, when it is possible to yield ourselves. The existence of the soul, of charioteers and chariots and of winged horses is immaterial. They did not exist for Plato, not even the charioteer and chariot; for certainly a charioteer driving his chariot across the whole heaven was for Plato precisely what he is for us. He was unreal for Plato as he is for us. Plato, however, could yield himself, was free to yield himself, to this gorgeous nonsense. We cannot yield ourselves. We are not free to yield ourselves.

Just as the difficulty is not a difficulty about unreal things, since the imagination accepts them, and since the poetry of the passage is, for us, wholly the poetry of the unreal, so it is not an emotional difficulty. Something else than the imagination is moved by the statement that the horses of the gods are all of them noble, and of noble breed or origin. The statement is a moving statement and is intended to be so. It is insistent and its insistence moves us. Its insistence is the insistence of a speaker, in this case Socrates, who, for the moment, feels delight, even if a casual delight, in the nobility and noble breed. Those images of nobility instantly become nobility itself and determine the emotional level at which the next page or two are to be read. The figure does not lose its vitality because of any failure of feeling on Plato's part. He does not communicate nobility coldly. His horses are not marble horses, the reference to their breed saves them from being that. The fact that the horses are not marble horses helps, moreover, to save the charioteer from being, say, a creature of cloud. The result is that we recognize, even if we cannot realize, the feelings of the robust poet clearly and fluently noting the images in his mind and by means of his robustness, clearness and fluency communicating much more than the images themselves. Yet we do not quite yield. We cannot. We do not feel free.

In trying to find out what it is that stands between Plato's figure and ourselves, we have to accept the idea that, however legendary it appears to be, it has had its vicissitudes. The history of a figure of speech or the history of an idea, such as the idea of nobility, cannot be very different from the history of anything else. It is the episodes that are of interest, and here the episode is that of our diffidence. By us and ourselves, I mean you and me; and yet not you and me as individuals but as representatives of a state of mind. Adams in his work on Vico makes the remark that the true history of the human race is a history of its progressive mental states. It is a remark of interest in this relation. We may assume that in the history of Plato's figure there have been incessant changes of response; that these changes have been psychological changes, and that our own diffidence is simply one more state of mind due to such a change.

The specific question is partly as to the nature of the change and partly as to the cause of it. In nature, the change is as follows: The imagination loses vitality as it ceases to adhere to what is real. When it adheres to the unreal and intensifies what is unreal, while its first effect may be extraordinary, that effect is the maximum effect that it will ever have. In Plato's figure, his imagination does not adhere to what is real. On the contrary, having created something unreal, it adheres to it and intensifies its unreality. Its first effect, its effect at first reading, is its maximum effect, when the imagination, being moved, puts us in the place of the charioteer, before the reason checks us. The case is, then, that we concede that the figure is all imagination. At the same time, we say that it has not the slightest meaning for us, except for its nobility. As to that, while we are moved by it, we are moved as observers. We recognize it perfectly. We do not realize it. We understand the feeling of it, the robust feeling, clearly and fluently communicated. Yet we understand it rather than participate in it.

As to the cause of the change, it is the loss of the figure's vitality. The reason why this particular figure has lost its vitality is that, in it, the imagination adheres to what is unreal. What happened, as we were traversing the whole heaven, is that the imagination lost its power to sustain us. It has the strength of reality or none at all.

2

What has just been said demonstrates that there are degrees of the imagination, as, for example, degrees of vitality and, therefore, of intensity. It is an implication that there are degrees of reality. The discourse about the two elements seems endless. For my own part, I intend merely to follow, in a very hasty way, the fortunes of the idea of nobility as a characteristic of the imagination, and even as its symbol or alter ego, through several of the episodes in its history, in order to determine, if possible, what its fate has been and what has determined its fate. This can be done only on the basis of the relation between the imagination and reality. What has been said in respect to the figure of the charioteer illustrates this.

I should like now to go on to other illustrations of the relation between the imagination and reality and particularly to illustrations that constitute episodes in the history of the idea of nobility. It would be agreeable to pass directly from the charioteer and his winged horses to Don Quixote. It would be like a return from what Plato calls "the back of heaven" to one's own spot. Nevertheless, there is Verrocchio (as one among others) with his statue of Bartolommeo Colleoni, in Venice, standing in the way. I have not selected him as a Neo-Platonist to relate us back from a modern time to Plato's time, although he does in fact so relate us, just as through Leonardo, his pupil, he strengthens the relationship. I have selected him because there, on the edge of the world in which we live today, he established a form of such nobility that it has never ceased to magnify us in our own eyes. It is like the form of an invincible man, who has come, slowly and boldly, through every warlike opposition of the past and who moves in our midst without dropping the bridle of the powerful horse from his hand, without taking off his helmet and without relaxing the attitude of a warrior of noble origin. What man on whose side the horseman fought could ever be anything but fearless, anything but indomitable? One feels the passion of rhetoric begin to stir and even to grow furious; and one thinks that, after all, the noble style, in whatever it creates, merely perpetuates the noble style. In this statue, the apposition between the imagination and reality is too favorable to the imagination. Our difficulty is not primarily with any detail. It is primarily with the whole. The point is not so much to analyze the difficulty as to determine whether we share it, to find out whether it exists, whether we regard this specimen of the genius of Verrocchio and of the Renaissance as a bit of uncommon panache, no longer quite the appropriate thing outdoors, or whether we regard it, in the language of Dr. Richards, as something inexhaustible to meditation or, to speak for myself, as a thing of a nobility responsive to the most minute demand. It seems, nowadays, what it may very well not have seemed a few years ago, a little overpowering, a little magnificent.

Undoubtedly, Don Quixote could be Bartolommeo Colleoni in Spain. The tradition of Italy is the tradition of the imagination. The tradition of Spain is the tradition of reality. There is no apparent reason why the reverse should not be true. If this is a just observation, it indicates that the relation between the imagination and reality is a question, more or less, of precise equilibrium. Thus it is not a question of the difference between grotesque extremes. My purpose is not to contrast Colleoni with Don Quixote. It is to say that one passed into the other, that one became and was the other. The difference between them is that Verrocchio believed in one kind of nobility and Cervantes, if he believed in any, believed in another kind. With Verrocchio it was an affair of the noble style, whatever his prepossession respecting the nobility of man as a real animal may have been. With Cervantes, nobility was not a thing of the imagination. It was a part of reality, it was something that exists in life, something so true to us that it is in danger of ceasing to exist, if we isolate it, something in the mind of a precarious tenure. These may be words. Certainly, however, Cervantes sought to set right the balance between the imagination and reality. As we come closer to our own times in Don Quixote and as we are drawn together by the intelligence common to the two periods, we may derive so much satisfaction from the restoration of reality as to become wholly prejudiced against the imagination. This is to reach a conclusion prematurely, let alone that it may be to reach a conclusion in respect to something as to which no conclusion is possible or desirable.

There is in Washington, in Lafayette Square, which is the square on which the White House faces, a statue of Andrew Jackson, riding a horse with one of the most beautiful tails in the world. General Jackson is raising his hat in a gay gesture, saluting the ladies of his generation. One looks at this work of Clark Mills and thinks of the remark of Bertrand Russell that to acquire immunity to eloquence is of the utmost importance to the citizens of a democracy. We are bound to think that Colleoni, as a mercenary, was a much less formidable man than General Jackson, that he meant less to fewer people and that, if Verrocchio could have applied his prodigious poetry to Jackson, the whole American outlook today might be imperial. This work is a work of fancy. Dr. Richards cites Coleridge's theory of fancy as opposed to imagination. Fancy is an activity of the mind which puts things together of choice, *not* the will, as a principle of the mind's being, striving to realize itself in knowing itself. Fancy, then, is an exercise of selection from among objects already supplied by association, a selection made for purposes which are not then and therein being shaped but have been already fixed. We are concerned then with an object occupying a position as remarkable as any that can be found in the United States in which there is not the slightest trace of the imagination. Treating this work as typical, it is obvious that the American will as a principle of the mind's being is easily satisfied in its efforts to realize itself in knowing itself. The statue may be dismissed, not without speaking of it again as a thing that at least makes us conscious of ourselves as we were, if not as we are. To that extent, it helps us to know ourselves. It helps us to know ourselves as we were and that helps us to know ourselves as we are. The statue is neither of the imagination nor of reality. That it is a work of fancy precludes it from being a work of the imagination. A glance at it shows it to be unreal. The bearing of this is that there can be works, and this includes poems, in which neither the imagination nor reality is present.

The other day I was reading a note about an American artist

who was said to have "turned his back on the aesthetic whims and theories of the day, and established headquarters in lower Manhattan." Accompanying this note was a reproduction of a painting called *Wooden Horses*. It is a painting of a merry-go-round, possibly of several of them. One of the horses seems to be prancing. The others are going lickety-split, each one struggling to get the bit in his teeth. The horse in the center of the picture, painted yellow, has two riders, one a man, dressed in a carnival costume, who is seated in the saddle, the other a blonde, who is seated well up the horse's neck. The man has his arms under the girl's arms. He holds himself stiffly in order to keep his cigar out of the girl's hair. Her feet are in a second and shorter set of stirrups. She has the legs of a hammer-thrower. It is clear that the couple are accustomed to wooden horses and like them. A little behind them is a younger girl riding alone. She has a strong body and streaming hair. She wears a short-sleeved, red waist, a white skirt and an emphatic bracelet of pink coral. She has her eyes on the man's arms. Still farther behind, there is another girl. One does not see much more of her than her head. Her lips are painted bright red. It seems that it would be better if someone were to hold her on her horse. We, here, are not interested in any aspect of this picture except that it is a picture of ribald and hilarious reality. It is a picture wholly favorable to what is real. It is not without imagination and it is far from being without aesthetic theory.

3

These illustrations of the relation between the imagination and reality are an outline on the basis of which to indicate a tendency. Their usefulness is this: that they help to make clear, what no one may ever have doubted, that just as in this or that work the degrees of the imagination and of reality may vary, so this variation may exist as between the works of one age and the works of another. What I have said up to this point amounts to this: that the idea of nobility exists in art today only in degenerate forms or in a much diminished state, if, in fact, it exists at all or otherwise than on sufferance; that this is due to failure in the relation between the imagination and reality. I should now like to add that this failure is due, in turn, to the pressure of reality.

A variation between the sound of words in one age and the sound of words in another age is an instance of the pressure of reality. Take the statement by Bateson that a language, considered semantically, evolves through a series of conflicts between the denotative and the connotative forces in words; between an asceticism tending to kill language by stripping words of all association and a hedonism tending to kill language by dissipating their sense in a multiplicity of associations. These conflicts are nothing more than changes in the relation between the imagination and reality. Bateson describes the seventeenth century in England as predominately a connotative period. The use of words in connotative senses was denounced by Locke and Hobbes, who desired a mathematical plainness; in short, perspicuous words. There followed in the eighteenth century an era of poetic diction. This was not the language of the age but a language of poetry peculiar to itself. In time, Wordsworth came to write the preface to the second edition of the *Lyrical Ballads* (1800), in which he said that the first volume had been published, "as an experiment, which, I hoped, might be of some use to ascertain how far, by fitting to metrical arrangement a selection of the real language of man in a state of vivid sensation, that sort of pleasure and that quantity of pleasure may be imparted, which a Poet may rationally endeavour to impart."

As the nineteenth century progressed, language once more became connotative. While there have been intermediate reactions, this tendency toward the connotative is the tendency today. The interest in semantics is evidence of this. In the case of some of our prose writers, as, for example, Joyce, the language, in quite different ways, is wholly connotative. When we say that Locke and Hobbes denounced the connotative use of words as an abuse, and when we speak of reactions and reforms, we are speaking, on the one hand, of a failure of the imagination to adhere to reality, and, on the other, of a use of language favorable to reality. The statement that the tendency toward the connotative is the tendency today is disputable. The general movement in the arts, that is to say, in painting and in music, has been the other way. It is hard to say that the tendency is toward the connotative in the use of words without also saying that the tendency is toward the imagination in other directions. The interest in the subconscious and in surrealism shows the tendency toward the imaginative. Boileau's remark that Descartes had cut poetry's throat is a remark that could have been made respecting a great many people during the last hundred years, and of no one more aptly than of Freud, who, as it happens, was familiar with it and repeats it in his *Future of an Illusion*. The object of that essay was to suggest a surrender to reality. His premise was that it is the unmistakable character of the present situation not that the promises of religion have become smaller but that they appear less credible to people. He notes the decline of religious belief and disagrees with the argument that man cannot in general do without the consolation of what he calls the religious illusion and that without it he would not endure the cruelty of reality. His conclusion is that man must venture at last into the hostile world and that this may be called education to reality. There is much more in that essay inimical to poetry and not least the observation in one of the final pages that "The voice of the intellect is a soft one, but it does not rest until it has gained a hearing." This, I fear, is intended to be the voice of the realist.

A tendency in language toward the connotative might very well parallel a tendency in other arts toward the denotative. We have just seen that that is in fact the situation. I suppose that the present always appears to be an illogical complication. The language of Joyce goes along with the dilapidations of Braque and Picasso and the music of the Austrians. To the extent that this painting and this music are the work of men who regard it as part of the science of painting and the science of music it is the work of realists. Actually its effect is that of the imagination, just as the effect of abstract painting is so often that of the imagination, although that may be different. Busoni said, in a letter to his wife, "I have made the painful discovery that nobody loves and feels music." Very likely, the reason there is a tendency in language toward the connotative today is that there are many who love it and feel it. It may be that Braque and Picasso love and feel painting and that Schön-berg loves and feels music, although it seems that what they love and feel is something else.

A tendency toward the connotative, whether in language or elsewhere, cannot continue against the pressure of reality. If it is the pressure of reality that controls poetry, then the immediacy of various theories of poetry is not what it was. For instance, when Rostrevor Hamilton says, "The object of contemplation is the highly complex and unified content of consciousness, which comes into being through the developing subjective attitude of the percipient," he has in mind no such "content of consciousness" as every newspaper reader experiences today.

By way of further illustration, let me quote from Croce's Oxford lecture of 1933. He said: "If . . . poetry is intuition and expression, the fusion of sound and imagery, what is the material which takes on the form of sound and imagery? It is the whole man: the man who thinks and wills, and loves, and hates; who is strong and weak, sublime and pathetic, good and wicked; man in the exultation and agony of living; and together with the man, integral with him, it is all nature in its perpetual labour of evolution. . . . Poetry . . . is the triumph of contemplation. . . . Poetic genius chooses a strait path in which passion is calmed and calm is passionate."

Croce cannot have been thinking of a world in which all normal life is at least in suspense, or, if you like, under blockage. He was thinking of normal human experience.

Quite apart from the abnormal aspect of everyday life today, there is the normal aspect of it. The spirit of negation has been so active, so confident and so intolerant that the commonplaces about the romantic provoke us to wonder if our salvation, if the way out, is not the romantic. All the great things have been denied and we live in an intricacy of new and local mythologies, political, economic, poetic, which are asserted with an ever-enlarging incoherence. This is accompanied by an absence of any authority except force, operative or imminent. What has been called the disparagement of reason is an instance of the absence of authority. We pick up the radio and find that comedians regard the public use of words of more than two syllables as funny. We read of the opening of the National Gallery at Washington and we are convinced, in the end, that the pictures are counterfeit, that museums are impositions and that Mr. Mellon was a monster. We turn to a recent translation of Kierkegaard and we find him saying: "A great deal has been said about poetry reconciling one with existence; rather it might be said that it arouses one against existence; for poetry is unjust to men . . . it has use only for the elect, but that is a poor sort of reconciliation. I will take the case of sickness. Aesthetics replies proudly and quite consistently, 'That cannot be employed, poetry must not become a hospital.' Aesthetics culminates . . . by regarding sickness in accordance with the principle enunciated by Friedrich Schlegel: 'Nur Gesundheit ist liebenswürdig.' (Health alone is lovable.)"

The enormous influence of education in giving everyone a little learning, and in giving large groups considerably more: something of history, something of philosophy, something of literature; the expansion of the middle class with its common preference for realistic satisfactions; the penetration of the masses of people by the ideas of liberal thinkers, even when that penetration is indirect, as by the reporting of the reasons why people oppose the ideas that they oppose,—these are normal aspects of everyday life. The way we live and the way we work alike cast us out on reality. If fifty private houses were to be built in New York this year, it would be a phenomenon. We no longer live in homes but in housing projects and this is so whether the project is literally a project or a club, a dormitory, a camp or an apartment in River House. It is not only that there are more of us and that we are actually close together. We are close together in every way. We lie in bed and listen to a broadcast from Cairo, and so on. There is no distance. We are intimate with people we have never seen and, unhappily, they are intimate with us. Democritus plucked his eye out because he could not look at a woman without thinking of her as a woman. If he had read a few of our novels, he would have torn himself to pieces. Dr. Richards has noted "the widespread increase in the aptitude of the average mind for self-dissolving introspection, the generally heightened awareness of the goings-on of our own minds, *merely as goings-on*." This is nothing to the generally heightened awareness of the goings-on of other people's minds, *merely as goings-on*. The way we work is a good deal more difficult for the imagination than the highly civilized revolution that is occurring in respect to work indicates. It is, in the main, a revolution for more pay. We have been assured, by every visitor, that the American businessman is absorbed in his business and there is nothing to be gained by disputing it. As for the workers, it is enough to say that the word has grown to be literary. They have become, at their work, in the face of the machines, something approximating an abstraction, an energy. The time must be coming when, as they leave the factories, they will be passed through an air-chamber or a bar to revive them for riot and reading. I am sorry to have to add that to one that thinks, as Dr. Richards thinks, that poetry is the supreme use of language, some of the foreign universities in relation to our own appear to be, so far as the things of the imagination are concerned, as Verrocchio is to the sculptor of the statue of General Jackson.

These, nevertheless, are not the things that I had in mind when I spoke of the pressure of reality. These constitute the drift of incidents, to which we accustom ourselves as to the weather. Materialism is an old story and an indifferent one. Robert Wolseley said: "True genius . . . will enter into the hardest and dryest thing, enrich the most barren Soyl, and inform the meanest and most uncomely matter . . . the baser, the emptier, the obscurer, the fouler, and the less susceptible of Ornament the subject appears to be, the more is the Poet's Praise . . . who, as Horace says of Homer, can fetch Light out of Smoak, Roses out of Dunghills, and give a kind of Life to the Inanimate . . ." (Preface to Rochester's *Valentinian*, 1685, *English Association Essays and Studies 1939*). By the pressure of reality, I mean the pressure of an external event or events on the consciousness to the exclusion of any power of contemplation. The definition ought to be exact and, as it is, may be merely pretentious. But when one is trying to think of a whole generation and of a world at war, and trying at the same time to see what is happening to the imagination, particularly if one believes that that is what matters most, the plainest statement of what is happening can easily appear to be an affectation.

For more than ten years now, there has been an extraordinary pressure of news—let us say, news incomparably more pretentious than any description of it, news, at first, of the collapse of our system, or, call it, of life; then of news of a new world, but of a new world so uncertain that one did not know anything whatever of its nature, and does not know now, and could not tell whether it was to be all-English, all-German, all-Russian, all-Japanese, or all-American, and cannot tell now; and finally news of a war, which was a renewal of what, if it was not the greatest war, became such by this continuation. And for more than ten years, the consciousness of the world has concentrated on events which have made the ordinary movement of life seem to be the movement of people in the intervals of a storm. The disclosures of the impermanence of the past suggested, and suggest, an impermanence of the future. Little of what we have believed has been true. Only the prophecies are true. The present is an opportunity to repent. This is familiar enough. The war is only a part of a war-like whole. It is not possible to look backward and to see that the same thing was true in the past. It is a question of pressure, and pressure is incalculable and eludes the historian. The Napoleonic era is regarded as having had little or no effect on the poets and the novelists who lived in it. But Coleridge and Wordsworth and Sir Walter Scott and Jane Austen did not have to put up with Napoleon and Marx and Europe, Asia and Africa all at one time. It seems possible to say that they knew of the events of their day much as we know of the bombings in the interior of China and not at all as we know of the bombings of London, or, rather, as we should know of the bombings of Toronto or Montreal. Another part of the war-like whole to which we do not respond quite as we do to the news of war is the income tax. The blanks are specimens of mathematical prose. They titillate the instinct of self-preservation in a class in which that instinct has been forgotten. Virginia Woolf thought that the income tax, if it continued, would benefit poets by enlarging their vocabularies and I dare say that she was right.

If it is not possible to assert that the Napoleonic era was the end of one era in the history of the imagination and the beginning of another, one comes closer to the truth by making that assertion in respect to the French Revolution. The defeat or triumph of Hitler are parts of a war-like whole but the fate of an individual is different from the fate of a society. Rightly or wrongly, we feel that the fate of a society is involved in the orderly disorders of the present time. We are confronting, therefore, a set of events, not only beyond our power to tranquillize them in the mind, beyond our power to reduce them and metamorphose them, but events that stir the emotions to violence, that engage us in what is direct and immediate and real, and events that involve the concepts and sanctions that are the order of our lives and may involve our very lives; and these events are occurring persistently with increasing omen, in what may be called our presence. These are the things that I had in mind when I spoke of the pressure of reality, a pressure great enough and prolonged enough to bring about the end of one era in the history of the imagination and, if so, then great enough to bring about the beginning of another. It is one of the peculiarities of the imagination that it is always at the end of an era. What happens is that it is always attaching itself to a new reality, and adhering to it. It is not that there is a new imagination but that there is a new reality. The pressure of reality may, of course, be less than the general pressure that I have described. It exists for individuals according to the circumstances of their lives or according to the characteristics of their minds. To sum it up, the pressure of reality is, I think, the determining factor in the artistic character of an era and, as well, the determining factor in the artistic character of an individual. The resistance to this pressure or its evasion in the case of individuals of extraordinary imagination cancels the pressure so far as those individuals are concerned.

4

Suppose we try, now, to construct the figure of a poet, a possible poet. He cannot be a charioteer traversing vacant space, however ethereal. He must have lived all of the last two thousand years, and longer, and he must have instructed himself, as best he could, as he went along. He will have thought that Virgil, Dante, Shakespeare, Milton placed themselves in remote lands and in remote ages; that their men and women were the dead—and not the dead lying in the earth, but the dead still living in their remote lands and in their remote ages, and living in the earth or under it, or in the heavens—and he will wonder at those huge imaginations, in which what is remote becomes near, and what is dead lives with an intensity beyond any experience of life. He will consider that although he has himself witnessed, during the long period of his life, a general transition to reality, his own measure as a poet, in spite of all the passions of all the lovers of the truth, is the measure of his power to abstract himself, and to withdraw with him into his abstraction the reality on which the lovers of truth insist. He must be able to abstract himself and also to abstract reality, which he does by placing it in his imagination. He knows perfectly that he cannot be too noble a rider, that he cannot rise up loftily in helmet and armor on a horse of imposing bronze. He will think again of Milton and of what was said about him: that "the necessity of writing for one's living blunts the appreciation of writing when it bears the mark of perfection. Its quality disconcerts our hasty writers; they are ready to condemn it as preciosity and affectation. And if to them the musical and creative powers of words convey little pleasure, how out of date and irrelevant they must find the . . . music of Milton's verse." Don Quixote will make it imperative for him to make a choice, to come to a decision regarding the imagination and reality; and he will find that it is not a choice of one over the other and not a decision that divides them, but something subtler, a recognition that here, too, as between these poles, the universal interdependence exists, and hence his choice and his decision must be that they are equal and inseparable. To take a single instance: When Horatio says,

> Now cracks a noble heart. Good night, sweet prince,
> And flights of angels sing thee to thy rest!

are not the imagination and reality equal and inseparable? Above all, he will not forget General Jackson or the picture of the *Wooden Horses*.

I said of the picture that it was a work in which everything was favorable to reality. I hope that the use of that bare word has been enough. But without regard to its range of meaning in thought, it includes all its natural images, and its connotations are without limit. Bergson describes the visual perception of a motionless object as the most stable of internal states. He says: "The object may remain the same, I may look at it from the same side, at the same angle, in the same light; nevertheless, the vision I now have of it differs from that which I have just had, even if only because the one is an instant later than the other. My memory is there, which conveys something of the past into the present."

Dr. Joad's comment on this is: "Similarly with external things. Every body, every quality of a body resolves itself into an enormous number of vibrations, movements, changes. What is it that vibrates, moves, is changed? There is no answer. Philosophy has long dismissed the notion of substance and modern physics has endorsed the dismissal. . . . How, then, does the world come to appear to us as a collection of solid, static objects extended in space? Because of the intellect, which presents us with a false view of it."

The poet has his own meaning for reality, and the painter has, and the musician has; and besides what it means to the intelligence and to the senses, it means something to everyone, so to speak. Notwithstanding this, the word in its general sense, which is the sense in which I have used it, adapts itself instantly. The subject-matter of poetry is not that "collection of solid, static objects extended in space" but the life that is lived in the scene that it composes; and so reality is not that external scene but the life that is lived in it. Reality is things as they are. The general sense of the word proliferates its special senses. It is a jungle in itself. As in the case of a jungle, everything that makes it up is pretty much of one color. First, then, there is the reality that is taken for granted, that is latent and, on the whole, ignored. It is the comfortable American state of life of the eighties, the nineties and the first ten years of the present century. Next, there is the reality that has ceased to be indifferent, the years when the Victorians had been disposed of and intellectual minorities and social minorities began to take their place and to convert our state of life to something that might not be final. This much more vital reality made the life that had preceded it look like a volume of Ackermann's colored plates or one of Töpfer's books of sketches in Switzerland. I am trying to give the feel of it. It was the reality of twenty or thirty years ago. I say that it was a vital reality. The phrase gives a false impression. It was vital in the sense of being tense, of being instinct with the fatal or with what might be the fatal. The minorities began to convince us that the Victorians had left nothing behind. The Russians followed the Victorians, and the Germans, in their way, followed the Russians. The British Empire, directly or indirectly, was what was left and as to that one could not be sure whether it was a shield or a target. Reality then became violent and so remains. This much ought to be said to make it a little clearer that in speaking of the pressure of reality, I am thinking of life in a state of violence, not physically violent, as yet, for us in America, but physically violent for millions of our friends and for still more millions of our enemies and spiritually violent, it may be said, for everyone alive.

A possible poet must be a poet capable of resisting or evading the pressure of the reality of this last degree, with the knowledge that the degree of today may become a deadlier degree tomorrow. There is, however, no point to dramatizing the future in advance of the fact. I confine myself to the outline of a possible poet, with only the slightest sketch of his background.

5

Here I am, well-advanced in my paper, with everything of interest that I started out to say remaining to be said. I am interested in the nature of poetry and I have stated its nature, from one of the many points of view from which it is possible to state it. It is an interdependence of the imagination and reality as equals. This is not a definition, since it is incomplete. But it states the nature of poetry. Then I am interested in the role of the poet and this is paramount. In this area of my subject I might be expected to speak of the social, that is to say sociological or political, obligation of the poet. He has none. That he must be contemporaneous is as old as Longinus and I dare say older. But that he *is* contemporaneous is almost inevitable. How contemporaneous in the direct sense in which being contemporaneous is intended were the four great poets of whom I spoke a moment ago? I do not think that a poet owes any more as a social obligation than he owes as a moral obligation, and if there is anything concerning poetry about which people agree it is that the role of the poet is not to be found in morals. I cannot say what that wide agreement amounts to because the agreement (in which I do not join) that the poet is under a social obligation is equally wide. Reality is life and life is society and the imagination and reality; that is to say, the imagination and society are inseparable. That is pre-eminently true in the case of the poetic drama. The poetic drama needs a terrible genius before it is anything more than a literary relic. Besides the theater has forgotten that it could ever be terrible. It is not one of the instruments of fate, decidedly. Yes: the all-commanding subject-matter of poetry is life, the never-ceasing source. But it is not a social obligation. One does not love and go back to one's ancient mother as a social obligation. One goes back out of a suasion not to be denied. Unquestionably if a social movement moved one deeply enough, its moving poems would follow. No politician can command the imagination, directing it to do this or that. Stalin might grind his teeth the whole of a Russian winter and yet all the poets in the Soviets might remain silent the following spring. He might excite their imaginations by something he said or did. He would not command them. He is singularly free from that "cult of pomp," which is the comic side of the European disaster; and that means as much as anything to us. The truth is that the social obligation so closely urged is a phase of the pressure of reality which a poet (in the absence of dramatic poets) is bound to resist or evade today. Dante in Purgatory and Paradise was still the voice of the Middle Ages but not through fulfilling any social obligation. Since that is the role most frequently urged, if that role is eliminated, and if a possible poet is left facing life without any categorical exactions upon him, what then? What is his function? Certainly it is not to lead people out of the confusion in which they find themselves. Nor is it, I think, to comfort them while they follow their leaders to and fro. I think that his function is to make his imagination theirs and that he fulfills himself only as he sees his imagination become the light in the minds of others. His role, in short, is to help people to live their lives. Time and time again it has been said that he may not address himself to an élite. I think he may. There is not a poet whom we prize living today that does not address himself to an élite. The poet will continue to do this: to address himself to an élite even in a classless society, unless, perhaps, this exposes him to imprisonment or exile. In that event he is likely not to address himself to anyone at all. He may, like Shostakovich, content himself with pretence. He will, nevertheless, still be addressing himself to an élite, for all poets address themselves to someone and it is of the essence of that instinct, and it seems to amount to an instinct, that it should be to an élite, not to a drab but to a woman with the hair of a pythoness, not to a chamber of commerce but to a gallery of one's own, if there are enough of one's own to fill a gallery. And that élite, if it responds, not out of complaisance, but because the poet has quickened it, because he has educed from it that for which it was searching in itself and in the life around it and which it had not yet quite found, will thereafter do for the poet what he cannot do for himself, that is to say, receive his poetry.

I repeat that his role is to help people to live their lives. He has had immensely to do with giving life whatever savor it possesses. He has had to do with whatever the imagination and the senses have made of the world. He has, in fact, had to do with life except as the intellect has had to do with it and, as to that, no one is needed to tell us that poetry and philosophy are akin. I want to repeat for two reasons a number of observations made by Charles Mauron. The first reason is that these observations tell us what it is that a poet does to help people to live their lives and the second is that they prepare the way for a word concerning escapism. They are: that the artist transforms us into epicures; that he has to discover the possible work of art in the real world, then to extract it, when he does not himself compose it entirely; that he is *un amoureux perpétuel* of the world that he contemplates and thereby enriches; that art sets out to express the human soul; and finally that everything like a firm grasp of reality is eliminated from the aesthetic field. With these aphorisms in mind, how is it possible to condemn escapism? The poetic process is psychologically an escapist process. The chatter about escapism is, to my way of thinking, merely common cant. My own remarks about resisting or evading the pressure of reality mean escapism, if analyzed. Escapism has a pejorative sense, which it cannot be supposed that I include in the sense in which I use the word. The pejorative sense applies where the poet is not attached to reality, where the imagination does not adhere to reality, which, for my part, I regard as fundamental. If we go back to the collection of solid, static objects extended in space, which Dr. Joad posited, and if we say that the space is blank space, nowhere, without color, and that the objects, though solid, have no shadows and, though static, exert a mournful power, and, without elaborating this complete poverty, if suddenly we hear a different and familiar description of the place:

> This City now doth, like a garment, wear
> The beauty of the morning, silent bare,
> Ships, towers, domes, theatres, and temples lie
> Open unto the fields, and to the sky;
> All bright and glittering in the smokeless air;

if we have this experience, we know how poets help people to live their lives. This illustration must serve for all the rest. There is, in fact, a world of poetry indistinguishable from the world in which we live, or, I ought to say, no doubt, from the world in which we shall come to live, since what makes the poet the potent figure that he is, or was, or ought to be, is that he creates the world to which we turn incessantly and without knowing it and that he gives to life the supreme fictions without which we are unable to conceive of it.

And what about the sound of words? What about nobility, of which the fortunes were to be a kind of test of the value of the poet? I do not know of anything that will appear to have suffered more from the passage of time than the music of poetry and that has suffered less. The deepening need for words to express our thoughts and feelings which, we are sure, are all the truth that we shall ever experience, having no illusions, makes us listen to words when we hear them, loving them and feeling them, makes us search the sound of them, for a finality, a perfection, an unalterable vibration, which it is only within the power of the acutest poet to give them. Those of us who may have been thinking of the path of poetry, those who understand that words are thoughts and not only our own thoughts but the thoughts of men and women ignorant of what it is that they are thinking, must be conscious of this: that, above everything else, poetry is words; and that words, above everything else, are, in poetry, sounds. This being so, my time and yours might have been better spent if I had been less interested in trying to give our possible poet an identity and less interested in trying to appoint him to his place. But unless I had done these things, it might have been thought that I was rhetorical, when I was speaking in the simplest way about things of such importance that nothing is more so. A poet's words are of things that do not exist without the words. Thus, the image of the charioteer and of the winged horses, which has been held to be precious for all of time that matters, was created by words of things that never existed without the words. A description of Verrocchio's statue could be the integration of an illusion equal to the statue itself. Poetry is a revelation in words by means of the words. Croce was not speaking of poetry in particular when he said that language is perpetual creation. About nobility I cannot be sure that the decline, not to say the disappearance of nobility is anything more than a maladjustment between the imagination and reality. We have been a little insane about the truth. We have had an obsession. In its ultimate extension, the truth about which we have been insane will lead us to look beyond the truth to something in which the imagination will be the dominant complement. It is not only that the imagination adheres to reality, but, also, that reality adheres to the imagination and that the interdependence is essential. We may emerge from our *bassesse* and, if we do, how would it happen if not by the intervention of some fortune of the mind? And what would that fortune of the mind happen to be? It might be only commonsense but even that, a commonsense beyond the truth, would be a nobility of long descent.

The poet refuses to allow his task to be set for him. He denies that he has a task and considers that the organization of materia poetica is a contradiction in terms. Yet the imagination gives to everything that it touches a peculiarity, and it seems to me that the peculiarity of the imagination is nobility, of which there are many degrees. This inherent nobility is the natural source of another, which our extremely headstrong generation regards as false and decadent. I mean that nobility which is our spiritual height and depth; and while I know how difficult it is to express it, nevertheless I am bound to give a sense of it. Nothing could be more evasive and inaccessible. Nothing distorts itself and seeks disguise more quickly. There is a shame of disclosing it and in its definite presentations a horror of it. But there it is. The fact that it is there is what makes it possible to invite to the reading and writing of poetry men of intelligence and desire for life. I am not thinking of the ethical or the sonorous or at all of the manner of it. The manner of it is, in fact, its difficulty, which each man must feel each day differently, for himself. I am not thinking of the solemn, the portentous or demoded. On the other hand, I am evading a definition. If it is defined, it will be fixed and it must not be fixed. As in the case of an external thing, nobility resolves itself into an enormous number of vibrations, movements, changes. To fix it is to put an end to it. Let me show it to you unfixed.

Late last year Epstein exhibited some of his flower paintings at the Leicester Galleries in London. A commentator in *Apollo* said: "*How with this rage can beauty hold a plea* . . . The quotation from Shakespeare's 65th sonnet prefaces the catalogue. . . . It would be apropos to any other flower paintings than Mr. Epstein's. His make no pretence to fragility. They shout, explode all over the picture space and generally oppose the rage of the world with such a rage of form and colour as no flower in nature or pigment has done since Van Gogh."

What ferocious beauty the line from Shakespeare puts on when used under such circumstances! While it has its modulation of despair, it holds its plea and its plea is noble. There is no element more conspicuously absent from contemporary poetry than nobility. There is no element that poets have sought after, more curiously and more piously, certain of its obscure existence. Its voice is one of the inarticulate voices which it is their business to overhear and to record. The nobility of rhetoric is, of course, a lifeless nobility. Pareto's epigram that history is a cemetery of aristocracies easily becomes another: that poetry is a cemetery of nobilities. For the sensitive poet, conscious of negations, nothing is more difficult than the affirmations of nobility and yet there is nothing that he requires of himself more persistently, since in them and in their kind, alone, are to be found those sanctions that are the reasons for his being and for that occasional ecstasy, or ecstatic freedom of the mind, which is his special privilege.

It is hard to think of a thing more out of time than nobility. Looked at plainly it seems false and dead and ugly. To look at it at all makes us realize sharply that in our present, in the presence of our reality, the past looks false and is, therefore, dead and is, therefore, ugly; and we turn away from it as from something repulsive and particularly from the characteristic that it has a way of assuming: something that was noble in its day, grandeur that was, the rhetorical once. But as a wave is a force and not the water of which it is composed, which is never the same, so nobility is a force and not the manifestations of which it is composed, which are never the same. Possibly this description of it as a force will do more than anything else I can have said about it to reconcile you to it. It is not an artifice that the mind has added to human nature. The mind has added nothing to human nature. It is a violence from within that protects us from a violence without. It is the imagination pressing back against the pressure of reality. It seems, in the last analysis, to have something to do with our self-preservation; and that, no doubt, is why the expression of it, the sound of its words, helps us to live our lives.

The Figure of the Youth
as Virile Poet

I

IT APPEARS that what is central to philosophy is its least valu-
able part. Note the three scraps that follow. First, part of
a letter from Henry Bradley to Robert Bridges, as follows:

> My own attitude towards all philosophies old and new,
> is very sceptical. Not that I despise philosophy or phi-
> losophers; but I feel that the universe of being is too
> vast to be comprehended even by the greatest of the
> sons of Adam. We do get, I believe, glimpses of the real
> problems, perhaps even of the real solutions; but when
> we have formulated our questions, I fear we have always
> substituted illusory problems for the real ones.

This was in reply to a letter from Bridges, in which Bridges
appears to have commented on Bergson. Then, second, it is
Bergson that Paul Valéry called

> *peut-être l'un des derniers hommes qui auront exclusive-
> ment, profondément et supérieurement pensé, dans une
> époque du monde où le monde va pensant et méditant de
> moins en moins. . . . Bergson semble déjà appartenir à
> un âge révolu, et son nom est le dernier grand nom de
> l'histoire de l'intelligence européenne.*

And yet, third, it is of Bergson's *L'Evolution Créatrice* that
William James said in a letter to Bergson himself:

> You may be amused at the comparison, but in finishing
> it I found the same after-taste remaining as after finish-
> ing *Madame Bovary*, such a flavor of persistent *euphony*.

2

If these expressions speak for any considerable number of
people and, therefore, if any considerable number of people

feel this way about the truth and about what may be called
the official view of being (since philosophic truth may be said
to be the official view), we cannot expect much in respect to
poetry, assuming that we define poetry as an unofficial view
of being. This is a much larger definition of poetry than it is
usual to make. But just as the nature of the truth changes,
perhaps for no more significant reason than that philosophers
live and die, so the nature of poetry changes, perhaps for no
more significant reason than that poets come and go. It is so
easy to say in a universe of life and death that the reason itself
lives and dies and, if so, that the imagination lives and dies no
less.

Once on a packet on his way to Germany Coleridge was
asked to join a party of Danes and drink with them. He
says:

> I went, and found some excellent wines and a dessert of
> grapes with a pine-apple. The Danes had christened me
> Doctor Teology, and dressed as I was all in black, with
> large shoes and black worsted stockings, I might cer-
> tainly have passed very well for a Methodist missionary.
> However I disclaimed my title. What then may you be
> . . . *Un philosophe*, perhaps? It was at that time in my
> life in which of all possible names and characters I had
> the greatest disgust to that of *un philosophe*. . . . The
> Dane then informed me that all in the present party were
> Philosophers likewise. . . . We drank and talked and
> sung, till we talked and sung altogether; and then we
> rose and danced on the deck a set of dances.

As poetry goes, as the imagination goes, as the approach to
truth, or, say, to being by way of the imagination goes, Cole-
ridge is one of the great figures. Even so, just as William James
found in Bergson a persistent euphony, so we find in Cole-
ridge, dressed in black, with large shoes and black worsted
stockings, dancing on the deck of a Hamburg packet, a man
who may be said to have been defining poetry all his life in
definitions that are valid enough but which no longer impress
us primarily by their validity.

To define poetry as an unofficial view of being places it in
contrast with philosophy and at the same time establishes the

relationship between the two. In philosophy we attempt to approach truth through the reason. Obviously this is a statement of convenience. If we say that in poetry we attempt to approach truth through the imagination, this, too, is a statement of convenience. We must conceive of poetry as at least the equal of philosophy. If truth is the object of both and if any considerable number of people feel very sceptical of all philosophers, then, to be brief about it, a still more considerable number of people must feel very sceptical of all poets. Since we expect rational ideas to satisfy the reason and imaginative ideas to satisfy the imagination, it follows that if we are sceptical of rational ideas it is because they do not satisfy the reason and if we are sceptical of imaginative ideas it is because they do not satisfy the imagination. If a rational idea does not satisfy the imagination, it may, nevertheless, satisfy the reason. If an imaginative idea does not satisfy the reason, we regard the fact as in the nature of things. If an imaginative idea does not satisfy the imagination, our expectation of it is not fulfilled. On the other hand, and finally, if an imaginative idea satisfies the imagination, we are indifferent to the fact that it does not satisfy the reason, although we concede that it would be complete, as an idea, if, in addition to satisfying the imagination, it also satisfied the reason. From this analysis, we deduce that an idea that satisfies both the reason and the imagination, if it happened, for instance, to be an idea of God, would establish a divine beginning and end for us which, at the moment, the reason, singly, at best proposes and on which, at the moment, the imagination, singly, merely meditates. This is an illustration. It seems to be elementary, from this point of view, that the poet, in order to fulfill himself, must accomplish a poetry that satisfies both the reason and the imagination. It does not follow that in the long run the poet will find himself in the position in which the philosopher now finds himself. On the contrary, if the end of the philosopher is despair, the end of the poet is fulfillment, since the poet finds a sanction for life in poetry that satisfies the imagination. Thus, poetry, which we have been thinking of as at least the equal of philosophy, may be its superior. Yet the area of definition is almost an area of apologetics. The look of it may change a little if we consider not that the definition has not yet been found but that there is none.

3

Certainly the definition has not yet been found. You will not find it in such works as those on the art of poetry by Aristotle and Horace. In his edition of Aristotle's work Principal Fyfe says that Aristotle did not even appreciate poetry. In the time of Aristotle, there was no such word as literature in Greek. Yet today poetry is literature more often than not; for poetry partakes of what may be called the tendency to become literature. Life itself partakes of this tendency, which is a phase of the growth of sophistication. Sophistication, in turn, is a phase of the development of civilization. Aristotle understood poetry to be imitation particularly of action in drama. In Chapter 6, Aristotle states the parts of tragedy, among them thought and character, which are not to be confused. He says that character in a play is that which reveals the moral purpose of the agents, i.e., the sort of thing they seek or avoid—hence, there is no room for character in a speech on a purely indifferent subject. The annotation of the editor is this:

> A man who chooses, e.g., vengeance rather than safety reveals his character by exercise of Will. A man who at dinner chooses grouse rather than rabbit reveals nothing, because no sane man would choose otherwise.

This sort of thing has nothing to do with poetry. With our sense of the imaginative today, we are bound to consider a language that did not contain a word for literature as extraordinary even though the language was the language of Plato. With us it is not a paradox to say that poetry and literature are close together. Although there is no definition of poetry, there are impressions, approximations. Shelley gives us an approximation when he gives us a definition in what he calls "a general sense." He speaks of poetry as created by "that imperial faculty whose throne is curtained within the invisible nature of man." He says that a poem is the very image of life expressed in its eternal truth. It is "indeed something divine. It is at once the centre and circumference of knowledge . . . the record of the best and happiest moments of the happiest and best minds . . . it arrests the vanishing apparitions which haunt the interlunations of life." In spite of the absence of a definition and in spite of the impressions and approximations we are never at a loss to recognize poetry. As a consequence it is easy for us to propose a center of poetry, a *vis* or *noeud vital*, to which, in the absence of a definition, all the variations of definition are peripheral. Sometimes we think that a psychology of poetry has found its way to the center. We say that poetry is metamorphosis and we come to see in a few lines descriptive of an eye, a hand, a stick, the essence of the matter, and we see it so definitely that we say that if the philosopher comes to nothing because he fails, the poet may come to nothing because he succeeds. The philosopher fails to discover. Suppose the poet discovered and had the power thereafter at will and by intelligence to reconstruct us by his transformations. He would also have the power to destroy us. If there was, or if we believed that there was, a center, it would be absurd to fear or to avoid its discovery.

Since we have no difficulty in recognizing poetry and since, at the same time, we say that it is not an attainable acme, not some breath from an altitude, not something that awaits discovery, after which it will not be subject to chance, we may be accounting for it if we say that it is a process of the personality of the poet. One does not have to be a cardinal to make the point. To say that it is a process of the personality of the poet does not mean that it involves the poet as subject. Aristotle said: "The poet should say very little *in propria persona.*" Without stopping to discuss what might be discussed for so long, note that the principle so stated by Aristotle is cited in relation to the point that poetry is a process of the personality of the poet. This is the element, the force, that keeps poetry a living thing, the modernizing and ever-modern influence. The statement that the process does not involve the poet as subject, to the extent to which that is true, precludes direct egotism. On the other hand, without indirect egotism there can be no poetry. There can be no poetry without the personality of the poet, and that, quite simply, is why the definition of poetry has not been found and why, in short, there is none. In one of the really remarkable books of the day, *The Life of Forms in Art*, Henri Focillon says:

> Human consciousness is in perpetual pursuit of a language and a style. To assume consciousness is at once to assume form. Even at levels far below the zone of definition and clarity, forms, measures and relationships exist. The chief characteristic of the mind is to be constantly describing *itself*.

This activity is indirect egotism. The mind of the poet describes itself as constantly in his poems as the mind of the sculptor describes itself in his forms, or as the mind of Cézanne described itself in his "psychological landscapes." We are talking about something a good deal more comprehensive than the temperament of the artist as that is usually spoken of. We are concerned with the whole personality and, in effect, we are saying that the poet who writes the heroic poem that will satisfy all there is of us and all of us in time to come, will accomplish it by the power of his reason, the force of his imagination and, in addition, the effortless and inescapable process of his own individuality.

It was of the temperament of the artist that Cézanne spoke so frequently in his letters, and while we mean something more, so, it seems, did Cézanne. He said:

> Primary force alone, *id est* temperament, can bring a person to the end he must attain.

Again:

> With a small temperament one can be very much of a painter. It is sufficient to have a sense of art. . . . Therefore institutions, pensions, honours can only be made for cretins, rogues and rascals.

And again, this time to Emile Bernard:

> Your letters are precious to me . . . because their arrival lifts me out of the monotony which is caused by the incessant . . . search for the sole and unique aim. . . . I am able to describe to you again . . . the realization

of that part of nature which, coming into our line of vision, gives the picture. Now the theme to develop is that—whatever our temperament or power in the presence of nature may be—we must render the image of what we see.

And, finally, to his son:

Obviously one must succeed in feeling for oneself and in expressing oneself sufficiently.

4

An attempt has been made to equate poetry with philosophy, and to do this with an indication of the possibility that an advantage, in the long run, may lie with poetry; and yet it has been said that poetry is personal. If it is personal in a pejorative sense its value is slight and it is not the equal of philosophy. What we have under observation, however, is the creative process, the personality of the poet, his individuality, as an element in the creative process; and by process of the personality of the poet we mean, to select what may seem to be a curious particular, the incidence of the nervous sensitiveness of the poet in the act of creating the poem and, generally speaking, the physical and mental factors that condition him as an individual. If a man's nerves shrink from loud sounds, they are quite likely to shrink from strong colors and he will be found preferring a drizzle in Venice to a hard rain in Hartford. Everything is of a piece. If he composes music it will be music agreeable to his own nerves. Yet it is commonly thought that the artist is independent of his work. In his chapter on "Forms in the Realm of the Mind," M. Focillon speaks of a vocation of substances, or technical destiny, to which there is a corresponding vocation of minds; that is to say, a certain order of forms corresponds to a certain order of minds. These things imply an element of change. Thus a vocation recognizes its material by foresight, before experience. As an example of this, he refers to the first state of the *Prisons* of Piranesi as skeletal. But "twenty years later, Piranesi returned to these etchings, and on taking them up again, he poured into them shadow after shadow, until one might say that he excavated this astonishing darkness not from the brazen plates, but from the living rock of some subterranean world." The way a poet feels when he is writing, or after he has written, a poem that completely accomplishes his purpose is evidence of the personal nature of his activity. To describe it by exaggerating it, he shares the transformation, not to say apotheosis, accomplished by the poem. It must be this experience that makes him think of poetry as possibly a phase of metaphysics; and it must be this experience that teases him with that sense of the possibility of a remote, a mystical *vis* or *noeud vital* to which reference has already been made. In *The Two Sources of Morality and Religion*, Bergson speaks of the morality of aspiration. It implicitly contains, he says,

> the feeling of progress. The emotion . . . is the enthusiasm of a forward movement. . . . But antecedent to this metaphysical theory . . . are the simpler representations . . . of the founders of religion, the mystics and the saints. . . . They begin by saying that what they experience is a feeling of liberation. . . .

The feeling is not a feeling peculiar to exquisite or (perhaps, as better) precise realization, and hence confined to poets who exceed us in nature as they do in speech. There is nothing rare about it although it may extend to degrees of rarity. On the contrary, just as Bergson refers to the simpler representations of aspiration occurring in the lives of the saints, so we may refer to the simpler representations of an aspiration (not the same, yet not wholly unlike) occurring in the lives of those who have just written their first essential poems. After all, the young man or young woman who has written a few poems and who wants to read them is merely the voluble convert or the person looking in a mirror who sees suddenly the traces of an unexpected genealogy. We are interested in this transformation primarily on the part of the poet. Yet it is a thing that communicates itself to the reader. Anyone who has read a long poem day after day as, for example, *The Faerie Queene*, knows how the poem comes to possess the reader and how it naturalizes him in its own imagination and liberates him there.

This sense of liberation may be examined specifically in relation to the experience of writing a poem that completely accomplishes the purpose of the poet. Bergson had in mind religious aspiration. The poet who experiences what was once called inspiration experiences both aspiration and inspiration. But that is not a difference, for it is clear that Bergson intended to include in aspiration not only desire but the fulfillment of desire, not only the petition but the harmonious decree. What is true of the experience of the poet is no doubt true of the experience of the painter, of the musician and of any artist. If, then, when we speak of liberation, we mean an exodus; if when we speak of justification, we mean a kind of justice of which we had not known and on which we had not counted; if when we experience a sense of purification, we can think of the establishing of a self, it is certain that the experience of the poet is of no less a degree than the experience of the mystic and we may be certain that in the case of poets, the peers of saints, those experiences are of no less a degree than the experiences of the saints themselves. It is a question of the nature of the experience. It is not a question of identifying or relating dissimilar figures; that is to say, it is not a question of making saints out of poets or poets out of saints.

In this state of elevation we feel perfectly adapted to the idea that moves and *l'oiseau qui chante*. The identity of the feeling is subject to discussion and, from this, it follows that its value is debatable. It may be dismissed, on the one hand, as a commonplace aesthetic satisfaction; and, on the other hand, if we say that the idea of God is merely a poetic idea, even if the supreme poetic idea, and that our notions of heaven and hell are merely poetry not so called, even if poetry that involves us vitally, the feeling of deliverance, of a release, of a perfection touched, of a vocation so that all men may know the truth and that the truth may set them free—if we say these things and if we are able to see the poet who achieved God and placed Him in His seat in heaven in all His glory, the poet himself, still in the ecstasy of the poem that completely accomplished his purpose, would have seemed, whether young or old, whether in rags or ceremonial robe, a man who needed what he had created, uttering the hymns of joy that followed his creation. This may be a gross exaggeration of a very simple matter. But perhaps that remark is true of many of the more prodigious things of life and death.

5

The centuries have a way of being male. Without pretend-
ing to say whether they get this character from their good
heroes or their bad ones, it is certain that they get it, in part,
from their philosophers and poets. It is curious, looking back
at them, to see how much of the impression that they leave
has been derived from the progress of thought in their time
and from the abundance of the arts, including poetry, left
behind and how little of it comes from prouder and much
noisier things. Thus, when we think of the seventeenth cen-
tury, it is to be remarked how much of the strength of its
appearance is associated with the idea that this was a time
when the incredible suffered most at the hands of the credible.
We think of it as a period of hard thinking. We have only their
records and memories by which to recall such eras, not the
sight and sound of those that lived in them preserved in an
eternity of dust and dirt. When we look back at the face of
the seventeenth century, it is at the rigorous face of the rig-
orous thinker and, say, the Miltonic image of a poet, severe
and determined. In effect, what we are remembering is the
rather haggard background of the incredible, the imagination
without intelligence, from which a younger figure is emerg-
ing, stepping forward in the company of a muse of its own,
still half-beast and somehow more than human, a kind of sister
of the Minotaur. This younger figure is the intelligence that
endures. It is the imagination of the son still bearing the an-
tique imagination of the father. It is the clear intelligence of
the young man still bearing the burden of the obscurities of
the intelligence of the old. It is the spirit out of its own self,
not out of some surrounding myth, delineating with accurate
speech the complications of which it is composed. For this
Aeneas, it is the past that is Anchises.

The incredible is not a part of poetic truth. On the contrary,
what concerns us in poetry, as in everything else, is the belief
of credible people in credible things. It follows that poetic
truth is the truth of credible things, not so much that it is
actually so, as that it must be so. It is toward that alone that
it is possible for the intelligence to move. In one of his letters,
Xavier Doudan says: *"Il y a longtemps que je pense que celui*

qui n'aurait que des idées claires serait assurément un sot." The reply to this is that it is impossible to conceive of a man who has nothing but clear ideas; for our nature is an illimitable space through which the intelligence moves without coming to an end. The incredible is inexhaustible but, fortunately, it is not always the same. We come, in this way, to understand that the moment of exaltation that the poet experiences when he writes a poem that completely accomplishes his purpose, is a moment of victory over the incredible, a moment of purity that does not become any the less pure because, as what was incredible is eliminated, something newly credible takes its place. As we come to the point at which it is necessary to be explicit in respect to poetic truth, note that, if we say that the philosopher pursues the truth in one way and the poet in another, it is implied that both are pursuing the same thing, and we overlook the fact that they are pursuing two different parts of a whole. It is as if we said that the end of logic, mathematics, physics, reason and imagination is all one. In short, it is as if we said that there is no difference between philosophic truth and poetic truth. There is a difference between them and it is the difference between logical and empirical knowledge. Since philosophers do not agree in respect to what constitutes philosophic truth, as Bertrand Russell (if any illustration whatever is necessary) demonstrates in his *Inquiry into Meaning and Truth*, even in the casual comment that truth as a static concept is to be discarded, it may not be of much use to improvise a definition of poetic truth. Nevertheless, it may be said that poetic truth is an agreement with reality, brought about by the imagination of a man disposed to be strongly influenced by his imagination, which he believes, for a time, to be true, expressed in terms of his emotions or, since it is less of a restriction to say so, in terms of his own personality. And so stated, the difference between philosophic truth and poetic truth appears to become final. As to the definition itself, it is an expedient for getting on. We shall come back to the nature of poetic truth very shortly.

In the most propitious climate and in the midst of life's virtues, the simple figure of the youth as virile poet is always surrounded by a cloud of double characters, against whose thought and speech it is imperative that he should remain on constant guard. These are the poetic philosophers and the philosophical poets. Mme. de Staël said: *"Nos meilleurs poètes lyriques, en France, ce sont peut-être nos grands prosateurs, Bossuet, Pascal, Fénelon, Buffon, Jean-Jacques. . . ."* M. Claudel added Rabelais, Chateaubriand, even Balzac, and when he did so, M. René Fernandat said: *"On remarquera que M. Claudel a supprimé les 'peut-être' de Mme. de Staël."* In English the poetic aspect of Bunyan is quite commonly recognized. This is an occasion to call attention to William Penn as an English poet, although he may never have written a line of verse. But the illustration of Descartes is irresistible. To speak of figures like Descartes as double characters is an inconceivable difficulty. In his exegesis of *The Discourse on Method*, Leon Roth says:

> His vision showed him first the "dictionary," then the "poets," and only afterwards the *est et non*; and his "rationalism," like the "anti-rationalism" of Pascal, was the product of a struggle not always completely successful. What less "rationalistic" could there be than the early thought preserved by Baillet from the *Olympica* (one may note in passing the poetical names of all these early works): "There are sentences in the writings of the poets more serious than in those of the philosophers. . . . There are in us, as in a flint, seeds of knowledge. Philosophers adduce them through the reason; poets strike them out from the imagination, and these are the brighter." It was the "rationalist" Voltaire who first called attention to the "poetic" in Descartes. . . . To the casual reader there is nothing more remarkable than the careless richness of his style. It is full of similes drawn not only from the arts, like architecture, painting and the stage, but also from the familiar scenes of ordinary and country life. . . . And this not only in his early writing. It is apparent even in his latest published work, the scientific analysis of the "passions of the soul," and it was Voltaire again who commented first on the fact that the last thing from his pen was a ballet written for the Queen of Sweden.

The philosopher proves that the philosopher exists. The poet merely enjoys existence. The philosopher thinks of the world as an enormous pastiche or, as he puts it, the world is as the percipient. Thus Kant says that the objects of perception are conditioned by the nature of the mind as to their form. But the poet says that, whatever it may be, *la vie est plus belle que les idées.* One needs hardly to be told that men more or less irrational are only more or less rational; so that it was not surprising to find Raymond Mortimer saying in the *New Statesman* that the "thoughts" of Shakespeare or Raleigh or Spenser were in fact only contemporary commonplaces and that it was a Victorian habit to praise poets as thinkers, since their "thoughts are usually borrowed or confused." But do we come away from Shakespeare with the sense that we have been reading contemporary commonplaces? Long ago, Sarah Bernhardt was playing Hamlet. When she came to the soliloquy "To be or not to be," she half turned her back on the audience and slowly weaving one hand in a small circle above her head and regarding it, she said, with deliberation and as from the depths of a hallucination:

> *D'être ou ne pas d'être, c'est là la question . . .*

and one followed her, lost in the intricate metamorphosis of thoughts that passed through the mind with a gallantry, an accuracy of abundance, a crowding and pressing of direction, which, for thoughts that were both borrowed and confused, cancelled the borrowing and obliterated the confusion.

There is a life apart from politics. It is this life that the youth as virile poet lives, in a kind of radiant and productive atmosphere. It is the life of that atmosphere. There the philosopher is an alien. The pleasure that the poet has there is a pleasure of agreement with the radiant and productive world in which he lives. It is an agreement that Mallarmé found in the sound of

> *Le vierge, le vivace et le bel aujourd'hui*

and that Hopkins found in the color of

> The thunder-purple seabeach plumèd purple-of-thunder.

The indirect purpose or, perhaps, it would be better to say, inverted effect of soliloquies in hell and of most celestial poems and, in a general sense, of all music played on the terraces of the audiences of the moon, seems to be to produce an agreement with reality. It is the *mundo* of the imagination in which the imaginative man delights and not the gaunt world of the reason. The pleasure is the pleasure of powers that create a truth that cannot be arrived at by the reason alone, a truth that the poet recognizes by sensation. The morality of the poet's radiant and productive atmosphere is the morality of the right sensation.

6

I have compared poetry and philosophy; I have made a point of the degree to which poetry is personal, both in its origin and in its end, and have spoken of the typical exhilaration that appears to be inseparable from genuine poetic activity; I have said that the general progress from the incredible to the credible was a progress in which poetry has participated; I have improvised a definition of poetic truth and have spoken of the integrity and peculiarity of the poetic character. Summed up, our position at the moment is that the poet must get rid of the hieratic in everything that concerns him and must move constantly in the direction of the credible. He must create his unreal out of what is real.

If we consider the nature of our experience when we are in agreement with reality, we find, for one thing, that we cease to be metaphysicians. William James said:

> Most of them [i.e., metaphysicians] have been invalids. I am one, can't sleep, can't make a decision, can't buy a horse, can't do anything that befits a man; and yet you say from my photograph that I must be a second General Sherman, only greater and better! All right! I love you for the fond delusion.

For all the reasons stated by William James, and for many more, and in spite of M. Jacques Maritain, we do not want to be metaphysicians. In the crowd around the simple figure of the youth as virile poet, there are metaphysicians, among the others. And having ceased to be metaphysicians, even though we have acquired something from them as from all men, and standing in the radiant and productive atmosphere, and examining first one detail of that world, one particular, and then another, as we find them by chance, and observing many things that seem to be poetry without any intervention on our part, as, for example, the blue sky, and noting, in any case, that the imagination never brings anything into the world but that, on the contrary, like the personality of the poet in the act of creating, it is no more than a process, and desiring with all the power of our desire not to write falsely, do we not begin to think of the possibility that poetry is only reality, after all, and that poetic truth is a factual truth, seen, it may be, by those whose range in the perception of fact—that is, whose sensibility—is greater than our own? From that point of view, the truth that we experience when we are in agreement with reality is the truth of fact. In consequence, when men, baffled by philosophic truth, turn to poetic truth, they return to their starting-point, they return to fact, not, it ought to be clear, to bare fact (or call it absolute fact), but to fact possibly beyond their perception in the first instance and outside the normal range of their sensibility. What we have called elevation and elation on the part of the poet, which he communicates to the reader, may be not so much elevation as an incandescence of the intelligence and so more than ever a triumph over the incredible. Here as part of the purification that all of us undergo as we approach any central purity, and that we feel in its presence, we can say:

> No longer do I believe that there is a mystic muse,
> sister of the Minotaur. This is another of the monsters
> I had for nurse, whom I have wasted. I am myself a part
> of what is real, and it is my own speech and the strength
> of it, this only, that I hear or ever shall.

These words may very well be an inscription above the portal to what lies ahead. But if poetic truth means fact and if fact includes the whole of it as it is between the extreme poles of sensibility, we are talking about a thing as extensible as it is ambiguous. We have excluded absolute fact as an element of poetic truth. But this has been done arbitrarily and with a sense of absolute fact as fact destitute of any imaginative aspect whatever. Unhappily the more destitute it becomes the more it begins to be precious. We must limit ourselves to saying that there are so many things which, as they are, and without any intervention of the imagination, seem to be imaginative objects that it is no doubt true that absolute fact includes everything that the imagination includes. This is our intimidating thesis.

One sees demonstrations of this everywhere. For example, if we close our eyes and think of a place where it would be pleasant to spend a holiday, and if there slide across the black eyes, like a setting on a stage, a rock that sparkles, a blue sea that lashes, and hemlocks in which the sun can merely fumble, this inevitably demonstrates, since the rock and sea, the wood and sun are those that have been familiar to us in Maine, that much of the world of fact is the equivalent of the world of the imagination, because it looks like it. Here we are on the border of the question of the relationship of the imagination and memory, which we avoid. It is important to believe that the visible is the equivalent of the invisible; and once we believe it, we have destroyed the imagination; that is to say, we have destroyed the false imagination, the false conception of the imagination as some incalculable *vates* within us, unhappy Rodomontade. One is often tempted to say that the best definition of poetry is that poetry is the sum of its attributes. So, here, we may say that the best definition of true imagination is that it is the sum of our faculties. Poetry is the scholar's art. The acute intelligence of the imagination, the illimitable resources of its memory, its power to possess the moment it perceives—if we were speaking of light itself, and thinking of the relationship between objects and light, no further demonstration would be necessary. Like light, it adds nothing, except itself. What light requires a day to do, and by day I mean a kind of Biblical revolution of time, the imagination does in the twinkling of an eye. It colors, increases, brings to a beginning and end, invents languages, crushes men and, for that matter, gods in its hands, it says to women more than it is possible to say, it rescues all of us from what we have called absolute fact and while it does these things, and more, it makes sure that

> *. . . la mandoline jase,*
> *Parmi les frissons de brise.*

Having identified poetic truth as the truth of fact, since fact includes poetic fact, that is to say: the indefinite number of actual things that are indistinguishable from objects of the imagination; and having, as we hope, washed the imagination clean, we may now return, once again, to the figure of the youth as virile poet and join him, or try to do so, in coming to the decision, on which, for him and for us, too, so much depends. At what level of the truth shall he compose his poems? That is the question on which he is reflecting, as he sits in the radiant and productive atmosphere, which is his life, surrounded not only by double characters and metaphysicians, but by many men and many kinds of men, by many women and many children and many kinds of women and of children. The question concerns the function of the poet today and tomorrow, but makes no pretence beyond. He is able to read the inscription on the portal and he repeats:

> I am myself a part of what is real and it is my own speech and the strength of it, this only, that I hear or ever shall.

He says, so that we can all hear him:

> I am the truth, since I am part of what is real, but neither more nor less than those around me. And I am imagination, in a leaden time and in a world that does not move for the weight of its own heaviness.

Can there be the slightest doubt what the decision will be? Can we suppose for a moment that he will be content merely to make notes, merely to copy Katahdin, when, with his sense of the heaviness of the world, he feels his own power to lift, or help to lift, that heaviness away? Can we think that he will elect anything except to exercise his power to the full and at its height, meaning by this as part of what is real, to rely on his imagination, to make his own imagination that of those who have none, or little?

And how will he do this? It is not possible to say how an

imaginative person will do a thing. Having made an election, he will be faithful to the election that he has made. Having elected to exercise his power to the full and at its height, and having identified his power as the power of the imagination, he may begin its exercise by studying it in exercise and proceed little by little, as he becomes his own master, to those violences which are the maturity of his desires. The character of the crisis through which we are passing today, the reason why we live in a leaden time, was summed up in a note on Klaus Mann's recent book on Gide, as follows:

> The main problem which Gide tries to solve—the crisis of our time—is the reconciliation of the inalienable rights of the individual to personal development and the necessity for the diminution of the misery of the masses.

When the poet has converted this into his own terms: the figure of the youth as virile poet and the community growing day by day more and more colossal, the consciousness of his function, if he is a serious artist, is a measure of his obligation. And so is the consciousness of his history. In the *Reflections on History* of Jakob Burckhardt, there are some pages of notes on the historical consideration of poetry. Burckhardt thought (citing Schopenhauer and Aristotle) that poetry achieves more for the knowledge of human nature than history. Burckhardt considers the status of poetry at various epochs, among various peoples and classes, asking each time *who* is singing or writing, and for *whom*. Poetry is the voice of religion, prophecy, mythology, history, national life and inexplicably, for him, of literature. He says:

> It is a matter for great surprise that Virgil, in those circumstances, could occupy his high rank, could dominate all the age which followed and become a mythical figure. How infinitely great are the gradations of existence from the epic rhapsodist to the novelist of today!

This was written seventy-five years ago. The present generation of poets is not accustomed to measure itself by obligations of such weight nor to think of itself as Burckhardt seems to have thought of epic bards or, to choose another example at random, of the writers of hymns, for he speaks of "the Protestant hymn as the supreme religious expression, especially of the seventeenth century."

The poet reflecting on his course, which is the same thing as a reflection by him and by us, on the course of poetry, will decide to do as the imagination bids, because he has no choice, if he is to remain a poet. Poetry is the imagination of life. A poem is a particular of life thought of for so long that one's thought has become an inseparable part of it or a particular of life so intensely felt that the feeling has entered into it. When, therefore, we say that the world is a compact of real things so like the unreal things of the imagination that they are indistinguishable from one another and when, by way of illustration, we cite, say, the blue sky, we can be sure that the thing cited is always something that, whether by thinking or feeling, has become a part of our vital experience of life, even though we are not aware of it. It is easy to suppose that few people realize on that occasion, which comes to all of us, when we look at the blue sky for the first time, that is to say: not merely see it, but look at it and experience it and for the first time have a sense that we live in the center of a physical poetry, a geography that would be intolerable except for the non-geography that exists there—few people realize that they are looking at the world of their own thoughts and the world of their own feelings. On that occasion, the blue sky is a particular of life that we have thought of often, even though unconsciously, and that we have felt intensely in those crystallizations of freshness that we no more remember than we remember this or that gust of wind in spring or autumn. The experiences of thinking and feeling accumulate particularly in the abnormal ranges of sensibility; so that, to use a bit of M. Focillon's personal language, while the "normative type" of poet is likely to be concerned with pretty much the same facts as those with which the genius, or, rather, the youth as virile poet, is concerned, the genius, because of the abnormal ranges of his sensibility, not only accumulates experiences with greater rapidity, but accumulates experiences and qualities of experience accessible only in the extreme ranges of sensibility.

But genius is not our concern. We are trying to define what we mean by the imagination of life, and, in addition, by that special illumination, special abundance and severity of abundance, virtue in the midst of indulgence and order in disorder that is involved in the idea of virility. We have been referring constantly to the simple figure of the youth, in his character of poet, as virile poet. The reason for this is that if, for the poet, the imagination is paramount, and if he dwells apart in his imagination, as the philosopher dwells in his reason, and as the priest dwells in his belief, the masculine nature that we propose for one that must be the master of our lives will be lost as, for example, in the folds of the garments of the ghost or ghosts of Aristotle. As we say these things, there begins to develop, in addition to the figure that has been seated in our midst, composed, in the radiant and productive atmosphere with which we have surrounded him, an intimation of what he is thinking as he reflects on the imagination of life, determined to be its master and ours. He is thinking of those facts of experience of which all of us have thought and which all of us have felt with such intensity, and he says:

Inexplicable sister of the Minotaur, enigma and mask, although I am part of what is real, hear me and recognize me as part of the unreal. I am the truth but the truth of that imagination of life in which with unfamiliar motion and manner you guide me in those exchanges of speech in which your words are mine, mine yours.

III

Three Academic Pieces

I

THE ACCURACY of accurate letters is an accuracy with respect to the structure of reality.

Thus, if we desire to formulate an accurate theory of poetry, we find it necessary to examine the structure of reality, because reality is the central reference for poetry. By way of accomplishing this, suppose we examine one of the significant components of the structure of reality—that is to say, the resemblance between things.

First, then, as to the resemblance between things in nature, it should be observed that resemblance constitutes a relation between them since, in some sense, all things resemble each other. Take, for example, a beach extending as far as the eye can reach, bordered, on the one hand, by trees and, on the other, by the sea. The sky is cloudless and the sun is red. In what sense do the objects in this scene resemble each other? There is enough green in the sea to relate it to the palms. There is enough of the sky reflected in the water to create a resemblance, in some sense, between them. The sand is yellow between the green and the blue. In short, the light alone creates a unity not only in the recedings of distance, where differences become invisible, but also in the contacts of closer sight. So, too, sufficiently generalized, each man resembles all other men, each woman resembles all other women, this year resembles last year. The beginning of time will, no doubt, resemble the end of time. One world is said to resemble another.

A moment ago the resemblance between things was spoken of as one of the significant components of the structure of reality. It is significant because it creates the relation just described. It binds together. It is the base of appearance. In nature, however, the relation is between two or more of the parts of reality. In metaphor (and this word is used as a symbol for the single aspect of poetry with which we are now concerned—that is to say, the creation of resemblance by the imagination, even though metamorphosis might be a better word)—in metaphor, the resemblance may be, first, between two or more parts of reality; second, between something real and something imagined or, what is the same thing, between something imagined and something real as, for example, between music and whatever may be evoked by it; and, third, between two imagined things as when we say that God is good, since the statement involves a resemblance between two concepts, a concept of God and a concept of goodness.

We are not dealing with identity. Both in nature and in metaphor identity is the vanishing-point of resemblance. After all, if a man's exact double entered a room, seated himself and spoke the words that were in the man's mind, it would remain a resemblance. James Wardrop, in *Signature*, said recently:

> The business of the press is to furnish an indefinite pub-
> lic with a potentially indefinite number of identical texts.

Nature is not mechanical to that extent for all its mornings and evenings, for all its inhabitants of China or India or Russia, for all its waves, or its leaves, or its hands. Its prodigy is not identity but resemblance and its universe of reproduction is not an assembly line but an incessant creation. Because this is so in nature, it is so in metaphor.

Nor are we dealing with imitation. The difference between imitation and resemblance is a nicety. An imitation may be described as an identity manqué. It is artificial. It is not fortuitous as a true metaphor is. If it is an imitation of something in nature, it may even surpass identity and assume a praeter-nature. It may very well escape the derogatory. If it is an imitation of something in metaphor, it is lifeless and that, finally, is what is wrong with it. Resemblance in metaphor is an activity of the imagination; and in metaphor the imagination is life. In Chinese metaphor, there is a group of subjects to which poets used to address themselves, just as early Western painters and etchers used to address themselves to such a subject as the Virgin crowned by Angels. The variations in these themes were not imitations, nor identities, but resemblances.

In reality, there is a level of resemblance, which is the level of nature. In metaphor, there is no such level. If there were it would be the level of resemblance of the imagination, which has no such level. If, to our surprise, we should meet a monsieur who told us that he was from another world, and if he had in fact all the indicia of divinity, the luminous body, the nimbus, the heraldic stigmata, we should recognize him as above the level of nature but not as above the level of the imagination. So, too, if, to our surprise, we should meet one of these morons whose remarks are so conspicuous a part of the folk-lore of the world of the radio—remarks made without using either the tongue or the brain, spouted much like the spoutings of small whales—we should recognize him as below the level of nature but not as below the level of the imagination. It is not, however, a question of above or below but simply of beyond. Level is an abbreviated form of level of resemblance. The statement that the imagination has no level of resemblance is not to be taken as a statement that the imagination itself has no limits. The imagination is deceptive in this respect. There is a limit to its power to surpass resemblance and that limit is to be found in nature. The imagination is able to manipulate nature as by creating three legs and five arms but it is not able to create a totally new nature as, for instance, a new element with creatures indigenous thereto, their costumes and cuisines. Any discussion of level is a discussion of balance as well. Thus, a false exaggeration is a disturbing of the balance between reality and the imagination.

Resemblances between one object and another as between one brick and another, one egg and another, are elementary. There are many objects which in respect to what they suggest resemble other objects and we may include here, as objects, people. Thus, in addition to the fact that one man resembles all other men, something about one man may make him resemble some other particular man and this is true even when the something about him is detached from him, as his wig. The wig of a particular man reminds us of some other particular man and resembles him. A strand of a child's hair brings back the whole child and in that way resembles the child. There must be vast numbers of things within this category. Apparently objects of sentiment most easily prove the existence of this kind of resemblance: something in a locket, one's grandfather's high beaver hat, one's grandmother's handwoven blankets. One may find intimations of immortality in an object on the mantelpiece; and these intimations are as real in the mind in which they occur as the mantelpiece itself. Even if they are only a part of an adult make-believe, the whole point is that the structure of reality because of the range of resemblances that it contains is measurably an adult make-believe. Perhaps the whole field of connotation is based on resemblance. Perhaps resemblance which seems to be related so closely to the imagination is related even more closely to the intelligence, of which perceptions of resemblance are effortless accelerations.

What has just been said shows that there are private resemblances. The resemblance of the baby's shoes to the baby, by suggestion, is likely to be a resemblance that exists for one or two alone. A public resemblance, by contrast, like the resemblance of the profile of a mountain to the profile of General Washington, exists for that great class of people who co-exist with the great ferns in public gardens, amplified music and minor education. What our eyes behold may well be the text of life but one's meditations on the text and the disclosures of these meditations are no less a part of the structure of reality.

It quite seems as if there is an activity that makes one thing resemble another (possibly as a phase of the police power of conformity). What the eye beholds may be the text of life. It is, nevertheless, a text that we do not write. The eye does not beget in resemblance. It sees. But the mind begets in resemblance as the painter begets in representation; that is to say, as the painter makes his world within a world; or as the musician begets in music, in the obvious small pieces having to do with gardens in the rain or the fountains of Rome and in the obvious larger pieces having to do with the sea, Brazilian night or those woods in the neighborhood of Vienna in which the hunter was accustomed to blow his horn and in which, also, yesterday, the birds sang preludes to the atom bomb. It is not difficult, having once predicated such an activity, to attribute it to a desire for resemblance. What a ghastly situation it would be if the world of the dead was actually different from the world of the living and, if as life ends, instead of passing to a former Victorian sphere, we passed into a land in which none of our problems had been solved, after all, and nothing resembled anything we have ever known and nothing resembled anything else in shape, in color, in sound, in look or otherwise. To say farewell to our generation and to look forward to a continuation in a Jerusalem of pure surrealism would account for the taste for oblivion.

The study of the activity of resemblance is an approach to the understanding of poetry. Poetry is a satisfying of the desire for resemblance. As the mere satisfying of a desire, it is pleasurable. But poetry if it did nothing but satisfy a desire would not rise above the level of many lesser things. Its singularity is that in the act of satisfying the desire for resemblance it touches the sense of reality, it enhances the sense of reality, heightens it, intensifies it. If resemblance is described as a partial similarity between two dissimilar things, it complements and reinforces that which the two dissimilar things have in common. It makes it brilliant. When the similarity is between things of adequate dignity, the resemblance may be said to transfigure or to sublimate them. Take, for example, the resemblance between reality and any projection of it in belief or in metaphor. What is it that these two have in common? Is not the glory of the idea of any future state a relation between a present and a future glory? The brilliance of earth is the brilliance of every paradise. However, not all poetry attempts such grandiose transfiguration. Everyone can call to mind a variety of figures and see clearly how these resemblances please and why; how inevitably they heighten our sense of reality. The images in Ecclesiastes:

> Or ever
> the silver cord be loosed, or the golden bowl be broken,
> or the pitcher be broken at the fountain, or the wheel
> broken at the cistern—

these images are not the language of reality, they are the symbolic language of metamorphosis, or resemblance, of poetry, but they relate to reality and they intensify our sense of it and they give us the pleasure of "lentor and solemnity" in respect to the most commonplace objects. These images have a special interest, as a group of images in harmony with each other. In both prose and poetry, images come willingly but, usually, although there is a relation between the subject of the images there is no relation between the images themselves. A group of images in harmony with each other would constitute a poem within, or above, a poem. The suggestion sounds euphuistic. If the desire for resemblance is the desire to enjoy reality, it may be no less true that the desire to enjoy reality, an acute enough desire today, is the desire for elegance. Euphuism had its origin in the desire for elegance and it was euphuism that was a season in the sun for metaphor. A school of literary ascetics denying itself any indulgence in resemblances would, necessarily, fall back on reality and vent all its relish there. The metaphorical school, in the end, does the same thing.

The proliferation of resemblances extends an object. The point at which this process begins, or rather at which this growth begins, is the point at which ambiguity has been reached. The ambiguity that is so favorable to the poetic mind is precisely the ambiguity favorable to resemblance. In this ambiguity, the intensification of reality by resemblance increases realization and this increased realization is pleasurable. It is as if a man who lived indoors should go outdoors on a day of sympathetic weather. His realization of the weather would exceed that of a man who lives outdoors. It might, in fact, be intense enough to convert the real world about him into an imagined world. In short, a sense of reality keen enough to be in excess of the normal sense of reality creates a reality of its own. Here what matters is that the intensification of the sense of reality creates a resemblance: that reality of its own is a reality. This may be going round a circle, first clockwise, then anti-clockwise. If the savor of life is the savor of reality, the fact will establish itself whichever way one approaches it.

The relations between the ego and reality must be left largely on the margin. Yet Narcissus did not expect, when he looked in the stream, to find in his hair a serpent coiled to strike, nor, when he looked in his own eyes there, to be met by a look of hate, nor, in general, to discover himself at the center of an inexplicable ugliness from which he would be bound to avert himself. On the contrary, he sought out his image everywhere because it was the principle of his nature to do so and, to go a step beyond that, because it was the principle of his nature, as it is of ours, to expect to find pleasure in what he found. Narcissism, then, involves something beyond the prime sense of the word. It involves, also, this principle, that as we seek out our resemblances we expect to find pleasure in doing so; that is to say, in what we find. So strong is that expectation that we find nothing else. What is true of the observations of ourselves is equally true of the observations of resemblances between other things having no relation to us. We say that the sea, when it expands in a calm and immense reflection of the sky, resembles the sky, and this statement gives us pleasure. We enjoy the resemblance for the same reason that, if it were possible to look into the sea as into glass and if we should do so and suddenly should behold there some extraordinary transfiguration of ourselves, the experience would strike us as one of those amiable revelations that nature occasionally vouchsafes to favorites. So, when we think of arpeggios, we think of opening wings and the effect of the resemblance is pleasurable. When we read Ecclesiastes the effect of the symbols is pleasurable because as symbols they are resemblances and as resemblances they are pleasurable and they are pleasurable because it is a principle of our nature that they should be, the principle being not something derived from Narcissism since Narcissism itself is merely an evidence of the operation of the principle that we expect to find pleasure in resemblances.

We have been trying to get at a truth about poetry, to get at one of the principles that compose the theory of poetry. It comes to this, that poetry is a part of the structure of reality. If this has been demonstrated, it pretty much amounts to saying that the structure of poetry and the structure of reality are one or, in effect, that poetry and reality are one, or should be. This may be less thesis than hypothesis. Yet hypotheses relating to poetry, although they may appear to be very distant illuminations, could be the fires of fate, if rhetoric ever meant anything.

There is a gradus ad Metaphoram. The nature of a metaphor is, like the nature of a play, comic, tragic, tragic-comic and so on. It may be poetic. A poetic metaphor—that is to say, a metaphor poetic in a sense more specific than the sense in which poetry and metaphor are one—appears to be poetry at its source. It is. At least it is poetry at one of its sources although not necessarily the most fecundating. But the steps to this particular abstraction, the gradus ad Metaphoram in respect to the general sense in which poetry and metaphor are one, are, like the ascent to any of the abstractions that interest us importantly, an ascent through illusion which gathers round us more closely and thickly, as we might expect it to do, the more we penetrate it.

In the fewest possible words since, as between resemblances, one is always a little more nearly perfect than another and since, from this, it is easy for perfectionism of a sort to evolve, it is not too extravagant to think of resemblances and of the repetitions of resemblances as a source of the ideal. In short, metaphor has its aspect of the ideal. This aspect of it cannot be dismissed merely because we think that we have long since outlived the ideal. The truth is that we are constantly outliving it and yet the ideal itself remains alive with an enormous life.

2

SOMEONE PUTS A PINEAPPLE TOGETHER

I

O juventes, O filii, he contemplates
A wholly artificial nature, in which
The profusion of metaphor has been increased.

It is something on a table that he sees,
The root of a form, as of this fruit, a fund,
The angel at the center of this rind,

This husk of Cuba, tufted emerald,
Himself, may be, the irreducible X
At the bottom of imagined artifice,

Its inhabitant and elect expositor.
It is as if there were three planets: the sun,
The moon and the imagination, or, say,

Day, night and man and his endless effigies.
If he sees an object on a table, much like
A jar of the shoots of an infant country, green

And bright, or like a venerable urn,
Which, from the ash within it, fortifies
A green that is the ash of what green is,

He sees it in this tangent of himself.
And in this tangent it becomes a thing
Of weight, on which the weightless rests: from which

The ephemeras of the tangent swarm, the chance
Concourse of planetary originals,
Yet, as it seems, of human residence.

II

He must say nothing of the fruit that is
Not true, nor think it, less. He must defy
The metaphor that murders metaphor.

He seeks as image a second of the self,
Made subtle by truth's most jealous subtlety,
Like the true light of the truest sun, the true

Power in the waving of the wand of the moon,
Whose shining is the intelligence of our sleep.
He seeks an image certain as meaning is

To sound, sound's substance and executant,
The particular tingle in a proclamation
That makes it say the little thing it says,

Below the prerogative jumble. The fruit so seen
As a part of the nature that he contemplates
Is fertile with more than changes of the light

On the table or in the colors of the room.
Its propagations are more erudite,
Like precious scholia jotted down in the dark.

Did not the age that bore him bear him among
Its infiltrations? There had been an age
When a pineapple on the table was enough,

Without the forfeit scholar coming in,
Without his enlargings and pale arrondissements,
Without the furious roar in his capital.

Green had, those days, its own implacable sting.
But now a habit of the truth had formed
To protect him in a privacy, in which

The scholar, captious, told him what he could
Of there, where the truth was not the respect of one,
But always of many things. He had not to be told

Of the incredible subjects of poetry.
He was willing they should remain incredible,
Because the incredible, also, has its truth,

Its tuft of emerald that is real, for all
Its invitation to false metaphor.
The incredible gave him a purpose to believe.

III

How thick this gobbet is with overlays,
The double fruit of boisterous epicures,
Like the same orange repeating on one tree

A single self. Divest reality
Of its propriety. Admit the shaft
Of that third planet to the table and then:

1. The hut stands by itself beneath the palms.
2. Out of their bottle the green genii come.
3. A vine has climbed the other side of the wall.

4. The sea is spouting upward out of rocks.
5. The symbol of feasts and of oblivion . . .
6. White sky, pink sun, trees on a distant peak.

7. These lozenges are nailed-up lattices.
8. The owl sits humped. It has a hundred eyes.
9. The coconut and cockerel in one.

10. This is how yesterday's volcano looks.
11. There is an island Palahude by name—
12. An uncivil shape like a gigantic haw.

These casual exfoliations are
Of the tropic of resemblance, sprigs
Of Capricorn or as the sign demands,

Apposites, to the slightest edge, of the whole
Undescribed composition of the sugar-cone,
Shiftings of an inchoate crystal tableau,

The momentary footings of a climb
Up the pineapple, a table Alp and yet
An Alp, a purple Southern mountain bisqued

With the molten mixings of related things,
Cat's taste possibly or possibly Danish lore,
The small luxuriations that portend

Universal delusions of universal grandeurs,
The slight incipiencies, of which the form,
At last, is the pineapple on the table or else

An object the sum of its complications, seen
And unseen. This is everybody's world.
Here the total artifice reveals itself

As the total reality. Therefore it is
One says even of the odor of this fruit,
That steeps the room, quickly, then not at all,

It is more than the odor of this core of earth
And water. It is that which is distilled
In the prolific ellipses that we know,

In the planes that tilt hard revelations on
The eye, a geometric glitter, tiltings
As of sections collecting toward the greenest cone.

3

OF IDEAL TIME AND CHOICE

Since thirty mornings are required to make
A day of which we say, this is the day
That we desired, a day of blank, blue wheels,

Involving the four corners of the sky,
Lapised and lacqued and freely emeraldine
In the space it fills, the silent motioner

There, of clear, revolving crystalline;
Since thirty summers are needed for a year
And thirty years, in the galaxies of birth,

Are time for counting and remembering,
And fill the earth with young men centuries old
And old men, who have chosen, and are cold

Because what they have chosen is their choice
No more and because they lack the will to tell
A matin gold from gold of Hesperus

The dot, the pale pole of resemblances
Experienced yet not well seen; of how
Much choosing is the final choice made up,

And who shall speak it, what child or wanderer
Or woman weeping in a room or man,
The last man given for epitome,

Upon whose lips the dissertation sounds,
And in what place, what exultant terminal,
And at what time both of the year and day;

And what heroic nature of what text
Shall be the celebration in the words
Of that oration, the happiest sense in which

A world agrees, thought's compromise, resolved
At last, the center of resemblance, found
Under the bones of time's philosophers?

The orator will say that we ourselves
Stand at the center of ideal time,
The inhuman making choice of a human self.

IV

About One of
Marianne Moore's Poems

MY PURPOSE is to bring together one of Miss Moore's poems and a paper, "On Poetic Truth," by H. D. Lewis. The poem, "He 'Digesteth Harde Yron,'" has just been reprinted in the *Partisan Reader*. The paper is to be found in the July number (1946) of *Philosophy, the Journal of the British Institute of Philosophy* (Macmillan, London).

I

Mr. Lewis begins by saying that poetry has to do with reality in its most individual aspect. An isolated fact, cut loose from the universe, has no significance for the poet. It derives its significance from the reality to which it belongs. To see things in their true perspective, we require to draw very extensively upon experiences that are past. All that we see and hear is given a meaning in this way. There is in reality an aspect of individuality at which every form of rational explanation stops short. Now, in his *Euphues*, Lyly repeats the following bit of folk-lore:

> Let them both remember that the Estridge
> digesteth harde yron to preserve his health.

The "Estridge," then, is the subject of Miss Moore's poem. In the second stanza she says:

> This bird watches his chicks with
> a maternal concentration, after
>   he has sat on the eggs
>   at night six weeks, his legs
> their only weapon of defense.

The *Encyclopaedia Britannica* says of the ostrich:

Extremely fleet of foot, when brought to bay the ostrich
uses its strong legs with great effect. Several hens com-
bine to lay their eggs in one nest, and on these the cock
sits by night, while the females relieve one another by
day.

Somehow, there is a difference between Miss Moore's bird
and the bird of the *Encyclopaedia*. This difference grows when
she describes her bird as

> The friend
> of hippotigers and wild
> asses, it is as
> though schooled by them he was
>
> the best of the unflying
> pegasi.

The difference signalizes a transition from one reality to an-
other. It is the reality of Miss Moore that is the individual
reality. That of the *Encyclopaedia* is the reality of isolated fact.
Miss Moore's reality is significant. An aesthetic integration is
a reality.

Nowhere in the poem does she speak directly of the subject
of the poem by its name. She calls it "the camel-sparrow" and
"the large sparrow Xenophon saw walking by a stream," "the
bird," "quadruped-like bird" and

> alert gargantuan
> little-winged, magnificently
> speedy running-bird.

This, too, marks a difference. To confront fact in its total
bleakness is for any poet a completely baffling experience. Re-
ality is not the thing but the aspect of the thing. At first read-
ing, this poem has an extraordinarily factual appearance. But
it is, after all, an abstraction. Mr. Lewis says that for Plato the
only reality that mattered is exemplified best for us in the
principles of mathematics. The aim of our lives should be to
draw ourselves away as much as possible from the unsubstan-
tial, fluctuating facts of the world about us and establish some
communion with the objects which are apprehended by

thought and not sense. This was the source of Plato's asceti-
cism. To the extent that Miss Moore finds only allusion tol-
erable she shares that asceticism. While she shares it she does
so only as it may be necessary for her to do so in order to
establish a particular reality or, better, a reality of her own
particulars: the "overt" reality of Mr. Lewis. Take, for ex-
ample, her particulars of the bird's egg. She says:

> The egg piously shown
> as Leda's very own
> from which Castor and Pollux hatched,
> was an ostrich-egg.

Again she speaks of

> jewel-
> gorgeous ugly egg-shell
> goblet.

It is obvious from these few quotations that Miss Moore has
already found an individual reality in the ostrich and again in
its egg. After all, it is the subject in poetry that releases the
energy of the poet.

Mr. Lewis says that poetry has to do with matter that is
foreign and alien. It is never familiar to us in the way in which
Plato wished the conquests of the mind to be familiar. On the
contrary its function, the need which it meets and which has
to be met in some way in every age that is not to become
decadent or barbarous, is precisely this contact with reality as
it impinges upon us from outside, the sense that we can touch
and feel a solid reality which does not wholly dissolve itself
into the conceptions of our own minds. It is the individual
and particular that does this. No fact is a bare fact, no indi-
vidual fact is a universe in itself. Is not Miss Moore creating
or finding and revealing some such reality in the stanza that
follows?

> Six hundred ostrich-brains served
> at one banquet, the ostrich-plume-tipped tent
> and desert spear . . .
> eight pairs of ostriches

> in harness, dramatize a
>   meaning always missed
>   by the externalist.

Here the sparrow-camel is all pomp and ceremony, a part of justice of which it was not only the symbol, as Miss Moore says, but also the source of its panoply and the delicacy of its feasts; that is to say, a part of unprecedented experience.

Miss Moore's finical phraseology is an element in her procedure. These lines illustrate this:

> Although the aepyornis
> or roc that lives in Madagascar, and
>   the moa are extinct

and

> Heroism is exhausting.

But what irrevocably detaches her from the *Encyclopaedia* is the irony of the following:

> How
> could he, prized for plumes and eggs and young, used
>   even as a riding-
> beast, respect men hiding
> actorlike in ostrich-skins, with
> the right hand making the neck move
>   as if alive and
>   from a bag the left hand
>
> strewing grain, that ostriches
> might be decoyed and killed!

and the delighted observation of the following:

> whose comic duckling head on its
> great neck, revolves with compass-
>   needle nervousness,
>   when he stands guard, in S-
>
> like foragings as he is
> preening the down on his leaden-skinned back.

The gist of the poem is that the camel-sparrow has escaped the greed that has led to the extinction of other birds linked to it in size, by its solicitude for its own welfare and that of its chicks. Considering the great purposes that poetry must serve, the interest of the poem is not in its meaning but in this, that it illustrates the achieving of an individual reality. Mr. Lewis has some very agreeable things to say about meaning. He says that the extraction of a meaning from a poem and appraisement of it by rational standards of truth have mainly been due to enthusiasm for moral or religious truth. He protests against the abstraction of this content from the whole and appraisement of it by other than aesthetic standards. The "something said" is important, but it is important for the poem only in so far as the saying of that particular something in a special way is a revelation of reality. He says:

> If I am right, the essence of art is insight of a special
> kind into reality.

Moreover, if he is right, the question as to Miss Moore's poem is not in respect to its meaning but in respect to its potency as a work of art. Does it make us so aware of the reality with which it is concerned, because of the poignancy and penetration of the poet, that it forces something upon our consciousness? The reality so imposed need not be a great reality.

Of course, if it does, it serves our purpose quite as certainly as a less modest poem would serve it. It is here, Mr. Lewis concludes, that the affinity of art and religion is most evident today. He says that both have to mediate for us a reality not ourselves and that this is what the poet does and that the supreme virtue here is humility, for the humble are they that move about the world with the lure of the real in their hearts.

2

Life, not the artist, creates or reveals reality: time and experience in the poet, in the painter. During this last September, I visited the old Zeller house in the Tulpehocken, in Pennsylvania. This family of religious refugees came to this country in 1709, lived for some fifteen or twenty years in the

Scoharie region in New York and then went down the Susquehanna to the valley in which the house was built. Over the door there is an architectural cartouche of the cross with palm-branches below, placed there, no doubt, to indicate that the house and those that lived in it were consecrated to the glory of God. From this doorway they faced the hills that were part of the frame of their valley, the familiar shelter in which they spent their laborious lives, happy in the faith and worship in which they rejoiced. Their reality consisted of both the visible and the invisible. On another occasion, a man went with me to visit Christ Church near Stouchsburg. This stout old Lutheran felt about his church very much as the Irish are said to feel about God. Kate O'Brien says that in Ireland God is a member of the family. The man told me that last spring a scovy duck had built her nest in the chimney of the church. When, finally, her brood was hatched, the ducklings came out of a stove in one of the rooms in the basement of the church. There were six of them and they are alive today on the sexton's farm. When the committee of the church in charge of the building was making its plans last spring, this true lover of his church agreed to paint the fence around the adjoining graveyard. In part, this fence consisted of cast-iron spears. He painted the spear-head silver and the staves black, one by one, week after week, until the job was done. Yet obviously this man's reality is the church-building but as a fellow-existence, of a sort.

As we drove along the road, we met one of the Lutheran's friends, who had been leader of the choir in Trinity Tulpehocken Reformed Church for more than a generation. He had wrapped his throat up in flannel because, he said, one of his tendons was sore. At choir-practice the night before, the hymns for the Sunday service had been selected. He was on his way to the church to put the numbers in the rack. When he had done this, he went with us to the old graveyard of this church. This was an enclosure of about an acre, possibly a little more. The wall was of limestone about four feet high, weather-beaten, barren, bald. In the graveyard were possibly eight or ten sheep, the color of the wall and of many of the gravestones and even of some of the tufts of grass, bleached and silvery in the hard sunlight. The droppings of the sheep fertilized the soil. There were a few cedars here and there but these only accentuated the sense of abandonment and destitution, the sense that, after all, the vast mausoleum of human memory is emptier than one had supposed. Near by stood the manse, also of limestone, apparently vacant, the upper part of each window white with the half-drawn blind, the lower part black with the vacantness of the place. Although the two elderly men were in a way a diversion from the solitude, there could not be any effective diversion from the reality that time and experience had created here, the desolation that penetrated one like something final. Later, when I had returned to New York, I went to the exhibition of books in the Morgan Library held by the American Institute of Graphic Arts. The brilliant pages from Poland, France, Finland and so on, books of tales, of poetry, of folk-lore, were as if the barren reality that I had just experienced had suddenly taken color, become alive and from a single thing become many things and people, vivid, active, intently trying out a thousand characters and illuminations.

3

It is true that Mr. Lewis contemplates a reality adequate to the profound necessities of life today. But it is no less true that it is easier to try to recognize it or something like it or the possible beginnings of it than to achieve it on that scale. Thus, the field in poetry is as great as it is in anything else. Nothing illustrates this better and nothing illustrates the importance of poetry better than this possibility that within it there may yet be found a reality adequate to the profound necessities of life today or for that matter any day. Miss Moore's poem is an instance of method and is not an example beyond the scale intended by her. She may well say:

> *Que ce n'est pas grand merveille de voir que l'Ostruche digére le fer, veu que les poulles n'en font pas moins.*

For she is not a proud spirit. It may be that proud spirits love only the lion or the elephant with its howdah. Miss Moore, however, loves all animals, fierce or mild, ancient or modern.

When she observes them she is transported into the presence of a recognizable reality, because, as it happens, she has the faculty of digesting the "harde yron" of appearance.

V

Effects of Analogy

THE SUPREME example of analogy in English is *Pilgrim's Progress*. This overwhelms us with direct analogy, that is to say: the personifications of allegory. Thus, in the Second Part where Christiana and young Mercy are on their way toward the Caelestial Country with Christiana's children to rejoin Christian, they come at evening to the house of the Interpreter. After the Interpreter has shown them his house he leads them into his garden and

> as they were coming in from abroad, they espied a little robin with a great spider in his mouth. So they looked, and Mercy wondred; but Christiana said, what a disparagement is it to such a little pretty bird as the robin-redbreast is, he being also a bird above many that loveth to maintain a kind of sociableness with man; I had thought they had lived upon crums of bread, or upon other such harmless matter. I like him worse than I did.
>
> The Interpreter then replied, This robin is an emblem very apt to set forth some professors by; for to sight they are as this robin, pretty of note colour and carriage. They seem also to have a very great love for professors that are sincere; and above all other to desire to sociate with, and to be in their company, as if they could live upon the good man's crums. They pretend also that therefore it is that they frequent the house of the godly, and the appointments of the Lord; but when they are by themselves, as the robin, they can catch and gobble up spiders, they can change their diet, drink iniquity, and swallow down sin like water.

In French, the supreme example of analogy is, probably, the *Fables* of La Fontaine. Of these, none is better known than the fable of "The Crow and the Fox," which goes, in the translation of Edward Marsh, as follows:

A Crow sat perched upon an oak,
And in his beak he held a cheese.
A fox snuffed up the savoury breeze,
And thus in honey'd accent spoke:
"O Prince of Crows, such grace of mien
Has never in these parts been seen.
If but your song be half as good,
You are the Phoenix of the wood!"
The Crow, beside himself with pleasure,
And eager to display his voice,
Opened his beak, and dropt his treasure.
The Fox was on it in a trice.
"Learn, sir," said he, "that flatterers live
On those who swallow what they say.
A cheese is not too much to give
For such a piece of sound advice!"
The Crow, ashamed t'have been such easy prey,
Swore, though too late, he shouldn't catch him twice.

As we read Bunyan we are distracted by the double sense
of the analogy and we are rather less engaged by the symbols
than we are by what is symbolized. The other meaning divides
our attention and this diminishes our enjoyment of the story.
But of such an indisputable masterpiece it must be true that
one reader, oblivious of the other meaning, reads it for the
story and another reader, oblivious of the story, reads it for
the other meaning; and that each finds in perfection what he
wants. But there is a third reader, one for whom the story
and the other meaning should come together like two aspects
that combine to produce a third or, if they do not combine,
inter-act, so that one influences the other and produces an
effect similar in kind to the prismatic formations that occur
about us in nature in the case of reflections and refractions.
Bunyan nowhere produces these prismatic crystallizations. As
for such things, he might as well be a collection of primitive
woodcuts. In La Fontaine, there is a difference. We are not
distracted. Our attention is on the symbol, which is interesting
in itself. The other meaning does not dog the symbol like its
shadow. It is not attached to it. Here the effect of analogy
almost ceases to exist and the reason for this is, of course, that

we are not particularly conscious of it. We do not have to stand up to it and take it. It is like a play of thought, some trophy that we ourselves gather, some meaning that we ourselves supply. It is like a pleasant shadow, faint and volatile. In Bunyan, it is the other meaning that is the solid matter; in La Fontaine, the solid matter is the story. The difference may be a national difference. We are interested in it only as a difference.

2

Commonly, analogy is a term in logic. Susan Stebbing in her *Logic in Practice* says:

> Inference by analogy consists in inferring that, since two cases are alike in certain respects, they will also be alike in some other respect. For example, since Mars resembles the Earth in certain respects, we infer that Mars also is inhabited. This may be a very risky inference, for Mars differs from the Earth in some respects, and these differences may be relevant to the property of being inhabited.

Now, we are not thinking, here, of analogy in this narrow sense. We are thinking of it as likeness, as resemblance between parallels and yet parallels that are parallels only in the imagination, and we are thinking of it in its relation to poetry. Finally we are thinking of it from the point of view of the effect it produces. The other day, Kenneth Burke, in the course of a review of Rosemond Tuve's *Elizabethan and Metaphysical Imagery*, referred to the introduction of rhetoric into the analysis of imagery. He said that it gave a clear picture of the ways in which logic, rhetoric and poetic are interwoven

> in contrast with the doctrines of those who would confine logic to science, rhetoric to propaganda or advertising, and thus leave for poetic a few spontaneous sensations not much higher in the intellectual scale than the twitchings of a decerebrated frog.

The analogy between the spontaneous sensations of a poet and the muscular twitchings of a decerebrated frog communicated Mr. Burke's antipathy to the doctrines on which he was commenting and was a way of characterizing those doctrines as at once futile, ugly and ludicrous. His analogy had its source in a feeling of scorn and took the form of an image that expressed his scorn. In short, his image had its origin in an emotion, was charged with that emotion and became the medium for communicating it. Thus, it belongs to that large class of images of emotional origin in which the nature of the image is analogous to the nature of the emotion from which it springs; and when one speaks of images, one means analogies. If, then, an emotional image or, say, an emotional analogy communicates the emotion that generates it, its effect is to arouse the same emotion in others. There is nothing of this in the sort of analogy that we find in *Pilgrim's Progress*. The very scale and deliberateness of allegory are against it. To be sure, *Pilgrim's Progress* is prose. In a long poem, so many emotions, so many sensations, are stirred up into activity that, after a time, the reader finds himself in a state of such sensibility that it cannot be said that the scale and deliberateness of allegory fail to produce an emotional effect. A prolonged reading of Spenser's *Faerie Queene*, for instance, creates just such a state of sensibility. In general, long poems have this attribute, derived from their very length, assuming that they have been charged throughout with the emotions of the poet.

In order to see how true it is that in images of emotional origin the image partakes of the nature of the emotion, let us analyze a passage from one of the poems of Allen Tate. He is looking at a young woman dead in her bed. He says:

> For look you how her body stiffly lies
> Just as she left it, unprepared to stay,
> The posture waiting on the sleeping eyes,
> While the body's life, deep as a covered well,
> Instinctive as the wind, busy as May,
> Burns out a secret passageway to hell.

He is moved by the ghastliness and ghostliness of the body before him. He communicates the ghastliness by a direct statement: her body stiffly lies. But the ghostliness he communicates by making of the posture one of death's attendants. The thoughts of life and death commingle. Under the hidden im-

age of the tomb, her spirit is instinctive as the wind in its blind
and fateful freedom.

A scene not too dissimilar gives rise to a different feeling in
John Crowe Ransom. In his *Bells for John Whiteside's Daugh-
ter*, he begins by describing her quizzically and yet as a little
old lady who used to harry the geese on her pond and, with
a rod, make them rise:

> But now go the bells, and we are ready,
> In our house we are sternly stopped
> To say we are vexed at her brown study,
> Lying so primly propped.

What is it that Mr. Ransom feels at the sight of John
Whiteside's daughter, dead, except the same quizzicality that
he felt at the sight of her alive? He communicates this in a
quizzical image of death as a brown study, but as a brown
study vexing in the case of one that lies so primly propped.
Neither Mr. Tate nor Mr. Ransom is an emotional poet. Nor
with such men is it a question of degree. Rather, their sensi-
bilities have large orbits.

We have not been dealing, up to this point, with the
appositeness of figures of speech but with their emotional
authenticity, which they have the power to propagate. The
emotional analogy is only one. When St. Matthew in his
Gospel says that Jesus went about all the cities, teaching and
preaching, and that

> when he saw the multitudes, he was moved with com-
> passion on them, because they . . . were scattered
> abroad, as sheep having no shepherd,

the analogy between the multitudes scattered abroad and
sheep having no shepherd is not an emotional analogy. On
the contrary, it is as if Matthew had poised himself if only for
an instant, had invoked his imagination and had made a choice
of what it offered to his mind, a choice based on the degree
of the appositeness of the image. He could do this without
being notably deliberate because the imagination does not re-
quire for its projections the same amount of time that the
reason requires. I spoke a moment ago of a reader for whom

the two elements of an analogy should combine to produce a third. There is still another reader for whom the effect of analogy is the effect of the degree of appositeness, for whom the imaginative projection, the imaginative deviation, raises the question of rightness, as if in the vast association of ideas there existed for every object its appointed objectification. In such a case, the object and its image become inseparable. It follows that for this fourth reader the effect of analogy is the effect of consummation. The example from Matthew is not only a good example, but a familiar one. One almost equally familiar is from the Greek Anthology, in Professor Mackail's translation:

> Even as a vine on her dry pole I support myself now
> on a staff and death calls me to Hades.

This epigram has about it something of the modern sense of epigram. Leonidas does not compare himself to a vine on her dry pole without a certain slyness. The image is not only that of the old man wandering on the edge of night. It includes, also, something of his tatteredness, something of the weather-beaten figure of the vagabond, which by its eccentricity arouses the sense of pathos but not the feeling of sorrow. These two citations, the one of sheep having no shepherd and the other of the vine on her dry pole, quite adequately illustrate the discipline that comes from appositeness in the highest degree.

It is primarily a discipline of rightness. The poet is constantly concerned with two theories. One relates to the imagination as a power within him not so much to destroy reality at will as to put it to his own uses. He comes to feel that his imagination is not wholly his own but that it may be part of a much larger, much more potent imagination, which it is his affair to try to get at. For this reason, he pushes on and lives, or tries to live, as Paul Valéry did, on the verge of consciousness. This often results in poetry that is marginal, subliminal. The same theory exists in relation to prose, to painting and other arts. The second theory relates to the imagination as a power within him to have such insights into reality as will make it possible for him to be sufficient as a poet in the very center of consciousness. This results, or should result, in a central poetry. Dr. Whitehead concluded his *Modes of Thought* by saying:

> . . . the purpose of philosophy is to rationalize mysticism. . . . Philosophy is akin to poetry, and both of them seek to express that ultimate good sense which we term civilization.

The proponents of the first theory believe that it will be a part of their achievement to have created the poetry of the future. It may be that the poetry of the future will be to the poetry of the present what the poetry of the present is to the ballad. The proponents of the second theory believe that to create the poetry of the present is an incalculable difficulty, which rarely is achieved, fully and robustly, by anyone. They think that there is enough and more than enough to do with what faces us and concerns us directly and that in poetry as an art, and, for that matter, in any art, the central problem is always the problem of reality. The adherents of the imagination are mystics to begin with and pass from one mysticism to another. The adherents of the central are also mystics to begin with. But all their desire and all their ambition is to press away from mysticism toward that ultimate good sense which we term civilization. The analogy of Matthew and the image of Leonidas are particles of that ultimate good sense.

In departing from the finality and rightness of two ancient specimens, let us make use of a third for the purpose of pointing out that it is not possible to measure the distances away from rightness except in the roughest manner nor to indicate anything more than crude differences of effect. Virgil, in the first book of the *Georgics*, in Day Lewis' translation, says:

> Winter's an off-time
> For farmers . . .
>   and they forget their worries;
> Just as, when ships in cargo have come to port at last,
> Glad to be home the sailors adorn their poops with
>   garlands.

This expresses an analogy between farmers after a summer and sailors after a voyage, fortified by secondary analogies between the worries of farmers and the trials of sailors, between crops and cargoes and between harvesting and making port. It is therefore a figure over which Virgil did something more than poise himself for an instant. It is a considered elaboration, a prototype of the considered elaborations with which in the eighteenth century, say, English poets were accustomed to embellish their pages. It does not click. If it is apposite at all it is only after we have thought about it and by that time we have lost interest in it. It is one of the multitude of figures of speech that are merely idle. It does not raise any question of taste. Nothing in Virgil could. One remembers the description of Virgil as the delight of all men of taste. Nevertheless, to go back to Allen Tate, it is just not a thing that

    . . . strikes like a hawk the crouching hare.

It would not be hard to find elsewhere examples of analogy displaying this or that defect, artificiality, incongruity, lack of definition. This is not an anatomy of metaphor. Nor is it an attempt to do more than to single out a few of the effects of analogy. The field must be one which has already been examined, for other purposes, by literary critics and historians, writers on aesthetics, psychologists, Freudians. Poetry is almost incredibly one of the effects of analogy. This statement involves much more than the analogy of figures of speech, since otherwise poetry would be little more than a trick. But it is almost incredibly the outcome of figures of speech or, what is the same thing, the outcome of the operation of one imagination on another through the instrumentality of the figures. To identify poetry and metaphor or metamorphosis is merely to abbreviate the last remark. There is always an analogy between nature and the imagination, and possibly poetry is merely the strange rhetoric of that parallel: a rhetoric in which the feeling of one man is communicated to another in words of the exquisite appositeness that takes away all their verbality.

3

Another mode of analogy is to be found in the personality of the poet. But this mode is no more limited to the poet than the mode of metaphor is so limited. This mode proposes for study the poet's sense of the world as the source of poetry.

The corporeal world exists as the common denominator of the incorporeal worlds of its inhabitants. If there are people who live only in the corporeal world, enjoying the wind and the weather and supplying standards of normality, there are other people who are not so sure of the wind and the weather and who supply standards of abnormality. It is the poet's sense of the world that is the poet's world. The corporeal world, the familiar world of the commonplace, in short, our world, is one sense of the analogy that develops between our world and the world of the poet. The poet's sense of the world is the other sense. It is the analogy between these two senses that concerns us.

We could not speak of our world as something to be distinguished from the poet's sense of it unless we objectified it and recognized it as having an existence apart from the projection of his personality, as land and sea, sky and cloud. He himself desires to make the distinction as part of the process of realizing himself. Once the distinction has been made, it becomes an instrument for the exploration of poetry. By means of it we can determine the relation of the poet to his subject. This would be simple if he wrote about his own world. We could compare it with ours. But what he writes about is his sense of our world. If he is a melancholy person he gives us a melancholy sense of our world. By way of illustration, here is a passage from James Thomson's *The City of Dreadful Night*:

> We do not ask a longer term of strife,
> > Weakness and weariness and nameless woes:
> We do not claim renewed and endless life
> > When this which is our torment here shall close,
> An everlasting conscious inanition!
> We yearn for speedy death in full fruition,
> > Dateless oblivion and divine repose.

On the other hand, a stronger man, Walt Whitman, in *A Clear Midnight* gives us this:

> This is thy hour, O soul, thy free flight into the wordless,
> Away from books, away from art, the day erased, the
> > lesson done,

Thee fully forth emerging, silent, gazing, pondering the
    themes thou lovest best,
Night, sleep, death and the stars.

The illustrations are endless but really none is required.

A man's sense of the world is born with him and persists,
and penetrates the ameliorations of education and experience
of life. His species is as fixed as his genus. For each man, then,
certain subjects are congenital. Now, the poet manifests his
personality, first of all, by his choice of subject. Temperament
is a more explicit word than personality and would no doubt
be the exact word to use, since it emphasizes the manner of
thinking and feeling. It is agreeable to think of the poet as a
whole biological mechanism and not as a subordinate mech-
anism within that larger one. Temperament, too, has attracted
a pejorative meaning. It should be clear that in dealing with
the choice of subject we are dealing with one of the vital fac-
tors in poetry or in any art. Great numbers of poets come and
go who have never had a subject at all. What is true of poets
in this respect is equally true of painters, as the existence of
schools of painters all doing more or less the same thing at
the same time demonstrates. The leader of the school has a
subject. But his followers merely have his subject. Thus Pi-
casso has a subject, a subject that devours him and devastates
his region. Possibly a better illustration would be one that is
less intimidating. Whether we like it or not, all of us who have
radios or who go to the movies hear a great deal of popular
music. Usually this is music without a subject. You have only
to tabulate the titles of the songs you hear over a short period
of time to convince yourself of this. The titles are trivial,
catchy, trite and silly. Love is not a subject unless the writer
of the song is in love. A man peddles love-songs because it is
easier to do than it is to peddle coconuts, and this is as true
of the man who writes the words as it is of the man who writes
the music.

What is the poet's subject? It is his sense of the world. For
him, it is inevitable and inexhaustible. If he departs from it he
becomes artificial and laborious and while his artifice may be
skillful and his labor perceptive no one knows better than he
that what he is doing, under such circumstances, is not essen-

tial to him. It may help him to feel that it may be essential to someone else. But this justification, though it might justify what he does in the eyes of all the world, would never quite justify him in his own eyes. There is nothing of selfishness in this. It is often said of a man that his work is autobiographical in spite of every subterfuge. It cannot be otherwise. Certainly, from the point of view from which we are now regarding it, it cannot be otherwise, even though it may be totally without reference to himself. There was a time when the ivory tower was merely a place of seclusion, like a cottage on a hill-top or a cabin by the sea. Today, it is a kind of lock-up of which our intellectual constables are the appointed wardens. Is it not time that someone questioned this degradation, not for the purpose of restoring the isolation of the tower but in order to establish the integrity of its builder? Our rowdy gun-men may not appreciate what comes from that tower. Others do. Was there ever any poetry more wholly the poetry of the ivory tower than the poetry of Mallarmé? Was there ever any music more wholly the music of the ivory tower than the music of Debussy?

The truth is that a man's sense of the world dictates his subjects to him and that this sense is derived from his personality, his temperament, over which he has little control and possibly none, except superficially. It is not a literary problem. It is the problem of his mind and nerves. These sayings are another form of the saying that poets are born not made. A poet writes of twilight because he shrinks from noon-day. He writes about the country because he dislikes the city, and he likes the one and dislikes the other because of some trait of mind or nerves; that is to say, because of something in himself that influences his thinking and feeling. So seen, the poet and his subject are inseparable. There are stresses that he invites; there are stresses that he avoids. There are colors that have the blandest effect on him; there are others with which he can do nothing but find fault. In music he likes the strings. But the horn shocks him. A flat landscape extending in all directions to immense distances placates him. But he shrugs his shoulders at mountains. One young woman seems to be someone that he would like to know; another seems to be someone that he must know without fail.

Recently, a very great deal has been said about the relation of the poet to his community and to other people, and as the propaganda on behalf of the community and other people gathers momentum a great deal more will be said. But if a poet's subject is congenital this is beside the point. Or is it? The ivory tower was offensive if the man who lived in it wrote, there, of himself for himself. It was not offensive if he used it because he could do nothing without concentration, as no one can, and because, there, he could most effectively struggle to get at his subject, even if his subject happened to be the community and other people, and nothing else. It may be that the poet's congenital subject is precisely the community and other people. If it is not, he may have to ask Shostakovich and Prokofiev and their fellow musicians and such writers as Michael Zoshchenko what to do next. These men, who backslide once in so often, should know. They are experienced.

The second way by which a poet manifests his personality is by his style. This is too well understood to permit discussion. What has just been said with respect to choice of subject applies equally to style. The individual dialect of a poet who happens to have one, analogous to the speech common to his time and place and yet not that common speech, is in the same position as the language of poetry generally when the language of poetry generally is not the common speech. Both produce effects singular to analogy. Beyond that the dialect is not in point.

A man's sense of the world may be only his own or it may be the sense of many people. Whatever it is it involves his fate. It may involve only his own or it may involve that of many people. The measure of the poet is the measure of his sense of the world and of the extent to which it involves the sense of other people. We have to stop and think now and then of what he writes as implicit with that significance. Thus in the lines of Leonidas:

Even as a vine on her dry pole I support myself now
on a staff and death calls me to Hades

we have to think of the reality and to read the lines as one having the reality at heart: an old man at that point at which antiquity begins to resume what everything else has left behind; or if you think of the lines as a figuration of despair on the part of the poet, and it is possible to change them into such a figuration, to read them as lines communicating a feeling that it was not within the poet's power to suppress.

4

Still another mode of analogy is to be found in the music of poetry. It is a bit old hat and romantic and, no doubt at all, the dated forms are intolerable. In recent years, poetry began to change character about the time when painting began to change character. Each lost a certain euphrasy. But, after all, the music of poetry has not come to an end. Is not Eliot a musical poet? Listen to part of what the lamp hummed of the moon in *Rhapsody on a Windy Night*:

> A washed-out smallpox cracks her face,
> Her hand twists a paper rose,
> That smells of dust and old Cologne,
> She is alone
> With all the old nocturnal smells
> That cross and cross across her brain.
> The reminiscence comes
> Of sunless dry geraniums
> And dust in crevices,
> Smells of chestnuts in the streets
> And female smells in shuttered rooms
> And cigarettes in corridors
> And cocktail smells in bars.

This is a specimen of what is meant by music today. It contains rhymes at irregular intervals and it is intensely cadenced. But yesterday, or the day before, the time from which the use of the word "music" in relation to poetry has come down to us, music meant something else. It meant metrical poetry with regular rhyme schemes repeated stanza after stanza. All of the stanzas were alike in form. As a result of this, what with the repetitions of the beats of the lines, and the constant and recurring harmonious sounds, there actually was a music. But with the disappearance of all this, the use of the word "music" in relation to poetry is as I said a moment ago a bit old hat:

anachronistic. Yet the passage from Eliot was musical. It is simply that there has been a change in the nature of what we mean by music. It is like the change from Haydn to a voice intoning. It is like the voice of an actor reciting or declaiming or of some other figure concealed, so that we cannot identify him, who speaks with a measured voice which is often disturbed by his feeling for what he says. There is no accompaniment. If occasionally the poet touches the triangle or one of the cymbals, he does it only because he feels like doing it. Instead of a musician we have an orator whose speech sometimes resembles music. We have an eloquence and it is that eloquence that we call music every day, without having much cause to think about it.

What has this music to do with analogy? When we hear the music of one of the great narrative musicians, as it tells its tale, it is like finding our way through the dark not by the aid of any sense but by an instinct that makes it possible for us to move quickly when the music moves quickly, slowly when the music moves slowly. It is a speed that carries us on and through every winding, once more to the world outside of the music at its conclusion. It affects our sight of what we see and leaves it ambiguous, somewhat like one thing, somewhat like another. In the meantime the tale is being told and the music excites us and we identify it with the story and it becomes the story and the speed with which we are following it. When it is over, we are aware that we have had an experience very much like the story just as if we had participated in what took place. It is exactly as if we had listened with complete sympathy to an emotional recital. The music was a communication of emotion. It would not have been different if it had been the music of poetry or the voice of the protagonist telling the tale or speaking out his sense of the world. How many things we should have found like in either case!

5

I have spoken of several kinds of analogy. I began with the personifications of Bunyan and the animalizations of La Fontaine. I then spoke of emotional images, taking illustrations from several sources, principally Kenneth Burke. Next I spoke of what may be called voluntary images, quoting from St. Matthew, Leonidas of Tarentum and Virgil. Finally I spoke of what may be called involuntary images, quoting from James Thomson and Walt Whitman and referring to music. It is time, therefore, to attempt a few generalizations, slight as the data may be. Accordingly, our first generalization is this: Every image is the elaboration of a particular of the subject of the image. If this is true it is a realistic explanation of the origin of images. Let us go back to the quotation from St. Matthew. Jesus went about all the cities, teaching and preaching, and

> when he saw the multitudes, he was moved with com-
> passion on them, because they . . . were scattered
> abroad, as sheep having no shepherd.

The analogy between men and sheep does not exist under all circumstances. There came into Matthew's mind in respect to Jesus going about, teaching and preaching, the thought that Jesus was a shepherd and immediately the multitudes scattered abroad and sheep having that particular in common became interchangeable. The image is an elaboration of the particular of the shepherd. In the lines from Leonidas:

> Even as a vine on her dry pole I support myself now
> on a staff and death calls me to Hades

the particular is the staff. This becomes the dry pole, and the vine follows after. There is no analogy between a vine and an old man under all circumstances. But when one supports itself on a dry pole and the other on a staff, the case is different. Two casual illustrations are not enough to establish a principle. But they are enough to suggest the possibility of a principle.

Our second generalization, based on even slighter data, and proposed in the same experimental way, is this: Every image is a restatement of the subject of the image in the terms of an attitude. The metaphor from Kenneth Burke illustrates this. Since it has already been analyzed, I merely refer to it. If there is any merit to what was said about the sense of the world, that also illustrates the principle.

Our third generalization is this: Every image is an intervention on the part of the image-maker. One does not feel the need of so many reservations, if of any, in the case of this principle. But then of the three it is the one that matters least. It refers to the sense of the world, as the second principle did, and it could be said to be a phase of the second principle, if it did not refer to style in addition to the sense of the world. The second principle does not refer to style.

It is time, too, to attempt a few simplifications of the whole subject by way of summing it up and of coming to an end. With one or two exceptions, all of the examples that we have made use of have been pictorial. The image has been descriptive or explanatory of the subject of the image. To say the same thing another way, the thing stated has been accompanied by a restatement and the restatement has illustrated and given definition to the thing stated. The thing stated and the restatement have constituted an analogy. The venerable, the fundamental books of the human spirit are vast collections of such analogies and it is the analogies that have helped to make these books what they are. The pictorializations of poetry include much more than figures of speech. We have not been studying images, but, however crudely, analogies, of which images are merely a part. Analogies are much the larger subject. And analogies are elusive. Take the case of a man for whom reality is enough, as, at the end of his life, he returns to it like a man returning from Nowhere to his village and to everything there that is tangible and visible, which he has come to cherish and wants to be near. He sees without images. But is he not seeing a clarified reality of his own? Does he not dwell in an analogy? His imageless world is, after all, of the same sort as a world full of the obvious analogies of happiness or unhappiness, innocence or tragedy, thoughtlessness or the heaviness of the mind. In any case, these are the pictorializations of men, for whom the world exists as a world and for whom life exists as life, the objects of their passions, the objects before which they come and speak, with intense choosing, words that we remember and make our own. Their words have made a world that transcends the world and a life livable in that transcendence. It is a transcendence achieved by means of the minor effects of figurations and the major effects of the poet's sense of the world and of the motive music of his poems and it is the imaginative dynamism of all these analogies together. Thus poetry becomes and is a transcendent analogue composed of the particulars of reality, created by the poet's sense of the world, that is to say, his attitude, as he intervenes and interposes the appearances of that sense.

VI

Imagination as Value

IT DOES not seem possible to say of the imagination that it has a certain single characteristic which of itself gives it a certain single value as, for example, good or evil. To say such a thing would be the same thing as to say that the reason is good or evil or, for that matter, that human nature is good or evil. Since that is my first point, let us discuss it.

Pascal called the imagination the mistress of the world. But as he seems never to have spoken well of it, it is certain that he did not use this phrase to speak well of it. He called it the deceptive element in man, the mistress of error and duplicity and yet not always that, since there would be an infallible measure of truth if there were an infallible measure of untruth. But being most often false, it gives no sign of its quality and indicates in the same way both the true and the false. A little farther on in his *Pensées* he speaks of magistrates, their red robes, their ermines in which they swathe themselves, like furry cats, the palaces in which they sit in judgment, the fleurs-de-lis, and the whole necessary, august apparatus. He says, and he enjoys his own malice in saying it, that if medical men did not have their cassocks and the mules they wore and if doctors did not have their square hats and robes four times too large, they would never have been able to dupe the world, which is incapable of resisting so genuine a display. He refers to soldiers and kings, of whom he speaks with complete caution and re-spect, saying that they establish themselves by force, the others "par grimace." He justifies monarchs by the strength they possess and says that it is necessary to have a well-defined reason to regard like anyone else the Grand Seigneur sur-rounded, in his superb seraglio, by forty thousand janissaries.

However this may be, if respect for magistrates can be es-tablished by their robes and ermines and if justice can be made to prevail by the appearance of the seats of justice and if vast populations can be brought to live peacefully in their homes and to lie down at night with a sense of security and to get up in the morning confident that the great machine of organized society is ready to carry them on, merely by dressing a few men in uniform and sending them out to patrol the streets, the sort of thing that was the object of Pascal's ridicule and that was, to his way of thinking, an evil, or something of an evil, becomes to our way of thinking a potent good. The truth is, of course, that we do not really control vast populations in this way. Pascal knew perfectly well that the chancellor had force behind him. If he felt in his day that medicine was an imaginary science, he would not feel so today. After all, Pascal's understanding of the imagination was a part of his understanding of everything else. As he lay dying, he experienced a violent convulsion. His sister, who attended him, described the scene. He had repeatedly asked that he might receive communion. His sister wrote:

> God, who wished to reward a desire so fervent and so just, suspended this convulsion as by a miracle and restored his judgment completely as in the perfection of his health, in a manner that the parish priest, entering into his room with the sacrament, cried to him: "Here is he whom you have so much desired." These words completely roused him and as the priest approached to give him communion, he made an effort, he raised himself half way without help to receive it with more respect; and the priest having interrogated him, following the custom, on the principal mysteries of the faith, he responded distinctly: "Yes, monsieur, I believe all that with all my heart." Then he received the sacred wafer and extreme unction with feelings so tender that he poured out tears. He replied to everything, thanked the priest and as the priest blessed him with the holy ciborium, he said, "Let God never forsake me."

Thus, in the very act of dying, he clung to what he himself had called the delusive faculty. When I said a moment ago that he had never spoken well of it, I did not overlook the fact that "this superb power, the enemy of reason," to use his own words, did not, and could not, always seem the same to him. In a moment of indifference, he said that the imagination disposes all things and that it is the imagination that creates beauty, justice and happiness. In these various ways, the example of Pascal demonstrates how the good of the imagination may be evil and its evil good. The imagination is the power of the mind over the possibilities of things; but if this constitutes a certain single characteristic, it is the source not of a certain single value but of as many values as reside in the possibilities of things.

A second difficulty about value is the difference between the imagination as metaphysics and as a power of the mind over external objects, that is to say, reality. Ernst Cassirer in his *An Essay on Man* says:

> In romantic thought the theory of poetic imagination had reached its climax. Imagination is no longer that special human activity which builds up the human world of art. It now has universal metaphysical value. Poetic imagination is the only clue to reality. Fichte's idealism is based upon his conception of "productive imagination." Schelling declared in his *System of Transcendental Idealism* that art is the consummation of philosophy. In nature, in morality, in history we are still living in the propylaeum of philosophical wisdom; in art we enter into the sanctuary itself. The true poem is not the work of the individual artist; it is the universe itself, the one work of art which is forever perfecting itself.

Professor Cassirer speaks of this as "exuberant and ecstatic praise of poetic imagination." In addition, it is the language of what he calls "romantic thought" and by romantic thought he means metaphysics. When I speak of the power of the mind over external objects I have in mind, as external objects, works of art as, for example, the sculptures of Michelangelo with what Walter Pater calls "their wonderful strength verging, as in the things of the imagination great strength always does, on what is singular or strange," or, in architecture, the formidable public buildings of the British or the architecture and decoration of churches, as, say, in the case of the Jesuit church at Lucerne, where one might so easily pass from the real to the visionary without consciousness of change. Imagination, as metaphysics, leads us in one direction and, as art, in another.

When we consider the imagination as metaphysics, we re-

alize that it is in the nature of the imagination itself that we
should be quick to accept it as the only clue to reality. But
alas! we are no sooner so disposed than we encounter the
logical positivists. In *Language, Truth and Logic*, Professor
Ayer says that

> it is fashionable to speak of the metaphysician as a kind
> of misplaced poet. As his statements have no literal
> meaning, they are not subject to any criteria of truth or
> falsehood; but they may still seem to express, or arouse,
> emotions, and thus be subject to ethical or aesthetic
> standards. And it is suggested that they may have con-
> siderable value, as means of moral inspiration, or even
> as works of art. In this way, an attempt is made to
> compensate the metaphysician for his extrusion from
> philosophy.

It appears from this that the imagination as metaphysics, from
the point of view of the logical positivist, has at least seeming
values. During the last few months, the *New Statesman* of
London has been publishing letters growing out of a letter
sent to it by a visitor to Oxford, who reported that Professor
Ayer's book had "acquired almost the status of a philosophic
Bible." This led Professor Joad to look up the book and see
for himself. He reported that the book teaches that

> If . . . God is a metaphysical term, if, that is to say,
> He belongs to a reality which transcends the world of
> sense-experience . . . to say that He exists is neither true
> nor false. This position . . . is neither atheist nor ag-
> nostic; it cuts deeper than either, by asserting that all
> talk about God, whether pro or anti, is twaddle.

What is true of one metaphysical term is true of all.

Then, too, before going on, we must somehow cleanse the
imagination of the romantic. We feel, without being particu-
larly intelligent about it, that the imagination as metaphysics
will survive logical positivism unscathed. At the same time, we
feel, and with the sharpest possible intelligence, that it is not
worthy to survive if it is to be identified with the romantic.
The imagination is one of the great human powers. The ro-
mantic belittles it. The imagination is the liberty of the mind.

The romantic is a failure to make use of that liberty. It is to the imagination what sentimentality is to feeling. It is a failure of the imagination precisely as sentimentality is a failure of feeling. The imagination is the only genius. It is intrepid and eager and the extreme of its achievement lies in abstraction. The achievement of the romantic, on the contrary, lies in minor wish-fulfillments and it is incapable of abstraction. In any case and without continuing to contrast the two things, one wants to elicit a sense of the imagination as something vital. In that sense one must deal with it as metaphysics.

If we escape destruction at the hands of the logical positivists and if we cleanse the imagination of the taint of the romantic, we still face Freud. What would he have said of the imagination as the clue to reality and of a culture based on the imagination? Before jumping to the conclusion that at last there is no escape, is it not possible that he might have said that in a civilization based on science there could be a science of illusions? He does in fact say that "So long as a man's early years are influenced by the religious thought-inhibition . . . as well as by the sexual one, we cannot really say what he is actually like." If when the primacy of the intelligence has been achieved, one can really say what a man is actually like, what could be more natural than a science of illusions? Moreover, if the imagination is not quite the clue to reality now, might it not become so then? As for the present, what have we, if we do not have science, except the imagination? And who is to say of its deliberate fictions arising out of the contemporary mind that they are not the forerunners of some such science? There is more than the romantic in the statement that the true work of art, whatever it may be, is not the work of the individual artist. It is time and it is place, as these perfect themselves.

To regard the imagination as metaphysics is to think of it as part of life, and to think of it as part of life is to realize the extent of artifice. We live in the mind. One way of demonstrating what it means to live in the mind is to imagine a discussion of the world between two people born blind, able to describe their images, so far as they have images, without the use of images derived from other people. It would not be our world that would be discussed. Still another illustration may help. A man in Paris does not imagine the same sort of thing that a native of Uganda imagines. If each could transmit his imagination to the other, so that the man in Paris, lying awake at night, could suddenly hear a footfall that meant the presence of some inimical and merciless monstrosity, and if the man in Uganda found himself in, say, the Muenster at Basel and experienced what is to be experienced there, what words would the Parisian find to forestall his fate and what understanding would the Ugandan have of his incredible delirium? If we live in the mind, we live with the imagination. It is a commonplace to realize the extent of artifice in the external world and to say that Florence is more imaginative than Dublin, that blue and white Munich is more imaginative than white and green Havana, and so on; or to say that, in this town, no single public object of the imagination exists, while in the Vatican City, say, no public object exists that is not an object of the imagination. What is engaging us at the moment has nothing to do with the external world. We are concerned with the extent of artifice within us and, almost parenthetically, with the question of its value.

What, then, is it to live in the mind with the imagination, yet not too near to the fountains of its rhetoric, so that one does not have a consciousness only of grandeurs, of incessant departures from the idiom and of inherent altitudes? Only the reason stands between it and the reality for which the two are engaged in a struggle. We have no particular interest in this struggle because we know that it will continue to go on and that there will never be an outcome. We lose sight of it until Pascal, or someone else, reminds us of it. We say that it is merely a routine and the more we think about it the less able we are to see that it has any heroic aspects or that the spirit is at stake or that it may involve the loss of the world. Is there in fact any struggle at all and is the idea of one merely a bit of academic junk? Do not the two carry on together in the mind like two brothers or two sisters or even like young Darby and young Joan? Darby says, "It is often true that what is most rational appears to be most imaginative, as in the case of Picasso." Joan replies, "It is often true, also, that what is most imaginative appears to be most rational, as in the case of Joyce. Life is hard and dear and it is the hardness that makes it dear." And Darby says, "Speaking of Joyce and the co-existence of opposites, do you remember the story that Joyce tells of Pascal in *Portrait of the Artist as a Young Man*? Stephen said:

> —Pascal, if I remember rightly, would not suffer his mother to kiss him as he feared the contact of her sex—
> —Pascal was a pig—said Cranby.
> —Aloysius Gonzaga, I think, was of the same mind—Stephen said.
> —And he was another pig then—said Cranby.
> —The church calls him a saint—Stephen objected."

How is it that we should be speaking of the prize of the spirit and of the loss, or gain, of the world, in connection with the relations between reason and the imagination? It may be historically true that the reason of a few men has always been the reason of the world. Notwithstanding this, we live today in a time dominated by great masses of men and, while the reason of a few men may underlie what they do, they act as their imaginations impel them to act. The world may, certainly, be lost to the poet but it is not lost to the imagination. I speak of the poet because we think of him as the orator of the imagination. And I say that the world is lost to him, certainly, because, for one thing, the great poems of heaven and hell have been written and the great poem of the earth remains to be written. I suppose it is that poem that will constitute the true prize of the spirit and that until it is written many lesser things will be so regarded, including conquests that are not unimaginable. One wants to consider the imagination on its most momentous scale. Today this scale is not the scale of poetry, nor of any form of literature or art. It is the scale of international politics and in particular of communism. Communism is not the measure of humanity. But I limit myself to an allusion to it as a phenomenon of the imagination. Surely the diffusion of communism exhibits imagination on its most momentous scale. This is because whether or not communism is the measure of humanity, the words themselves echo back to us that it has for the present taken the measure of an important part of humanity. With the collapse of other beliefs, this grubby faith promises a practicable earthly paradise. The only earthly paradise that even the best of other faiths has been able to promise has been one in man's noblest image and this has always required an imagination that has not yet been included in the fortunes of mankind.

The difference between an imagination that is engaged by the materialism of communism and one that is engaged by the projects of idealism is a difference in nature. It is not that the imagination is versatile but that there are different imaginations. The commonest idea of an imaginative object is something large. But apparently with the Japanese it is the other way round and with them the commonest idea of an imaginative object is something small. With the Hindu it appears to be something vermicular, with the Chinese, something round and with the Dutch, something square. If these evidences do not establish the point, it can hardly be because the point needs establishing. A comparison between the Bible and poetry is relevant. It cannot be said that the Bible, the most widely distributed book in the world, is the poorest. Nor can it be said that it owes its distribution to the poetry it contains. If poetry should address itself to the same needs and aspirations, the same hopes and fears, to which the Bible addresses itself, it might rival it in distribution. Poetry does not address itself to beliefs. Nor could it ever invent an ancient world full of figures that had been known and become endeared to its readers for centuries. Consequently, when critics of poetry call upon it to do some of the things that the Bible does, they overlook the certainty that the Biblical imagination is one thing and the poetic imagination, inevitably, something else. We cannot look at the past or the future except by means of the imagination but again the imagination of backward glances is one thing and the imagination of looks ahead something else. Even the psychologists concede this present particular, for, with them, memory involves a reproductive power, and looks ahead involve a creative power: the power of our expectations. When we speak of the life of the imagination, we do not mean man's life as it is affected by his imagination but the life of the faculty itself. Accordingly, when we think of the permeation of man's life by the imagination, we must not think of it as a life permeated by a single thing but by a class of things. We use our imagination with respect to every man of whom we take notice when by a glance we make up our mind about him. The differences so defined entail differences of value. The imagination that is satisfied by politics, whatever the nature of the politics, has not the same value as the imagination that seeks to satisfy, say, the universal mind, which, in the case of a poet, would be the imagination that tries to penetrate to basic images, basic emotions, and so to compose a fundamental poetry even older than the ancient world. Perhaps one drifts off into rhetoric here, but then there is nothing more congenial than that to the imagination.

Of imaginative life as social form, let me distinguish at once between everyday living and the activity of cultural organization. A theater is a social form but it is also a cultural organization and it is not my purpose to discuss the imagination as an institution. Having in mind the extent to which the imagination pervades life, it seems curious that it does not pervade, or even create, social form more widely. It is an activity like seeing things or hearing things or any other sensory activity. Perhaps, if one collected instances of imaginative life as social form over a period of time, one might amass a prodigious number from among the customs of our lives. Our social attitudes, social distinctions and the insignia of social distinctions are instances. A ceremonious baptism, a ceremonious wedding, a ceremonious funeral are instances. It takes very little, however, to make a social form arising from the imagination stand out from the normal, and the fact that a form is abnormal is an argument for its suppression. Normal people do not accept something abnormal because it has its origin in an abnormal force like the imagination nor at all until they have somehow normalized it as by familiarity. Costume is an instance of imaginative life as social form. At the same time it is an instance of the acceptance of something incessantly abnormal by reducing it to the normal. It cannot be said that life as we live it from day to day wears an imaginative aspect. On the other hand, it can be said that the aspect of life as we live it from day to day conceals the imagination as social form. No one doubts that the forms of daily living secrete within themselves an infinite variety of things intelligible only to anthropologists nor that lives, like our own, lived after

an incalculable number of preceding lives and in the accu-
mulation of what they have left behind are socially compli-
cated even when they appear to be socially innocent. To me,
the accumulation of lives at a university has seemed to be a
subject that might disclose something extraordinary. What is
the residual effect of the years we spend at a university, the
years of imaginative life, if ever in our lives there are such
years, on the social form of our own future and on the social
form of the future of the world of which we are part, when
compared with the effects of our later economic and political
years?

The discussion of the imagination as metaphysics has led us
off a little to one side. This is justified, however, by the con-
siderations, first, that the operation of the imagination in life
is more significant than its operation in or in relation to works
of art or perhaps I should have said, from the beginning, in
arts and letters; second, that the imagination penetrates life;
and finally, that its value as metaphysics is not the same as its
value in arts and letters. In spite of the prevalence of the imag-
ination in life, it is probably true that the discussion of it in
that relation is incomparably less frequent and less intelligent
than the discussion of it in relation to arts and letters. The
constant discussion of imagination and reality is largely a dis-
cussion not for the purposes of life but for the purposes of
arts and letters. I suppose that the reason for this is that few
people would turn to the imagination, knowingly, in life,
while few people would turn to anything else, knowingly, in
arts and letters. In life what is important is the truth as it is,
while in arts and letters what is important is the truth as we
see it. There is a real difference here even though people turn
to the imagination without knowing it in life and to reality
without knowing it in arts and letters. There are other possible
variations of that theme but the theme itself is there. Again
in life the function of the imagination is so varied that it is
not well-defined as it is in arts and letters. In life one hesitates
when one speaks of the value of the imagination. Its value in
arts and letters is aesthetic. Most men's lives are thrust upon
them. The existence of aesthetic value in lives that are forced
on those that live them is an improbable sort of thing. There
can be lives, nevertheless, which exist by the deliberate choice

of those that live them. To use a single illustration: it may be assumed that the life of Professor Santayana is a life in which the function of the imagination has had a function similar to its function in any deliberate work of art or letters. We have only to think of this present phase of it, in which, in his old age, he dwells in the head of the world, in the company of devoted women, in their convent, and in the company of familiar saints, whose presence does so much to make any convent an appropriate refuge for a generous and human philosopher. To repeat, there can be lives in which the value of the imagination is the same as its value in arts and letters and I exclude from consideration as part of that statement any thought of poverty or wealth, being a *bauer* or being a king, and so on, as irrelevant.

The values of which it is common to think in relation to life are ethical values or moral values. The Victorians thought of these values in relation to arts and letters. It may be that the Russians mean to do about as the Victorians did, that is to say, think of the values of life in relation to arts and letters. A social value is simply an ethical value expressed by a member of the party. Between the wars, we lived, it may be said, in an era when some attempt was made to apply the value of arts and letters to life. These excursions of values beyond their spheres are part of a process which it is unnecessary to delineate. They are like the weather. We suffer from it and enjoy it and never quite know the one feeling from the other. It may, also, be altogether wrong to speak of the excursions of values beyond their spheres, since the question of the existence of spheres and the question of what is appropriate to them are not settled. Thus, something said the other day, that "An objective theory of value is needed in philosophy which does not depend upon unanalysable intuitions but relates goodness, truth and beauty to human needs in society," has a provocative sound. It is so easy for the poet to say that a learned man must go on being a learned man but that a poet respects no knowledge except his own and, again, that the poet does not yield to the priest. What the poet has in mind, when he says things of this sort, is that poetic value is an intrinsic value. It is not the value of knowledge. It is not the value of faith. It is the value of the imagination. The poet tries to exemplify it, in part, as I have tried to exemplify it here, by identifying it with an imaginative activity that diffuses itself throughout our lives. I say exemplify and not justify, because poetic value is an intuitional value and because intuitional values cannot be justified. We cannot very well speak of spheres of value and the transmission of a value, commonly considered appropriate to one sphere, to another, and allude to the peculiarity of roles, as the poet's role, without reminding ourselves that we are speaking of a thing in continual flux. There is no field in which this is more apparent than painting. Again, there is no field in which it is more constantly and more intelligently the subject of discussion than painting. The permissible reality in painting wavers with an insistence which is itself a value. One might just as well say the permissible imagination. It is as if the painter carried on with himself a continual argument as to whether what delights us in the exercise of the mind is what we produce or whether it is the exercise of a power of the mind.

A generation ago we should have said that the imagination is an aspect of the conflict between man and nature. Today we are more likely to say that it is an aspect of the conflict between man and organized society. It is part of our security. It enables us to live our own lives. We have it because we do not have enough without it. This may not be true as to each one of us, for certainly there are those for whom reality and the reason are enough. It is true of us as a race. A single, strong imagination is like a single, strong reason in this, that the extreme good of each is a spiritual good. It is not possible to say, as between the two, which is paramount. For that matter it is not always possible to say that they are two. When does a building stop being a product of the reason and become a product of the imagination? If we raise a building to an imaginative height, then the building becomes an imaginative building since height in itself is imaginative. It is the moderator of life as metempsychosis was of death. Nietzsche walked in the Alps in the caresses of reality. We ourselves crawl out of our offices and classrooms and become alert at the opera. Or we sit listening to music as in an imagination in which we believe. If the imagination is the faculty by which we import the unreal into what is real, its value is the value

of the way of thinking by which we project the idea of God
into the idea of man. It creates images that are independent
of their originals since nothing is more certain than that the
imagination is agreeable to the imagination. When one's aunt
in California writes that the geraniums are up to her second-
story window, we soon have them running over the roof. All
this diversity, which I have intentionally piled up in confusion
in this paragraph, is typical of the imagination. It may suggest
that the imagination is the ignorance of the mind. Yet the
imagination changes as the mind changes. I know an Italian
who was a shepherd in Italy as a boy. He described his day's
work. He said that at evening he was so tired he would lie
down under a tree like a dog. This image was, of course, an
image of his own dog. It was easy for him to say how tired
he was by using the image of his tired dog. But given another
mind, given the mind of a man of strong powers, accustomed
to thought, accustomed to the essays of the imagination, and
the whole imaginative substance changes. It is as if one could
say that the imagination lives as the mind lives. The primitiv-
ism disappears. The Platonic resolution of diversity appears.
The world is no longer an extraneous object, full of other
extraneous objects, but an image. In the last analysis, it is with
this image of the world that we are vitally concerned. We
should not say, however, that the chief object of the imagi-
nation is to produce such an image. Among so many objects,
it would be the merest improvisation to say of one, even
though it is one with which we are vitally concerned, that it
is the chief. The next step would be to assert that a particular
image was the chief image. Again, it would be the merest
improvisation to say of any image of the world, even though
it was an image with which a vast accumulation of imagina-
tions had been content, that it was the chief image. The imag-
ination itself would not remain content with it nor allow us
to do so. It is the irrepressible revolutionist.

In spite of the confusion of values and the diversity of as-
pects, one arrives eventually face to face with arts and letters.
I could take advantage of the pictures from the Kaiser Frie-
drich Museum in Berlin, which are being exhibited through-
out the country and which many of you, no doubt, have seen.

The pictures by Poussin are not the most marvelous pictures in this collection. Yet, considered as objects of the imagination, how completely they validate Gide's: "We must approach Poussin little by little" and how firmly they sustain the statement made a few moments ago that the imagination is the only genius. There is also among these pictures a Giorgione, the portrait of a young man, head and shoulders, in a blue-purple blouse, or if not blue-purple, then a blue of extraordinary enhancings. Vasari said of Giorgione that he painted nothing that he had not seen in nature. This portrait is an instance of a real object that is at the same time an imaginative object. It has about it an imaginative bigness of diction. We know that in poetry bigness and gaiety are precious characteristics of the diction. This portrait transfers that principle to painting. The subject is severe but its embellishment, though no less severe, is big and gay and one feels in the presence of this work that one is also in the presence of an abundant and joyous spirit, instantly perceptible in what may be called the diction of the portrait. I could also take advantage, so far as letters are concerned, of a few first books of poems or a few first novels. One turns to first works of the imagination with the same expectation with which one turns to last works of the reason. But I am afraid that although one is, at last, face to face with arts and letters and, therefore, in the presence of particulars beyond particularization, it is prudent to limit discussion to a single point.

My final point, then, is that the imagination is the power that enables us to perceive the normal in the abnormal, the opposite of chaos in chaos. It does this every day in arts and letters. This may seem to be a merely capricious statement; for ordinarily we regard the imagination as abnormal per se. That point of view was approached in the reference to the academic struggle between reason and the imagination and again in the reference to the relation between the imagination and social form. The disposition toward a point of view derogatory to the imagination is an aversion to the abnormal. We see it in the common attitude toward modern arts and letters. The exploits of Rimbaud in poetry, if Rimbaud can any longer be called modern, and of Kafka in prose are deliberate exploits of the abnormal. It is natural for us to identify the imagination with those that extend its abnormality. It is like identifying liberty with those that abuse it. A literature overfull of abnormality and, certainly, present-day European literature, as one knows it, seems to be a literature full of abnormality, gives the reason an appearance of normality to which it is not, solely, entitled. The truth seems to be that we live in concepts of the imagination before the reason has established them. If this is true, then reason is simply the methodizer of the imagination. It may be that the imagination is a miracle of logic and that its exquisite divinations are calculations beyond analysis, as the conclusions of the reason are calculations wholly within analysis. If so, one understands perfectly the remark that "in the service of love and imagination nothing can be too lavish, too sublime or too festive." In the statement that we live in concepts of the imagination before the reason has established them, the word "concepts" means concepts of normality. Further, the statement that the imagination is the power that enables us to perceive the normal in the abnormal is a form of repetition of this statement. One statement does not demonstrate the other. The two statements together imply that the instantaneous disclosures of living are disclosures of the normal. This will seem absurd to those that insist on the solitude and misery and terror of the world. They will ask of what value is the imagination to them; and if their experience is to be considered, how is it possible to deny that they live in an imagination of evil? Is evil normal or abnormal? And how do the exquisite divinations of the poets and for that matter even the "aureoles of the saints" help them? But when we speak of perceiving the normal we have in mind the instinctive integrations which are the reason for living. Of what value is anything to the solitary and those that live in misery and terror, except the imagination?

Jean Paulhan, a Frenchman and a writer, is a man of great sense. He is a native of the region of Tarbes. Tarbes is a town in southwestern France in the High Pyrenees. Marshal Foch was born there. An equestrian statue of the Marshal stands there, high in the air, on a pedestal. In his *Les Fleurs de Tarbes*, Jean Paulhan says:

One sees at the entrance of the public garden of Tarbes, this sign:

It is forbidden
To enter into the garden
Carrying flowers.

He goes on to say:

One finds it, also, in our time at the portal of literature. Nevertheless, it would be agreeable to see the girls of Tarbes (and the young writers) carrying a rose, a red poppy, an armful of red poppies.

I repeat that Jean Paulhan is a man of great sense. But to be able to see the portal of literature, that is to say: the portal of the imagination, as a scene of normal love and normal beauty is, of itself, a feat of great imagination. It is the vista a man sees, seated in the public garden of his native town, near by some effigy of a figure celebrated in the normal world, as he considers that the chief problems of any artist, as of any man, are the problems of the normal and that he needs, in order to solve them, everything that the imagination has to give.

VII

The Relations Between Poetry and Painting

I

ROGER FRY concluded a note on Claude by saying that "few of us live so strenuously as never to feel a sense of nostalgia for that Saturnian reign to which Virgil and Claude can waft us." He spoke in that same note of Corot and Whistler and Chinese landscape and certainly he might just as well have spoken, in relation to Claude, of many poets, as, for example, Chénier or Wordsworth. This is simply the analogy between two different forms of poetry. It might be better to say that it is the identity of poetry revealed as between poetry in words and poetry in paint.

Poetry, however, is not limited to Virgilian landscape, nor painting to Claude. We find the poetry of mankind in the figures of the old men of Shakespeare, say, and the old men of Rembrandt; or in the figures of Biblical women, on the one hand, and of the madonnas of all Europe, on the other; and it is easy to wonder whether the poetry of children has not been created by the poetry of the Child, until one stops to think how much of the poetry of the whole world is the poetry of children, both as they are and as they have been written of and painted, as if they were the creatures of a dimension in which life and poetry are one. The poetry of humanity is, of course, to be found everywhere.

There is a universal poetry that is reflected in everything. This remark approaches the idea of Baudelaire that there exists an unascertained and fundamental aesthetic, or order, of which poetry and painting are manifestations, but of which, for that matter, sculpture or music or any other aesthetic realization would equally be a manifestation. Generalizations as expansive as these: that there is a universal poetry that is reflected in everything or that there may be a fundamental aesthetic of which poetry and painting are related but dissimilar manifestations, are speculative. One is better satisfied by particulars.

740

No poet can have failed to recognize how often a detail, a propos or remark, in respect to painting, applies also to poetry. The truth is that there seems to exist a corpus of remarks in respect to painting, most often the remarks of painters themselves, which are as significant to poets as to painters. All of these details, to the extent that they have meaning for poets as well as for painters, are specific instances of relations between poetry and painting. I suppose, therefore, that it would be possible to study poetry by studying painting or that one could become a painter after one had become a poet, not to speak of carrying on in both métiers at once, with the economy of genius, as Blake did. Let me illustrate this point of the double value (and one might well call it the multifold value) of sayings for painters that mean as much for poets because they are, after all, sayings about art. Does not the saying of Picasso that a picture is a horde of destructions also say that a poem is a horde of destructions? When Braque says "The senses deform, the mind forms," he is speaking to poet, painter, musician and sculptor. Just as poets can be affected by the sayings of painters, so can painters be affected by the sayings of poets and so can both be affected by sayings addressed to neither. For many examples, see Miss Sitwell's *Poet's Note-Book*. These details come together so subtly and so minutely that the existence of relations is lost sight of. This, in turn, dissipates the idea of their existence.

2

We may regard the subject, then, from two points of view, the first from the point of view of the man whose center is painting, whether or not he is a painter, the second from the point of view of the man whose center is poetry, whether or not he is a poet. To make use of the point of view of the man whose center is painting let me refer to the chapter in Leo Stein's *Appreciation* entitled "On Reading Poetry and Seeing Pictures." He says that, when he was a child, he became aware of composition in nature and gradually realized that art and composition are one. He began to experiment as follows:

I put on the table . . . an earthenware plate . . . and

this I looked at every day for minutes or for hours. I had in mind to see it as a picture, and waited for it to become one. In time it did. The change came suddenly when the plate as an inventorial object . . . a certain shape, certain colors applied to it . . . went over into a composition to which all these elements were merely contributory. The painted composition on the plate ceased to be *on* it but became a part of a larger composition which was the plate as a whole. I had made a beginning to seeing pictorially.

What had been begun was carried out in all directions. I wanted to be able to see anything *as* a composition and found that it was possible to do this.

He improvised a definition of art: that it is nature seen in the light of its significance, and recognizing that this significance was one of forms he added "formal" to "significance."

Turning to education in hearing, he observed that there is nothing comparable to the practice in composition that the visible world offers. By composition he meant the compositional use of words: the use of their existential meanings. Composition was his passion. He considered that a formally complete picture is one in which all the parts are so related to one another that they all imply each other. Finally he said, "an excellent illustration is the line from Wordsworth's Michael . . . 'And never lifted up a single stone.' " One might say of a lazy workman, "He's been out there, just loafing, for an hour and never lifted up a single stone," and no one would think this great poetry. . . . These lines would have no existential value; they would simply call attention to the lazy workman. But the compositional use by Wordsworth of his line makes it something entirely different. These simple words become weighted with the tragedy of the old shepherd, and are saturated with poetry. Their referential importance is slight, for the importance of the action to which they refer is not in the action itself, but in the meaning; and that meaning is borne by the words. Therefore this is a line of great poetry.

The selection of composition as a common denominator of poetry and painting is the selection of a technical characteristic by a man whose center was painting, even granting that he was not a man whom one thinks of as a technician. Poetry and painting alike create through composition.

Now, a poet looking for an analogy between poetry and painting and trying to take the point of view of a man whose center is poetry begins with a sense that the technical pervades painting to such a degree that the two are identified. This is untrue, since, if painting was purely technical, that conception of it would exclude the artist as a person. I want to say something, therefore, based on the sensibility of the poet and of the painter. I am not quite sure that I know what is meant by sensibility. I suppose that it means feeling or, as we say, the feelings. I know what is meant by nervous sensibility, as, when at a concert, the auditors, having composed themselves and resting there attentively, hear suddenly an outburst on the trumpets from which they shrink by way of a nervous reaction. The satisfaction that we have when we look out and find that it is a fine day or when we are looking at one of the limpid vistas of Corot in the pays de Corot seems to be something else. It is commonly said that the origins of poetry are to be found in the sensibility. We began with the conjunction of Claude and Virgil, noting how one evoked the other. Such evocations are attributable to similarities of sensibility. If, in Claude, we find ourselves in the realm of Saturn, the ruler of the world in a golden age of innocence and plenty, and if, in Virgil, we find ourselves in the same realm, we recognize that there is, as between Claude and Virgil, an identity of sensibility. Yet if one questions the dogma that the origins of poetry are to be found in the sensibility and if one says that a fortunate poem or a fortunate painting is a synthesis of exceptional concentration (that degree of concentration that has a lucidity of its own, in which we see clearly what we want to do and do it instantly and perfectly), we find that the operative force within us does not, in fact, seem to be the sensibility, that is to say, the feelings. It seems to be a constructive faculty, that derives its energy more from the imagination than from the sensibility. I have spoken of questioning, not of denying. The mind retains experience, so that long after the experience, long after the winter clearness of a January morning, long after the limpid vistas of Corot, that faculty within us of which I have spoken makes its own constructions out of that experience. If it merely reconstructed the experience or repeated for us our sensations in the face of it, it would be the memory. What it really does is to use it as material with which it does whatever it wills. This is the typical function of the imagination which always makes use of the familiar to produce the unfamiliar. What these remarks seem to involve is the substitution for the idea of inspiration of the idea of an effort of the mind not dependent on the vicissitudes of the sensibility. It is so completely possible to sit at one's table and without the help of the agitation of the feelings to write plays of incomparable enhancement that that is precisely what Shakespeare did. He was not dependent on the fortuities of inspiration. It is not the least part of his glory that one can say of him, the greater the thinker the greater the poet. It would come nearer the mark to say the greater the mind the greater the poet, because the evil of thinking as poetry is not the same thing as the good of thinking in poetry. The point is that the poet does his job by virtue of an effort of the mind. In doing so, he is in rapport with the painter, who does his job, with respect to the problems of form and color, which confront him incessantly, not by inspiration, but by imagination or by the miraculous kind of reason that the imagination sometimes promotes. In short, these two arts, poetry and painting, have in common a laborious element, which, when it is exercised, is not only a labor but a consummation as well. For proof of this let me set side by side the poetry in the prose of Proust, taken from his vast novel, and the painting, by chance, of Jacques Villon. As to Proust, I quote a paragraph from Professor Saurat:

> Another province he has added to literature is the description of those eternal moments in which we are lifted out of the drab world. . . . The madeleine dipped in tea, the steeples of Martinville, some trees on a road, a perfume of wild flowers, a vision of light and shade on trees, a spoon clinking on a plate that is like a railway man's hammer on the wheels of the train from which the trees were seen, a stiff napkin in an hotel, an inequality in two stones in Venice and the disjointment in the yard of the Guermantes' town house. . . .

As to Villon: shortly before I began to write these notes I dropped into the Carré Gallery in New York to see an exhibition of paintings which included about a dozen works by him. I was immediately conscious of the presence of the enchantments of intelligence in all his prismatic material. A woman lying in a hammock was transformed into a complex of planes and tones, radiant, vaporous, exact. A tea-pot and a cup or two took their place in a reality composed wholly of things unreal. These works were *deliciae* of the spirit as distinguished from *delectationes* of the senses and this was so because one found in them the labor of calculation, the appetite for perfection.

3

One of the characteristics of modern art is that it is uncompromising. In this it resembles modern politics, and perhaps it would appear on study, including a study of the rights of man and of women's hats and dresses, that everything modern, or possibly merely new, is, in the nature of things, uncompromising. It is especially uncompromising in respect to precinct. One of the De Goncourts said that nothing in the world hears as many silly things said as a picture in a museum; and in thinking about that remark one has to bear in mind that in the days of the De Goncourts there was no such thing as a museum of modern art. A really modern definition of modern art, instead of making concessions, fixes limits which grow smaller and smaller as time passes and more often than not come to include one man alone, just as if there should be scrawled across the façade of the building in which we now are, the words *Cézanne delineavit*. Another characteristic of modern art is that it is plausible. It has a reason for everything. Even the lack of a reason becomes a reason. Picasso expresses surprise that people should ask what a picture means and says that pictures are not intended to have meanings. This explains everything. Still another characteristic of modern art is that it is bigoted. Every painter who can be defined as a modern painter becomes, by virtue of that definition, a freeman of the world of art and hence the equal of any other modern painter. We recognize that they differ one from another but in any event they are not to be judged except by other modern painters.

We have this inability (not mere unwillingness) to compromise, this same plausibility and bigotry in modern poetry. To exhibit this, let me divide modern poetry into two classes, one that is modern in respect to what it says, the other that is modern in respect to form. The first kind is not interested primarily in form. The second is. The first kind is interested in form but it accepts a banality of form as incidental to its language. Its justification is that in expressing thought or feeling in poetry the purpose of the poet must be to subordinate the mode of expression, that, while the value of the poem as a poem depends on expression, it depends primarily on what is expressed. Whether the poet is modern or ancient, living or dead, is, in the last analysis, a question of what he is talking about, whether of things modern or ancient, living or dead. The counterpart of Villon in poetry, writing as he paints, would concern himself with like things (but not necessarily confining himself to them), creating the same sense of aesthetic certainty, the same sense of exquisite realization and the same sense of being modern and living. One sees a good deal of poetry, thanks, perhaps, to Mallarmé's *Un Coup de Dés*, in which the exploitation of form involves nothing more than the use of small letters for capitals, eccentric line-endings, too little or too much punctuation and similar aberrations. These have nothing to do with being alive. They have nothing to do with the conflict between the poet and that of which his poems are made. They are neither "bonne soupe" nor "beau langage."

What I have said of both classes of modern poetry is inadequate as to both. As to the first, which permits a banality of form, it is even harmful, as suggesting that it possesses less of the artifice of the poet than the second. Each of these two classes is intransigent as to the other. If one is disposed to think well of the class that stands on what it has to say, one has only to think of Gide's remark, "Without the unequaled beauty of his prose, who would continue to interest himself in Bossuet?" The division between the two classes, the division, say, between Valéry and Apollinaire, is the same division into factions that we find everywhere in modern painting. But aesthetic creeds, like other creeds, are the certain evidences of exertions to find the truth. I have tried to say no more than was necessary to evince the relations, in which we are interested, as they exist in the manifestations of today. What, when all is said and done, is the significance of the existence of such relations? Or is it enough to note them? The question is not the same as the question of the significance of art. We do not have to be told of the significance of art. "It is art," said Henry James, "which makes life, makes interest, makes importance . . . and I know of no substitute whatever for the force and beauty of its process." The world about us would be desolate except for the world within us. There is the same interchange between these two worlds that there is between one art and another, migratory passings to and fro, quickenings, Promethean liberations and discoveries.

Yet it may be that just as the senses are no respecters of reality, so the faculties are no respecters of the arts. On the other hand, it may be that we are dealing with something that has no significance, something that is the result of imitation. Quatremère de Quincy distinguished between the poet and the painter as between two imitators, one moral, the other physical. There are imitations within imitations and the relations between poetry and painting may present nothing more. This idea makes it possible, at least, to see more than one side of the subject.

4

All of the relations of which I have spoken are themselves related in the deduction that the vis poetica, the power of poetry, leaves its mark on whatever it touches. The mark of poetry creates the resemblance of poetry as between the most disparate things and unites them all in its recognizable virtue. There is one relation between poetry and painting which does not participate in the common mark of common origin. It is the paramount relation that exists between poetry and people in general and between painting and people in general. I have not overlooked the possibility that, when this evening's subject was suggested, it was intended that the discussion should be limited to the relations between modern poetry and modern painting. This would have involved much tinkling of familiar cymbals. In so far as it would have called for a comparison of this poet and that painter, this school and that school, it would have been fragmentary and beyond my competence. It seems to me that the subject of modern relations is best to be approached as a whole. The paramount relation between poetry and painting today, between modern man and modern art is simply this: that in an age in which disbelief is so profoundly prevalent or, if not disbelief, indifference to questions of belief, poetry and painting, and the arts in general, are, in their measure, a compensation for what has been lost. Men feel that the imagination is the next greatest power to faith: the reigning prince. Consequently their interest in the imagination and its work is to be regarded not as a phase of humanism but as a vital self-assertion in a world in which nothing but the self remains, if that remains. So regarded, the study of the imagination and the study of reality come to appear to be purified, aggrandized, fateful. How much stature, even vatic stature, this conception gives the poet! He need not exercise this dignity in vatic works. How much authenticity, even orphic authenticity, it gives to the painter! He need not display this authenticity in orphic works. It should be enough for him that that to which he has given his life should be so enriched by such an access of value. Poet and painter alike live and work in the midst of a generation that is experiencing essential poverty in spite of fortune. The extension of the mind beyond the range of the mind, the projection of reality beyond reality, the determination to cover the ground, whatever it may be, the determination not to be confined, the recapture of excitement and intensity of interest, the enlargement of the spirit at every time, in every way, these are the unities, the relations, to be summarized as paramount now. It is not material whether these relations exist consciously or unconsciously. One goes back to the coercing influences of time and place. It is possible to be subjected to a lofty purpose and not to know it. But I think that most men of any degree of sophistication, most poets, most painters know it.

When we look back at the period of French classicism in the seventeenth century, we have no difficulty in seeing it as a whole. It is not so easy to see one's own time that way.

Pretty much all of the seventeenth century, in France, at least, can be summed up in that one word: classicism. The paintings of Poussin, Claude's contemporary, are the inevitable paintings of the generation of Racine. If it had been a time when dramatists used the detailed scene directions that we expect today, the directions of Racine would have left one wondering whether one was reading the description of a scene or the description of one of Poussin's works. The practice confined them to the briefest generalization. Thus, after the list of persons in *King Lear*, Shakespeare added only two words: "Scene: Britain." Yet even so, the directions of Racine, for all their brevity, suggest Poussin. That a common quality is to be detected in such simple things exhibits the extent of the interpenetration persuasively. The direction for *Britannicus* is "The scene is at Rome, in a chamber of the palace of Nero"; for *Iphigénie en Aulide*, "The scene is at Aulis, before the tent of Agamemnon"; for *Phèdre*, "The scene is at Trézène, a town of the Peloponnesus"; for *Esther*, "The scene is at Susa, in the palais of Assuérus"; and for *Athalie*, "The scene is in the temple of Jerusalem, in a vestibule of the apartment of the grand priest."

Our own time, and by this I mean the last two or three generations, including our own, can be summed up in a way that brings into unity an immense number of details by saying of it that it is a time in which the search for the supreme truth has been a search in reality or through reality or even a search for some supremely acceptable fiction. Juan Gris began some notes on his painting by saying: "The world from which I extract the elements of reality is not visual but imaginative." The history of this attitude in literature and particularly in poetry, in France, has been traced by Marcel Raymond in his *From Baudelaire to Surrealism*. I say particularly in poetry because there are associated with it the names of Baudelaire, Rimbaud, Mallarmé and Valéry. In painting, its history is the history of modern painting. Moreover, I say in France because, in France, the theory of poetry is not abstract as it so often is with us, when we have any theory at all, but is a normal activity of the poet's mind in surroundings where he must engage in such activity or be extirpated. Thus necessity develops an awareness and a sense of fatality which give to poetry values not to be reproduced by indifference and chance. To the man who is seeking the sanction of life in poetry, the namby-pamby is an intolerable dissipation. The theory of poetry, that is to say, the total of the theories of poetry, often seems to become in time a mystical theology or, more simply, a mystique. The reason for this must by now be clear. The reason is the same reason why the pictures in a museum of modern art often seem to become in time a mystical aesthetic, a prodigious search of appearance, as if to find a way of saying and of establishing that all things, whether below or above appearance, are one and that it is only through reality, in which they are reflected or, it may be, joined together, that we can reach them. Under such stress, reality changes from substance to subtlety, a subtlety in which it was natural for Cézanne to say: "I see planes bestriding each other and sometimes straight lines seem to me to fall" or "Planes in color. . . . The colored area where shimmer the souls of the planes, in the blaze of the kindled prism, the meeting of planes in the sunlight." The conversion of our *Lumpenwelt* went far beyond this. It was from the point of view of another subtlety that Klee could write: "But he is one chosen that today comes near to the secret places where original law fosters all evolution. And what artist would not establish himself there where the organic center of all movement in time and space—which he calls the mind or heart of creation—determines every function." Conceding that this sounds a bit like sacerdotal jargon, that is not too much to allow to those that have helped to create a new reality, a modern reality, since what has been created is nothing less.

This reality is, also, the momentous world of poetry. Its instantaneities are the familiar intelligence of poets, although it has been the intelligence of another ambiance. Simone Weil in *La Pesanteur et La Grâce* has a chapter on what she calls decreation. She says that decreation is making pass from the created to the uncreated, but that destruction is making pass from the created to nothingness. Modern reality is a reality of decreation, in which our revelations are not the revelations of belief, but the precious portents of our own powers. The greatest truth we could hope to discover, in whatever field we discovered it, is that man's truth is the final resolution of everything. Poets and painters alike today make that assumption and this is what gives them the validity and serious dignity that become them as among those that seek wisdom, seek understanding. I am elevating this a little, because I am trying to generalize and because it is incredible that one should speak of the aspirations of the last two or three generations without a degree of elevation. Sometimes it seems the other way. Sometimes we hear it said that in the eighteenth century there were no poets and that the painters—Chardin, Fragonard, Watteau—were élégants and nothing more; that in the nineteenth century the last great poet was the man that looked most like one and that the whole Pierian sodality had better have been fed to the dogs. It occasionally seems like that today. It must seem as it may. In the logic of events, the only wrong would be to attempt to falsify the logic, to be disloyal to the truth. It would be tragic not to realize the extent of man's dependence on the arts. The kind of world that might result from too exclusive a dependence on them has been questioned, as if the discipline of the arts was in no sense a moral discipline. We have not to discuss that here. It is enough to have brought poetry and painting into relation as sources of our present conception of reality, without asserting that they are the sole sources, and as supports of a kind of life, which it seems to be worth living, with their support, even if doing so is only a stage in the endless study of an existence, which is the heroic subject of all study.

UNCOLLECTED PROSE

The Thessalians

The old age of the land of Japhet came down from the night frosted Olympus and finds her piteous and solitary. When from the exhausted east the morn-day light spreads her luminous mists and the ancient sun frost bathed in the Hydaspian flood sends his gray to the west, when the unpruned wood, black and dripping from slumbrous cold, hears the first slight piping of the lark, that land alone doth cry: Alas! unhappy day!

For her, indeed, the time is out of joint; for her, indeed, the hour is full of fear. O year of shame, O shoal of honor! She sees her chambers desolate, her portals foul. She sees a weakling king of unskilled hand, she sees without her gates the ranks of foreign powers, but still she stands a David 'gainst a score of Goliaths. The speaker referred to the heroes, the gods and the scholars in well turned sentences, and continuing, said: "O admirable diplomacy that deprives men of their rights! O excellent peoples that admit of this! O mighty lords that outface a weakened state! I fear the earth has been undone, when Christians espouse a selfish cause, when men of war turn argosies of trade and soldiers, traffickers. If that is not apostacy, if that is not dishonor, I would as leave call thieving, giving, and despotism, charity.

"As a rock withstands a bruising flood, so Greece withstands the schemes of conspirators. This state it took a thousand years to build, and now an hour degrades it to the dust.

"The hills on land are rifted shaggy as before, the vales at sea are everlasting. It is only men that change. Have they, then, from their very age, lost all their sinews, and fallen far asunder?

"Let not the straightened foreheads of fools, like as the king and prince of Greece, conduct the strife, but may the earth give up her sons, men high and ranking, full of state; let these turn counsellors to her. Though Greece should fall, though she should mourn and die, let every fleet that sweeps the central blue, let every ship that sails the utmost sphere of seas, let every arm, let every breast, let every man defend the cross forever."

The Reading Eagle, June 24, 1897

A Day in February

The warm afternoon beat against his windows courageously, and his face was hidden in a book whose leaves were following one another to the end. He was unconsciously enjoying the sun upon his back, though he probably imputed his good humor to the philosophy he was reading, and was quite unaware that, after all, any philosophy was a sin on such a day. When he first came to college, he had been tall and fresh, but, as he piled up theme upon theme and thesis upon thesis, a slight bend became noticeable in his shoulders, and he felt empty and unambitious; for the few steps that carried him every day to two or three recitations were not to be compared with the walks he had taken at home, alone on the roads, free and high spirited.

But somehow his former buoyancy would occasionally assert itself, like a clear spot in the confusion of his studies, and then he would wonder at the change that had taken place— the change from his old life of poetic impulse to this new existence of libraries and lectures. And when the philosophy had run out, and the book had been put on his shelves, he thrust his hands into his pockets and walked to the window. The afternoon was still full and diaphanous, and he stood there longer, perhaps, than he had intended; for he knew that whatever time he gave to the mere gazing at things was lost to Science and his own Wisdom.

It was unaccountable, but suddenly he threw the window open. A deep stream of sweet air poured into his room, suffusing him with a pleasure in it and a delight which was downright treachery to his courses. He was thinking to himself that this was one of those first warm days, premonitions of Spring, which stray into the calendar now and then despite the weather bureau; and with that thought came others of a certain hill in Pennsylvania, of a certain grove of maples, and of a certain house which he knew as home on vacations and in summer time. He also thought that now would be a good time to rest an hour and be himself again. But the wind that was so sweet to him was gone. It had blown into the dry corners, rustled the curtains, passed over his pictures, and turned over the things on his table—the things which had frightened and driven it away, things covered with economic calculations and mathematical designs. That made him remember that it was still winter.

But winter or no winter, he found that his work was disagreeable and he lost faith in it. What did he care to know of the religion of the mound builders, or of the antiquity of a legend which was not worth the telling? Of what interest to him was it to know the technical kind of reasoning that had induced Caesar to adorn Rome with theatres, when he felt the throbbing in his blood of new life, new love? His industry seemed worthless so far as he himself was concerned; it seemed like the building of a house of cards when what he desired were castles in Spain. It is not to be wondered at, therefore, that this tall, eager form that had been buried in philosophy a moment ago, suddenly buttoned up its coat, threw on a cap, and started out of doors.

On the street all the old fervor came back into his blood, his face, his gait. He swung along under the trees, feeling as though he had accomplished some meritorious deed, like a knight in street clothes. He saw fellows with whom he had been accustomed to review History and compose English, and he nodded in a high, exuberant way. When he found the houses getting thin, he turned back again, his eyes bright, his cheeks burning. The work he had left seemed shallow, and he resolved that after this he would be less Faust than Pan. Then, when he was in his room again, he pitched a stack of writing into a waste basket and, bowing to an imaginary person, he said: "Ah, old man, old fellow, you don't know, you haven't any idea how glad I am to meet you again."

The Harvard Advocate, March 6, 1899

Editorials on the Fence Question

Putting a fence around the Yard strikes us as being the easiest way of achieving order out of chaos. One reason we have spread out through Cambridge in such a loose fashion is that we have had no point of concentration, the Yard, as it now stands, extending wherever you choose to have it extend. For instance, it is still a question whether the unknown land back of Sever is part of our geography. But a fence would settle all this; it would bring about a definite spot and turn it into a point around which new buildings could cluster. In addition to this, a fence would unquestionably bring back to the Yard some of the prestige which it has lost. To be within the walls would soon come to be an envious position; and thus the yard would regain the hold on our imaginations which it is gradually losing. For these reasons, we think that a fence would be about the best thing that could be built by those whose aim it is to improve our present conditions.

March 24, 1900

We come back to the question of the fence because it is one of much importance. Only recently it has been proposed to have a sort of combination structure, half solid wall, half open iron work. It would seem as though the hodge-podge that already afflicts us were not enough, and that, instead of attempting to give the yard an exterior if not an interior uniformity, we were to continue patching to the end. The object of the solid walls would be to hide the rear of such buildings as Holworthy Hall and the Boylston Laboratory. Now, if the backs of these buildings are unsightly,—and certainly they are not all that they might be,—it seems to us that the best way to give them some sort of decency would not be to put a wall up in front of them, since the wall would merely hide the defect, and not get rid of it. The easiest way of getting around the difficulty would be to use the iron fence because it could be so constructed as to catch the eye pleasantly rather than stop it abruptly; besides, the spaces between the fence and the walls could be planted with shrubbery and small trees. It may be urged that the wall would give room for memorials; but certainly bronze tablets fitted into the iron openings would be as satisfactory as marble ones fitted into the bricks. Let us

by all means have all wall or all fence—preferably the latter.
No more architectural potpourri.

April 13, 1900

———

As between the Memorial Society and the architect in re-
gard to the "Proposed Enclosure of the Yard" we side with
the architect: "we regard the fence simply as an enclosure."
The Memorial Society considers "open iron panel work, ex-
tending through the entire height of the fence" as homely.
We should have said simple and dignified. They think the iron
palings appearing "in long stretches would be irresistibly op-
pressive." Why would they be more oppressive than "a low
wall, say three and a half feet high"; that would stretch as far
as the eye could reach? Why would they be more oppressive
than memorial tablets of all grades of elaborateness set in the
wall at haphazard? We agree that "we should have simply a
useful enclosure"; but we fail to see how we are to have it if
the Memorial Society makes its point. The iron work fence
seems to us to be the only one so far suggested that is both
"appropriate and pleasing." It must be remembered that its
"more or less massive pillars of masonry" would soon be over-
grown with ivy and that their massiveness would then be a
delight to the eye. The great danger of any fence is that it will
modernize the Yard; but the iron enclosure seems to us to be
the least likely to effect this evil. Neither will it mar the vistas
of the Yard; nor fail to be "beautiful and interesting." We are,
then, in favor of a fence that shall be simply an enclosure both
dignified and consistent; and we believe that the iron panel
fence nearest approaches this ideal. We are glad that the Cor-
poration has accepted Mr. McKim's design.

To return to the subject of the memorial tablets we must
say that we are against having them put in the fence at all.
For some time past all the important buildings that have been
erected have been memorials—until it has become the fashion
to memorialize. The Yard which was once a purely college

affair has become lugubrious with its architectural "pomp of woe." Every other thing one sees is in memory of somebody. Of course this may seem a rather heartless point of view on our part, but certainly there should be other incentives to generosity than death; just as there should be buildings which one could look at and live in without a pang. Let us keep the fence free, then, from the memorial tablets. It would be absurd to have a line of mournful "bas-reliefs, inscriptions and coats of arms" extending around the yard. If the various sections were contributed by classes the years of the classes in Roman numerals at the bases of the sections would be perfectly justifiable; or, if private donors assisted, the object of their gifts might be briefly stated—but we should deplore any "elaborateness." The fence must be utilitarian, not gorgeously commemorative; it must be attractive not depressing.

After all the importance of the fence cannot be overestimated. We have referred to the subject several times before, and we pointed out the sense of seclusion that the fence would bring to those who dwelt in the Yard. The *Monthly* in an extremely well-considered editorial in its last number casually brings up this side of the question a second time. But it does not seem to recognize the connection between the quality of seclusion and the character of the fence. The least degree of difference will change seclusion to confinement if not imprisonment; and, if the fence is of the importance claimed for it, then this delicate matter in connection with it is worth discussing. Figures II and III in the *Monthly* supplement show enclosures with too much wall. While these walls lend strength to the enclosure one must not forget that it is not intended to be a defence or a bastion. Besides these walls have a disagreeable heaviness and weighty look. They would make the Yard seem impregnable. They are harsh and uninviting. The seclusion the fence is meant to secure is not a seclusion of aloofness but of distinct whereabouts, of separateness.

Four Characters

I.

"As a horseman I never hed a match. My ol' horse, Gold Dust—eh? You remember her? Well, she *was* a horse. Never had a match either—because I knew jes' how to treat her. Why, sir, I've been about horses ever since I was born. I remember jes' as well as not, as though 't was only the other day, how my ol' Gold Dust slipped once. Up she went an' down she came an' I lay in the gutter. Oh, Golly! I jumps up an' finds the blood pourin' out my forehead into my eyes, an' then I staggers to a tree an' sinks down on the curbstone. Oh, Golly! I set there and watched the men tryin' to get ol' Gold Dust to her feet. One of 'em gives her a kick; another says, 'Oh,' he says, 'Get up, you damn horse.' But ol' Gold Dust lies there on her side, her breath scattering the dust about her nostrils. By 'n by I jumps up an' gets on my knees in front of her and lifts her head in my hands an' says, 'Ol' Gold Dust, don't you know me?' Oh, Golly, I plead with that horse. 'Don't you know me, ol' Gold Dust?' I says. I patted him, oh, jes' like a little lamb. 'Don't you know me?' I kept askin' an' askin'. An my tongue was like the Ba'm of Gilead. You know in the winter when I can't do nothin' else I sell powder for polishin' medals, tin cups an' the like. Why, I can get a tin cup so bright—I did once. I went to Andy Wiggses' an' called his wife out on the porch. I asked her if she had an ol' black tin cup. Oh, Mighty, how she looked! Then she laughed an' hunted one for me in a closet. Well, I polished an' polished an' held the cup up to her an' finally the sun struck it an' it shone like silver. But Wiggses is Wiggses an' I had my trouble for my reward. My tongue's like the Ba'm of Gilead, but, Mighty! you can't sell anything to Wiggses. What! ol' Gold Dust? oh, he's been dead ten years now, I s'pose. He died right there in the street that day. He never got up. Why once——"

II.

I was sitting on a fence at the edge of a clover field. There was not a single cloud in the sky and the whole atmosphere was very clear, bringing all the hilly perspectives into splendid prominence. The horizon was blue, rimmed, in the east, with a light pink mistiness; in the west, with a warm yellowish red that gradually died into thin whiteness. No star appeared until eight o'clock, and even then I could hardly make out the one I had probably been mistaking for Jupiter. Close at hand on a tall spray of blackberry bushes a robin was swinging in the wind, his throat pouring forth a song of ravishing beauty. While I was listening a middle-sized farmer came along and stopped at my side. His clothes were covered with splotches of clay from the field he had been ploughing. He was about to speak to me when suddenly he heard the robin who was quite lost in the ecstasy of his song. The farmer looked about until his eye caught sight of the bird. He stared at it wonderingly.

"Just listen to thet robin a'hollerin' over there," he said.

III.

One night I met a friend of mine who was a reporter for a newspaper. He was looking up a death. I went with him. We climbed up the filthy stairs of a tenement house and knocked at the door of a room on the third floor. A woman of about seventy or seventy-five years of age answered the knock. She stood back and closed the door after us as we entered.

"I am a reporter for the *Times*," said my friend. "I believe a man named Bigsby died here to-night. Can you give me any information?"

The old woman nodded, and with short little steps walked to the stove, which stood against a wall of the room. She pushed a kettle of boiling, steaming water to the back part of the stove, then returned to the table where we were standing, bent down and looked up under the shade of a feeble lamp, shaking it to get more light.

"Yes, he died here to-night. That's him."

She picked up the lamp and walked across the room to a dark corner. Two chairs had been connected with an ironing board, and on this board lay the body of an old man covered with a bed-cloth.

"That's my husband," continued the woman, pulling the

cloth away from his face. "He's eighty years old, and that's pretty old, isn't it? We've always been here in this room. I took in washing, and Bigsby would sit around and smoke his pipe. No, I don't think he had any relatives—except myself."

She pulled the cloth back over the thin, sunken features, put the lamp on the table, and went over to the stove again.

"Won't you have some tea?" she asked. I'm just going to make some. Bigsby hated it."

We thanked her and started to go.

"I will light you to the stairs," she said. As she crossed the room the lamp lit up the hovel, and we saw a bed that had not been visible before. It was made of a tattered mattress with straw sticking out at the edges. It was perfectly bare, without pillow or sheet.

IV.

"When my father was alive the garden extended for a half square all around the house. We had countless servants,— Diksy and Tom and Helen and May. May was my governess; I believe she is companion to Mrs. Arnold Arms now. You may have noticed when you came in that the doorway and vestibule are copies of the doorway and vestibule of the Temple of the Winds,—a weakness of my father's. Poor dad! He had this very room"—it was a room in the attic: the woodwork was painted brown; the wallpaper was a faded green, stained with gray where the rain had leaked through the half-ruined roof—"he had this very room painted in imitation of the Ducal Palace in Venice. I have never been to Venice; father died the summer I meant to go. But some of my friends say the imitation is quite remarkable, although I don't care much. And the garden!—the garden! How we used to dance there in the summer evenings!—with the trees bright with little lanterns, and the rosebushes tied up with ribbons, and the sweetest orchestra of guitars and mandolins hidden somewhere in the foliage. And all our friends! But I had to sell first this, then that, until now there is nothing left. You should have seen the halls and the parlor!—no boarders then. The room below this used to be one of the guest-chambers. Mrs. Arnold Arms lived there a whole winter. What would she say if she could see grimy little Smith with his boxes and books piled up where she sat and passed her mornings! We were very happy then. I used to bring May into the room, and she would read to us together. And downstairs there was a dining-room, with a high white ceiling and a golden chandelier. Well, you will see it if you decide to come. You will see your fellow-boarders, too. There will be a seamstress and an artist, and Smith, and an electrician. But you will see, you will see!"

The Harvard Advocate, June 16, 1900

Cattle Kings of Florida

Saddle bags filled with gold left lying on the front porch or even in the stable!

Coffee cans or kitchen pots filled to the brim with the yellow Spanish coins and left unguarded on kitchen shelves of isolated ranch homes!

Such tales told by the few surviving pioneer cattle kings of Florida contrast strangely with present day customs. A single gold coin is more or less of a curiosity today while anyone in Atlanta, or Florida either, with a sizable bag of gold would watch it with a shot gun until they could procure an armored car to move it to the deposit vaults of some bank.

And yet the Florida tales are true, as any old time cow hunter who trailed the herds down to Punta Rassa in the '70s and '80s will testify. The little port a few miles from Fort Myers, on the Gulf of Mexico, is only a cable station with a few fishing racks now, but in the early days it saw thousands of Florida's free range cattle rafted out to Spanish ships bound for Havana and in turn saw thousands of Spain's golden coins turned over to the cattle barons who lived on scattered and unfenced ranches in the interior.

Fort Myers itself wasn't much of a town then and didn't offer many facilities for recreation. Some of the early cattle-men, the Tolles and the Hendrys and a few others made their homes there, but most of them poured the gold into their saddle bags and after a few drinks around mounted their shaggy and tired looking ponies and rode northward toward Polk or DeSoto Counties.

Although their mounts had several times the speed and spirit their appearances indicated, it usually took several days to cover the trail back home. Camp was made by the cattlemen wherever nightfall found them and the tired riders would dump their saddle bags wherever it was handiest. If a friend dropped in after camp was made and wanted to borrow money, or if the cattle owner owed him money, the visitor was frequently told to find the saddle bags and count out what he needed or what was due him.

Honesty wasn't questioned in money matters on the range. From all reports, the cattle kings would and did steal cows from each other. But stealing money was taboo among the home folks and tourists and other visiting gentry were still practically unknown in Florida below Jacksonville and St. Augustine.

One of the famous cattle kings of this period was Jacob Summerlin, a cowboy philanthropist of the early days whose generosity made him rather a patron saint of the south Florida range, and who left eternal monuments to his credit in Bartow and Orlando.

There are many still living who knew Summerlin personally and he has several descendants still residing in Polk County. Innumerable stories are told of his saddle pockets filled with gold and how any tale of distress or want, particularly on the part of widow or orphan, always found him digging out a handful of coins for the unfortunate one.

Despite his wealth he was said to have always dressed only in the cotton trousers and shirt, leather boots and five-gallon hat of the range. Thus, without any outward manifestation of having any money it was said to be a favorite trick of his to ride into some settler's yard where he was not known and beg a meal for himself and his horse. If the family was hospitable, as practically all pioneer families were, he would keep up his disguise until leaving; then he would give each child a Spanish ten-dollar gold piece; and if he had learned during his visit that the family lacked any particular necessity which money could buy, that would be forthcoming, too.

Summerlin was said to have been an orphan boy and to

have had practically no schooling. That he deeply missed his lack of an opportunity for a higher education was shown when he purchased a large tract of land near the heart of Bartow, county seat of Polk County, and deeded it to trustees to sell in city lots and "form a free school for the poor white children." Schools up to that time in south Florida had been largely operated under the fee system, with few but the children of the well-to-do able to attend. Summerlin's donation financed the erection of the first brick school building in the southern portion of the state and initiated the free school system through the entire region, for, although his first intention was only a school for the poor children who could not attend the fee schools, his idea was enlarged upon by the trustees and a public school opened. The main public school in Bartow today is still known as Summerlin Institute, although, of course, it is now supported entirely by tax money.

Summerlin also donated ten-acre tracts of land within the town to each of the then established churches of Bartow and gave the town of Orlando the land surrounding many of the beautiful little lakes, forming the basis of Orlando's present park system around its lake shores—one of its chief claims to fame.

Another instance illustrating conditions when the Cuban cattle trade was booming was related to the writer some years ago by the late T. L. Wilson, of Bartow, who, before his death, became one of the most prominent attorneys and bankers of south Florida and was well known in Atlanta through his activities as a member of the war finance board appointed by President Woodrow Wilson.

Colonel Wilson was the son of a farmer and small cattleman who came from Georgia just after the War Between the States. "Tom" grew up as a pioneer Cracker boy without much book learning but with a pretty thorough knowledge of the out-of-doors. He started out to become a cattle king on his own account and had acquired a herd of a couple of hundred head by the time he was 18.

But one stormy night while he was riding herd down in the cypress flats and palmetto prairies near the present site of Immokalee, in Collier County, one thing went wrong after another. The cattle stampeded at every lightning flash. His horse slipped and fell with him half a dozen times while he was working in the dark. Wet and muddy and cold he stuck it out until daylight and then turned the job over to the cow hand he had riding with him with the brief remark that he was through with bovine playmates forever, or words to that effect.

He rode into Fort Myers, reaching the home of an uncle there after the family had gone to bed. He woke his relative up and after a short explanation of the situation, offered him his herd at the market price, saying he was going to take the money and study law.

The uncle didn't think much of his nephew's decision. In a land where most of the crime concerned shooting matches, and the shootees unable to go to court after it was over as a usual thing, he didn't see much promise in becoming a lawyer. But he agreed to buy the cattle if the boy insisted on selling.

"You'll see my saddlebags on the porch as you go out," he said. "I just sold a bunch at Punta Rassa this morning and am pretty tired, so I won't get up. You count out your money and go ahead, if you're bound you won't spend the night."

Mr. Wilson counted out the nearly two thousand dollars that his cattle came to and left for home. And he stated that there was probably a thousand dollars more still in the bags left on the porch for the night.

The youth never regretted his change of profession from a financial viewpoint at least. He went direct from the range to Washington and Lee University at Lexington, and was said to have been one of the two men ever to complete the law course there in one year, and that without even a complete grammar school education. He was admitted to the bar before he was 21 by a special act of the Florida legislature, and from that time on his success justified his choice of a career.

The old order of cattle raising began to change generally after the Spanish-American war. Cuba settled down under its new regime and began to raise more of its own beef. Florida's own steady growth furnished a constantly increasing home market, but at the same time the new towns and farms and groves springing up all over the former vast open range cut into the pasturage and made it more difficult and costly to handle the big herds.

Many of the cattle kings held on. Most of the big ones had built up very sizable fortunes when the yellow coins from Spain were rolling in so freely. Some of them went into other activities as the changes became more marked. Others who felt that they could not be satisfied with any other life began to alter their methods. Many voluntarily fenced their vast pastures long before the townsfolk and grove owners began to advocate a fence law in the more settled regions.

The old careless days of half a century ago with their easy money will probably never return, but the manner in which the Florida cattle industry is adapting itself to the new conditions indicates that it will be a big business there for a long time to come.

The Atlanta Journal, December 14, 1930

On "The Emperor of Ice Cream"

I think I should select from my poems as my favorite *The Emperor of Ice Cream*. This wears a deliberately commonplace costume, and yet seems to me to contain something of the essential gaudiness of poetry; that is the reason why I like it. I do not remember the circumstances under which this poem was written, unless this means the state of mind from which it came. I dislike niggling, and like letting myself go. Poems of this sort are the pleasantest on which to look back, because they seem to remain fresher than others. This represented what was in my mind at the moment, with the least possible manipulation.

Fifty Poets: An American Auto-Anthology, 1933

Williams

The slightly tobaccoy odor of autumn is perceptible in these pages. Williams is past fifty.

There are so many things to say about him. The first is that he is a romantic poet. This will horrify him. Yet the proof is everywhere. Take the first poem, ALL THE FANCY THINGS. What gives this its distinction is the image of the woman, once a girl in Puerto Rico in the old Spanish days, now solitary and growing old, not knowing what to do with herself, remembering. Of course, this is romantic in the accepted sense, and Williams is rarely romantic in the accepted sense.

The man has spent his life in rejecting the accepted sense of things. In that, most of all, his romantic temperament appears. But it is not enough merely to reject: what matters is the reason for rejection. The reason is that Williams has a romantic of his own. His strong spirit makes its own demands and delights to try its strength.

It will be observed that the lonely figure in ALL THE FANCY THINGS and the person addressed in BRILLIANT SAD SUN have been slightly sentimentalized. In order to understand Williams at all, it is necessary to say at once that he has a sentimental side. Except for that, this book would not exist and its character would not be what it is. THE COD HEAD is a bit of pure sentimentalization; so is THE BULL. Sentiment has such an abhorrent name that one hesitates. But if what vitalizes Williams has an abhorrent name, its obviously generative function in his case may help to change its reputation. What Williams gives, on the whole, is not sentiment but the reaction from sentiment, or, rather, a little sentiment, very little, together with acute reaction.

His passion for the anti-poetic is a blood passion and not a passion of the inkpot. The anti-poetic is his spirit's cure. He needs it as a naked man needs shelter or as an animal needs salt. To a man with a sentimental side the anti-poetic is that truth, that reality to which all of us are forever fleeing.

The anti-poetic has many aspects. The aspect to which a poet is addicted is a test of his validity. Its merely rhetorical aspect is valueless. As an affectation it is a commonplace. As a scourge it has a little more meaning. But as a phase of a man's spirit, as a source of salvation, now, in the midst of a baffled generation, as one looks out of the window at Rutherford or Passaic, or as one walks the streets of New York, the anti-poetic acquires an extraordinary potency, especially if one's nature possesses that side so attractive to the Furies.

Something of the unreal is necessary to fecundate the real; something of the sentimental is necessary to fecundate the anti-poetic. Williams, by nature, is more of a realist than is commonly true in the case of a poet. One might, at this point, set oneself up as the Linnaeus of aesthetics, assigning a female rôle to the unused tent in THE ATTIC WHICH IS DESIRE, and a male rôle to the soda sign; and generally speaking one might run through these pages and point out how often the essential poetry is the result of the conjunction of the unreal and the real, the sentimental and the anti-poetic, the constant inter-action of two opposites. This seems to define Williams and his poetry.

All poets are, to some extent, romantic poets. Thus, the poet who least supposes himself to be so is often altogether so. For instance, no one except a *surréaliste* himself would hesitate to characterize that whole school as romantic, dyed through and through with the most authentic purple. What, then, is a romantic poet now-a-days? He happens to be one who still dwells in an ivory tower, but who insists that life there would be intolerable except for the fact that one has, from the top, such an exceptional view of the public dump and the advertising signs of Snider's Catsup, Ivory Soap and Chevrolet Cars; he is the hermit who dwells alone with the sun and moon, but insists on taking a rotten newspaper. While Williams shares a good deal of this with his contemporaries in the manner and for the reason indicated, the attempt to define him and his work is not to be taken as an attempt to define anyone or anything else.

So defined, Williams looks a bit like that grand old plaster cast, Lessing's Laocoon: the realist struggling to escape from the serpents of the unreal.

He is commonly identified by externals. He includes here specimens of abortive rhythms, words on several levels, ideas without logic, and similar minor matters, which, when all is said, are merely the diversions of the prophet between morn-ing and evening song. It will be found that he has made some veritable additions to the corpus of poetry, which certainly is no more sacred to anyone than to him. His special use of the anti-poetic is an example of this. The ambiguity produced by bareness is another. The implied image, as in YOUNG SYCA-

MORE, the serpent that leaps up in one's imagination at his prompting, is an addition to imagism, a phase of realism which Williams has always found congenial. In respect to manner he is a virtuoso. He writes of flowers exquisitely. But these things may merely be mentioned. Williams himself, a kind of Diogenes of contemporary poetry, is a much more vital matter. The truth is that, if one had not chanced to regard him as Laocoon, one could have done very well by him as Diogenes.

Preface to William Carlos Williams' *Collected Poems 1921–1931*, 1934

Response to an Enquiry

1. *Do you intend your poetry to be useful to yourself or others?*
2. *Do you think there can now be a use for narrative poetry?*
3. *Do you wait for a spontaneous impulse before writing a poem; if so, is this impulse verbal or visual?*
4. *Have you been influenced by Freud and how do you regard him?*
5. *Do you take your stand with any political or politico-economic party or creed?*
6. *As a poet what distinguishes you, do you think, from an ordinary man?*

1. Not consciously. Perhaps I don't like the word useful.
2. There can now be a use for poetry of any sort. It depends on the poet.
3. Most often. While the immediate impulse is verbal, there is, no doubt, a group of impulses.
4. No. I have not read Freud except the *Interpretation*.
5. I am afraid that I don't.
6. Inability to see much point to the life of an ordinary man. The chances are an ordinary man himself sees very little point to it.

New Verse, October 1934

Martha Champion

Miss Champion begins by being an artist. The trouble she takes about small letters in place of capitals and about the relations between her lines and about punctuation; the indifference to what she is writing about as compared to the way in which she writes about it; the pleasure she finds in lines like

> Intent and bright
> Like tenderness

and

> Wave-slap on the shore.
> Grief is slow,
> Which overtakes me here;

these things are manifestly the affairs of an artist. If it is the *Farewell of Meleager* translated by Mackail in *Select Epigrams* (8:XIV):

> No longer will I . . . inhabit the
> hill-tops: what is there sweet, what
> desirable in the mountains? Daphnis
> is dead . . . I will dwell here in the
> city

that is the source of *After Meleager*, Miss Champion's paraphrase which changes the tone of the Anthology to the tone of today is again the affair of an artist.

Youngish artists have a way of being melancholy. It may be that this is merely a symptom of the distress they feel at the absence of definition. They have no very distinct outline either of themselves or of the abstractions that bedevil them. They are, in short, likely to be a bit baffled. Thus to Miss Champion the idea of the twisting of love, which might involve all sorts of implications, has exclusively an artistic implication. The elaboration of the metaphor in *Fragmenta I* interests her without regard to its insignificance. In *Fragmenta II*, a subject that might have been profoundly felt, there are, in the absence of feeling, the phrases:

> towering plains

> Divides the waves
> Like solitude

> sweet-crumbling pebbles;

and in *Perseid* the melancholy of what chance have we is confused with

> giddy Charlestoning deft houses.

If Miss Champion happened to be setting out to think about the twisting of love, or to think about farewells to Daphnis or Daphne or her Uncle Charles or Mrs. Mistlebacher, or about separation, or grief and its assuaging, or the oddity of man measuring himself against things against which the Perseids do so poorly as, say the Hotel Pierre; or if she meant to feel these things to the depths or felt them whether or not she meant to do so; or if she did not mean to think about them or to be moved by them in the least but to use them for the sounds they might provoke, the sensations as of color or the opportunities for strange conjunctions to which they might give rise, as

> dark seas,
> And silly clouds

and

> feeble stars . . .
> bent, hatted chimneys;

if she meant to do any one of these things and meant it persistently so that her will involved everything for her, that would be one thing; but if she did not quite know what she meant to do and did a little of all of them, that would be something infinitely more complicated and difficult and defeating and discouraging. None of Miss Champion's themes is a clear theme lustily treated.

Yet there is nothing more delightful in poetry than the sort of sensitiveness that Miss Champion possesses when it is put to the lusty uses to which she seems capable of putting it. The

> crooked noises

and

> we finger a dead mouse in this house

of *Poem* are fascinating.

Trial Balances, 1935

A Poet That Matters

The tall pages of *Selected Poems* by Marianne Moore are the papers of a scrupulous spirit. The merely fastidious spirit *à la mode* is likely to be on the verge of suffocation from hyperaesthesia. But Miss Moore's is an unaffected, witty, colloquial sort of spirit. In *The Fish*, for instance, the lines move with the rhythm of sea-fans waving to and fro under water. They are lines of exquisite propriety. Yet in this poem she uses what appears, aesthetically, to be most inapposite language:

> "All
>   external
>   marks of abuse are present on this
>   defiant edifice—
>   all the physical features of."

Everywhere in the book there is this enhancing diversity. In consequence, one has more often than not a sense of invigoration not usually communicated by the merely fastidious.

That Miss Moore is scrupulous, the lines just quoted demonstrate. *All* and *external* are rhymes enough for anyone that finds full rhymes to be crude. The same thing is true of *this* and *edifice*. Thus, the lines which at first glance appeared to contain no rhymes whatever, have on a second look a more intricate appearance. Moreover, the units of the lines are syllables and not feet; the first line contains one syllable; the second three; the third nine; the fourth six; the last eight. This scheme is repeated with exactness throughout the poem. It is this scheme that requires Miss Moore to end the stanza with *of*, and that occasionally requires her to pass, elsewhere, from one line to the next in the middle of a word. If the verse is not to be free, its alternative is to be rigid. Finally, in printing the lines, the first two have been set well to the left, the next two have been set in a little to the right and the last has been set in still farther to the right. Now, all these things contribute to the effect of the stanza. The light rhymes please one unconsciously. The exactness with which the syllables are repeated, the larger recurrences as the stanzas are repeated, the indentations which arrest the eye, even if slightly: all these things assist in creating and in modulating the rhythm. In addition, Miss Moore instinctively relates sounds. There is a relation between the groups of letters *ext, ks, phys*. The *i*'s in *defiant edifice* are related. As these relations change, not only the sounds change, but the colours, the texture, the effects also change.

The poem with which the book opens, *The Steeple-Jack*, is highly characteristic. The lines and stanzas flow innocently. Nevertheless, throughout the dozen stanzas the lines repeat themselves, syllable by syllable, without variation. The stanzas are mechanisms. Yet instead of producing a mechanical effect, they produce an effect of ease. In one of her poems Miss Moore writes of

> ". . . intermingled echoes
> struck from thin glasses successively at random—."

In *The Steeple-Jack* she writes of

> "a sea the purple of the peacock's neck is
>   paled to greenish azure as Dürer changed
> the pine green of the Tyrol to peacock blue."

The strong sounds of *the purple of the peacock's neck* contrast and intermingle with the lighter sounds of *paled to greenish azure* and return again to the strong sounds of the last line. The colours of the first and second lines acquire a quality from their association with the word Dürer and the image of Dürer and the pine green and peacock blue of the last line owe something to the word Tyrol and the image of the Tyrol. This is not at all going too finely into minutiae. For with Miss Moore these things lie on the surface.

The Steeple-Jack serves, too, to illustrate what interests Miss Moore. The point of the poem is a view of the common-place. The view is that of Dürer or of Miss Moore in the mask or mood of Dürer, or, more definitely, perhaps, under the stimulus of Dürer. The common-place is, say, a New England fishing-village. Whatever the poem may do for Dürer or for the village, it does many happy things for Miss Moore and for those who delight in her. Obviously, having in mind the subject-matter of the poem, Miss Moore *donne dans le romanesque*. Consciously, the point of the poem may have been something wholly casual. It may lie in the words

> "it is a privilege to see so
> much confusion."

Consciously, it may have had no more point than the wish to make note of observations made while in the cloud of a mood. That is Miss Moore's method. Subject, with her, is often incidental. There are in *The Steeple-Jack* the following creatures: eight stranded whales, a fish, sea-gulls, the peacock of the peacock's neck referred to a moment ago, a guinea, a twenty-five pound lobster, an exotic serpent (by allusion), a ring-lizard, a snake (also by allusion), a crocodile, cats, cobras, rats, the diffident little newt and a spider. This is a modest collection. Miss Moore makes the most lavish snake-charmer look like a visitor. The people in the poem are Dürer;

> "The college student
> named Ambrose sits on the hill-side
> with his not-native books and hat
> and sees boats
>
> at sea progress white and rigid as if in
> a groove";

and C. J. Poole, Steeple-Jack, with one or two references to others. Poole is merely a sign on the sidewalk with his name on it. The last stanza is:—

> "It could not be dangerous to be living
> in a town like this, of simple people,
> who have a steeple-jack placing danger signs by
> the church
> while he is gilding the solid-
> pointed star, which on a steeple
> stands for hope."

Stendhal in his *Pensées* said:

> "Le bel esprit comme on sait fut de tout
> temps l'ennemi le plus perfide du génie."

Miss Moore's wit, however, does not in the least imperil what she is about. Out of her whales and the college student and Poole and the danger signs she composes a poem simple, radiant with imagination, contemporaneous, displaying everywhere her sensitive handling. The poem leaves one indubitably convinced that she leans to the romantic.

And so she should, with a difference. In *The Steeple-Jack* she observes the fog on the sea-side flowers and trees

> "so that you have
> the tropics at first hand: the trumpet vine . . .
> or moon vines trained on fishing-twine."

She then writes

> ". . . There are no banyans, frangipani nor
> jack-fruit trees; nor an exotic serpent
> life."

If she had said in so many words that there were banyans, frangipani, and so on, she would have been romantic in the sense in which the romantic is a relic of the imagination. She hybridises the thing by a negative. That is one way. Equally she hybridises it by association. Moon-vines are moon-vines and tedious. But moon-vines trained on fishing-twine are something else and they are as perfectly as it is possible for anything to be what interests Miss Moore. They are an intermingling. The imagination grasps at such things and sates itself, instantaneously, in them. Yet clearly they are romantic. At this point one very well might stop for definitions. It is clear enough, without all that, to say that the romantic in the pejorative sense merely connotes obsolescence, but that the word has, or should have, another sense. Thus, when A. E. Powell in *The Romantic Theory of Poetry* writes of the romantic poet,

"He seeks to reproduce for us the feeling as it lives within himself; and for the sake of a feeling which he thinks interesting or important he will insert passages which contribute nothing to the effect of the work as a whole," she is surely not thinking of the romantic in a derogatory sense. True, when Professor Babbitt speaks of the romantic, he means the romantic. Romantic objects are things, like garden furniture or colonial lingerie or, not to burden the imagination, country millinery.

Yes, but the romantic in its other sense, meaning always the living and at the same time the imaginative, the youthful, the delicate and a variety of things which it is not necessary to try to particularise at the moment, constitutes the vital element in poetry. It is absurd to wince at being called a romantic poet. Unless one is that, one is not a poet at all. That, of course, does not mean banyans and frangipani; and it cannot for long mean no banyans and no frangipani. Just what it means, Miss Moore's book discloses. It means, now-a-days, an uncommon intelligence. It means in a time like our own of violent feelings, equally violent feelings and the most skilful expression of the genuine. Miss Moore's lines,

> "the shadows of the Alps
> imprisoning in their folds like flies in amber, the rhythms
> of the skating rink"

might so easily have been pottered over and nullified; and how hilarious, how skilful they are! Only the other day there was a comment on "Samuel Prout's romantic renderings of mediaeval fountains." The commentator was far from meaning mediaeval renderings of romantic fountains. For him Prout's renderings were romantic because they delighted him and since the imagination does not often delight in the same thing twice, it may be assumed that by romantic he meant something that was, for his particular imagination, an indulgence and a satisfaction.

Professor Babbitt says that

> "a thing is romantic when, as Aristotle would say, it is wonderful rather than probable . . . A thing is romantic when it is strange, unexpected, intense, superlative, extreme, unique, etc."

It must also be living. It must always be living. It is in the sense of living intensity, living singularity that it is the vital element in poetry. The most brilliant instance of the romantic in this sense is Mr. Eliot, who incessantly revives the past and creates the future. It is a process of cross-fertilisation, an immense process, all arts considered, of hybridisation. Mr. Eliot's *Prelude* with the smell of steaks in passageways, is an instance, in the sense that the smell of steaks in the Parnassian air is a thing perfectly fulfilling Professor Babbitt's specifications. Hamlet in modern dress is another instance of hybridisation. Any playing of a well-known concerto by an unknown artist is another. Miss Moore's book is a collection of just that. It is not a matter of phrases, nor of odd-looking lines, nor of poems from which one must wholly take, giving anything whatsoever at one's peril. Poetry for her is "a place for the genuine." If the conception of the poet as a creature ferocious with ornamental fury survives anywhere except in the school books, it badly needs a few pungent footnotes. We do not want "high-sounding interpretation." We want to understand. We want, as she says,

"imaginary gardens with real toads in them."

The very conjunction of imaginary gardens and real toads is one more specimen of the romantic of Miss Moore. Above all things she demands

"the raw material of poetry in
all its rawness."

She demands the romantic that is genuine, that is living, the enriching poetic reality.

Miss Moore's form is not the quirk of a self-conscious writer. She is not a writer. She is a woman who has profound needs. In any project for poetry (and one wishes that the world of tailors, plasterers, barkeepers could bring itself to accept poets in a matter-of-fact way) the first effort should be devoted to establishing that poets are men and women, not writers. Miss Moore may have had more than one reason for adding in the *Notes* appended to her book that in *Peter*, the hero "built for the midnight grass-party," was a

"Cat owned by Miss Magdalen Heuber and
Miss Maria Weniger."

But this amusing stroke is, after all, a bit of probity, whatever else it may be. That Miss Moore uses her wit is a bit of probity.

The romantic that falsifies is rot and that is true even though the romantic inevitably falsifies: it falsifies but it does not vitiate. It is an association of the true and the false. It is not the true. It is not the false. It is both. The school of poetry that believes in sticking to the facts would be stoned if it was not sticking to the facts in a world in which there are no facts: or some such thing.

This brings one round to a final word. Miss Moore's *emportements* are few. Instead of being intentionally one of the most original of contemporary or modern poets, she is merely one of the most truthful. People with a passion for the truth are always original. She says:

"Truth is no Apollo."

She has thought much about people and about poetry, and the truth, and she has done this with all the energy of an intense mind and imagination and this book is the significant result. It contains the veritable thing.

Life and Letters To-day, December 2, 1935

In Memory of Harriet Monroe

Her job brought Miss Monroe into contact with the most ferocious egoists. I mean poets in general. You could see her shrewd understanding adapt itself to her visitors. When they had left her office she remained just as amiable. There must be many of her contributors to whom she gave the feeling not only that she liked their poems, but that she liked them personally, as she usually did.

No one could have been more agreeable, yet she had not a trace of the busy welcomer. She wanted more time so that she might know you better. She would go along to lunch and then invite you to her house for dinner. She did the most she could for you and gave you the best she had. To cite not too exalted an instance, I remember that on one occasion she produced after dinner as a liqueur a small bottle of whiskey which she said was something like ninety years old, almost colonial, as if stored up for that particular winter's night.

We had the pleasure of seeing her on several occasions in Hartford, where again she impressed us with her sincerity and good will.

All this reflected itself in POETRY, which might so easily have become something less than it was: something less in the sense of being the organ of a group or mode, or of having a rigid any-other standard. It was notably a magazine of many people; it was the widest possible. She made it so. She liked to be among people; in a group she was always most eager. It was not merely courtesy that made her think well and speak well of others; she did it because she enjoyed doing it.

Poetry, December 1936

The Irrational Element in Poetry

I

To begin with, the expression: the irrational element in poetry, is much too general to be serviceable. After one has thought about it a bit it spreads out. Then too we are at the moment so beset by the din made by the surrealists and sur-rationalists, and so preoccupied in reading about them that we may become confused by these romantic scholars and think of them as the sole exemplars of the irrational today. Certainly, they exemplify one aspect of it. Primarily, however, what I have in mind when I speak of the irrational element in poetry is the transaction between reality and the sensibility of the poet from which poetry springs.

II

I am not competent to discuss reality as a philosopher. All of us understand what is meant by the transposition of an objective reality to a subjective reality. The transaction between reality and the sensibility of the poet is precisely that. A day or two before Thanksgiving we had a light fall of snow in Hartford. It melted a little by day and then froze again at night, forming a thin, bright crust over the grass. At the same time, the moon was almost full. I awoke once several hours before daylight and as I lay in bed I heard the steps of a cat running over the snow under my window almost inaudibly. The faintness and strangeness of the sound made on me one of those impressions which one so often seizes as pretexts for poetry. I suppose that in such a case one is merely expressing one's sensibility and that the reason why this expression takes the form of poetry is that it takes whatever form one is able to give it. The poet is able to give it the form of poetry because poetry is the medium of his personal sensibility. This is not the same thing as saying that a poet writes poetry because he writes poetry, although it sounds much like it. A poet writes poetry because he is a poet; and he is not a poet because he is a poet but because of his personal sensibility. What gives a man his personal sensibility I don't know and it does not matter because no one knows. Poets continue to be born not made and cannot, I am afraid, be predetermined. While, on the one hand, if they could be predetermined, they might long since have become extinct, they might, on the other hand, have changed life from what it is today into one of those transformations in which they delight, and they might have seen to it that they greatly multiplied themselves there.

III

There is, of course, a history of the irrational element in poetry, which is, after all, merely a chapter of the history of the irrational in the arts generally. With the irrational in a pathological sense we are not concerned. Fuseli used to eat raw beef at night before going to bed in order that his dreams might attain a beefy violence otherwise lacking. Nor are we concerned with that sort of thing; nor with any irrationality provoked by prayer, whiskey, fasting, opium, or the hope of publicity. The Gothic novels of eighteenth-century England are no longer irrational. They are merely boring. What interests us is a particular process in the rational mind which we recognize as irrational in the sense that it takes place unaccountably. Or, rather, I should say that what interests us is not so much the Hegelian process as what comes of it. We should probably be much more intelligently interested if from the history of the irrational there had developed a tradition. It is easy to brush aside the irrational with the statement that we are rational beings, Aristotelians and not brutes. But it is becoming easier every day to say that we are irrational beings; that all irrationality is not of a piece and that the only reason why it does not yet have a tradition is that its tradition is in progress. When I was here at Harvard, a long time ago, it was a commonplace to say that all the poetry had been written and all the paintings painted. It may be something of that sort that first interested us in the irrational. One of the great figures in the world since then has been Freud. While he is responsible for very little in poetry, as compared, for example, with his effect elsewhere, he has given the irrational a legitimacy that it never had before. More portentous influences have been Mallarmé and Rimbaud.

IV

It may be that my subject expressed with greater nicety is irrational manifestations of the irrational element in poetry; for if the irrational element is merely poetic energy, it is to be found wherever poetry is to be found. One such manifestation is the disclosure of the individuality of the poet. It is unlikely that this disclosure is ever visible as plainly to anyone as to the poet himself. In the first of the poems that I shall read to you in a moment or two the subject that I had in mind was the effect of the depression on the interest in art. I wanted a confronting of the world as it had been imagined in art and as it was then in fact. If I dropped into a gallery I found that I had no interest in what I saw. The air was charged with anxieties and tensions. To look at pictures there was the same thing as to play the piano in Madrid this afternoon. I was as capable of making observations and of jotting them down as anyone else; and if that is what I had wished to do, I could have done it. I wanted to deal with exactly such a subject and I chose that as a bit of reality, actuality, the contemporaneous. But I wanted the result to be poetry so far as I was able to write poetry. To be specific, I wanted to apply my own sensibility to something perfectly matter-of-fact. The result would be a disclosure of my own sensibility or individuality, as I called it a moment ago, certainly to myself. The poem is called "The Old Woman and the Statue." The old woman is a symbol of those who suffered during the depression and the statue is a symbol of art, although in several poems of which *Owl's Clover*, the book from which I shall read, consists, the statue is a variable symbol. While there is nothing automatic about the poem, nevertheless it has an automatic aspect in the sense that it is what I wanted it to be without knowing before it was written what I wanted it to be, even though I knew before it was written what I wanted to do. If each of us is a biological mechanism, each poet is a poetic mechanism. To the extent that what he produces is mechanical: that is to say, beyond his power to change, it is irrational. Perhaps I do not mean wholly beyond his power to change, for he might, by an effort of the will, change it. With that in mind, I mean beyond likelihood of change so long as he is being himself. This happens in the case of every poet.

V

I think, too, that the choice of subject-matter is a completely irrational thing, provided a poet leaves himself any freedom of choice. If you are an imagist, you make a choice of subjects that is obviously limited. The same thing is true if you are anything else in particular and profess rigidly. But if you elect to remain free and to go about in the world experiencing whatever you happen to experience, as most people do, even when they insist that they do not, either your choice of subjects is fortuitous or the identity of the circumstances under which the choice is made is imperceptible. Lyric poets are bothered by spring and romantic poets by autumn. As a man becomes familiar with his own poetry, it becomes as obsolete for himself as for anyone else. From this it follows that one of the motives in writing is renewal. This undoubtedly affects the choice of subjects as definitely as it affects changes in rhythm, diction and manner. It is elementary that we vary rhythms instinctively. We say that we perfect diction. We simply grow tired. Manner is something that has not yet been disengaged adequately. It does not mean style; it means the attitude of the writer, his bearing rather than his point of view. His bearing toward what? Not toward anything in particular, simply his pose. He hears the cat on the snow. The running feet set the rhythm. There is no subject beyond the cat running on the snow in the moonlight. He grows completely tired of the thing, wants a subject, thought, feeling, his whole manner changes. All these things enter into the choice of subject. The man who has been brought up in an artificial school becomes intemperately real. The Mallarmiste becomes the proletarian novelist. All this is irrational. If the choice of subject was predictable it would be rational. Now, just as the choice of subject is unpredictable at the outset, so its development, after it has been chosen, is unpredictable. One is always writing about two things at the same time in poetry and it is this that produces the tension characteristic of poetry. One is the true subject and the other is the poetry of the subject. The difficulty of sticking to the true subject, when it is the poetry of the subject that is paramount in one's mind, need only be mentioned to be understood. In a poet who makes the true subject paramount and who merely embellishes it, the subject is constant and the development orderly. If the poetry of the subject is paramount, the true subject is not constant nor its development orderly. This is true in the case of Proust and Joyce, for example, in modern prose.

VI

Why does one write poetry? I have already stated a number of reasons, among them these: because one is impelled to do so by personal sensibility and also because one grows tired of the monotony of one's imagination, say, and sets out to find variety. In his discourse before the Academy, ten years or more ago, M. Brémond elucidated a mystical motive and made it clear that, in his opinion, one writes poetry to find God. I should like to consider this in conjunction with what might better be considered separately, and that is the question of meaning in poetry. M. Brémond proposed the identity of poetry and prayer, and followed Bergson in relying, in the last analysis, on faith. M. Brémond eliminated reason as the essential element in poetry. Poetry in which the irrational element dominated was pure poetry. M. Brémond himself does not permit any looseness in the expression pure poetry, which he confines to a very small body of poetry, as he should, if the lines in which he recognizes it are as precious to his spirit as they appear to be. In spite of M. Brémond, pure poetry is a term that has grown to be descriptive of poetry in which not the true subject but the poetry of the subject is paramount. All mystics approach God through the irrational. Pure poetry is both mystical and irrational. If we descend a little from this height and apply the looser and broader definition of pure poetry, it is possible to say that, while it can lie in the temperament of very few of us to write poetry in order to find God, it is probably the purpose of each of us to write poetry to find the good which, in the Platonic sense, is synonymous with God. One writes poetry, then, in order to approach the good in what is harmonious and orderly. Or, simply, one writes poetry out of a delight in the harmonious and orderly. If it is true that the most abstract painters paint herrings and apples, it is no less true that the poets who most urgently search the world for the sanctions of life, for that which makes life so prodigiously worth living, may find their solutions in a duck in a pond or in the wind on a winter night. It is conceivable that a poet may arise of such scope that he can set the abstraction on which so much depends to music. In the meantime we have to live by the literature we have or are able to produce. I say live by literature, because literature is the better part of life, provided it is based on life itself. From this point of view, the meaning of poetry involves us profoundly. It does not follow that poetry that is irrational in origin is not communicable poetry. The pure poetry of M. Brémond is irrational in origin. Yet it communicates so much that M. Brémond regards it as supreme. Because most of us are incapable of sharing the experiences of M. Brémond, we have to be content with less. When we find in poetry that which gives us a momentary existence on an exquisite plane, is it necessary to ask the meaning of the poem? If the poem had a meaning and if its explanation destroyed the illusion, should we have gained or lost? Take, for instance, the poem of Rimbaud, one of *Les Illuminations*, entitled "Beaten Tracks." I quote Miss Rootham's translation:

On the right the summer dawn wakes the leaves, the mists and the sounds in this corner of the park. The slopes on the left clasp in their purple shade the myriad deep-cut tracks of the damp highway. A procession from fairyland passes by. There are chariots loaded with animals of gilded wood, with masts and canvas painted in many colors, drawn by twenty galloping piebald circus-ponies; and children and men on most astonishing beasts; there are twenty vehicles, embossed, and decked with flags and flowers like coaches of by-gone days, as coaches out of a fairytale; they are full of children dressed up for a suburban pastoral. There are even coffins under their night-dark canopies and sable plumes, drawn by trotting mares, blue and black.

I do not know what images the poem has created. M. Delahaye says that the poem was prompted by an American circus which visited Charleville, where Rimbaud lived as a boy, in 1868 or 1869. What is the effect of this explanation? I need not answer that. Miss Sitwell wrote the introduction to the collection of Miss Rootham's translations of the poems of Rimbaud. Something that she said in the course of that introduction illustrates the way the true subject supersedes the nominal subject. She said:

How different was this life [of the slum] from that sheltered and even rather stuffy life of perpetual Sundays that he had led when he was a little boy in Charleville, and on these ever-recurring days of tight clothing and prayer, when Madame Rimbaud had escorted him, his brother and two sisters, to the eleven o'clock Mass, along the bright light dust-powdery roads, under trees whose great glossy brilliant leaves and huge pink flowers that seemed like heavenly transfigurations of society ladies, appeared to be shaking with laughter at the sober procession.

Miss Sitwell herself could not say whether the eleven o'clock Mass suggested the bright light flowers or whether the society ladies came into her mind with the great glossy brilliant leaves and were merely trapped there by the huge pink flowers, or whether they came with the huge pink flowers. It might depend upon whether, in Miss Sitwell's mind, society ladies are, on the one hand, great glossy and brilliant, or, on the other hand, huge and pink. Here the true subject was the brilliance and color of an impression.

VII

The pressure of the contemporaneous from the time of the beginning of the World War to the present time has been constant and extreme. No one can have lived apart in a happy oblivion. For a long time before the war nothing was more common. In those days the sea was full of yachts and the yachts were full of millionaires. It was a time when only maniacs had disturbing things to say. The period was like a stage-setting that since then has been taken down and trucked away. It had been taken down by the end of the war, even though it took ten years of struggle with the consequences of the peace to bring about a realization of that fact. People said that if the war continued it would end civilization, just as they say now that another such war will end civilization. It is one thing to talk about the end of civilization and another to feel that the thing is not merely possible but measurably probable. If you are not a communist, has not civilization ended in Russia? If you are not a Nazi, has it not ended in Germany? We no sooner say that it never can happen here than we recognize that we say it without any illusions. We are preoccupied with events, even when we do not observe them closely. We have a sense of upheaval. We feel threatened. We look from an uncertain present toward a more uncertain future. One feels the desire to collect oneself against all this in poetry as well as in politics. If politics is nearer to each of us because of the pressure of the contemporaneous, poetry, in its way, is no less so and for the same reason. Does anyone suppose that the vast mass of people in this country was moved at the last election by rational considerations? Giving reason as much credit as the radio, there still remains the certainty that so great a movement was emotional and, if emotional, irrational. The trouble is that the greater the pressure of the contemporaneous, the greater the resistance. Resistance is the opposite of escape. The poet who wishes to contemplate the good in the midst of confusion is like the mystic who wishes to contemplate God in the midst of evil. There can be no thought of escape. Both the poet and the mystic may establish themselves on herrings and apples. The painter may establish himself on a guitar, a copy of *Figaro* and a dish of melons. These are fortifyings, although irrational ones. The only possible resistance to the pressure of the contemporaneous is a matter of herrings and apples or, to be less definite, the contemporaneous itself. In poetry, to that extent, the subject is not the contemporaneous, because that is only the nominal subject, but the poetry of the contemporaneous. Resistance to the pressure of ominous and destructive circumstance consists of its conversion, so far as possible, into a different, an explicable, an amenable circumstance.

VIII

M. Charles Mauron says that a man may be characterized by his obsessions. We are obsessed by the irrational. This is because we expect the irrational to liberate us from the rational. In a note on Picasso with the tell-tale title of "Social Fact and Cosmic Vision," Christian Zervos says:

> The explosion of his spirit has destroyed the barriers which art . . . impressed on the imagination. Poetry has come forward with all that it has of the acute, the enigmatical, the strange sense which sees in life not only an image of reality but which conceives of life as a mystery that wraps us round everywhere.

To take Picasso as the modern one happens to think of, it may be said of him that his spirit is the spirit of any artist that seeks to be free. A superior obsession of all such spirits is the obsession of freedom. There is, however, no longer much excuse for explosions for, as in painting, so in poetry, you can do as you please. You can compose poetry in whatever form you like. If it seems a seventeenth-century habit to begin lines with capital letters, you can go in for the liquid transitions of greater simplicity; and so on. It is not that nobody cares. It matters immensely. The slightest sound matters. The most momentary rhythm matters. You can do as you please, yet everything matters. You are free, but your freedom must be consonant with the freedom of others. To insist for a moment on the point of sound. We no longer like Poe's tintinnabulations. You are free to tintinnabulate if you like. But others are equally free to put their hands over their ears. Life may not be a cosmic mystery that wraps us round everywhere. You have somehow to know the sound that is the exact sound;

and you do in fact know, without knowing how. Your knowl-
edge is irrational. In that sense life is mysterious; and if it is
mysterious at all, I suppose that it is cosmically mysterious. I
hope that we agree that it is at least mysterious. What is true
of sounds is true of everything: the feeling for words, without
regard to their sound, for example. There is, in short, an un-
written rhetoric that is always changing and to which the poet
must always be turning. That is the book in which he learns
that the desire for literature is the desire for life. The incessant
desire for freedom in literature or in any of the arts is a desire
for freedom in life. The desire is irrational. The result is the
irrational searching the irrational, a conspicuously happy state
of affairs, if you are so inclined.

Those who are so inclined and without reserve say: The
least fastidiousness in the pursuit of the irrational is to be re-
pudiated as an abomination. Rational beings are canaille. In-
stead of seeing, we should make excavations in the eye; instead
of hearing, we should juxtapose sounds in an emotional clit-
ter-clatter.

This seems to be freedom for freedom's sake. If we say that
we desire freedom when we are already free, it seems clear
that we have in mind a freedom not previously experienced.
Yet is not this an attitude toward life resembling the poet's
attitude toward reality? In spite of the cynicisms that occur to
us as we hear of such things, a freedom not previously expe-
rienced, a poetry not previously conceived of, may occur with
the suddenness inherent in poetic metamorphosis. For poets,
that possibility is the ultimate obsession. They purge them-
selves before reality, in the meantime, in what they intend to
be saintly exercises.

You will remember the letter written by Rimbaud to M.
Delahaye, in which he said:

> It is necessary to be a seer, to make oneself a seer. The poet makes
> himself a seer by a long, immense and reasoned unruliness of the
> senses. . . . He attains the unknown.

IX

Let me say a final word about the irrational as part of the
dynamics of poetry. The irrational bears the same relation to

the rational that the unknown bears to the known. In an age as harsh as it is intelligent, phrases about the unknown are quickly dismissed. I do not for a moment mean to indulge in mystical rhetoric, since for my part, I have no patience with that sort of thing. That the unknown as the source of knowledge, as the object of thought, is part of the dynamics of the known does not permit of denial. It is the unknown that excites the ardor of scholars, who, in the known alone, would shrivel up with boredom. We accept the unknown even when we are most skeptical. We may resent the consideration of it by any except the most lucid minds; but when so considered, it has seductions more powerful and more profound than those of the known.

Just so, there are those who, having never yet been convinced that the rational has quite made us divine, are willing to assume the efficacy of the irrational in that respect. The rational mind, dealing with the known, expects to find it glistening in a familiar ether. What it really finds is the unknown always behind and beyond the known, giving it the appearance, at best, of chiaroscuro. There are, naturally, charlatans of the irrational. That, however, does not require us to identify the irrational with the charlatans. I should not want to be misunderstood as having the poets of surrealism in mind. They concentrate their prowess in a technique which seems singularly limited but which, for all that, exhibits the dynamic influence of the irrational. They are extraordinarily alive and that they make it possible for us to read poetry that seems filled with gaiety and youth, just when we were beginning to despair of gaiety and youth, is immensely to the good. One test of their dynamic quality and, therefore, of their dynamic effect, is that they make other forms seem obsolete. They, in time, will be absorbed, with the result that what is now so concentrated, so inconsequential in the restrictions of a technique, so provincial, will give and take and become part of the process of give and take of which the growth of poetry consists.

Those who seek for the freshness and strangeness of poetry in fresh and strange places do so because of an intense need. The need of the poet for poetry is a dynamic cause of the poetry that he writes. By the aid of the irrational he finds joy in the irrational. When we speak of fluctuations of taste, we are speaking of evidences of the operation of the irrational. Such changes are irrational. They reflect the effects of poetic energy; for where there are no fluctuations, poetic energy is absent. Clearly, I use the word irrational more or less indifferently, as between its several senses. It will be time enough to adopt a more systematic usage, when the critique of the irrational comes to be written, by whomever it may be that this potent subject ultimately engages. We must expect in the future incessant activity by the irrational and in the field of the irrational. The advances thus to be made would be all the greater if the character of the poet was not so casual and intermittent a character. The poet cannot profess the irrational as the priest professes the unknown. The poet's role is broader, because he must be possessed, along with everything else, by the earth and by men in their earthy implications. For the poet, the irrational is elemental; but neither poetry nor life is commonly at its dynamic utmost. We know Sweeney as he is and, for the most part, prefer him that way and without too much effulgence and, no doubt, always shall.

Lecture delivered at Harvard University, December 8, 1936

Insurance and Social Change

If each of us could put his hand on money whenever money was necessary: to repair any damage, to meet any emergency, we should all be willing to stop so far as money goes. To be certain of a regular income, as in the case of social security, is not the same thing as to be able to repair any damage, or to meet any emergency. Obviously, in a world in which insurance had become perfect, the case of social security would be a minor case. In short, universal insurance or insurance for all is not the same thing as ubiquitous insurance or insurance for everything.

The significance of a business is not wholly an affair of its statistics. This note is written lightly and is intended to touch the imagination, because that seems to be the best way to come quickly to the point. The objective of all of us is to live in a world in which nothing unpleasant can happen. Our prime instinct is to go on indefinitely like the wax flowers on the mantelpiece. Insurance is the most easily understood geometry for calculating how to bring the thing about.

The truth is that we may well be entering an insurance era. Compare the man who, as an individual, insures his dwelling against fire with that personality of the first plane who, at a stroke, insures all dwellings against fire; and who, without stopping to think about it, insures not only the lives of all those that live in the dwellings, but insures all people against all happenings of everyday life, even the worm in the apple or the piano out of tune. These are instances of insurance as it exists; and if they were not, there would be Lloyds or the future. There is no difference between the worm in the apple and the tack in the can of sardines, and not the slightest difference between the piano out of tune and a person disabled.

It helps us to see the actual world to visualize a fantastic world. Thus, when Mr. Wells creates a world of machines, a matter-of-fact truth about the world in which we live becomes clear for all the fiction. When he passes from the international to the interstellar, we hug the purely local. In the same way it helps us to see insurance in the midst of social change to imagine a world in which insurance had been made perfect. In such a world we should be certain of an income. Out of the income we should be able, by the payment of a trivial premium, to protect ourselves, our families and our property against everything. The procedure would necessarily be simple: Probably the dropping of a penny each morning in a box at the corner nearest one's place of residence on the way to one's place of employment. Each of us would have a personal or peculiar penny. What is the difference between a personal penny and a social security number? The circle just stated: income, insurance, the thing that happens and income again, would widen and soon become income, insurance, the thing that fails to happen and income again. In other words, not only would all our losses be made good, but all our wishes would come true.

If Mr. Wells has preferred the machine to insurance as his field, he has only left insurance to others. How far have others

gone? The Italians have a quasi-governmental insurance or-
ganization, known as the National Insurance Institute, which
came into being as the result of a national law passed in 1912.
A consular report says . . .

The law was passed in pursuance of a proposal of a state monopoly
of life insurance made the same year by Premier Giolitti. The avowed
purposes of this proposal were to make monopoly profits available
for social welfare expenditure and to enable the employment of state
guarantees to stimulate increase of life insurance in Italy.

This does not mean, however, that private companies have
been required to cease operations. In 1923 the Fascist govern-
ment issued a decree permitting private companies to operate
under conditions; and the fact is that private companies, both
domestic and foreign, are in operation at the present time,
although it is said that they operate under severe competitive
handicaps. It is not surprising to hear it reported that ap-
proximately half of the life insurance in the Kingdom is in the
Institute. Private companies must cede or reinsure substantial
parts of their business to the Institute. Note, too, that in Italy
postal officials are among those that sell life insurance.

Liability insurance, or civil responsibility business, as they
call it, is not so attractive a subject for the monopolistically-
minded politician, and this field remains in Italy a field for
private enterprise. There is little to be said about fire insurance
in Italy, where virtually all buildings are constructed chiefly
of non-combustible materials. The government has a monop-
oly of obligatory social insurance (Cassa Nazionale per le
Assicurazioni Sociali, of Rome). Social insurance relates to
disability, tuberculosis, old age and unemployment. The
funds of Cassa Nazionale are invested largely in public
works.

In Germany private companies survive, but under a super-
vision described as "a continuous supervision of the whole
business management whereby the Supervision Board may to
a great extent act at its own decision". There are compulsory
standard rules relating, for example, even to bookkeeping. As
the field of insurance expands, and as the interest of the gov-
ernment in it becomes intensified to a point approaching
identity, supervision justifiably becomes increasingly more se-

vere. If this would be true in normal circumstances, it is all the more true in a period in which exhaustion has been an aggressive force.

In England, a Parliamentary committee on obligatory insurance has only recently reported in favor of a licensing system in which the approval of companies will be vested in other companies which will contribute to a central fund. Losses from the insolvency of any company will be payable from the central fund. Third party losses, uncollectible because of the operation of conditions, will also be payable from the central fund.

In the vast monopoly of Communism, insurance is itself a monopoly. The organization, Gosstrakh, is a state department and, by government decree, no other organization has the right to do an insurance business in the territory of the Soviets. This would put insurance agents on a footing with letter carriers or government employees generally, if it were not for the fact that, in Russia, everybody is on the same footing. Gosstrakh issues policies in several foreign companies which are its correspondents.

These very inadequate glimpses of the situation in those European countries where social pressure has been most acute and social and political change most marked indicate that, as the social mass seeks to maintain itself, it relies more and more on insurance and treats it as of such significance that the preservation of the insurers becomes a governmental function or a highly important object of governmental solicitude. Moreover, the government, in turn, avails itself of insurance not only in its social and political aspects but, in some directions, itself becomes an insurer and opens to its requirements the huge accumulation of funds from that source, which it applies, sometimes to social purposes, sometimes to general purposes, its own credit taking the place of reserves.

We shall never live in a world quite so mechanical as the one that Mr. Wells has imagined, nor in a world in which insurance has been made perfect, and where we can buy peace and prosperity as readily and as cheaply as we can buy the morning newspaper. All the same, we have advanced remarkably; and future advances seem to be not fantastic but certain. It is all a question of remaining solvent, a question of making a reasonable profit. Agents have as much at stake as any group in the making of a reasonable profit. Even if the point is considered from the view of the nationalization of the business, it is not to be supposed that any government can maintain an entire population indefinitely at a loss. If private companies can continue to expand with profit, no question of nationalization, except in regulatory and certain social aspects, is likely to arise under our system.

Under other systems, that is to say, under both Fascist and Communist systems, the finely-tailored agent, wearing a boutonniere, gives way to the letter carrier. In a late number of the Accident Company's Confidential Bulletin, it was said that . . .

Cemeteries have been found by a number of offices to be a very definite market for the Hartford's All Risk Securities Policy.

This observation would apply to the Hartford's policies generally under Communism and, to some extent, under Fascism. In short, then, the activities of the insurance business are likely, the greater and more significant they are, to make one reflect on the possibilities of nationalization, particularly in a period of unrest and the changes incident to unrest, a period so easily to be regarded as a period of transition. Yet the greater these activities are: that is to say, the more they are adapted to the changing needs of changing times (provided they are conducted at a profit) the more certain they are to endure on the existing basis. But this exacts of each of us all that each of us, in his own job, has to give.

The Hartford Agent, October 1937

Surety and Fidelity Claims

People suppose, since there is so much human interest in selling Fuller brushes or sorting postcards in a post office, that the same thing must be true of handling fidelity and surety claims. After all, over a period of time, you spend an immense amount of money, millions.

But, actually, you never see a dollar. You sign a lot of drafts.

You see surprisingly few people. You do the greater part of your work either in your own office or in lawyers' offices. You don't even see the country; you see law offices and hotel rooms. You try to do your traveling at night and often do it night after night. You wind up by knowing every county court house in the United States.

In particular, people suppose that there must be an immense amount of dishonesty in the way claims are made. Yet every man knows that he will have to establish his claim. Besides, to make a dishonest claim requires an intention to defraud the company. The danger from ignorance is far greater. A claim man is constantly separating the good from the bad. Some of the bad is due to a disposition to claim everything and let the company look after itself; some of it is due to improper constructions placed on language used by the company; some of it is due to a willingness to make a nuisance of yourself unless you are bought off. But most of it is due to ignorance. "Read your policy" relates to ignorance.

The major activity of a fidelity and surety claim department lies, of course, in paying claims. This involves much more than merely drawing drafts. It involves making sure that there has been a loss; that the company is liable for it; that you are discharging the liability by the payment, and that you are protecting whatever is available by way of salvage. There is nothing cut and dried about any of these things; you adapt yourself to each case.

A bookkeeper makes false entries in his books and keeps a memorandum of them and of the amounts embezzled by him. You make sure of the loss by checking. It may seem morbid of an embezzler to keep a memorandum, yet many of them do. It may be mere neatness. Public officials seem to be a little less fastidious. They collect taxes without making records. In such a case we look for people with receipts. Tellers in savings banks take money from their cash and make charges against inactive accounts. In such a case the bank tries to persuade depositors to bring in their books. A filling station man asks you to pay him a large sum of money under a bond for a contractor conditioned for the payment of labor and materials. You find that part of the bill covers gasoline supplied to the contractor's wife for her personal car, that part of it is for repairs ordered by a man who rented a truck to a sub-contractor, and you pay the balance. These are instances of determining that there has been a loss.

You find that, while a sheriff failed to make a levy on property belonging to a judgment debtor and specifically called to his attention, this occurred in October in one term of office, while you did not become liable until January in another term of office. One of the next of kin sues you on the bond of an administrator. The administrator has been in office for a few months only and neither he nor you are subject to suit. A boy sues you on a bond for his mother as his guardian; you find that he has released his mother. A manufacturer of cement sues you for $80,000 on a bond which ordinarily would protect him. His right to sue you is based on a statute which limits the time for suit. It is too late and besides the manufacturer has taken $65,000 from payments made to him by the contractor out of the proceeds of the job covered by your bond and has applied the money (as he is free to do) to a balance due on a job not bonded by you. You contest the suit and defeat the claim. These are instances in which the company is not liable.

You have a bond guaranteeing that an electrician will pay his bills. The bond is for $1,000. His books show that he owes $3,000 and, if his books are incorrect, he may owe twice as much. You are threatened by suits; how are you to proceed? A family is killed by fumes from a gas stove in a cabin in a tourist camp. If the husband died first, his estate goes to A, B and C; if the wife died first, the husband's estate goes to X, Y and Z. The estate amounts to $50,000. You are on the bond of the administrator of the husband's estate. The $50,000 consisted of cash on deposit in a bank which failed several years after you gave your bond. A, B and C will settle for $10,000, but X, Y and Z want $50,000. What had you better do? You are on a very large bond for a woman as executrix of her husband's estate. She has not accounted and you are unable to form any idea respecting her ability to account. What is more, she does not reside in the jurisdiction of the court, and you are not at all sure even that she exists. She was represented by lawyers who are willing to tell you what they know if you will first pay them the fee which she has failed to pay. They want, say, $25,000. You do not know whether what they will tell you will clear you or will disclose a liability for some hundreds of thousands of dollars. Shall you pay the $25,000? A contractor asks you to lend him a week's payroll for a few days or to pay off an accumulation of bills until he collects the amount of an estimate, within a week or two. To do so will not cut down the amount of your liability; shall you do it? These are instances of questions relating to payments as discharging or not discharging the company's liability.

Then there is salvage: People would not so commonly be required to give bonds if they had money. This means that people are required to give bonds because they don't have money. From this point of view, the saying among claim men that often the only salvage recoverable lies in an advantageous settlement, is true. In any case, the recovering of salvage is closely involved with the treatment of claims. A man investigating a claim investigates at the same time the chance of getting the money back. The possibility of recovering salvage frequently dictates the kind of papers to take when settling. It is an essential part of the claim man's job to lay the foundation for the recovery of salvage, if that is at all possible, in every case handled by him.

A man in the home office tends to conduct his business on the basis of the papers that come before him. After twenty-five years or more of that sort of thing, he finds it difficult sometimes to distinguish himself from the papers he handles and comes almost to believe that he and his papers constitute a single creature, consisting principally of hands and eyes: lots of hands and lots of eyes. Fortunately, this singular creature yields to more mature types: fortunately, because a business alive and expanding in other respects must be alive and expanding equally in respect to claims. The truth is that the most conspicuous element from the point of view of human interest in the handling of claims is the claim man himself.

The Eastern Underwriter, March 25, 1938

Response to an Enquiry

1. *Do you think a representative "American poetry" exists now, distinct from English poetry, that an "American tradition" is in process of creation? To put the question another way, do you think the American Renaissance of 1912 and the following years had permanent value?*

2. *Do you regard yourself as part of the "American tradition," as an American poet, regional or national; or as a poet simply, dissociated from nationality?*

3. *Do you think the poetry written by Americans during the last ten years shows any line of development (progression)?*

Question 1—

The relationship between Americans is at least approximately racial, and does not pretend to be anything else. We have the country in common, even if we do not always have each other. This does not make for tradition. In the case of any poem professing to be an American poem, most Englishmen would be competent to determine for themselves, by now, whether it was genuinely American. In short, there exists a clear sense of what is American. Conceding that we are racially a bit tentative, does not the sense of what we are answer your question? The less said about permanent values now-a-days, the better.

Question 2—

I should not say that I was flagrantly American, but I hope that I am American.

Question 3—

The older poets have to be considered as individuals; the younger poets, whom it is easier to see as a group, lack a leader. After all, the fury of poetry always comes from the presence of a madman or two and, at the moment, all the madmen are politicians.

Twentieth Century Verse, September–October 1938

A Note on Poetry

My intention in poetry is to write poetry: to reach and express that which, without any particular definition, everyone recognizes to be poetry, and to do this because I feel the need of doing it.

There is such a complete freedom now-a-days in respect to technique that I am rather inclined to disregard form so long as I am free and can express myself freely. I don't know of anything, respecting form, that makes much difference. The essential thing in form is to be free in whatever form is used. A free form does not assure freedom. As a form, it is just one more form. So that it comes to this, I suppose, that I believe in freedom regardless of form.

The Oxford Anthology of American Literature, 1938

Homage to T. S. Eliot

I don't know what there is (any longer) to say about Eliot. His prodigious reputation is a great difficulty.

While that sort of thing: more or less complete acceptance of it, helps to create the poetry of any poet, it also helps to destroy it.

Occasionally I pick up Eliot's poems and read them, eliminating from my mind all thought of his standing. It is like having an opportunity to see, in an out of the way place, a painting that has made a great stir: for example, it is like having a Giotto in what is called a breakfast nook.

Reading Eliot out of the pew, so to speak, goes on keeping one young. He remains an upright ascetic in a world that has grown exceedingly floppy and is growing floppier.

The Harvard Advocate, December 1938

Notes on Jean Labasque

I

It seems that painting based on the man and having a moral axis would be likely to possess a strong literary element. Mr. Labasque agrees. It would also be likely to be allegorical in nature. Since allegory is so conspicuous in moral or architectural painting, it may be that Mr. Labasque is preoccupied with "civic" painting, "civic" art. Thus, his moral and social interests would lead to a role for him, as a "civic" artist. *Préface à une peinture* read in the light of this comment contains many accents justifying the comment.

II

Mr. Labasque shows a passionate admiration for the work of Rousseau and, by inference, for the work of any primitive deriving from popular art. He works for the people or, at least, finds those that do so congenial. He is interested in communal synthesis. He is hostile to the egocentric. He believes in the human, the simple in art that springs from despair, hope, joy, emotion specified by him.

III

What he does not appear to concede is the interest in painting (from the point of view of Cézanne) on the part of the public, and in poetry. Even though the amateur is ignorant of the technique of painting (for example, the manner in which Cézanne composes), the fact remains that there is a vast amount of art criticism, art history, etc., in circulation and that this has created (or that it fosters) a class of people who "live" in this sort of thing, whether from snobbism or otherwise; and certainly there are many much better reasons than snobbism, and perfectly legitimate ones. Impressionism, in so far as the public was concerned, was a poetic movement. The parasitic developments following it were different. But if the only really great thing in modern art: impressionism, was poetic, the poetic is not to be flipped away because that particular poetic expression is *vieux jeu*.

1938–1941?

The Situation in American Writing: Seven Questions

1. *Are you conscious, in your own writing, of the existence of a "usable past"? Is this mostly American? What figures would you designate as elements in it? Would you say, for example, that Henry James's work is more relevant to the present and future of American writing than Walt Whitman's?*

2. *Do you think of yourself as writing for a definite audience? If so, how would you describe this audience? Would you say that the audience for serious American writing has grown or contracted in the last ten years?*

3. *Do you place much value on the criticism your work has received? Would you agree that the corruption of the literary supplements by advertising—in the case of the newspapers—and political pressures—in the case of the liberal weeklies—has made serious literary criticism an isolated cult?*

4. *Have you found it possible to make a living by writing the sort of thing you want to, and without the aid of such crutches as teaching and editorial work? Do you think there is any place in our present economic system for literature as a profession?*

5. *Do you find, in retrospect, that your writing reveals any allegiance to any group, class, organization, region, religion, or system of thought, or do you conceive of it as mainly the expression of yourself as an individual?*

6. *How would you describe the political tendency of American writing as a whole since 1930? How do you feel about it yourself? Are you sympathetic to the current tendency towards what may be called "literary nationalism"—a renewed emphasis, largely uncritical, on the specifically "American" elements in our culture?*

7. *Have you considered the question of your attitude towards the possible entry of the United States into the next world war? What do you think the responsibilities of writers in general are when and if war comes?*

1. The material of the imagination is reality and reality can be nothing else except the usable past. In my own case this is wholly an American past. However, it does not follow that this or that particular figure of the past is relevant to the future. It is just as easy to be diffident about James as it is to be diffident about Whitman. I suppose you have chosen these two figures as symbols; neither of them means anything to me. The projections of the past are as incalculable as the stock market; otherwise it would be nothing but a bore.

2. I do not visualize any audience. To me poetry is one of the sanctions of life and I write it because it helps me to accept and validate my experience. Writing poetry is one thing; publishing it is another. Often I wish that I did not publish it, because the act of publishing it invokes a seriousness different from the seriousness of writing it. I think that the audience for serious American writing must have grown in the last ten years.

3. Much of the criticism one receives is a good deal keener than people who have not been subjected to the same thing can know. Besides, critics are perhaps the most important part of one's audience. I doubt if business and political pressures influence the criticism of poetry to any considerable extent. The Marxist point of view is exclusive, and I suppose that extremists encounter a good deal of opposition, but that there is anything corrupt about the opposition is something else.

4. I have not tried to make a living by writing. However, the fact that writers commonly take advantage of "such crutches as teaching and editorial work" is nothing that entitles writers to indulge themselves in spasms of self-pity. Most people avail themselves of crutches of one sort or another: lawyers promote business enterprises; doctors marry rich women and buy and sell securities. I think that there is a place in the present economic system for literature as a profession.

5. Unquestionably and notwithstanding the fact that I indulge in a good deal of abstraction, I do not regard my poems as mainly an expression of myself, nor as modern in the sense in which that unpleasant commonplace is so frequently used. Still, some time ago, when I sent one of my books to an honest man in England, he wrote to me saying that he found

it personal and modern, and that these qualities were not his dish of tea.

6. I don't believe in factitious Americanism. An American has to be an American because there is nothing else for him to be and also, I hope, because it would not matter if there was. Even so, I believe in forgetting about it except as a quality, a savor.

7. I don't think that the United States should enter into the next world war, if there is to be another, unless it does so with the idea of dominating the world that comes out of it, or unless it is required to enter it in self-defense. The question respecting the responsibility of writers in war is a very theoretical question respecting an extremely practical state of affairs. A war is a military state of affairs, not a literary one. Conceding that the propagandists don't agree, does it matter that they don't agree? The role of the writer in war remains the fundamental role of the writer intensified and concentrated.

Partisan Review, Summer 1939

Concerning a Chair of Poetry

MEMORANDUM

The first step toward a Chair of Poetry is to try to fix an outline of one's intentions. One does not intend a literary course, except as the theory of poetry is a part of the theory of literature. The intention is not to read poetry from archaic to contemporary; nor is the intention to teach the writing of poetry. And, by way of a final negation, the intention is not to foster a cult.

What is intended is to study the theory of poetry in relation to what poetry has been and in relation to what it ought to be. Its literature is a part of it, and only a part of it. For this purpose, poetry means not the language of poetry but the thing itself, wherever it may be found. It does not mean verse any more than philosophy means prose. The subject-matter of poetry is the thing to be ascertained. Offhand, the subject-matter is what comes to mind when one says of the month of August . . .

"Thou art not August, unless I make thee so".

It is the aspects of the world and of men and women that have been added to them by poetry. These aspects are difficult to recognize and to measure.

While aesthetic ideas are commonplaces in this field, its import is not the import of the superficial. The major poetic idea in the world is and always has been the idea of God. One of the visible movements of the modern imagination is the movement away from the idea of God. The poetry that created the idea of God will either adapt it to our different intelligence, or create a substitute for it, or make it unnecessary. These alternatives probably mean the same thing, but the intention is not to foster a cult. The knowledge of poetry is a part of philosophy, and a part of science; the import of poetry is the import of the spirit. The figures of the essential poets should be spiritual figures. The comedy of life or the tragedy of life as the material of an art, and the mold of life as the object of its creation are contemplated.

The delicacy and significance of all this disclose that there is nothing of the sort in existence, and that to establish it would require the collaboration of men themselves acute and significant. The Chair would be either a brilliant center or pretty much nothing at all. It could not be improvised. The founder of such a Chair might well invite the collaboration of a small group to prepare the course. Or if a potent enough man could be found, the course could be developed over a period of years starting under such a man who, as he found his way, would be finding what was needed. The holder of the Chair would necessarily have to be a man of a dynamic mind and, in this field, something of a scholar and very much of an original force. A man like Dr. Santayana illustrates the character, although in him the religious and the philosophic are too dominant. He is merely cited as an illustration. It is possible that a man like T. S. Eliot illustrates the character, except that I regard him as a negative rather than a positive force. I don't think that it would be difficult to find the really serious man that is required.

If it is objected that any attraction in this scheme of things is that of an academic novelty, the answer must be that it must be an odd civilization in which poetry is not the equal of philosophy, for which many universities largely exist. It would not be initiating the study of the true nature of poetry; it would merely be initiating its study in a high academic sense, certainly in America.

Again, if it is objected that poetry is, after all, the field of exceptional people, the answer is that it has to be: it has no choice. That is one of the things that deprives it of the prestige that it would have if seen in proper perspective.

Again, if it is objected that this is carrying humanism to a point beyond which it ought to be carried in time of so much socialistic agitation, the answer must be that humanism is one thing and socialism is another, and that the mere act of distinguishing between the two should be helpful to preserve humanism and possibly to benefit socialism.

The fundamental objection is that this would be a course in illusion. I think that this requires no answer.

October 15, 1940

Note for "This Is My Best"

Poems may have, for their author, values not apparent to one who reads them. In the following group the poem, *Domination of Black*, was only one of a projected series and it has, therefore, for its author, a value as referring to many poems never actually written, which it cannot possibly have for anyone else. Other poems, *In The Carolinas* and *The Load of Sugar Cane*, for example, revive times and places on which the poems are the slightest possible notes. Thus, a personal choice of poems is obscure. This group is a personal choice and not a critical choice. It contains a good many more poems from my first book than from my last, although the poems in my last book are no doubt more important than those in my first book, more important because, as one grows older, one's objectives become clearer.

The themes of life are the themes of poetry. It seems to be, so clearly, that what is the end of life for the politician or the philosopher, say, ought to be the end of life for the poet, and that his important poems ought to be the poems of the achievement of that end. But poetry is neither politics nor philosophy. Poetry is poetry, and one's objective as a poet is to achieve poetry, precisely as one's objective in music is to achieve music. There are poets who would regard that as a scandal and who would say that a poem that had no importance except its importance as poetry had no importance at all, and that a poet who had no objective except to achieve poetry was a fribble and something less than a man of reason. We have a curious way, however, of being dependent on unexpected things, and among these are the unexpected transformations of poetry. Perhaps the poems gathered together here will illustrate these remarks. The period during which they were written, the last twenty years, has been terribly alive, and these poems have been at least related to that life.

August 10, 1942

Epitaphiana

For almost two hundred years the Stevens family was associated with the North and Southampton Reformed Church at Churchville, in Bucks County, Pennsylvania. The first few photographs are photographs of the exterior and interior of the present building of that church and of the cemetery adjoining it. The church was organized in 1710. Its first ministers were sent out from Holland and preached in Dutch to what were essentially Dutch congregations. Its early records were in Dutch.

The first Stevens in Bucks County, Abraham, was active in the church. His son John (recorded as Johannes) married

Saartje Stoothof there in 1763. Their grandson, Benjamin Stevens, was superintendent of its Sunday School for forty years. Benjamin Stevens' grandson, also Benjamin Stevens, had the gold-headed cane that was presented to his grandfather when he gave up his work in the Sunday School, and this is now in the possession of his daughter. The church was a vital center for all of them. Benjamin Stevens and his wife, Elizabeth Barcalow, and her parents, Garret Barcalow and his wife, Eleanor Hogeland, and many of their relatives and friends, are buried in this cemetery. A history of the church was printed in a pamphlet issued in 1935. The original Dutch burial ground was not at Churchville but at Feasterville. Here some of the Kroesens and John Stevens and his wife, Saartje Stoothof, are buried. At least one picture of this ancient burial ground is included here. References to these cemeteries in the genealogy of the Stevens family are, of course, based on actual visits by the genealogist.

The photographs were made in October, 1943, by Sylvia Salmi, of New York, who spent several days in Bucks County for that purpose. The landscapes are not pictures of Stevens farms, but merely show the kind of country in which the members of the family spent their lives.

1943

Introduction to Samuel French Morse's "Time of Year"

What is there about a book of first poems that immediately interests us? For one thing, it is possible that we are going to have a fresh opportunity to become aware that the people in the world, and the objects in it, and the world as a whole, are not absolute things, but, on the contrary, are the phenomena of perception. In short, it is possible that a new poet is that special person at our elbow with his special, possibly even extraordinary, perception, to whom Thoreau refers at the end of the passage from 'Autumnal Tints,' with which Mr. Morse introduces his collection. Since the perception of life is life itself, a book containing the first poems of a poet new to us has a natural and intense attraction.

This is true even if, as we turn the pages, we find them a little obstinate. But they could hardly be anything else. If we were all alike; if we were millions of people saying do, re, mi in unison, one poet would be enough and Hesiod himself would do very well. Everything he said would be in no need of expounding or would have been expounded long ago. But we are not all alike and everything needs expounding all the time because, as people live and die, each one perceiving life and death for himself, and mostly by and in himself, there develops a curiosity about the perceptions of others. This is what makes it possible to go on saying new things about old things. The fact is that the saying of new things in new ways is grateful to us. If a bootblack says that he was so tired that he lay down like a dog under a tree, he is saying a new thing about an old thing, in a new way. His new way is not a literary novelty; it is an unaffected statement of his perception of the thing.

Poems written with this in mind will often not possess, nor be intended to possess, either emotion or the music of emotion. Instead, they will possess, and be intended to possess, the 'moral beauty' that Mr. Venturi spoke of recently as being present in the painting of Cezanne. As the writer of such poems becomes more and more the master of his own poetry: that is to say, as he becomes better able to realize his individual perceptions, and as he acquires faith in his function as poet, he is likely to project the rigors of his early work into what he does later. So that his early work really discloses his identity.

What, then, is the identity of Mr. Morse? It is something that he is serious about poetry. The passage from Thoreau demonstrates that, and so do the three or four words from Job which, in the Bible, follow the verse in which Job cries

Or seest thou as man seeth?

But what is his exact character as a poet? One of his poems, 'The Track into the Swamp,' relates to one of the abandoned roads, the lost roads, of which New England is so full. We have been accustomed to think that at the far end of such roads the ghosts of the Transcendentalists still live. Obviously they do not live at this end. Mr. Morse is not the ghost of a Transcendentalist. If he has any use at all for Kant, it is to keep up the window in which the cord is broken. He is anti-transcendental.

His subject is the particulars of experience. He is a realist; he tries to get at New England experience, at New England past and present, at New England foxes and snow and thunderheads. When he generalizes, as in 'End of a Year,' his synthesis is essentially a New England synthesis. He writes about his own people and his own objects as closely as possible according to his own perception. This rectitude characterizes everything that he does.

1943

"There was a mother chicken"

There was a mother chicken had three little chickies. The oldest one: a boy chickie, was called Mr. Haff; the next oldest one was called David-Holly, and the baby was called Clover-Smelly.

Once the mother chicken had to be away from home for a period of time. She took the little chickies to their grandmother. She asked their grandmother whether she would take care of them. The grandmother said "I will do the best I can but three little chickies are a good deal to take care of". The mother chicken asked the grandmother whether she could not get some one to help her. She said that she had a neighbor, Mr. Rooster, who was as amiable as he was handsome, and who was fond of music, especially crowing.

Mr. Rooster agreed to assist the grandmother. He tried to teach the little chickies how to crow. He had no trouble with Mr. Haff, because Mr. Haff was a boy chickie and could crow very well. He taught him to crow this way: Ki-ki-ri-ki, Ko-ko-ro-ko, Koo-koo-roo-koo.

He had some trouble with David-Holly every time he tried to teach David-Holly. David-Holly was a boy chickie and could crow very well. He could not teach Clover-Smelly to crow at all because she was just a baby.

After a while the mother chickie came back and Mr. Rooster showed her how well he had taught Mr. Haff and David-Holly to crow. The mother chicken was so pleased and so happy and she liked Mr. Rooster so much that she asked him to become her husband, and so they were married and lived happily together in a little house of their own.

1943?

A Ceremony

In the sixteen hundreds, three brothers left Holland to seek their fortunes. One found his way to Ceylon where he took up life with a herd of elephants. In his discourse before the elephants, he said that he was human, believing that this alone would be enough to establish himself among them. But the tradition of men among elephants was not the same as it was among men themselves; and the elephants concluding that man in general was less worthy of his tradition among other men than of his tradition among elephants condemned him and trampled him to death.

The second brother went to Brazil. Leaving the Dutch fort near Belem and pushing up the Amazon to a remote position, he was attacked by Indians, who had never before seen a Dutchman. When taken prisoner, he tried to procure his liberty by indicating, as best he could, that he was not an enemy, that in spite of many differences he and they were or could be friends and allies. The Indians, notwithstanding a tradition among them respecting Spaniards, determined to spare his life. They disarmed him and kept him a prisoner until his death. They held off from him, since they had no single tradition in common; and when they buried him they built a mound for him far from their own.

The third brother came to New Netherland and bought a farm at New Utrecht. He became a neighbor of people who had left Holland when he was a boy, to whom he brought letters and news from home and word of parents and friends. He had come from Leyden and was welcome, as any one from an old land is welcome among those that have left it and know it and know him. His merely being what he was composed of him and for him a tradition that was recognized. On his death he was buried under the altar of his church.

The ghosts of these three men met at dinner a long time later. The first ghost said of his discourse before the elephants that the appeal to tradition is not an appeal that can be made to barbarians, whether elephants or otherwise, since it is predicated on something that is held in common honor; and that it is this holding in common honor that gives it compulsion. The second ghost said of his dumb-show in the presence of the Indians that tradition is not ourselves imitating ourselves. If it was that, it would be what is left of the past and nothing more. Tradition is more than the memory and the customs of the memory. It is life's experiment made knowingly. The third ghost said that tradition is something that awakens a sense not only of that to which it relates but of itself. Thus when he had brought news of the university at Leyden to the fiscaal in New Amsterdam, when he had delivered messages from the many uncles who had stayed at home, when he had described the new banners in the old church, it was not only that the exiles to whom he spoke were back in Holland again, but that they felt a pride in having been, or of being still, a part of that of which such things could be said. The third ghost said that it is that pride, that warmth of feeling about many things, not only great things but also things small and dear to us, things held in common honor by those that have gone before us and by ourselves, that awaken a sense that tradition is like the revelations of an instinct.

At this moment, there entered into the room in which the three ghosts were having their dinner, together with a much larger company of persons dining there, as if they were a single body or society, a group of men carrying a kind of litter, on which they bore an ancient bird of lead, a cock desperate to be abroad with all his feathers fighting the wind. At this gallant sight, the whole company rose to salute the procession waving their napkins in the air in a storm, in the midst of which the three ghosts suddenly vanished.

FANFARE IN THE MODE
OF
MYNHEER VAN DONK

PROCESSION

1944

Response to an Enquiry

What do you believe to be the major problem or problems facing the young writer in America today?

Today, in America, all rôles yield to that of the politician.

The rôle of the poet may be fixed by contrasting it to that of the politician. The poet absorbs the general life: the public life. The politician is absorbed by it. The poet is individual. The politician is general. It is the personal in the poet that is the origin of his poetry. If this is true respecting the relation of the poet to the public life and respecting the origin of his poetry, it follows that the first phase of his problem is himself.

This does not mean that he is a private figure. On the other hand, it does mean that he must not allow himself to be absorbed as the politician is absorbed. He must remain individual. As individual he must remain free. The politician expects everyone to be absorbed as he himself is absorbed. This expectation is part of the sabotage of the individual. The second phase of the poet's problem, then, is to maintain his freedom, the only condition in which he can hope to produce significant poetry.

If people are to become dependent on poetry for any of the fundamental satisfactions, poetry must have an increasing intellectual scope and power. This is a time for the highest poetry. We never understood the world less than we do now nor, as we understand it, liked it less. We never wanted to understand it more nor needed to like it more. These are the intense compulsions that challenge the poet as the appreciatory creator of values and beliefs. That, finally, states the problem.

I have not touched on form which, although significant, is not vital today, as substance is. When one is an inherent part of the other, form, too, is vital.

The Yale Literary Magazine, Spring 1946

Rubbings of Reality

If a man writes a little every day, as Williams does, or used to do, it may be that he is merely practicing in order to make perfect. On the other hand he may be practicing in order to get at his subject. If his subject is, say, a sense, a mood, an integration, and if his representation is faint or obscure, and if he practices in order to overcome his faintness or obscurity, what he really does is to bring, or try to bring, his subject into that degree of focus at which he sees it, for a moment, as it is and at which he is able to represent it in exact definition.

A man does not spend his life doing this sort of thing unless doing it is something he needs to do. One of the sanctions of the writer is that he is doing something that he needs to do. The need is not the desire to accomplish through writing something not incidental to the writing itself. Thus a political or a religious writer writes for political or religious reasons. Williams writes, I think, in order to write. He needs to write.

What is the nature of this need? What does a man do when he delineates the images of reality? Obviously, the need is a general need and the activity a general activity. It is of our nature that we proceed from the chromatic to the clear, from the unknown to the known. Accordingly the writer who practices in order to make perfect is really practicing to get at his subject and, in that exercise, is participating in a universal activity. He is obeying his nature. Imagism (as one of Williams' many involvements, however long ago) is not something superficial. It obeys an instinct. Moreover, imagism is an ancient phase of poetry. It is something permanent. Williams is a writer to whom writing is the grinding of a glass, the polishing of a lens by means of which he hopes to be able to see clearly. His delineations are trials. They are rubbings of reality.

The modern world is the result of such activity on a grand scale, not particularly in writing but in everything. It may be said, for instance, that communism is an effort to improve the human focus. The work of Picasso is an attempt to get at his subject, an attempt to achieve a reality of the intelligence. But the world of the past was equally the result of such activity. Thus the German pietists of the early 1700's who came to Pennsylvania to live in the caves of the Wissahickon and to dwell in solitude and meditation were proceeding, in their way, from the chromatic to the clear. Is not Williams in a sense a literary pietist, chastening himself, incessantly, along the Passaic?

This is an intellectual *tenue*. It is easy to see how underneath the chaos of life today and at the bottom of all the disintegrations there is the need to see, to understand: and, in so far as one is not completely baffled, to re-create. This is not emotional. It springs from the belief that we have only our own intelligence on which to rely. This manifests itself in many ways, in every living art as in every living phase of politics or science. If we could suddenly re-make the world on the basis of our own intelligence, see it clearly and represent it without faintness or obscurity, Williams' poems would have a place there.

Briarcliff Quarterly, October 1946

Homage to Henry Church

As I saw him in New York, although he was withdrawn, he was eager to make friends and it was clear that his friendships were precious to him. This sort of duality: being withdrawn and at the same time being eager to make friends, was characteristic of him. Thus, in New York, he seemed to be essentially of Paris and, very likely, in Paris, he seemed to be essentially of New York. He was a simple man who had little interest in things that were not complex. He was a plain man who lived in a certain luxury which he ignored. He was most literate yet had only a few books on his table. He had read philosophy for forty years but it seemed to be, for him, pretty much a substitute for fiction. Ideas were the bread of life to him, but, although I saw him frequently, what he actually enjoyed was not the discussion of ideas, but casual conversations. When Mrs. Church and he and I would meet to go somewhere for lunch he would appear to be as hungry as a wolf. Nevertheless he would choose what he wanted fastidiously and be most abstemious in what he ate of it. He would study a wine list a long time and then drink a single sip.

He came all smiles to our meetings. Perhaps he had been reading Nietzsche until two or three o'clock that morning and had slept late and was looking forward to coming out of his hotel into the bright sunshine of the New York streets. At this moment, he was the sedentary man on the go; he was the man who had spent half the night in reflection recovering himself and almost willing to chatter, almost but not quite. He liked to be still in the midst of activity.

Because of the existence in him of these opposites, two things followed, one, that he seemed often to be an enigma and, the other, when one realized the truth about him, that he was always a potential figure. Here was an American who lived in France, or, say, a Frenchman who made long visits to America; a man who had studied music but never mentioned the subject; a man who loved the hurly-burly of New York and yet shrank from what was aggressive and over-robust; a native, so to speak, of Versailles who liked the oil derricks on the lawns of houses in Oklahoma. He clung to his American origin faithfully and affectionately, to the elderly cousin who lived alone with cats and plants, to the cousin in business who was so obviously dear to him. He was not in the least sentimental. It was Chicago that impressed him. He looked at this country as a foreigner looks at it.

In the end this delineates a figure more than potential. He was as eager to make friends of life as he was to make friends of people and this he had accomplished to an extraordinary degree.

Fall 1947

The Shaper

Paul Rosenfeld was a shaper who lived a life of shaping, that is to say, a *Schöpfer*, who lived for the sake of *Schöpfung*. Perhaps there existed for him an ideal *Schöpfung*, a world composed of music, but which did not whirl round in music alone; or of painting, but which did not expand in color and form alone; or of poetry, but which did not limit itself to the *explication orphique* of the poet. But whether or not there was an ideal *Schöpfung*, in which everything coalesced, toward which everything converged, the truth about him seems to be that he was incessantly engaged or involved or attracted by the activity of shaping.

This is the life of the artist, whether the artist be the young sculptor or the old politician, or, say, sociologist; whether the artist be the young Spanish painter or the barbarian statesman. Thus, if the uncertainty in the case of Rosenfeld suggested by the words "engaged or involved or attracted" had been a certainty, if the shaping had been the obsession of a single shape, if the fascinated interest had become a determination of the will to be executed with all the *Schöpferkraft* of which he was capable, we should have said, afterward, that this urbane and somewhat placid figure had not really surprised us. The uninterrupted activity of shaping dissipated the possibility of an ultimate shape.

This constant shaping, as distinguished from constancy of shape, is characteristic of the poet. Rosenfeld appears to have been too eagerly sensitive to the figures about him to be able to isolate himself or to permit himself to be isolated, in any single shaping of his own. He was the young man (for a long time) of eager intelligence, conscious of the creative forces of his generation and delighting in them. In a way, he lived and spoke in constant praise of his generation. It may be that his generation as a whole was the ideal *Schöpfung* to which Rosenfeld has been related. He was conscious of his generation as a whole and while he may have praised it without thinking that that was what he was doing, he would have done it just the same had it occurred to him because, although he itemized, the sum of the items was his generation. In short, he saw the world in his character as poet. To be explicit, he delighted in and praised the poetry in the activity of the young sculptor, the young painter, and so on.

To be still more explicit, his character as poet made it easy and natural for him to give character to the young poet, the most inchoate of human beings and yet potentially the most choate. If it should not be quite true that poets are born, not made, it seems certain that if made they must be made shortly after being born. Even then they lose character quickly. The existence of certain figures checks this loss of character. The figure most likely to do this seems to be that of the perfectly normal creature who is touched by poetry, the man of intelligence who discloses by his interest and sympathy that poetry is something significant to him. Rosenfeld was such a character.

He was not the critic angered by the idea that poetry is so much twaddle fit for fools. He was a poet himself; and he would as soon have thought that philosophy is the nonsense of apt comedians. As a member of a group, as a familiar figure, without eccentricity, saying and writing things of understanding, he communicated confidence and discipline, and a sense of the necessity of both; and in that, too, he was shaping, helping to give shape, to those to whom that meant becoming choate.

Paul Rosenfeld: Voyager in the Arts, 1948

John Crowe Ransom: Tennessean

What John Crowe Ransom does is to make a legend of reality. One picks up a sense of his personality in its native condition without any of the trophies of his experience as an outsider. It might be clearer to say before any of the trophies, etc., instead of without, because the reality of which he makes a legend is the reality of Tennessee. They say that there are even more Ransoms in Tennessee than Tates in Kentucky. However that may be, the more there are of you, the more you possess and the more you are possessed. To be a Ransom in Tennessee is something more precious than it is easy to say.

There are scholars who have never been anybody anywhere
and never will be. Mr. Ransom is not one of them. It is hard
in speaking of this sort of thing to keep on the right side.
When one speaks of the personality of the Tennessean, the
exact sense one has of the words cannot be conveyed hastily.
The Tennessean is not the New Englander. He is not the
Westerner. He is not even the Southerner. He lives in a land
of his own as endeared and as beloved as any in the world,
and among a people, whose chief characteristic is its raciness.
He would say that he lives in Tennessee and among the Ten-
nesseans and it would be the same thing. I don't in the least
mean anything romantic. On the contrary, I mean a real land
and a real people and I mean Mr. Ransom as the instinct and
expression of them.

One turns with something like ferocity toward a land that
one loves, to which one is really and essentially native, to de-
mand that it surrender, reveal, that in itself which one loves.
This is a vital affair, not an affair of the heart (as it may be in
one's first poems), but an affair of the whole being (as in one's
last poems), a fundamental affair of life, or, rather, an affair of
fundamental life; so that one's cry of O Jerusalem becomes
little by little a cry to something a little nearer and nearer until
at last one cries out to a living name, a living place, a living
thing, and in crying out confesses openly all the bitter secre-
tions of experience. This is why trivial things often touch us
intensely. It is why the sight of an old berry patch, a new
growth in the woods in the spring, the particular things on
display at a farmers' market, as, for example, the trays of poor
apples, the few boxes of black-eyed peas, the bags of dried
corn, have an emotional power over us that for a moment is
more than we can control.

There are men who are not content merely to acknowledge
these emotions. There are men who must understand them,
who isolate them in order to understand them. Once they
understand them it may be said that they cease to be natives.
They become outsiders. Yet it is certain that, at will, they be-
come insiders again. In ceasing to be natives they have become
insiders and outsiders at once. And where this happens to a
man whose life is that of the thinker, the poet, the philoso-
pher, the teacher, and in a broad generalized sense, the artist,

while his activity may appear to be that of the outsider, the insider remains as the base of his character, the essential person, something fixed, the play of his thoughts, that on which he lavishes his sense of the prodigious and the legendary, the material of his imagination.

Mr. Ransom's poems are composed of Tennessee. It would not necessarily be the case that the poems of a native of another land would be composed of that land. But a Tennessean has no choice. O Jerusalem. O Appalachia. Above everything else Mr. Ransom's poems are not composed of the books he has read, of the academies he has seen, of the halls and columns and carvings on the columns, the stairs and towers and doorways and tombs, the wise old men and the weak young men of nowhere in particular, going nowhere at all. He himself comes out of a region dense with a life of its own, so individualized that he can tell a fellow countryman by a thousand things and not know how he does it. It is not a question of his being bold enough to be himself. He is of that hard stuff on which a mountain has been bearing down for a long time with such a weight that its impress on him has passed into everything he does and passes, through him, outward, a long distance.

But it is as a legend. As he grew into an outsider without ceasing to be an insider, it was as if everything to which he was native took on a special quality, an exact identity, a microscopic reality, which, only for what it was, had a value because it was wholly free from his outsidedness. This is what happens to things we love. He picked it up and took it with him. He drew a picture of it, many pictures of it, in his books. The greater the value he set on it, the dearer it became, the more closely he sought out its precise line and look, the more it became a legend, the peculiar legend of things as they are when they are as we want them to be, without any of the pastiche of which the presence vulgarizes so many legends and possibly everything legendary in things, not as they are, but as we should like them to be.

The Sewanee Review, Summer 1948

The State of American Writing, 1948:
Seven Questions

1. *What, in your opinion, are the new literary tendencies or figures, if any, that have emerged in the forties? How does the literary atmosphere of this decade compare with that of the thirties? In what way, too, does the present period differ from the first postwar period? Can the differences between the two postwar periods be defined in relation to the European situation?*

2. *Do you think that American middlebrow culture has grown more powerful in this decade? In what relation does this middlebrow tendency stand to serious writing—does it threaten or bolster it?*

3. *What is the meaning of the literary revivals (James, Forster, Fitzgerald, etc.) that have taken place of late? Is this a publishing phenomenon or is it an organic literary interest in the sense that the rediscovered writers of the past are in some way truly expressive of current literary needs?*

4. *It is the general opinion that, unlike the twenties, this is not a period of experiment in language and form. If that is true, what significance can be attached to this fact? Does present writing base itself on the earlier experimentation, in the sense that it has creatively assimilated it, or can it be said that the earlier experimentation came to a dead end?*

5. *In the twenties most writers were free-lancers, whereas now many make their living by teaching in universities. Has this change affected the tone and mood of literature in our time? Can it with justice be said that American writing has grown more academic since the twenties?*

6. *In recent decades serious literary criticism has shown a special bent for the analysis and interpretation of poetry. What is the significance of this concentration at a time when poetry itself has had an ever-diminishing audience? Would literature benefit from a critical concern, equally intense, with other genres of writing? In our time, when the fate of culture as a whole is called into question, does the basic meaning of the literary effort stand in need of reexamination?*

7. *What is the effect on American writing of the growing tension between Soviet Communism and the democratic coun-*

tries? How are cultural interests affected by this struggle and do you think a writer should involve himself in it (as writer? as person?) to the point of commitment?

These answers are limited to parts of questions 4, 6 and 7 and to poetry.

Experiment in language. Poetry is nothing if it is not experiment in language. A recent remark by de Rougemont,

"Le vrai superstitieux se moque des superstitions comme le vrai poète des sujets et des mots poétiques,"

explains this. The poet records his experience as poet in subjects and words which are part of that experience. He knows that nothing but the truth of that experience means anything to him or to anyone else. Experiment in respect to subjects and words is the effort on his part to record the truth of that experience.

In this statement the experience is central and experiment is the struggle with the experience and here experiment, also, is central. But often there is little, even no, experience and here experiment is merely experiment. The opinion that, unlike the twenties, this is not a period of experiment seems to be right in respect to experience in both senses. In respect to central experiment, the experience of the poet as poet may be too much or too little for him to record as yet: too much and too immediate or too little and not near enough; and so it may never be recorded at all. In respect to experiment that is merely experiment, this seems, in the circumstances, to be a pastime proper for Nero's children's children.

If these things are fluctuations of literary modes, what is the cause of the fluctuations? It may be simply our experience of life. To sum this up, central experiment is one of the constants of the spirit which is inherent in a true record of experience. But experiment for the sake of experiment has no such significance. Our present experience of life is too violent to be congenial to experiment in either sense. There is also the consideration that the present time succeeds a time of experiment. Theoretically a period of attempts at a world revolution should destroy or endanger all stationary poetic subjects and words and be favorable in the highest degree to the recording of fresh experience. But the vivification of reality has not yet occurred in spite of the excitement. Only the excitement has occurred.

Experiment in form. So, too, experiment in form is one of the constants of the spirit. Much of what has been said about subjects and words applies to form. There is, however, a usage with respect to form as if form in poetry was a derivative of plastic shape. The tendency to visualize form is illustrated by the way a reference to form becomes a reference to the appearance of the poem on the page as in the case of a poem in the shape of a pear, say, or a poem without any shape at all. Such trivialities show that the record of a man's experience in the modern world is not a derivative of plastic shape. Modern poetry is not a privilege of heteroclites. Poetic form in its proper sense is a question of what appears within the poem itself. It seems worth while to isolate this because it is always form in its inimical senses that destroys poetry. By inimical senses one means the trivialities. By appearance within the poem itself one means the things created and existing there. The trivialities matter little today and most people concede that poetic form is not a question of literary mode.

About poetry. It is not necessary to answer the last question relating to the fate of culture in order to consider the present position of poetry. That question implies that an understanding of the basic meaning of literary effort involves the fate of culture. Certainly a critical concern with poetry involves an understanding of the basic meaning of literary effort. Perhaps the present interest in the analysis and interpretation of poetry is in itself an attempt to get at the basic meaning of literary effort.

It seems that poetic order is potentially as significant as philosophic order. Accordingly, it is natural to project the idea of a theory of poetry that would be pretty much the same thing as a theory of the world based on a coordination of the poetic aspects of the world. Such an idea completely changes the significance of poetry. It does what poetry itself does, that is to say, it leads to a fresh conception of the world. The sense of this latent significance exists. Many sensitive readers of poetry, without being mystics or romantics or metaphysicians, feel that there probably is available in reality something accessible through a theory of poetry which would make a profound difference in our sense of the world. The interest in the analysis and interpretation of poetry is the same thing as an interest in poetry itself. For that reason it is not possible to speak of an enlarged audience for the analysis and interpretation of poetry and at the same time of a diminishing audience for poetry itself. The analysis and interpretation of poetry are perceptions of poetry.

You may not regard these answers as responsive to questions that contemplate literary tendencies, literary atmosphere, literary interest, literary criticism, and so on. One's interest is, however, an interest in life and in reality. From this point of view it is easy to say that the basic meaning of literary effort, and, therefore, of poetry, is with reference to life and reality and not with reference to politics. The basic meaning of the effort of any man to record his experience as poet is to produce poetry, not politics. The poet must stand or fall by poetry. In the conflict between the poet and the politician the chief honor the poet can hope for is that of remaining himself. Life and reality, on the one hand, and politics, on the other, notwithstanding the activity of politics, are not interchangeable terms. They are not the same thing, whatever the Russians may pretend.

Partisan Review, August 1948

A Comment on Meaning in Poetry

Things that have their origin in the imagination or in the emotions (poems) very often have meanings that differ in nature from the meanings of things that have their origin in reason. They have imaginative or emotional meanings, not rational meanings, and they communicate these meanings to people who are susceptible to imaginative or emotional meanings. They may communicate nothing at all to people who are open only to rational meanings. In short, things that have their origin in the imagination or in the emotions very often take on a form that is ambiguous or uncertain. It is not possible to attach a single, rational meaning to such things without destroying the imaginative or emotional ambiguity or uncertainty that is inherent in them and that is why poets do not like to explain. That the meanings given by others are sometimes meanings not intended by the poet or that were never present in his mind does not impair them as meanings. On the inside cover of the album of Mahler's Fifth Symphony recently issued by Columbia there is a note on the meanings of that work. Bruno Walter, however, says that he never heard Mahler intimate that the symphony had any meanings except the meanings of the music. Does this impair the meanings of the commentators as meanings? Certainly this music had no single meaning which alone was the meaning intended and to which one is bound to penetrate. If it had, what justification could the composer have had for concealing it? The score with its markings contains any meaning that imaginative and sensitive listeners find in it. It takes very little to experience the variety in everything. The poet, the musician, both have explicit meanings but they express them in the forms these take and not in explanation.

The Explicator, November 1948

Marcel Gromaire

Catalogues for exhibitions of pictures are the natural habitat of the prose-poem. But in the case of Marcel Gromaire one feels that the need for definition comes first.

Gromaire was born in 1892 in the Département du Nord. This is the Département farthest North East in France beginning at the edge of the North Sea and running, in a narrow strip of farms and factories, half of the whole length of the Belgian border. It is a region in which the relationship with the Belgian of the present and, more particularly, the kinship with the Fleming of the past are strong, so strong, in the case of Gromaire that one's immediate impression of his work is that it is work typical of the mystical realism of a Northerner. One does not usually think of Frenchmen as mystical realists or Northerners.

Yet, for all that, Gromaire is very much of a Frenchman. He lives in Paris and has his atelier there. The paintings shown in the present exhibition are paintings of his maturity. He is now fifty-seven. Some critics have spoken of elements in his work derived from Matisse and Soutine and others have denied these derivations. Certainly, Gromaire is in no way derivative. His principal characteristic is that he is just the opposite. These oddly hallucinatory tableaux (in the English sense) are the pictures of a determined man, somewhat possessed, predestined and, because of these characteristics, also rebellious. Being rebellious is being oneself and being oneself is not being one of the automata of one's time. In consequence of being himself, Gromaire's appearances come to us, one by one, as he experiences them and not as part of the day's great, common flocks and herds and shoals of things alike.

One thing that he is determined about is substance. This is one of the truths about Gromaire. He himself speaks of "la recherche de la substance": the pursuit of substance. By substance he means the spiritual fund of the picture, the fund originating in the thought and feeling of the artist and perceptible in the painting. He does not mean the picture as itself a spiritual fund, except in that objective way. He speaks of "la qualité des oeuvres, qui est leur vie même et leur pensée profonde": the property of works which is their very life and profound meaning. He speaks of the human spirit seeking its own architecture, its own "mesure" that will enable it to be in harmony with the world. It is from the intensity, the passion, of this search that the quality of works is derived, not from the codes and manuals of painting compiled by doctrinaires and conformist pedagogues. And this is the quality sought after by the clairvoyant spectator. These remarks illustrate Gromaire's mystical side.

At the same time he postulates an "art directement social" which transmits itself to the spectator without mediation or explanation, as much by reason of its "chimie intérieure": sublimation, say, as by the idea which it materializes; social in the sense of something that affects the march of events, fixes the ephemeral sensation and makes it possible for this sensation "grâce à cette pérennité conquise, d'agir sur le futur et sur le comportement humain," makes it possible for the ephemeral sensation, thanks to this acquired characteristic of being perennial, to act on the future and on human behavior. This is not the language of the individual escapist. On the contrary it is that of a painter who visualizes a great epoch for his art, in which painting instead of being "un jeu désespéré": a spiritless game, will be as he says "un don continu et fraternel, la présence de l'homme et du rhythme universel qui nous régit" or, paraphrased, a brother's constant giving, a human association and the activity of the universal rhythm that dominates us.

These statements of theory define Gromaire in his own words. They help us to look at his pictures as they are: heterodox, slightly grim (an orthodox element in anything intended to be social comment), dense in color, as becomes a Goth, rugged with realism (what one expects of pictures much thought over and not exclusively sensory or abstract), uncompromising, in the idiom of Verhaeren, endowed with the strength that comes from participation in life's struggle, full of the mesmeric presence of meanings below the surface, things not of the school of Paris, but of some harsher, more fundamental zone—and one need only have in mind, say, much of Europe, much of everywhere, always.

Gromaire: Exhibition of Paintings, Louis Carré Gallery, 1949

Response to an Enquiry

1. Is it nonsense to talk of a typical American poem? If not, what, in your opinion, are the qualities which tend to distinguish a poem as 'American'?

2. Do you consider that the language of American poetry (vocabulary, use of vocabulary, metric, cadences, syntax, punctuation) differs notably from that of English poetry? Is this difference (if any) fortuitous, or does it correspond to some underlying difference of sensibility?

3. Has American poetry been affected by those trends in English poetry in the thirties typified by the work of Auden, Spender, Day Lewis and MacNeice?

4. Has American poetry been affected by the romanticism now prevalent in English poetry, and represented in varying ways by the work of Dylan Thomas, George Barker, The New Apocalypse, Personalism, and the later poetry of Miss Edith Sitwell?

1. At bottom this question is whether there is such a thing as an American. If there is, the poems that he writes are American poems. And a typical American poem is merely a matter of choice as between one of his poems and another. It must be as easy to distinguish an American poem from a Maori poem as it is to distinguish an American from a Maori. While it is not always so easy to distinguish an American poem from an English poem, after all would *Snow-Bound* sound quite like an English poem to you? Would you be likely to mistake *Leaves of Grass* for something English? *Snow-Bound* is a typical American poem. The poems in *Leaves of Grass* are typical American poems. Even if a difference was not to be found in anything else, it could be found in what we write about. We live in two different physical worlds and it is not nonsense to think that that matters.

2. No. At the same time, I think that there is an underlying difference of sensibility. We use the same language in pretty much the same way that you do, in print. While there are variations in vocabulary and no doubt variations in other respects, the difference, in print, is not notable.

3. My answer to this is included in my answer to 4.

4. Undoubtedly American poetry has been enriched by all of the poets mentioned in questions 3 and 4. I think that Americans find English poetry extremely to their liking. We give ourselves up to it, not at all because it is English, but because in the minute differences between it and our own poetry we find something that has a poetic value in itself.

Modern American Poetry, 1950

Three Paraphrases from Léon-Paul Fargue

I should like to close this program by turning, now, for a very few minutes, to the work of someone else, a Frenchman, Léon-Paul Fargue, who lived as a poet all his life in Paris and died there two or three years ago. As a boy of eight or nine he was a member of Mallarmé's class in English at the Collège Rollin and ten years or more thereafter became one of those that were accustomed to gather in Mallarmé's apartment. He was a friend of Paul Valéry for fifty years. I suppose it could be said that during the greater part of the last half-century he knew everyone in Paris having to do with poetry. It is not possible to comment on his work beyond saying that most of his poems were prose poems. Claudine Chonez in a study that she made of him for the series, *Poètes d'Aujourd'hui*, Poets of To-Day, speaks (p. 66) of the solemnity of his strophe, of its somewhat ritual, not to say theatrical character. I shall read paraphrases of two of the poems contained in *Poèmes* (1912), his first book of importance, and the one best liked, and also of a page of his prose from *Portraits de Famille* (1947). I call these translations paraphrases because, in order to carry over the sense of cadence, paraphrase seemed more useful than literal translation.

Dans un quartier (*Poèmes* p. 59)

In a quarter made drowsy by the odor of its gardens and of its trees, the ramp of dreams, in the distance, accelerates and retards its chords, a little, in the autumn weather . . .

What gorgeous aspects cluster over their pale Calvary! What gestures evoke the chants of latent and unrealized dreams! What hands have opened penetrations into landscapes where things remembered come to sight like the perspectives of roofs seen by lightning . . .

A road lamp bides its time at the end of the gravel walk that leads to the villa lost beneath the leaves, in which a light rain still drips.

The angel is there, no doubt, at the keyboard, under the plume of the shade; and his noble visage, and his hands, on which the rings put forth touches toward the light, are bright with a steadfast flame.

The bird troubled by some secret of the Islands, and yet concealing it, picks up its song, in its basketry of gold!

A terrace of autumn. A white villa placed like something on the watch at the terminal of the walk in the bitter odor. A thought as of gold falls down with sad descent. The blinds have been drawn in the rooms in which the idylls are dead.

Un odeur nocturne (*Poèmes*, p. 90)

A fragrance of night, not to be defined, that brings on an obscure doubt, exquisite, tender, comes by the open window into the room where I am at work . . .

My cat watches the darkness, as rigid as a jug. A fortune of subtle seeing looks at me through its green eyes . . .

The lamp sings its slight song quietly, subdued as the song one hears in a shell. The lamp reaches out its placating hands. In its aureole, I hear the litanies, the choruses and the responses of flies. It lights up the flowers at the edge of the terrace. The nearest ones come forward timidly to see me, like a troop of dwarfs that discover an ogre . . .

The minute violin of a mosquito goes on and on. One could believe that a person was playing alone in a house at a remote distance . . . Insects fall with a sidewise fall and writhe gently on the table. A butterfly yellow as a wisp of straw drags itself along the little yellow valley that is my book . . .

A big clock outdoors intones drearily. Memories take motion like children dancing in a ring . . .

The cat stretches itself to the uttermost. Its nose traces in the air an imperceptible evolution. A fly fastens its scissors in the lamp . . .

Kitchen clatter mounts in a back-yard. Argumentative voices play at pigeon-vole. A carriage starts up and away. A train chugs at the next station. A long whistle rises far-off . . .

I think of someone whom I love, who is so little to be so separated, perhaps beyond the lands covered by the night, beyond the profundities of water. I am not able to engage her glance . . .

Segonzac Ou L'Artiste (*Portraits de Famille* 171)

Between the things of these twenty years, between the sensations of these twenty years and the eye of Segonzac, there have been exchanges, secret, puissant, unerring, which he has inscribed in lasting stone. His faces, his portraits, his Morin, whom he loves like a son, his strolls around circuses, his bathers of Saint-Tropez, his heads of calves, his willows and his harvests sometimes, for me, finish by having the documentary value of postage-stamps. What I want to say is that they illustrate messages of precise origin, well-defined sensations, about which it is impossible to be mistaken. For me, the true artist appears to be like that: he is a witness. Sometimes a guide. Through him should shine the time that inspired him, of which he has disengaged in traits of fire the special symbols, the forms, the views, the spiritual habit as well as the positions of trees or of villages that belong to this time round the carrousel. That the National Library has now hastened to recognize in Segonzac this social role and this talent compounded of instinct and authority, shows that our poor old country is far from being down and out.

I read recently in a review these lines over which I meditated: "What is left today of the misty sheets of water of Corot, of those glades where the gold of the sun filtered, rich and clear, through the foliage woven by Courbet, and of these celebrated slopes of the Seine, so Second Empire, of Renoir, of Manet, and of Monet. What is left of the rose and blue snows of Monet?

"Yes: but where are last year's snows?"

What is left? Well, for one thing, men like Segonzac, who carry on, quite simply, who lead tradition by the hand, up to the point where it meets what is modern. A modernity which they pass through without becoming too splashed up, always to find again, on the appointed day, the durable, the classic, the incontestable.

Read at YMHA Poetry Center, New York, 1951

On Receiving the Gold Medal from the Poetry Society of America

I am happy to receive this evening's medal and grateful that a society occupying the position of the Poetry Society of America should think me worthy of this award. Thank you. That the medal should be presented in the name of a young poet makes it all the more precious, since, among all the images of the poet, the purest is that of the young poet.

We are, here, a group of people who regard poetry as one of the sanctions of life. We believe it to be a vital engagement between the imagination and reality. The outcome of that engagement, if successful, is fulfillment. We say, also, that poetry is an instrument of the will to perceive the innumerable accords, whether of the imagination or of reality, that make life a thing different from what it would be without such insights. If we are right, then, from this serious point of view, the act of bestowing an honor on a poet is equal to the honor of receiving it.

The other day, in the middle of January, as I was taking a walk in Elizabeth Park, in Hartford, I saw a little distance across the snow a group of automobiles that had pulled up on one side of the road. A dozen people or more got out of them. They took off their coats and threw them together in a pile on the asphalt. It was then possible to see that this was a wedding party. Often in the summer, particularly on Saturday mornings, one sees such parties there. They come to have photographs taken in the gardens. But these people had come in January. The bride stood up in white satin covered with a veil. An ornament in her hair caught the sunlight and sparkled brightly in the cold wind. The bridesmaids were dressed in dark crimson gowns with low necks. They carried armfuls of chrysanthemums. One of the men stood in the snow taking pictures of the bride, then of the bride surrounded by the bridesmaids, and so on, until nothing more was possible. Now, this bride with her gauze and glitter was the genius of poetry. The only thing wrong with her was that she was out of place.

What is the apt locale of the genius of poetry? As it happens, she creates her own locale as she goes along. Unlike the bride, she recognizes that she cannot impose herself on the scene. She is the spirit of visible and invisible change. She knows that if poetry is one of the sanctions of life, if it is truly a vital engagement between man and his environment of the world, if it is genuinely a means by which to achieve balance and measure in our circumstances, it is something major and not minor; and that if it is something major it must have its place with other major things. And knowing this and in consequence of it, she has herself chosen as her only apt locale in a final sense the love and thought of the poet, where everything she does is right and reasonable. Her power to change is so great that out of the love and thought of individual poets she makes the love and thought of the poet, the single image. Out of that which is often untutored and seemingly incapable of being tutored, insensible to custom and law, marginal, grotesque, without a past, the creation of unfortunate chance, she evolves a power that dominates life, a central force so subtle and so familiar that its presence is most often unrealized. Individual poets, whatever their imperfections may be, are driven all their lives by that inner companion of the conscience which is, after all, the genius of poetry in their hearts and minds. I speak of a companion of the conscience because to every faithful poet the faithful poem is an act of conscience.

The answer I have given to the question as to the apt locale of the genius of poetry is also the answer to the question as to the position of poetry in the world today. There is no doubt that poetry does in fact exist for the thoughtful young man in Basel or the votary in Naples. The Marxians, and for that matter a good many other people, think of it in terms of its social impact. In one direction it moves toward the ultimate things of pure poetry; in the other it speaks to great numbers of people of themselves, making extraordinary texts and memorable music out of what they feel and know. In both cases it makes itself manifest in a kind of speech that comes from secrecy. Its position is always an inner position, never certain, never fixed. It is to be found beneath the poet's word and deep within the reader's eye in those chambers in which the genius of poetry sits alone with her candle in a moving solitude.

I shall read two short poems from *Parts of a World*.

January 24, 1951

On Receiving the National Book Award for Poetry

Mr.   , Ladies and Gentlemen:
Not long ago I was listening to a conversation between two

men about modern poetry. One said to the other "Do you really think that any of these fellows are as good, say, as Sir Walter Scott?" Now, how many of you when you go home tonight are likely to sit down and read The Lady of the Lake? Sir Walter Scott's poetry is like the scenery of a play that has come to an end. It is scenery that has been trucked away and stored somewhere on the horizon or just a little below. In short, the world of Sir Walter Scott no longer exists. It means nothing to compare a modern poet with the poet of a century or more ago. It is not a question of comparative goodness. It is like comparing a modern soldier, say, with an ancient one, like comparing Eisenhower with Agamemnon.

I have just used the words "a modern poet". These words are intended to mean nothing more than a poet of the present time. The word "modern" to whatever it may be attached, as, for example, a modern publisher or a bookseller with a modern shop, usually implies a sense of modishness. A modern painter is more than likely to be the product of a movement. A modern musician sounds like one the moment you hear him. However that may be, what a modern poet desires, above everything else, is to be nothing more than a poet of the present time. I think it may be said that he considers his function to be this: to find, by means of his own thought and feeling, what seems to him to be the poetry of his time as differentiated from the poetry of the time of Sir Walter Scott, or the poetry of any other time, and to state it in a manner that effectively discloses it to his readers.

I say that he is to find it by his own thought and feeling; and the reason for this is that the only place for him to find it is in the thought and feeling of other people of which he becomes aware through his own thought and feeling. Becoming aware does not always mean becoming consciously aware. His awareness may be limited to instinct. There is about every poet a vast world of other people from which he derives himself and through himself his poetry. What he derives from his generation he returns to his generation, as best he can. His poetry is theirs and theirs is his, because of the interaction between the poet and his time, which publishers, booksellers and printers do more than any others in the world to broaden and deepen.

I am happy to receive this afternoon's award and appreciate the honor that has been done me. I should like to thank the book industry for its great generosity. At the same time, I should like to thank the panel of judges of the poetry division for the pleasure they have given me and for their good will which is itself a distinction.

March 6, 1951

On Receiving an Honorary Degree from Bard College

Mr. President, Ladies and Gentlemen:

The act of conferring an honor on a poet is a poetic act. By a poetic act I mean an act that is a projection of poetry into reality. The act of conferring an academic honor on a poet is a poetic act specifically because it engages all those that participate in it with at least the idea of poetry, for at least a moment, that is to say it engages them with something that is unreal, as if they had opened a door and stepped into another dimension full of the potentialities of any dimension not immediately calculable. What is unreal here is the idea of poetry and the projection of that idea into this present place. To choose this immediate act as an illustration of the poetic act is a choice of expediency only.

The act should be observed for a moment. When we go to the corner to catch a bus or walk down the block to post a letter, our acts in doing these things are direct. But when we gather together and become engaged with something unreal our act is not so much the act of gathering together as it is the act of becoming engaged with something unreal. We do this sort of thing on a large scale when we go to church on Sunday, when we celebrate days like Christmas or the much more impressive days of the end of Lent. On Easter the great ghost of what we call the next world invades and vivifies this present world, so that Easter seems like a day of two lights, one the sunlight of the bare and physical end of winter, the other the double light. However, we find the poetic act in lesser and everyday things, as for example, in the mere act of looking at a photograph of someone who is absent or in writing a letter to a person at a distance, or even in thinking of a remote figure, as when Virgil, in the last lines of the last of the Georgics, thinks of Caesar and of the fact that while the poet was writing his poem

> . . . great Caesar fired his lightnings and conquered
> By deep Euphrates.

As to this last example, it is an instance of one of the commonplaces of the romantic. Just as in space the air envelops objects far away with an ever-deepening blue, so in the dimension of the poetic act the unreal increasingly subtilizes experience and varies appearance. The real is constantly being engulfed in the unreal. But I want to be quite sure that you recognize that I am talking about something existing, not about something purely poetic; and for that reason I add one or two more examples from actuality. The act of thinking of the life of the rich is a poetic act and this seems to be true whether one thinks of it with liking or with dislike. The same thing may be said of the act of thinking of the life of the poor. Most of us do not share the life of either the one or the other and for that reason both are unreal. It is possible, too, to think of the national economy as a poetico-economy; and surely for millions of men and women the act of joining the armed forces is measurably a poetic act, since for all of them it is a deviation from the normal, impelled by senses and necessities inoperative on the ordinary level of life. The activity of the unreal in reality, that is to say, the activities of poetry in every day life, would be like the activity of an hallucination in the mind, except for this, that the examples cited have been cited as poetic acts in the course of the visible life about us. An awareness of poetic acts may change our sense of the texture of life, but it does not falsify the texture of life. When Joan of Arc said:

> Have no fear: what I do, I do by command.
> My brothers of Paradise tell me what I have to do.

those words were the words of an hallucination. No matter what her brothers of Paradise drove her to do, what she did was never a poetic act of faith in reality because it could not be.

The important question is: what is the significance of the poetic act or, in short, what is the philosophy of what we are talking about? I am thinking of it in terms of meaning and value for the poet. Ordinarily the poet is associated with the word, not with the act; and ordinarily the word collects its strength from the imagination or, with its aid, from reality. The poet finds that as between these two sources: the imagination and reality, the imagination is false, whatever else may be said of it, and reality is true; and being concerned that poetry should be a thing of vital and virile importance, he commits himself to reality, which then becomes his inescapable and ever-present difficulty and inamorata. In any event, he has lost nothing; for the imagination, while it might have led him to purities beyond definition, never yet progressed except by particulars. Having gained the world, the imaginative remains available to him in respect to all the particulars of the world. Instead of having lost anything, he has gained a sense of direction and a certainty of understanding. He has strengthened himself to resist the bogus. He has become like a man who can see what he wants to see and touch what he wants to touch. In all his poems with all their enchantments for the poet himself, there is the final enchantment that they are true. The significance of the poetic act then is that it is evidence. It is instance and illustration. It is an illumination of a surface, the movement of a self in the rock. Above all it is a new engagement with life. It is that miracle to which the true faith of the poet attaches itself.

Mr. President, I have tried to portray, in a few words, the way of the poet as the way of the truth and I have tried to say that the need to follow this way is a need of his nature and that, at least for this generation, it is a way through reality. That sums it up. I am happy to receive the degree that you have been generous enough to confer on me. I appreciate the honor and thank you for it and for your courtesy and for the courtesy and hospitality of Bard College.

March 30, 1951

Two or Three Ideas

My first proposition is that the style of a poem and the poem itself are one.

One of the better known poems in *Fleurs du Mal* is the one (XII) entitled *La Vie Antérieure* or *Former Life*. It begins with the line:

> J'ai longtemps habité sous de vastes portiques

or

> A long time I lived beneath tremendous porches.

It continues:

> Which the salt-sea suns tinged with a thousand fires
> And which great columns, upright and majestic,
> At evening, made resemble basalt grottoes.

The poem concerns the life among the images, sounds and colors of those calm, sensual presences

> At the center of azure, of waves, of brilliances,

and so on. I have chosen this poem to illustrate my first proposition, because it happens to be a poem in which the poem itself is immediately recognizable without reference to the manner in which it is rendered. If the style and the poem are one, one ought to choose, for the purpose of illustration, a poem that illustrates this as, for example, Yeats' *Lake-Isle of Innisfree*. To choose a French poem which has to be translated is to choose an example in which the style is lost in the paraphrase of translation. On the other hand, Baudelaire's poem is useful because it identifies what is meant by the poem itself. The idea of an earlier life is like the idea of a later life, or like the idea of a different life, part of the classic repertory of poetic ideas. It is part of one's inherited store of poetic subjects. Precisely, then, because it is traditional and because we understand its romantic nature and know what to expect from it, we are suddenly and profoundly touched when we hear it declaimed by a voice that says:

> I lived, for long, under huge porticoes.

It is as if we had stepped into a ruin and were startled by a flight of birds that rose as we entered. The familiar experience is made unfamiliar and from that time on, whenever we think of that particular scene, we remember how we held our breath and how the hungry doves of another world rose out of nothingness and whistled away. We stand looking at a remembered habitation. All old dwelling-places are subject to these transmogrifications and the experience of all of us includes a succession of old dwelling-places: abodes of the imagination, ancestral or memories of places that never existed. It is plain that when, in this world of weak feeling and blank thinking, in which we are face to face with the poem every moment of time, we encounter some integration of the poem that pierces and dazzles us, the effect is an effect of style and not of the poem itself or at least not of the poem alone. The effective integration is not a disengaging of the subject. It is a question of the style in which the subject is presented.

Although I have limited myself to an instance of the relation between style and the familiar, one gets the same result in considering the relation between style and its own creations, that is between style and the unfamiliar. What we are really considering here are the creations of modern art and modern literature. If one keeps in mind the fact that most poets who have something to say are content with what they say and that most poets who have little or nothing to say are concerned primarily with the way in which they say it, the importance of this discussion becomes clear. I do not mean to imply that the poets who have something to say are the poets that matter; for obviously if it is true that the style of a poem and the poem itself are one, it follows that, in considering style and its own creations, that is to say, the relation between style and the unfamiliar, it may be, or become, that the poets who have little or nothing to say are, or will be, the poets that matter. Today, painters who have something to say are less admired than painters who seem to have little or nothing to say but who do at least believe that style and the painting are one. The inclination toward arbitrary or schematic constructions in poetry is, from the point of view of style, very strong; and certainly if these constructions were effective it would be true that the style and the poem were one.

In the light of this first idea the prejudice in favor of plain English, for instance, comes to nothing. I have never been able to see why what is called Anglo-Saxon should have the right to higgle and haggle all over the page, contesting the right of other words. If a poem seems to require a hierophantic phrase, the phrase should pass. This is a way of saying that one of the consequences of the ordination of style is not to limit it, but to enlarge it, not to impoverish it, but to enrich and liberate it.

The second idea relates to poetry and the gods, both ancient and modern, both foreign and domestic. To simplify, I shall speak only of the ancient and the foreign gods. I do not mean to refer to them in their religious aspects but as creations of the imagination; and I suppose that as with all creations of the imagination I have been thinking of them from the point of view of style, that is to say of their style. When we think of Jove, while we take him for granted as the symbol of omnipotence, the ruler of mankind, we do not fear him. He does have a superhuman size, but at least not so superhuman as to amaze and intimidate us. He has a large head and a beard and is a relic, a relic that makes a kindly impression on us and reminds us of stories that we have heard about him. All of the noble images of all of the gods have been profound and most of them have been forgotten. To speak of the origin and end of gods is not a light matter. It is to speak of the origin and end of eras of human belief. And while it is easy to look back on those that have disappeared as if they were the playthings of cosmic make-believe, and on those that made petitions to them and honored them and received their benefits as legendary innocents, we are bound, nevertheless, to concede that the gods were personae of a peremptory elevation and glory. It would be wrong to look back to them as if they had existed in some indigence of the spirit. They were in fact, as we see them now, the clear giants of a vivid time, who in the style of their beings made the style of the gods and the gods themselves one.

This brings me to the third idea, which is this: In an age of disbelief, or, what is the same thing, in a time that is largely humanistic, in one sense or another, it is for the poet to supply the satisfactions of belief, in his measure and in his style. I say in his measure to indicate that the figures of the philosopher, the artist, the teacher, the moralist and other figures, including the poet, find themselves, in such a time, to be figures of an importance greatly enhanced by the requirements both of the individual and of society; and I say in his style by way of confining the poet to his role and thereby of intensifying that role. It is this that I want to talk about today. I want to try to formulate a conception of perfection in poetry with reference to the present time and the near future and to speculate on the activities possible to it as it deploys itself throughout the lives of men and women. I think of it as a role of the utmost seriousness. It is, for one thing, a spiritual role. One might stop to draw an ideal portrait of the poet. But that would be parenthetical. In any case, we do not say that the philosopher, the artist or the teacher is to take the place of the gods. Just so, we do not say that the poet is to take the place of the gods.

To see the gods dispelled in mid-air and dissolve like clouds is one of the great human experiences. It is not as if they had gone over the horizon to disappear for a time; nor as if they had been overcome by other gods of greater power and profounder knowledge. It is simply that they came to nothing. Since we have always shared all things with them and have always had a part of their strength and, certainly, all of their knowledge, we shared likewise this experience of annihilation. It was their annihilation, not ours, and yet it left us feeling that in a measure we, too, had been annihilated. It left us feeling dispossessed and alone in a solitude, like children without parents, in a home that seemed deserted, in which the amical rooms and halls had taken on a look of hardness and emptiness. What was most extraordinary is that they left no mementoes behind, no thrones, no mystic rings, no texts either of the soil or of the soul. It was as if they had never inhabited the earth. There was no crying out for their return. They were not forgotten because they had been a part of the glory of the earth. At the same time, no man ever muttered a petition in his heart for the restoration of those unreal shapes. There was always in every man the increasingly human self, which instead of remaining the observer, the non-participant, the delinquent, became constantly more and more all there was or so it seemed; and whether it was so or merely seemed so still left it for him to resolve life and the world in his own terms.

Thinking about the end of the gods creates singular attitudes in the mind of the thinker. One attitude is that the gods of classical mythology were merely aesthetic projections. They were not the objects of belief. They were expressions of delight. Perhaps delight is too active a word. It is true that they were engaged with the future world and the immortality of the soul. It is true, also, that they were the objects of veneration and therefore of religious dignity and sanctity. But in the blue air of the Mediterranean these white and a little colossal figures had a special propriety, a special felicity. Could they have been created for that propriety, that felicity? Notwithstanding their divinity, they were close to the people among whom they moved. Is it one of the normal activities of humanity, in the solitude of reality and in the unworthy treatment of solitude, to create companions, a little colossal as I have said, who, if not superficially explicative, are, at least, assumed to be full of the secret of things and who in any event bear in themselves even, if they do not always wear it, the peculiar majesty of mankind's sense of worth, neither too much nor too little? To a people of high intelligence, whose gods have benefited by having been accepted and addressed by the superior minds of a superior world, the symbolic paraphernalia of the very great becomes unnecessary and the very great become the very natural. However all that may be, the celestial atmosphere of these deities, their ultimate remote celestial residences are not matters of chance. Their fundamental glory is the fundamental glory of men and women, who being in need of it create it, elevate it, without too much searching of its identity.

The people, not the priests, made the gods. The personages of immortality were something more than the conceptions of priests, although they may have picked up many of the conceits of priests. Who were the priests? Who have always been the high priests of any of the gods? Certainly not those officials or generations of officials who administered rites and observed rituals. The great and true priest of Apollo was he that composed the most moving of Apollo's hymns. The really illustrious archimandrite of Zeus was the one that made the being of Zeus people the whole of Olympus and the Olympian land, just as the only marvelous bishops of heaven have always been those that made it seem like heaven. I said a moment ago that we had not forgotten the gods. What is it that we remember of them? In the case of those masculine do we remember their ethics or is it their port and mien, their size, their color, not to speak of their adventures, that we remember? In the case of those feminine do we remember, as in the case of Diana, their fabulous chastity or their beauty? Do we remember those masculine in any way differently than the way in which we remember Ulysses and other men of supreme interest and excellence? In the case of those feminine do we remember Venus in any way differently from the way in which we remember Penelope and other women of much mark and feeling? In short, while the priests helped to realize the gods, it was the people that spoke of them and to them and heard their replies.

Let us stop now and restate the ideas which we are considering in relation to one another. The first is that the style of a poem and the poem itself are one; the second is that the style of the gods and the gods themselves are one; the third is that in an age of disbelief, when the gods have come to an end, when we think of them as the aesthetic projections of a time that has passed, men turn to a fundamental glory of their own and from that create a style of bearing themselves in reality. They create a new style of a new bearing in a new reality. This third idea, then, may be made to conform to the way in which the other two have been expressed by saying that the style of men and men themselves are one. Now, if the style of a poem and the poem itself are one; if the style of the gods and the gods themselves are one; and if the style of men and men themselves are one; and if there is any true relation between these propositions, it might well be the case that the parts of these propositions are interchangeable. Thus, it might be true that the style of a poem and the gods themselves are one; or that the style of the gods and the style of men are one; or that the style of a poem and the style of men are one. As we hear these things said, without having time to think about them, it sounds as if they might be true, at least as if there might be something to them. Most of us are prepared to listen patiently to talk of the identity of the gods and men. But where does the poem come in? And if my answer to that is that I am concerned primarily with the poem and that my purpose this morning is to elevate the poem to the level of one of the major significances of life and to equate it, for the purpose or discussion, with gods and men, I hope it will be clear that it comes in as the central interest, the fresh and foremost object.

If in the minds of men creativeness was the same thing as creation in the natural world, if a spiritual planet matched the sun, or if without any question of a spiritual planet, the light and warmth of spring revitalized all our faculties, as in a measure they do, all the bearings one takes, all the propositions one formulates would be within the scope of that particular domination. The trouble is, however, that men in general do not create in light and warmth alone. They create in darkness and coldness. They create when they are hopeless, in the midst of antagonisms, when they are wrong, when their powers are no longer subject to their control. They create as the ministers of evil. Here in New England at this very moment nothing but good seems to be returning; and in that good, particularly if we ignore the difference between men and the natural world, how easy it is suddenly to believe in the poem as one has never believed in it before, suddenly to require of it a meaning beyond what its words can possibly say, a sound beyond any giving of the ear, a motion beyond our previous knowledge of feeling. And, of course, our three ideas have not only to be thought of as deriving what they have in common from the intricacies of human nature as distinguished from what the things of the natural world have in common, derived from strengths like light and warmth. They have to be thought of with reference to the meaning of style. Style is not something applied. It is something inherent, something that permeates. It is of the nature of that in which it is found, whether the poem, the manner of a god, the bearing of a man. It is not a dress. It may be said to be a voice that is inevitable. A man has no choice about his style. When he says I am my style the truth reminds him that it is his style that is himself. If he says, as my poem is, so are my gods and so am I, the truth remains quiet and broods on what he has said. He knows that the gods of China are always Chinese; that the gods of Greece are always Greeks and that all gods are created in the images of their creators; and he sees in these circumstances the operation of a style, a basic law. He observes the uniform enhancement of all things within the category of the imagination. He sees, in the struggle between the perfectible and the imperfectible, how the perfectible prevails, even though it falls short of perfection.

It is no doubt true that the creative faculties operate alike on poems, gods and men up to a point. They are always the same faculties. One might even say that the things created are always the same things. In case of a universal artist, all of his productions are his peculiar own. When we are dealing with racial units of the creative faculties all of the productions of one unit resemble one another. We say of a painting that it is Florentine. But we say the same thing and with equal certainty of a piece of sculpture. There is no difficulty in arguing about the poems, gods and men of Egypt or India that they look alike. But if the gods of India disappeared would not the poems of India and the men of India still remain alike. And if there were no poems, a new race of poets would produce poems that would take the place of the gods that had disappeared. What, then, is the nature of poetry in a time of disbelief? The truistic nature of some of the things that I have said shows how the free-will of the poet is limited. They demonstrate that the poetry of the future can never be anything purely eccentric and dissociated. The poetry of the present cannot be purely eccentric and dissociated. Eccentric and dissociated poetry is poetry that tries to exist or is intended to exist separately from the poem, that is to say in a style that is not identical with the poem. It never achieves anything more than a shallow mannerism, like something seen in a glass. Now, a time of disbelief is precisely a time in which the frequency of detached styles is greatest. I am not quite happy about the word detached. By detached, I mean the unsuccessful, the ineffective, the arbitrary, the literary, the non-umbilical, that which in its highest degree would still be words. For the style of the poem and the poem itself to be one there must be a mating and a marriage, not an arid love-song.

Yes: but the gods—how they come into it and make it a delicious subject, as if we were here together wasting our time on something that appears to be whimsical but turns out to be essential. They give to the subject just that degree of effulgence and excess, no more, no less, that the subject requires. Our first proposition, that the style of a poem and the poem itself are one was a definition of perfection in poetry. In the presence of the gods, or of their images, we are in the presence of perfection in created beings. The gods are a definition of perfection in ideal creatures. These remarks expound the second proposition that the style of the gods and the gods themselves are one. The exhilaration of their existence, their freedom from fate, their access to station, their liberty to command fix them in an atmosphere which thrills us as we share it with them. But these are merely attributes. What matters is their manner, their style, which tells us at once that they are as we wished them to be, that they have fulfilled us, that they are us but purified, magnified, in an expansion. It is their style that makes them gods, not merely privileged beings. It is their style most of all that fulfills themselves. If they lost all their privileges, their freedom from fate, their liberty to command, and yet still retained their style, they would still be gods, however destitute. That alone would destroy them, which deprived them of their style. When the time came for them to go, it was a time when their aesthetic had become invalid in the presence not of a greater aesthetic of the same kind, but of a different aesthetic, of which from the point of view of greatness, the difference was that of an intenser humanity. The style of the gods is derived from men. The style of the gods is derived from the style of men.

One has to pierce through the dithyrambic impressions that talk of the gods makes to the reality of what is being said. What is being said must be true and the truth of it must be seen. But the truth about the poet in a time of disbelief is not that he must turn evangelist. After all, he shares the disbelief of his time. He does not turn to Paris or Rome for relief from the monotony of reality. He turns to himself and he denies that reality was ever monotonous except in comparison. He asserts that the source of comparison having been eliminated, reality is returned, as if a shadow had passed and drawn after it and taken away whatever coating had concealed what lay beneath it. Yet the revelation of reality is not a part peculiar to a time of disbelief or, if it is, it is so in a sense singular to that time. Perhaps, the revelation of reality takes on a special meaning, without effort or consciousness on the part of the poet, at such a time. Why should a poem not change in sense when there is a fluctuation of the whole of appearance? Or why should it not change when we realize that the indifferent experience of life is the unique experience, the item of ecstasy which we have been isolating and reserving for another time and place, loftier and more secluded. There is inherent in the words *the revelation of reality* a suggestion that there is a reality of or within or beneath the surface of reality. There are many such realities through which poets constantly pass to and fro, without noticing the imaginary lines that divide one from the other. We were face to face with such a transition at the outset, for Baudelaire's line

A long time I passed beneath an entrance roof

opens like a voice heard in a theatre and a theatre is a reality within a reality. The most provocative of all realities is that reality of which we never lose sight but never see solely as it is. The revelation of that particular reality or of that particular category of realities is like a series of paintings of some natural object affected, as the appearance of any natural object is affected, by the passage of time, and the changes that ensue, not least in the painter. That the revelation of reality has a character or quality peculiar to this time or that or, what is intended to be the same thing, that it is affected by states of mind, is elementary. The line from Baudelaire will not have the same effect on everyone at all times, any more than it will continue to have the same effect on the same person constantly. I remember that when a friend of mine in Ireland quoted the line, a few years ago, in a letter, my feeling about it was that it was a good instance of the value of knowing people of different educations. The chances are that my friend in Dublin and I have done much the same reading. The chances are, also, that we have retained many different things. For instance, this man had chosen Giorgione as the painter that meant most to him. For my own part, Giorgione would not have occurred to me. I should like you to be sure that in speaking of the revelation of reality I am not attempting to forecast the poetry of the future. It would be logical to conclude that, since a time of disbelief is also a time of truthloving and since I have emphasized that I recognize that what I am trying to say is nothing unless it is true and that the truth of it must be seen, I think that the main characteristic of the poetry of the future or the near future will be an absence of the poetic. I do not think that. I cannot see what value it would have if I did, except as a value to me personally. If there is a logic that controls poetry, which everything that I have been saying may illustrate, it is not the narrow logic that exists on the level of prophecy. That there is a larger logic I have no doubt. But certainly it has to be large enough to allow for a good many irrelevancies.

One of the irrelevancies is the romantic. It looks like something completely contemptible in the light of literary intellectualism and cynicism. The romantic, however, has a way of renewing itself. It can be said of the romantic, just as it can be said of the imagination, that it can never effectively touch the same thing twice in the same way. It is partly because the romantic will not be what has been romantic in the past that it is preposterous to think of confining poetry hereafter to the revelation of reality. The whole effort of the imagination is toward the production of the romantic. When, therefore, the romantic is in abeyance, when it is discredited, it remains true that there is always an unknown romantic and that the imagination will not be forever denied. There is something a little romantic about the idea that the style of a poem and the poem itself are one. It seems to be a much more broadly romantic thing to say that the style of the gods and the gods themselves are one. It is completely romantic to say that the style of men and men themselves are one. To collect and collate these ideas of disparate things may seem to pass beyond the romantic to the fantastic. I hope, however, that you will agree that if each one of these ideas is valid separately, or more or less valid, it is permissible to have brought them together as a collective source of suppositions. What is romantic in all of them is the idea of style which I have not defined in any sense uniformly common to all three. A poem is a restricted creation of the imagination. The gods are the creation of the imagination at its utmost. Men are a part of reality. The gradations of romance noticeable as the sense of style is used with reference to these three, one by one, are relevant to the difficulties of the imagination in a truth-loving time. These difficulties exist only as one foresees them. They may never exist at all. An age in which the imagination might be expected to become part of time's *rejectamenta* may behold it established and protected and enthroned on one of the few ever-surviving thrones; and, to our surprise, we may find posted in the portico of its eternal dwelling, on the chief portal, among the morning's ordinances, three regulations which if they were once rules of art will then have become rules of conduct. By that time the one that will matter most is likely to be the last, that the style of man is man himself, which is about what we have been saying.

It comes to this that we use the same faculties when we write poetry that we use when we create gods or when we fix the bearing of men in reality. That this is obvious does not make the statement less. On the contrary, it makes the statement more, because its obviousness is that of the truth; and in things that are central to us the last sanction is that of the truth. The three ideas are sources of perfection. They are of such a nature that they are instances of aesthetic ideas tantamount to moral ideas, a subject precious in itself but beyond our scope today. For today, they mean that however one time may differ from another, there are always available to us the faculties of the past, but always vitally new and strong, as the sources of perfection today and tomorrow. The unity of style and the poem itself is a unity of language and life that exposes both in a supreme sense. Its collation with the unity of style and the gods and the unity of style and men is intended to demonstrate this.

Lecture at Mount Holyoke College, April 28, 1951

A Collect of Philosophy

It is often the case that the concepts of philosophy are poetic. I thought, therefore, that you might like to consider the poetic nature of at least a few philosophic ideas. I have in mind ideas that are inherently poetic, as, for example, the concept of the infinity of the world. But when I wrote to Jean Wahl, who is both a poet and a philosopher, about ideas that are inherently poetic, he said immediately that no ideas are inherently poetic, that the poetic nature of any idea depends on the mind through which it passes. This is as true of the poetic aspect of nature as it is of the poetic aspect of ideas. The sun rises and sets every day and yet it brings to few men and to those men only infrequently a sense of the universe of space. However, the idea of the infinity of the world, which is the same thing as a sense of the universe of space, is an idea that we are willing to accept as inherently poetic even at moments when it means nothing at all, just as we are willing to assume that the rising and the setting of the sun are inherently poetic, even at moments when we are indifferent to them. The idea of the infinity of the world is a poetic idea because it gives the imagination sudden life. Bruno became the orator of the Copernican theory. He said,

By this knowledge we are loosened from the chains of a most narrow dungeon, and set at liberty to rove in a more august empire; we are removed from presumptuous boundaries and poverty to the innumerable riches of an infinite space, of so worthy a field, and of such beautiful worlds. . . . It is not reasonable to believe that any part of the world is without a soul, life, sensation and organic structure. From this infinite All, full of beauty and splendor, from the vast worlds which circle above us to the sparkling dust of stars beyond, the conclusion is drawn that there are an infinity of creatures, a vast multitude, which, each in its degree, mirrors forth the splendor, wisdom and excellence of the divine beauty. . . . There is but one celestial expanse, where the stars choir forth unbroken harmony.

If this is sixteenth century philosophy, it is, equally, sixteenth century poetry. One understands why Victor Hugo said, in his time, that the stars are no longer mentionable in poetry. The remark also illustrates Jean Wahl's point that that is poetic which the mind conceives to be so.

I

It will help to define what is intended by the poetic nature

of concepts of philosophy to speak of a few of the things that
are not intended. One of these things is a poetic way of think-
ing on the part of the philosopher. For the moment, I do not
refer to a poetic way of writing as, for example, in the case of
Plato and in modern times of Nietzsche, say, or Bergson.
There is a poetic style or way of thinking. A poet's natural
way of thinking is by way of figures, and while this includes
figures of speech it also includes examples, illustrations and
parallel cases generally. Take Leibniz, for instance. The follow-
ing passage from his *Theodicy* is a compact of figurations:

> We know a very small part of eternity, which is immeasurable in its
> extent. . . . Nevertheless from so slight an experience we rashly
> judge regarding the immeasurable and eternal, like men who, having
> been born and brought up in prison, or perhaps in the subterranean
> salt mines of the Sarmatians, should think that there is no other light
> in the world than that of the feeble lamp which hardly suffices to
> direct their steps. If you look at a very beautiful picture, having cov-
> ered up the whole of it except a very small part, what will it present
> to your sight . . . but a confused mass of colors, laid on without
> selection and without art? . . . The experience of the eyes in painting
> corresponds to that of the ears in music. Eminent composers very
> often mingle discords with harmonies so as . . . to prick the hearer,
> who becomes anxious as to what is going to happen, and is so much
> the more pleased when presently all is restored to order; (just as) . . .
> we delight in the show of danger that is connected with performances
> on the tight-rope, or sword-dancing; and we ourselves in jest half let
> go a little boy, as if about to throw him from us, like the ape which
> carried Christiern, king of Denmark, while still an infant in swaddling
> clothes, and then, as in jest, relieved the anxiety of every one by
> bringing him safely back to his cradle.

We associate the name of Leibniz with his *Monadology*. He
held that reality consists of a mass of monads, like bees cling-
ing to a branch, although for him the branch was merely a
different set of monads. Bertrand Russell said that Leibniz'
monads were gods. Monad by monad, then, by way of the
course of an immense unity, he achieved God. The concept
of this monadic creation seems to be the disappointing pro-
duction of a poet manqué. Leibniz had a poet's manner of
thinking but there was something a little too methodical
about it. He had none of the enthusiasm of Bruno. There are
those who regard a world of monads as poetic. Certainly the

idea transforms reality. Moreover, in a system of monads, we come, in the end, to a man who is not only a man but sea and mountain, too, and to a God who is not only all these: man and sea and mountain but a God as well. Yet the idea seems to be completely lacking in anything securely lofty. Leibniz was a poet without flash. It is worth while stopping to think about him a moment because with all the equipage of a poet he never exposed any of a poet's brilliant excess in accomplishment. This may be because he was too intent on exposing something else and because he wanted his figures of speech to be the most understandable that would serve. It is worth while stopping to think of him because he stands for a class: the philosopher afraid of ornament. Men engaged in the elucidation of obscurity might well feel a horror of the metaphor. But the class I have in mind is the class to which metaphor is native and inescapable, which chooses to make its metaphors plain, and thinks from the true abundance of its thought. The disposition to metaphor cannot be kept concealed by the choice of metaphor; and one cannot help thinking that the presence of discipline is as much of an intrusion as the absence of it and, in the case of a man of genius, a deprivation and destruction. For a comparison between thinking like a philosopher and thinking like a poet, compare the quality of the image of the resemblance between the tension produced by a composer and the tension produced by a performer on the tight-rope with the quality of the image used by Jowett in his introduction to the *Phaedo*:

Is the soul related to the body as sight to the eye, or as the boatman to his boat?

Poets and philosophers often think alike, as we shall see. For the present, we must deny ourselves the definitions of poetry which are exceeded only by the definitions of philosophy. Leibniz, to sum it up, was a man who thought like a poet but did not write like one, although that seems strangely impossible; and, in consequence, his *Monadology* instead of standing as one of the world's revelations looks like a curious machine, several centuries old.

Another thing not intended is a poetic way of writing. If thinking in a poetic way is not the same thing as writing in a

poetic way, so writing in a poetic way is not the same thing
as having ideas that are inherently poetic conceptions. This is
an accurate statement in the sense in which I mean it. Yet
Plato wrote in a poetic way and certainly the doctrines of
which he was so constantly prolific are with great frequency
concepts poetic per se. When I say that writing in a poetic
way is not the same thing as having ideas that are inherently
poetic concepts, I mean that the formidable poetry of
Nietzsche, for example, ultimately leaves us with the formi-
dable poetry of Nietzsche and little more. In the case of Berg-
son, we have a poetry of language, which made William James
complain of its incessant euphony. But we also have the *élan
vital*. In the case of Santayana, who was an exquisite and
memorable poet in the days when he was, also, a young phi-
losopher, the exquisite and memorable way in which he has
always said things has given so much delight that we accept
what he says as we accept our own civilization. His pages are
part of the *douceur de vivre* and do not offer themselves for
sensational summary.

Nor are we interested in philosophic poetry, as, for example,
the poetry of Lucretius, some of the poetry of Milton and
some of the poetry of Pope, and those pages of Wordsworth,
which have done so much to strengthen the critics of poetry
in their attacks on the poetry of thought. Theoretically, the
poetry of thought should be the supreme poetry. Hegel called
poetry the art of arts, specifically because in poetry the ma-
terial of which the poem is made, that is to say, the language
of the poem, is wholly subordinated to the idea. A poem in
which the poet has chosen for his subject a philosophic theme
should result in the poem of poems. That the wing of poetry
should also be the rushing wing of meaning seems to be an
extreme aesthetic good; and so in time and perhaps, in other
politics, it may come to be. It is very easy to imagine a poetry
of ideas in which the particulars of reality would be shadows
among the poem's disclosures. If we are to dismiss from po-
etry expectations of that nature, we might equally well dismiss
from philosophy all the profound expectations on which it is
based. Of course, poems like the *De Rerum Natura* and the
Essay on Man do not stir us particularly one way or the other,
that is to say, either as poetry or as philosophy. The great

poetry I have projected is a compensation of time to come. In our consideration of the poetic aspect of philosophy it is enough to dismiss the philosophic poem as irrelevant and yet, at the same time, to point out the perfection latent in it. After all, Socrates left descendants and one of them, in his youth, may choose to be concerned with the self, not in the sense common to youthful poets, but in the major sense common to the descendants of Socrates. Paul Weiss says in his *Nature and Man* that every object in the universe has some pertinence to the self. That is the sense of the self common to the descendants of Socrates.

When one says that the poetry of thought should be the supreme poetry and when one considers with what thought has been concerned throughout so many ages, the themes of supreme poetry are not hard to identify. Dr. Weiss, who was kind enough to write several letters to me last summer in relation to this paper, sent me a formulation of central doctrines to assist in the selecting of ideas which I have described as inherently poetic. I quote from one of these letters because to do so is like turning the pages of one of those books of the future about which I have been speculating. He said,

Plato: all things participate in the good; all beings love what they do not have, to wit, the good. Aristotle: all beings strive to realize their peculiar goods, already exemplified in some being somewhere in the natural world. St. Francis and St. Bonaventure: all beings have at least a trace of God in them. St. Thomas Aquinas: all existence is owed to God. Descartes: all bodies are machines. Leibniz: the world is at once the best and most rational of worlds; all the things we know in experience are combinations of spirits. Spinoza: all things happen by necessity; all things are in God. Kant: to be free is to be moral, and to be moral is to be free. Hegel: negation is a force; the absolute works out its own destiny; what comes to be is right.

Dr. Weiss did not limit himself to these formulations. He recognized that they were over-simplified. He said,

If by a poetic view we mean one which probes beneath those used in daily living, or one which cuts across the divisions which are normative to ordinary discourse, then all philosophy must be said to be poetic in conception and doctrine. It writes a cosmic poetry in prose, making use of such abstract terms as being, individuality, causality, etc. in order to talk about the presuppositions of all there is.

That all philosophy is poetic in conception and doctrine is no more true than that all poetry is philosophic in conception and doctrine. But if it was true, it would not mean that the object of all philosophic study is to achieve poetry. It would only mean what I have intended from the beginning and that is that it is often the case that the concepts of philosophy are poetic. Dr. Weiss' last remark is a statement of one of the reasons why that is true. Certainly a sense of the infinity of the world is a sense of something cosmic. It is cosmic poetry because it makes us realize in the same way in which an escape from all our limitations would make us realize that we are creatures, not of a part, which is our every day limitation, but of a whole for which, for the most part, we have as yet no language. This sudden change of a lesser life for a greater one is like a change of winter for spring or any other transmutation of poetry. Not all philosophy probes beneath daily living. Does the philosophy of science? Not all the abridgments of abstraction draw us away into metaphysical spheres. Was John Locke a mystic? It is true that philosophy is poetic in conception and doctrine to the extent that the ideas of philosophy may be described as poetic concepts. It is true all the way and not merely to an extent as Dr. Weiss puts it. To the extent stated, however, it demonstrates itself and nothing more is required. A realization of the infinity of the world is equally a perception of philosophy and a typical metamorphosis of poetry.

II

Essentially what I intend is that it shall be as if the philosophers had no knowledge of poetry and suddenly discovered it in their search for whatever it is that they are searching for and gave the name of poetry to that which they discovered. Whether one arrives at the idea of God as a philosopher or as a poet matters greatly. The philosopher if he sees God himself as a philosopher, and he usually does, adorns him with the regalia and immanences with which it would be natural for a poet to adorn him. There are levels of thought or vision where everything is poetic. But there are levels of philosophy and for that matter of poetry where nothing is poetic. Our object is to stay on the levels where everything is poetic and to give attention to what we find there, that is to say, to identify at least a few philosophic ideas that are inherently poetic and to comment on them, one by one and, then, in general. We have already noticed the idea of the infinity of the world and the somewhat furious poetry that it brought about in Bruno and we have spoken of Leibniz' world of monads or spirits. Before we stop to look at another eccentric philosophic apparatus on the grand scale in the *World As Will* of Schopenhauer, let us take a look or two at some of the poetic concepts that have resulted from the study of perception.

According to the traditional views of sensory perception, we do not see the world immediately but only as the result of a process of seeing and after the completion of that process, that is to say, we never see the world except the moment after. Thus, we are constantly observing the past. Here is an idea, not the result of poetic thinking and entirely without poetic intention, which instantly changes the face of the world. Its effect is that of an almost inappreciable change of which, nevertheless, we remain acutely conscious. The material world, for all the assurances of the eye, has become immaterial. It has become an image in the mind. The solid earth disappears and the whole atmosphere is subtilized not by the arrival of some venerable beam of light from an almost hypothetical star but by a breach of reality. What we see is not an external world but an image of it and hence an internal world. Berkeley rushed into this breach. He said,

It is indeed an opinion strangely prevailing amongst men, that houses, mountains, rivers, and in a word all sensible objects, have an existence, natural or real, distinct from their being perceived by the understanding. But with how great an assurance and acquiescence soever this principle may be entertained in the world, yet whoever shall find in his heart to call it in question may, if I mistake not, perceive it to involve a manifest contradiction. For what are the forementioned objects but the things we perceive by sense? And what do we perceive besides our own ideas or sensations? And is it not plainly repugnant that any one of these, or any combination of them, should exist unperceived?

This was only one phase of Berkeley's philosophy. We are not interested, here, in following it beyond this stage. The point is that poetry is to a large extent an art of perception and that the problems of perception as they are developed in philosophy resemble similar problems in poetry. It may be said that to the extent that the analysis of perception in philosophy leads to ideas that are poetic the problems are identical. Whitehead has an important chapter related to this, "The Romantic Reaction," in his *Science And The Modern World*. He refers particularly to Wordsworth and Shelley. We have time only to mention this and, for the sake of disclosing another part of what he calls "the perceptual field," to quote one or two sentences, as follows:

My theory involves the entire abandonment of the notion that simple location is the primary way in which things are involved in space-time. In a certain sense, everything is everywhere at all times, for every location involves an aspect of itself in every other location. Thus every spatio-temporal standpoint mirrors the world.

These words are pretty obviously words from a level where everything is poetic, as if the statement that every location involves an aspect of itself in every other location produced in the imagination a universal iridescence, a dithering of presences and, say, a complex of differences.

I spoke a moment ago of the *World As Will*. Many of the ideas with which we are concerned have been very briefly summarized by Rogers in his *A Student's History of Philosophy*. I shall make use of his summary of Schopenhauer, as I have made use, elsewhere in this paper, of others of his summaries. He says,

While the world is illusion, mere appearance, there exists behind it a reality which appears—the thing-in-itself of Kant. . . . Is this thing really unknowable, however, as Kant had claimed? . . . Schopenhauer . . . agrees that we cannot reach it by the pathway of the reason. . . . Our insight into its nature is rather the outcome of a direct intuition of genius. . . . Now the inner essence of man's nature is *will*. It is as will that the reality of his own body comes home to him immediately. The various parts of the body are the visible expression of desires; teeth, throat and bowels are objectified hunger; the brain is the will to know, the foot the will to go, the stomach the will to digest. It is only as a secondary outcome of this original activity that the thought life arises. We think in order to do; the active impulse precedes, and is the necessary basis for, any conscious motion.

And this insight, once attained, throws a flood of light on the outer world. The eternally striving, energizing power which is working everywhere in the universe—in the instinct of the animal, the life process of the plant, the blind force of inorganic matter—what is this but the will that underlies all existence . . . . Reality, then, is will . . . We must leave out of our conception of the universal will that action for intelligent ends which characterizes human willing. . . . The will is thus far deeper seated than the intellect; it is the blind man carrying on his shoulders the lame man who can see.

These words depict, in the imagination, a text of the grotesque, both human and inhuman. It is the text of a poem although not a happy one. It is, in a way, the same poem as the poem of Leibniz although the terms are different. It is the cosmic poem of the ascent into heaven. I suppose that some kinds of faith require logical, even though fantastic, structures of this kind to support them on the way of that ascent. The number of ways of passing between the traditional two fixed points of man's life, that is to say, of passing from the self to God, is fixed only by the limitations of space, which is limitless. The eternal philosopher is the eternal pilgrim on that road. It is difficult to take him seriously when he relies on the evidence of the teeth, the throat and the bowels. Yet in the one poem that is unimpeachably divine, the poem of the ascent into heaven, it is possible to say that there can be no faults, since it is precisely the faults of life that this poem enables us to leave behind. If the idea of God is the ultimate poetic idea, then the idea of the ascent into heaven is only a little below it. Conceding that not all philosophy is concerned with this particular poem, nevertheless a great deal of it is, and always has been, and the philosophy of Schopenhauer is. The poets of that theme find things on the way and what they find on the way often interests as much as what they find in the end. Thus, Samuel Alexander in *Space, Time And Deity* finds the order of compresence. He says,

What is of importance is the recognition that in any experience the mind enjoys itself and contemplates its object or its object is contemplated, and that these two existences, the act of mind and the object as they are in the experience, are distinct existences united by the relation of compresence. The experience is a piece of the world consisting of these two existences in their togetherness. The one existence, the enjoyed, enjoys itself, or experiences itself as an enjoyment; the other existence, the contemplated, is experienced by the enjoyed. The enjoyed and the contemplated are together.

Dr. Alexander expresses himself with the same straining for the utmost exactness in the words he uses as the straining of a poet for like exactness.

As a matter of fact, it is what philosophers find on the way that constitutes the body of philosophy for if the end is appointed in advance neither logic nor the lack of it can affect their passage. Jean Wahl wrote to me, saying

> I am just now reading the *Méditations Cartesiennes* by Husserl. Very dry. But he affirms that there is an enormous (ungeheueres) a priori in our minds, an inexhaustible infinity of a priori. He speaks of the approach to the unapproachable.

This enormous a priori is potentially as poetic a concept as the idea of the infinity of the world. Jean Wahl spoke, also, of other things in which you might be interested: of Pascal in a frightened mood saying *"Le silence de ces espaces infinis m'effraie,"* adding appropriately that in Victor Hugo one might find echoes of that idea. He quoted again from Pascal: *"La sphère dont le centre est partout et la circonférence est nulle part,"* as a concept belonging to our category. He spoke of the idea of the ricorsi of Vico; the idea of the Ewiges Wiederkehr of Nietzsche; the idea of freedom as developed in the French philosopher Lequier; the idea of *"les vérités éternelles"* of Malebranche. He particularly suggested the poems of Traherne. We have, however, excluded poems of philosophic intentions from our discussion. He had spoken in an earlier letter of Novalis influenced by the ideas of Fichte; Hölderlin influencing, in his opinion, the young Hegel; Shelley influenced by Plato; Blake; Mallarmé influenced by the Kabbala and Hegel. But these were all poets and I was approaching the subject the other way and with a different end in view. I was not interested in the philosophy of poets but in the poetry of philosophers. He made many other suggestions which I am happy to acknowledge for there is no one, what with his immense reading, to whom I could be more easily or more willingly indebted. I am not a philosopher.

Jean Paulhan sent some notes. He said,

It seems to me that the old psychological theory of perception considered as a true hallucination is the very type of the call to poetry. . . . The first word of the philosophy of the sciences, today, is that science has no value except its effectiveness and that nothing, absolutely nothing, constitutes an assurance that the external world resembles the idea that we form of it. Is that a poetic idea? Anti-poetic, rather, in that it is opposite to the confidence which the poet, by nature, reposes, and invites us to repose, in the world. Let us say that it needs poetry to rise above itself; hence that it is an invitation to much poetry. It is an indirect way of being poetic.

Later on, he expressed himself as thinking that the philosophy of the sciences would lend itself better to the kind of poetry that I am trying to specify. His attitude toward the problem was not that of a man looking at the past but that of a man looking at the present and asking himself whether the concepts of the philosophy of the sciences are poetic. He said,

It is admitted, since Planck, that determinism—the relation of cause to effect—exists, or so it seems, on the human scale, only by means of an aggregate of statistical compensations and as the physicists say, by virtue of macroscopic approximations. (There is much to dream about in these macroscopic approximations.) As to the true nature of corpuscular or quantic phenomena, well, try to imagine them. No one has yet succeeded. But the poets—it is possible.

And later, because his mind had been engaged by the subject, he sent a last word. He said,

It comes to this that philosophers (particularly the philosophers of science) make, not discoveries but hypotheses that may be called poetic. Thus Louis de Broglie admits that progress in physics is, at the moment, in suspense because we do not have the words or the images that are essential to us. But to create illuminations, images, words, that is the very reason for being of poets.

III

Let us see, now, what deductions can be made from all this material.

First of all, since a similarity has been established between poets and philosophers and since it can no longer be necessary to argue that a measure of identity exists between them, what is the fundamental respect that separates them. The habit of forming concepts unites them. The use to which they put their ideas separates them. By the habit of forming concepts, I do not, of course, mean merely thinking, for all men have in common the habit of thinking. The habit of forming concepts is a habit of the mind by which it probes for an integration. Where we see the results of that habit in the works of philosophers we may think that it is a habit which they share with no one else. This is untrue. The habit of probing for an integration seems to be part of the general will to order. We must, therefore, go a step farther and look for the respect that separates the poet and the philosopher in the kind of integrations for which they search. The philosopher searches for an integration for its own sake, as, for example, Plato's idea that knowledge is recollection or that the soul is a harmony; the poet searches for an integration that shall be not so much sufficient in itself as sufficient for some quality that it possesses, such as its insight, its evocative power or its appearance in the eye of the imagination. The philosopher intends his integration to be fateful; the poet intends his to be effective.

And yet these integrations, although different from each other, have something in common, such as, say, a characteristic of the depth or distance at which they have been found, a facture of the level or position of the mind or, if you like, of a level or position of the feelings, because in the excitement of bringing things about it is not always easy to say whether one is thinking or feeling or doing both at the same time. The probing of the philosopher is deliberate, as the history of the part that logic has played in philosophy demonstrates. Yet one finds it simple to assume that the philosopher more or less often experiences the same miraculous shortenings of mental processes that the poet experiences. The whole scheme of the world as will may very well have occurred to Schopenhauer in an instant. The time he spent afterward in the explication of that instant is another matter. The idea of the Hegelian state, one of the masterpieces of idealism, may very well have come into Hegel's mind effortlessly and as a whole, as distinct from its details, in the same way that the gist of a poem comes into the poet's mind and takes possession of it. It remains true, however, that the probing of the philosopher is deliberate. On the other hand, the probing of the poet is fortuitous. I am speaking of the time before he has found his subject, because, once he has found his subject, that is to say, once he has achieved the integration for which he has been probing, he becomes as deliberate, in his own way, as the philosopher. Up to the point at which he has found his subject, the state of vague receptivity in which he goes about resembles one part of something that is dependent on another part, which he is not quite able to specify. In any case, it is misleading to speak of the depth or distance at which their integrations are found, or of the level or position of the mind or feelings, if the fact is that they probe in different spheres and if, in their different spheres, they move about by means of different motions. It may be said that the philosopher probes the sphere or spheres of perception and that he moves about therein like someone intent on making sure of every foot of the way. If the poet moves about in the same sphere or spheres, and occasionally he may, he is light-footed. He is intent on what he sees and hears and the sense of the certainty of the presences about him is as nothing to the presences themselves. The philosopher's native sphere is only a metaphysical one. The poet's native sphere is the sphere of which du Bellay wrote: "my village . . . my own small house . . .

My Gaulish Loire more than the Latin Tiber,
My tiny Lyré more than the Palatine hill,
And more than sea-salt air, the sweet air of Anjou."

This seductive quotation takes one away from the sphere of perception a little too abruptly and too completely; for, after all, the philosopher, also, has a solid land that he loves. The poet's native sphere, to speak more accurately, is what he can make of the world.

The uses to which the philosopher and the poet put the world are different and the ends that they have in mind are different. This statement raises the question of the final cause of philosophy and the final cause of poetry. The answers to this question are as countless as the definitions of philosophy and poetry. The other day I read a phrase in Alain: "the history of doctrines." These words give us a single sense and an inadequate sense of what philosophy is. If I say that poetry constantly requires a new station, it is a way, and an inadequate way, of saying what poetry is. To define philosophy and to define poetry are parts of the repertory of the mind. They are classic exercises. This could not be true if the definitions were adequate. In view of this difficulty about definitions, any discussion of the final causes of philosophy and poetry must be limited, here, to pointing out the relation between the question of purposes and the miscellany of definitions. And yet for all the different kinds of philosophy it is possible to generalize and to say that the philosopher's world is intended to be a world, which yet remains to be discovered and which, at bottom, the philosophers probably hope will always remain to be discovered and that the poet's world is intended to be a world, which yet remains to be celebrated and which, at bottom, the poets probably hope will always remain to be celebrated. If the philosopher's world is this present world plus thought, then the poet's world is this present world plus imagination. If we think of the philosopher and the poet as raised to their highest exponents and made competent to realize everything that the figures of the philosopher and the poet, as projected in the mind of their creator, were capable of or, in other words, if we magnify them, what would they compose, by way of fulfilling not only themselves but also by way of fulfilling the aims of their creator? This brings us face to face once more with all the definitions. But whatever they composed, they could not compose the same thing and, perhaps, we should wonder what had ever led us to believe that they were close together.

Yet we should never be able to get away, even under this extreme magnifying, from the sense that they had in common the idea of creating confidence in the world:

la confiance que le poète fait naturellement—et nous invite à faire—au monde.

The confidence of the philosopher might be a certainty with respect to something to be left behind. The confidence of the poet might be a more immediate certainty. These are ancient routines. The means used by philosophers and poets alike change and disappear. Other means take their place. An immense amount of philosophy is no longer part of our thought and yet perpetuates itself. The soul and Leibniz' swarms of spirits and Schopenhauer's manifestations of will, which appear to us to be eccentric conceptions, are not junk. Thus the soul lives as the self. When we read the *Phaedo*, we stand in the presence of Socrates, in the chamber in which he is shortly to die and we listen to him as he expounds his ideas concerning immortality. We observe that his confidence in the immortality of what was really Socrates was no less a confidence in the world, in which he reclined and spoke, a hostile and a fatal world. When we look over the shoulder of Jean Paulhan, in Paris, while he writes of *"la confiance . . . au monde"* and stop to consider what a happy phrase that is, we wonder whether we shall have the courage to repeat it, until we understand that there is no alternative. So many words other than confidence might have been used—words of understanding, words of reconciliation, of enchantment, even of forgetfulness. But none of them would have penetrated to our needs more surely than the word confidence.

The most significant deduction possible relates to the question of supremacy as between philosophy and poetry. If we say that philosophy is supreme, this means that the reason is supreme over the imagination. But is it? Does not philosophy carry us to a point at which there is nothing left except the imagination? If we rely on the imagination (or, say, intuition), to carry us beyond that point, and if the imagination succeeds in carrying us beyond that point (as in respect to the idea of God, if we conceive of the idea of God as this world's capital idea), then the imagination is supreme, because its powers have shown themselves to be greater than the powers of the reason. Philosophers, however, are not limited to the reason and, as the concepts, to which I have referred, show, their ideas are often triumphs of the imagination. To call attention to ideas in which the reason and the imagination have been acting in concert is a way of saying that when they act in concert they are supreme and is not the same thing as to say that one is supreme over the other. I might have cited the idea of God when I was speaking of the infinity of the world, of the infinite spaces, which terrified Pascal, the most devout of believers and, in the same abandonment to the superlative, the most profound of thinkers; and it would have been possible, in that case, to conclude what I have to say by placing here at the end a figure which would leave the question of supremacy a question too difficult to attempt to solve. In his words about the sphere of which the center is everywhere and the circumference nowhere, which I quoted a moment ago, we have an instance of words in which traces of the reason and traces of the imagination are mingled together.

However, instead of placing at the end the figure of Pascal, let me place here the figure of Planck. I recognize that Pascal was a much greater human being. On the other hand, Planck, who died only four years ago at Göttingen, at the age of ninety, was a much truer symbol of ourselves; and in that true role is a more significant figure for us than the remote and almost fictitious figure of Pascal. I referred to him earlier and in relation to the quantum theory. There has recently been published in Europe a group of his posthumous texts, of which one is a thesis on "The Concept of Causality in Physics." He was, of course, the patriarch of all modern physicists. André George published a note on these last writings of this great scholar in *Les Nouvelles Littéraires*, which I summarize to the extent that it is in point, particularly in respect to the thesis on causality. He says:

. . . The last pages of the thesis are quite curious. One feels there, as it were, a supreme hesitation; the believer henceforth is no longer able to conceal a certain trouble. The most convinced determinist, Planck declares, in so many words, is not able to satisfy himself entirely with such an interpretation. For, in the end, a universal principle like the rigorous causal bond between two successive events ought to be independent of man. It is a principle of cosmic importance, it ought to be an absolute. Now, Planck not only recognizes that it is part of human aptitude to foresee events but to foresee them by means of science, 'the provisional and changing creation of the power of the imagination.' How then liberate the concept from such an anthropomorphic hypothesis? Only an intelligence external to man, 'not constituting a part of nature,' would be able to liberate it. This supra-natural intelligence would act through the deterministic power . . . Planck thereupon concludes that the law of causality is neither true nor false. It is a working hypothesis.

George says, finally, that this conclusion is far away from the rigid concept, firmly determinist, which seemed up to now to constitute Planck's belief. He calls it a nuance but a nuance of importance, worth being signalized.

I think we may fairly say that it is a nuance of the imagination, one of those unwilled and innumerable nuances of the imagination that we find so often in the works of philosophers and so constantly in the works of poets. It is unexpected to have to recognize even in Planck the presence of the poet. It is as if in a study of modern man we predicated the greatness of poetry as the final measure of his stature, as if his willingness to believe beyond belief was what had made him modern and was always certain to keep him so.

Moody Lecture, University of Chicago, November 16, 1951

A Note on "Les Plus Belles Pages"

Apparently the poem means that the conjunction of milkman and moonlight is the equivalent of the conjunction of logician and saint. What it really means is that the inter-relation between things is what makes them fecund. Interaction is the source of potency. Sex is an illustration. But the principle is not confined to the illustration. The milkman and the moonlight are an illustration. The two people, the three horses etc. are illustrations. The principle finds its best illustration in the interaction of our faculties or of our thoughts and emotions. Aquinas is a chance example: a figure of great modern interest, whose special force seems to come from the interaction between his prodigious logic and his prodigious love of god. The idea that his theology, as such, is involved, is dismissed in the last line. That the example is not of scholarly choice is indicated by the title. But the title also means that les plus belles pages are those in which things do not stand alone but are operative as the result of interaction, interrelation. This is an idea of some consequence, not a casual improvisation. The interrelation between reality and the imagination is the basis of the character of literature. The interrelation between reality and the emotions is the basis of the vitality of literature, between reality and thought the basis of its power.

1952

Raoul Dufy

Raoul Dufy's sudden death in March, 1953, was like a rip in the rainbow. His work for the lithographs in the present portfolio had been completed. The collection was far advanced toward its appearance. It was based on his largest and most significant fresco. It had engaged him seriously for a long period of time. He regarded it as a typical and sympathetic undertaking and he looked forward to its publication as a kind of radiant realization. But this realization of the spirit of the artist was destined to be a realization on the part of others after his death. The work reveals Dufy, on a scale beyond comparison with anything else he has done, exploiting, as artist, the world we know and the world of what we know, which are always the same. It is an exploitation of fact by a man of elevation. It is a surface of prose changeable with the luster of poetry and thought.

The lithographs enable us to see how Dufy, for all the documentation that was inevitable, for all the ten supernumeraries from the *Comédie-Française* who posed for him, for all the costuming, for all the full year of study and observation, prevails, in the end, purely as artist; and how all the ideas, documentation, study and observation, of which the original fresco was composed, are subdued, finally, by Dufy's sense; and seeing this clearly, seeing how the artist is enabled to carry lightly the burden imposed on him by a great work, until, when it is finished, we have, not a memorial of work but the happiness of the artist who has achieved what he wanted to achieve as artist (and in this case the peculiar *allégresse* associated with Dufy's name), we experience a confidence that in the many futures of knowledge, the artist will always come through as one of the masters of his particular time.

Dufy was asked to do a mural painting for the electricity pavilion at the International Exposition at Paris in 1937. For this purpose he produced a work about thirty feet high and a little less than two hundred feet wide, in which he traced the history of light and power from pastoral time to the present time. He included figures as large as life of the principal characters who, in the course of history, and this means universal history, contributed by their discoveries or inventions to the coming on of electricity, its uses and the engineering incidental thereto. To overcome the notion of electricity as an abstraction, he symbolized it as *La Fée Electricité*, a fay rather plump and wholesome from the American point of view respecting fays and, perhaps, an improvement on that point of view. Now, what is Dufy's attitude toward all this material? It is the same attitude to which he has accustomed us in his work generally. His personalizing of the scenes that have interested him has always been slight. He has never forged blatant Dufyisms out of what he saw. There was never any melodrama and, although there was poetry, it was pretty much the radiance of exact prose, a gaiety of strokes like a gaiety of words. In consequence, this epic of *La Fée Electricité*, composed, episodically, day by day, over a long period of time, has all the interest and meaning of a simple prose narrative. Yet it is a scroll of poetry in its truth and the implications of its truth. Dufy does not engage in "the dire delight, negative and cantankerous, of men who are lacking in sense". He remains steadfast in his own intelligence delineating and allowing history to crowd its figures upon him. An artist has no being who has no identity. Here in this large work one finds the identity that we recognize as Dufy, engaged in all the delectations that make up his identity, extended and prolonged. He is not speculating about the future of the world, the potentialities of changes inherent in knowledge nor the integrity of the artist. These are glosses. He is not discursive. He knows that everything depends on concentration. He concentrates effortlessly on what is within his focus, so that it is natural for the highest point of his painting to be a collection of electrical machinery in a power plant in Paris, say, instead of some sparkling fantasy acted by his planetary heroine.

The lithographs are original works. To reproduce the original fresco it had to be done over again. When he painted the work for the first time Dufy had to enlarge everything. After the work had been schematized and reduced, Dufy repainted it for this portfolio, in its new scale, making a few changes, as, for example, eliminating figures which in the process of

reduction had become too small. The lithographs are the only
form in which the work is available, short of the construction
of a special building to contain the fresco itself.

Near the figure of Goethe there is a quotation from one of
Goethe's letters, as follows:

> I shall turn myself toward the artisans—chemistry—The hour of
> the beautiful has gone by; today, misery and implacable necessity lay
> claim to our time.

That approach to the modern goes far back, as the litho-
graphs show; but regardless of the degree of remoteness the
words of Goethe, or similar words, have always been in the
air above the approach. Today more than ever those words
are heard on the approach to what is presently modern, since
the finality of what is modern is never fully and ultimately
attainable. At the moment, the approach is precise, taking
nothing for granted. Dufy's *La Fée Electricité* is most defi-
nitely a union of drudge and dazzling angel.

The intelligence is part of the comedy of life. It was not
only that Dufy tried to dress each of the many figures that
appear in his fresco in clothes that were appropriate and which
they might have worn; nor that he had a scholar from the
Sorbonne tutor him a little in respect to electricity; nor that
he visited various central electric stations throughout France;
it was not only that he tried to grasp the truth. He tried, also,
to express his own intelligence respecting these things, that is:
to produce a painting that interests us by its reality and which,
in these lithographs, gives us an experience as with a multitude
of actualities, an experience intense and yet without extrava-
gance. The lithographs leave us feeling that the dissipations
of life inevitably arrange themselves in a final scene, a scene
that fills us with optimism and satisfaction as the characters
leave the stage with all the lights burning. Is not that, after
all, the chief effect of this pageant? Is it not the principal thing
that the individuality of Dufy should be the coordinating force
and high issue of all these details? And is not this high issue
one of those choices of the intelligence of an artist who, by
making this choice, goes forward with the train of his char-
acters, of whom he is really one, committed to the same pur-
pose? These great blues of Dufy are a kind of assertion of

strength. They create a human self-confidence, as if one had known from the beginning the eventual denouement of knowledge, so long postponed and so incredible.

Raoul Dufy, 1953

Autobiographical Statement for the "New York Herald-Tribune Book Review"

I have no set way of working. A great deal of my poetry has been written while I have been out walking. Walking helps me to concentrate and I suppose that, somehow or other, my own movement gets into the movement of the poems. I have to jot things down as I go along since, otherwise, by the time I got to the end of the poem I should have forgotten the beginning. Often, when I reach the office, I hand my notes to my stenographer who does a better job frequently at deciphering them than I should be able to do myself. Then I pull and tug at the typed script until I have the thing the way I want it, when I put it away for a week or two until I have forgotten about it and can take it up as if it was something entirely fresh. If it satisfies me at that time, that is the end of it.

When you speak of play, I should speak of relaxation. I like most to go to New York for a day and I like the ride to and fro, whether it is in a train or in a car, almost as much as I like being in New York. Then, for me, it is a great relaxation to stop reading. This last summer I made up my mind not to read a thing for several months and only this last week-end I made up my mind not even to put on my glasses, and stuck to it. It adds tremendously to the leisure and space of life not to pick up a book every time one sits down. With all, there is constantly a good deal of walking even though, nowadays, it is only a small fraction of what I used to do, when I could walk up Broadway from Chambers Street to Grace Church in a shade under eighteen minutes and thought nothing at all of walking up the Palisades on Sundays to Nyack and sometimes a long way beyond. If I stopped at Nyack, I could cross to

Beacon and be back in New York in good time for dinner.
But, if I went beyond, I had to come back on the West shore,
which was not the same thing.

                                                    September 20, 1954

The Whole Man: Perspectives, Horizons

The subject of "The Whole Man" would have excited the
attention of Professor Whitehead. One of his constant con-
cerns was with the effect of types of individuals or groups on
society and, in the long run, this was a concern with civili-
zation. For example, he said, "College faculties are going to
want watching. . . . I don't need to tell you that there is a
good deal of sniffing on this, the Harvard College and grad-
uate schools side of the Charles River, sniffing at the new
Harvard School of Business Administration on the opposite
bank. . . . If the American universities were up to their job
they would be taking business in hand and teaching it ethics
and professional standards."

These remarks illustrate the existence of a relation between
an imaginative thinker like Professor Whitehead and business.
To consider the effect of his presence as a member of the
board of directors of a corporation of national scope or, for
that matter, as a member of the executive committee of one
of the larger unions, makes a dazzling parenthesis. I am trying
to make a point by citing Professor Whitehead as an example
of an all-round man, because I do not think the definition of
an all-round man necessarily includes a man of any actual tech-
nical business experience. He need not be a banker who col-
lects books or a manufacturer who reads philosophy. It is a
question of breadth of character and, say, diversity of faculties.
In order to establish in your minds Professor Whitehead's
right to the title, let me quote him again: "The mischief of
elevating the type that has aptitude for economic advancement
is that it denies the superior forms of aptitude which exist in
quite humble people. Who shall say that to live kindly and
graciously and meet one's problems bravely from day to day

is not a great art, or that those who can do it are not great artists. Aesthetics are understood in too restricted a sense."

This sketches for you a man who did as much as any man can do to qualify as an all-round man. He began life as a mathematician and ended it as a philosopher. He is a wholly contemporaneous figure although no longer alive. My quotations are from his Dialogues as recorded by Lucien Price.

Last week I received a letter, greetings on my seventy-fifth birthday, from a young scholar, a Korean. When he was at New Haven, he used to come up to Hartford and the two of us would go out to Elizabeth Park, in Hartford, and sit on a bench by the pond and talk about poetry. He did not wait for the ducks to bring him ideas but always had in mind questions that disclosed his familiarity with the experience of poetry. He spoke in the most natural English. He is now studying in Switzerland at Fribourg, from where his letter came. It was written in what appeared to be the most natural French. Apparently they prize all-round young men in Korea, too. In his letter, he said, "Seventy-five years is not a great deal, when one thinks that the poets and philosophers of the Far East, nourishing themselves only on the mist, have been able to prolong life up to one hundred and even one hundred and fifty years. Historians tell us that they have then been able to enter into fairyland, which is beyond our comprehension today."

That is my idea of a specialist. If these venerable men, by reducing themselves to skin and bones and by meditation prolonged year after year, could perceive final harmony in what all the world would concede to be final form, they would be supreme in life's most magnificent adventure. But they would still be specialists. They would, of course, be specialists in precisely that respect which led us to regard Professor Whitehead as a specimen of the all-round man.

There is an inevitable rapport between all men who seek the truth and who hope, thereby, to be made free and to remain free. I, for one, do not regard the all-round man as the apt opposite of the vertical man. It is illusory so to regard him. There is not the same contradistinction that would exist, say, between the horizontal and the vertical or between the latitudinal and the longitudinal. What really exists is the difference between the theorist and the technician, the difference between Hamlet and Horatio, the difference between the man who can talk about pictures and the man who can afford to buy them. None of these differences involve direct and total opposites. The best technician, the purest mechanic, is necessarily something of a theorist. Hamlet was far more pushing than Horatio ever thought of being, when it came to the point. More often than the satirists admit, the man who can afford to buy pictures is entirely competent to take their measure and at the same time to take the measure both of the artist and of the dealer.

Admitting, however, that human nature contains no built-in iron curtains, the relation of the theorist to society is one thing and the relation of the technician is another. They do not make their impacts by what they have in common but by that in which they differ. The community does not reflect their likenesses but their unlikenesses. If we personalize a university, it corresponds to the all-round man. It is a complex of theorists and of some exceedingly vertical characters. As a whole, however, it is articulate only through its theorists. The world is the world through its theorists. Their function is to conceive of the whole and, from the center of their immense perspectives, to tell us about it. If we say that the basic consideration underlying this evening's discussion is that there are grades of importance in the multitude of man's concerns and that things of first importance must have precedence over things of secondary or lesser importance, it becomes clear that the man who applies himself to considerations of first importance must have precedence over the man who applies himself to things of secondary or lesser importance. This does not require demonstration. Let me try, nevertheless. Modern art often seems to be an attempt to bridge the gap between fact and miracle. To succeed in doing this, if it can be done at all, seems to be exclusively the task of the specialist, that is to say, the painter. If we want to build a bridge, we are bound to employ a bridge builder. It would not help us to invoke even the ghost of Professor Whitehead, which is, no doubt, an exceedingly able-bodied ghost. Sooner or later, however, some all-round man is going to think about this particular bit of bridge building. He will say that there is a kind of corollary to the relation between the theorist and the technician (or if you prefer between the humanist and the scientist) and the relation between art, on the one hand, and painting, on the other. It seems likely that modern art will be affected more by what he has to say by way of approval, if he should approve, or by way of disapproval, if he should disapprove, than by what the painters themselves will have to say.

I suppose it is true that nothing keeps painting alive from one time to another except its form. What is true of painting is no less true of poetry and music. Form alone and of itself is an ever-youthful, ever-vital beauty. The vigor of art perpetuates itself through generations of form. But if the vigor of art is itself formless, and since it is merely a principle it must be, its form comes from those in whom the principle is active, so that generations of form come from generations of men. The all-round man is certain to scrutinize form as he scrutinizes men, that is to say, in relation to all past form. It is inevitable that, from his scrutiny of past form, some ideal should have been created, whether it is derived from something actual in the past or something desired to become actual in the future. Modern art is inescapably framed within these large horizons, which, certainly, are not the horizons of a school, whether of time or place. I repeat that what is true of painting is no less true of poetry and music. The principle of poetry is not confined to its form however definitely it may be contained therein. The principle of music would be an addition to humanity if it were not humanity itself, in other than human form, and while this hyperbole is certain to be repulsive to a good many people, still it may stand. This is the life of the arts which the all-round man thinks of in relation to life itself.

You may be saying that I am going beyond the intentions of this evening's general subject, that I am changing the man with more interests than one into a figure slightly fabulous and also that I am changing the specialist, who is, after all, a creature of necessity, into an illiberal bigot; and that the figures with whom we are really concerned are the educated, intelligent, widely experienced man on the one hand, and the educated, intelligent, less widely experienced man on the other. The trouble is that a man's scope may be independent of his education, intelligence, and experience. Furthermore, one may at least express uncertainty about this scope always having a relation to his effect on society. Notwithstanding this, I prefer my slightly fabulous creature of thought and my technician. As to the latter, it may be said that the ever-increasing mass of people could not live together in the world without the technician and that the elevating of the level of life for people in general is, in all except its concept, a technical problem. The all-round man was in his heyday, in this country, a hundred and fifty or even two hundred years ago. Looking back at them, many of our original political philosophers seem to have been just such all-round men: Franklin, Washington, Jefferson, Madison. There were no technicians, or few. A city the size of New York today could not exist without technicians. We live here today by the aid of types living a century and more apart. What a many-sided man Dr. Benjamin Rush of Philadelphia seems to us to have been. In what a leisurely, spacious city he lived. Did Dr. Rush have much choice about it? Could Philadelphia have been anything but what it was? Could Franklin, Washington, Jefferson, Madison have lived different lives? If we account for our technicians by saying that they are part of the struggle for survival, can we account for our all-round men in any other way? Are the all-round men any less the result of pressure than the technicians? What pressure? What other pressure could it be than the pressure of society itself, the developing forces, the demands and permissions of people adapting themselves to the circumstances in which they find themselves, devising the formulae of civilized existence? The human struggle, however, is immensely more than the mere struggle to survive that these questions suggest.

It is possible to conceive of a neo-Platonic republic in which technicians would be political and moral neuters. In such a republic, one class would be the class of all-round men: the general thinkers, the over-all thinkers, men capable of different sights, the sturdy fathers of that very republic and the authors of its political and moral declarations. Since most of us are technicians on at least one side or, say, to some extent, those in whom we reposed the profoundest confidence would actually be few, perhaps a group composed of men with minds like the rapacious and benign mind of Professor Whitehead. To be ruled by thought, in reality to govern ourselves by the truth or to be able to feel that we were being governed by the truth, would be a great satisfaction, as things go. The great modern faith, the key to an understanding of our times, is faith in the truth and particularly in the idea that the truth is attainable, and that a free civilization based on the truth, in general and in detail, is no less attainable.

Paper presented at American Federation of Arts convention,
October 21, 1954

On Receiving the National Book Award for Poetry

When a poet comes out of his cavern or wherever it is that he secretes himself, even if it is a law office or a place of business, and suddenly finds himself confronted by a great crowd of people, the last thing in the world that enters his mind is to thank those who are responsible for his being there. And this is particularly true if the crowd has come not so much on his account as on account, say, of a novelist or some other figure, who is, as a rule, better known to it than any poet. And yet the crowd will have come to some extent on his account, because the poet exercises a power over life, by expressing life, just as the novelist does; and I am by no means sure that the poet does not exercise this power at more levels than the novelist, with more colors, with as much perception and certainly with more music, not merely verbal music, but the rhythms and tones of human feeling.

I think then that the first thing that a poet should do as he comes out of his cavern is to put on the strength of his particular calling as a poet, to address himself to what Rilke called the mighty burden of poetry and to have the courage to say that, in his sense of things, the significance of poetry is second to none. We can never have great poetry unless we believe that poetry serves great ends. We must recognize this from the beginning so that it will affect everything we do. Our belief in the greatness of poetry is a vital part of its greatness, an implicit part of the belief of others in its greatness. Now, at seventy-five, as I look back on the little that I have done and as I turn the pages of my own poems gathered together in a single volume, I have no choice except to paraphrase the old verse that says that it is not what I am, but what I aspired to be that comforts me. It is not what I have written but what I should like to have written that constitutes my true poems, the uncollected poems which I have not had the strength to realize.

Humble as my actual contribution to poetry may be and however modest my experience of poetry has been, I have learned through that contribution and by the aid of that experience of the greatness that lay beyond, the power over the mind that lies in the mind itself, the incalculable expanse of the imagination as it reflects itself in us and about us. This is the precious scope which every poet seeks to achieve as best he can.

Awards and honors have nothing to do with this. The role of awards and honors in the life of a poet is simply to bring him back to reality, to remind him, in the midst of all his hopes for poetry, that he lives in the world of Darwin and not in the world of Plato. He does not accept them as a true satisfaction because there is no true satisfaction for the poet but poetry itself. He accepts them as tokens of the community that exists between poetry on the one hand and men and women on the other. He accepts them not for their immediate meaning but as symbols and it is their secondary value that makes him the richer for having received them.

And having said this much, I feel better able to express my obligation to this body and to the judges for the privilege of being here today and for the honor they have done me and to say that I am grateful to them and thank them. And I am grateful to my publisher, Alfred Knopf, and his staff, and thank them for the notably handsome job they made of the *Collected Poems.*

January 25, 1955

A Footnote to Saul Bellow's "Pains and Gains"

Some years ago a cable car in San Francisco let go and by the time it arrived at the foot of California Street the passengers were all over the place. A man who had not seen what had happened came out of a side street and went to the nearest victim and asked him what it was all about. The man who was lying in the street said to him, "Well, there has been an accident and we are waiting for the adjuster for the street car company to turn up." "Do you mind," said the newcomer, "if I lie down with you."

Semi-Colon, Spring 1955

On Walt Whitman

I suppose that you think of Whitman as one who lived in Brooklyn. But that was a totally different Brooklyn from the Brooklyn of today. I always think of him as one who lived in Camden and rode around Philadelphia on open street cars. If he was up front, he would be lounging with one foot on the running-board. If he was in back, he would have both feet on the rail.

Nocturne, Spring 1955

Two Prefaces

Gloire du long Désir, Idées

Denis Saurat refers to *Eupalinos* as Valéry's "prose masterpiece," not meaning more, however, than that it was one of a number of masterpieces by Valéry in prose, not to speak of his masterpieces in verse. He cites a brief passage or two and then says, "You have to go back to Bossuet to find such writing in prose." It is easy to believe this of *Eupalinos* if you give yourself up to some of the more rhetorical episodes. There is, for example, the passage in which Socrates speaks of the chance that had placed in his hands an object which became, for him, the source of reflections on the difference between constructing and knowing. Phaedrus asked him to help him to see the object, and thereupon Socrates said:

Well then, Phaedrus, this is how it was. I was walking on the very edge of the sea. I was following an endless shore. . . . This is not a dream I am telling you. I was going I know not whither, overflowing with life, half-intoxicated by my youth. The air, deliciously rude and pure, pressing against my face and limbs, confronted me—an impalpable hero that I must vanquish in order to advance. And this resistance, ever overcome, made of me, too, at every step an imaginary hero, victorious over the wind, and rich in energies that were ever reborn, ever equal to the power of the invisible adversary. . . . That is just what youth is. I trod firmly the winding beach, beaten and hardened by the waves. All things around me were simple and pure: the sky, the sand, the water.

Merely to share the balance and the imagery of these words is to share the particular exhilaration of the experience itself. Then, too, toward the close of the work, in the speech in which Socrates states the conclusions to which the speakers have been brought, he substitutes for oral exhilaration the exhilaration that comes from the progression of the mind. Only enough of this true apostrophe can be cited to identify it. Socrates says to Phaedrus:

O coeternal with me in death, faultless friend, and diamond of sincerity, hear then:

It served no purpose, I fear, to seek this God, whom I have tried all my life to discover, by pursuing him through the realm of thought alone; by demanding him of that most variable and most ignoble sense of the just and the unjust, and by urging him to surrender to the solicitings of the most refined dialectic. The God that one so finds is but a word born of words, and returns to the word. For the reply we make to ourselves is assuredly never anything other than the question itself; and every question put by the mind to the mind is only, and can only be, a piece of simplicity. But on the contrary, it is in acts, and in the combination of acts, that we ought to find the most immediate feeling of the presence of the divine, and the best use for that part of our strength that is unnecessary for living, and seems to be reserved for the pursuits of an indefinable object that infinitely transcends us.

Valéry himself has commented on the work. In a letter to Paul Souday written in 1923, he said:

I was asked to write a text for the album *Architectures*, which is a collection of engravings and plans. Since this text was to be magnificently printed in folio format and fitted in exactly with the decoration and pagination of the work, I was requested to limit its size quite precisely to 115,800 *letters* . . . 115,800 characters! It is true, the characters were to be sumptuous.

I accepted. My dialogue was at first too long. I shortened it; and then a little too short—I lengthened it. I came to find these exigencies very interesting, though it is possible that the text itself may have suffered a little in consequence.

After all, the sculptors never complained who were obliged to house their Olympian personages inside the obtuse triangle of pediments! . . .

There is, also, a letter to Dontenville, *inspecteur d'Académie*, written in 1934. The letter to Paul Souday was written a few months after the composition of *Eupalinos*. The letter to Dontenville was written after the lapse of ten years. Valéry, referring again to the requirement of 115,800 characters, said:

This rigor, at first astounding and repellent, albeit required of a man accustomed enough to the rigor of poems in fixed form, made this man wonder at first—but then find that the peculiar condition proposed to him might be easily enough satisfied by employing the very elastic form of the *dialogue*. (An insignificant rejoinder, introduced or cut out, allows us after a few fumblings to conform with fixed requirements of measurement.) The adjustment was, in effect, easily made in the proofs.

The vast proof sheets I received gave me the strange impression that I had in my hands a work of the sixteenth century and was 400 years dead.

The name of Eupalinos was taken by me from the article "Architecture" in the *Encyclopédie Berthelot*, when I was looking for the name of an architect. I since learned, from a study by the learned Hellenist Bidez (of Ghent), that Eupalinos, an engineer more than an architect, dug canals and built scarcely any temples; I gave him my ideas, as I did Socrates and Phaedrus. Moreover, I have never been in Greece; and as for Greek, I have unfortunately remained the most indifferent of scholars, getting lost in the original text of Plato and finding him, in the translations, terribly long and often boring. . . .

Since Valéry describes Eupalinos as of Megara, and since it was at Megara that the school of Euclid flourished, Valéry's ascription of the name of Eupalinos to the *Encyclopédie Ber-*

thelot dispels the idea of any relation between Eupalinos and Euclid. Finally, to return to the letter to Paul Souday, Valéry said of "these dialogues":

They are works made to order, in which I have not managed or known how to establish a true thought in its most favorable light. I should have tried to show that pure thought and the search for truth in itself can only ever aspire to the discovery or the construction of some *form*.

What, then, are the ideas that Valéry has chosen to be discussed by the shades of Socrates and his friend Phaedrus, as they meet, in our time, in their "dim habitation" on the bank of Ilissus? They are alone and remain alone. Eupalinos does not appear and takes no part in the discussion, unless, as he is spoken of, an image of him passes, like the shade of a shade. The talk is prolonged, and during its course, one or the other speaker propounds ideas. If we attempt to group a number of the ideas propounded, we have something like the following:

There are no details in execution.

Nothing beautiful is separable from life, and life is that which dies.

We must now know what is truly beautiful, what is ugly; what befits man; what can fill him with wonder without confounding him, possess him without stupefying him. . . . It is that which puts him, without effort, above his own nature.

By dint of constructing, . . . I truly believe that I have constructed myself. . . . To construct oneself, to know oneself—are these two distinct acts or not?

What is important for me above all else is to obtain from *that which is going to be*, that it should with all the vigor of its newness satisfy the reasonable requirements of *that which has been*.

O body of mine . . . keep watch over my work. . . . Grant me to find in thy alliance the feeling of what is true; temper, strengthen, and confirm my thoughts.

No geometry without the word.

Nothing can beguile, nothing attract us, . . . nothing by us is chosen from among the multitude of things, and causes a stir in our souls, that was not in some sort pre-existent in our being or secretly awaited by our nature.

An artist is worth a thousand centuries.

Man . . . fabricates by abstraction.

Man can act only because he can ignore.

That which makes and that which is made are indivisible.

The greatest liberty is born of the greatest rigor.

Man's deepest glances are those that go out to the void. They converge beyond the All.

If, then, the universe is the effect of some act; that act itself, the effect of a Being, and of a need, a thought, a knowledge, and a power which belong to that Being, it is then only by an act that you can rejoin the grand design, and undertake the imitation of that which has made all things. And that is to put oneself in the most natural way in the very place of the God.

Now, of all acts the most complete is that of constructing.

But the constructor whom I am now bringing to the fore . . . takes as the starting point of his act, the very point where the god had left off. . . . Here I am, says the Constructor, I am the act.

Must I be silent, Phaedrus?—So you will never know what temples, what theaters, I should have conceived in the pure Socratic style! . . . And exercising an ever stricter control over my mind, at the highest point I should have realized the operation of transforming a quarry and a forest into an edifice, into splendid equilibriums! . . .

Then out of raw materials I was going to put together my structures entirely ordained for the life and joy of the rosy race of men. . . . But you shall learn no more. You can conceive only the old Socrates, and your stubborn shade. . . .

This is the substance of the dialogue between Socrates and Phaedrus, or, at least, these sayings, taken from their talk, indicate what they have been talking about. And what in fact have they been talking about? And why is Valéry justified when, in his closing words, Socrates says: ". . . all that we have been saying is as much a natural sport of the silence of these nether regions as the fantasy of some rhetorician of the other world who has used us as puppets!" Have we been listening to the talk of men or of puppets? These questions are parts of the fundamental question, What should the shades of men talk about, or in any case what may they be expected, categorically, to talk about, in the Elysian fields? Socrates answers this question in the following manner:

Think you not that we ought now to employ this boundless leisure which death leaves us, in judging and rejudging ourselves unwearyingly, revising, correcting, attempting other answers to the events that took place, seeking, in fine, to defend ourselves by illusions against nonexistence, as the living do against their existence?

This Socratic question (and answer) seems empty. The Elysian fields would be the merest penal habitude, if existence in them was not as absolute as it is supposed to be eternal and if our disillusioned shades were dependent, there, on some fresh illusion to be engendered by them for themselves in that transparent realm. It cannot be said freely that Valéry himself fails to exhibit Socrates and Phaedrus engaged in any such discussion, for as the talk begins to reach its end, there emerges from it an Anti-Socrates, to whom an Anti-Phaedrus is listening, as if their conversation had been, after all, a process of judging and rejudging what they had done in the past, with the object of arriving at a state of mind equivalent to an illusion. The dialogue does not create this impression. It does not seem to us, as we read it, that we are concerned with the fortunes of the selves of Socrates and Phaedrus, notwithstanding that that would be a great concern.

We might well expect an existence after death to consist of the revelation of the truth about life, whether the revelation was instantaneous, complete, and dazzling, or whether it was a continuity of discoveries made at will. Hence when a conversation between Socrates and Phaedrus after death occurs, we somehow expect it to consist of resolutions of our severest philosophical or religious difficulties, or of some of them. The present dialogue, however, is a discussion of aesthetics. It may even be said to be the apotheosis of aesthetics, which is not at all what we have had in mind as that which phantoms talk about. It makes the scene seem more like a place in provincial France than either an archaeological or poetic afterworld. In view of Valéry's reference to "the very admirable Stephanos," it is clear that the scene is the afterworld of today, since Mallarmé died in 1898. The trouble is that our sense of what ought to be discussed in the afterworld is derived from specimens that have fallen into disuse. Analysis of the point would be irrelevant. It seems enough to suppose that to the extent that the dead exist in the mind of the living, they discuss whatever the living discuss, although it cannot be said that they do it in quite the same way, since when Phaedrus told Socrates how Socrates, if he had been an architect, would have surpassed "our most famous builders," Eupalinos included, Socrates replied: "Phaedrus, I beg of you! . . . This subtle matter of which we are now made does not permit of our laughing. I feel I ought to laugh, but I cannot. . . . So refrain!"

This elevation of aesthetics is typical of Valéry's thought. It is itself an act of construction. It is not an imbalance attributable to his nature as a poet. It is a consequence of reasonable conviction on his part. His partiality for architecture was instinctive and declared itself in his youthful *Introduction to the Method of Leonardo da Vinci.* It was not an artificiality contrived to please the company of architects who had commanded *Eupalinos.* It seems most natural that a thinker who had traced so much of man's art to man's body should extend man's art itself to the place of God and in that way should relate man's body to God, in the manner in which this is done in *Eupalinos.* Socrates said: "I cannot think that there exists more than one Sovereign Good."

Phaedrus then spoke of what Eupalinos had said concerning forms and appearances. He repeated the words of Eupalinos:

Listen, Phaedrus . . . that little temple, which I built for Hermes, a few steps from here, if you could know what it means to me!—There where the passer-by sees but an elegant chapel—'t is but a trifle: four columns, a very simple style—there I have enshrined the memory of a bright day in my life. O sweet metamorphosis! This delicate temple, none knows it, is the mathematical image of a girl of Corinth, whom I happily loved. It reproduces faithfully the proportions that were peculiarly hers. It lives for me! It gives me back what I have given it. . . .

Eupalinos had then spoken of buildings that are mute, of others that speak, and of others that sing, for which he gave the reasons.

Socrates interrupted Phaedrus with a reference to his prison, which he called "a drab and indifferent place in itself." But he added, "In truth, dear Phaedrus, I never had a prison other than my body."

Eupalinos had gone on to speak to Phaedrus of the effect on the spirit of the sites of ports: ". . . the presence of the

pure horizon, the waxing and the waning of a sail, the emo-
tion that comes of being severed from the earth, the begin-
ning of perils, the sparkling threshold of lands unknown." He
did not profess to be able to connect up an analysis with an
ecstasy. He said:

I feel my need of beauty, proportionate to my unknown resources,
engendering of itself alone forms that give it satisfaction. I desire with
my whole being. . . . The powers assemble. The powers of the soul,
as you know, come strangely up out of the night. . . . By force of
illusion they advance to the very borders of the real. I summon them,
I adjure them by my silence. . . .

He continued:

O Phaedrus, when I design a dwelling (whether it be for the gods,
or for a man), and when I lovingly seek its form, . . . I confess, how
strange soever it may appear to you, *that it seems to me my body is
playing its part in the game.*

Eupalinos ended with the prayer to his body, which Socrates
called "an unexampled prayer," when Phaedrus repeated it.
It is Socrates himself—in the apostrophe to Phaedrus, begin-
ning "O coeternal with me in death," in the closing pages of
the dialogue—who says that man by his acts puts himself in
the place of God, not meaning that he becomes God but that
he puts himself in the very place of God: *la place même du
Dieu.*

It follows that for Eupalinos and for men like him what they
do is their approach to the divine and that the true under-
standing of their craft and the total need that they feel to try
to arrive at a true understanding of it and also at an exact
practice of it are immeasurably the most important things in
the world, through which the world itself comes to the place
of the divine. The present work has to be read with all this in
mind. Any rigorous intellectual discipline in respect to some-
thing significant is a discipline in respect to everything signif-
icant. Valéry's own discipline appears in every page of the
dialogue. The need to understand uncommon things and to
manifest that understanding in common things shows itself
constantly. The modeling of the cluster of roses is an instance.
The comparison of the object found on the shore of the sea,

a natural object, with an object made by man is another. The parable of the Phoenician and how he went about making a ship is a third. It is the parable of the artist. The image of the Phoenician's boat recalled to Socrates ". . . the black, loose-flapping sails of the vessel with its load of priests, which as it labored back from Delos, dragging on its oars. . . ."

At this, Phaedrus exclaimed, "How little you seem to relish living your beautiful life over again!"

Socrates then asked, "Is there anything vainer than the shadow of a sage?"

And Phaedrus said, "A sage himself." The image of the man of action makes the shade of the man of thought regret his life. It is, in a way, the triumphant image of the constructor as it faces the image of the man of thought. Perhaps on his own grounds, it was Valéry, for all his life of study, full of the sea, watching the departure of the Phoenician's supreme boat on its maiden voyage: "Her scarlet cheeks took all the kisses that leapt up to meet her on her course; the well-stretched triangles of her full, hard sails held down her quarter to the wave. . . ."

Is it not possible that one of the most perceptive texts of modern times, although neither immense nor varied, and containing little of life and the nature of man, is yet a masterpiece? Within the limits of the work, Valéry expresses ideas relevant to the thought of his time as it came to consider, with an unprecedented interest, the problems of art. In the dialogue, Socrates speaks of these expatiations as if with a nuance of their triviality. As he continued to probe, his interest heightened to such an extent that he lost his own traditional character; and in this, he became part of the new time in which his shade comes close to us. The nuance of triviality had vanished by the time he reached the noble speech beginning "O coeternal with me in death," when he was ready to say:

The Demiurge was pursuing his own designs, which do not concern his creatures. The converse of this must come to pass. He was not concerned about the troubles that were bound to spring from that very separation which he diverted or perhaps bored himself with making. He has given you the means of living, and even of enjoying many things, but not generally those which you particularly want.

But I come after him. I am he who conceives what you desire a trifle more exactly than you do yourselves. . . . I shall make mistakes sometimes, and we shall have some ruins; but one can always very profitably look upon a work that has failed as a step which brings us nearer to the most beautiful.

In the end, Socrates had become the constructor, and if he had, then Valéry had. The thinker had become the creator. Jean Wahl might have diminished this to a defense mechanism. Perhaps it was an appearance of what Alain called the inimitable visage of the artist. To be a little more exact in quoting Alain, one should say that the creator had asserted its parentage of the thinker, for Alain had spoken of thought as the daughter of poetry in a passage peculiarly applicable to Valéry. He had said that of all the indicators of thought the most sensitive were poets, first because they take risks a little further than logic permits; also because the rule they adopt always carries them a little beyond what they hoped for. Mallarmé and Valéry announce a new climate of thought. They want clear enigmas, those that are developable, that is to say, mathematical. Alain says:

And if it is true, as I believe, that Thought, daughter of Poetry, resembles her mother, we shall see everywhere a clarity of details, a clarity won by conquest, in the place of our vague aspirations; and the young will make us see another manner of believing—which will be a refusal to believe.

Eupalinos is a work of this "clarity of details." This is its precise description. In it Valéry made language itself a constructor, until Socrates asked:

What is there more mysterious than clarity? . . . What more capricious than the way in which light and shade are distributed over hours and over men? . . . Orpheuslike we build, by means of the word, temples of wisdom and science that may suffice for all reasonable creatures. This great art requires of us an admirably exact language.

It has been said that Rilke, who translated so much of Valéry, including *Eupalinos*, felt an intense interest, as a poet, in the language of the work. The page on music—". . . a mobile edifice, incessantly renewed and reconstructed within itself, and entirely dedicated to the transformations of a soul"; the page on the sea shore—"This frontier between Neptune and Earth"; the page on in the beginning—"In the beginning

. . . there was what is: the mountains and the forests . . ."—
are pages of true poetry. It was natural for such pages to give
Rilke pleasure. But what impressed him was what he called
the composure and finality of Valéry's language. Rilke read
Eupalinos when it came out in the *Nouvelle Revue française*,
and his translation of it was the last work he did before he died.

It seems sometimes, in the fluidity of the dialogue, as if the
discussion was casual and fortuitous or, say, Socratic. But a
discussion over which the mind of Socrates presides derives
much of its vitality from this characteristic, so that when the
talk is over, we have a sense of extended and noble unity, a
sense of large and long-considered form.

Chose légère, ailée, sacrée

In 1930, Louis Séchan published a work on *La Danse
grecque antique*, which contained a chapter on Valéry's *Dance
and the Soul*. M. Séchan was Professor of Greek Language
and Literature at the University of Montpellier. He sent a copy
of this book to Valéry, who acknowledged it in a letter, which
it seems worth while to copy at length, as follows:

I thank you greatly for your attention in sending me your fine work
on Greek dancing. I learn from it many things I ignored—and even
ignored about myself. Your kind chapter on my little dialogue gen-
erously attributes to me much more erudition than I ever possessed.
Neither Callimachus nor Lucian, Xenophon nor the Parthenia was
known to me; and would not in any case have been of much use to
me. Documents in general impede rather than help me. They result
in difficulties for me, and consequently in peculiar solutions, in all
those compositions in which history must play some part.

In reality, I confined myself to dipping into Emmanuel at the Li-
brary, and I left open on my table the book of Marey which I have
had for the last thirty years. Those outline drawings of jumping and
walking, some memories of ballets were my essential resources. The
flutist does come from the Throne. The head compact like a pine
cone from a living dancer.

The constant thought of the Dialogue is physiological—from the
digestive troubles of the prelude-beginning to the final swoon. Man
is slave to the sympathetic and pneumogastric nerves. Sumptuary sen-
sations, the gestures of luxury, and spectacular thoughts exist only by
the good favor of these tyrants of our vegetative life. Dance is the
type of the runaway.

As for the form of the whole, I have tried to make of the Dialogue itself a sort of ballet of which the Image and the Idea are Coryphaeus in turn. The abstract and the sensible take the lead alternately and unite in the final vertigo.

To sum up: I in no degree strove for historic or technical rigor (and for very good reason). I freely introduced what I needed to maintain my Ballet and vary its figures. This extended to *the ideas themselves*. Here they are *means*. It is true that this idea (that ideas are means) is familiar to me, and perhaps *substantial*. It leads on, moreover, to wicked thoughts about philosophy (cf. "Leonardo and the Philosophers," which I published last year).

I should never have planned to write on the dance, to which I had never given serious thought. Moreover, I considered—and I still do—that Mallarmé had exhausted the subject in so far as it belongs to literature. This conviction made me first refuse the invitation of the *Revue musicale*. Other reasons made me resolve to accept it. What Mallarmé had prodigiously written then became a peculiar condition of my work. I must neither ignore him nor espouse his thought too closely. I adopted the line of introducing, amid the divers interpretations which the three characters give of the dance, the one whose formulation and incomparable demonstration through style are to be found in the *Divagations*.

I have explained myself at considerable length. But I feel I owe this to one who has been such an attentive and even fervent critic of my Dialogue. You have perfectly presented its spirit, which, in truth, is neither *this* nor *that*—neither with Plato, nor according to Nietzsche, but an act of transformation.

The nature of M. Séchan's book can be gathered from Valéry's comment on it. M. Séchan thought that Valéry's attitude toward *Dance and the Soul* as something fortuitous was typical of Valéry. He discussed Mallarmé's remarks in *Divagations* on the dance as corporeal writing or hieroglyphic, and he dwelt on the resemblance between the dance and the meditations of the spirit in moments of tension. He referred to the analysis of *Dance and the Soul* by Paul Souday in the latter's work on Valéry and, in particular, to the contrasting conceptions of the dance by the persons taking part in the present dialogue, thus: the conception of Eryximachus (the Eryximachus of Plato's *Symposium*) that the dance is purely sensory; the conception of Phaedrus (the Phaedrus of *Eupalinos*) that the dance is psychologically evocative; and the conception of

Socrates, which reconciles the other two, that the dance is an interpretation of a secret and physical order. And finally M. Séchan speaks of the fact that both Schopenhauer and Nietzsche were influential forces at the time when Valéry was maturing. But he regards *Dance and the Soul* as Apollonian rather than Dionysian, because as Apollonian it corresponds better with the Greek genius. It is, in fact, possible, if only because Valéry published *Eupalinos* and *Dance and the Soul* together and because they seem to be inseparable companions, that Valéry had a sense that *Eupalinos* was Apollonian and that *Dance and the Soul* was Dionysian. On the other hand, it is certain that Valéry's own genius was Apollonian and that the Dionysian did not comport with it, and, with that, the subject may be dismissed.

Dance and the Soul is a lesser work than *Eupalinos*, since it does not contain the proliferation of ideas which characterizes *Eupalinos*. Socrates is always and everywhere proliferation. In this dialogue, however, he confines himself to the proliferation of a single idea. He asks repeatedly the question, "O my friends, what in truth is dance?" and again, "But what then is dance, and what can steps say?" and again, "O my friends, I am only asking you what is dance. . . ."

While these questions are being asked, a dance is going on, a ballet is being danced. The scene is a banqueting place with a banquet in course. There are servants serving food and no end of wine. The persons are Socrates, Phaedrus, and Eryximachus, great numbers of multicolored groups of smiling figures, whirling and dissolving in enchanted sequences, Athikte, the *première danseuse*, who is commencing, the *musiciennes*, one of whom, coral-rose, is blowing an enormous shell, another, a tall flute-player, who denotes the measure with her toe. Socrates is conscious of ideas that come to him as he watches Athikte and observes the majesty of her movements. Eryximachus exclaims: "Dear Socrates, she teaches us that which we do, showing clearly to our souls that which our bodies accomplish obscurely."

Phaedrus adds: "In which respect this dancer would, according to you, have something Socratic, teaching us, in the matter of walking, to know ourselves a little better."

These remarks illustrate the constant allusions to the dancers which keep the reader of the dialogue in the presence of the dancers. He hears the voices of the speakers and watches the movements of the dancers at one and the same time, without the least confusion, as he would do in reality; and as his interest in what is being said grows greater as the discussion approaches its resolutions, and as his absorption in the spectacle becomes deeper with his increased understanding of it and because of the momentum toward the ultimate climax, he realizes, for the first time, the excitement of a meaning as it is revealed at once in thought and in act.

The work is regenerative. M. Séchan quoted the words of Plato on the poet: *chose légère, ailée, sacrée.* These words apply equally to Valéry's text. Here again we have what we had in *Eupalinos,* the body as source and the act in relation to the body. Socrates says to Eryximachus:

Do you not see then, Eryximachus, that among all intoxications the noblest, the one most inimical to that great tedium, is the intoxication due to acts? Our acts, and more particularly those of our acts which set our bodies in motion, may bring us into a strange and admirable state. . . .

Still speaking to Eryximachus, he made a gesture in the direction of

. . . that ardent Athikte, who divides and gathers herself together again, who rises and falls, so promptly opening out and closing in, and who appears to belong to constellations other than ours—seems to live, completely at ease, in an element comparable to fire—in a most subtle essence of music and movement, wherein she breathes boundless energy, while she participates with all her being in the pure and immediate violence of extreme felicity.

As he continues, he says what sums up his argument and sums up the whole work:

If we compare our grave and weighty condition with the state of that sparkling salamander, does it not seem to you that our ordinary acts, begotten by our successive needs, and our gestures and incidental movements are like coarse materials, like an impure stuff of duration—whilst that exaltation and that vibration of life, that supremacy of tension, that transport into the highest agility one is capable of, have the virtues and the potencies of flame; and that the shames, the worries, the sillinesses, and the monotonous foods of existence are consumed within it, making what is divine in a mortal woman shine before our eyes?

There is a series of speeches by Socrates in the closing pages of the dialogue which are full of the noble rhetoric of the truth. But they are still rhetoric; and it is the presence of this rhetoric of the truth that makes the work regenerative. It is rhetoric to say: "In a sonorous world, resonant and rebounding, this intense festival of the body in the presence of our souls offers light and joy. . . . All is more solemn, all more light, all more lively, all stronger; all is possible in another way; all can begin again indefinitely. . . ." So, too, it is rhetoric to say: "I hear the clash of all the glittering arms of life! . . . The cymbals crush in our ears any utterance of secret thoughts. They resound like kisses from lips of bronze. . . ." It is, however, this rhetoric, the eloquent expression of that which is precisely true, that gives what it expresses an irresistible compulsion as when Socrates says: "A body, by its simple force, and its act, is powerful enough to alter the nature of things more profoundly than ever the mind in its speculations and dreams was able to do!"

While Socrates is pronouncing his subtle and solemn words, our eyes remain fastened on Athikte, while she tries to make us see that which Socrates is seeking to tell us. She moves through jewels, makes gestures like scintillations, filches impossible attitudes from nature, so that Eryximachus says, "Instant engenders form, and form makes the instant visible." She continues to dance until she falls. When she has fallen and lies, white, on the ground, she says something to herself, the simplest possible thing. Phaedrus asks what it is and Eryximachus replies, "She said: 'How well I feel!' "—a remark immense with everything that Socrates himself had been saying a moment or two before. She has spoken in a rhetoric which achieves the pathetic essential almost without speech. It is obvious that this degree of agitation has been reached in what is, after all, an exegetical work, through the form of the work. Valéry's slim and cadenced French adds its own vitality to the original. It seems enough to present the work in this brief manner. André Levinson said in relation to *Dance and the Soul*: "To explain a thing is to deform it; to think is to substitute what is arbitrary for the unknowable truth." What *Dance and the Soul* requires is not so much explanation as— what Valéry called M. Séchan—attentive and fervent critics or, say, readers, willing to experience the transformation which knowing a little about themselves brings about as by miracle or, say, by art.

Man has many ways to attain the divine, and the way of Eupalinos and the way of Athikte and the various ways of Paul Valéry are only a few of them.

Dialogues, by Paul Valéry, 1956

Connecticut Composed

The thrift and frugality of the Connecticut Yankee were necessary to life in the Colony and still are. They were imposed on him by the character of the natural world in which he had come to live, which has not changed. It required thrift and frugality to live in Connecticut and still does. And now after three centuries or more of this tradition, the people of the state are proud of it. They are proud of the kind of strength of character which they have derived from this necessity, proud of the intelligent ingenuity with which they faced their many hardships and with which they rose to the high general level of intelligence and dignified style of living that is now so characteristic of them. The other day, early in April, when the weather was still bleak and everything still had the look of winter, I went from Hartford to Boston, on the railroad by way of Willimantic. Everything seemed gray, bleached and derelict and the word derelict kept repeating itself as part of the activity of the train. But this was a precious ride through the character of the state. The soil everywhere seemed thin and difficult and every cutting and open pit disclosed gravel and rocks, in which only the young pine trees seemed to do well. There were chicken farms, some of them abandoned, and there were cow-barns. The great barns of other states do not exist. There were orchards of apples and peaches. Yet in this sparse landscape with its old houses of gray and white there were other houses, smaller, fresher, more fastidious.

And spring was coming on. It was as if the people whose houses I was seeing shared the strength that was beginning to assert itself. The man who loves New England and particularly the spare region of Connecticut loves it precisely because of the spare colors, the thin lights, the delicacy and slightness of the beauty of the place. The dry grass on the thin surfaces would soon change to a lime-like green and later to an emerald brilliant in a sunlight never too full. When the spring was at its height we should have a water-color not an oil and we should all feel that we had had a hand in the painting of it, if only in choosing to live there where it existed. Now, when all the primitive difficulties of getting started have been overcome, we live in the tradition which is the true mythology of the region and we breathe in with every breath the joy of having ourselves been created by what has been endured and mastered in the past. We think of the state not only as a matrix, but as a very mother, above all in the spring, when the reward of discipline is visible and tangible, or seems to be. We seem to be conscious then, more than at any other time, of the extent to which those who helped to prepare each present season are part of it, and of the extent to which the nature of the land is part of them and of ourselves.

There are only some two million people living in the state, which is the third smallest state in the country. Of these a quarter of a million are foreign born. Of those who were born in the state, many are the children of parents who were themselves foreign-born, or of parents whose parents, generation back of generation, were foreign-born. All of us together constitute the existing community. Those who descend from earlier generations know that the forces that moulded them are today moulding those who descend from later generations. The children look alike. There are no foreigners in Connecticut. Once you are here you are or you are on your way to become a Yankee. I was not myself born in the state. It is not that I am a native but that I feel like one. It interests me to think of our sea-coast—the coast-line of Connecticut, much of it merely the coast of Long Island Sound. I like to think

of all the small ports and harbors on that coast, the little fish-
ing towns; also the towns up and down the Connecticut River,
the anchorages of the whalers. Those who did not do too well
at making livings in Connecticut made their livings in China or
the Marquesas or Jamaica and used the banks of the Connecti-
cut River as the sites of their dwellings and of the gazebos in the
gardens of their dwellings, in which they sat and planned and
fostered the temples and universities and the many practical
enterprises to which their imaginations were addicted.

But that was when they had come home. There is nothing
that gives the feel of Connecticut like coming home to it. I
am not thinking of the thousands of commuters who come
home to it every night from New York; nor even, since it is
not a question of distance, of those returning after remoter
and longer absences. It is easy to see the picture in the mind
of those who are far away as if the state was a single metrop-
olis, in the way they say that England is a park. Truly Con-
necticut is much like a single metropolis, highly industrial,
with factories and mills and shops and schools and homes
spread out everywhere, with a few major concentrations in
Bridgeport, New Haven, Hartford, New London. One could
say in a few words simply that Connecticut is an industrial and
business center. That would leave out the salt-water of Noank
and Stonington, the hills in which the various Cornwalls are
situated, the sense of being on high land, of being on a large
plateau, at Pomfret, the rare rich fields over East, the heights
and depths of our Western and part of our Northern borders,
the special countries of the Housatonic and the Thames. Yet
to return to these places would not be quite what I had in
mind when I spoke of the coming home that gives one the
feel of Connecticut. What I had in mind was something
deeper that nothing can ever change or remove. It is a ques-
tion of coming home to the American self in the sort of place
in which it was formed. Going back to Connecticut is a return
to an origin. And as it happens, it is an origin which many
men all over the world, both those who have been part of us
and those who have not, share in common: an origin of har-
dihood, good faith and good will.

Script for "This Is America" radio series, April 1955

FROM THE NOTEBOOKS

1915?

Schemata

I.

A vivid fruit in vivid atmosphere.

II.

Wear only your golden masks tonight.

III.

Land of pine and marble.

IV.

Good worm . . . . .

V.

Diamond on the slipper of her naked ghost.

VI.

Is it a goat, or a cock, you chase now, skeleton death?

VII.

The old marble is gray in the rain.

VIII.

A weaving of the slow shadow-wheel.

IX.

The hairy saints of the north.

X.

Mrs. Burbank's cakes.

XI.

Time on time's revenges.

1918?

from *Adagia*

I

Happiness is an acquisition.

Progress in any aspect is a movement through changes of terminology.

The highest pursuit is the pursuit of happiness on earth.

L'art d'être heureuse.

Goethe's *General-Beichte* was written of another who "spake three thousand proverbs, and his songs were a thousand and five. From Goethe proverbs poured incessantly."
    Goethe: Felkin O. Univ. P. 1932.

Each age is a pigeon-hole.

The stream of consciousness is individual; the stream of life is total. Or, the stream of consciousness is individual; the stream of life, total.

To give a sense of the freshness or vividness of life is a valid purpose for poetry. A didactic purpose justifies itself in the mind of the teacher; a philosophical purpose justifies itself in the mind of the philosopher. It is not that one purpose is as justifiable as another but that some purposes are pure others impure. Seek those purposes that are purely the purposes of the pure poet.

The poet makes silk dresses out of worms.

The public of the poet. The public of the organist is the church in which he improvises.

Authors are actors, books are theatres.

An attractive view: The aspects of earth of interest to a poet are the casual ones, as light or color, images.

Definitions are relative. The notion of absolutes is relative.

Life is an affair of people not of places. But for me life is an affair of places and that is the trouble.

Wisdom asks nothing more.

Parfait Martinique: coffee mousse, rum on top, a little cream on top of that.

Literature is the better part of life. To this it seems inevitably necessary to add provided life is the better part of literature.

Thought is an infection. In the case of certain thoughts it becomes an epidemic.

After one has abandoned a belief in god, poetry is that essence which takes its place as life's redemption.

Art, broadly, is the form of life or the sound or color of life. Considered as form (in the abstract) it is often indistinguishable from life itself.

The poet seems to confer his identity on the reader. It is easiest to recognize this when listening to music—I mean this sort of thing: the transference.

A poem is a meteor.

An evening's thought is like a day of clear weather.

The loss of a language creates confusion or dumbness.

The collecting of poetry from one's experience as one goes along is not the same thing as merely writing poetry.

A grandiose subject is not an assurance of a grandiose effect but, most likely, of the opposite.

As life grows more terrible, its literature grows more terrible.

Poetry and materia poetica are interchangeable terms.

The imagination wishes to be indulged.

A new meaning is the equivalent of a new word.

Poetry is not personal.

The earth is not a building but a body.

Manner is an additional element.

Poetry is a form of melancholia. Or rather, in melancholy it is one of the "aultres choses solatieuses."

The poet must come at least as the miraculous beast and, at his best, as the miraculous man.

Life cannot be based on a thesis, since, by nature, it is based on instinct. A thesis, however, is usually present and living is the struggle between thesis and instinct.

Weather is a sense of nature. Poetry is a sense.

There are two opposites: the poetry of rhetoric and the poetry of experience.

The poet must put the same degree of intentness into his poetry as, for example, the traveller into his adventure, the painter into his painting.

The bare image and the image as a symbol are the contrast: the image without meaning and the image as meaning. When the image is used to suggest something else, it is secondary. Poetry, as an imaginative thing, consists of more than lies on the surface.

Politics is the struggle for existence.

One has a sensibility range beyond which nothing really exists for one. And in each this is different.

In poetry, you must love the words, the ideas and images and rhythms with all your capacity to love anything at all.

The individual partakes of the whole. Except in extraordinary cases he never adds to it.

It is the belief and not the god that counts.

Things seen are things as seen. Absolute real.

Not all objects are equal.

What we see in the mind is as real to us as what we see by the eye.

The mind is the most powerful thing in the world.

There is nothing in life except what one thinks of it.

A new future is good business.

Poetry is a form of melancholia.

There is nothing beautiful in life except life.

There is no wing like meaning.

Poetry is not a personal matter.

Poetry is a means of redemption.

Sentimentality is a failure of feeling.

The imagination is the romantic.

Poetry is not the same thing as the imagination taken alone. Nothing is itself taken alone. Things are because of interrelations or interactions.

The final belief is to believe in a fiction, which you know to be a fiction, there being nothing else. The exquisite truth is to know that it is a fiction and that you believe in it willingly.

I

All of our ideas come from the natural world: Trees = umbrellas.

II

There is nothing so offensive to a man of intellectual principle as unprincipled thinking.

Wine and music are not good until afternoon. But poetry is like prayer in that it is most effective in solitude and in the times of solitude as, for example, in the earliest morning.

Intolerance respecting other people's religion is toleration itself in comparison with intolerance respecting other people's art.

The great objective is the truth not only of the poem but of poetry.

Poetry is a poetic conception, however expressed. A poem is poetry expressed in words. But in a poem there is a poetry of words. Obviously, a poem may consist of several poetries.

That part of the truth of the world that has its origin in the feelings.

The exposition of a theory of poetry involves comparison with other theories and the analysis of all.

Ethics are no more a part of poetry than they are of painting.

Poetry is the expression of the experience of poetry.

Values other than those merely of the eye and ear.

Seelensfriede durch dichtung.

The ideal is the actual become anaemic. The romantic is often pretty much the same thing.

As the reason destroys, the poet must create.

The exquisite environment of fact. The final poem will be the poem of fact in the language of fact. But it will be the poem of fact not realized before.

We live in the mind.

A poet must have something by nature and he must know more about the world by reason thereof.

The poet feels *abundantly* the poetry of everything.

To live in the world but outside of existing conceptions of it.

It is the explanations of things that we make to ourselves that disclose our character:

The subjects of one's poems are the symbols of one's self or of one of one's selves.

Poetry has to be something more than a conception of the mind. It has to be a revelation of nature. Conceptions are artificial. Perceptions are essential.

A poem should be part of one's sense of life.

To read a poem should be an experience, like experiencing an act.

There is no difference between god and his temple.

War is the periodical failure of politics.

Money is a kind of poetry.

Poetry is an effort of a dissatisfied man to find satisfaction through words, occasionally of the dissatisfied thinker to find satisfaction through his emotions.

It is not every day that the world arranges itself in a poem.

The death of one god is the death of all.

In the presence of extraordinary actuality, consciousness takes the place of imagination.

Everything tends to become real; or everything moves in the direction of reality.

There is an intensely pejorative aspect of the idea of the real. The opposite should be the case. Its own poetry is actual.

One does not write for any reader except one.

Every man dies his own death.

The writer who is content to destroy is on a plane with the writer who is content to translate. Both are parasites.

The thing said must be the poem not the language used in saying it. At its best the poem consists of both elements.

A poet looks at the world somewhat as a man looks at a woman.

To have nothing to say and to say it in a tragic manner is not the same thing as to have something to say.

The poem is a nature created by the poet.

The aesthetic order includes all other orders but is not limited to them.

Religion is dependent on faith. But aesthetics is independent of faith. The relative positions of the two might be reversed. It is possible to establish aesthetics in the individual mind as immeasurably a greater thing than religion. Its present state is the result of the difficulty of establishing it except in the individual mind.

La vie est plus belle que les idées.

Perhaps there is a degree of perception at which what is real and what is imagined are one: a state of clairvoyant observation, accessible or possibly accessible to the poet or, say, the acutest poet.

The ultimate value is reality.

Realism is a corruption of reality.

Perhaps it is of more value to infuriate philosophers than to go along with them.

The world is the only thing fit to think about.

All history is modern history.

Poetry is the sum of its attributes.

I don't think we should insist that the poet is normal or, for that matter, that anybody is.

This happy creature— It is he that invented the Gods. It is he that put into their mouths the only words they have ever spoken.

Poetry is a purging of the world's poverty and change and evil and death. It is a present perfecting, a satisfaction in the irremediable poverty of life.

Poetry is the scholar's art.

The thing seen becomes the thing unseen. The opposite is, or seems to be, impossible.

To study and to understand the fictive world is the function of the poet.

When one is young everything is physical; when one is old everything is psychic.

Hermit of poetry.

Which is correct: whether, if I respect my ancestors I am bound to respect myself or if I respect myself I am bound to respect my ancestors?

Meine Seele muss Prachtung haben.

The most beautiful (the only beautiful) (beautiful is an inadequate and temporizing improvisation) thing in the world is, of course, the world itself. This is so not only logically but categorically.

I believe in the image.

The tongue is an eye.

God is a symbol for something that can as well take other forms, as, for example, the form of high poetry.

The satisfactions of nature.

The time will come when poems like Paradise will seem like very *triste* contraptions.

The poet is a stronger life.

The great conquest is the conquest of reality. It is not to present life, for a moment, as it might have been.

A poem is a pheasant.

How has the human spirit ever survived the terrific literature with which it has had to contend?

The gold dome of things is the perfected spirit.

Reality is a vacuum.

All men are murderers.

Poetry is metaphor.

The word must be the thing it represents otherwise it is a symbol. It is a question of identity.

When the mind is like a hall in which thought is like a voice speaking, the voice is always that of some one else.

In dramatic poetry the imagination attaches itself to a heightened reality. Degrees or planes of reality.

It is necessary to propose an enigma to the mind. The mind always proposes a solution.

There must be something of the peasant in every poet.

Aristotle is a skeleton.

The body is the great poem.

The purpose of poetry is to contribute to man's happiness.

There is a basic literature of which poetry is an essential part.

How things seem now is always a question of sensibility.

Man is an eternal sophomore.

It is necessary to any originality to have the courage to be an amateur.

Life is the elimination of what is dead.

The fundamental difficulty in any art is the problem of the normal.

The poet is the priest of the invisible.

Society is a sea.

Metaphor creates a new reality from which the original appears to be unreal.

The transition from make believe for one's self to make believe for others is the beginning, or the end, of poetry in the individual.

The acquisitions of poetry are fortuitous: trouvailles. (Hence, its disorder.)

Exhibitionism attaches and is not inherent.

Romanticism is to poetry what the decorative is to painting.

The great poem is the disengaging of (a) reality.

The eye sees less than the tongue says. The tongue says less than the mind thinks.

Reality is the motif.

We have to step boldly into man's interior world or not at all.

A living poetry that deals with everything or none.

To touch with the imagination in respect to reality.

The World Reduced to One Thing

Genealogy is the science of correcting other genealogists' mistakes.

The poet must not adapt his experience to that of the philosopher.

It is manner that becomes stale.

Description is an element, like air or water.

The reading of a poem should be an experience. Its writing must be all the more so.

A poem is a café. (Restoration.)

Poets acquire humanity.

Thought tends to collect in pools.

The reason is a part of nature and is controlled by it.

Life is not people and scene but thought and feeling.

In the world of words, the imagination is one of the forces of nature.

Life is not free from its forms.

The poet comes to words as nature comes to dry sticks.

Words are the only melodeon.

Bringing out the music of the eccentric sounds of words is no different in principle from bringing out their form & its eccentricities (Cummings): language as the material of poetry not its mere medium or instrument.

We have made too much of life. A journal of life is rarely a journal of happiness.

Since man made the world, the inevitable god is the beggar.

Poetry sometimes crowns the search for happiness. It is itself a search for happiness.

God is a postulate of the ego.

Esthétique is the measure of a civilization: not the sole measure, but a measure.

Poetry must resist the intelligence almost successfully.

The romantic exists in precision as well as in imprecision.

Literature is based not on life but on propositions about life, of which this is one.

Life is a composite of the propositions about it.

A change of style is a change of subject.

Poetry is the statement of a relation between a man and the world.

The feeling or the insight is that which quickens the words, not the other way round.

A man cannot search life for unprecedented experiences.

In children it is not the imitation that pleases us, but our perception of it. In later life, the pejorative aspect of imitation discloses its inherent unpleasantness. To give pleasure an imitation must have been studied as an imitation and then it pleases us as art.

Everything accomplishes itself: fulfills itself.

The imagination is not the only co-relation of reality. Science etc.

The romantic is the first phase of (a non-pejorative) lunacy.

The full flower of the actual, not the California fruit of the ideal.

In the end, the esthetic is completely crushed and destroyed by the inability of the observer who has himself been crushed to have any feeling for it left.

The world is myself. Life is myself.

II

God is in me or else is not at all (does not exist).

The world is a force, not a presence.

Loss of faith is growth.

People take the place of thoughts.

Life lived on the basis of opinion is more nearly life than life lived without opinion.

Thought is life.

Everyone takes sides in social change if it is profound enough.

Poetry is not limited to a single effect, as, for example, overt reality.

Poetry is a search for the inexplicable.

Poems are new subjects.

Ignorance is one of the sources of poetry.

Poetry is a pheasant disappearing in the brush.

We never arrive intellectually. But emotionally we arrive constantly (as in poetry, happiness, high mountains, vistas).

The imagination consumes & exhausts some element of reality.

The poet is a god or The young poet is a god. The old poet is a tramp.

If the mind is the most terrible force in the world, it is, also, the only force that defends us against terror. (or)

The mind is the most terrible force in the world principally in this that it is the only force that can defend us against itself. The modern world is based on this pensée.

The poet represents the mind in the act of defending us against itself.

Quaere, whether the residual satisfaction in a poem is the intellectual one.

No man is a hero to anyone that knows him.

On the bearing of the poet:
  1. The prestige of the poet is part of the prestige of poetry.
  2. The prestige of poetry is essential to the prestige of the poet.

The world is at the mercy of the strongest mind in it whether that strength is the strength of sanity or insanity, cunning or good-will.

Every poem is a poem within a poem: the poem of the idea within the poem of the words.

The poetic view of life is larger than any of its poems (a larger thing than any poem); and to recognize this is the beginning of the recognition of the poetic spirit.

On the death of some men the world reverts to ignorance.

Poetry is the gaiety/joy of language.

Words are everything else in the world.

Only a noble people evolve a noble God.

If the answer is frivolous, the question was frivolous.

Unless life is interesting, there is nothing left (or, unless life is made interesting).

The interest of life is experienced by participating and by being part, not by observing nor by thinking.

Eventually an imaginary world is entirely without interest.

To be at the end of fact is not to be at the beginning of the imagination but it is to be at the end of both.

To sit in a park and listen to the locusts; to sit in a park and hear church-bells—two pasts or one present and one past?

What is meant by interest? Is it a form of liking?

One cannot spend one's time in being modern when there are so many more important things to be.

The man who asks questions seeks only to reach a point where it will no longer be necessary for him to ask questions.

I have no life except in poetry. No doubt that would be true if my whole life was free for poetry.

The more intensely one feels something that one likes the more one is willing for it to be what it is.

The mind is not equal to the demands of oratory, poetry etc.

There is a nature that absorbs the mixedness of metaphors.

The world of the poet depends on the world that he has contemplated.

Poetry is a health.

Poetry is great only as it exploits great ideas or what is often the same thing great feelings.

Imagination applied to the whole world is vapid in comparison to imagination applied to a detail.

It is easier to copy than to think, hence fashion. Besides a community of originals is not a community.

There must be some wing on which to fly.

Poetry is a cure of the mind.

Most modern reproducers of life, even including the camera, really repudiate it. We gulp down evil, choke at good.

We like the world because we do.

The mind that in heaven created the earth and the mind that on earth created heaven were, as it happened, one.

Nothing could be more inappropriate to American literature than its English source since the Americans are not British in sensibility.

Poetry is a response to the daily necessity of getting the world right.

A poem should stimulate the sense of living and of being alive.

Reality is the spirit's true center.

A poem need not have a meaning and like most things in nature often does not have.

Newness (not novelty) may be the highest individual value in poetry. Even in the meretricious sense of newness a new poetry has value.

There is nothing in the world greater than reality. In this predicament we have to accept reality itself as the only genius.

Man is the imagination or rather the imagination is man.

To "subtilize experience" = to apprehend the complexity of the world, to perceive the intricacy of appearance.

Poetry is often a revelation of the elements of appearance.

Literature is the abnormal creating an illusion of the normal.

Poetry is a renovation of experience. Originality is an escape from repetition.

The theory of poetry is the life of poetry. Christianity is an exhausted culture.

Feed my lambs (on the bread of living) . . . The glory of god is the glory of the world . . . To find the spiritual in reality . . . To be concerned with reality.

The theory of poetry is the theory of life.

Reality is the object seen in its greatest common sense.

Poetry constantly requires a new relation.

Reality is not what it is. It consists of the many realities which it can be made into.

What reality lacks is a *noeud vital* with life.

French and English constitute a single language.

One's ignorance is one's chief asset.

Proposita:
   1. God and the imagination are one.
   2. The thing imagined is the imaginer.
The second equals the thing imagined and the imaginer are one. Hence, I suppose, the imaginer is God.

The greatest piece of fiction: Greek mythology. Classical my-thology but Greek above Latin.

Poetry is, (and should be,) for the poet, a source of pleasure and satisfaction, not a source of honors.

1930?–1955

from *Sur Plusieurs Beaux Sujects*

Success as the result of industry is a peasant ideal.

Success is to be happy with the wise.

Suppose any man whose spirit has survived had consulted his contemporaries as to what to do, or what to think, or what music to write, and so on.

In the long run the truth does not matter.

It should be said of poetry that it is essentially romantic as if one were recognizing the truth about poetry for the first time. Although the romantic is referred to, most often, in a pejor-ative sense, this sense attaches, or should attach, not to the romantic in general but to some phase of the romantic that has become stale. Just as there is always a romantic that is potent, so there is always a romantic that is impotent.

For myself, the indefinite, the impersonal, atmospheres and oceans and, above all, the principle of order are precisely what I love; and I don't see why, for a philosopher, they should not be the ultimate inamorata. The premise to Storrs is that the universe is explicable only in terms of humanity.

Ex Divina Pulchritudine esse omnium Derivatur, and, above all, poetry. And in reflecting on this think of it in connection with the association of poetry and pleasure and, also, in con-nection with l'instinct du bonheur. If happiness is in our selves, divine pulchritude is in our selves and poetry is a rev-elation or a contact.

Poetry creates a fictitious existence on an exquisite plane. This definition must vary as the plane varies, an exquisite plane being merely illustrative.

An objection to originality in poetry is an objection to poetry itself because originality is of the essence of the thing. Renard wrote to Rostand that one of his books was "jeune, surprenant, émouvant et joli." The original is the surprenant, even the émouvant.

1932?–1936?

Materia Poetica

I

Merit in poets is as boring as merit in people.

II

It is life that one is trying to get at in poetry.

III

The poet confers his identity on the reader. He cannot do this if he intrudes personally.

IV

Accuracy of observation is the equivalent of accuracy of thinking.

V

Collecting poetry from one's experience as one goes along is not the same thing as merely writing poetry.

VI

The relation of art to life is of the first importance especially in a skeptical age since, in the absence of a belief in God, the mind turns to its own creations and examines them, not alone from the aesthetic point of view, but for what they reveal, for what they validate and invalidate, for the support that they give.

VII

Art involves vastly more than the sense of beauty.

VIII

Life is the reflection of literature.

IX

Usage is everything. (Les idées sont destinées à être deformées à l'usage. Georges Braque, Verve, No. 2).

X

The romantic cannot be seen through; it is for the moment willingly not seen through.

XI

A dead romantic is a falsification.

XII

Poetry is a means of redemption.

XIII

Poetry may be an aspect of melancholia. At least, in melancholy, it is one of the "aultres choses solatieuses."

XIV

The poet must come, at his worst, as the miraculous beast and, at his best, as the miraculous man.

XV

(Poet,) feed my lambs.

XVI

The real is only the base. But it is the base.

XVII

The poem reveals itself only to the ignorant man.

XVIII

The relation between the poetry of experience and the poetry of rhetoric is not the same thing as the relation between the poetry of reality and that of the imagination. Experience, at least in the case of a poet of any scope, is much broader than reality.

XIX

To a large extent, the problems of poets are the problems of painters and poets must often turn to the literature of painting for a discussion of their own problems.

XX

Abstraction is a part of idealism. It is in that sense that it is ugly.

XXI

In poetry, at least, the imagination must not detach itself from reality.

XXII

Not all objects are equal. The vice of imagism was that it did not recognize this.

XXIII

All poetry is experimental poetry.

XXIV

Each of us has a sensibility range beyond which nothing exists. In each this is different.

XXV

In poetry, you must love the words, the ideas, the images and the rhythms with all your capacity, to love anything at all.

XXVI

A journey in space equals a journey in time.

XXVII

Poetry must be irrational.

XXVIII

The purpose of poetry is to make life complete in itself.

XXIX

Poetry increases the feeling for reality.

XXX

Consider:
    a. That the whole world is material for poetry;
    b. That there is not a specifically poetic material.

XXXI

One reads poetry with one's nerves.

XXXII

The poet is the intermediary between people and the world in which they live and, also, between people as between themselves; but not between people and some other world.

XXXIII

The essential fault of surrealism is that it invents without discovering. To make a clam play an accordion is to invent not to discover. The observation of the unconscious, so far as it can be observed, should reveal things of which we have previously been unconscious, not the familiar things of which we have been conscious plus imagination.

XXXIV

The imagination does not add to reality.

XXXV

The great well of poetry is not other poetry but prose: reality. However it requires a poet to perceive the poetry in reality.

XXXVI

At the moments when one's terror of life should be greatest (when one is young or old) one is usually insensible to it. Some such thing is true of the most profoundly poetic moments. This is the origin of sentimentality, which is a failure of feeling.

XXXVII

Poetry is reality and thought or feeling.

XXXVIII

If one believes in poetry then questions of principle become vital questions. In any case, if there is nothing except reality and art, the mere statement of that fact discloses the significance of art.

XXXIX

The dichotomy is not between realists and artists. There must be few pure realists and few pure artists. We are hybrids absorbed in hybrid literature.

1940

———

Gaiety in poetry is a precious characteristic but it should be a characteristic of the diction.

Poetic Exercises of 1948

Das Leben Als Glockenspiel. The world is a clock
The fire-flies are in the air, above the tree-tops,
On the night of June twelfth
In spite of a month of vicious weather.
It will thunder in July.
There is a continuing explosion of chimes.

Reality is a cliché
From which we escape by metaphor
It is only au pays de la métaphore
Qu'on est poète.

The degrees of metaphor
The absolute object slightly turned
Is a metaphor of the object.

Some objects are less susceptible to metaphor than others. The whole world is less susceptible to metaphor than a tea-cup is.

There is no such thing as a metaphor of a metaphor. One does not progress through metaphors. Thus reality is the in-dispensable element of each metaphor. When I say that man is a god it is very easy to see that if I say also that a god is something else, god has become reality.

Illegible events.

Poetry seeks out the relation of men to facts.

The imagination is man's power over nature. Query

Imagination is the only genius. Query

Relation of the German to his Forest.

How to change real objects without the aid of metaphor. By feeling, style etc.

Poetry as manifestation of the relationship that man creates between himself & reality.

The momentum of the mind is all toward abstraction.

Approchons-nous de Poussin peu à peu. A. Gide

The imagination of the blind man cannot be the extension of an externality he has never seen. (Berkeley)

Imagination *per se*. Berkeley
Imagination as amusement & pleasure

The serious pursuit of pleasure & the pleasure worthy of se-rious pursuit.

The effect of the imagination on the works of artists is a dif-ferent subject from that in which I am interested. In art its effect is the production of qualities: as strength (Pater, Michael Angelo) and its value is a question of the value of those qualities. In life it produces things and its value is a question of the value of those things as, for example, the value of works of art.

1948?

———

There are two arch-types of poets, of whom it is possible to take Homer as an illustration of the narrative type and Plato, regardless of the consideration that he did not write in verse, as an illustration of the reflective type.

1948?

JOURNALS AND LETTERS

From the Journals

December, 27 (1898)

Yesterday afternoon I took a walk alone over Mount Penn starting from Stony Creek and going through the trees to the Tower and down from that to the city, avoiding paths as much as possible. The edge of the woods from Stony Creek was very tangled with long, green, thorny tendrils of wild-roses. The ground at that foot of the hill was marshy in spots, elsewhere the leaves were matted and laid by the weight of a snow which had melted. Clusters of green ferns spread here and there. There were some brilliant spots of moss and every now and then I would start at a piece of dead white birch stirred by my foot which looked very much like a frozen snake. I found a large snail, some yellow dandelions and a weed of some sort, heavy-grey on the face but deep purple on the under side. At the top of the hill I sat down on a pile of rocks with my back to the city and my face towards a deep, rough valley in the East. The city was smoky and noisy but the country depths were prodigiously still except for a shout now and then from some children in the woods on the slope of the hill and once the trembling rumble of an unnatural train down on the horizon. I forget what I was thinking of—except that I wondered why people took books into the woods to read in summertime when there was so much else to be read there that one could not find in books. I was also struck by the curious effect of the sunlight on the tops of the trees while so much darkness lay under the limbs. Coming home I saw the sun go down behind a veil of grime. It was rather terrifying I confess from an allegorical point of view. But that is usually the case with allegory.

———

In the evening Lee Smith, Livingood, Will Dunigan and I called on the Savages. We talked about Livingood's theory that a man who writes poetry in many cases will be found to be a poor singer, that an artist may not enjoy poetry, that an orator may not enjoy music—in short that any emotion expressed in one form of art tends to exclude the possibility of its expression through any other.

June 15.

I came to New York yesterday. Stopped at the Astor House. At three in the afternoon I called at *Commercial-Advertiser* presented a letter from Copeland to Carl Hovey who introduced me to Steffens a Californian, the city editor. I also called at *Evening Sun* and made an appointment for Monday next. At half-past six dined with Rodman Gilder and his "Aunt Julia"—a witty, old lady of some avoirdupois and watery eyes who was disappointed because the sherbet was pineapple instead of orange. After dinner hurried to the East River Park in Yorkville and wrote up a band concert for the *Advertiser.*

This morning I called to see Charles Scribner who was not at his office. And Arthur Goodrich of the Macmillan Company with whom I am to take lunch.

———

Goodrich took me to lunch at the Players Club—an interesting place where one sees celebrities. We sat on the verandah. Nearby was Reid the artist—I think it is Reid although now I see the word in black and white it may be Read. The walls of the house are covered with mementoes of the stage and actors. It is a near approach to Bohemia.

I called at Scribners' again and found Charles Scribner in his offices. He is a plain man with a keen face. He was pleasant to me and put my name down. Speaking of pleasantness, I must give the preference to Goodrich who although a stranger treated me like an old friend.

———

The house I am living in is a boarding-house kept by two unmarried Frenchwomen. The elder, about thirty years of age, has a bosom a foot and a half thick. No wonder the French are amorous with such accommodation for lovers. The younger, about twenty-eight years of age, is of more moderate proportions. She has dark rings under her eyes. I have just slaughtered two bugs in a wall of my room. They were lice! Dinner next—wherever I can find it—with an aimless evening to follow.

———

Took dinner in a little restaurant—poached eggs, coffee and three crusts of bread—a week ago my belly was swagging with strawberries. Bought a couple of newspapers from a little fellow with blue eyes who was selling *Journals* and *Worlds* & who had to ransack the neighborhood for the ones I wanted. As I came back to my room the steps of the street for squares were covered with boarders etc. leaning on railings and picking their teeth. The end of the street was ablaze with a cloud of dust lit by the sun. All around me were tall office buildings closed up for the night. The curtains were drawn and the faces of the buildings looked hard and cruel and lifeless. This street of mine is a wonderful thing. Just now the voices of children manage to come through my window from out it, over the roofs and through the walls.

———

All New York, as I have seen it, is for sale—and I think the parts I have seen are the parts that make New York what it is. It is dominated by necessity. Everything has its price—from Vice to Virtue. I do not like it and unless I get some position that is unusually attractive I shall not stay. What is there to keep me, for example, in a place where all Beauty is on exhibition, all Power a tool of Selfishness, and all Generosity a source of Vanity? New York is a field of tireless and antagonistic interests—undoubtedly fascinating but horribly unreal. Everybody is looking at everybody else—a foolish crowd walking on mirrors. I am rather glad to be here for the short time that I intend to stay—it makes me appreciate the opposite of it all. Thank Heaven the winds are not generated in Yorkville, or the clouds manufactured in Harlem. What a price they would bring!

———

The carpet on the floor of my room is gray set off with pink roses. In the bath room is a rug with the figure of a peacock woven in it—blue and scarlet, and black, and green, and gold. And on the paper of my wall are designs of fleur-de-lis and forget-me-not. Flowers and birds enough of rags and paper— but no more. In this Eden, made spicey with the smoke of my pipe which hangs heavy in the ceiling, in this Paradise ringing with the bells of streetcars and the bustle of fellow-boarders heard through the thin partitions, in this Elysium of Elysiums I now shall lay me down.

―――

I shall say my prayers up the chimney. That is their only chance of getting above the housetops.

―――

I have just looked out of the window to see whether there were any stray tramps on the roof. I'faith, there were stars in heaven.

1900

March 11, 1901.
The streets are blue with mist this morning.

―――

Went home last Thursday for a few hours—first time since Xmas. Reading looked the acme of dullness & I was glad, therefore, to get back to this electric town which I adore. I had a good long talk with the old man in which he did most of the talking. One's ideas don't get much of a chance under such conditions. However he's a wise man. We talked about the law which he has been urging me to take up. I hesitated— because this literary life, as it is called, is the one I always had as an ideal & I am not quite ready to give it up because it has not been all that I wanted it to be. The other day, after returning to New-York, I called on John Phillips of McClure, Phillips and had a talk about the publishing business. P. is philosophical and serious & yet, I think, a person of no imagination—or little. He told me that the business was chiefly clerical—unpleasant fact—& that I could hardly expect to live on my wages—etc. etc. I was considerably jarred by the time he got through. The mirage I had fancied disappeared & I found myself as usual in the desert—where I invariably land. However, I've made a market for Mss—if it's at all worth while!

I've been giving "Olivia" a rest for a short time—so as to be able to inspect it as it should be inspected, before I start it.

The mist outside has grown visibly thicker since I wrote the above. The season is changing.

Sunday. August 10.

I've had a handsome day of it and am contented again. Left the house after breakfast and went by ferry and trolley to Hackensack over in Jersey. From H. I walked 5½ miles on the Spring Valley road, then 4 miles to Ridgewood, then another mile to Hoboken and back towards town 7 miles more to Paterson: 17½ in all, a good day's jaunt at this time of the year. Came from Paterson to Hoboken by trolley and then home. In the early part of the day I saw some very respectable country which, as usual, set me contemplating. I love to walk along with a slight wind playing in the trees about me and think over a thousand and one odds and ends. Last night I spent an hour in the dark transept of St. Patrick's Cathedral where I go now and then in my more lonely moods. An old argument with me is that the true religious force in the world is not the church but the world itself: the mysterious callings of Nature and our responses. What incessant murmurs fill that ever-laboring, tireless church! But to-day in my walk I thought that after all there is no conflict of forces but rather a contrast. In the cathedral I felt one presence; on the highway I felt another. Two different deities presented themselves; and, though I have only cloudy visions of either, yet I now feel the distinction between them. The priest in me worshipped one God at one shrine; the poet another God at another shrine.

The priest worshipped Mercy and Love; the poet, Beauty and Might. In the shadows of the church I could hear the prayers of men and women; in the shadows of the trees nothing human mingled with Divinity. As I sat dreaming with the Congregation I felt how the glittering altar worked on my senses stimulating and consoling them; and as I went tramping through the fields and woods I beheld every leaf and blade of grass revealing or rather betokening the Invisible.

1902

Thursday

Hosey & I have had the best two days of the whole trip, I think. We started about two o'clock on Tuesday afternoon with the mare of Hosey's for the foot of our Gibraltar. Near Lake No. 2 we started several grouse & both of us rushed after them into the bush. The mare followed. On trying to chase her back she gave us a devil of a chase; first up-hill & then downward on the trail towards camp. Hosey nipped her. Further up along the trail I shot a partridge, & near the first trap, beyond the dead-fall, pumped a bullet into a porcupine's belly (stupid beast). We camped in some tall timber on a foot-hill. The moon covered all the hills with a violet haze & looked through our trees in a strangely distant way. I was awake practically all night. At daybreak, & after I had watched the progress of innumerable stars, Hosey started with the tea-pot in search of water. We were off about six in a great sweat. The slope we ascended seemed interminable & we had barely reached the last swell of rocks when Hosey caught sight of a lion. We chased it over the summit but without getting a shot. A moment later I caught sight of a splendid goat watching us from the top of a higher ridge. We crept along as well as we could & finally got within reach. But we were by that time in a shaky position & the goat was a good distance below. I aimed but was afraid to shoot off my gun, since I had all I could do to keep my balance—not to speak of banging away with a 45–90. Then Hosey took a hand & fired four shots, whereupon the goat gambolled away like a lamb in May. I caught him trying to get up hill & struck near him. This was our last shot.

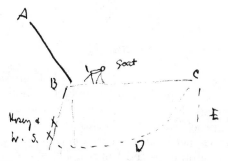

If Hosey had gone to B & cut off the goat's escape up A & if I had gone via D to C, we might have had a better chance. We both went to B & the goat went to C & down to E & we had to fire down a precipice & missed.

It being bitter cold we decided to come down. I had been walking on snow and quite à propos. The air suddenly darkened & we had a ripping little storm. The trail down hill was the most terrible I have ever travelled. At no time could one have fallen more than ten feet; but it was a difficult thing not to fall ten feet every minute. I thought I had broken my left knee-cap after one jolt; but beyond weakening & stiffening the leg no harm was done. I left a good part of my shoes on the way. Well, we reached our starting point, had some venison & prunes & cold tea & started for camp. The confounded mare had slipped her noose & so we had to carry our blankets home strapped over our rifles. We've had a happy time!

———

The upper slopes of the mountains are radiant with red & blue wild flowers & the rocks are covered with lichens—yellow, orange, red; brown & green.

September 3, 1903

Letters

To Elsie Moll

Dear Bo-Bo:—   Thursday Evening
  Secret *memoires*: go back to the bicycle period, for example—and before that to the age of the velocipede. Yes: I had a red velocipede that broke in half once going over a gutter in front of Butcher Deems (where the fruit store is now, beyond the Auditorium)—and I hurt my back and stayed away from school.—On Sundays, in those days, I used to wear patent leather pumps with silver buckles on 'em—and go to Sunday school and listen to old Mrs. Keeley, who had wept with joy over every page in the Bible.—It seems now that the First Presbyterian church was very important: oyster suppers, picnics, festivals. I used to like to sit back of the organ and watch the pump-handle go up and down.—That was before John McGowan, the hatter, became a deacon.—The bicycle period had its adventures: a ride to Ephrata was like an excursion into an unmapped country; and one trip to Womelsdorf and back was incredible.—In summer-time I was up very early and often walked through Hessian Camp before breakfast. Sometimes I rode out to Leisz' bridge and back—I remember a huge cob-web between the rails of a fence sparkling with dew.—And I had a pirate period somewhere. I used to "hop" coal-trains and ride up the Lebanon Valley and stone farmhouses and steal pumpkins and so on—with a really tough crowd.—Then I took to swimming. For three or four summers I did nothing else. We went all morning, all afternoon and all evening and I was as black as a boy could be. I think there are some photographs of all that at home—somebody had a camera. I must try to find them.—I could swim for hours without resting and, in fact, can still. Bob Bushing and I were chummy then—and Felix North and "Gawk" Schmucker.—We used to lie on the stone-walls of the locks and bake ourselves by the hour, and roll into the water to cool.—I always walked a great deal, mostly alone, and mostly on the hill, rambling along the side of the mountain.—When

I began to read, many things changed. My room was the third
floor front. I used to stay up to all hours—although I had
never, up to that time, been up all night. I had a pipe with a
very small bowl and a long, straight stem. There never was a
better.—Those were the days when I read Poe and Hawthorne
and all the things one ought to read (unlike "Cousin
Phillis"—the book I am reading now.)—And I studied hard—
very.—You know I took *all* the prizes at school! (Isn't it an
abominable confession?) No doubt, mother still has the gold
medal I won for spouting at the Academy—picture in the
Eagle, and all that—just as the school-boy orators of to-day
are puffed up.—At High School, I played foot-ball every fall—
left end. We generally won at home and lost when we were
away. In one game at Harrisburg the score was fifty-two to
nothing, against us. But the other team was made up of
giants.—The only other member of the team that I recall is
"Tod" Kaufman, a half-back. He has something to do with
the *Herald* and still calls me Pat, which was my name then.
Most of the fellows called me Pat.—I never attended class-
meetings and never knew any of the girls belonging to the
class. Well, perhaps I did; but they do not come back to me
now.—I sang in Christ Cathedral choir for about two years,
soprano and, later, alto—worked at Sternberg's for two weeks,
once—at the Reading Hardware Company for two months.
(Father was an officer of the company—my working did not
interfere with swimming.)—And I went to the World's Fair,
and to school in Brooklyn for a while, and sometimes to the
Zoo in Philadelphia.—When I was very young, "mamma"
used to go shopping to New-York and we would meet her at
the station—and then there would be boxes of candy to open
at home. We used to spend months at a time at the old hotel
at Ephrata, summer after summer, and "papa" would come
on Saturday nights with baskets of fruit—peaches and pears,
which would be given to us during the week.—Sometimes an
uncle from Saint Paul visited us. He could talk French and
had big dollars in his pockets, some of which went into
mine.—Then there was a time when I went very much with
Johnny Richards and Arthur Roland. They were "bad": poker
(for matches) and cigarettes.—The truth is, I have never
thought much about those early days and certainly never set

them in order. I was distinctly a rowdy—and there are still gossips to tell of it, although Aunt Emmy Schmucker who had all the scandal at her fingers ends no longer lives to tell. When Jones', near you, moved into their new house, they gave a blow-out which Aunt Emmy attended. She ate so much that she was sick the next day and stayed in bed. After that she never got up. Soon she knew she was dying. She asked mother to ask me to see her and when I went she kissed me good-bye.—With her, went infinite tittle-tattle. But she made the most of life, while she had it.—My first year away from home, at Cambridge, made an enormous difference in everything. Since then I have been home comparatively little and, but for you, I think I should have drifted quite out of it, as the town grew strange and the few friends I had became fewer still.—But the years at college will do for another time.—Your own recollections interested me so much that I have followed your lead. Bye!

Pat.

January 21, 1909

To Elsie Moll

My dear Rose-cap:—   Thursday Evening

It was a disappointment to me last week not to have written you a letter "for Saturday and Sunday". To-morrow evening I expect to go to the Academy of Design. Therefore I must write this evening, to avoid a repetition of last week. It is just twenty-nine minutes of twelve! Fancy sitting down to write a letter—and a longish one—at such an hour. But I want you to have a letter.—You wonder what I have been doing tonight. Well, I continued my superficial study of Mr. Okakura's book, and read a great deal besides. Then I went to an exhibition (getting there at nine.) It was an exhibition chiefly of tapestry. But there were some antiquated musical instruments that were amusing. One had sixteen strings. There were lutes inlaid with mother of pearl and there were French cornemeuses.—I saw two cabinets of carved jade—whatever that may be. I know it is highly prized but I don't altogether see

why.—Shall I send a picture or two to make a private exhi-
bition for you? Well, here they are, and all from the Chinese,
painted centuries ago:

> "pale orange, green and crimson, and white,
> and gold, and brown;"

and,

> "deep lapis-lazuli and orange, and opaque
> green, fawn-color, black, and gold;"

and,

> "lapis blue and vermilion, white, and gold
> and green."

I do not know if you feel as I do about a place so remote and
unknown as China—the irreality of it. So much so, that the
little realities of it seem wonderful and beyond belief.—I have
just been reading about the Chinese feeling about landscape.
Just as we have certain traditional subjects that our artists
delight to portray (like "Washington Crossing the Delaware"
or "Mother and Child" etc. etc!) so the Chinese have certain
aspects of nature, of landscape, that have become tradi-
tional.—A list of those aspects would be as fascinating as those
lists of "Pleasant Things" I used to send. Here is the list
(upon my soul!)—

The Evening Bell from a Distant Temple
Sunset Glow over a Fishing Village
Fine Weather after Storm at a Lonely Mountain Town
Homeward-bound Boats off a Distant Shore
The Autumn Moon over Lake Tung-t'ing
Wild Geese on a Sandy Plain
Night Rain in Hsiao-Hsiang.

This is one of the most curious things I ever saw, because it is so
comprehensive. Any twilight picture is included under the first
title, for example. "It is just that silent hour when travellers say
to themselves, 'The day is done', and to their ears comes from
the distance the expected sound of the evening bell."—And
last of all in my package of strange things from the East, a
little poem written centuries ago by Wang-an-shih:

"It is midnight; all is silent in the house;
the water-clock has stopped. But I am
unable to sleep because of the beauty of the
trembling shapes of the spring-flowers, thrown
by the moon upon the blind."

I don't know of anything more beautiful than that anywhere, or more Chinese—and Master Green-cap bows to Wang-An-shih. No: Wang-An-shih is sleeping, and may not be disturbed.—I am going to poke around more or less in the dust of Asia for a week or two and have no idea what I shall disturb and bring to light.—Curious thing, how little we know about Asia, and all that. It makes me wild to learn it all in a night.—But Asia (a brief flight from Picardy—as the mind flies) will do for some other time.—I expect to read the week out and to walk on Sunday. Finer than all books is this full, gusty air. How specially bright it blows the stars in the first hour of evening! I noticed it to-night, just as it was growing dark. There were at least a dozen big, golden stars—that seem to belong to March, more than to the general sky.—And I wish my Sunday walk might be with you. You said in your letter to-day that if it was more convenient for me not to come at Easter—why, I should tell you. You are not twitting me, Bo-Bo, are you?

Your

Wallace

March 18, 1909

To Harriet Monroe

Dear Miss Monroe: Sunday Evening
   A further postponement will defer my seeing you for about a month. From to-day's train:

I

The cows are down in the meadows, now, for the first time.
The sheep are grazing under the thin trees.
My fortune is high.
All this makes me happy.

II
FICKLE CONCEPT
Another season of illusion and belief and ease.

III
FIRST POEM FOR THE MEDITATION OF INFANTS
Gather together the stones around the tree and
    let the tree gather its leaves and fruit.

IV
Earth-creatures, two-legged years, suns, winters . . .

V
POUPÉE DE POUPÉES
She was not the child of religion or science
Created by a god or by earth.
She was the creature of her own minds.

VI
Certainties cutting the centuries

Je vous assure, madame, q'une promenade à travers le soot-
deposit qu'est Indianapolis est une chose véritablement
étrange. Je viens de finir une belle promenade. Le jour aprés
demain je serai à Pittsburg d'ou je partirai pour Hartford. Au
revoir.

Recevez, madame, etc.

April 25, 1920

To Alice Corbin Henderson

Dear Mrs. Henderson: March 27, 1922.
    My poems seem so simple and natural to me that I am never
able to understand how they may seem otherwise to anyone
else. They are not intended to be either deep, dark or mys-
terious. Whatever can be expressed can be expressed clearly.
Epater les savants is as trifling as épater les bourgeois. But one
cannot always say a thing clearly and retain the poetry of what
one is saying. For instance, at the moment I am writing a

thing called Palace of the Blondes Who Read Books of Moonlight. Now that means precisely what it says. If I said: this poem is a momentary cure for poverty; it raises a class to its highest exponent, to the satisfaction of its imagination of what it would like to be; it inflames and placates desire—and so on, I should convey the same idea but I should not write a poem. Now, the disbeliever in the Palace of the Babies is the mood of the disenchanted in the presence of the enchanted (I hate like the devil to write like this). The doctor of Geneva is the confined philosopher actual facing the illimitable (his field) in realism. The bland old gentleman who does the talking to the bland and credulous old ladies about him, with whom he is having tea anywhere—at the Palaz of Hoon if you like, is simply explaining everybody in terms of himself. The Cuban is the person fostered by interiors: comfortable sofas etc who cannot keep exteriors out. There was a time when the country really made me ill, more or less. And there was a very good friend of mine who stayed indoors from June to September one summer. No joke. Imagine the American sky or any intense as savage blue as the Indian and so much for that. Addressing Clouds is an actual address to the clouds. The gloomy grammarians and funest philosophers are the clouds themselves. What could be simpler? Of course, it all depends on the point of view. People scent symbolism as if something of their own realism and reason must, like the blood of an Englishman, be somewhere concealed. You can imagine people accustomed to potatoes studying apples with the idea that unless the apples somehow contain potatoes they are unreasonable. Such people have poignant difficulties with zinnias and pies. We regard Chaplin throwing pies as a simple phenomenon but a writer in the *Beacon*, published in Oxford, raised his eyebrows at what he called pelting with puddings. I know that we agree about this in general. Your difficulty, no doubt, in my own case, or in any specific case, is simple lack of familiarity with my point of view. My things are all perfectly direct and mean just what they say even when that may seem a bit neither here nor there. I have had nothing recent from Alfred Kreymborg. He separated from Loeb, spent the winter at Rapallo, where Gordon Craig and Max Beerbohm are spending their old age, and will be back here, I daresay, shortly. I thought Williams' last book very slight—very. Charming but such a tame savage, such a personal impersonal. Marianne Moore's book meant very little to me. She concerns herself so much with form, and concerns herself by evading it, that I cannot arouse myself about her worth. There is a curious lack of substance in so many of these things, even after conceding that substance may be a matter of nuances, sounds, colors etc instead of eighteenth-century avoirdupois. There appears to be little going on in New-York. This year's Independent Show is a poor thing but it has grown almost fashionable and attracts large crowds. The independent scholar is what is lacking. Independence is nothing unless it is liberty to personality, to thought etc. Independence to do as you please is my idea of being out of a job. Besides, of course, there isn't a damned bit of independence about it. You must do as the independents do or be a laughing-stock. Just so, you must do as the academicians do or be a laughing stock. It is as well to live in Hartford or Santa Fe and not be bothered by any public even the public of a small group of friends. The only real independence is to pull people by the ears and not be pulled by them, if it comes to a choice, and it does come to a choice, if you care what people think. I have a good deal of correspondence with people abroad and receive quite a number of magazines from London and Paris. The thing is the same everywhere. John Rodker is trying to interest me in buying a Wyndham Lewis, writes about his latest manner as being something amazing and refers me to the reproductions in the last number of the *Tyro*. Fancy the swank of Wyndham Lewis. I know of only one real literary Deadwood Dick at the present time and that is Robert McAlmon. Awful stuff—but such pep! Yvor Winters sent me a copy of his recent attenuations. I like Winters, I suppose, because he likes me but he doesn't exactly smell of whiskey and I expect nothing from him. So many people play tunes on their finger-nails and think they are making the welkin ring. However, this sort of thing is not my forte. By the way, Carl Sandburg was here not long ago. I expected to swallow my Adam's apple when he began to sing but the truth is that I enjoyed it immensely. I often inquire about you and it has been a great pleasure to hear of your recovery. It seemed such a spunky thing for you to go down to New Mexico and such a superb thing for Mr. Henderson and the whole family to go with you and for the whole lot of you to go right on as before. Mrs. Stevens is perfectly happy here—likes it, I know, much better than she liked New-York. Sincerest good wishes to all of you.

Very sincerely yours,

To Alice Corbin Henderson

Dear Mrs. Henderson: Hartford, November 27.

I had noticed that Mr. Henderson was having a show in New-York, before receiving your note. I shall try to see it and him the next time I go down. There is only one possible hitch and that is Mrs. Stevens, a fascinating creature whom one cannot exactly get away from. Eliot's poem is, of course, the rage. As poetry it is surely negligible. What it may be in other respects is a large subject on which one could talk for a month. If it is the supreme cry of despair it is Eliot's and not his generation's. Personally, I think it's a bore.

With kindest personal regards,

1922

To Marianne Moore

Dear Miss Moore:

Sometime ago The Dial sent me Gorham Munson's note in your November number. I ought to have thanked you, and Munson too; but there are a lot of things one ought to do. Generally, people look at it the other way: there are a lot of things one ought not to do. And I feel sure that one of the things I ought not to do is to review Williams' book. What Columbus discovered is nothing to what Williams is looking

for. However much I might like to try to make that out—
evolve a mainland from his leaves, scents and floating bottles
and boxes—there is a baby at home. All lights are out at nine.
At present there are no poems, no reviews. I am sorry. Perhaps
one is better off in bed anyhow on cold nights.

                                                    Sincerely,
November nineteenth
Nineteen Twenty-five.

To William Carlos Williams

Dear Williams   Hartford, September 7/27
   I return the cartolina postale di poste italiane da Rapallo,
yes. Many thanks. But believe me, signor, I'm as busy as the
grand Mussolini himself. I rise at day-break, shave etc; at six
I start to exercise; at seven I massage and bathe; at eight I
dabble with a therapeutic breakfast; from eight-thirty to nine-
thirty I walk down-town, work all day . . . go to bed at nine.
How should I write poetry, think it, feel it? Mon Dieu, I am
happy if I can find time to read a few lines, yours, Pound's,
anybody's. I am humble before Pound's request. But the
above is the above.

                                      Always sincerely yours,

To Ronald Lane Latimer

Dear Mr. Latimer: November 26, 1935
   The music of poetry which creates its own fictions is one of
the "sisterhood of the living dead". It is a muse; all of the
muses are of that sisterhood. But then I cannot say, at this dis-
tance of time, that I specifically meant the muses; this is just an
explanation. I don't think that I meant anything definitely ex-
cept all the things that live in memory and imagination.
   Titles with me are, of course, of the highest importance.
Some years ago a student of Wesleyan came up to the office.

Apparently he had been given the job of writing a paper on HARMONIUM. He was under the impression that there was no relation whatever between the titles and the poems. Possibly the relation is not as direct and as literal as it ought to be. Very often the title occurs to me before anything else occurs to me. This is not uncommon; I knew a man in New York who ought to know who once told me that many more people have written the first chapters of novels than have written the rest of them, and that still more people have given their novels titles without having given them any bodies.

When you ask about a pattern of metaphors you are asking about the sort of thing with which one constantly experiments. For instance, I am very much afraid that what you like in my poetry is just the sort of thing that you ought not to like: say, its music or color. If that is true, then an appropriate experiment would be to write poetry without music and without color.* But so many of these experiments come to nothing. If they were highly successful, well and good, but they so rarely are.

I suppose that the explanation for the bursts of freedom is nothing more than this: that when one is thinking one's way the pattern becomes small and complex, but when one has reached a point and finds it possible to move emotionally one goes ahead rapidly. One of the most difficult things in writing poetry is to know what one's subject is. Most people know what it is and do not write poetry, because they are so conscious of that one thing. One's subject is always poetry, or should be. But sometimes it becomes a little more definite and fluid, and then the thing goes ahead rapidly.

Yours very truly,

———

The paper has arrived and I shall return it to you in a day or two. So, too, Mr. Warren's book has arrived, although I have had time only to glance at it. Mr. Warren is an extremely interesting poet & I look forward to reading his book with care, as soon as I have the time. I went to Cambridge for the Yale game last weekend and am badly in need of about a week's sleep.

W. S.

*In music, this would give you Schönberg.

To Leonard C. van Geyzel

Dear Mr. Van Geyzel: December 31, 1937

If I say that I think that you made a very good choice of things to send, I am sure that I shall be saying more in that exact way than if I let myself go.

Very likely you have read Ashley Gibson's CINNAMON AND FRANGIPANNI: In the first paragraph he puts a taboo on ebony elephants and the sort of thing that tourists pick up and, curiously, he speaks of precisely the things that you have sent as being things most truly representative of Ceylon. It is, of course, difficult for anyone on this side of the earth to realize with any definiteness just what Ceylon is like. But I think that your box, with your very interesting letter, together with a book or two, helps to create a pretty clear impression. Gibson's book to which I have just referred, is very badly written; and yet, in spite of all the adjectives and literary familiarities, it strikes one as being full of the actual thing. I have picked up a copy of de Croisset's FÉERIE CINGHA-LAISE, but have not had time even to cut the pages. After I picked up this copy, I noticed an edition illustrated with colored woodcuts in a book catalogue from Paris, for which I have sent.

Both Mrs. Stevens and Holly were delighted with the necklaces; both of them are light in color. Holly, my daughter, was particularly pleased. As you can imagine, it makes a great spread on the floor to set all these things out, together with the other gifts that pile in at Christmas time. The living room has been full of the odor of the fans.

The box reached New York somewhat earlier than you had forecast. I had arranged to have it sent to Hartford in bond. This was because I thought there might be some trouble about the milk punch and the jaggery. But the men in the Customs Office here in Hartford were very decent about it, and classified all these things as preserves. I did not send the box home until a day or two before Christmas, and did not see its contents until we opened it on Christmas morning. Since I did not want to write to you until after I had seen the things themselves, I thought it best to send you a wire so that you would know that your efforts had been successful. The only thing that was at all scratched was one of the cans of jaggery; fortunately, the other two were perfectly intact.

I selected as my own the Buddha, which is so simple and explicit that I like to have it in my room. At night, when my windows are open and the air is like ice, this particular Buddha must wish that I put a postage stamp on him and send him back to Colombo.

I am having woodapple jelly and your tea every morning for breakfast. The jelly, which smells almost as good as it tastes, is not unlike a home-made guava jelly, although it is very much unlike the sort of guava jelly that is not home-made.

Thank you, which means not so much for the painstaking care with which you made a choice as for your kindness in taking the trouble.

When summer comes round I shall be wanting to do something of this sort again, but in some other place, say, Java or Hong Kong or Siam. Do you know of anyone in any of those places to whom I could write as I wrote to you, and who would be likely to take my letter in the same spirit in which you took it? I am not trying to work my way round the world on the basis of other people's courtesy; I should be quite willing to pay for the trouble. I say this because you might know some one who would be glad to be on the lookout over a period of time for interesting odds and ends. I should be glad to supply the money for this in advance. The great difficulty is to find people of taste: people who are really interested in doing this sort of thing as part of the interest of living.

Let me repeat my willingness to be of service to you at any time over here. And thanks again.

Very truly yours,

To C. L. Daughtry

Dear Daughtry: November 24, 1941
   Many thanks for the persimmons. These meant more to me than you can imagine. I have far more things to eat and far more things to drink than are good for me. I indulge in abstemious spells merely to keep my balance.
   Wild persimmons make one feel like a hungry man in the woods. As I ate them, I thought of opossums and birds, and the antique Japanese prints in black and white, in which monkeys are eating persimmons in bare trees. There is nothing more desolate than a persimmon tree, with the old ripe fruit hanging on it. As you see, there is such a thing as being a spiritual epicure.

                                                             Yours,

To William Carlos Williams

Dear Bill: January 22, 1942.
   Thanks for your postcard. I am just getting under way. Twenty or thirty years from now I expect to be really well oiled. Don't worry about my gray hair. Whenever I ring for a stenographer she comes in with a pistol strapped around her belt.
   Best regards young feller and best wishes,

To Harvey Breit

Dear Mr. Breit: August 8, 1942
   Your letter making the most of the situation (which for your sake I regret) is quite the nicest and most human thing I know about you. In return for it, let me say this:
   I have been away the last day or two and, while away, visited the Dutch Church at Kingston: the Reformed Protestant

Dutch Church. This is one of the most beautiful churches that I know of. It is improved by the fact that it has a pleasant janitor with a red nose: merely a red nose, not a red nose due to drink. But having a red nose subdues one.

The janitor told me that at one time there were nine judges in the congregation and that often the whole nine of them were there together at a service, sitting in their separate pews. One of them was Judge Alton Parker; another was Judge Gilbert Hasbrouck. Now, Judge Hasbrouck was as well known in Kingston as Martin Luther was in Wittenberg.

The janitor gave me a pamphlet containing an extract from studies relating to the Reformed Church. The pamphlet consists of an article by Judge Hasbrouck on this particular church. It starts out with this . . .

> "Indeed when Spinoza's great logic went search-
> ing for God it found Him in a predicate of sub-
> stance."

The material thing: the predicate of substance in this case, was this church: the very building. Now, if a lawyer as eminent as Judge Hasbrouck went to church because it made it possible for him to touch, to see, etc., the very predicate of substance, do you think he was anything except a poet? He was only one of nine of them, so that, instead of nine judges, there were nine poets in the congregation, all of them struggling to get at the predicate of substance, although not all of them struggled to do so through Spinoza's great logic.

Another thing that this episode makes clear is that Spinoza's great logic was appreciated only the other day in Kingston; and, still more, that lawyers very often make use of their particular faculties to satisfy their particular desires.

Very truly yours,

To Jane MacFarland Stone

Dear Jane: November 2, 1943
I am returning today the album, with everything in it. I have had copies made of the picture of my father as a boy,

also of the picture of him with a beard and, finally, I have had a copy made of one of the pictures of my mother. These are all that I care to have for my own purposes. Many of these pictures I know as well as I know my own hands and I must say that it gives me no particular pleasure to see them. Looking at them is somewhat the reverse of looking at the picture of my father taken in April, 1910, which was, I believe, only a few months before his death. When I look at the pictures of the children and then consider that I am able to think of their lives as wholes, the thing becomes disturbing. It is like standing by and watching people come into the world, live for a while and then go out of it again. It isn't that it makes me feel old, because I don't feel old; I feel young. And it isn't that I think of all these lives as having ended before they had really matured. It just upsets me; I have not thought about it long enough to know why. But obviously one reason for returning the album to you is that I expect to be happier with this selection that I have made than if I had all of these pictures constantly before me. I mean to think well of everyone in my family and if there are any of them that were not as fortunate as the others or, say, as they might have been, I mean to forget that. When I think of my father's pride and of all the anxiety that he must have felt, and then look at this last picture of him in which he seems so completely defeated, the feeling isn't anything that I want to renew. I very much prefer to look at him and think of him in his prime. The truth is that I rather think that, seeing him as a whole, I understand him better perhaps than he understood himself, and that I can really look into his heart in which he must have concealed so many things. I say this because he was one of the most uncommunicative of men. Had he been more selfish than he was, everything would have been different for him, so that I am bound to think well of him.

I shall write you again by and by. This is merely to tell you that the album is on its way.

Yours,

To José Rodríguez Feo

Dear Mr. Rodríguez-Feo: June 20, 1945

When I saw your letter this morning I thought it was going to tell me when you intended to be in this country, and I was disappointed. Even though there appears to be a vast difference between us in respect to age, I am most interested in finding how much alike we are. For example, you are now interested in Stendhal. This is an intermittent interest; it comes back to you throughout life every few years. For me, Stendhal is the embodiment of the principle of prose. I don't mean literary reality, but reason in its more amiable aspects. No doubt Stendhal will survive Flaubert, because Stendhal is a point of reference for the mature, while Flaubert is a point of reference for the artist, and perhaps for the immature. Flaubert takes possession of the immature and almost developes a sense of maturity and of competence and strength. However, there is an enormous amount of dust gathered about Stendhal. I have a number of odds and ends of his that are not to be found everywhere, but I have never made any attempt to collect any of the material relating to him. This has been much overdone.

I like to hear you say "Pooh!" when you speak of Charles Henri Ford. The young man who knows a little more about books, or a little more about music than his neighbor is likely to be rather hard to bear. But the young man who knows a little more about painting than his neighbor is impossible. As a matter of fact, I don't think that Ford knows much about anything; he is completely impossible. All the same, he is clever and he has created for himself a sphere in which everything approves of him and is as he wants it to be. He is having the best time in the world, and always has had, but he is as untamed a snob as ever breathed, and VIEW is a monument not to silliness but to snobbery and in particular the snobbery of the young man who knows a little more about painting than his neighbor, in the sense that he knows an artist or two. God is gracious to some very peculiar people. The hard part about all this is that I have promised Ford a poem or two.

The poem, or poems, that I shall send to you will have to

be written during the summer, because I have been busy with something else and, besides, I almost always dislike anything that I do that doesn't fly in the window. Perhaps this has some bearing on what you call "the monotony of elegance". To live in Cuba, to think a little in the morning and afterward to work in the garden for an hour or two, then to have lunch and to read all afternoon and then, with your wife or someone else's wife, fill the house with fresh roses, to play a little Berlioz (this is the current combination at home: Berlioz and roses) might very well create all manner of doubts after a week or two. But when you are a little older, and have your business or your job to look after, and when there is quite enough to worry about all the time, and when you don't have time to think and the weeds grow in the garden a good deal more savagely than you could ever have supposed, and you no longer read because it doesn't seem worth while, but you do at the end of the day play a record or two, that is something quite different. Reality is the great *fond*, and it is because it is that the purely literary amounts to so little. Moreover, in the world of actuality, in spite of all I have just said, one is always living a little out of it. There is a precious sentence in Henry James, for whom everyday life was not much more than the mere business of living, but, all the same, he separated himself from it. The sentence is . . .

> "To live *in* the world of creation—to get into it and stay in it—to frequent it and haunt it—to *think* intensely and fruitfully—to woo combinations and inspirations into being by a depth and continuity of attention and meditation—this is the only thing."

I am going to Cambridge next week to read a poem there at the exercises of Phi Beta Kappa, which are in a general way part of the Commencement activities.

I hope you received the copy of VOICES that I sent you. I am always happy to hear from you.

Very sincerely yours,

To Charles Norman

Dear Mr. Norman: November 9, 1945

I prefer not to take part in your symposium on Pound and although I am going to say a word or two about the thing, I don't want to be quoted or referred to in any way.

It seems to me that since Pound's liberty, not to say even his life, may be at stake, he ought to be consulted about this sort of thing. After all, he might shrink from the idea of your doing what you propose to do. Then again, he may be guilty and he may admit it. He is an eccentric person. I don't suppose there is the slightest doubt that he did what he is said to have done. While he may have many excuses, I must say that I don't consider the fact that he is a man of genius as an excuse. Surely, such men are subject to the common disciplines.

There are a number of things that could well be said in his defense. But each one of these things is so very debatable, that one would not care to say them, without having thought them out most carefully. One such possibility is that the acts of propagandists should not entail the same consequences as the acts of a spy or informer because no one attaches really serious importance to propaganda. I still don't smoke Camels, don't eat Wheaties and don't use Sweetheart soap. I don't believe that the law of treason should apply to chatter on the radio when it is recognizably chatter.

At the same time, that remark illustrates what I said a moment ago, that the things that might be said in Pound's defense are things that ought to be carefully thought out. His motives might be significant. Yet, it is entirely possible that Pound deliberately and maliciously undertook to injure this country. Don't you think it worthwhile waiting until you know why he did what he did before rallying to his defense?

I repeat that the question of his distinction seems to me to be completely irrelevant. If his poetry is in point, then so are Tokyo Rose's singing and wise-cracking. If when he comes over, he wants help and shows that he is entitled to it, then I, for one, should be very glad to help him and I mean that in a practical way and do anything possible for him.

I write this way because I think it highly likely that Pound has very good personal friends who will rally around him. They might well resent just this sort of thing that you propose to do, but I know nothing about it. I merely want to keep out of it.

This letter is not to be quoted or used in any way.

Yours very truly,

To Allen Tate

Dear Allen: April 6, 1948

There isn't a chance of my taking part in a poetry festival. The other day I read a paper somewhere. As we walked down the aisle to get on the platform, I felt more like an elephant at every step. When we had taken our seats on the platform, I noticed that the reading desk was low and said that that would make it necessary for me to stoop as I read. The result would be that my voice would go in the wrong direction. Consequently, the other man went over to the reading desk and began to screw something in the pedestal to elevate the desk to a decent height. This made everyone laugh. I can only say: not on your life.

I look forward to seeing you one of these days. My opportunities for seeing friends are few and far between.

Sincerely yours,

To Thomas McGreevy

Dear Mr. McGreevy: December 8, 1948.

My correspondence with friends has been in a bad way. But I enjoy your letters so much that I can take no further chances. I have not even been able as yet to pay my respects to Mrs. Church, who is of course in New York. My wife and I were there for several days last week. I made no effort to see anyone, spending my spare time walking in the open air of which I felt the greatest need. I had taken with me a shopping list for Christmas which I tore up. What a superb freedom it is to cut oneself loose from all ties and all errands and to carry no parcels for a change.

I am going to carry that freedom forward in this present short letter and skip all past correspondence and the news, if there is any news. In any case, the London periodical that was going to publish the poems has been shot to pieces. I cannot find out what has become of the poems which makes me feel that they thought them too rotten to spend postage on them. This does me good. One should constantly confront the machinations of the devil and the contumely of his courts. These confrontations make one shrink back into one's own virtue. The poet must always desire the pure good of poetry just as the sinner desires only the pure good of the blood of the land. Without thee, O Sophia, what value has anything? The poet lives only in and for the world of poetry. Nicht wahr?

New York was not at its best. In Radio City they have erected a Christmas tree, fir or spruce, 90' high at the edge of the ice rink. The rink was crawling with skaters. And on Park Avenue they were erecting a line of trees which will shortly be covered with lights in the evening. Yet the weather was too mild and reminded one of the past instead of the future. And over and above all this and under and around it and right in the middle of it was the feeling that the whole world makes Christmas a bit of a farce this year. If there is any shield against conspiracy, Santa Claus is not the man to hold it.

I dropped into one or two bookshops where I know people. It was impossible to interest myself in anything. I kept away from the galleries. Salesmen disguised as catalogues or as chairs get on one's nerves. Matisse has a collection of Dubuffet's drawings which I should like to have seen because I recently had some correspondence with Dubuffet. Wildenstein has a large collection of Courbet. These are the two poles of feeling over here now: fantasy on one hand and realism on the other: evasion and evasion. Here in Hartford is an exhibition of an American landscapist of a century ago: Thomas Cole. This man gives one something. But he also shocks one's dreams. For all that, I like to hold on to anything that seems to have a definite American past even though the American trees may be growing by the side of queer Parthenons set, say, in the neighborhood of Niagara Falls. One is so homeless over here in such things and something really American is like meeting a beautiful cousin or, for that matter, even one's mother for the first time.

I suppose the greatest satisfaction which we had from our trip was the arrival home. We went into the kitchen, sat there drinking milk and eating cookies. The next day was Sunday and it was not necessary for us to get up before sunrise. Getting up after sunrise at this time of year is one of the few luxuries that are left to us.

This is not much. Yet it is a little in spite of everything.

Sincerely yours,

To Barbara Church

Dear Mrs. Church: April 27, 1950.

I hope, and expect, to be down on May 11. Apparently the war is already on in New York. While it is probably inevitable, I don't believe it is going to take place for the present. It is not possible for a radio man to say things simply—and in any case as news passes along it becomes increasingly inaccurate. For my own part, I listen only to Groucho Marx, Jack Benny and Leopold Stokowski. At my ripe age, the world begins to seem a little thin. To thicken it, I need a great deal more than excitement. Perhaps the idea of more is merely another illusion. This year the coming of Spring has left me cold. We do not really have Spring in Hartford and I say this although we had a large bouquet of daffodils and jonquils on the table for dinner last night. Over night in the warmth and stillness of the house they filled the dining-room with fragrance. All the same, we never have the brilliance of Spring here, although we always expect it—and sometimes, perhaps for a day—. I continue to receive letters about the Bollingen award and, among them, letters from people that I knew when I was a boy and who were themselves boys then. This has been a really moving experience: to find that people one had long ago forgotten were still alive, one man 73, another 78, and here am

I practically unchipped and completely uncracked. But, also, this experience reveals the occasionally frightening aspect of the past, into which so many that we have known have disappeared, almost as if they had never been real. We become too deeply engaged with life to have it disappear like that. My dear old boy Judge Powell of Atlanta (77) has written to suggest that I come down for a picnic. He is, and says he is, an extrovert and extroverts live only in the present. I expect to be highly extrovert at your party, if I come, much more, of course, than it was necessary to be at the Sweeneys, who were always in a position to shove me off the terrace if it seemed best.

Very sincerely yours,

To Robert Pack

Dear Mr. Pack: December 28, 1954.

At the top of page 16 of your paper you say: "Mr. Stevens' work does not really lead anywhere." This is not quite the same thing as get anywhere and I realize that you say this in connection with a differentiation between a work without a plot and a work with a plot. Still, without regard to any other consideration, if it meant to me what it meant to me, it might very well mean the same thing to anybody else. That a man's work should remain indefinite is often intentional. For instance, in projecting a supreme fiction, I cannot imagine anything more fatal than to state it definitely and incautiously. For a long time, I have thought of adding other sections to the NOTES and one in particular: *It Must Be Human*. But I think that it would be wrong not to leave well enough alone.

I don't mean to try to exercise the slightest restraint on what you say. Say what you will. But we are dealing with poetry, not with philosophy. The last thing in the world that I should want to do would be to formulate a system.

Sincerely yours,

To Samuel French Morse

Dear Sam: July 5, 1955.

I have been back in the office for two weeks, coming at 10:00 and leaving at 1:30 and doing very little in the meantime except seeing people who want to know how I feel. As a matter of fact, I should be very much better off at Avery Convalescent Hospital than I am under the present circumstances because living there was putting no one to any trouble and because it was cool and comfortable and, finally, because during the thirty-one days that I spent there I was able to retain everything that I ate. But they don't expect you to stay indefinitely. Many nights I slept under a winter blanket. Of course, there is a vast difference between this appalling July heat and the weather that we had while I was there. This heat is something that you never have in Maine; if you do, it cools off at night. Here when you go upstairs at night the house is like an oven. But somehow we survive.

There is no chance, I think, of any new poems. Most of the time when I am at home I drowse. I am without energy even to read the numerous things that are sent to me. On Saturday, in one day, I received two volumes of poetry in English and one manuscript in French. I just can't bother myself about these things while I am as limp as I am now. I have had a number of people write to me for poems and have had to say no to all of them. My principal object at the present time is to get back on my feet.

Call me up when you return to Hartford. I have not been to the Canoe Club now for a long time and believe that even a single Martini would be a disaster. The most I might be able to do would be to go and sit on the porch and drink lemonade and I should be glad to do that one of these days because I always loved the porch over there. But I know nothing about their lemonade.

With my best to all of you, I am

                                        Sincerely yours,

CHRONOLOGY

NOTE ON THE TEXTS

NOTES

INDEXES

Chronology

Elizabeth Stevens and family. Delivers prize-winning oration "The Greatest Need of the Age" at Reading Boys' School in December.

1897–98 Graduates Reading Boys' School in June; delivers oration "The Thessalians." Enters Harvard as special three-year student in September. In Cambridge, lives in boarding house where he will room for next three years. Develops interest in Chinese and Japanese art which he shares with Harvard friends Arthur Pope (future director of Fogg Museum) and poets Witter Bynner and Arthur Davison Ficke.

1898–1900 Poem "Autumn" appears in Reading Boys' School magazine *The Red and Black* in January 1898. Studies composition with literary historian Barrett Wendell, who encourages keeping of journal, and English literature with Charles Townsend Copeland; also studies French and German literature. Reads letters of Edward FitzGerald and classical scholar Benjamin Jowett; begins journal with epigraph from Jowett: "If I live I ought to speak my mind." Contributes poetry and short stories to Harvard magazines, sometimes under pseudonyms. During spring term composes sonnet sequence for satisfaction of "long theme" assignment; meets George Santayana. Joins staff of *Harvard Advocate* at invitation of Witter Bynner. Works on *Reading Times* over summer 1899. Grandmother Stevens dies in September. Becomes president of *Harvard Advocate*. Completes three-year program at Harvard; goes to New York in June 1900 and on father's advice seeks work in publishing or journalism. Stays in cheap boarding house; writes article about funeral service of Stephen Crane on June 28. Accepts job working overnight shift at *New-York Tribune*. Moves in July to small apartment at 37 West 9th Street; covers political campaigns for *Tribune*. Becomes avid playgoer, and is especially impressed by performance of Sarah Bernhardt as Hamlet.

1901 Proposes to father that he resign from *Tribune* and devote himself to writing; father urges him to take up law. In February, moves to East 24th Street and experiments with playwriting. Enters New York Law School in fall. Father suffers nervous collapse and takes six-month rest cure.

1902–3 During summer vacation in 1902, clerks at New York office of W. G. Peckham. Begins taking long walks in the country on weekends, and recording his observations in journal. At year's end resolves to abstain from drinking and "to write something every night—be it no more than a line to sing or a page to read." Graduates from law school in June 1903 and continues clerkship with Peckham. Accompanies Peckham on seven-week hunting trip to British Columbia in summer of 1903.

1904   Admitted to New York bar in June. In Reading for summer, is introduced to Elsie Viola Kachel Moll (born 1886), a piano teacher who also works selling sheet music and playing piano in local department store. Returns to New York, where he starts law practice with Lyman Ward; it soon fails. Periodically visits Reading to see Elsie, and writes to her often.

1905–7   Moves to East Orange, New Jersey, in May 1905. Works at various law offices; makes business trips to Midwest and Southwest. Moves to Fordham Heights in the Bronx in October 1906. Reading during this period includes *The Greek Anthology*, Propertius, Catullus, Horace, the Bible, books on Indian and Japanese culture, Boswell's *Life of Samuel Johnson*, Leopardi, Keats, Balzac's *La Peau de Chagrin*, Schopenhauer, and Ibsen. Out of work from July to November 1907, spends most of his time in Reading; moves back to Greenwich Village in December.

1908   Begins work in January at American Bonding Company; establishes contacts in insurance business. Presents Elsie with manuscript collection "A Book of Verses" for her birthday on June 5. Quarrels with father over family's disapproval of Elsie; on November visit to Reading does not see family. Proposes marriage to Elsie at Christmas, presenting her with Tiffany diamond engagement ring.

1909–10 Writes almost daily to Elsie; letters include childhood memories as well as current impressions. Presents Elsie with "The Little June Book," a second collection of verses. Marries Elsie on September 21, 1909, at Grace Lutheran Church in Reading (his family does not attend ceremony). After honeymoon in Massachusetts, they settle in apartment at 441 West 21st Street, leased from sculptor Adolph Alexander Weinman. (Elsie, discontented in New York, frequently returns to Reading to stay with mother.)

1911–12   Father dies July 14, 1911. Stevens, who had not spoken with him since quarrel over his marriage, returns to Reading for funeral. Upset at being passed up for a promotion in August, but dismisses Elsie's suggestion that they return to Reading where he can start a business: "I fully intend to continue along my present line—because it gives me a living and because it seems to offer possibilities. I am far from being a genius—and must rely on hard and faithful work." Mother, ill since father's death, dies July 16, 1912.

1913   Elsie spends summer in Poconos; Stevens visits on weekends whenever possible and learns to play golf. Writes poetry regularly again after break of several years. Leaves American Bonding Company in August for Equitable Surety Company, having acquired specialty in fidelity and surety bonds; buys baby grand paino.

1914–15   Named resident vice-president, second in charge of Equitable's New York branch, in February 1914. Composes poems including "Peter Quince at the Clavier," "The Silver Plough-Boy," "Disillusionment of Ten O'Clock," and "Sunday Morning." Contributes eight poems (published as "Carnet de Voyage") to September issue of *Trend*, edited by Harvard friend Pitts Sanborn. Receives encouragement from Harriet Monroe, editor of *Poetry*, and Alfred Kreymborg, poet and editor of *Others*. Renews association with Harvard friend Walter Conrad Arensberg, an art collector and poet; attends salon evenings at Arensberg's apartment. Through Arensberg and others, introduced to circle of writers, artists, and musicians that includes William Carlos Williams, Mina Loy, Carl Van Vechten, Donald Evans, Albert Gleizes, Francis Picabia, Marcel Duchamp, and Edgard Varèse. Begins contributing poems regularly to little magazines including *Poetry*, *Others*, *Rogue*, *Soil*, and *The Little Review*.

1916   After unexpected failure of Equitable, takes position in March with Hartford Accident and Indemnity Company; assigned to handle surety claims and oversee legal affairs of expanding bond department (within two years, a separate fidelity and surety claims department is established which Stevens will head for the rest of his life). Becomes officer of subsidiary Hartford Livestock Insurance Company and moves to Hartford, Connecticut, in May. Travels on business for most of year, visiting St. Paul, Minneapolis, Chicago, Atlanta, Jacksonville, Miami. Writes regularly to Elsie and composes poems; verse play *Three Travelers Watch a Sunrise* wins prize from *Poetry* in May.

1917   Composes another play, *Carlos Among the Candles*, commissioned by Wisconsin Players (it is performed once at Neighborhood Playhouse in New York in October). Continues to travel extensively while Elsie manages move to apartment at 210 Farmington Avenue in Hartford, where they will live until 1924.

1918–19   On business in Chicago in March 1918, visits Harriet Monroe at *Poetry* offices; meets Carl Sandburg. His sister Mary Katharine, a Red Cross volunteer in France, dies of effects of mastoiditis in May 1919.

1920–21   Does not attend sole performance of *Three Travelers* at Provincetown Playhouse in New York in February 1920. Away on business for two months in spring, in Erie, Youngstown, and Cleveland. Wins Helen Haire Levinson Prize ($200) in November 1920 for group of poems published in *Poetry* under rubric "Pecksniffiana." Corresponds with writers and friends in Europe, including Robert McAlmon, John Rodker, Ferdinand Reyher, and Pitts Sanborn. (When Reyher criticizes prevalence of free verse, Stevens responds: "Why do you scorn free verse? Isn't it the only kind of verse now being written which has any aesthetic impulse back of it?") Composes "From the Journal of Crispin" in December 1921, and submits it for Blindman Prize judged by Amy Lowell.

1922   Travels to Florida in early January with Arthur Powell, a business acquaintance from Atlanta; stays on Biscayne Bay and Long Key ("one of the choicest places I have ever been to"), fishing with Powell and friends. (Forms close friendship with Powell, and in future years makes annual winter visits to Florida with him and other colleagues.) Visits Havana. After Blindman Prize goes to Grace Hazard Conkling, revises "Crispin" as "The Comedian as the Letter C." At suggestion of Carl Van Vechten, gathers poems for a volume, and manuscript is accepted for publication by Alfred A. Knopf. Receives visit from William Carlos Williams in August.

1923   Proposes "The Grand Poem: Preliminary Minutiae" as title for book, but after discussion with Knopf agrees on *Harmonium*; it is published in September. Leaves in October on first extended holiday with Elsie since marriage, embarking on cruise to Havana, then through Panama Canal, past Tehuantepec to California; they tour in California and return overland, stopping to visit Witter Bynner in New Mexico.

1924   Pleased by Marianne Moore's positive review of *Harmonium* in January *Dial*. Daughter Holly Bright Stevens born August 10. Family moves to house at 735 Farmington Avenue in West Hartford.

1925   Receives visit in October from Archibald MacLeish. Writes to Marianne Moore in November, in response to her request for a review, ". . . there is a baby at home. All lights are out at nine. At present there are no poems, no reviews." Spends Christmas season in Florida with family.

1926   Begins experiencing blurred vision; diagnosed in October as acromegalic and overweight, with high blood pressure; advised to reduce, exercise, and moderate use of alcohol.

1927–28   Visits Florida on business in May. In August, Williams forwards letter from Ezra Pound requesting poems for publication; Stevens responds with account of a daily routine leaving no time for poetry and little time for reading. Writes Marianne Moore: "The extreme irregularity of my life makes poetry out of the question, for the present, except for momentary violences." At end of 1927 is told that as a result of his strict regimen he is anemic and underweight; receives favorable medical report in October 1928.

1929–30   Composes a few poems. Holly enters Oxford School, which she will attend until 1941. Takes holiday in Atlantic City with Elsie and Holly in September 1930.

1931   Revised edition of *Harmonium* published by Knopf. Corresponds with R. P. Blackmur, who is at work on critical essay about Stevens' poetry. Begins purchasing books and paintings from Parisian bookseller Anatole Vidal, with whom he will deal regularly (after Vidal's death in 1944, will continue buying from his daughter, Paule Vidal).

1932–33   Writes to Monroe in August: "Whatever else I do, I do not write poetry nowadays." Buys house at 118 Westerly Terrace in Hartford and moves in in September. Hires full-time housekeeper who also helps care for Holly.

1934   After long hiatus, new poems ("things more or less improvised") appear in journals. Writes introduction for William Carlos Williams' *Collected Poems, 1921–1931*. Is made a vice-president of the Hartford.

1935   Meets and spends time with Robert Frost in Key West. Discouraged by Elsie from drinking at home, becomes connoisseur of teas; frequently joins friends for martinis at the Canoe Club in Hartford. Ronald Lane Latimer's Alcestis Press publishes limited edition of *Ideas of Order* in August. Begins working on poetic sequence *Owl's Clover*.

1936   Provokes drunken fight with Ernest Hemingway while in Key West in February; breaks right hand in two places from hitting Hemingway's jaw, and is knocked down; the two make up before Stevens leaves (tells Elsie he fell down a flight of stairs). *Ideas of Order* published by Knopf in October; favorable reviews acknowledge Stevens as major American poet. In fall, along with brother John, begins to support ailing brother Garrett Jr. *Owl's Clover* published by Alcestis Press in November; reads portions of it, along with lecture "The Irrational Element in Poetry," at Harvard in December. Wins poetry prize from *The Nation* for "The Men That Are Falling."

1937–38   *The Man with the Blue Guitar* (containing a shortened version of *Owl's Clover*) published by Knopf in October. Contributes poems regularly to periodicals. Unable to afford winter trips to Florida and summer holidays because of support to Garrett Jr. Begins correspondence in 1938 with Ceylonese planter Leonard van Geyzel. Garrett Jr. dies on November 3, 1938; Stevens continues to help his widow, Sarah.

1939   Travels during summer with Elsie and Holly in Maine and New York, where they visit World's Fair and attend theater. Acknowledges good wishes for his birthday, noting "a poet should be 30 not 60. It is incredible to me that I am 60." Forms close friendship with wealthy arts patron Henry Church and his wife, Barbara. (Church, who edits French-language magazine *Mesures*, introduces him to intellectual circle that includes philosopher Jean Wahl, poet Frederick Morgan, and Guggenheim Museum director James Johnson Sweeney.)

1940   Spends several weeks in February with family in Key West, which he now finds "too furiously literary"; dines there with Robert Frost. Writes prolifically on return (describes himself as "at one of those stages when it is hard to get away from one's thoughts"). Corresponds at length with Henry Church about proposal to establish poetry chair at Harvard. Brother John dies July 9; mother-in-law killed in auto accident in August. Pursues growing interest in genealogy. Gives Holly a red convertible for her sixteenth birthday. Corresponds extensively about his poetry with critic Hi Simons: "It is a habit of mind with me to be thinking of some substitute for religion. . . . My trouble, and the trouble of a great many people, is the loss of belief in the sort of God in Whom we were all brought up to believe."

1941   Reads extensively in philosophy and literary criticism, including Vico, Descartes, Hegel, and I. A. Richards. Delivers lecture "The Noble Rider and the Sound of Words" at Princeton in May. Holly enters Vassar.

1942   During summer Holly announces she does not want to continue at Vassar, but Stevens persuades her to return. *Parts of a World* published by Knopf in September; limited edition of poetic sequence "Notes Toward a Supreme Fiction" published by Cummington Press in October. Upset when Holly leaves Vassar at year's end; finds her a job as clerk at Aetna Life Insurance Company.

1943   Sister Elizabeth dies in February. At Entretiens de Pontigny conference (seminar bringing together European and American intellectuals) at Mount Holyoke in August, delivers lecture "The Figure of the Youth as Virile Poet," and meets Marianne Moore for first time. Unhappy about Holly's relationship with repairman John Hanchak, whom he refuses to allow in the house; she moves to local boarding house. Refuses two invitations to read poetry: "I am not a troubadour and I think the public reading of poetry is something particularly ghastly."

1944 Pleased by Knopf's invitation in April to do another volume; devotes summer to poetry. Quarrels with Holly when she tells him of her engagement to Hanchak, whom she marries August 5. Begins correspondence with Cuban poet José Rodríguez Feo.

1945 Declines Robert Penn Warren's invitation to record for Library of Congress archive, claiming he does not read well. Delivers "Description Without Place" as Phi Beta Kappa poem at Harvard in June. Cummington Press publishes limited edition of *Esthétique du Mal* in July. Declines to contribute to symposium on treason case against Ezra Pound in newspaper *PM*. Becomes fellow of National Institute of Arts and Letters in December.

1946 Receives Harriet Monroe Poetry Award in June. Spends three weeks in late summer in Pennsylvania with Elsie, including several days in Reading ("we found the place really unbearable and we left almost immediately without seeing a single one of the few relatives of mine who still live there"). Sees eye doctor about vision problems in December.

1947 Delivers "Three Academic Pieces" at Harvard in February. *Transport to Summer* published in March; strongly favorable reviews appear throughout the year. Meets José Rodríguez Feo in New York. Henry Church dies suddenly on April 4; Stevens attends funeral (remains close to widow Barbara Church for remainder of his life). Grandson Peter Reed Hanchak born April 26. Dines with *Partisan Review* editors and contributors despite lack of sympathy with their left-wing politics. Receives honorary doctorate from Wesleyan in June; Cummington Press publishes *Three Academic Pieces* in December.

1948   Delivers lectures in March at Yale ("Effects of Analogy")
        and in September at Columbia ("Imagination as Value").
        Holly begins divorce proceedings (finalized 1951). Devel-
        ops interest in work of French painter Jean Dubuffet after
        attending his first New York show in December. Gratified
        by end-of-year royalty check from Knopf, the largest he
        has ever received.

1949   From March through June works on long poem "An Or-
        dinary Evening in New Haven"; reads in November at
        Connecticut Academy of Arts and Sciences. Immensely
        pleased by arrival of Pierre Tal Coat painting from Paris
        (inspires poem "Angel Surrounded by Paysans"); writes
        catalogue introduction for exhibition by Marcel Gromaire.

1950   Receives Bollingen Prize in March. Works on "The Rock"
        in early spring. Visited at Hartford office by Marianne
        Moore in July; sees her regularly over next several years.
        (Requests that Moore make selection for British edition
        of *Selected Poems*, but she declines.) *The Auroras of Au-
        tumn* published in September; Knopf announces reissue of
        all Stevens' earlier volumes.

1951   Delivers lecture "The Relations Between Poetry and
        Painting" at Museum of Modern Art in January, begin-
        ning a demanding schedule of speaking engagements. Re-
        ceives National Book Award in March for *The Auroras of
        Autumn*. Lectures at Mount Holyoke in April; attends fif-
        tieth reunion of Harvard class in June, pleased by second
        honorary doctorate. Corresponds with Korean writer
        Peter Lee and meets poet Richard Wilbur. Prose collection
        The Necessary Angel published in November. Delivers "A
        Collect of Philosophy" as Moody Lecture at University of
        Chicago in November; disappointed when philosopher
        Paul Weiss rejects it for publication in *The Review of
        Metaphysics*. Serves as judge for National Book Awards in
        December.

1952   Reads at Wellesley in January; later in month serves on
        Bollingen committee, which awards prize to Marianne
        Moore for *Collected Poems* (will also serve on committee
        in 1953 and 1954). Reads at Harvard in May. Grieved by
        news of Santayana's death in Rome in September.

1953   *Selected Poems* published in England by Faber and Faber
            in February. Corresponds with Harvard professor Renato
            Poggioli, who is preparing Italian translation of his poems.
            Declines to speak at memorial for Dylan Thomas ("an ut-
            terly improvident person").

1954   Records reading of poems for Harvard Library. Delivers
            "The Sail of Ulysses" as Phi Beta Kappa poem at Colum-
            bia in May. *Collected Poems* published in October, coin-
            ciding with Stevens' 75th birthday; guests at celebration
            at Harmonie Club in New York include Conrad Aiken,
            Louise Bogan, James Merrill, Marianne Moore, Delmore
            Schwartz, Lionel Trilling, and Carl Van Vechten. Reads at
            Vassar and YMHA in New York in November. Declines
            invitation by Archibald MacLeish to be Charles Eliot Nor-
            ton professor of poetry at Harvard for 1955–56. Pleased by
            "avalanche of cards" at Christmas.

1955   Learns in early January that Yale will award him honorary
            degree in June (the "greatest prize for a Harvard man").
            Elsie suffers stroke on January 14. Receives National Book
            Award for second time at January 25 ceremony. In April,
            gastrointestinal tests reveals diverticulitis. Before entering
            hospital completes "Connecticut Composed" for Voice of
            America broadcast and writes poems " 'A mythology re-
            flects its region' " and "Of Mere Being." Surgery on April
            26 discloses advanced stomach cancer; remains in St. Fran-
            cis Hospital in Hartford for more than three weeks. Learns
            in May that he has won Pulitzer Prize. After leaving hos-
            pital spends short time at home; moves to Avery Conva-
            lescent Hospital for a month, then goes home, before
            returning in July to the Avery and then to St. Francis.
            Maintains good humor; recites Longfellow to nurses; re-
            peatedly recollects to Holly details of 1903 trip to British
            Columbia. Dies on morning of August 2. After brief ser-
            vice at James T. Pratt Funeral Home, buried in Cedar Hill
            Cemetery, Hartford, on August 4.

Note on the Texts

This volume contains six published collections of poetry by Wallace Stevens, *Harmonium* (1923), *Ideas of Order* (1936), *The Man with the Blue Guitar* (1937), *Parts of a World* (1942), *Transport to Summer* (1947), and *The Auroras of Autumn* (1950), as well as four additional groupings of poetry: the 14 poems added by Stevens to the 1931 edition of *Harmonium*; the 25 poems Stevens collected for the first time in "The Rock," the final section of *The Collected Poems of Wallace Stevens* (1954); a section titled "Late Poems" that includes 29 poems written after the publication of *The Collected Poems of Wallace Stevens* (or that perhaps were inadvertently omitted from the *Collected Poems*); and a selection of 94 poems, sequences of poems, manuscript books of poetry, and poetic translations that were never collected by Stevens, arranged in the approximate order of their composition. Following the poems, this volume presents three plays, *Three Travelers Watch a Sunrise*, *Carlos Among the Candles*, and *Bowl, Cat and Broomstick*; a collection of essays, *The Necessary Angel: Essays on Reality and the Imagination* (1951); a selection of 49 essays, articles, prefaces, and other prose writings that were never collected by Stevens; seven selections from his notebooks; and a section containing five journal entries, written between 1898 and 1903, and 20 letters, written between 1909 and 1955.

In July 1922 Carl Van Vechten wrote to Stevens, suggesting that he prepare a collection of his poetry for publication. Stevens replied that he felt "frightfully uncertain about a book," but he soon reached an agreement with Alfred A. Knopf for its publication and completed work on the manuscript in November. In March 1923 Stevens wrote to his publisher suggesting that the book be titled "The Grand Poem: Preliminary Minutiae," but in a telegram sent to Knopf on May 18 he chose to use *Harmonium* as its title. *Harmonium* was published by Alfred A. Knopf on September 7, 1923, in a printing of 1,500 copies. The present volume prints the text of the 1923 first edition.

Knopf wrote to Stevens in the spring of 1930, asking him if he would like to add new poems to *Harmonium* when it was reprinted. Stevens responded on October 16, 1930, with a list of 14 poems and specified that they be inserted into the collection after "Nomad Exquisite" (page 77.1–15 in this volume) and before "Tea" (p. 77.16–24). He also requested that three poems from the 1923 edition, "The Silver Plough-Boy," "Exposition of the Contents of a Cab," and "Architecture," be omitted from the new edition. The second edition of *Harmonium*, which incorporated these changes, was published by

Alfred A. Knopf on July 24, 1931. The present volume places the 14 poems that were added to *Harmonium* in a separate section, arranged in the order in which they appeared in the 1931 edition; the texts printed here are taken from that edition.

In 1934 Ronald Lane Latimer, the editor of the quarterly poetry magazine *Alcestis*, wrote to Stevens proposing to publish a new collection of his poetry in a limited edition. Stevens agreed, subject to obtaining the consent of Knopf, who, under the terms of the contract for *Harmonium*, had the option to publish Stevens' next book. Knopf agreed to the publication of a collection by Alcestis Press, and Stevens chose 33 poems for inclusion in the volume. *Ideas of Order* was published by the Alcestis Press on August 12, 1935, in an edition of 165 copies. When Knopf subsequently offered to publish a trade edition of the book, Stevens agreed, writing in a letter of March 23, 1936: "I am grateful to you for your attitude. Of course it must be true that you do not publish poetry with the idea of making any money on it except in an occasionally fortunate instance. My relations with you have always been most agreeable and naturally I am happy to have you ask me to go on with you." Stevens added three poems, "Farewell to Florida," "Ghosts as Cocoons," and "A Postcard from the Volcano," to the Knopf edition and made changes in the poems that had appeared in the Alcestis edition. *Ideas of Order* was published by Alfred A. Knopf on October 19, 1936, in a printing of 1,000 copies. The present volume prints the text of the 1936 Knopf edition.

The Man with the Blue Guitar & Other Poems was published by Alfred A. Knopf on October 4, 1937, in a printing of 1,000 copies. Four long poems were collected in the volume, including a significantly revised and shortened version of "Owl's Clover," which had been previously published by the Alcestis Press on November 5, 1936, in an edition of 105 copies (the text of the Alcestis Press edition is printed on pp. 567–90 of this volume). The first edition of *The Man with the Blue Guitar* included on its colophon page a statement regarding the book's typographical design: "In some of the lines appear unusual blank spaces and extra-wide spacing of certain crucial words. By this experimental device the author wishes to indicate a desirable pause or emphasis suggested by the sense. In observing these rests the reader may feel by so much the closer to the poet's intention." Referring to this passage, Stevens wrote in a letter to Ronald Lane Latimer on September 16, 1937: "This is pure nonsense. I never said any such thing and have a horror of poetry pretending to be contemporaneous because of typographical queerness." The present volume prints the text of the 1937 Knopf first edition but does not reproduce the spacing used in its typographical design.

Parts of a World was published by Alfred A. Knopf on September

8, 1942, in a printing of 1,000 copies. The present volume prints the text of the first printing of the Knopf edition.

Transport to Summer was published by Alfred A. Knopf on March 20, 1947, in a printing of 1,750 copies. Two of the poems collected in the volume had been previously published in limited editions by The Cummington Press: "Notes toward a Supreme Fiction" in October 1942 (with a second edition in November 1943) and "Esthétique du Mal" in November 1945; Stevens made minor changes in both poems for their inclusion in the Knopf edition. The present volume prints the text of the first printing of the Knopf edition.

The Auroras of Autumn was published by Alfred A. Knopf on September 11, 1950, in a printing of 3,000 copies. One poem in the collection, "A Primitive Like an Orb," had been printed as a pamphlet by The Banyan Press in March 1948. This volume prints the text of the first printing of the Knopf edition.

In April 1954 Stevens agreed to Knopf's proposal to publish a collected edition of his poetry in honor of his seventy-fifth birthday on October 2, 1954, and asked that it include a section of new poems in addition to the poetry that had appeared in previously published volumes. Stevens initially proposed calling this section "Amber Umber," but then decided to use "The Rock" as its title. Six of the 25 poems included in "The Rock" had previously appeared in book form: "To an Old Philosopher in Rome," in *The Pocket Book of Modern Verse*, edited by Oscar Williams (1954); "Two Illustrations That the World Is What You Make It," "Prologues to What Is Possible," and "Song of Fixed Accord" in *New Poems by American Poets*, edited by Rolfe Humphries (1953); "Final Soliloquy of the Interior Paramour" in *Selected Poems*, published in London by Faber and Faber (1953); and "The River of Rivers in Connecticut," in both English and an Italian translation, in *Mattino Domenicale ed altre poesie* (1954). *The Collected Poems of Wallace Stevens* was published by Alfred A. Knopf on October 1, 1954, in a printing of 2,500 copies. The present volume prints texts of the poems in "The Rock" taken from the first printing of *The Collected Poems of Wallace Stevens*.

A letter Stevens wrote to Robert Pack on April 14, 1955, indicates that Stevens inadvertently omitted from *Collected Poems* at least one poem that he had intended to include in "The Rock." Stevens wrote, "I did not know that I had omitted *The Course of a Particular*. This was simply a mistake." After explaining that Knopf had used copies of previously published books to compile most of *Collected Poems*, Stevens continued, "I had, of course, to send him manuscripts of the poems in the last section of the book and if there is anything omitted, it is simply because I had not kept a copy of the manuscript or had misplaced it." The present volume includes, in a section titled "Late

Poems," the texts of 29 poems that were published in periodicals or anthologies, or were composed by Stevens, after he completed work on *The Auroras of Autumn*. The texts of 16 poems are taken from their initial publication in periodicals or anthologies. Four poems, "The Sail of Ulysses," "On the Way to the Bus," " 'A mythology reflects its region,' " and "Of Mere Being," were unpublished at the time of Stevens' death (all four poems have been published posthumously) and are printed in the present volume from typescript, or, in the case of "The Sail of Ulysses," a revised carbon typescript. Nine poems that were published in periodicals—"As at a Theatre," "The Desire to Make Love in a Pagoda," "Nuns Painting Water-Lilies," "The Role of the Idea in Poetry," "Americana," "The Souls of Women at Night" (all from *Wake*, Summer 1950); "Presence of an External Master of Knowledge" (*Times Literary Supplement*, September 17, 1954); "Conversation with Three Women of New England" (*Accent*, Autumn 1954); and "A Clear Day and No Memories" (*The Sewanee Review*, Winter 1955)—are printed from typescript because collation has shown that the periodical texts did not follow Stevens' punctuation.

In addition to the poems that he included in various collections of his work, Stevens published other poems that he chose not to collect (poems that originally appeared in various periodicals, anthologies, pamphlets, and limited editions). He also left unpublished poems, written before 1950, in typescript and holograph manuscript (these poems have all been published posthumously). Of the 94 items selected for inclusion in the section of this volume titled "Uncollected Poems," the texts of 42 poems are taken from their periodical publication. Three poems are taken from their initial publication in anthologies, and one poem is taken from its initial publication as a pamphlet. The text of "Owl's Clover" presented in this section is taken from the limited edition published by the Alcestis Press on November 5, 1936. The texts of 24 poems are printed from holograph manuscripts, including the sequence of 14 sonnets Stevens wrote in 1899 while a student at Harvard, some of which were later published in periodicals (see note 482.16 in this volume), and the poetic translation "Instant of Clearness," which was published as "Moment of Light" in *Modern School*, October 1918, in a text which omitted one line and reversed the order of two other lines. Four poems are printed from the holograph manuscripts of letters written by Stevens. "A Book of Verses" and "The Little June Book," which Stevens presented as birthday gifts to Elsie Moll in 1908 and 1909, are printed from the holograph originals (Stevens later published in periodicals versions of some of the poems included in these two manuscript books; see notes 522.1 and 525.1). Nine poems are printed from typescript, and the texts of eight poems are printed from books published after Stevens' death because no other texts of these poems are available. The texts of "Self-Respect," "To Miss Gage," and "From a Vagabond" are taken from Holly Stevens, *Souvenirs and Prophecies: The Young Wallace Stevens* (1966); the text of " 'If I love thee, I am thine,' " is taken from *Letters of Wallace Stevens*, selected and edited by Holly Stevens (1966); the text of " 'I have lived so long with the rhetoricians' " is taken from Robert Buttel, *Wallace Stevens: The Making of Harmonium* (1967); and the text of "First Warmth" is taken from Wallace Stevens, *Opus Posthumous*, edited by Samuel French Morse (1957). "Phases" is printed from A. Walton Litz, *Introspective Voyager: The Poetic Development of Wallace Stevens* (1972); Litz uses a holograph manuscript, a partial typescript, and the portions of the poem that were published in *Poetry* in November 1914 to establish a text of the poem (see note 525.9). "Lettres d'un Soldat" is taken from the revised edition of *Opus Posthumous*, edited by Milton J. Bates (1989), which uses typescript and the text established by Litz in *Introspective Voyager* to establish a text of this sequence of poems, portions of which were published in *Poetry* in May 1918 (see note 538.8).

Stevens wrote three plays, two of which were published in periodicals during his lifetime. *Three Travelers Watch a Sunrise* appeared in *Poetry* in July 1916, and *Carlos Among the Candles* was published in *Poetry* in December 1917; the text printed in the present volume are taken from their original periodical appearances. *Bowl, Cat and Broomstick* (which has been published posthumously) is printed from the typescript, WAS 4118, in the Huntington Library, San Marino, California, and from Samuel French Morse, "A Note on 'Bowl, Cat and Broomstick'," *The Wallace Stevens Journal* (1978), which presents the text of a page missing from the typescript in the Huntington (this typescript page corresponds to page 622.11–37 in the present volume.)

The Necessary Angel: Essays on Reality and the Imagination was published by Alfred A. Knopf on November 12, 1951, in a printing of 3,000 copies, and includes two poems, "Someone Puts a Pineapple Together" and "Of Ideal Time and Choice," which Stevens did not collect in book form elsewhere. All seven of the essays included in the volume had been previously published: "The Noble Rider and the Sound of Words" in *The Language of Poetry*, edited by Allen Tate (1942); "The Figure of the Youth as Virile Poet" in *The Sewanee Review*, Autumn 1944; "Three Academic Pieces" in *Partisan Review*, May–June 1947, and in a limited edition published by The Cummington Press on December 8, 1947 (in both of these versions, the prose piece appeared under the title "The Realm of Resemblance"); "About One of Marianne Moore's Poems" in *Quarterly Review of Literature*, Summer 1948; "Effects of Analogy" in *The Yale Review*,

September 1948; "Imagination as Value" in *English Institute Essays 1948*, edited by D. A. Robertson, Jr. (1949); and "The Relations Between Poetry and Painting" in a pamphlet published by the Museum of Modern Art, New York, in 1951. This volume presents the text of the first printing of the Knopf edition.

The section of the present volume titled "Uncollected Prose" contains a selection of 49 prose pieces, written by Stevens between 1897 and 1955, that were never collected by him in book form. Of these pieces, the texts of 22 are taken from their original periodical publication. Eight pieces are printed from their initial publication in anthologies or as prefaces to books. Three pieces, "Epitaphiana," "Marcel Gromaire," and "Raoul Dufy," are printed from their initial appearance in pamphlets or exhibition catalogs. The text of "A Note on 'Les Plus Belles Pages' " is taken from the holograph manuscript. "The Irrational Element in Poetry" and "Notes on Jean Labasque" are printed from *Opus Posthumous*, edited by Samuel French Morse (1957), which presents texts based on source material whose present location is unknown. The texts of 13 pieces are printed from typescript, including four pieces that were published in some form during Stevens' lifetime. Three of them were published in versions that omit material contained in the typescripts submitted by Stevens: "Note for *This Is My Best*" appeared in *This Is My Best*, edited by Whit Burnett (1942); the "Autobiographical Statement" appeared as "Wallace Stevens: Walker" in the *New York Herald-Tribune Book Review*, October 24, 1954; and "Connecticut Composed" appeared as "This Is Connecticut" in the *Hartford Courant*, July 21, 1955. The fourth, "Homage to Henry Church," was published in a French translation as "Portrait" in *Homage à Henry Church* (1948). Of the nine pieces printed from typescript that were not published during Stevens' lifetime, one, "There was a mother chicken," is printed here for the first time; the remaining eight have all been published posthumously.

This volume prints seven selections from Stevens' notebooks, one of which, "Materia Poetica," was published during his lifetime (all of the material in the other six sections has been published posthumously). Stevens submitted "Materia Poetica," an arrangement of 39 aphorisms, to *View* in 1940. The first 22 aphorisms appeared in the September 1940 number of the magazine in the order in which Stevens had arranged them, but the remainder were printed in the October 1942 number in a rearranged order and without the roman numerals Stevens had used to enumerate them. This volume prints the text of "Materia Poetica" from the typescript prepared by Stevens. The selections from *Sur Plusieurs Beaux Sujets* are taken from *Sur Plusieurs Beaux Sujets: Wallace Stevens' Commonplace Book*, edited by Milton J. Bates (1989), and the text of "Schemata" is taken from typescript; the four remaining selections are taken from holograph manuscript.

The texts of the journal entries and letters presented in this volume are taken from holograph manuscript and typescript (this material has been previously published, sometimes in excerpted or edited form).

The following is a list of the poems and prose writings included in the present volume in the sections titled "Late Poems," "Uncollected Poems," "Uncollected Prose," "From the Notebooks," and "Journals and Letters," giving the source of each text. Descriptive titles supplied in the present volume for some of the poems and prose writings appear within quotation marks. The most common sources of manuscript material are indicated by these abbreviations:

Beinecke   Yale Collection of American Literature, Beinecke Rare Book and Manuscript Library, Yale University Library, New Haven, Connecticut. Reprinted by permission.

Huntington   Huntington Library, San Marino, California. Reprinted by permission.

Ransom   Harry Ransom Humanities Research Center, University of Texas at Austin. Reprinted by permission.

Regenstein   Special Collections, Joseph Regenstein Library, University of Chicago, Chicago, Illinois. Reprinted by permission.

LATE POEMS

The Sick Man. *Accent*, Spring 1950.
As at a Theatre. Typescript, *Huntington*. WAS 4142.
The Desire to Make Love in a Pagoda. Typescript, *Huntington*. WAS 4142.
Nuns Painting Water-Lilies. Typescript, *Huntington*. WAS 4142.
The Role of the Idea in Poetry. Typescript, *Huntington*. WAS 4142.
Americana. Typescript, *Huntington*. WAS 4142.
The Souls of Women at Night. Typescript, *Huntington*. WAS 4142.
A Discovery of Thought. *Imagi*, Summer 1950.
The Course of a Particular. *Hudson Review*, Spring 1951.
How Now, O, Brightener . . . *Shenandoah*, Spring 1952.
The Dove in Spring. *7 Arts # Two*, edited by Fernando Puma (Garden City, N.Y.: Permabooks, 1954).
Farewell Without a Guitar. *New World Writing* (New York: New American Library, 1954).
The Sail of Ulysses. Revised carbon typescript, *Huntington*. WAS 4228.
Presence of an External Master of Knowledge. Typescript, *Huntington*. WAS 2409.

A Child Asleep in Its Own Life. *Times Literary Supplement*, September 17, 1954.

Two Letters. *Vogue*, October 1, 1954.

Conversation with Three Women of New England. Typescript, *Huntington*. WAS 4124.

Dinner Bell in the Woods. *Perspective*, Autumn 1954.

Reality Is an Activity of the Most August Imagination. *Perspective*, Autumn 1954.

On the Way to the Bus. Typescript, *Huntington*. WAS 4206.

The Region November. *Zero*, Spring 1956.

Solitaire Under the Oaks. *The Sewanee Review*, Winter 1955.

Local Objects. *The Sewanee Review*, Winter 1955.

Artificial Populations. *The Sewanee Review*, Winter 1955.

A Clear Day and No Memories. Typescript, *Huntington*. WAS 4122.

Banjo Boomer. *Atlantic Monthly*, March 1955.

July Mountain. *Atlantic Monthly*, April 1955.

"A mythology reflects its region." Typescript, *Huntington*. WAS 4193.

Of Mere Being. Typescript, *Huntington*. WAS 4205.

UNCOLLECTED POEMS

Autumn. *The Red and Black*, January 1898.

Who Lies Dead? *The Harvard Advocate*, November 28, 1898.

Vita Mea. *The Harvard Advocate*, December 12, 1898.

Self-Respect. Holly Stevens, *Souvenirs and Prophecies: The Young Wallace Stevens* (New York: Alfred A. Knopf, 1977), 23.

Sonnets. Holograph manuscript, *Huntington*. WAS 8.

Song ("She loves me or loves me not"). *The Harvard Advocate*, March 13, 1899.

"You say this is the iris?" Holograph manuscript, *Huntington*. WAS 7.

Imitation of Sidney: To Stella (Miss B?). Holograph manuscript, *Huntington*. WAS 8.

Quatrain ("Go not, young cloud"). *The Harvard Advocate*, November 13, 1899.

To the Morn. *Harvard Monthly*, December 1899 (signed "Hillary Harness").

Song ("Ah yes! beyond these barren walls"). *The Harvard Advocate*, March 10, 1900.

Outside the Hospital. *The Harvard Advocate*, March 24, 1900 (signed "R. Jerries").

Street Songs. *The Harvard Advocate*, April 3, 1900.

Ode. Pamphlet, Harvard Class of '01, Junior Dinner, May 1, 1900. Reprinted with permission of Harvard University Archives.

Night-Song. *The Harvard Advocate*, May 10, 1900 (signed "Kenneth Malone").

Ballade of the Pink Parasol. *The Harvard Advocate*, May 23, 1900 (signed "Carrol More").

Quatrain ("He sought the music"). *The Harvard Advocate*, June 2, 1900 (signed "Henry Marshall").

A Window in the Slums. Holograph manuscript, *Huntington*. WAS 8.

Sonnet ("Build up the walls about me"). Holograph manuscript, *Huntington*. WAS 8.

To Miss Gage. Holly Stevens, *Souvenirs and Prophecies: The Young Wallace Stevens* (New York: Alfred A. Knopf, 1977), 103.

"If I love thee, I am thine." *Letters of Wallace Stevens*, selected and edited by Holly Stevens (New York: Alfred A. Knopf, 1966), 94.

"Elsie's mirror only shows." Holograph manuscript of letter to Elsie Moll, April 12, 1907, *Huntington*. WAS 1773.

From a Vagabond. Holly Stevens, *Souvenirs and Prophecies: The Young Wallace Stevens* (New York: Alfred A. Knopf. 1977), 186–87.

A Book of Verses. Holograph manuscript, *Huntington*. WAS 24.

Chiaroscuro. Holograph manuscript, *Huntington*. WAS 4120.

In a Garden. Holograph manuscript of letter to Elsie Moll, January 31, 1909, *Huntington*. WAS 1812.

The Little June Book. Holograph manuscript, *Huntington*. WAS 25.

Colors. Holograph manuscript, *Huntington*. WAS 4165.

Testamentum. Holograph manuscript, *Huntington*. WAS 4165.

Sonnet from the Book of Regrets. Holograph manuscript of letter to Elsie Moll, July 25, 1909, *Huntington*. WAS 1878.

A Valentine. Holograph manuscript of letter to Elsie Stevens, February 14, 1910, *Huntington*. WAS 1775.

Dolls. Holograph manuscript, *Huntington*. WAS 4131.

Infernale. Typescript, *Huntington*. WAS 4131.

"All things imagined are of earth compact." Holograph manuscript, *Huntington*. WAS 4102.

L'Essor Saccadé. Holograph manuscript, *Huntington*. WAS 4139.

An Exercise for Professor X. Holograph manuscript, *Huntington*. WAS 4141.

Headache. Holograph manuscript, *Huntington*. WAS 4157.

"I have lived so long with the rhetoricians." Robert Buttel, *Wallace Stevens: The Making of Harmonium* (Princeton, N.J.: Princeton University Press, 1967), 183.

"The night-wind of August." Holograph manuscript, *Huntington*. WAS 4198.

To Madame Alda, Singing a Song, in a White Gown. Typescript, *Huntington*. WAS 4250.

Carnet de Voyage. *The Trend*, September 1914.

From a Junk. *The Trend*, November 1914.

Home Again. *The Trend*, November 1914.

Phases. A. Walton Litz, *Introspective Voyager: The Poetic Development of Wallace Stevens* (New York: Oxford University Press, 1972), 305–9.

Blanche McCarthy. Typescript, *Huntington*. WAS 4115.

For an Old Woman in a Wig. Holograph manuscript, *Huntington*. WAS 4150.

The Florist Wears Knee-Breeches. *Others*, March 1916.

Song ("There are great things doing . . ."). *Others*, March 1916.

Inscription for a Monument. *Others*, March 1916.

Bowl. *Others*, March 1916.

Primordia. *The Soil*, January 1917.

Meditation. *Others*, December 1917.

Gray Room. *Others*, December 1917.

Lettres d'un Soldat. Wallace Stevens, *Opus Posthumous*, revised, enlarged, and corrected edition, edited by Milton J. Bates (New York: Alfred A. Knopf, 1989), 29–36.

Instant of Clearness. Holograph manuscript, Special Collections, Van Pelt-Dietrich Library, University of Pennsylvania.

The Naked Eye of the Aunt. Holograph manuscript, *Huntington*. WAS 4194.

Peter Parasol. *Poetry*, October 1919.

Piano Practice at the Academy of the Holy Angels. Holograph manuscript, Harriet Monroe Library of Modern Poetry, *Regenstein*.

The Indigo Glass in the Grass. *Poetry*, October 1919.

Anecdote of the Prince of Peacocks. Holograph manuscript, *Huntington*. WAS 4107.

Anecdote of the Abnormal. Holograph manuscript, *Huntington*. WAS 4106.

Romance for a Demoiselle Lying in the Grass. Holograph manuscript, *Huntington*. WAS 4226.

Lulu Gay. *Contact*, 1921.

Lulu Morose. *Contact*, 1921.

This Vast Inelegance. Typescript, *Huntington*. WAS 4246.

Saturday Night at the Chiropodist's. Holograph manuscript, *Huntington*. WAS 4231.

Mandolin and Liqueurs. *The Chapbook*, April 1923.

The Shape of the Coroner. *The Measure*, May 1923.

Red Loves Kit. *The Measure*, August 1924.

"Though Valentine brings love." Holograph manuscript, *Huntington*. WAS 4248.

Metropolitan Melancholy. Holograph manuscript, Harriet Monroe Library of Modern Poetry, *Regenstein*.

Annual Gaiety. *Modern American Poetry: A Critical Anthology*, fourth revised edition, edited by Louis Untermeyer (New York: Harcourt Brace, 1930).

Good Man, Bad Woman. *Poetry*, October 1932.

The Woman Who Blamed Life on a Spaniard. *Contempo*, December 15, 1932.

Secret Man. *Modern Things*, edited by Parker Tyler (New York: The Galleon Press, 1934).

What They Call Red Cherry Pie. *Alcestis*, October 1934.

Hieroglyphica. *Direction*, Autumn 1934.

The Drum-Majors in the Labor Day Parade. *Smoke*, Autumn 1934.

Polo Ponies Practicing. *Westminster Magazine*, Autumn 1934.

The Widow. Typescript, Ronald Latimer Papers, Modern Poetry Collections, *Regenstein*.

Lytton Strachey, Also, Enters into Heaven. *The Rocking-Horse*, Spring 1935.

Agenda. *Smoke*, Summer, 1935.

Table Talk. Typescript, *Huntington*. WAS 4243.

A Room on a Garden. Typescript, *Huntington*. WAS 4227.

Owl's Clover. *Owl's Clover* (New York: Alcestis Press, 1936).

Communications of Meaning. *Trend*, March 1942.

One of Those Hibiscuses of Damozels. *Trend*, March 1942.

Outside of Wedlock. *Trend*, March 1942.

Desire & the Object. *Accent*, Summer 1942.

This as Including That. Typescript, *Huntington*. WAS 4245.

Tradition. *The Saint Nicholas Society of the City of New York* (New York: Saint Nicholas Society, 1945), 17–19.

Memorandum. *Poetry Quarterly*, Winter 1947.

First Warmth. Wallace Stevens, *Opus Posthumous*, edited by Samuel French Morse (New York: Alfred A. Knopf, 1957), 89–90.

As You Leave the Room. Typescript, *Huntington*. WAS 4111.

UNCOLLECTED PROSE

The Thessalians. *The Reading Eagle*, June 24, 1897.

A Day in February. *The Harvard Advocate*, March 6, 1899.

"Editorials on the Fence Question." *The Harvard Advocate*, March 24, 1900; April 13, 1900; June 16, 1900.

Four Characters. *The Harvard Advocate*, June 16, 1900.

Cattle Kings of Florida. *The Atlanta Journal*, December 14, 1930.

"On 'The Emperor of Ice Cream.' " *Fifty Poets: An American Auto Anthology*, edited by William Rose Benét (New York: Duffield and Green, 1933).

Williams. William Carlos Williams, *Collected Poems 1921–1931* (New York: The Objectivist Press, 1934).

"Response to an Enquiry." *New Verse*, October 1934.

"Martha Champion." *Trial Balances*, edited by Ann Winslow (New York: Macmillan, 1935).

A Poet That Matters. *Life and Letters To-day*, December 2, 1935.

"In Memory of Harriet Monroe." *Poetry*, December 1936.

The Irrational Element in Poetry. Wallace Stevens, *Opus Posthumous*, edited by Samuel French Morse (New York: Alfred A. Knopf, 1957), 216–29.

Insurance and Social Change. *The Hartford Agent*, October 1937.

Surety and Fidelity Claims. *The Eastern Underwriter*, March 25, 1938.

"Response to an Enquiry." *Twentieth Century Verse*, September–October 1938.

A Note on Poetry. *The Oxford Anthology of American Literature*, edited by William Rose Benét and Norman Holmes Pearson (New York: Oxford University Press, 1938).

"Homage to T.S. Eliot." *The Harvard Advocate*, December 1938.

Notes on Jean Labasque. Wallace Stevens, *Opus Posthumous*, edited by Samuel French Morse (New York: Alfred A. Knopf, 1957) 292–93.

The Situation in American Writing: Seven Questions. *Partisan Review*, Summer 1939.

"Concerning a Chair of Poetry." Typescript enclosed in letter to Henry Church, October 15, 1940, *Huntington*. WAS 3479.

"Note for *This Is My Best*." Typescript, Manuscripts Division, Department of Rare Books and Special Collections, Princeton University Libraries. Reprinted by permission.

Epitaphiana. Facsimile reproduction of pamphlet privately printed for Stevens, J. M. Edelstein, *Wallace Stevens: A Descriptive Bibliography* (Pittsburgh: University of Pittsburgh Press, 1973), 53.

"Introduction to Samuel French Morse's *Time of Year*." Samuel French Morse, *Time of Year* (Cummington, Mass.: The Cummington Press, 1943).

"There was a mother chicken." Typescript, *Huntington*. WAS 4244.

A Ceremony. Typescript, *Huntington*. WAS 4119.

"Response to an Enquiry." *The Yale Literary Magazine*, Spring 1946.

Rubbings of Reality. *Briarcliff Quarterly*, October 1946.

"Homage to Henry Church." Typescript enclosed in letter to Barbara Church, November 12, 1947, *Huntington*. WAS 3562.

The Shaper. *Paul Rosenfeld: Voyager in the Arts*, edited by Jerome Mellquist and Lucie Wiese (New York: Creative Age Press, 1948).

John Crowe Ransom: Tennessean. *The Sewanee Review*, Summer 1948.

The State of American Writing, 1948: Seven Questions. *Partisan Review*, August 1948.

"A Comment on Meaning in Poetry." *The Explicator*, November 1948.

Marcel Gromaire. *Gromaire: Exhibition of Paintings, December 5–31, 1949*, exhibition catalog, Louis Carré Gallery, New York.

"Response to an Enquiry." *Modern American Poetry*, edited by B. Rajan (London: Dennis Dobson, 1950).

"Three Paraphrases from Léon-Paul Fargue." Typescript, *Huntington*. WAS 4211.

"On Receiving the Gold Medal from the Poetry Society of America." Typescript, *Huntington*. WAS 4100.

"On Receiving the National Book Award for Poetry." Typescript, *Huntington*. WAS 4098.

"On Receiving an Honorary Degree from Bard College." Typescript, *Huntington*. WAS 4097.

Two or Three Ideas. *The CEA Critic*, Supplement, October 1951.

A Collect of Philosophy. Typescript, *Huntington*. WAS 4123.

"A Note on 'Les Plus Belles Pages.' " Holograph manuscript, Houghton Library, Harvard University. Reprinted by permission.

Raoul Dufy. *Raoul Dufy*, promotional pamphlet (New York: Pierre Berès, Inc., 1953).

"Autobiographical Statement for the *New York Herald-Tribune Book Review*." Typescript enclosed in letter to Irita Van Doren, September 20, 1954, *Huntington*. WAS 2676.

The Whole Man: Perspectives, Horizons. *Yale Review*, Winter 1955.

"On Receiving the National Book Award for Poetry." Typescript, *Beinecke*.

A Footnote to Saul Bellow's "Pains and Gains." *Semi-Colon*, Spring 1955.

"On Walt Whitman." *Nocturne*, Spring 1955.

Two Prefaces. Paul Valéry, *Dialogues* (New York: Pantheon Books, 1956).

Connecticut Composed. Typescript, *Huntington*. WAS 2306.

FROM THE NOTEBOOKS

Untitled note (sonnet titles). Holograph manuscript, *Huntington*. WAS 4216.

Schemata. Typescript, *Huntington*. WAS 4232.

from *Adagia*. Holograph manuscript, *Huntington*. WAS 70.

from *Sur Plusieurs Beaux Sujects*. *Sur Plusieurs Beaux Sujects: Wallace Stevens' Commonplace Book*, edited by Milton J. Bates (Stanford and San Marino: Stanford University Press and Huntington Library, 1989). Copyright © 1989 by the Henry E. Huntington Library and Art Gallery. Reprinted by permission.

Materia Poetica. Typescript, *Huntington*. WAS 4190.

"Gaiety in poetry is a precious characteristic . . ." Holograph manuscript, *Huntington*. WAS 72.

"There are two arch-types of poets . . ." Holograph manuscript, *Huntington*. WAS 72.

JOURNALS AND LETTERS

December 27, 1898. *Huntington*. WAS 7.

June 15, 1900. *Huntington*. WAS 8.

March 11, 1901. *Huntington*. WAS 8.

August 10, 1902. *Huntington*. WAS 9.

September 3, 1903. *Huntington*. WAS 9.

To Elsie Moll, January 21, 1909. *Huntington*. WAS 1809.

To Elsie Moll, March 18, 1909. *Huntington*. WAS 1831.

To Harriet Monroe, April 25, 1920. Holograph manuscript, *Regenstein*.

To Alice Corbin Henderson, March 27, 1922. Holograph manuscript, *Ransom*.

To Alice Corbin Henderson, November 17, 1922. Holograph manuscript, *Ransom*.

To Marianne Moore, November 19, 1925. Typescript, *Beinecke*.

To William Carlos Williams, September 7, 1927. Holograph manuscript, *Beinecke*.

To Ronald Lane Latimer, November 26, 1935. Typescript, *Regenstein*.

To Leonard C. van Geyzel, December 31, 1937. Typescript, Dartmouth College Library. Reprinted by permission.

To C.L. Daughtry, November 24, 1941. Typescript, *Huntington*. WAS 510.

To William Carlos Williams, January 22, 1942. Typescript, *Beinecke*.

To Harvey Breit, August 8, 1942. Typescript, *Huntington*. WAS 216.

To Jane MacFarland Stone, November 2, 1943. Typescript, *Huntington*. WAS 2761.

To José Rodríguez Feo, June 20, 1945. Typescript, Houghton Library, Harvard University. Reprinted by permission.

To Charles Norman, November 9, 1945. Typescript, *Ransom*.

To Allen Tate, April 6, 1948. Typescript, Manuscripts Division, Department of Rare Books and Special Collections, Princeton University Libraries. Reprinted by permission.

To Thomas McGreevy, December 8, 1948. Typescript, *Huntington.* WAS 189.

To Barbara Church, April 27, 1950. Holograph manuscript, *Huntington.* WAS 3734.

To Robert Pack, December 28, 1954. Typescript, *Huntington.* WAS 1369.

To Samuel French Morse, July 5, 1955. Typescript, *Huntington.* WAS 1275.

The following is a list of pages where a stanza break coincides with the foot of the page (except where such breaks are apparent from the regular stanzaic structure of the poem): 15, 24, 33, 43, 47, 107, 111, 115, 154, 191, 222, 229, 233, 280, 284, 286, 293, 314, 428, 481, 485, 492, 497, 516, 525, 555.

This volume presents the texts of the printings, typescripts, and manuscripts chosen for inclusion here but does not attempt to reproduce features of their typographic design or visual style. The texts are printed without alteration, except for the correction of typographical errors and slips of the pen. Spelling, punctuation, and capitalization are sometimes expressive features, and they are not altered, even when inconsistent or irregular. Some of the errors listed here have been determined by collating copy-texts against alternate versions. The following is a list of typographical and handwriting errors corrected, cited by page and line number: 11.16, Yangste; 35.18, philactary; 41.14, province; 52.10–11, flesh, / And; 57.12, atttains; 124.28, pistache; 145.6, thinks.; 164.15, reclame; 165.23, hand; 209.12, it not; 294.8, Molíere; 304.14–15, Resemblances / Of; 331.26, green; 331.28, us; 331.29, breathed; 331.31, complete, 332.4, pedagogues; 349.6–7, it, // discover; 444.16, rendezvous.; 446.20, rock; 506.10, intervenes; 565.15, Dixhuitieme; 568.9, sounds; 580.2, pampeluned; 595.5, traditino; 595.20, didstance; 625.21, pauses).; 671.24, Cezanne; 691.8, reason; 702.10, sepyornis; 750.14, sublety; 750.14, sublety; 755.21, trafficers; 761.29, an,; 762.24, *Times*"; 763.7, wont; 764.17, contrasts; 766.28, apponted; 766.40, lightening; 794.3, mantlepiece; 808.9, is; 822.38, democraitc; 830.10, Aujourdhui; 832.22, Yes; 832.22, years; 837.7, Ceasar; 838.14, innamorata; 840.20, it; 895.14, whereit; 915.8, wise; 915.12, matter; 915.22, dont; 916.4, emouvant; 916.5, emouvant; 926.14, *Advertiser*; 926.32, are,; 926.32, accomodation; 929.4 its; 931.13, done I.

Notes

In the notes below, the reference numbers denote page and line of this volume (the line count includes titles and headings). No note is made for material included in standard desk-reference books such as Webster's *Collegiate*, *Biographical*, and *Geographical* dictionaries. Biblical references are keyed to the King James Version. For further background and references to other studies, see: *Letters of Wallace Stevens* (New York: Alfred A. Knopf, 1966), ed. Holly Stevens; Wallace Stevens, *Opus Posthumous* (New York: Alfred A. Knopf, revised, enlarged, and corrected edition, 1989), ed. Milton J. Bates; *Sur Plusieurs Beaux Sujects: Wallace Stevens' Commonplace Book* (Stanford and San Marino: Stanford University Press and Huntington Library, 1989), ed. Milton J. Bates; Peter Brazeau, *Parts of a World: Wallace Stevens Remembered* (San Francisco: North Point Press, 1985); *Wallace Stevens: A Celebration* (Princeton: Princeton University Press, 1980), ed. Frank Doggett and Robert Buttel; J.M. Edelstein, *Wallace Stevens: A Descriptive Bibliography* (Pittsburgh: University of Pittsburgh Press, 1973); A. Walton Litz, *Introspective Voyager: The Poetic Development of Wallace Stevens* (New York: Oxford University Press, 1972); Joan Richardson, *Wallace Stevens: The Early Years, 1879–1923* and *Wallace Stevens: The Later Years, 1923–1955* (New York: William Morrow, 1986 and 1988); Holly Stevens, *Souvenirs and Prophecies: The Young Wallace Stevens* (New York: Alfred A. Knopf, 1977).

HARMONIUM

4.7   *In the Carolinas*]   First published as section 7 of "Primordia" (page 536.7–16 in this volume).

6.2   Oh, la . . . le pauvre!]   Oh, there . . . the poor thing!

11.12   *connaissance*]   Knowledge.

14.25–29   *Williams . . . part!*]   The complete text of William Carlos Williams' "El Hombre" (1917).

17.1–3   *Cy . . . Vierges*]   Old French: "Here Is Depicted Saint Ursula and the Eleven Thousand Virgins."

22.1   *The Comedian . . . C*]   An early version of this poem titled "From the Journal of Crispin" was submitted for the Blindman Prize in 1921 but was not published in Stevens' lifetime:

From the Journal of Crispin

I.

The World without Imagination.

Nota: Man is the intelligence of his soil,
The sovereign ghost. As such, the Socrates
Of snails, musician of pears, principium
And lex. Sed quaeritur: Is this same wig
Of things, this nincompated pedagogue,
The sceptre of the unregenerate sea?
Crispin at sea creates a touch of doubt.
An eye most apt in gelatines and jupes,
Berries of villages, a barber's eye,
This eye of land, of simple salad-beds,
Of honest quilts, the eye of Crispin, hangs
On porpoises, that hung on apricots,
And on silentious porpoises, whose snouts
Dibble in waves that are mustachios,
Inscrutable hair in an inscrutable world.

One eats one paté, even of salt, quotha.
It is not so much that one's mythology
Is blotched by the sea. It was a boresome book,
From which one trilled orations of the west,
Based on the prints of Jupiter. Rostrum.
A snug hibernal from this sea and salt,
This century of wind in a single puff.
What counts is the mythology of self.
That's blotched beyond unblotching. Crispin,
The lutanist of fleas, the knave, the thane,
The ribboned stick, the bellowing breeches, cloak
Of China, cap of Spain, imperative haw
Of hum, inquisitorial botanist,
And general lexicographer of mute
And maidenly greenhorns, now beholds himself,
A skinny sailor peering in sea-glass.
What word split up the clickering syllables
And storming under multitudinous tones
Is name for this short-shanks in all this brunt?
Crispin is washed away by magnitude.
The whole of life that still remains in him
Dwindles to one sound strumming in his ear,
Ubiquitous concussion, slap and sigh,
Polyphony beyond his baton's thrust.

Can Crispin stem verboseness in the sea,
The old age of a watery realist,
Triton, dissolved in shifting diaphanes
Of blue and green? A wordy, watery age
That whispers to the sun's compassion, makes

A convocation, nightly, of the sea-stars,
And on the clopping foot-ways of the moon
Lies grovelling. Triton incomplicate with that
Which made him Triton, nothing left of him,
Except in faint, memorial gesturings,
That are like arms and shoulders in the waves,
Here, something in the rise and fall of wind,
That seems hallucinating horn, and here,
And everywhere upon the deep, in caves,
And down the long sea-eddies, his despair,
That is a voice, both of remembering
And of forgetfulness, in alternate strain.
Just so an ancient Crispin is dissolved.
The valet in the tempest is annulled.
Bordeaux to Yucatan, Havana next,
And then to Carolina. Simple jaunt.
Yet Crispin, mere minuscule in the gales,
Appoints his manner to the turbulence.
The salt hangs on his spirit like a frost,
The dead brine melts within him like a dew
Of winter, until nothing of himself
Remains, except some starker, barer self
In a starker, barer world, in which the sun
Is not the sun because it never shines
With bland complaisance on pale parasols,
Beetles, in chapels, on the chaste bouquets.
Against the shepherds' pipes a trumpet brays
Celestial sneering boisterously. Crispin
Becomes an introspective voyager.

Here is the veritable ding an sich, at last.
Crispin confronting it. A vocable thing,
But with a voice belched out of hoary darks
Noway resembling his. A visible thing,
And excepting negligible Triton, free
From the inescapable shadow of himself,
That lies elsewhere around him. Severance
Is clear. The last distortion of romance
Deserts the insatiable egotist. The sea
Severs not only lands but also selves.
Here is no help before reality.
Crispin beholds and Crispin is made new.
The imagination, here, no more evades,
In poems of plums, the strict austerity
Of one vast, subjugating, final tone.
The drenching of stale lives no more descends.
What is this gaudy, gusty panoply?
Out of what swift destruction does it spring?
It is caparison of wind and cloud
And something given to make whole among
The ruses that are shattered by the large.

II.

Concerning the Thunderstorms of Yucatan.

They say they still scratch sonnets in the south,
The bards of Capricorn. Medicaments
Against the weather. Useful laxatives.
Petrarch is the academy of youth
In Yucatan. The Maya sonneteers
Of the Caribbean amphitheatre,
In spite of hawk and falcon, green toucan,
And jay, still to the bulbul make their plea,
As if raspberry tanagers in palms,
High up in orange air, were barbarous.

But Crispin is too destitute to find
In any book the succor that he needs.
He is not padre in a curricle,
Thumbing opuscules, brooding on their musk.
He is a man made vivid by the sea,
A man come out of luminous traversing,
Much trumpeted, made desperately clear,
Fresh from discoveries of tidal skies,
To whom oracular rockings give no rest.
Into a savage color he goes on.

How greatly he has grown in his demesne,
This auditor of insects! He that saw
The stride of vanishing autumn in a park
By way of decorous melancholy; he
That wrote his couplet yearly to the spring,
As dissertation of profound delight,
Stopping, on voyage, in the land of snakes,
Finds his vicissitudes have much enlarged
His apprehension, made him intricate
In moody rucks, and difficult and strange
In all desires, his destitution's mark.
Qua interludo: Crispin, if he could,
Would chant assuaging Virgil and recite
In the oratory of his breast, the rhymes
That drop down Ariosto's benison.
And be in this as other freeman are,
Sonorous nutshells. This he cannot do.
His violence is for aggrandizement
And not for stupor, such as music makes
For sleepers halfway waking. He perceives
That coolness for his heat comes suddenly,
And only, in the fables he would write
With his own quill, in its indigenous dew,
Of an aesthetic tough, diverse, untamed,
Incredible to prudes, the mint of dirt,
Green barbarism turning paradigm.
Crispin foresees a curious promenade

Or, nobler, senses elemental fate,
And elemental potencies and pangs,
And beautiful barenesses, as yet unseen.
These are the snowy fables he would write,
Making the most of savagery of palms,
Of moonlight on the thick, cadaverous bloom
That yuccas breed, and of the panther's tread.
An artful, most affectionate emigrant,
From Cytherea and its learned doves,
Or else nearby, become a loyal scribe.
The fabulous and its intrinsic verse
Come like two spirits parleying, adorned
In radiance from the Atlantic coign,
For Crispin and his quill to catechize.
But they come parleying of such an earth,
So thick with sides and jagged lops of green,
So intertwined with serpent-kin encoiled
Among the purple tufts, the scarlet crowns,
Scenting the jungle in their refuges,
So streaked with yellow, blue and green and red
In beak and bud and fruity gobbet-skins,
That earth is like a jostling festival
Of seeds grown fat, too juicily opulent,
Expanding in the gold's maternal warmth.

So much for that. For one compelled to nose
Through much locution for the savory sense,
Crispin is tireless at his task. He hears
A new reality in parrot-sqwawks.
But let that pass, since Crispin aims at more,
An umbelliferous fact. Now, as this droll
Discoverer walks round the harbor streets
Inspecting the cabildo, the façade
Of the cathedral, making notes, he hears
A rumbling, west of Mexico, it seems,
Approaching like a gasconade of drums.
The white cabildo darkens, the façade,
As sullen as the sky, is swallowed up
In swift, successive shadows, dolefully.
The rumbling broadens as it falls. The wind
Tempestuous clarion, with heavy cry,
Comes bluntly thundering, more terrible
Than the revenge of music on bassoons.
Gesticulating lightning, mystical,
Makes pallid flitter. Crispin, here, takes flight.
An annotator has his scruples, too.
He kneels in the cathedral with the rest,
This connoisseur of elemental fate,
Aware of exquisite thought. The storm is one
Of many proclamations of the kind,
Proclaiming something harsher than he learned

From hearing signboards whimper in cold nights
Or seeing the midsummer artifice
Of heat upon his pane. This is the span
Of force, the umbelliferous fact, the note
Of Vulcan, that a valet seeks to own,
The thing that sanctions his most eloquent phrase.

And while the torrent on the roof still drones
Crispin arraigns the Mexican sonneteers,
Because his soul feels the Andean breath.
Can fourteen laboring mules, like theirs,
In spite of gorgeous leathers, gurgling bells,
Convey his being through the land? A more condign
Contraption must appear. Crispin is free,
And more than free, elate, intent, profound
And studious of a self possessing him,
That was not in him in the crusty town,
From which he sailed. Beyond him, westward, lie
The mountainous ridges, purple balustrades,
In which the thunder lapsing in its clap,
Lets down gigantic quavers of its voice,
For Crispin to vociferate again.

III.

Approaching Carolina.

The book of moonlight is not written yet,
Nor half begun, but, when it is, leave room
For Crispin, fagot in the lunar fire,
Who, in the hubbub of his pilgrimage
Through sweating changes, never can forget
That wakefulness, or meditating sleep,
In which the sulky strophes willingly
Bear up, in time, the somnolent, deep songs.
Leave room, therefore, in that unwritten book
For the legendary moonlight that once burned
In Crispin's mind above a continent.
America was always north to him,
A northern west or western north, but north,
And thereby polar, polar-purple, chilled
And lank, rising and slumping from a sea
Of hardy foam, receding flatly, spread
In endless ledges, glittering, submerged
And cold in a boreal mistiness of the moon.
The spring came there in clinking pannicles
Of half-dissolving frost, the summer came,
If ever, whisked and wet, not ripening
Before the winter's vacancy returned.
The myrtle, if the myrtle ever bloomed,
Was like a glacial pink upon the air,
The green palmettoes in crepuscular ice

Clipped frigidly blue-black meridians,
Morose chiaroscuro, gauntly drawn.
A feverish conception that derived
From early writs and marginal heraldry.

The poet, seeking the true poem, seeks,
As Crispin seeks, the simplifying fact,
The common truth. Crispin, however, sees
How many poems he denies himself
In his observant progress, lesser things
Than the relentless contact he desires,
How many sea-masks he ignores, what sounds
He closes from his tempering ear, what thoughts,
Like jades affecting the sequestered bride,
He banishes, what descants he foregoes.
Perhaps the Arctic moonlight really gave
The liaison, the blissful liaison,
Between himself and his environment,
Which was, and is, chief motive, first delight,
For him, and not for him alone. It seemed
Illusive, faint, more mist than moon, perverse,
Wrong as a divagation to Pekin,
One more frustration, beautiful, perhaps,
To beauty's exorcist, who postulates
The vulgar as his theme, his hymn and flight,
A passionately niggling nightingale.
Moonlight is an evasion, or, if not,
A minor meeting, facile, delicate,
Chanson evoking vague, inaudible words.
Crispin is avid for the strenuous strokes
That clang from a directer touch, the clear
Vibration rising from a daylight bell,
Minutely traceable to the latest reach.
Imagination soon exhausts itself
In artifice too tenuous to sustain
The vaporous moth upon its fickle wings.
Crispin conceives his Odyssey to be
An up and down in these two elements,
A fluctuating between sun and moon,
A sally into gold and scarlet forms,
As on this voyage, out of goblinry,
And then retirement like a sinking down
To sleep, among its violet feints and rest
And turning back to the indulgences
That in the moonlight have their habitude.
But let these backward lapses, if they will,
Grind their seductions on him, Crispin knows
It is a flourishing tropic he requires
For his refreshment, an abundant zone,
Prickly and obdurate, dense, harmonious
Yet with a harmony not rarefied

Nor fined for the inhibited instruments
Of over-civil stops. And thus he tossed
Between a Carolina of old time,
A little juvenile, an ancient whim,
And the visible, circumspect presentment drawn
From what he saw across his vessel's prow.

He comes. The poetic hero without palms
Or jugglery, without regalia.
And as he comes he sees that it is spring,
A time abhorrent to the nihilist
Or searcher for the fecund minimum.
The moonlight fiction vanishes and spring,
Although contending featly in its veils,
Irised in dew and early fragrancies
Is gemmy marionnette to him that seeks
A sinewy nakedness. A river bears
The vessel inward. Crispin tilts his nose
To inhale the rancid rosin, burly smells
Of dampened lumber, emanations blown
From warehouse doors, the gustiness of ropes,
Decays of sacks, and all the arrant stinks
That help him round his rude aesthetic out.
He savors rankness like a sensualist.
He notes the marshy ground around the dock,
The crawling railroad spur, the rotten fence,
That makes enclosure, a periphery
Of bales, machines and tools and tanks and men,
Directing whistles, puffing engines, cranes,
Provocative paraphernalia to his mind.
A short way off the city starts to climb,
At first in alleys which the lilacs line,
Abruptly, then, to the cobbled merchant streets,
The shops of chandlers, tailors, bakers, cooks,
The Coca Cola-bars, the barber-poles,
The Strand and Harold Lloyd, the lawyers' row,
The Citizens' Bank, two tea rooms, and a church.
Crispin is happy in this metropole.
If the lilacs give the alleys a young air
Of sentiment, the alleys in exchange
Make gifts of no less worthy ironies.
If poems are transmutations of plain shops,
By aid of starlight, distance, wind, war, death,
Are not these doldrums poems in themselves,
These trophies of wind and war? At just what point
Do barber-poles become burlesque or cease
To be? Are bakers what the poets will,
Supernal artisans or muffin men,
Or do they have, on poets' minds, more influence
Than poets know? Are they one moment flour,
Another pearl? The Citizens' Bank becomes

Palladian and then the Citizens' Bank
Again. The flimsiest tea room fluctuates
Through crystal changes. Even Harold Lloyd
Proposes antic Harlequin. The bars infect
The sensitive. Crispin revitalized
Makes these researches faithfully, a wide
Curriculum for the marvelous sophomore.
They purify. They make him see how much
Of what he sees he never sees at all.
He grips more closely the essential prose
As being, in a world so falsified,
The one integrity for him, the one
Discovery still possible to make,
To which all poems are incident, unless
That prose should wear a poem's guise at last.

IV.
The Idea of a Colony.

Nota: His soil is man's intelligence.
That's better. That's worth crossing seas to find.
Crispin in one laconic phrase lays bare
His cloudy drift and plans a colony.
Exit the mental moonlight, exit lex,
Rex and principium, exit the whole
Shebang. Exeunt omnes. Here is prose
More exquisite than any tumbling verse,
A still new continent in which to dwell.
What was the purpose of his pilgrimage,
Whatever shape it took in Crispin's mind,
If not, when all is said, to drive away
The shadow of his fellows from the skies,
And, from their stale intelligence released,
To make a new intelligence prevail.
Hence his despite of Mexican sonneteers,
Evoking lauras in the thunderstorms.
Hence the reverberations in the words
Of his first central hymns. Hence his intent
Analysis of barber-poles and shops,
Invaluable trivia, tests of the strength,
Of his aesthetic, his philosophy,
The more invidious, the more desired.
The florist asking aid from cabbages,
The rich man going bare, the paladin
Afraid, the blind man as astronomer,
The appointed power unwielded from disdain.

His western voyage ends and it begins.
The torment of fastidious thought abates,
Another, still more bellicose, comes on.
Crispin delineates his progeny:
A race of natives in a primitive land,

But primitive because it is more true
To its begetting than its patriarch,
A race obedient to its origins
And from the obstinate scrutiny of its land,
And in its land's own wit and mood and mask,
Evolving the conjectural resonance
Of voice, the flying youthfulness of form,
Of a spirit to be singer of the song
That Crispin formulates but cannot sing.
It comes to that. This late discoverer
Discovers for himself what idler men
And less ambitious sires have dawdled with.
He, therefore, writes his prolegomena
And, being full of the caprice, inscribes
Commingled souvenirs and prophecies.
He makes a singular collation. Thus:
The natives of the rain are rainy men.
Although they paint effulgent, azure lakes,
And April hillsides wooded white and pink,
Their azure has a cloudy edge, their white
And pink, the water bright that dogwood bears.
And in their music showering sounds intone.
This is as certain as their cherry-ripe
Pips in the fruit-men in the month of May.
Virgins on Volcan del Fuego wear
That Volcan in their bosoms as they wear
Its nibs upon their fingers. They adorn
Their weavings with its iridescent threads.
They shut its fury in each bangle-blaze.
On what strange froth does the gross Indian dote
What Eden sapling gum, what honeyed gore,
What pulpy dram distilled of innocence,
That streaking gold should speak in him
Or bask within his images and words?
If these rude instances impeach themselves
By force of rudeness, let the burgher say
If he is burgher by his will. Burgher,
He is, by will, but not his own. He dwells
A part of wilful dwellings that impose
Alike his morning and his evening prayer.
His town exhales its mother breath for him
And this he breathes, a candid bellows-boy,
According to canon. Let the principle
Be plain. For application Crispin strives,
Abhorring Turk as Esquimau, the lute
As the marimba, the magnolia as rose.

Upon these premises Crispin propounds
And propagates. His colony extends
From the big-rimmed snow-star over Canada,
To the dusk of a whistling south below the south,

A comprehensive island hemisphere.
And here he plants his colonists. The man
In Mississippi, waking among pines,
Shall be pine-spokesman. The responsive man,
Planting his pristine cores in Florida,
Shall prick thereof, not on the psaltery,
But on the banjo's categorical gut,
Tuck tuck, while the flamingos flap his bays.
Sepulchral señors, bibbing pale mescal,
Oblivious to the Aztec almanacs,
Shall make the intricate Sierra scan
In polysyllabled vernacular.
The dark Brazilian in his red café,
Musing immaculate, pampean dits,
Shall scrawl a vigilant anthology,
Not based on Camoëns, but flushed and full,
For surfeit in his leaner, lusting years,
For something to make answer when he calls
And be to him his lucent paramour.
These are the broadest instances. Crispin,
Progenitor of such extensive scope,
Is not indifferent to smart detail.
The melon shall have apposite ritual,
Performed in verd apparel, and the peach,
When its black branches germinate, belle day,
Shall have an incantation, and again,
When piled on salvers its aroma steeps
The summer, it shall have a sacrament
And celebration. Shrewd novitiates
Shall be the clerks of our experience.

These bland excursions into time to come,
Related in romance to backward flights,
However prodigal, however proud,
Contain in their afflatus the reproach
That first drove Crispin to his wandering.
He could not be content with counterfeit,
With masquerade of thought, with hapless words
That must belie the racking masquerade,
With fictive flourishes that preordained
His passions' permit, hang of coat, degree
Of buttons, measure of his salt. Such trash
Might help the blind, not him, serenely sly.
It irked beyond his patience. Hence it was,
Preferring text to gloss, he humbly served
Grotesque apprenticeship to chance event,
A clown, perhaps, but an aspiring clown.
There is a monotonous babbling in our dreams
That makes them our dependent heirs, the heirs
Of dreamers buried in our sleep, and not
The oncoming fantasies of better birth.

> The apprentice knows these dreamers. If he dreams
> Their dreams, he does it in a gingerly way.
> All dreams are vexing. Let them be expunged.
> But let the rabbit run, the cock declaim.
> His colony may not arrive. The site
> Exists. So much is sure. And what is sure
> In our abundance is his seignory.
> His journal, at best, concerns himself,
> Nudging and noting, wary to divulge
> Without digression, so that when he comes
> To search himself, in the familiar glass
> To which the lordliest traveler returns,
> Crispin may take the tableau cheerfully.
> Trinket pasticcio, flaunting skyey sheets,
> With Crispin as the tiptoe cozener?
> No, no: veracious page on page, exact.
> As Crispin in his attic shapes the book
> That will contain him, he requires this end:
> The book shall discourse of himself alone,
> Of what he was, and why, and of his place,
> And of its fitful pomp and parentage.
> Thereafter he may stalk in other spheres.

22.7   Sed quaeritur] But it is asked.

23.37   ding an sich] Thing in itself.

26.8   cabildo] Chapter house.

35.22   halidom . . . unbraided femes] Holy place, sanctuary (literally "holy dome"); untarnished, undamaged women or wives.

44.24   Funest] Doleful; portending death or evil.

52.14   Thridding] Variant of threading.

58.16   *Six Significant Landscapes*] A manuscript version titled "Eight Significant Landscapes" includes the two additional stanzas printed in the notes below.

59.29   V] This stanza is number "VI" in "Eight Significant Landscapes," where "V" reads:

> Wrestle with morning-glories,
> O muscles!
> It is useless to contend
> With falling mountains.

60.1   VI] This stanza is number "VIII" in "Eight Significant Landscapes," where "VII" reads:

> Crenellations of mountains
> Cut like strummed zithers;
> But dead trees do not resemble
> Beaten drums.

66.1   *Architecture*] Titled "Architecture for the Adoration of Beauty" in *The Little Review* (Dec. 1918).

66.4–5   chastel . . . pensée] Castle of chastity, / Of thought.

68.16–17   *Elle . . . Mondes*] She knew all the legends of Paradise and all the stories of Poland; *La Revue des Deux Mondes* (*Review of Two Worlds*), a leading literary journal.

68.19   Voragine] Jacobus de Voragine, author of the medieval ecclesiastical manual *Legenda aurea* (*The Golden Legend*), with lives of saints.

72.10   *Peter Quince*] Carpenter and play-director in Shakespeare's *A Midsummer Night's Dream*.

72.20   elders . . . Susanna] In the Apocryphal "History of Susanna."

77.25   *To the . . . Wind*] First published as the conclusion of "Primordia" (page 537.1–5 in this volume).

POEMS ADDED TO HARMONIUM

81.10   The malady . . . quotidian] In a version of the poem published in *The New Republic* (Sept. 14, 1921), this line is followed by four additional lines: "Perhaps, if summer ever came to rest / And lengthened, deepened, comforted, caressed / Through days like oceans in obsidian // Horizons full of night's midsummer blaze;".

81.18–82.12   *The Death . . . Superhuman*] "The Death of a Soldier," "Negation," and "The Surprises of the Superhuman" were originally parts of "Lettres d'un Soldat" (see pages 544.11–23, 543.7–17, 541.15–21, and note 538.8).

82.15   Übermenschlichkeit] Superhumanness.

83.6   *C'était . . . âme.*] It was my child, my jewel, my soul.

83.25   *C'était . . . or.*] It was my celestial brother, my life, my gold.

84.13   *C'était . . . amour.*] It was my ecstasy and my love.

85.3   *C'était . . . divine.*] It was my faith, divine nonchalance.

85.22   *C'était . . . l'ignominie.*] It was my bastard spirit, shame.

86.2   Capitán . . . geloso] Profound (deep) captain, jealous captain.

86.8   Bellissimo, pomposo] Most beautiful, grand (magnificent).

87.11, 15   *Soupe Aux Perles . . . Sans*] Soup With Pearls. *Sans*, Without.

87.12   ginger and fromage] In a version of the poem published in *The Measure* (April 1923), this reads: "cheese and guava peels".

89.10, 14   *Scène Flétrie . . . Fleurie*] Faded Scene. *Fleurie*, Flowery.

89.16   Pinakothek]   Picture gallery.

89.17   *Lunar Paraphrase*]   Originally part of "Lettres d'un Soldat" (see page 542.1–13 and note 538.8).

91.1   *The Public Square*]   Titled "How the Constable Carried the Pot Across the Public Square" in *The Measure* (April 1923).

93.13   *Indian River*]   First published as section 9 of "Primordia" (page 536.28–35 in this volume).

IDEAS OF ORDER

95.1   IDEAS OF ORDER]   A statement by Stevens on the dust jacket of the 1936 Knopf edition reads:

> We think of changes occurring today as economic changes, involving political and social changes. Such changes raise questions of political and social order.
> While it is inevitable that a poet should be concerned with such questions, this book, although it reflects them, is primarily concerned with ideas of order of a different nature, as, for example, the dependence of the individual, confronting the elimination of established ideas, on the general sense of order; the idea of order created by individual concepts, as of the poet, in "The Idea of Order at Key West"; the idea of order arising from the practice of any art, as of poetry in "Sailing after Lunch."
> The book is essentially a book of pure poetry. I believe that, in any society, the poet should be the exponent of the imagination of that society. *Ideas of Order* attempts to illustrate the role of the imagination in life, and particularly in life at present. The more realistic life may be, the more it needs the stimulus of the imagination.

99.4   *pejorative*]   In a letter to Ronald Lane Latimer (March 12, 1935), in which he enclosed a copy of this poem, Stevens wrote: " . . . while I am against explanations, the thing is an abridgement of at least a temporary theory of poetry. When people speak of the romantic, they do so in what the French commonly call a *pejorative* sense. But poetry is essentially romantic, only the romantic of poetry must be something constantly new and, therefore, just the opposite of what is spoken of as the romantic."

110.1   *riva*]   Seashore, bank.

111.3   MARIO ROSSI]   Italian philosopher, author, and teacher.

114.15   *mille fiori*]   Thousand flowers.

117.25   nouveautés]   Novelties.

119.20   *Anglais . . . Florence*]   Englishman Dead in Florence.

122.27   Ananke]   In Greek literature, necessity or fate personified.

124.30   *Cochon!*]   French: Pig!

127.19   *Encore . . . bonheur.*]   One more moment of happiness.

129.20   I have never . . . beneath]   In a version of the poem published
in *The Hound and Horn* (Winter 1932), this line is followed by an additional
line: "The stillness that comes to me out of this, beneath".

130.6   Jim . . . Margaret]   James and Margaret Powell; the "singer" en-
tertained at one of the New York nightspots they visited with Stevens.

THE MAN WITH THE BLUE GUITAR

133.1–2   THE MAN . . . GUITAR]   A statement by Stevens on the dust
jacket of the 1937 Knopf edition reads:

> In one group, *Owl's Clover*, while the poems reflect what was then going
> on in the world, that reflection is merely for the purpose of seizing and
> stating what makes life intelligible and desirable in the midst of great
> change and great confusion. The effect of *Owl's Clover* is to emphasize the
> opposition between things as they are and things imagined; in short, to
> isolate poetry.
>
> Since this is of significance, if we are entering a period in which poetry
> may be of first importance to the spirit, I have been making notes on the
> subject in the form of short poems during the past winter. These short
> poems, some thirty of them, form the other group, *The Man with the Blue
> Guitar*, from which the book takes its title. This group deals with the
> incessant conjunctions between things as they are and things imagined.
> Although the blue guitar is a symbol of the imagination, it is used most
> often simply as reference to the individuality of the poet, meaning by the
> poet any man of imagination.

135.1   *The Man . . . Guitar*]   An early manuscript version of "The Man
with the Blue Guitar" includes six poems that Stevens dropped in revisions.
The first of these (numbered "III" in the manuscript) was later titled "Com-
munications of Meaning" and published as part of "Five Grotesque Pieces"
(see page 591.31 and note). The other omitted poems, which were not pub-
lished in Stevens' lifetime, are printed below from the revised edition of *Opus
Posthumous*:

VII

The day is green and the wind is young.
The world is young and I play my guitar.

The skeletons sit on the wall. They drop
Red mango peels and I play my guitar.

The gate is not jasper. It is not bone.
It is mud, and mud baked long in the sun,

An eighteenth century fern or two
And the dewiest beads of insipid fruit

And honey from thorns and I play my guitar.
The negress with laundry passes me by.

The boatman goes humming. He smokes a cigar
And I play my guitar. The vines have grown wild.

The oranges glitter as part of the sky.
A tiara from Cohen's, this summer sea.

IX

A letter for the ignorant.
The dithering goes on. I read.

"The myths in which we recognize
Ourselves, incessantly revealed,

Keep us concealed." Things as they are
Stand jabbering. But to catch the word,

To know completely we have heard,
To pick it on the blue guitar—

I read. "The subject of poetry
Is poetry, things as they are."

We hear them on the blue guitar.
The poet picks them as they are,

But picks them on a blue guitar,
A guitar that makes things as they are.

X

But then things never really are.
How does it matter how I play

Or what I color what I say?
It all depends on inter-play

Or inter-play and inter-say,
Like tweedle-dum and tweedle-dee,

Or ti-ri-la and ti-ri-li
And these I play on my guitar

And leave the final atmosphere
To the imagination of the engineer.

I could not find it if I would.
I would not find it if I could.

I cannot say what things I play,
Because I play things as they are

And since they are not as they are,
I play them on a blue guitar.

XI

I play them on a blue guitar
And then things are not as they are.

The shaping of the instrument
Distorts the shape of what I meant,

Which takes a shape by accident.
Yet what I mean I always say.

The accident is how I play.
I still intend things as they are.

The greenish quaverings of day
Quiver upon the blue guitar.

XXI

To ride an old mule round the keys—
Mature emotional gesture, that—

Blond weather. One is born a saint,
Complete in wind-sucked poverty,

In such an air, poor as one's mule.
Here, if there was a peak to climb,

One could watch the blue sea's blueness flow
And blacken into indigo.

But squint and squeak, where no people are:
On suck a peak, the blue guitar—

Blond weather. Give the mule his hay.
True, things are people as they are.

141.23–24   "hoard / Of destructions"]   Cf. Christian Zervos' "Conversation with Picasso" (*Cahiers d'art*, vol. X, 1935) in which Picasso is quoted as saying that in the past, pictures were completed in stages and were a sum of additions, but that in his case "a picture is a sum of destructions. I make a picture—then I destroy it. In the end, though, nothing is lost: the red I removed from one place turns up somewhere else." Cf. also *The Necessary Angel*, page 741.15–17 in this volume.

145.20   Dichtung und Wahrheit]   Poetry and Truth (title of Goethe's autobiographical account of events that shaped his development as an artist).

149.3   fantoche]   Puppet, marionette.

161.34   Ananke]   See note 122.27.

170.35   gaudium]   Joy, delight.

172.18   celui . . . pleure]   The one who sings and cries.

PARTS OF A WORLD

178.8   Corazon]   Heart, spirit.

187.34   Vidal]   Anatole Vidal, a book and art dealer in Paris; Stevens owned a Jean Labasque portrait of him.

187.35   *Qui . . . banales*]   Who doesn't give a hoot about pretty banalities.

188.2   *Je tâche . . . poète.*]   "I try, while remaining precise, to be a poet," in *Le Journal de Jules Renard 1897–1910*.

191.6   Encore . . . dieux]   Again, again, again the gods . . .

196.32   le plus pur]   The purest.

200.15   Calypso's isle]   Ogygia, ruled by the nymph Calypso, goddess of silence, in Homer's *Odyssey*.

203.8   *Duft*]   Smell, fragrance, perfume.

222.13   *Les Plus . . . Pages*]   "The Most Beautiful Pages" (name of a series of books of extracts from French writers).

224.20   douce campagna]   Sweet country.

231.22   Ercole]   Hercules.

232.30–31   *la belle . . . crinolines*]   The beauty in crinolines.

234.11   *Montrachet-le-Jardin*]   A white wine.

236.21   friseured]   French *friser* means to curl, to frizz.

244.4   *Examination . . . War*]   A manuscript at the Houghton Library, Harvard University, contains a stanza numbered "III" that is not included in published versions of this poem:

> The words are in the way and thoughts are.
> Forgetful of death in war, there rises
> From the middens of life, rotten and acrid,
> A race that is a hero, entirely
> Without heroic words, heroic
> Hybrids impossible to the wardens
> Within us. False hybrids and false heroes,
> Half men and half new, modern monsters . . .
> The hero is the man who is himself, who
> As a man among other men, divested
> Of attributes, naked of myth, true,
> Not true to this or that, but true, knows
> The frame of the hero. Yet, willingly, he
> Becomes the hero without heroics.

Another two omitted stanzas (for which no manuscript source is now known to be extant) were published in the first edition of *Opus Posthumous* (1957):

> An immense drum rolls through a clamor of people.
> The women with eyes like opals vanish
> And men look inwardly, for the emblem:
> The star-yplaited, visible sanction,
> The strength of death or triumph. Oheu!
> That the choice should come on them so early.
> They had hardly grown to know the sunshine,

Before the sun brought them that destruction
And with it, the antiquest wishing
To bear virile grace before their fellows,
Regardless of gods that were praised in goldness
And triple chime . . . The self-same rhythm
Moves in lamenting and the fatal,
The bold, obedience to Ananke.

It is the common man against evil,
Now. War as a punishment. The hero
As hangman, a little sick of blood, of
The deep sigh with which the hanging ends, close
To his gorge, hangman, once helmet-maker
And headsman and trumpeteer and feather
In casque and scaffold orator, fortified
By gestures of a mortal perfection.
What misanthrope, impugning heroica,
Maligning his costumes and disputing
His roles, would leave to the clouds the righting,
The immediate and intolerable need
Of the very body instinctively crying
A challenge to a final solution.

247.35   sua voluntate]   Of one's own accord.

TRANSPORT TO SUMMER

264.8   Liadoff]   Anatoly Liadoff, or Lyadov (1855–1914), Russian composer and collector of folk songs.

268.13   *Poesie Abrutie*]   Besotted Poetry.

276.2   Palabra]   Palaver, talk, speech.

276.9   Durand-Ruel's]   Art gallery in Paris and New York.

279.5   Livre . . . Nature]   Book of All Sorts of Flowers Following (in the Style of) Nature.

293.21   *Paisant*]   Obsolete form of "peasant."

307.23   Tinicum . . . Cohansey]   Island in the Delaware River near Philadelphia, settled 1643, and Cohansey Bridge, settled 1686 (later Bridgeton, New Jersey).

310.11   Perkiomen]   A fishing creek near Feasterville, Pennsylvania.

320.5   Tulpehocken]   Parish in Pennsylvania where Stevens' maternal great-great-grandfather Franz Zeller lived.

320.18   San Miguel de los Baños]   Cuban spa known for its mineral waters.

320.19   Hermosas]   Identified by Stevens as "a variety of roses. Of course, I don't know that Hermosas grow at San Miguel . . . probably nobody knows. Besides, the San Miguel of the poem is a spiritual not a physical place" (in a letter dated December 10, 1946, to José Rodríguez Feo, who was translating the poem).

323.27   Oley]   Town northeast of Reading, Pennsylvania.

326.13–14   *douceurs, / Tristesses*]   . . . comforts, / Sorrows.

334.8   Schwärmerei]   (Gushing) rapture.

340.7   là-bas]   Over there.

349.21   violent]   In the Cummington Press edition of *Notes Toward a Supreme Fiction* (1942; 1943), this reads "violet".

THE AURORAS OF AUTUMN

363.19   *so blau . . . so lind*]   So blue; so soft (mild, gentle).

363.20   *Und so lau*]   And so tepid.

363.21   *Of clay . . . made*]   This and the italicized phrases at 363.22 (*hear . . . core*), 363.26 (*And a . . . there.*), and 364.3–4 (*And live . . . glade.*) are from William Butler Yeats' "The Lake Isle of Innisfree."

368.22   Swatara]   A Pennsylvania creek that joins the Susquehanna.

375.17   *Kinder-Scenen*]   Scenes from childhood.

376.13   *Celle . . . Héaulmiette*]   She Who Was Héaulmiette.

382.11–16   *Papini . . . Poets*]   Papini (1881–1956), Italian philosopher and author, *Lettere agli uomini del papa Celestino sesto*, ch. 10.

389.3–12   *Tom McGreevy . . . Tarbert*]   McGreevy (1893–1967), born in Tarbert on the River Shannon, was a poet, art critic, and director of the Irish National Gallery; Mal Bay, north of Tarbert, is referred to in his poem "Recessional" (1934).

390.9   *Puella Parvula*]   Little Girl.

391.8–13   *Mother . . . words of José*]   The italicized words are from José Rodríguez Feo's letter to Stevens, dated September 21, 1948.

391.17   Varadero]   In Cuba.

391.20   *Olalla . . . blanco*]   Federico Garcia Lorca, "Martirio de Santa Olalla" ("Martyrdom of Saint Eulalia"), III.22: "Eulalia white in the white."

392.4   *retrato*]   Portrait.

394.26   enfantillages]   Childishnesses.

395.4   Peter the voyant]   Stevens' epithet for his grandson (French *voyant* means "seer").

397.1   *An Ordinary . . . New Haven*]   Stevens read an 11-canto version of this poem (I, VI, IX, XI, XII, XVI, XXII, XXVIII, XXX, XXXI, XXIX) at a meeting of the Connecticut Academy of Arts and Sciences on November 4, 1949.

398.28   bats]   Lumps, pieces (of a substance); flat round slabs of clay, the primary stage of making cups, bowls, or plates.

412.25   *C'est . . . regarde*]   It is always life that watches me.

419.23   Weisheit]   German: wisdom.

422.24   rex Impolitor]   King Inelegance (or Unpolished, Unadorned).

423.1   *Angel . . . Paysans*]   *Paysans* means peasants, countrymen. The poem is based on a painting by Pierre Tal Coat that Stevens acquired from Paule Vidal in September 1949. Stevens wrote her that he was calling it *Angel Surrounded by Peasants*, and, "The angel is the Venetian glass bowl on the left with the little spray of leaves in it. The peasants are the terrines, bottles and the glasses that surround it. This title alone tames it as a lump of sugar might tame a lion."

THE ROCK

429.22   *Lebensweisheitspielerei*]   Worldly Wisdom's Game.

441.23–27   *J'ai passe . . .* ENESCO]   "I have spent a great deal of time working with my violin, traveling. But nothing was ever able to suspend in me the composer's essential exercise—meditation . . . I live a continuing dream, which never stops, night or day." Enesco (1881–1955) was a Romanian violinist, conductor, and composer of the opera *Oedipus* (1936).

LATE POEMS

456.4   outre-terre]   Beyond the earth.

457.7   fraicheur]   Freshness, coolness.

462.13   *The Sail of Ulysses*]   Read at Phi Beta Kappa exercises at Columbia University on May 31, 1954.

463.35   Morningside]   Morningside Heights in New York City, the location of Columbia University.

476.25   decor]   In the first edition of *Opus Posthumous* (1957), this reads: "distance".

UNCOLLECTED POEMS

481.21   *Vita Mea*]   My Life.

482.8   *Self-Respect*]   This poem is erased in Stevens' journal (Dec. 17, 1898), but could still be read by Holly Stevens when preparing her book, *Souvenirs and Prophecies.*

482.16   *Sonnets*]   Stevens wrote this sequence of sonnets in his journal be-
tween February 22 and April 14, 1899. Six of them were eventually published:
I, *Harvard Monthly*, July 1899 (signed "John Morris 2nd"); II, *East & West*,
May 1900; VI, *Harvard Monthly*, March 1899; VII, *Harvard Advocate*, April
10, 1899; IX, *Harvard Monthly*, May 1899; and XIV, *Harvard Advocate*, May
23, 1900 (signed "R. Jerries").

497.25   *Sonnet*]   Stevens has drawn a line through this poem in the journal
entry (Oct. 21, 1900) from which it is taken, and added a note below: "Sorry
I wrote it—sorry I crossed it out."

498.12   *Miss Gage*]   Sybil Gage of Cambridge, Massachusetts, a friend of
Stevens.

499.15   *From a Vagabond*]   Stevens inscribed this poem and "To Elsie,
Xmas 1907" on the flyleaf of Bliss Carman and Richard Hovey's *Songs from
Vagabondia* (1894; the first of their three *Vagabondia* books).

507.12   *Home Again*]   A version of this poem was published in *The Trend*
(see page 525.1 in this volume).

510.2   *A Concert of Fishes*]   Published as section III of "Carnet de Voy-
age" (page 522.27 in this volume).

511.20–29   Man . . . spring in.]   Published as section VI of "Carnet de
Voyage" (page 523.23 in this volume).

511.29–512.4   She that . . . weep!]   Published as section IV of "Carnet de
Voyage" (page 523.7 in this volume).

515.2–9   I am . . . sing.]   Published as section V of "Carnet de Voyage"
(page 523.14 in this volume).

515.20–27   There . . . flows.]   Published as section VII, "Chinese
Rocket," in "Carnet de Voyage" (page 524.1 in this volume).

516.7, 15   *Colors, Testamentum*]   In Stevens' manuscript, these poems fol-
low a separate sheet that bears the title "Intermezzi."

518.1   *Infernale*]   In the margin of his original typescript, beside the final
line, Stevens has written "glistens through the air." A second typescript,
marked "The only copy" and sent to Ronald Lane Latimer on August 16,
1935, bears the title "The Guide of Alcestis"; in it, "naked" (at page 518.13 in
this volume) reads "living" and "Soaring Olympus glitters" (at 518.17) reads
"The soaring mountains glitter".

519.1   *L'Essor Saccadé*]   Bumpy (or choppy) flight.

522.1   *Carnet de Voyage*]   "Travel Log." Sections III–VII are drawn from
"The Little June Book" (see pages 510.2–515.27 and notes).

525.1   *Home Again*]   An earlier version was included in "A Book of
Verses" (page 507.12 in this volume).

525.9   *Phases*] Sections II–V of this group were published in a special "War Number" of *Poetry* (Nov. 1914).

525.10–11   *"La justice . . . accusée."*] "Justice without force is inconsistent, because the wicked are with us always; force without justice is inexcusable."

527.15   [ ]] Brackets indicate a missing portion of Stevens' typescript.

534.11   *Primordia*] Stevens drew on three poems in this group for *Harmonium* (see notes 4.7, 77.25, and 93.13).

538.8   *Lettres d'un Soldat*] Sections II–VI and VIII–XI, reprinted here from *Opus Posthumous*, were published in *Poetry* (May 1918). Four of the poems were also included, without their epigraphs, in the 1931 edition of *Harmonium* (see pages 81.18–82.12, 89.17, and notes).

538.8–16   *Lettres . . . Kshettryas!*] Stevens based his poem on *Lettres d'un soldat (août 1914-avril 1915)* (Paris, 1916; letters of Eugène Emmanuel Lemercier, a French soldier on the western front, to his mother). The quotation from Chevrillon's preface may be translated: "To fight with his brothers, in his place and rank, with his eyes wide open, without hope of glory or profit, and simply because this is the law, here is the commandment that the god gives to the warrior Arjuna when he doubts that he must turn away from the absolute toward the human nightmare of battle. . . . Simply, let Arjuna stretch his bow with the other Kshettryas!"

538.20–22   *Nous . . . fatalité*] "We are embarked on an adventure, without any dominant feeling, except perhaps a rather beautiful acceptance of fatality."

539.6–8   *Jamais . . . amie.*] "Never did the majesty of the night bring me such consolation than around this accumulation of trials. Glistening Venus is a friend to me."

539.24–25   *Ce . . . violence.*] "What is necessary is to recognize the love and the triumphant beauty of all violence."

540.18–20   *Jusqu'à . . . future.*] "Until this moment I have possessed a wisdom of renunciation, but now I want a Wisdom that accepts all and aims toward future action."

540.26–31   *Si . . . Graces*] "If you saw the confidence of the little animals of the woods, mice, field mice! The other day, in our leafy shelter, I followed the movements of these little beasts. They were as beautiful as a Japanese print, the inside of their ears pink like shells." / How God Dispenses Grace.

541.12–14   *J'ai . . . avons.*] "I have strong hope, but above all I have confidence in eternal justice, however much it might surprise our human idea of it."

541.15 *The Surprises . . . Superhuman*] Included in the 1931 edition of *Harmonium* (see page 82.12–18 and notes).

541.23–29 *au matin . . . paix.*] " . . . morning, in quarters / Such was the beauty of yesterday. I spoke to you of the preceding evenings, along the road, the moon designed an embroidery of the trees, the pathos of the hills, the pity of the houses one knew to be ruins, but which the night conjured up like an evocation of peace."

542.16–20 *Bien . . . universel.*] "My beloved Mother. . . . As for what concerns your heart, I have such confidence in your courage, that at the present time this certainty is my great comfort. I know that my mother has attained that freedom of the soul which permits contemplation of the universal spectacle."

543.3–6 *La seule . . . forme.*] "My only sanction is my conscience. We must submit to an impersonal justice, independent of any human aspect, and to a fate which is useful and harmonious no matter how horrible its form."

543.20–21 *Hier . . . vie!*] "Last night, returning to my barn, drunkenness, brawls, cries, songs and howling. Life!"

544.11 *La mort . . . naturelles.*] "The death of a soldier is close to natural things."

544.26–28 *J'ai . . . cri.*] "I forgot to tell you that the other evening, during the storm, I saw the cranes returning. A lull allowed me to hear their cry."

544.29–32 In a theatre . . . repertoire . . .] In another manuscript, this reads:

> The cranes return. The soldier hears their cry.
> No: not as if the jades of willow-tree
> Or river-fern came coloring the sky.
> But still the cranes return.
>
> The soldier hears their cry. He knows the fire
> That touches them—knows that he must not know
> Nor burden his endurance with desire.
> ~~But still the cranes return . . .~~
>
> Endurance that grows heavy from despair,
> Drowsed with the oblivion of oblivions—
> The chant of spring becomes an obsolete air—
> ~~But still~~ The cranes return . . .
>
> ~~Grows heavy from despair, too much alone~~
> ~~To feel the spring infusing its relief~~
> ~~In sleepiness, to resist that weight of sky.~~
> ~~But still the cranes return.~~

545.3–5   *Rien . . . terre.*]   "Nothing new from our hilltop which we con-
tinue to organize. . . . From time to time the pickaxe hits a wretched corpse
that the war torments even in the ground."

545.19   *Instant of Clearness*]   The French poem is titled "Instant de
clarté." In Stevens' manuscript, the title "Instant of Clearness" is canceled
and above it is written, in another hand, "Moment of Insight."

547.21–548.12   *The Naked Eye . . . dreams.*]   In the three-page manu-
script, "The Naked Eye of My Aunt" is on the first sheet, lines 547.22–32 (I
peopled . . . moon.) on the second, and lines 548.2–12 (Poets . . . dreams.)
on a third sheet that is headed "VIII." These stanzas are printed in *Opus
Posthumous*, revised edition, under the title "Stanzas for 'Le Monocle de Mon
Oncle'."

547.25   mon idée]   My idea.

548.15–16   *Aux. . .chevaux*]   To bulls God gives horns / And hard hoofs
to horses.

553.6   *This Vast Inelegance*]   In another typescript, the second and fourth
lines of this poem have been canceled.

561.18–562.5   *What They . . . Hieroglyphica*]   These poems were later pub-
lished, with some changes, in "Five Grotesque Pieces" (see notes 562.9–11 and
591.31–593.20).

562.9–11   Even if . . . Hey-di-ho]   Omitted in "Five Grotesque Pieces."

575.29   Schloss]   Castle.

580.33   Ananke]   See note 122.27.

591.24   gaudium]   See note 170.35.

591.31–593.20   *Communications . . . Wedlock*]   These poems were pub-
lished in a group titled "Five Grotesque Pieces" (*The Trend*, March 1942) that
included: "I / Communications of Meaning"; "II / One of Those Hibiscuses
of Damozels"; "III / Hieroglyphica" (see page 561.18); "IV / What They
Call Cherry Pie" (see page 562.5 and note); and "V / Outside of Wedlock."
An untitled version of "Communication of Meaning" (in which "palmy" at
591.32 reads "balmy" and "petals" at 592.4 reads "rose-leaves") occurs in a
draft of "The Man with the Blue Guitar" (see note 135.1).

593.19   Benjamin . . . Blandenah]   Stevens' grandfather was Benjamin
Stevens and his great-great grandmother, Blandina Janse van Woggelum
Stevens.

595.1   *Tradition*]   Composed at the request of the Saint Nicholas Society
of New York in commemoration of its 100th Paas (Easter) Festival, 1945.

596.24   Ephrata]   A Biblical name of Bethlehem and the name of a rural
borough of southeast Pennsylvania settled around 1730 by a semi-monastic

sect of celibate Seventh-day Baptists, followers of the German-born mystic Conrad Beissel (1690–1768).

597.1 Pravda] "Truth," the name of the official newspaper of the Communist Party of the Soviet Union.

597.10 *First Warmth*] Stevens inscribed this poem in Herbert Weinstock's copy of *Transport to Summer* (Weinstock was Stevens' editor at Knopf).

PLAYS

632.23 BROOMSTICK] Printed here as it appears in Stevens' typescript.

THE NECESSARY ANGEL

638.1–3 *I am* . . . AUTUMN] Page 423.14–15 in this volume.

639.14–16 Except . . . published] An acknowledgment follows the Introduction in the original edition: "*The Noble Rider and the Sound of Words* was read at Princeton, as one of a group of essays by several persons on *The Language of Poetry*, made possible by the interest and generosity of Mr. and Mrs. Henry Church, and was published by the Princeton University Press in 1942. *The Language of Poetry* was edited by Allen Tate. *The Figure of the Youth as Virile Poet* was read at the Entretiens de Pontigny, a conference held at Mount Holyoke College in 1943. The essay was published in *Sewanee Review* the following year. *Three Academic Pieces* was read at Harvard on the basis of the Morris Gray Fund. Later, in 1947, it was published by *Partisan Review* and also by Cummington Press. *About One of Marianne Moore's Poems* was published in *Quarterly Review of Literature* in 1948 in a number in honor of Miss Moore. *Effects of Analogy* was read as a Bergen lecture at Yale and was published a little later, in 1948, in the *Yale Review*. *Imagination as Value* was read at Columbia before the English Institute and was included in the volume of *English Institute Essays 1948* published by the Columbia University Press in 1949. *The Relations Between Poetry and Painting* was read in New York at the Museum of Modern Art in 1951 and was thereafter published by the museum as a pamphlet."

643.22–23 Coleridge . . . nonsense.] In a letter to John Thelwall (Dec. 31, 1796): "Now as to the Metaphysicians, Plato says, it is *Harmony*—he might as well have said, a fiddle stick's end—but I love Plato—his dear *gorgeous* Nonsense!"

645.11–12 Adams . . . Vico] H. P. Adams, *The Life and Writings of Giambattista Vico* (1935).

647.11–12 the language . . . meditation] English critic and poet I. A. Richards (1893–1979); this, and the quotations at 648.17–18 and 653.36–40, are from his *Coleridge on the Imagination* (1934).

648.40 American artist] Reginald Marsh (1898–1954).

650.5   Bateson] English editor and literary critic F. W. Bateson (1901–78).

651.6   Boileau's remark] The remark was attributed to Boileau (Nicolas Boileau-Despréaux, 1636–1711) by Jean-Baptiste Rousseau.

653.28   River House] Complex of large, expensive apartments between East 52nd and 53rd streets in Manhattan offered in the 1930s primarily to corporate executives.

658.3–10   Bergson describes . . . present."] Henri Bergson, *Creative Evolution* (1907), ch. 1.

658.11   Dr. Joad's] C. E. M. Joad (1891–1953), author and professor of psychology and philosophy at the University of London.

661.29   Charles Mauron] A French critic and author, Mauron (1899–1966) developed a "psychocritical" method of studying the psychology of creativity by searching texts for clues to the author's unconscious motivations.

661.35–36   *un amoureux perpétuel*] A constant lover.

662.16–20   This City . . . air] William Wordsworth, "Composed Upon Westminster Bridge, September 3, 1802," lines 4–8.

663.32   *bassesse*] Baseness.

666.18–24   Valéry . . . *européenne.*] "Discours sur *l'Evolution créatrice* de Bergson," *Lettres Francais* (Oct. 1941): "perhaps one of the last men to have given himself to thinking exclusively, profoundly and in a superior way in a time when most think and meditate less and less. . . . Bergson seems to belong to an age that has already passed, and his name is the last great name in the history of European intelligence."

667.13–28   Coleridge . . . set of dances.] "Satyrane's Letters," I, in *Biographia Literaria*, vol. II (1847).

669.6–7   edition . . . Fyfe] W. Hamilton Fyfe, *Aristotle's Art of Poetry: A Greek View of Poetry and Drama* (Oxford: Clarendon, 1934).

669.32–670.5   Shelley . . . life."] In "A Defense of Poetry" (posthumously published, 1840).

670.8–9   *vis* or *noeud vital*] Vital sticking point (literally, "screw") or nexus.

671.22–672.8   Cézanne . . . sufficiently] The four quotations are from the letters of Paul Cézanne (dated, respectively, Feb. 22, 1905, July 25, 1904, Oct. 23, 1903, Sept. 13, 1906).

674.22   *l'oiseau qui chante*] The bird who sings.

675.39–676.1   "*Il . . . sot.*"] "I have long thought that someone who only had clear ideas would have to be a fool," in the posthumously published *Lettres* (1879) of French critic Paul Doudan (1800–72).

677.2–4   Mme. de Staël . . . *Jean Jacques*]   "Our finest lyric poets, in France, are perhaps our great prose writers, Bossuet, Pascal, Fenelon, Buffon, Jean Jacques [Rousseau] . . . " (*L'Allemagne*, 1810).

677.6–7   Fernandat . . . *de Staël*]   "Observe that Claudel has omitted the 'perhaps' of Mme. de Staël" (*Autour de Paul Valery*).

677.20   Baillet]   Adrien Baillet (1679–1766), author of *La Vie de M. Descartes* (1751).

678.5–6   *la vie . . . idées*]   "Life is more beautiful than ideas."

678.33   *La vierge . . . aujourd'hui*]   "The virgin, vivacious, and beautiful today," line 1 of the second of Mallarmé's *Plusieurs Sonnets.*

678.34–35   Hopkins . . . purple-of-thunder]   Gerard Manley Hopkins, "Henry Purcell," line 12.

681.22   *vates*]   Seer, prophet, soothsayer.

681.33–34   Biblical . . . eye]   Cf. 1 Corinthians 15:51–52: "We shall not all sleep, but we shall all be changed, / In a moment, in the twinkling of an eye."

682.1–2   *la mandoline . . . brise*]   Paul Verlaine, *Fêtes Galantes* (1869), "Mandoline," last lines: "The mandolin chatters / Among the tremblings of the breeze."

683.9–14   a note . . . masses]   Enid Starkie's note (*The New Statesman*, May 22, 1943) on Mann's *André Gide* (1943).

692.35   gradus ad Metaphoram.]   Step to Metaphor.

693.21   O juventes, O filii]   O youths, O sons.

704.13   Kate O'Brien]   Irish author, playwright, and journalist (1897–1974).

705.33–34   *Que . . . moins.*]   "It is no great marvel to see that the Ostrich digests iron, since hens do no less."

710.27–34   Allen Tate . . . hell.]   "Inside and Outside" (1928), I.9–14.

712.11–12   Mackail's translation]   John W. Mackail, Oxford professor of poetry, *Select Epigrams from the Greek Anthology* (1907).

714.12–13   Allen Tate . . . hare.]   "Emblems" (1932), last line.

724.28   "par grimace."]   By making faces.

726.30–32   Walter Pater . . . strange,"]   In "The Poetry of Michelangelo" (1871).

734.13   *bauer*]   Peasant.

738.35 Jean Paulhan] Paulhan (1884–1968) was a critic, essayist, and editor of journals including *Nouvelle Revue Française* and, with Henry Church, *Mesures.*

741.15–17 saying of Picasso . . . destructions?] See note 141.23–24.

747.8–11 "It is art," . . . process."] In a letter to H. G. Wells (July 10, 1915).

747.20 Quatremère de Quincy] French antiquarian Antoine Chrysostom Quatremère de Quincy (1755–1849), author of *Dictionnaire d'architecture* (1788–1825; new ed., 1832).

750.33 *La Pesanteur . . . Grâce*] *Gravity and Grace* (1946).

UNCOLLECTED PROSE

755.1 *The Thessalians*] Stevens' commencement address at Reading Boys' High School.

772.1 *Martha Champion*] A graduate student at Columbia University, one of the 32 young poets whose works were published, with commentary by established writers, in *Trial Balances.*

772.14–22 Mackail . . . Anthology] See note 712.11–12.

776.6–7 *donne . . . romanesque*] Verges (encroaches) on the romantic.

777.2–3 "Le bel . . . génie."] "Wit, as everyone knows, has always been the worst enemy of genius."

778.2 Professor Babbitt] Literary critic Irving Babbitt (1865–1933), professor of French literature at Harvard.

785.31 Brémond] French historian and critic Henri Bremond (1865–1933); his works include *Pure Poetry* (1926) and *Prayer and Poetry* (1927).

787.13–14 M. Delahaye] Ernest Delahaye, a childhood friend of Rimbaud and author of *Rimbaud: l'artiste et l'être moral* (1923).

789.11 Charles Mauron] See note 661.29.

789.15 Christian Zervos] Zervos (1889–1970), a critic and historian of art and editor of *Cahiers d'art.*

790.31–32 letter . . . Delahaye] Actually in Rimbaud's letter to the poet Paul Demeny, dated May 15, 1871, known as the *lettre du voyant* (letter of the seer).

792.18 Sweeney] A character in poems of T. S. Eliot.

805.21 MEMORANDUM] Sent in a letter to Henry Church, who had queried Stevens about establishing a university chair of poetry.

807.24 *Note . . . Best"*] Sent with a list of 18 poems to Whit Burnett, who was preparing the anthology *This Is My Best* (1942); listed were: "Earthy

Anecdote," "In the Carolinas," "Domination of Black," "The Snow Man," "The Load of Sugar-Cane," "The Emperor of Ice-Cream," "Sunday Morning," "Anecdote of the Jar," "To the One of Fictive Music," "Dance of the Macabre Mice," "The Pleasures of Merely Circulating," "The Man with the Blue Guitar" (sections V, XV, XVII, XVIII, XXVIII), "Country Words," and "Asides on the Oboe." "Domination of Black" and a portion of the statement (808.4–15, "The themes . . . man of reason.") were included in the anthology.

808.23   *Epitaphiana*]   Stevens wrote this pamphlet to accompany a portfolio of photographs of Pennsylvania landscapes.

809.24   *Samuel French Morse's*]   A poet and critic; Morse would edit the first edition of *Opus Posthumous* (1957).

810.24   Mr. Venturi]   Art critic Lionello Venturi (1885–1961).

818.2   Paul Rosenfeld]   Rosenfeld (1890–1946) was a music, art, and literary critic, and an editor of *American Caravan*.

818.3   *Schöpfer . . . Schöpfung*]   Creator; creation.

823.7–9   de Rougemont . . . poétiques."]   Swiss essayist and moralist Denis de Rougemont (1906–85), "The truly superstitious scoffs at superstition just as the true poet at poetic subjects and words."

825.26   *A Comment . . . Poetry*]   Written in response to a letter from a reader of *The Explicator*, which had published two interpretations of "The Emperor of Ice-Cream" in its April 1948 number.

827.35   "chimie intérieure"]   Inner chemistry.

832.22   but where . . . snows?"]   Cf. François Villon (1431–c. 1465), *Ballade des dames du temps jadis* (*Ballad of Ladies of Times Past*): "Mais ou sont les neiges d'antan?"

834.32   poems . . . *World*]   Stevens read "A Rabbit as King of the Ghosts" and "The Candle a Saint."

839.4   *Fleurs du Mal*]   *Flowers of Evil* (1853) by Charles Baudelaire.

851.3   Jean Wahl]   French poet and philosopher (1888–1974).

853.27   Jowett . . . *Phaedo*]   Benjamin Jowett in his translations of Plato (5 vols., 1871–92).

854.18   *douceur de vivre*]   Sweetness of life.

854.38–39   *De Rerum Natura . . . Essay on Man*]   Philosophical poems by, respectively, Titus Lucretius Carus (c. 99–53 B.C.), *On the Nature of Things*, and Alexander Pope (1688–1744).

855.8   Paul Weiss]   Philosopher then teaching at Bryn Mawr.

857.26–38   Berkeley . . . unperceived?]   George Berkeley, *A Treatise concerning the Principles of Human Knowledge* (1710), I.

860.18–19   *"Le silence . . . m'effraie,"*]   "The silence of these infinite spaces terrifies me" (in Pascal's *Pensées*, 1607, *silence* reads *silence eternel*).

860.21–23   *"La sphère . . . part,"*]   "The sphere whose center is everywhere and circumference nowhere."

860.24–25   ricorsi . . . Ewiges Wiederkehr]   Recurrence . . . eternal return.

860.39   Jean Paulhan]   See note 738.35.

863.24–27   *du Bellay . . . Anjou."*]   Stevens' 1909 translation of the sonnet is on pages 516.21–517.10 in this volume.

864.33–34   *la confiance . . . monde.*]   The confidence that the poet has naturally—and invites us to have—in the world.

868.28   *allégresse*]   Lightness.

873.9   a young scholar]   Peter Lee.

879.1   *"Pains and Gains"*]   Bellow's story, which had appeared in the previous issue of *Semi-Colon*, concerns a woman who falls on a sidewalk and refuses to be helped up until she can establish grounds for a lawsuit.

879.22   *Gloire . . . Idées*]   "Glory of long desire, Ideas!"; a line from Mallarmé's "Prose: pour des Esseintes" that is quoted in *Eupalinos.*

889.13   *Chose . . . sacrée*]   "A light, winged, sacred thing," description of a poet in Plato's *Ion* that is quoted in Séchan.

894.13   Connecticut Composed]   Written for the United States Information Agency; a shorter version was broadcast as "This is Connecticut" over the Voice of America in July 1955.

FROM THE NOTEBOOKS

900.12   L'art . . . heureuse]   The art of being happy.

900.13–16   Goethe's . . . 1932]   Cf. the opening of Frederick W. Felkin's *Goethe: A Century After* (London: Oxford University Press, 1932).

902.6   "aultres choses solatieuses."]   Old French: other consoling things.

904.13   Seelensfriede durch dichtung]   Respite (peace of soul) through poetry.

906.7   La vie . . . idées]   Life is more beautiful than ideas.

907.5   Meine Seele . . . haben.]   My soul must have pomp.

908.24   trouvailles]   Discoveries.

914.25   *noeud vital*]   Vital nexus.

915.6   *Sur . . . Sujects*]   Stevens' commonplace book.

915.23   premise to Storrs] In the commonplace book, this entry is pre-
ceded by a quotation from Richard S. Storrs' *Divine Origin of Christianity
Indicated by Its Historical Effects* (1884): "The philosopher could not love the
indefinite and impersonal principle of order pervading the universe, any more
than he could love atmospheres or oceans."

915.25   Ex Divina . . . Derivatur] From Divine Beauty is derived the ex-
istence of all things.

915.28   l'instinct du bonheur] The instinct for happiness.

916.3–4   his books . . . joli] Edmond Rostand's *La Samaritaine* (1897):
"young, surprising, moving, and lovely."

917.6–7   Les idées . . . l'usage] Ideas are destined to be deformed
through use.

917.17   "aultres . . . solatieuses."] See note 902.6.

920.23   Das Leben Als Glockenspiel] Life as a glockenspiel.

920.31–32   au pays . . . poète] In the country of metaphor that one is a
poet.

921.22   Approchons-nous . . . peu] Let us approach Poussin little by
little.

JOURNALS AND LETTERS

925.3   (1898)] Printed here as it appears in the journal.

925.31   ——] Here and below, —— represents the mark made by Stevens
to separate consecutive journal entries.

929.6   "Olivia"] A four-act romantic comedy that Stevens had outlined.

930.11   Hosey] Hosea Locke, an "Adirondack woodsman" whom W. G.
Peckham had brought along on the camping trip to British Columbia.

937.11   POUPÉE DE POUPÉES] Doll of Dolls.

937.17–22   Je vous . . . Recevez] I assure you, madam, that a walk
through the soot-deposit that is Indianapolis is truly a strange thing. I've just
come back from a lovely walk. The day after tomorrow I will be in Pittsburgh
and from there leave for Hartford. Until then. / Receive . . . .

937.24   *Alice Corbin Henderson*] Poet and associate editor of *Poetry*,
1912–16; her husband was William Penhallow Henderson.

938.38   Alfred Kreymborg . . . Loeb] Kreymborg, a poet and playwright,
resigned in February 1922 from the little magazine *Broom* (1921–24), which
he and Harold Loeb had founded and co-edited in Rome.

939.1–3   Williams' . . . Moore's book] Williams' *Sour Grapes* (1921) and
Moore's *Poems* (1921).

939.25   John Rodker]   Rodker (1894–1955) was a poet and publisher of the
Ovid Press in England.

939.30   Robert McAlmon]   McAlmon (1895–1956) was an American ex-
patriate writer, publisher, and editor with William Carlos Williams of the little
magazine *Contact.*

940.13   Eliot's poem]   *The Waste Land* (first published in *Criterion*, Oct.
1922).

940.21   Gorham Munson's note]   "The Dandyism of Wallace Stevens."

940.26   Williams' book]   William Carlos Williams, *In the American Grain*
(1925).

941.11   cartolina . . . Rapallo.]   Italian postcard from Rapallo.

941.19   Pound's request]   Pound had requested, through Williams, a
poem from Stevens.

941.27   "sisterhood . . . dead."]   Cf. "To the One of Fictive Music,"
page 70.16 in this volume.

942.32   Mr. Warren's book]   Robert Penn Warren's *Thirty-Six Poems*
(1935), published by Lane's Alcestis Press.

943.1   *Leonard C. van Geyzel*]   Poet and translator of Singhalese poetry,
a descendant of Dutch settlers in Ceylon. Stevens wrote him in September
1937 at the suggestion of a mutual friend.

946.32   *Jane MacFarland Stone*]   Daughter of Stevens' sister, Elizabeth
MacFarland (d. Feb. 1943).

949.25–29   "To live . . . thing."]   From James' notebook entry dated
October 23, 1891.

949.30   poem]   "Description Without Place" (page 296.13 in this
volume).

950.3   symposium on Pound]   "The Case for and against Ezra Pound"
(*PM*, Nov. 25, 1945), edited by Norman, a journalist with the newspaper.
Pound was being returned to the United States to face charges of treason.

951.24   *Thomas McGreevy*]   See note 389.3–12.

954.14   *Robert Pack*]   Poet (b. 1929) and, later, an educator and director
of the Bread Loaf Writers' Conference in Vermont.

954.16–17   your paper . . . anywhere."]   "Wallace Stevens: The Secular
Mystery and the Comic Spirit" (*Western Review*, Autumn 1955); Pack emended
the sentence before it was published.

955.27   return]   Morse (see note 809.24) returned on August 2 to teach a
summer class at Trinity College.

Index of Poem Titles and First Lines

Index of Prose Titles

Library of Congress Cataloging-in-Publication Data

Stevens, Wallace, 1879–1955.
[Selections. 1997]
    Collected poetry and prose / Wallace Stevens.
        p.   cm. — (The library of America; 96)
    Includes bibliographical references and index.
    ISBN 1–883011–45–0 (alk. paper)
    1. Stevens, Wallace, 1879–1955 — Literary collections. I. Title.
II. Series.
PS3537.T4753A6 1997   97–7023
811′.52—dc21   CIP

This book is set in 10 point Linotron Galliard,
a face designed for photocomposition by Matthew Carter
and based on the sixteenth-century face Granjon. The paper is
acid-free Ecusta Nyalite and meets the requirements for permanence
of the American National Standards Institute. The binding
material is Brillianta, a woven rayon cloth made by
Van Heek-Scholco Textielfabrieken, Holland.
The composition is by The Clarinda
Company. Printing and binding by
R.R.Donnelley & Sons Company.
Designed by Bruce Campbell.